Teacher's Edition

Bible Truths

2

A Servant's Heart

Fourth Edition

bju press®

Greenville, South Carolina

Note: The fact that materials produced by other publishers may be referred to in this volume does not constitute an endorsement of the content or theological position of materials produced by such publishers. Any references and ancillary materials are listed as an aid to the student or the teacher and in an attempt to maintain the accepted academic standards of the publishing industry.

BIBLE TRUTHS 2 Teacher's Edition
A Servant's Heart
Fourth Edition

Coordinating Author
Daryl Kopp

Contributing Authors
Ann Larson
Eileen M. Berry

Third Edition Authors
Tammie D. Jacobs
Diane Brown
Nellie Ashe Cooper
Joanne Hall
Susan Jaeger
Lisa Marie Massato
Charlotta Pace
Karen Wooster

Third Edition Contributing Authors
Marianne Appleman
Eileen M. Berry
Lynnae A. Hadaway
Sharon Hambrick
Karin Wiley

Project Editor
Dennis Cone

Project Managers
Roxana P. Pérez de Keiser
Andrew Fry

Bible Integration
Bryan Smith, PhD
Brian Collins, MDiv

Design Coordinator
Dan VanLeeuwen

Page Layout
Carol Larson

Book Designer
Drew Fields

Cover Designer
Rita Golden

Media Transfer Specialist
James Frasier

Permissions
Rita Mitchell
Joyce Landis
Carla Thomas

Music Permissions
Megan Anthony
Kendra Zimmerman

© 2011 BJU Press
Greenville, South Carolina 29614

First edition © 1976 BJU Press
Second edition © 1981 BJU Press
Third edition © 1999 BJU Press

ISBN 978-1-59166-958-6 (Teacher's Edition with CD-ROM)

15 14 13 12 11 10 9 8 7 6 5 4 3

Teaching Goals

Teaching students to know, love, and live the Bible

This Teacher's Edition is a ready guide to help you ground your students in the Christian Faith by . . .

. . . teaching that the Bible is God's Word.
- Students are taught that Bible accounts are fact. The Bible is used as the final authority in all guided discussions.

. . . aiding students in recognizing their need of Christ as personal Savior.
- Lessons emphasize God's dealing with His people and the need of every individual to be saved.
- Students learn how to share the plan of salvation with others.

. . . encouraging Christlikeness in students.
- Application stories teach students by example what behaviors please and displease God.
- Students learn what steps of Christian obedience follow salvation.

. . . instilling a desire in students to know more about God.
- As students learn about the Word of God, they also learn about the God of the Word.
- Discussion questions after each Bible account focus on what the account teaches and how students should respond.

. . . promoting understanding and application of Bible knowledge to daily life.
- Students study the principles found in memory verses in every lesson.
- Students learn that God's Word has relevance to every part of their lives.
- Students see how lessons can change the way they believe, think, speak, and act.

. . . providing a systematic plan for the practice of Bible skills.
- The student textbook teaches skills such as reading the contents page, using a glossary, and understanding parts of a verse.
- Students use their Bibles to find information and interpret meaning.

. . . connecting Bible events with other historical events.
- Background information on Bible accounts provides a broader knowledge of Bible times.
- Students learn chronology of Bible events and characters by use of individual timelines.
- Students hear stories about noted Christians in history.

. . . correlating academic subjects with Bible teaching.
- Lessons are supplemented with optional connections, including history, art, science, English, writing, math, and drama.
- Everyday objects are used to teach Bible truths.

Contents

Instructional Materials

Student Materials

Student Worktext

The Worktext is a colorful companion to the Teacher's Edition. It reviews Bible accounts, provides practice of Bible study skills, and applies Bible knowledge to the lives of the students.

The appendix includes music for each of the ten unit hymns, maps of lands in Bible times, a listing of the Bible Truths for Christian Growth for this grade, a glossary of Bible terms, and an index. Activity pages correlate with the missionary story, the application novel, and Heroes of the Faith lessons. A complete listing of the Bible Truths for Christian Growth may be found on the Toolkit CD that accompanies the Teacher's Edition.

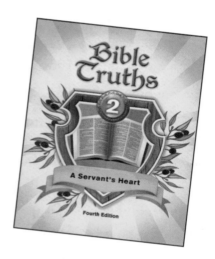

Tests

The test packet (sold separately) features a one or two-page test for each of the ten units. Also available is an answer key for easy grading.

Student Materials

Illustrated bookmarks help the student mark the locations of the memory verses studied in each unit. An individualized timeline aids the student in understanding the chronology of Bible characters and Heroes of the Faith. The bookmarks and student timeline materials are on the Toolkit CD and may be printed out on heavy paper or cardstock. (*Note:* There is some disagreement in certain areas of Old and New Testament chronology. The dates in this curriculum reflect our best interpretation of the evidence. It is not uncommon, however, for dates in conservative sources to vary minimally. This has no effect, of course, on the reliability of the biblical record; disagreement comes from our own limitations.)

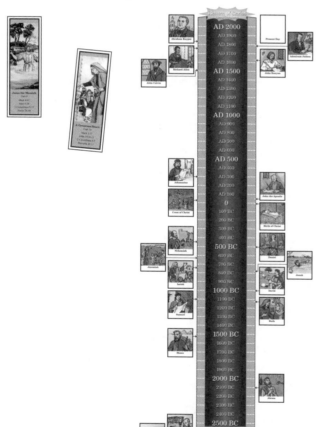

Miscellaneous School Supplies

For every lesson each student will need a Bible and his own copy of the Worktext. For various learning activities, he will need standard school supplies: crayons, colored pencils or markers, a highlighter, pencils, scissors, and glue. It is more convenient if each student has an individual copy of the missionary story *A Question of Yams* for use with the lessons in Unit 6.

Teacher Materials

Teacher's Edition

A Bible and this Teacher's Edition, which is the heart of this Bible program, are needed for every lesson.

The daily lesson plans are divided into thirty–six subunits (or weeks). Each subunit consists of four lessons. On the fifth day of the week, the students can attend chapel, do the Reinforcement and Enrichment activities from the Going Beyond section, and/or be evaluated on their knowledge of the Bible.

The thirty–six subunits are grouped into ten thematic units. Each unit begins with a Unit Overview providing introductory information for the teacher. Each Overview offers a short personal devotional for the teacher to use in self preparation before teaching that unit. It also contains a list of specified materials used to teach the lessons. The two pages immediately following the Unit Overview page feature a daily lesson plan chart for the Unit. Note that an abbreviated daily lesson plan chart for the entire second grade Bible curriculum can be found on pages xvi–xxv at the front of this book.

The appendix begins with the ten unit hymns (words and music) taught in the lessons and two additional songs that reinforce each unit theme.

Reproducible Activity Pages and Unit Review pages aid the teacher in presenting some lessons and provide the teacher and parents a convenient way to review the unit and prepare for the optional unit test. The appendix also includes a short Thanksgiving MiniUnit with three lesson plans and reproducible Activity Pages to be used in place of the regular Bible lesson.

The next two sections are the complete outline of Bible doctrines and the glossary, which contains definitions and pronunciations of Bible terms. The cumulative index provides a view of the topics taught in all six elementary grades. The Bible 2 index is specific to topics covered in second grade.

Toolkit CD

The Toolkit CD included with this Teacher's Edition provides a diagram of each unit bulletin board with some explanations. Also included on the CD are the visuals from the Teacher's Visual Packet, the hymns, the Activity Pages, and the Unit Reviews. The student materials section contains the student timeline and unit bookmarks. The entire set of the Bible Truths for Christian Growth questions and answers (for all six elementary grades) appear on the CD as well.

Music CD*

The recording presents the ten unit hymns sung by children with instrumental accompaniment. Accompaniment may be used without voices by adjusting the balance control.

*this item sold separately

Missionary Story*

The missionary story *A Question of Yams* is used in teaching some Unit 6 lessons. The book is written on a second-grade reading level so that students may read the chapters before the teacher discusses the story. Worktext pages are designed to accompany the teaching of this story.

Application Novel*

The application novel *Pelts and Promises* is used in teaching some of the Unit 10 lessons. Since the book is written above the second-grade reading level, the teacher will need to read the chapters aloud before discussing the story in class. Worktext pages are designed to accompany the teaching of this story.

Visual Packet*

The Visual Packet contains twenty-six colorful Info-Scenes to be used in the teaching of the lessons and classroom display. The classroom-sized timeline enhances the student's grasp of the chronology of the Bible characters and Heroes of the Faith studied in this book. The Bible TimeLine is vertical and can be placed on the back of a standard door. Also included are maps of Bible lands. (*Note:* Copies of the charts and maps are in the Worktext and the Toolkit CD.)

Lesson Features

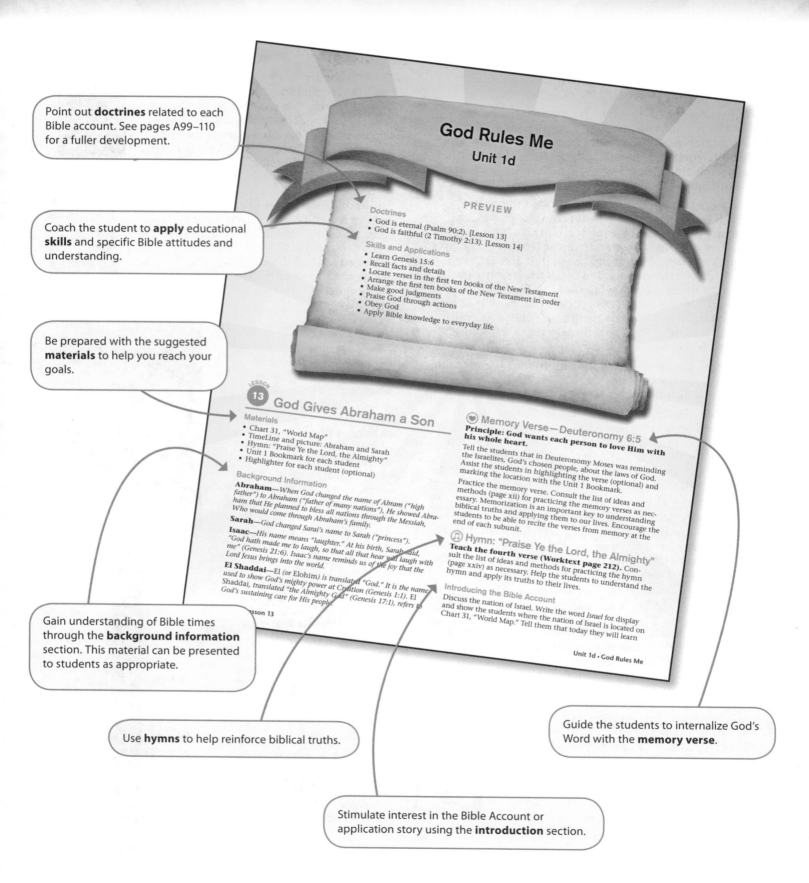

Point out **doctrines** related to each Bible account. See pages A99–110 for a fuller development.

Coach the student to **apply** educational **skills** and specific Bible attitudes and understanding.

Be prepared with the suggested **materials** to help you reach your goals.

Gain understanding of Bible times through the **background information** section. This material can be presented to students as appropriate.

Use **hymns** to help reinforce biblical truths.

Stimulate interest in the Bible Account or application story using the **introduction** section.

Guide the students to internalize God's Word with the **memory verse**.

God Rules Me
Unit 1d

PREVIEW

Doctrines
- God is eternal (Psalm 90:2). [Lesson 13]
- God is faithful (2 Timothy 2:13). [Lesson 14]

Skills and Applications
- Learn Genesis 15:6
- Recall facts and details
- Locate verses in the first ten books of the New Testament
- Arrange the first ten books of the New Testament in order
- Make good judgments
- Praise God through actions
- Obey God
- Apply Bible knowledge to everyday life

LESSON 13 — God Gives Abraham a Son

Materials
- Chart 31, "World Map"
- TimeLine and picture: Abraham and Sarah
- Hymn: "Praise Ye the Lord, the Almighty"
- Unit 1 Bookmark for each student
- Highlighter for each student (optional)

Background Information

Abraham—When God changed the name of Abram ("high father") to Abraham ("father of many nations"), He showed Abraham that He planned to bless all nations through the Messiah, Who would come through Abraham's family.

Sarah—God changed Sarai's name to Sarah ("princess").

Isaac—His name means "laughter." At his birth, Sarah said, "God hath made me to laugh, so that all that hear will laugh with me" (Genesis 21:6). Isaac's name reminds us of the joy that the Lord Jesus brings into the world.

El Shaddai—El (or Elohim) is translated "God." It is the name used to show God's mighty power at Creation (Genesis 1:1). El Shaddai, translated "the Almighty God" (Genesis 17:1), refers to God's sustaining care for His people.

Lesson 13

♥ Memory Verse—Deuteronomy 6:5

Principle: God wants each person to love Him with his whole heart.

Tell the students that in Deuteronomy Moses was reminding the Israelites, God's chosen people, about the laws of God. Assist the students in highlighting the verse (optional) and marking the location with the Unit 1 Bookmark.

Practice the memory verse. Consult the list of ideas and methods (page xii) for practicing the memory verses as necessary. Memorization is an important key to understanding biblical truths and applying them to our lives. Encourage the students to be able to recite the verses from memory at the end of each subunit.

♫ Hymn: "Praise Ye the Lord, the Almighty"

Teach the fourth verse (Worktext page 212). Consult the list of ideas and methods for practicing the hymn (page xxiv) as necessary. Help the students to understand the hymn and apply its truths to their lives.

Introducing the Bible Account

Discuss the nation of Israel. Write the word *Israel* for display and show the students where the nation of Israel is located on Chart 31, "World Map." Tell them that today they will learn

Unit 1d • God Rules Me

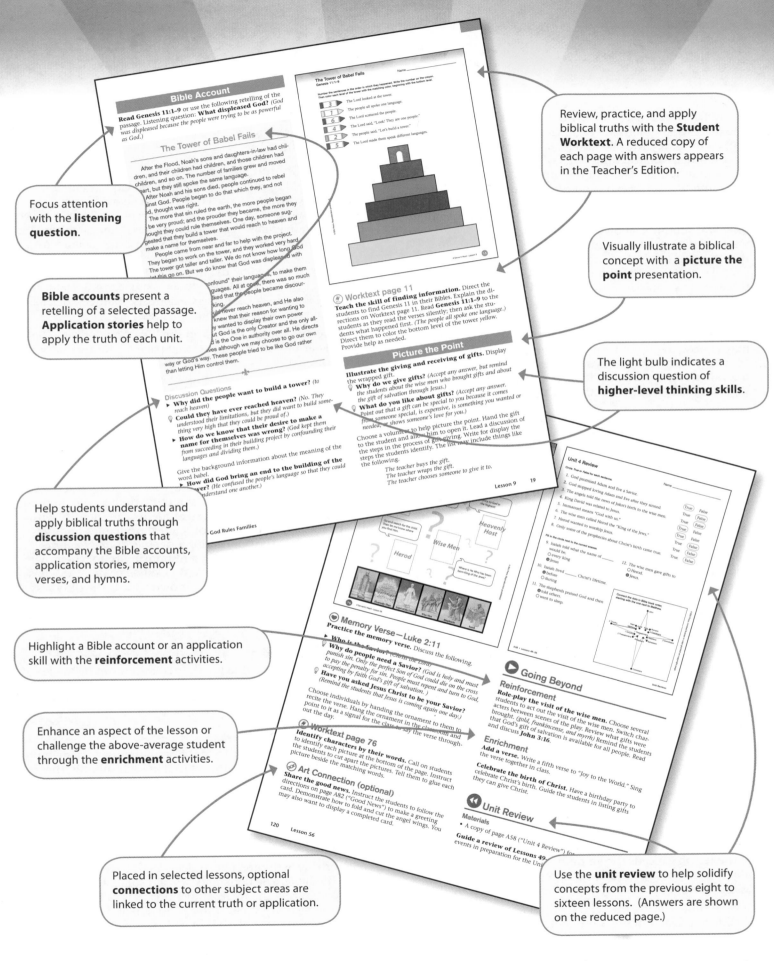

Review, practice, and apply biblical truths with the **Student Worktext**. A reduced copy of each page with answers appears in the Teacher's Edition.

Focus attention with the **listening question**.

Bible accounts present a retelling of a selected passage. **Application stories** help to apply the truth of each unit.

Visually illustrate a biblical concept with a **picture the point** presentation.

The light bulb indicates a discussion question of **higher-level thinking skills**.

Help students understand and apply biblical truths through **discussion questions** that accompany the Bible accounts, application stories, memory verses, and hymns.

Highlight a Bible account or an application skill with the **reinforcement** activities.

Enhance an aspect of the lesson or challenge the above-average student through the **enrichment** activities.

Placed in selected lessons, optional **connections** to other subject areas are linked to the current truth or application.

Use the **unit review** to help solidify concepts from the previous eight to sixteen lessons. (Answers are shown on the reduced page.)

Teaching Tips

In the Classroom or at Home

The daily lesson plans are organized into ten thematic units that survey the Old and New Testaments in chronological order. The teaching order of the units may be changed if desired. Eight of the units are divided into four subunits, with each subunit consisting of four lessons, allowing each unit to be taught in four weeks. Unit 4 (the Christmas unit) and Unit 8 (the Easter unit) contain only two subunits, allowing each unit to be taught in two weeks. You may have to adjust your teaching schedule so that you can teach these units at the appropriate time of year. An optional Thanksgiving MiniUnit consisting of three lessons appears in the appendix of this book.

Each subunit contains four days of lessons. The fifth day of each week is for those classes meeting with other classes for chapel. If your class does not have that option, you may choose to do the Reinforcement and Enrichment activities in the Going Beyond section. Teachers wanting to evaluate their students' Bible knowledge and application skills may also want to do this on the fifth day of the week.

At Church

This curriculum can be adapted for Sunday school or children's church. The teacher could choose to teach one subunit each Sunday. Depending on the length of the class, the teacher would choose a Bible account, an application story, one activity, the memory verse, and the hymn. Following this schedule, the teacher would complete one subunit each Sunday (approximately one unit each month) and a grade-level curriculum in thirty-six weeks. If the teacher desires, he can spend two Sundays teaching a subunit. This enables him to use all the Bible accounts and application stories, and most of the activities. The teacher would use one grade-level curriculum for an entire year. If the group in children's church includes several grades, teachers should alternate grade levels each year, repeating the cycle after three years.

Teaching Bible

The Bible accounts in the lessons are retellings from specific listed passages. When reading the Bible account aloud to the students, it is good to have a Bible open to the reference to help reinforce that this account is from God's Word. Instead of reading from the lesson, you may choose to read the Scripture aloud to the students or retell it in your own words.

During a typical week, two or three Bible accounts will be taught to the students. After reading or retelling the Bible account, it is important to discuss it and ask questions about it. In large part, this is where the development of further understanding takes place, opening the door to make application of Bible principles to the students' personal lives. For this purpose, if for any reason the time of the lesson exceeds the amount of available time, it is highly recommended to always present this section of the lesson in full and to shorten another element of the lesson.

Several times during the school year a lesson will feature the life and teachings of a prophet. The purpose of each Prophet Focus is to introduce some of the biblical prophets and their specific ministry: warning people of God's judgment, encouraging people to obey God, and foretelling Christ's birth.

Teaching Church History

A one-page biography of six people that God has used in shaping the history of the church is an added element of this curriculum. These are titled Heroes of the Faith, and the featured individuals were chosen because they established churches, wrote about God and His glory, and defended the Faith, some to the point of death. The Christian church today is still blessed by the impact of their ministries. These accounts help balance what students are learning about the accomplishments of explorers, scientists, mathematicians, government leaders, and sports heroes.

Students hear a story based on the life of one of these heroes in various units. An optional page in the appendix of the Worktext may be used to reinforce the information on each hero. A picture of each hero accompanies the timelines and may be attached to the appropriate time.

Teaching Christian Living

The application stories show students what behaviors please or displease God through examples of children in fictionalized stories. A missionary story and an application novel take the place of the short application stories in Units 6 and 10. Because you and your students read these books over a period of time, students will become more involved in the characters' lives. Students can identify with the characters' application of biblical principles in different situations. The application novel, *Pelts and Promises*, teaches students about taking responsibility for their own actions. The missionary story, *A Question of Yams*, teaches that God's way, rather than our own way, is the only way to live a satisfying life and glorify God. It is important that students learn how to apply their Bible knowledge to their personal lives so that they can live the Bible.

Picturing the Point

Sometimes a concept (e.g., reconciliation) can be made more understandable to students by using an object to visually illustrate the point. A few such teaching tools are suggested in the lessons.

Memorizing Bible Verses

Students need to understand the Scripture they are memorizing. As a new verse is introduced in each subunit, the teacher needs to explain it fully. The main principle of the verse is identified for the teacher and can be shared with the students. The memory verses relate to the unit themes, and the references are likewise noted on the unit bookmark. Students should look up and read the verses from their own Bibles. Verse visuals can be made and are helpful for memorizing Scripture, but students need to read Scripture from the Bible. The bookmark will aid students in locating the verse during the week. Students can use a highlighter to mark the memory verse. If this procedure is used throughout elementary school, the students will have a record of the verses they memorized at school.

Two keys to memorizing Bible verses are comprehension and frequent practice. Teachers should not expect that all the necessary practice needed is taking place at home. Practice time is provided during the Bible lesson. Some teachers find it helpful to draw five pictures for display in the morning and erase one picture every time students practice throughout the day. This ensures that the teacher and students remember to practice. Memorizing verses should be pleasant and positive, rather than a dreaded drill time.

You can adjust the amount of required memorization to meet the needs of the class. If the verse is too long, use only a portion of it. The verse can also be adjusted to meet the abilities of a specific student. [*Note:* A list of classroom and one-on-one methods for helping students learn, comprehend, and apply the memory verses is included on pages xii–xiii.]

The evaluation of Scripture memory is optional. Some teachers have students say verses aloud as a class, as small groups, or as individuals. Other teachers prepare verse quizzes with a limited number of blanks that the students complete, using words from a word bank. It is not necessary to assign a grade to this evaluation. Assigning letter grades to memory verses will often require the teacher to deviate from a strict percentage for the number of correct answers. It is more important for students to understand the meaning of the verse and be able to use it in their own lives than to know the verse word-perfect. Students should hide God's Word in their hearts, not just in their minds.

Singing
Most teachers and students have favorite songs. Because teachers and students are familiar with these and will want to continue to sing them during Bible time, only one hymn was chosen for each unit. Each unit hymn was selected for its potential and continued use for worship, inspiration, and growth in the students' lives. Some of these hymns contain adult phraseology, abstraction, and symbolism. Simple explanations are included to help you explain the meanings of these hymns. Additional songs for each unit appear with the unit hymn in the appendix of this book.

[*Note:* A list of methods to help students (both in the classroom and one-on-one) learn, comprehend, and apply the hymns is included on pages xiii–xiv.]

Praying
Prayer is an integral part of each school day. Use this time to teach students what prayer is and how God answers prayer. Prayer time may be during the Bible lesson, at the beginning of the school day, or at numerous times throughout the day. Invite students to share prayer requests from time to time. Two prayer journal pages are located at the back of the Student Worktext. Encourage students to record some of their classmates' prayer requests. (*Note:* Most second graders enjoy sharing prayer requests. The teacher may choose to limit the number of prayer requests made each day.)

Teaching Bible Study Skills
An important aspect of teaching the Bible is to teach how to use the Bible. Time is allotted for showing students how to use the contents page. Students use a glossary to look up Bible terms. They study the books of the Bible and learn which book contains specific Bible accounts (e.g., Creation and the Flood in Genesis, Moses's leading the Israelites out of Egypt in Exodus, God's talking to Samuel in 1 Samuel). Students actively use their Bibles to find information and interpret meaning.

Christian Worldview Shaping: Connections
The Bible teaches us much more than just how to behave—it shows us how to look at the world. It teaches us a Christian worldview. One element of that is to understand that all creation exists to declare God's glory. In this Bible curriculum, we highlight some connections between the Bible and other subjects studied in school. We see connections between the Bible and history by studying the different governmental, geographical, and cultural aspects presented. A mathematical connection is seen, for example, in the amount of money Zacchaeus returned to those he had cheated. The dryness or dampness of Gideon's fleece provides for a scientific discussion. The poetry of David lends itself to a study about literature, writing, and grammar.

God's goal is for us to study all things, not as disciplines isolated from His purpose, but as tools to help us see how all truth has its source in Him. Therefore, the Christian should study each aspect of our world with the end goal of glorifying some aspect of God's glorious character. Each activity and bit of knowledge, whether it's using the contents page or a glossary, reading a map, or writing a letter, should be mastered with the ultimate objective of God being glorified through His wisdom and creation.

Combining Grade Levels
Bible instruction is free of two considerations in combining grade levels: achievement testing and preparing students for the next grade level. When combining grades, consider the age of the students as well as the span of grades and adjust your teaching and requirements. Younger students need more explanations, less memory work, and more help in completing Worktext pages. Older students can review memory verses from previous weeks, complete Worktext pages independently, and apply the lessons further.

If you are teaching this curriculum to a group of first, second, and third graders, you will need to decide whether the first graders can easily memorize the verses. If not, assign only a phrase or choose one verse and work on it for two weeks. Both first and second graders need guidance in completing the Worktext pages. First graders may give answers orally while someone writes down their answers. Difficult pages such as those containing map skills may be omitted or be done in class. Let second and third graders locate and read aloud Scripture references. *A Question of Yams* may need to be read aloud for the first graders, but third graders may enjoy reading *Pelts and Promises* independently. Remember, the goal is not just to teach all students to know the Bible, but also to teach them to love it and live it as well.

Methods for Learning Verses and Hymns

Teaching a Verse to a Class

Teaching tips: Repetition is very important. Involve the senses when possible. Flashcards, markerboard, flannelgraph, posters, puppets, pictures, music, and physical movement aid comprehension and retention. Use variety and ask questions. Incentives for learning may include the use of charts, stickers, and points.

Knowledge

- Read or recite the verse silently, whispering, or with a normal voice.
- Divide it into parts.
- Choose different students, rows, or genders to say it.
- Choose students to say/recite it based on what they ate for breakfast; who is wearing a certain color; who lives within a certain distance from church/school; those with older or younger siblings; those with pets of a certain kind; those who have lived in another state; those whose names begin with A–L or M–Z; those whose birthdays fall in the first half of the year (January through June) or in the second half (July through December); those whose birth dates are between the first and fifteenth or the sixteenth and thirty-first of the month.
- Use visuals.
- Use hand motions.
- Allow those who can recite it to choose the next person to recite it.
- Teams of two or three say every other word.
- Say one word and ask what word follows it.
- Use the contents page to find the verse.
- Write the first letter of each word as a prompt for the word that comes next.
- Say it throughout the day.
- Allow students who achieve a certain goal to recite the verse.
- Instruct students to stand when a certain word from the verse is spoken.
- Write parts of the verse on strips of paper. Distribute the strips to several students. Allow them to line themselves up in order in the front of class.
- Toss a beanbag to a student who has recited the verse. He may toss the beanbag to another student who will then recite the verse. Continue as time allows.
- When students are familiar with the verse, form a circle and pass a ball around, allowing each student to say a word as he gets the ball. If a child does not know the word, he is "out."
- Write the verse in different colors. Those who are wearing those colors say that part or parts.
- Write each word of the verse on a strip of paper. Words may be used more than once. Put each strip in a bag and line the bags up at the front of the class. Divide the class in half and have a student from each team pick a bag. If he is able to say the words that come before and after that word, his team gets a point. The team with the most points wins.
- Divide the class into groups. Point to a student and ask what the second word is. Choose a student from another team and ask what the fifth word is. Then another student for the fourth word, and so on.
- Divide the class into groups. Begin to say the verse and stop before a certain word. Invite a volunteer to finish the verse. Begin the verse again but stop at a different word. Call on a student from another team. Repeat as desired.
- Ask students to identify the second word that begins with a certain letter. Repeat, using a different letter each time.
- Ask what is the first word with four (or any desired number of) letters.
- Recite the verse, starting in the seated position. Instruct each student to say one word of the verse, standing when he says it, and then being seated again. This method is easiest done in rows.
- Write the verse for display. Remove words one at a time and have the class say the verse, filling in words until all words are gone.

Comprehension

- Ask questions about the meanings of words.
- Ask questions about the Bible account and invite those who answer correctly to read or recite the verse.
- Act it out.
- Ask why any particular word is important.
- Ask students to identify someone they know who is a good example of the verse.
- Ask what they think the writer/speaker wanted the listeners to do, say, or think.
- Ask what the writer's/speaker's thoughts were.
- Ask if the writer/speaker was happy, sad, pleased, joyful, and so on.
- Instruct each student to write one question about the verse and take it home to ask a parent, guardian, Sunday school teacher, or other adult. (Sample questions: What does the word ___ mean? When should I do this? How often should I do this? Does this mean I should or shouldn't ___?)
- Instruct each student to write a statement about the verse and take it home to discuss with a parent, guardian, Sunday school teacher, or other adult. (Sample statements: I like this verse because it reminds me of . . .; This verse scares me because . . .; I can't obey this verse because . . .; This verse makes me happy because . . .; I don't know what this verse means because . . .)
- Ask what a synonym for ___ is.
- Ask what an antonym for ___ is.
- Ask if there are any phrases that sound like they mean the same thing.

Application

- Ask when it would be difficult or easy to obey this verse.
- Ask students to tell how they can obey it.
- Tell a story (real life or made up). Ask how this verse would apply to that situation.
- Ask, "What does this verse tell us we should think, do, or say when we go to [place] or when we do [activity]?"
- Ask how many times each student can do/say/be this in the next seven days.

Teaching a Verse One-on-One

Teaching tips: Repetition is very important. Involve the senses when possible. Flashcards, markerboard, flannelgraph, posters, puppets, pictures, music, and physical movement all aid comprehension and retention. Use variety and ask questions. Incentives for learning may include the use of charts, stickers, and points.

Knowledge

- Read or recite the verse silently, whispering, or in a normal voice.
- Divide it into parts: student and teacher alternate saying different parts or every other word.
- Use visuals.
- Use hand motions.
- Ask questions about the Bible account; if he answers correctly, he may say or recite the verse. After reciting it a certain number of times, reward him with a special activity.
- Say one word and ask what word follows it.
- Write the verse for display. Remove words one at a time and invite the student to say the verse, filling the word in until all words are gone.
- Use the contents page to find the verse.
- Write the first letter of each word as a prompt for what word comes next.
- Say the verse throughout the day.
- Allow him to say the verse if he achieves a certain goal.
- Select certain words. Recite the verse to him, instructing him to stand when those words are spoken.
- Write parts of the verse on strips of paper. Place strips on the table, and have him arrange them in order.
- Toss a beanbag back and forth as you each say alternating words.
- Write the verse in different colors. Have him say the parts that correspond to the colors of the clothing he is wearing.
- Write each word of the verse on a strip of paper. Words may be used more than once. Place each strip upside down (not in order). As he chooses each strip, he is to say the words that come before and after that word. Time him after he practices a few times.
- Ask the student what the second word is. Ask what the fifth word is. Then the fourth word, and so on.
- Say the verse and stop before a certain word. Ask the student to finish the verse. Do the same thing again but stop at a different word. Repeat as desired.
- Ask the student to identify the second word that begins with a certain letter. Repeat, using a different letter each time.
- Ask the student to identify the first word with four (or any desired number of) letters.

Comprehension and Application

[*See* Teaching a Verse to a Class]

Teaching a Hymn to a Class

Use of the Grade 2 music CD is encouraged as necessary for the first few times a new song or verse is presented.

Teaching tips: Repetition is very important. Involve the senses when possible. Flashcards, markerboard, flannelgraph, posters, puppets, pictures, music, and physical movement aid comprehension and retention. Use variety and ask questions. Incentives for learning may include the use of charts, stickers, and points.

Knowledge

- Sing the song silently, in a whisper, or with a normal voice.
- Read it instead of singing it at first.
- Lead the students in chanting and clapping the words in rhythm.
- Divide it into parts: students and teacher alternate singing different verses or the verse and chorus.
- Ask students to sing odd or even verses based on what they ate for breakfast; who is wearing a certain color; who lives within a certain distance from church/school; those with older or younger siblings; those with pets of a certain kind; those who have lived in another state; those whose names begin with A–L or M–Z; those whose birthdays fall in the first half of the year (January through June) or in the second half (July through December); or those whose birth dates are between the first and fifteenth or the sixteenth and thirty-first of the month.
- Use visuals.
- Use hand motions.
- Identify certain phrases in the song and direct the students to echo each phrase after you.
- Explain the meanings of key words and phrases.
- Ask questions about the Bible account. When a student answers correctly, his row may sing any portion.
- Sing the first couple of words of a verse, allowing students to guess which verse you are starting.
- Say one word and ask what word follows it.
- Write the verses or chorus for display and remove words one at a time. Invite the class to sing the selection, filling in the missing word(s). Repeat until all the words are gone.
- Write the first letter of each word as a prompt for the word that comes next.
- Sing it throughout the day before prayer.
- Allow students who achieve a certain goal to sing any portion.
- Instruct students to stand when a certain word of the song (previously chosen) is sung.
- Write parts of the verses or chorus on strips of paper. Distribute strips to several students. Allow them to line themselves up in order in the front of class.
- Act out the song or a particular verse.
- Write the verses and/or chorus in different colors. Those who are wearing those colors sing the corresponding verse(s) or chorus.
- Perform for another class.

Comprehension and Application
- Ask questions about the meanings of words.
- Ask when it would be difficult or easy to obey this song.
- Ask students to tell how they can obey it.
- Ask students to mention a person who is a good example of this verse.
- Ask what they think the writer/speaker wanted the listeners to do or think.
- Ask what the writer's/speaker's thoughts were.
- Ask if the writer/speaker was happy, sad, pleased, joyful, and so on.
- Ask why any particular word is important.

Teaching a Hymn One-on-One
Use of the Grade 2 music CD is encouraged as necessary for the first few times a new song or verse is presented.

Teaching tips: Repetition is very important. Involve the senses when possible. Flashcards, markerboard, flannelgraph, posters, puppets, pictures, music, and physical movement aid comprehension and retention. Use variety and ask questions. Incentives for learning may include the use of charts, stickers, and points.

Knowledge
- Sing or recite the hymn silently, in a whisper, or with a normal voice.
- Read it instead of singing it at first.
- Lead the student in chanting and clapping the words in rhythm.
- Divide it into parts: student and teacher alternate singing different verses or the verse and chorus.
- Use visuals.
- Use hand motions.
- Ask how words or phrases can be said in another way.
- Identify certain phrases in the song and direct your student to echo each phrase after you.

- Explain the meanings of key words and phrases.
- Ask questions about the Bible account: if he answers correctly, he may sing any portion.
- Sing the first couple of words of a verse and invite him to guess which verse it is.
- Say one word and ask what word follows it.
- Write the verses or chorus for display and remove several words. Invite him to sing that verse, filling in the words. Repeat until all the words are gone.
- Write the first letter of each word as a prompt for what word comes next.
- Sing it throughout the day before you pray.
- Allow him to sing it if he achieves a certain goal.
- Instruct your student to stand when a certain word of the song is sung.
- Write parts of the verse on strips of paper. Place strips on a table and have him arrange them in order.
- Act out the song or a particular verse.
- Write verses or chorus in different colors. Ask him to sing any of the phrases that correspond to the color of clothing he is wearing.
- Perform for an individual or group.

Comprehension and Application
[*See* Teaching a Hymn to a Class]

Leading a Child to Christ

One of the greatest desires of Christian teachers is to lead children to the Savior. God has called you to present the gospel to your students so that they may repent and trust Christ, thereby being acceptable to God through Christ.

Relying on the Holy Spirit, you should take advantage of the opportunities that arise during lessons for presenting the good news of Jesus Christ. Ask questions to personally apply the Ten Commandments to your students (e.g., What is sin? Have *you* ever (name sin)? Are *you* a sinner?) You may also ask questions to discern the child's sincerity or any misunderstanding he might have (e.g., What is the gospel? What does it mean to repent? Can you do anything to save yourself?). Read verses from your Bible. You may find the following outline helpful, especially when dealing individually with a child.

1. I have sinned (Romans 3:23).
    *   Sin is disobeying God's Word (1 John 3:4). I break the Ten Commandments (Exodus 20:2–17) by loving other people or things more than I love God, worshiping other things or people, using God's name lightly, disobeying and dishonoring my parents, lying, stealing, cheating, thinking harmful and sinful thoughts, or wanting something that belongs to somebody else.
    *   Therefore I am a sinner (Psalm 51:5; 58:3; Jeremiah 17:9).
    *   God is holy and must punish me for my sin (Isaiah 6:3; Romans 6:23).
    *   God hates sin, and there is nothing that I can do to get rid of my sin by myself (Titus 3:5; Romans 3:20, 28). I cannot make myself become a good person.

2. Jesus died for me (Romans 5:8).
    *   God loves me even though I am a sinner.
    *   He sent His Son, Jesus Christ, to die on the cross for me. Christ is sinless and did not deserve death. Because of His love for me, Christ took my sin on Himself and was punished in my place (1 Peter 2:24*a*; 1 Corinthians 15:3; John 1:29).
    *   God accepted Christ's death as the perfect substitution for the punishment of my sin (2 Corinthians 5:21).
    *   Three days later, God raised Jesus from the dead. Jesus Christ is alive today and offers salvation to all. This is the gospel of Jesus Christ: He died on the cross for our sins according to the Scriptures, and He rose again the third day according to the Scriptures (1 Corinthians 15:1–4; 2 Peter 3:9; 1 Timothy 2:4).

3. I need to put my trust in Jesus (Romans 10:9–10, 13–14*a*).
    *   I must repent (turn away from my sin) and trust only Jesus Christ for salvation (Mark 1:15).
    *   If I repent and believe in what Jesus has done, I am putting my trust in Jesus.
    *   Everyone who trusts in Jesus is forgiven of sin (Acts 2:21) and will live forever with God (John 3:16). I'm given His righteousness and become a new creation, with Christ living in me (2 Corinthians 5:21; Colossians 1:27).

If a child shows genuine interest and readiness, ask, "Are you ready to put your trust in Jesus and depend on only Christ for salvation?" If he says yes, then ask him to talk to God about this. Perhaps he will pray something like the following:

> "God, I know that I've sinned against You and that You hate sin, but that You also love me. I believe that Jesus died to pay for my sin and that He rose from the dead, so I put my trust in Jesus to forgive me and give me a home with You forever. In Jesus's name I pray. Amen."

Show the child how to know from God's Word that he is forgiven and in God's family (1 John 5:12–13; John 3:18; Galatians 4:4–7). Encourage him to follow Jesus by obeying Him each day. Tell him that whenever he sins, he will be forgiven as soon as he confesses those sins to God (1 John 1:9).

Unit 1 God Is My King

Hymn: "Praise Ye the Lord, the Almighty"

Theme, Memory Verse, and Principle	Lesson Number	TE Page	Worktext Page(s)	Appendix Page(s)	Lesson Title	Scripture or Focus
Unit 1a **God Rules Creation** Genesis 1:1 *God is the all-powerful Creator.*	1	4	1		The Beginning of All Things	Genesis 1:1–13
	2	6	2	A69–70	It is Perfect!	Genesis 1:14–31
	3	8	3	A71	Rest and Praise God!	Genesis 2:1–3
	4	9	4		Sin, Death, and God's Love	Application Story
Unit 1b **God Rules Nature** Genesis 6:8, 22 *God's favor on us should lead us to complete obedience.*	5	11	5–6	A72	Safe in the Ark with God	Genesis 6:1–22
	6	13	7		Atop Mount Ararat	Genesis 7:1–9:17
	7	15	8		God Blesses Trust	Application Story
	8	16	9–10	A73	Noah's Faith—God's Promise	Genesis 6–8
Unit 1c **God Rules Families** Deuteronomy 6:5 *God wants each person to love Him with his whole heart.*	9	18	11		The Tower of Babel Fails	Genesis 11:1–9
	10	20	12		God Chooses Abram	Genesis 12:1–13:18
	11	21	13–14	A74	Trust Obeys and Waits	Application Story
	12	23	15–16		Hero of the Faith: John Bunyan	Biography
Unit 1d **God Rules Me** Genesis 15:6 *God gives us righteousness by faith.*	13	26	17		God Gives Abraham a Son	Genesis 17:1–19; 21:1–8
	14	28	18		Abraham Gives to God	Genesis 22
	15	29	19–20		Worthy of Praise	Application Story
	16	31	21–22	A75, A55	Taste and See	Psalm 119:103

Unit 2   An Obedient Heart

Hymn: "Lead On, O King Eternal"

Theme, Memory Verse, and Principle	Lesson Number	TE Page	Worktext Page(s)	Appendix Page(s)	Lesson Title	Scripture or Focus
Unit 2a **Obedient Feet** Exodus 14:31 *God's display of power causes people to fear and believe.*	17	36	23–24		God Calls Moses	Exodus 3:1–4:17
	18	39	25–26		God Shows His Power	Exodus 4:29–12:51
	19	41	27		God Shows the Way	Exodus 13:21–14:31
	20	42	28		Called to Witness	Application Story
Unit 2b **Obedient Eyes** Exodus 32:26 *God hates sin. We should stand on God's side.*	21	45	29		The Ten Commandments	Exodus 19:1–20:17
	22	47	30		The Golden Calf	Exodus 32–33
	23	48	31		Rules Are for Our Good	Application Story
	24	50	32–34		Prophet Focus: Jonah	Jonah 1–4
Unit 2c **Obedient Speech** John 14:15 *If we love Christ, we will cheerfully obey the Bible.*	25	53	35–36		A Message for Balaam	Numbers 22:1–35
	26	55	37		Balaam and His Prophecy	Numbers 22:36–24:17
	27	57			Be Kind to One Another	Application Story
	28	58	38	A76	What Should You Say?	Proverbs 16:24
Unit 2d **Obedient Hands** Micah 6:8*b* *It is better to obey God than to have an outward appearance of worshiping Him.*	29	60	39		Jericho First	Joshua 1–6
	30	62	40		Victory and Defeat	Joshua 7
	31	63	41		Obey All the Way	Application Story
	32	64	42	A56	Who Disobeyed?	Joshua 7

Unit 3   A Humble Heart

Theme, Memory Verse, and Principle	Lesson Number	TE Page	Worktext Page(s)	Appendix Page(s)	Lesson Title	Scripture or Focus
Unit 3a **There Is Only One God** Isaiah 45:22 *There is only one God.*	33	70	43–44		God Calls Gideon	Judges 6:1–32
	34	72	45		Gideon's Assurance	Judges 6:33–7:14
	35	74	46–47		Gideon Serves the Lord	Judges 7:15–8:33
	36	75	48	A77	Obedience Is the Best Way	Application Story
Unit 3b **Humble Yourself Before God** 2 Chronicles 7:14 *The Lord calls us to humble ourselves before Him.*	37	78	49		Humbling Yourself	Application Story
	38	80	50		Samson Needs Humility	Judges 13–14
	39	81	51–53		Samson Reaps the Results of Pride	Judges 15–16
	40	84	54	A78	A Humble Spirit	Application Story
Unit 3c **Humble Yourself Before Others** Galatians 6:10 *Serve others, doing good to them.*	41	86	55–56		Ruth Has a Servant's Heart	Ruth 1–4
	42	89	57–58		Hannah Gives Her Gift	1 Samuel 1
	43	90	59	A79	Hero of the Faith: Richard Allen	Biography
	44	92	60		A Heart for Serving	Application Story
Unit 3d **Walk in a Spirit of Humility** 1 John 1:7 *Christians have fellowship and forgiveness when they live God's way.*	45	95	61	A80	God Speaks to Samuel	1 Samuel 2–3
	46	97	62–63		Samuel Speaks to the People	1 Samuel 12 Picture the Point
	47	99	64		God Can Change Sinful Attitudes	Application Story
	48	100		A57	Walking in Humility	Application Story

Unit 4   Birth of the Savior

Theme, Memory Verse, and Principle	Lesson Number	TE Page	Worktext Page(s)	Appendix Page(s)	Lesson Title	Scripture or Focus
Unit 4a **Foretelling Christ's Birth** Isaiah 9:6 *Christ's birth was foretold.*	49	106	65–66		We Need a Savior	Genesis 2:15–3:24
	50	108	67		Isaiah Prophesies About Christ	Isaiah 7:14–16
	51	109	68, 240	A81	Hero of the Faith: John Calvin	Biography
	52	112	69–70		Who Knew?	Application Story
Unit 4b **Christ's Birth** Luke 2:11 *God sent us a Savior.*	53	114	71–72		The Shepherds Seek Jesus	Luke 2:1–20
	54	116			The Gift	Application Story
	55	117	73–75		The Wise Men Seek Jesus	Matthew 2:1–13
	56	119	76	A82, A58	Giving Gifts	Picture the Point

Unit 5   A Serving Heart

Hymn: "Joy in Serving Jesus"

Theme, Memory Verse, and Principle	Lesson Number	TE Page	Worktext Page(s)	Appendix Page(s)	Lesson Title	Scripture or Focus
Unit 5a **God's Servants Know God** Mark 10:45 *We must serve God and minister to others.*	57	124	77–78		Jonathan Knew God	1 Samuel 12:14–14:23
	58	126	79		David Puts God First	1 Samuel 16–17
	59	128	81		Prophet Focus: Jeremiah	Jeremiah 18:1–10
	60	129	82		Putting God and Others First	Picture the Point Application Activity
Unit 5b **God's Servants Serve in Love** 1 Samuel 12:24 *Serve God from the heart.*	61	132	83–84	A83	A Prince and a Shepherd Serve Together	1 Samuel 18:1–11; 20:1–12
	62	135	85–86		King David Serves	1 Samuel 13:1–4; 2 Samuel 4:4; 9:1–13
	63	137	87–90		In Love Serve One Another	Galatians 5:13
	64	139			Thinking of Others	Application Story
Unit 5c **God Can Use Me** 1 Chronicles 28:20a *God will help me serve Him.*	65	141	91		God Uses a Servant Girl	2 Kings 5:1–4
	66	143	92–94		A Captain Becomes a Servant	2 Kings 5:5–16
	67	146	95–96		A Servant's Crown	Application Story
	68	148	97–98		God's People Serve Him	Romans 6:13
Unit 5d **God Wants Us to Work Together** Psalm 133:1 *God's servants should live together in peace.*	69	151	99–100	A84–86	Nehemiah Wants to Rebuild	Nehemiah 1:1–2:8
	70	154	101–2		Rebuilding Together	Nehemiah 2:9–6:19
	71	156	103–4		Helping Hands?	Application Story
	72	158	105–6	A59	Who Will Do God's Work?	One-Act Play

Unit 6   A Courageous Heart   Hymn: "Am I a Soldier of the Cross?"

Theme, Memory Verse, and Principle	Lesson Number	TE Page	Worktext Page(s)	Appendix Page(s)	Lesson Title	Scripture or Focus
Unit 6a **Courage to Trust God** Romans 8:28 *If we love God, we will understand that He works out the details of our lives for our good.*	73	164	107–8	A87	Esther Becomes Queen	Esther 1–4
	74	166	109–10		Esther Goes Before the King	Esther 5–10
	75	168	111–12		Character: What Was Mordecai Like?	Missionary Story
	76	170	246		All Things Work Together	Missionary Story
Unit 6b **Courage During Hard Times** Deuteronomy 31:6 *We can be courageous because God is with us.*	77	172	113–14	A87	God Gives Courage to Do Right	Daniel 3:1–30
	78	174	115, 241		Hero of the Faith: Adoniram Judson	Biography
	79	176	116, 247		Strength and Courage	Missionary Story
	80	178	117, 248		Before and After	Missionary Story
Unit 6c **Courage to Speak God's Word** Romans 1:16 *We should not be ashamed to tell others about the gospel of Jesus Christ.*	81	179	119–20		Daniel's Reputation	Daniel 5:1–16
	82	181	121	A87	A Message from God	Daniel 5:17–31
	83	182	122, 249		Whose Way?	Missionary Story
	84	183	250		God's Book	Missionary Story
Unit 6d **Courage to Live a Godly Life** Psalm 56:11 *When we put our trust in God, we do not need to fear what people can do to us.*	85	185	123–24		A Godly Man Keeps Praying	Daniel 6:1–15
	86	186	125–26	A87	God Protects Daniel	Daniel 6:16–28
	87	188	127, 251		Whose Laws?	Missionary Story
	88	190	128, 252	A88–89, A60	Trusting God	Missionary Story

Unit 7   A Forgiving Heart

Hymn: "Cleanse Me"

Theme, Memory Verse, and Principle	Lesson Number	TE Page	Worktext Page(s)	Appendix Page(s)	Lesson Title	Scripture or Focus
Unit 7a **I Need Forgiveness** Romans 3:10–11 *I am sinful. I need God's forgiveness.*	89	196	129		Trapped by Sin	Application Story
	90	197	130		The Freedom of Forgiveness	Application Story
	91	199	131–32		Two Short Prayers	Luke 18:9–14
	92	200	133–34	A90	Forgiven but Unforgiving	Matthew 18:21–35
Unit 7b **God Forgives Me** Ephesians 1:7 *God forgives me through Christ's sacrifice.*	93	203	135–36	A91–92	Jesus Forgives and Heals	Mark 2:1–12
	94	205	137–38		A New Person	Application Story
	95	207	139–40		Forgiveness and Love	Luke 7:36–50
	96	208		A93	Giving	Picture the Point
Unit 7c **I Accept God's Forgiveness** Psalm 103:12 *God's forgiveness is forever.*	97	210	141–42, 242		Hero of the Faith: Abraham Kuyper	Biography
	98	213	143–44		A Whole Family Is Saved	Acts 16:9–34
	99	214	145		Trust God's Word	Application Story
	100	215	146		Thankful for God's Goodness	Picture the Point Luke 17:11–19
Unit 7d **I Forgive Others** Matthew 6:14–15 *Forgive others as God forgives you.*	101	218	147–48		Forgiven	Philemon 1:8–21
	102	220	149–50		Two Sons, Two Sins	Luke 15:11–32
	103	222	151		Jesus Forgives the Most	Matthew 27:27–35
	104	223	152	A61–62	Learning to Forgive	Application Story

Unit 8   Easter: He Lives

Hymn: "What a Wonderful Savior"

Theme, Memory Verse, and Principle	Lesson Number	TE Page	Worktext Page(s)	Appendix Page(s)	Lesson Title	Scripture or Focus
Unit 8a **Christ's Crucifixion** Romans 5:8 *Jesus died for sinners.*	105	228	153–54		At the Cross	Matthew 27:32–44; Mark 15:21–32; Luke 23:26–43; John 19:17–27
	106	231	155–56		Jesus's Death and Burial	Matthew 27:45–66; Mark 15:33–47; Luke 23:44–56; John 19:28–42
	107	232	157–58		Reconciliation	Picture the Point
	108	234	159–60, 243		Hero of the Faith: Athanasius	Biography
Unit 8b **Christ's Resurrection** Matthew 28:6 *Christ rose from the dead.*	109	237	161–62		He Is Risen	Luke 24:1–12; John 20:1–18
	110	239	163		Jesus Appears to His Followers	Luke 24:13–53; John 21:1–14
	111	240	164		Jesus Christ, Our Mediator	Application Story
	112	242	165–66	A63	Reflecting God's Love	Picture the Point

Unit 9   Jesus the Messiah

Hymn: "Jesus Shall Reign"

Theme, Memory Verse, and Principle	Lesson Number	TE Page	Worktext Page(s)	Appendix Page(s)	Lesson Title	Scripture or Focus
Unit 9a **Jesus Is God** Mark 4:41 *Jesus is God.*	113	248	167–68		Jesus Calms the Storm	Mark 4:35–41
	114	250	169–71		Prayer and Faith	Application Story
	115	252	172		Jesus Raises Lazarus	John 11:1–45
	116	253		A94–95	God's Power	Psalm 126:3
Unit 9b **Jesus Is Man** John 6:38 *Jesus is our example.*	117	255	173		Jesus Was Baptized	Matthew 3; John 1:19–34
	118	257	174		Jesus Was Tempted	Matthew 4:1–11
	119	258	175		The Misery of Sin	Application Story
	120	260	176	A96	Turning from Temptation	1 Corinthians 10:13
Unit 9c **Jesus Is the Savior of the World** 2 Corinthians 5:17 *A saved person is a changed person.*	121	261	177–78		Nicodemus	John 3:1–21
	122	263	179–80		Zacchaeus	Luke 19:1–10
	123	266	181	A97	Tell the Good News	Application Story
	124	267	182		Prophet Focus: Isaiah	Prophet Focus
Unit 9d **Jesus Is the King of Kings** Psalm 24:10 *The Lord Jesus Christ is the King of Glory.*	125	270	183–84		Jesus, the Humble King	Matthew 21:1–11
	126	272	185–86		Jesus Is Coming Again!	Revelation 20–22
	127	274	187		Press On!	Application Story
	128	276	188	A98, A64	Jesus Shall Reign	Luke 1:32–33

Unit 10   A Generous Heart

Hymn: "Living for Jesus"

Theme, Memory Verse, and Principle	Lesson Number	TE Page	Worktext Page(s)	Appendix Page(s)	Lesson Title	Scripture or Focus
Unit 10a **I Give Myself to God** Mark 1:17 *Jesus wants to make believers "fishers of men."*	**129**	282	189–90		John the Baptist	Matthew 11:7–13; 14:3–12
	130	284	191–92		The Disciples Leave All	Mark 1:16–20; 2:13–17; 3:13–19; John 1:43–48
	131	286	193, 256		Beginning and Ending	Application Novel
	132	287	194, 257		Following Jesus	Application Novel
Unit 10b **God Gives to Me** John 14:2b–3 *Jesus is preparing a home for believers.*	**133**	289	195		Five Thousand Fed	Matthew 14:13–21
	134	291	196		Jesus Promises an Eternal Home	John 13:31–14:6
	135	292	197, 258		Heaven	Application Novel
	136	294	198, 259		Find It Quickly	Application Novel
Unit 10c **I Give My Possessions to God** 2 Corinthians 9:7 *We should give to God joyfully.*	**137**	296	199–200		The Widow Loves from Little	Mark 12:41–44
	138	298	201–2		Mary Loves from Much	Mark 14:3–9
	139	300	203, 260		Honoring Jesus	Application Novel
	140	301	204, 261		Giving	Application Novel
Unit 10d **I Give Myself to Others** Proverbs 20:11 *Children are known by their deeds.*	**141**	303	205–6		Dorcas: Doer of Good Deeds	Acts 9:36–43
	142	305	207–8		Paul, the Missionary	Acts 27:1–28:6
	143	307	209, 262		Followers of Jesus	Application Novel
	144	308	210, 263	A65–66	Where Is It?	Application Novel

1

God Is My King

OVERVIEW

Preparing the Teacher

Unit 1 introduces students to the sovereign power of God. Share with them the wonderful concept that the same God Who created everything also rules over families and individuals. Job stated that he had previously heard of God, but he now saw Him with spiritual eyes. Keep in mind that the students should become acquainted with the truth of God's existence and power and also acknowledge God's right to direct their lives. Read **Job 42:1–5**. Pray for guidance and wisdom as you undertake the joyous task of helping the students see God's sovereignty for themselves.

Preparing the Materials

Note: For all the lessons, the teacher will need a Bible, and each student will need a Bible and a Worktext.

  1—One sheet of blue and one sheet of green art paper [E]; verse visual— one sheet of blue and one sheet of green construction paper; Unit 1 Bookmark [E]

  2—Six sheets of art paper; transparency of page A69 ("Ancient Middle East") and a transparency overlay of page A70 ("The Middle East Today") [O]; transparency pens [O]

  3—Copy of page A71 ("God Created! I'm Glad!") [E, O]

Unit 1a Going Beyond—books with pictures of animals

  5—Picture of a five-story building and a picture of a school bus [O]; transparency of the ark designs from A72 ("God Designed the Ark")

  7—Toy boat

  8—Copy of page A73 ("God Is in Control") [E, O]

  10—Container of sand or sugar; sheet of sturdy paper (light construction paper or copier paper) [E]

  11—Transparent tape [E]; copy of page A74 ("God Rules Families") [E, O]

  12—Copy of *Pilgrim's Progress*

Unit 1c Going Beyond—copy of Romans 4:3 on small sheet of paper [E]

  16—Transparent tape [E]; copy of page A75 ("God Rules Me") [E, O]; copy of page A55 ("Unit 1 Review") [E]

Unit 1d Going Beyond—individual or family picture from each student; drawing paper [E]

[E] = for each student; [O] = optional

Unit 1　God Is My King

Hymn: "Praise Ye the Lord, the Almighty"

Theme, Memory Verse, and Principle	Lesson Number	TE Page	Worktext Page(s)	Appendix Page(s)	Lesson Title	Scripture or Focus
Unit 1a **God Rules Creation** Genesis 1:1 *God is the all-powerful Creator.*	1	4	1		The Beginning of All Things	Genesis 1:1–13
	2	6	2	A69–70	It is Perfect!	Genesis 1:14–31
	3	8	3	A71	Rest and Praise God!	Genesis 2:1–3
	4	9	4		Sin, Death, and God's Love	Application Story
Unit 1b **God Rules Nature** Genesis 6:8, 22 *God's favor on us should lead us to complete obedience.*	5	11	5–6	A72	Safe in the Ark with God	Genesis 6:1–22
	6	13	7		Atop Mount Ararat	Genesis 7:1–9:17
	7	15	8		God Blesses Trust	Application Story
	8	16	9–10	A73	Noah's Faith—God's Promise	Genesis 6–8
Unit 1c **God Rules Families** Deuteronomy 6:5 *God wants each person to love Him with his whole heart.*	9	18	11		The Tower of Babel Fails	Genesis 11:1–9
	10	20	12		God Chooses Abram	Genesis 12:1–13:18
	11	21	13–14	A74	Trust Obeys and Waits	Application Story
	12	23	15–16, 238		Hero of the Faith: John Bunyan	Biography
Unit 1d **God Rules Me** Genesis 15:6 *God gives us righteousness by faith.*	13	26	17		God Gives Abraham a Son	Genesis 17:1–19; 21:1–8
	14	28	18		Abraham Gives to God	Genesis 22
	15	29	19–20		Worthy of Praise	Application Story
	16	31	21–22	A75, A55	Taste and See	Psalm 119:103

Unit 1　God Is My King

Connections	Bible Doctrines	Skills/Applications
L1—TimeLine: day 1	**The Doctrine of God** *Existence of God* God has shown Himself in nature (Rom. 1:20).	**Practical** • Recall facts and details • Find information in the Bible • Follow directions
L2—World History	*Attributes of God* God is eternal (Ps. 90:2). God is all-powerful (Jer. 32:27; Matt. 19:26).	• Read a map • Read a timeline
L3—Art	God is faithful (2 Tim. 2:13). God is love (1 John 4:8).	• Sequence events • Interpret information • Read a genealogy chart • Make good judgments
	The Doctrine of Man *Original State of Man* God created man directly (Gen 2:7). Man has a will (Gen. 3:6).	**Foundational** • Realize that God hates sin • Know that God wants Christians to live by faith
L6—TimeLine: Noah World History	*Fall of Man* Man has a sinful nature (Rom. 5:12). Man lives in a corrupted environment (Rom. 8:22).	• Realize that man can do nothing good without God • Praise God through actions
	Redemption of Man Man has God's favor (Eph. 1:3).	**Personal** • Realize that God can always be trusted
L8—Art	**The Doctrine of Salvation** *Elements of Salvation* Man turns to God through repentance and faith (Mark 1:15).	• Realize that to trust and obey God brings joy • Understand and apply Bible knowledge to everyday life
L10—TimeLine: Abram		
L11—Art		
L13—TimeLine: Abraham and Sarah		
L16—Art		

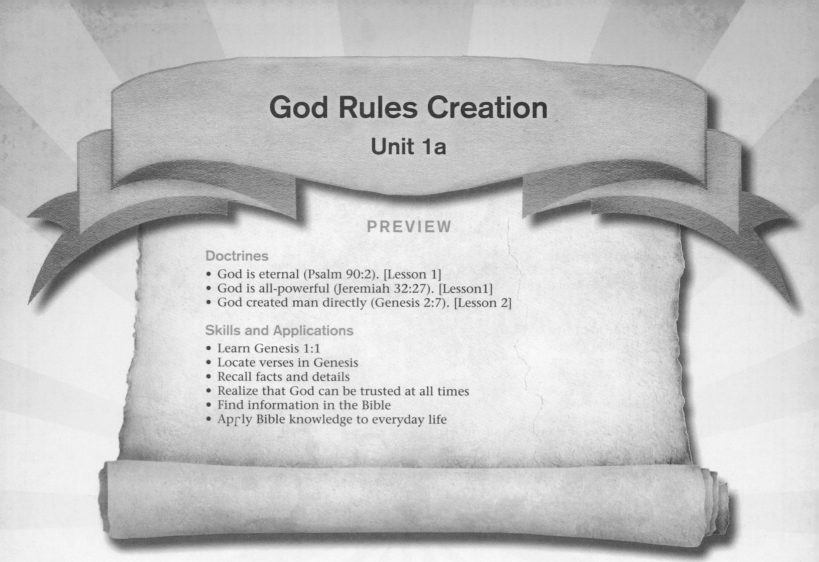

God Rules Creation
Unit 1a

PREVIEW

Doctrines

- God is eternal (Psalm 90:2). [Lesson 1]
- God is all-powerful (Jeremiah 32:27). [Lesson1]
- God created man directly (Genesis 2:7). [Lesson 2]

Skills and Applications

- Learn Genesis 1:1
- Locate verses in Genesis
- Recall facts and details
- Realize that God can be trusted at all times
- Find information in the Bible
- Apply Bible knowledge to everyday life

 LESSON 1

The Beginning of All Things

Materials

- TimeLine and cards for day 1 and present day
- Unit 1 Bookmark for each student
- Art paper for each student: one sheet of blue and one sheet of green
- Construction paper for verse visual: one green and one blue
- Highlighter for each student (optional)

Material	Location
Charts Maps InfoScenes TimeLine and pictures	Visual Packet (or the Visuals section of the Toolkit CD)
Student Bookmarks Student TimeLine and pictures	Student Materials section of the Toolkit CD
Music for teaching the unit hymns is found in the appendix of both this Teacher's Edition and the Student Worktext. A recording of children singing these hymns is available on CD. Included in the appendix of this Teacher's Edition are two additional hymns or songs for each unit. See listing on page A1.	

- Visual of Genesis 1:1 for a choral reading (optional): Write the verse on a sheet of blue construction paper and on a sheet of green construction paper. On the blue paper, underline the words *the heaven*. On the green paper, underline the words *and the earth*.

Introducing the Bible Account

Draw things in the sky and things on the earth.
Instruct the students to draw on the blue sheet of paper things that are in the sky (sun, moon, stars, birds) and to draw on the green sheet of paper things on the earth (trees, grass, animals, oceans, people). Ask the students whether they have just created those things. Explain that they have only the power to draw these things on paper. When God wanted there to be the sun, birds, animals, and everything else, He had the power to create them. He did not have anything to start with like paper and crayons. He created everything out of nothing.

Bible Account

Read Genesis 1:1–13 or use the following retelling of the passage. Listening question: **What is another name for the sky?** *(firmament)*

You may present the account in your own words to enhance your listeners' comprehension and attentiveness. Asking questions at various points in the account will help the students to understand and apply the truths of God's Word.

The Beginning of All Things

God does not have a birthday because He was never born. Time, as we measure it, did not exist until God created it.

God created the earth. At first, it was "without form." The Bible tells us that God made everything. God did not need any tools to make the world. He spoke, and the world was created because God's word is all-powerful.

First God made light. He said, "Let there be light," and there was light. God separated the light, which He called day, from the darkness, which He called night. That evening and morning were the first day. (The earth was still empty, but time had begun.)

On the second day, God made the firmament, or sky. He separated the waters below and the clouds above. God called the firmament heaven.

On the third day, God made the land, seas, and plants. He said that all the water should be "gathered together" to let the "dry land appear." And that's exactly what happened. That evening and morning were the third day.

❖

Discussion Questions

You may use the following questions as desired or create original questions to accomplish specific teaching goals and objectives. Questions marked with a pointer are literal questions. Those marked with a light bulb are interpretive, critical, or appreciative in nature.

▶ **On the first day of time, what did God create?** *(light; day and night)*

💡 **Why do you think God created day and night first?** *(Many answers are acceptable.)*

💡 **What is power?** *(Many answers are acceptable.)*

▶ **What did God create on the second day?** *(the sky)*

▶ **What did God create on the third day?** *(oceans, dry land, growing plant life)*

💡 **Which of the plants God created are your favorites?** *(Any answers of plant names are acceptable.)*

💡 **Did God need any of His creations for Himself?** *(no)* **How do you know He did not need them?** *(because He had existed before these things were created)*

💡 **Does God give us everything we need to do His will?** *(yes)*

💡 **How was God able to create without using materials that already existed?** *(God is all-powerful.)*

🕐 TimeLine

Introduce the history of time. Discuss when time began; then display the TimeLine. Place the day 1 picture on the TimeLine. Guide the students as they glue the picture of day 1 (from the Student Materials section of the Toolkit CD) on their TimeLines. Place the present day card (with the current year on it) on the TimeLine. Guide the students in writing the current year in the present day box and gluing it to their TimeLines.

The Beginning of All Things
Genesis 1:1–13   Name _____

Look at the contents box to the right to answer the questions.

On what page does Genesis begin? **1**

Exodus? **35**   Leviticus? **64**

Numbers? **85**   Deuteronomy? **115**

Contents	
Book	**Page Number**
Genesis	1
Exodus	35
Leviticus	64
Numbers	85
Deuteronomy	115

Use the words in the word bank to fill in the blanks.

What does the contents page in your Bible tell you?

Word Bank
books   page

It lists the names of the ___*books*___ of the Bible

and the ___*page*___ number on which each book starts.

When God spoke, He created. Use the words in the word bank to write what God created each day. You may use your Bible to help you.

Day 1
Let there be
___*light*___.

Day 2
God created the
___*heavens*___.

Day 3
Let there be
___*land*___
and
___*plants*___.

Word Bank
land   light   good
heavens   plants

God saw that what He had made was ___*good*___.

A Servant's Heart • Lesson 1   ①

📖 Bible Study Skills, Worktext page 1

Introduce students to the contents page in the Bible. Open your Bible and point out the contents page. Explain that it has two columns: the names of the books of the Bible, and the page number each book starts on. Invite the students to locate the contents pages in their Bibles. Direct them to use the "Contents" box and word banks in their Worktexts to answer the questions and fill in the blanks.

Read **Genesis 1:1** to the students. As you read, leave out selected words for the students to fill in.

Recall facts and details. Guide the students in completing the sentences about the days of Creation using the words in the word bank.

❤ Memory Verse—Genesis 1:1

Consult the list of ideas and methods (page xii) for practicing the memory verses as necessary. Memorization is an important key to understanding biblical truths and applying them to our lives. Encourage the students to be able to recite the verses from memory at the end of each subunit.

Principle: God is the all-powerful Creator. Tell the students that Genesis is the first book in the Bible and that the Creation account is found in chapter 1 of Genesis.

Distribute the Unit 1 Bookmark and direct the students to mark the location of the memory verse in their Bibles. If you

choose to let the students highlight their verses, explain that by the end of the school year they will have highlighted all the verses they have memorized together.

Discussion Questions

You may use the following questions as desired or create original questions to accomplish specific teaching goals and objectives. Questions marked with a pointer are literal questions. Those marked with a light bulb are interpretive, critical, or appreciative in nature.

💡 **Why do we memorize God's Word?** *(Many answers are acceptable, but explain that Psalm 119:11 tells us that hiding God's Word in our hearts will help us to not sin. Hopefully as we memorize verses, we will also know what they mean and use them to direct our lives.)*

💡 **What does God show you about Himself in Genesis 1:1?** *(God created everything. He is all-powerful.)*

💡 **Since God is all-powerful, how can He help you today wherever you are or go?** *(Many answers are acceptable, but lead the students in understanding that in a Christian's life there is no problem too big for God.)* **Give specific physical and spiritual examples as time permits.**

Practice the memory verse. Utilize the verse visuals or consult the list of ideas and methods (page xii) for practicing the memory verses.

LESSON 2 — It Is Perfect!

Materials

- Six sheets of art paper
- Verse visuals from the previous lesson (optional)
- A transparency of page A69 ("Ancient Middle East") and a transparency overlay of page A70 ("The Middle East Today"): Using transparency pens, outline or color the modern-day countries of Egypt, Lebanon, Syria, Iraq, Iran, Saudi Arabia, and Jordan on the overlay. (Transparencies will be used on an overhead projector during the optional History Connection.)

Background Information

Eden—*Scripture locates the Garden of Eden by its placement of the river that flowed out of it, breaking off into other branches. Because the Flood altered the land and waterways, we cannot know exactly where Eden was. The region that is now bordered by the present day Tigris and Euphrates Rivers is referred to as the cradle of civilization. This is due to the many archeological discoveries of the ancient world in that area. However, it is important to remember that these discoveries are of people who lived after the Flood and after the relocation of the rivers.*

Introducing the Bible Account

Review what God created on days 1–3. Discuss what God made on the first three days of Creation. Attach six sheets of art paper to the board. Draw a picture or choose three volunteers to draw a picture (on three sheets) representing God's creation as you review the first three days. Display the pictures at the front of the classroom during the Bible account. (*Note:* A mural can be made if you want all

the students to participate in drawing Creation pictures.) Ask the students what they think God created on the next three days. *(Many answers are acceptable.)*

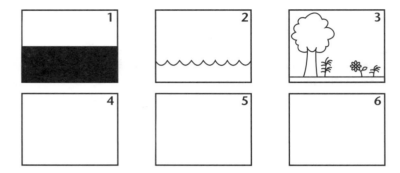

Bible Account

✓ **Read Genesis 1:14–31** or use the following retelling of the passage. You may present the account in your own words to enhance your listeners' comprehension and attentiveness. Asking questions at various points in the account will help the students to understand and apply the truths of God's Word. Listening question: **Why do you think God created man?** *(Answers will vary, but emphasize the fact that God is all-powerful and that He made man in His image to glorify Himself.)* After you read about what God created on day 4, choose several volunteers to draw that creation on the fourth sheet of paper on the board. Follow the same procedure after reading about days 5 and 6.

✓ It Is Perfect!

On the fourth day, God made the sun, moon, and stars in the sky. God made the sun to rule the day and the moon to rule the night. These lights measured days and years and provided light for the earth.

On the fifth day, God made birds, fish, and all sea creatures. He created every living creature that lives in the water. God blessed them and said, "Be fruitful, and multiply, and fill the waters and the seas." He also said that the birds should multiply on the earth.

On the sixth day, God made land animals, man, and woman. God made man from the dust of the ground, and woman from the man's rib.

Human beings are different and finer than any other of God's creatures because they were made in God's image. Humans were created perfect and sinless, enjoying unhindered fellowship with God. Unlike any other creation, people have souls that will live forever. God gave humans rule over all other creation on the earth. God told them that they would rule "over the fish of the sea, and over the fowl of the air, and over the cattle, and over all the earth." God looked over all His creation and saw that "it was very good."

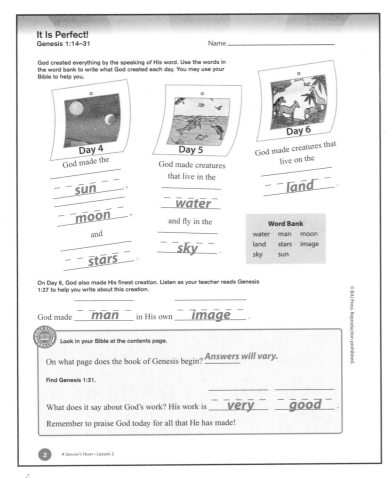

It Is Perfect!
Genesis 1:14–31

Name _____

God created everything by the speaking of His word. Use the words in the word bank to write what God created each day. You may use your Bible to help you.

Day 4
God made the

sun

moon

and

stars

Day 5
God made creatures that live in the

water

and fly in the

sky

Day 6
God made creatures that live on the

land

Word Bank

water	man	moon
land	stars	image
sky	sun	

On Day 6, God also made His finest creation. Listen as your teacher reads Genesis 1:27 to help you write about this creation.

God made _man_ in His own _image_ .

Look in your Bible at the contents page.

On what page does the book of Genesis begin? _Answers will vary._

Find Genesis 1:31.

What does it say about God's work? His work is _very_ _good_ .

Remember to praise God today for all that He has made!

2   A SERVANT'S HEART • Lesson 2

© BJU Press. Reproduction prohibited.

✓ Discussion Questions

You may use the following questions as desired or create original questions to accomplish specific teaching goals and objectives. Questions marked with a pointer are literal questions. Those marked with a light bulb are interpretive, critical, or appreciative in nature.

▸ **What non-living things did God put in His beautiful sky?** *(sun, moon, and stars)*

▸ **Why did God put the lights in the sky?** *(to measure days and years and to provide light and heat for the earth)*

💡 **There was a time when God used a special star to guide some men. Who were these men and where did the star guide them?** *(The wise men were guided to Bethlehem to see God's Son, Jesus.)*

▸ **What did God create to go in the waters?** *(fish and other creatures that live well in water)*

▸ **What living things did God create to go in the sky?** *(birds and other creatures that would live well in the sky)*

▸ **What did God create to live on the land?** *(animals)*

▸ **What was the finest and most amazing of God's creations?** *(humans)*

💡 **Every person has a birthday. Does God have a birthday?** *(No. God has no birthday because He is eternal.)*

▸ **What did God say humans were to rule over?** *(everything on the earth)*

💡 **Who rules over mankind?** *(God)*

💡 **Do you think humans are special to God?** *(yes)*

▸ **How did God make human beings different from all the other creations?** *(He made humans in His own image; people have souls that will live forever.)*

💡 **What does the creation story tell us about God?** *(that God is powerful and eternal)*

✓ 🚀 World History Connection (optional)

Discuss where Christ will reign from. Ask the students where Adam and Eve first lived. *(the Garden of Eden)* They were the only two human beings ever to see it. The only history we know about it is the Bible's description of it before the Flood. Though Genesis tells us where it was located, we can no longer identify that location because the whole topography of the earth was drastically changed during and after the Flood. We have no idea where the Garden of Eden was located in relation to the earth as we now observe it to be.

One thing we do know, however, is where the end of history will be. Display Chart 32, "Ancient Middle East." Point to Jerusalem, the capital of Israel. This area is included in the territory that God promised to Abraham thousands of years ago. Show transparency of page A69 ("Ancient Middle East") and point to Israel.

The nation of Israel is surrounded by countries that were or still are its enemies. Many of these countries have attacked Israel since modern Israel's inception as a nation in 1948. From prophecies in the Bible, we know that in the end times Israel's enemies will strive to destroy Israel so that it no longer exists. Overlay the first transparency with the colored transparency from Activity page A70, "The Middle East Today," indicating Israel's enemy neighbors which have shown hostilities to Israel. Other countries farther away are enemies of Israel as well.

Encourage your students to understand that just as God has controlled the history of the world, He will control the future of the world, securing Israel's continued existence. Though we don't know where history began, we do know where Christ will rule as King of the world in the end, even though that country is now surrounded by His enemies.

Encourage your students to trust their future to the King of heaven and earth, even though they will face discouragement in the future.

✓ ✏️ Worktext page 2

Recall facts and details. Review Creation days 4–6 using the pictures on the page. Direct the students to write what God created each day using the words from the word bank. Read aloud **Genesis 1:27** to help students complete the sentence about God's finest creation.

📖 Bible Study Skills

Teach the skill of using a contents page. Direct the students to find the contents page in their Bibles. Guide them in locating the verse listed at the bottom of page 2 (**Genesis 1:31**). After completing the questions, call on students to tell what they would like to praise God for today.

Memory Verse—Genesis 1:1

Practice the memory verse. Utilize the prepared visuals or consult the list of ideas and methods (page xii) for practicing the memory verses.

LESSON 3 Rest and Praise God!

Materials
- Hymn: "Praise Ye the Lord, the Almighty"
- A copy of page A71 ("God Created! I'm Glad!") for each student (optional)

Introducing the Bible Account

Guide a discussion about rest. Ask individual students to tell why we need to rest. *(Many answers are acceptable.)* Discuss whether you must sleep to rest.

Bible Account

Read Genesis 2:1–3 or use the following retelling of the passage. Listening question: **What did God make on the seventh day?** *(He didn't make anything; He rested.)*

Rest and Praise God!

God was pleased with His work when He was finished. The Bible tells us that God rested on the seventh day. God did not need to rest, but He did. God made a special day for us to stop everyday activities. We go to school for five days. What do you like to do on Saturdays? What do we do on Sundays? *[Accept any answer, but elicit that we go to church.]* We go to church because God wants us to set one day aside for Him. On this day we worship God. Just as God rested, we need a day of rest.

❖

Discussion Questions

▶ **When did God rest?** *(on day 7, when He was finished with Creation)*

💡 **What does it mean to worship God?** *(to show our love and reverence to God through attitude and actions)*

💡 **What are some things we do when we are not resting?** *(Answers will vary.)*

 Memory Verse—Genesis 1:1

Practice the verse. You may utilize the verse visuals, or consult the list of ideas on page xii.

Worktext page 3

Guide the finding of information. Demonstrate how to find in the verses what happened on day 7. Let students work independently to complete each sentence unless help is needed.

Guide an activity to relate Bible knowledge to actions. Show the students how to cross out the letters *d*, *m*,

---

Rest and Praise God!
Genesis 2:1–3

Name _____

Find Genesis 2:1–3 in your Bible. Complete the sentences.

God made everything in __6__ days.

On Day 7 He _ _ _ _ _ _ __rested__ _.

We also should work __6__ days and rest __1__ day.
The day of rest is also a special time to praise God.

To find who should praise God, cross out the letters d, m, and k (Psalm 150:6).

everything that hath breath

Let kmddkeverythingdmkkkthatmkhdk...dkmdbreathkdmmd... praise the Lord!

A Servant's Heart • Lesson 3 ③

---

and *k*. Give help to the students who need it. Discuss how we can praise God. *(by singing, by words of testimony about God's goodness, by talking to Him)*

🎵 Hymn: "Praise Ye the Lord, the Almighty"

Introduce the hymn. Tell the students that the writer of this hymn did not always love the Lord. One night, he and his friends went to a church service to make fun of the people there; instead, he was saved. Joachim Neander ended up writing more than sixty hymns during his lifetime. In this hymn, he paraphrased Psalm 103:1–6 and Psalm 150. You may choose to read these verses to your students.

Teach the first verse (Worktext page 212). Utilize the recording as necessary throughout the unit. Each verse of the hymn is on a separate track of the CD. A list of ideas and methods for practicing the hymn is given on page xii of this manual, with the goal of helping the students to understand the hymn and apply its truths to their lives.

▶ **What is the Lord King of?** *(Creation)*
▶ **What is God to us?** *(our health and salvation)*
▶ **Whose temple are we to draw near to?** *(God's)*
💡 **What is glad adoration?** *(joyful praise)*

✏️ Art Connection (optional)

Guide an activity to relate Bible knowledge to everyday life. Explain the directions for page A71 ("God Created! I'm Glad!"); then let the students work on their

---

pictures. After the drawings are complete, the students can place them on the Unit 1 bulletin board.

4 Sin, Death, and God's Love

Materials
- Hymn: "Praise Ye the Lord, the Almighty"

♥ Memory Verse—Genesis 1:1
Practice the memory verse.

Introducing the Application Story
Guide a discussion about pain, illness, and death. Allow volunteers to tell about times when they have experienced sickness and pain.

CCW - when the fire happened

Application Story

Read or tell the following story. You may tell the story in your own words to enhance your listeners' comprehension and attentiveness. Ask questions at various points in the story to help students understand and apply the concepts presented. Listening question: **Why are sickness, pain, and death in the world now?** *(They are the result of sin.)*

Tell God Your Worries

Matthew sat with his head on his hand, staring at the rocks in his mother's pretty garden. He had helped choose them and paint them and find just the right spots for them among the flowers. He sighed.

"What's that big sigh for?" his mother asked.

"Oh, nothing," he said.

She came down the steps and sat beside him on the grass. "Seemed like a big sigh for nothing, Matt."

He reached out and fingered the soft leaf of a white plant his mother called Lamb's Ear.

"Well," he said at last, "I'm worried about Grandpa."

"I see," said Mom. "Grandpa is very sick. But we'll go see him tonight at the hospital. Maybe you can make him a picture to hang by his bed."

Matthew nodded. "OK." But still he did not smile or look at his mother.

"Look how well these flowers are doing," his mother said. She picked up one and held it to her nose. "Think how wonderful the Garden of Eden must have been."

"That's just it," Matthew said. "Why is there so much pain and suffering? Why do people get sick and hurt so much, and die?"

Mom could see his tears. "It hurts to see Grandpa sick and weak," she said. "It wasn't always like this though. Long ago in the beginning, God made the world perfect. In fact, back then there was no sickness or death at all."

Matthew's forehead wrinkled, and he looked at his mom with wide eyes. "Well what happened that changed all of that?"

"In the Garden of Eden, the Devil lied to Eve and tempted her to disobey God. Satan told her that it would be better for

her if she disobeyed. Then both she and Adam disobeyed God." Mom paused. "The results were horrible."

Sitting up straight now, Matthew wiped away a tear. "Was that when pain and death started?" he asked.

"Yes, it was, Matthew. Adam and Eve knew right away that the results were dreadful. They changed; they were afraid of God, and they hid from Him."

"Did anything else happen?" Matthew asked.

"Yes," said Mom. "Before Adam sinned, God had told him that he would die if he disobeyed God. And ever since he sinned, pain, troubles, sickness, and death have been in the world. Adam's sin also affected the earth. Now there are problems like storms, droughts, floods, and earthquakes."

"Wow," Matthew said. "All of that because of one sin?"

"Yes. Sin is very serious. God sent Adam and Eve out of the Garden of Eden. They could never go back to it. Life became very hard from that point on."

Then Mom's face brightened into a smile. "But God still loved Adam and Eve, just as He loves us with an eternal love. That's why Christ came. He became sin for us, so we can have fellowship with God again—for all eternity. But there will still be sickness, pain, and death as long as we live. There is good news, though. God walks through troubles with people who have trusted Christ as Savior."

Matthew smiled. "Then, even though Grandpa is sick, God is with him, right? God knows all about it and is taking care of Grandpa?"

Mom stroked Matthew's hair. "Yes, Matthew. God cares for Grandpa more than we can imagine, and we can trust Him to do the best thing in Grandpa's life."

"Mom," Matthew asked, "can we pray for Grandpa right now? And then I want to draw a picture of me praying for him, so I can take it to him today."

"That's a wonderful idea, Matthew," Mom said with a smile. "That would remind him that God is taking care of him. Let's pray for Grandpa right now."

Discussion Questions
You may use the following questions as desired or create original questions to accomplish specific teaching goals and objectives. Questions marked with a pointer are literal questions. Those marked with a light bulb are interpretive, critical, or appreciative in nature.

▶ **Why was Matthew so worried?** *(His grandfather was sick.)*

▶ **How did pain, sickness, and death come to the world?** *(through Adam's sin)*

▶ **Did Satan tell Eve the truth?** *(No. Satan is a liar and will always tempt us to sin.)*

▶ **How do we know God loves us?** *(He tells us in the Bible, and He sent Jesus to die in our place.)*

▶ **What did Matthew decide to do?** *(He prayed for his grandpa instead of worrying.)*

💡 **Does God want us to worry?** *(Answers may vary. Elicit that we should pray about everything and trust in God's care as 1 Peter 5:7 instructs us.)*

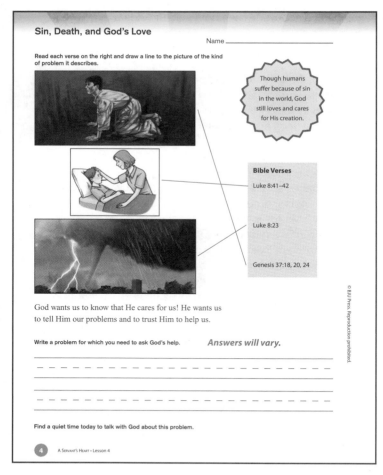

Sin, Death, and God's Love

Name _____

Read each verse on the right and draw a line to the picture of the kind of problem it describes.

Though humans suffer because of sin in the world, God still loves and cares for His creation.

Bible Verses

Luke 8:41–42

Luke 8:23

Genesis 37:18, 20, 24

God wants us to know that He cares for us! He wants us to tell Him our problems and to trust Him to help us.

Write a problem for which you need to ask God's help.   *Answers will vary.*

_____
_____
_____
_____

Find a quiet time today to talk with God about this problem.

4 A SERVANT'S HEART • Lesson 4

💡 **Will God help you with trials and pain?** *(Yes. Explain that we need to do what is right, and God will do what is right. See **Deuteronomy 32:4**.)*

🎵 **Hymn: "Praise Ye the Lord, the Almighty"**
Sing the first verse (Worktext page 212).

📖 **Bible Study Skills**
Review the first five books of the Old Testament. Direct the students to read the names of the first five books of the Old Testament together as they look at the contents page in their Bibles. Practice until they are able to recite them.

✍ **Worktext page 4**
Guide an activity matching verses with accompanying pictures. Read aloud or direct the students to read silently **Luke 8:41–42**. Instruct the students to draw a line from the reference to the corresponding picture. Follow the same procedure with the other references.

Apply Bible knowledge to everyday life. Read the directions and discuss how God wants to help with our problems. Let the students work independently unless help is needed. (*Note:* The ability to write sentences varies with second graders. Encourage each student to do his best even if he can write only a word or two.)

 **Going Beyond**

Reinforcement

Materials
• Verse visuals from Lesson 1

Explain God's power to a friend. Let a volunteer use the verse visuals to explain man's power compared to God's power, as you did in the Lesson 1 activity. Ask the student to explain what the earth was like and how God changed it by creating light on the first day. Repeat with other volunteers.

Enrichment

Materials
• Books with animal pictures

Research and report about unusual characteristics of some of God's creatures. Direct the students to look through some books about animals to find what they consider to be unusual characteristics of some creatures that God created. Encourage the students to record some of them and share them with the class.

God Rules Nature

Unit 1b

PREVIEW

Doctrines

- Man has a will (Genesis 3:6). [Lesson 5]
- Man has a sinful nature (Romans 5:12). [Lesson 5]
- Man lives in a corrupted environment (Romans 8:22). [Lesson 5]
- God has shown Himself in nature (Romans 1:20). [Lesson 6]
- God is love (1 John 4:8). [Lesson 6]

Skills and Applications

- Learn Genesis 6:8, 22
- Follow directions
- Read a map
- Read a timeline
- Locate verses in the first four books of the Old Testament and the first three books of the New Testament
- Organize seven books into belonging to either the Old or New Testament
- Realize that trusting and obeying God will bring joy
- Realize that God hates sin
- Apply Bible knowledge to everyday life

---

5 Safe in the Ark with God

Materials

- Chart 1, "Ark"
- Hymn: "Praise Ye the Lord, the Almighty"
- Unit 1 Bookmark for each student
- Highlighter for each student (optional)
- Picture of a five-story building and a picture of a school bus (optional)
- Transparency of the ark designs on page A72 ("God Designed the Ark") to be used on an overhead projector

Background Information

Dimensions of the Ark—*God gave Noah specific instructions to build the ark. Genesis 6:15 says that the ark was 300 cubits long, 50 cubits wide, and 30 cubits high. Using the standard of a royal cubit (20.4"), Noah's ark measured 510' long, 85' wide, and 51' high. The ark was one and two-thirds times the length of a football field and comparable in height to a five-story building.*

Over the years people who did not believe that the Bible is true thought it would have been impossible for Noah to build such a large ship. However, since God commanded this, we know that He enabled Noah to complete the task. The timing of God's warning about the Flood allowed sufficient time for Noah to build the ark before the rain started. It is possible that Noah employed others to help in the project. Considering these and other facts, we can understand how Noah was able to obey God completely in everything he was commanded to do.

Inside the Ark—*The ark was built with three stories, or floors. Air circulated through the windows at the top of the ark. The Bible does not tell us which floor Noah, his family, and the different animals lived on. It is thought by some that Noah, his family, and small animals lived on the top floor. Middle-sized animals would be kept on the middle floor. The large, heavy animals would then be on the bottom floor.*

Introducing the Bible Account

Introduce the account with the background information. Tell the students that God gave Noah very detailed

---

instructions about building the ark and then recorded them for us in the Bible. Use the background information to discuss further details about the ark.

Bible Account

Read Genesis 6:1–22 or use the following retelling of the passage. Listening question: **When did the following historical event take place?** *(many years after God created Adam and Eve)*

Safe in the Ark with God

Humans were created holy and perfect. They were made in God's image. They had a will and could choose whether or not to sin. Adam and Eve knew that if they sinned, they would die, but they still chose to disobey God. The earth changed; it was cursed because of their sin. With sin came death, disease, and sadness.

Adam and Eve obeyed God's command to multiply on the earth. They had children, and their children had children, and over time there were more and more people on the earth. "God saw that the wickedness of man was great in the earth." He was sorry that He had created humans. "It grieved him at his heart." All people are sinners, and when we do wicked things, it saddens God.

The Lord said, "I will destroy man whom I have created from the face of the earth." God decided to destroy every person and animal that He had created (except those in the ark) because mankind had forgotten about and ignored their Creator. God decided to destroy the entire earth and everything in it with a great flood.

One man, however, "found grace in the eyes of the Lord." God told him to build an ark for his family and two of every kind of animal on earth so that they would survive the flood. *[Display Chart 1, "Ark."]*

God told Noah to build an ark of wood, to make rooms in it, and to cover it with pitch (a sticky kind of coating that keeps water out). God gave Noah specific dimensions for the ark so that Noah would know how big to make it. The ark was very, very big. God said to make a roof and leave space for windows all around under the roof. God told Noah to make a door in the side of the ark and to make three stories (floors) inside the ark. For 120 years, Noah worked on the giant boat, doing "all that God commanded him."

❖

Discussion Questions

💡 **What happened as there were more and more people on the earth?** *(They didn't obey God; they did what they wanted to do and not what God told them to do.)*

💡 **If we do what we want instead of obeying God, what are we doing?** *(We are sinning.)* Discuss with your students that sin is disobeying God's commandments **(1 John 3:4)**.

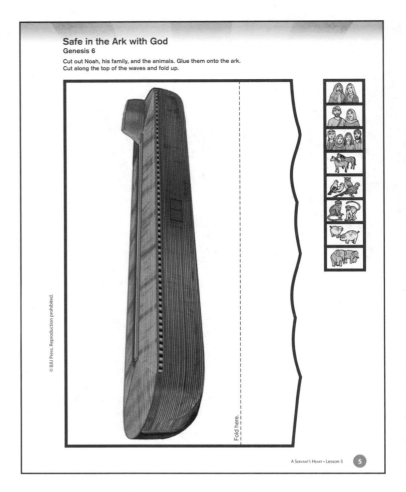

Safe in the Ark with God
Genesis 6
Cut out Noah, his family, and the animals. Glue them onto the ark.
Cut along the top of the waves and fold up.

© BJU Press. Reproduction prohibited.

Fold here.

A Servant's Heart • Lesson 5   5

▶ **How did God feel about the people's evil ways?** *(He felt sorry that He had created humans.)*

▶ **How was Noah different from other people?** *(He found grace in the eyes of God.)*

▶ **What did God tell Noah that He was going to do?** *(destroy all living things except Noah and his family and some of the animals)*

▶ **Did Noah obey God when he built the ark?** *(Yes. He did all that God had said to do.)*

🎵 Hymn: "Praise Ye the Lord, the Almighty"

Sing the first verse (Worktext page 212). Consult the list of ideas and methods for practicing the hymn (page xii) as necessary. Help the students to understand the hymn and apply its truths to their lives.

⊚ Worktext pages 5–6

Display the ark transparency. Display the transparency of the ark as the students look at the ark on page 5. Tell them that the ark was almost as tall as a five-story building and longer than thirteen school buses lined up end to end. If possible, go outside and look at a school bus and look at a five-story building. If this is not possible, use the pictures of the building and the school bus. Refer to the inside of the ark on the transparency to give the students an idea of what the ark was like inside.

Guide an activity for following directions. Explain to the students how to cut out the pictures of Noah, his family,

Safe in the Ark with God (continued)

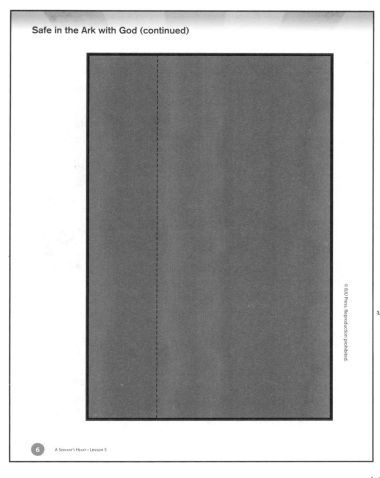

and the animals and to glue them onto the ark. Demonstrate how to cut the waves on the heavy dark line and to fold the waves on the dashed line up onto the ark.

♥ Memory Verses—Genesis 6:8, 22

Principle: God's favor on us should lead us to complete obedience.

Consult the list of ideas and methods (page xii) for practicing the memory verses as necessary. Memorization is an important key to understanding Biblical truths and applying them to our lives. Encourage the students to be able to recite the verses from memory at the end of each subunit.

Assist the students in highlighting verse 8 and marking the location with the Unit 1 Bookmark. Follow the same procedure for verse 22.

Discuss the meanings of the verses, helping the students to understand that grace is God's giving a person something good that the person does not deserve. God enabled Noah to accomplish this task by His grace. It is the same today. A person who is saved can obey God in every area of life only by trusting God's grace for obedience. God strengthens the Christian inside by His Spirit to help him obey and serve Him.

LESSON 6
Atop Mount Ararat

Materials

- TimeLine and picture: Noah
- Hymn: "Praise Ye the Lord, the Almighty"
- Chart 5, "Atop Mount Ararat"

♫ Hymn: "Praise Ye the Lord, the Almighty"

Sing the first verse with open Worktexts (page 212). Discuss how one of the descriptions of God in this hymn ("the King of creation") relates to the Flood. (*He controls all things because He made all things.*)

Background Information

Altar—*The first thing that Noah did after leaving the ark was to build an altar to thank God for sparing him and his family from destruction (**Genesis 8:20**). This is the first mention of altars in the Bible. People built altars for various reasons. Sometimes a person wanted to give thanks to God as Noah did. Other times people built altars to make a sacrifice for sin. Their sacrifice of blood on the altar asked for forgiveness. Sometimes people built altars to reaffirm their trust in God. Christians have the same needs today. We should thank God for His mercy, seek His forgiveness when we have sinned, and sometimes just express our love for Him.*

The Great Flood—*Adam knew that sin would lead to death. When he sinned, he suffered separation from God, the essence of spiritual death. Adam also began to die physically. Noah and his family survived the Flood because they were in the ark. God sent the terrible Flood to judge man's sin while saving Noah so that he could be a testimony to God's grace and repopulate the earth. If you have trusted Christ as your Savior, God wants you to be a testimony of His grace and to tell others how they can be saved from the punishment of their sin.*

The Landing of the Ark—*The Bible tells us that the ark stopped drifting and landed "upon the mountains of Ararat." Some mountains that are today called Ararat are located near the border of Iran and Turkey. Some people claim to have seen a ship or giant house lying in the ravines of Mount Ararat in Turkey. Over the years Bible scholars have explored this area trying to find the ark. Some scholars believe the ark no longer exists; others believe it is still in the mountains. We do not need evidence of the ark to believe the Bible account. Even if we never see it, we should tell others about God's great provision that saved Noah and his family from the worldwide judgment.*

Introducing the Bible Account

Guide a review about Noah building the ark. Ask the students to comment on the ark. *(Possible comments include that it was five stories tall, had windows and a door, and took 120 years to build, etc.)* Remind the students that Noah built the ark because God wanted to save him, his family, and some of the animals. Noah and his family were the only people who trusted God for safety.

Bible Account

Read Genesis 7:1–9:17 or use the following retelling of the passage. Listening question: **In what ways does God rule nature?** (*God sends or withholds the rain, the storms, and all*

other weather.) Direct the students to look at Worktext page 7 as they listen to the Bible account.

InfoScene: "Atop Mount Ararat"
Display Chart 5 from the Visual Packet for the students to refer to throughout this unit.

Atop Mount Ararat

After 120 years, Noah and his family had finished building the ark exactly as God commanded. Then it was time to put the animals into the ark.

Certain animals were to be used for sacrifices; God told Noah to take seven of each of these animals. Noah also took two of each of the animals not used for sacrifice—one male and one female.

After all the animals were inside, Noah, his wife, his sons, and his daughters-in-law entered the ark. When everyone was inside, God shut the door of the ark. Seven days later, "the waters of the flood were upon the earth."

This was the first rain on the earth. For forty days and forty nights it rained. The water level increased, and floated the ark above the surface of the earth. The water rose until it covered the mountains. Everything outside the ark died. The floodwaters lasted for 150 days. Then God sent a wind to decrease the water on the earth. The ark stopped drifting and rested on some mountains. About three months after the ark stopped drifting, the tops of the mountains could be seen. Forty days later, Noah opened the window in the ark and sent out a raven and a dove. The dove found no place to land, so it returned to the ark. After a week, Noah sent it out again and it came back with an olive leaf in its mouth. Another week later, Noah sent the dove a third time, and it did not come back. Noah knew that the earth was dry enough now. Noah removed the covering of the ark and saw the dry ground; then God told Noah to take his family and the animals out of the ark.

Discussion Questions

▶ **How long did it take Noah to build the ark?** *(120 years)*

▶ **When the ark was completed, what did Noah and his family do?** *(They put the creatures in the ark, and they went in also.)*

💡 **Where did the water that God sent come from?** *(above and below)*

How do you think Noah's family felt when they heard the rain stop? *(Several answers are acceptable, such as excited and curious.)*

▶ **What was the first thing Noah and his family did when they were out of the ark and on dry land?** *(They built an altar and sacrificed to God to show their gratitude.)*

💡 **What should you thank God for today?** *(Answers will vary.)*

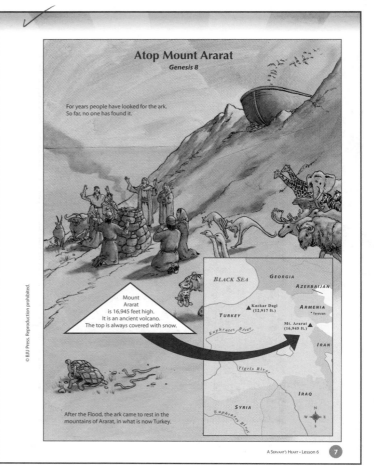

Atop Mount Ararat
Genesis 8

For years people have looked for the ark. So far, no one has found it.

© BJU Press. Reproduction prohibited.

Mount Ararat is 16,945 feet high. It is an ancient volcano. The top is always covered with snow.

BLACK SEA · GEORGIA · AZERBAIJAN · ARMENIA · *Yerevan* · TURKEY · Kackar Dagi (12,917 ft.) · Mt. Ararat (16,945 ft.) · IRAN · *Euphrates River* · *Tigris River* · IRAQ · SYRIA · *Euphrates River*

After the Flood, the ark came to rest in the mountains of Ararat, in what is now Turkey.

A Servant's Heart • Lesson 6   **7**

⏱ TimeLine
Add Noah to the TimeLine. Place the picture of Noah on the TimeLine (died ca. 2500 BC), pointing out the time that passed from day 1 of Creation until the approximate time of Noah's death. Guide the students as they glue their pictures of Noah from the Student Materials section of the ToolKit CD onto their TimeLines.

♥ Memory Verses—Genesis 6:8, 22
Practice the verses.

✏ World History Connection (optional)
Discuss the area shown by the map on Worktext page 7. You may share any of the following information about the Kurds and the Armenians.

Kurdistan—Kurdistan is an area located in the mountains of northern Iraq, northeastern Syria, eastern Turkey, and northwestern Iran. The Kurds have lived in this mountainous region for at least four thousand years. The Kurds have been fighting for freedom for a long time, but their only autonomous political entity is one province in Iraq.

Armenia—The Armenians have a unique language with its own alphabet, which they invented around AD 400. Even before that, Armenia was the first nation in the world to call itself officially a Christian nation (around AD 300). Armenia's mountainous terrain provided protection from the Greek, Persian, and Roman Empires. Although it used to be a republic in the Soviet Union, Armenia is now an independent country.

Armenian saw ark 1900 & 1905. climbed on it. & noahsark.it

Discuss the landing of the ark. Display Chart 31, "World Map," or a globe. Point out on the map where the students live, and then point out the locations of Iran, Armenia, and Turkey. Discuss further details about the landing of the ark using the background information. Explain the map on Worktext page 7.

LESSON 7 — God Blesses Trust

Materials
- Hymn: "Praise Ye the Lord, the Almighty"
- A toy boat

🎵 Hymn: "Praise Ye the Lord, the Almighty"

Teach the second verse (Worktext page 212). Consult the list of ideas and methods for practicing the hymn (page xii) as necessary. Help the students to understand the hymn and apply its truths to their lives.

Write the following phrases and sentences for display and explain them: "shelters thee under His wings," "gently sustaineth," and "Hast thou not seen / How thy desires e'er have been / Granted in what He ordaineth?" Explain the last words in each phrase: *reigneth, sustaineth, ordaineth*. Direct the students to sing through the second verse with the recording, asking them to stand as they hear or sing the phrases written for display.

Introducing the Application Story

Guide a discussion about trust. Noah trusted in God, and he therefore obeyed God. Noah had to obey God in order to build the ark correctly, which allowed him and his family to be completely safe inside the ark. God was their only security. When it started to rain, they had only God to trust. God kept them in that ark to save them, and they had to believe Him.

💡 **Is there anyone you really trust?** *God, family*
(*Call on volunteers to share names of people they trust [depend on, believe in].*)

💡 **Do you obey the people you trust?** (*Accept any answer. Remind them that Noah trusted and obeyed God.*)

Display the toy boat.

▶ **Have any of you ever been in a rowboat?** (*Allow students to describe what it was like to row it.*)

Application Story

Read or tell the following story. You may tell the story in your own words to enhance your listeners' comprehension and attentiveness. Ask questions at various points in the story to help students understand and apply the concepts presented. Listening question: **Whose instructions does Jonathan have to trust and obey?** (*Grandpa's*)

Jonathan Turns Around

Jonathan tightened his life jacket and sat down on the cold aluminum seat in Grandpa's boat. His insides felt cold too—an excited kind of cold.

Grandpa sat on the dock, untangling a fishing line. "Your dad caught his first bass when he was about your age," he said, "right here in this very lake."

Jonathan leaned forward. Grandpa worked the thin, silky-looking line with rough fingers.

"I've never even been in a boat before," he said. "Is the lake very deep?"

Grandpa gazed out over the water. "Maybe twenty-five feet at the deepest spot," he said. "No need to worry. Your life jacket will keep your head high and dry even if you fall out. And I'm not planning on flipping the boat," Grandpa said with a wink.

Jonathan scooted to the back seat as Grandpa climbed into the middle seat, where the oars were. "Whoa, wait a minute," Grandpa said. "I left my favorite fishing lure in the truck. Hold her steady, Jonathan. I'll be right back."

As soon as Grandpa stepped out, Jonathan felt the boat move slightly from its resting spot on the bank. Before he realized what was happening, the boat had drifted a few feet off shore.

Jonathan had seen Grandpa use the oars before. All he had to do was push the oars through the water a few times, and he could move the boat right back up beside the dock again. He climbed into the middle seat.

Jonathan grunted as he picked up the oars. They were heavier than he expected. They splashed as he let them down into the water. He leaned back and tugged, as he had seen Grandpa do. The boat was moving! He lifted the oars again, dropped them into the water and leaned back, and pulled.

Then he realized he wasn't getting closer to the dock. He was getting farther away. "Grandpa!" he called.

Maybe he wasn't rowing fast enough. He strained harder at the oars.

Grandpa turned around from the truck.

Jonathan!" he shouted. "Where do you think you're going? Bring the boat back in!"

Jonathan's voice shook as he called back. "I'm trying! The boat's going the wrong way!" Another pull with the oars carried him even farther from the dock. "I'm rowing as hard as I can!"

He put the oars down and tried to stand up. The little boat rocked wildly from side to side. Jonathan dropped down again and gripped the sides of the seat. The ripples in the water made small slapping sounds against the boat.

"Help!" he called in a weak voice. His throat felt tight. He bit his lips to keep back a sob.

"Okay, Jon, listen to me." Grandpa stood at the end of the dock, his voice steady and calm. "I'll tell you what to do. Just listen—and do what I say, all right?"

Jonathan nodded.

"You need to turn the boat around. Pick up the left oar. Just the left one."

Jonathan had to think for a moment about which one was on the left. He picked it up.

"Okay, easy does it. Start rowing with just that one. Leave the right one alone."

Jonathan obeyed. His eyes grew wide as he saw that the boat was turning, slowly, in a circle. Soon he was facing the opposite shore, with his back to Grandpa.

"Okay," Grandpa's voice said. "Pick up the other one, and row with both of them."

"But I'm headed the wrong way!"

"Trust me. Both oars, now."

Jonathan placed both oars in the water and pulled gently at first. The boat moved backward! He took a bigger stroke with the oars.

"You're doing great." Grandpa's quiet voice came from behind him. "Nice and straight. Keep it coming."

Three more strokes and he was there. "See, Son. You did it. You need to keep your back to the point where you want to end up. It may seem like you're all turned around, but you must trust the fact that if you row the right way, you'll end up in the right place." Grandpa gave him a big hug.

"You know, Jon, that's a lot like what the Bible says about life. We need to trust God's Word like you trusted me when I told you how to row. The Bible always directs us right. We just need to trust and obey."

"You sure were a big help, Grandpa," said Jonathan. "I was afraid and didn't know what to do."

"I'll tell you what," Grandpa said. "Sit right back down there. Anybody who obeys as well as you do can learn how to handle this boat in no time!"

❦

Discussion Questions

Why do you think Jonathan was excited to be going fishing with Grandpa? (*Many responses are acceptable such as he wanted to catch a fish, or he wanted to spend time with Grandpa.*)

How did the author let you know Jonathan's emotions? (*"His insides felt cold—an excited kind of cold."*)

What happened that caused Jonathan's trouble? (*The boat moved when Grandpa stepped out, and Jonathan started experimenting with the oars.*)

How did Jonathan get out of trouble? (*He did just what Grandpa said to do.*)

Do you think that if you obeyed God all the time, you would not have problems? (*Answers may vary, but explain that difficulties will always be part of life even when we obey. But we will not get ourselves into sinful problems.*)

♥ Memory Verses—Genesis 6:8, 22
Practice the verses.

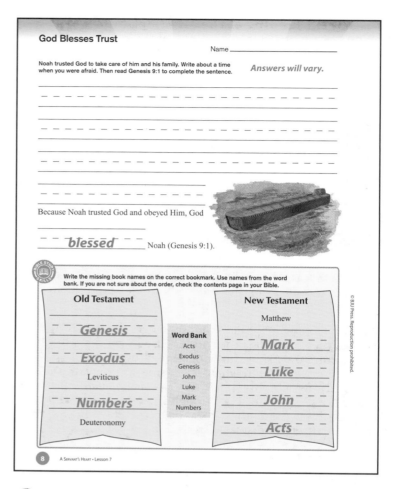

✏ Worktext page 8

Guide a discussion about fear. Share with the class a time when you were afraid. Allow the students to share some experiences they may have had while being afraid. Tell them to write about one experience. (*Note:* The ability to write sentences varies with second graders. Encourage each student to do his best even if he can write only a word or two.)

📖 Bible Study Skills

Teach the skill of using the contents page. Open your Bible to the contents page, and show the students both the Old and New Testament starting places. Direct the students to open their Bibles to the contents page, and follow along as you read the names of the first five books of each testament. Review how to use the contents page to find the locations of the books. Guide the students to write the book names on the bookmarks on Worktext page 8.

LESSON 8 Noah's Faith—God's Promise

Materials

- Hymn: "Praise Ye the Lord, the Almighty"
- Copy of page A73 ("God Is in Control") for each student (optional)

♥ Memory Verses—Genesis 6:8, 22
Review the verses.

Noah's Faith—God's Promise
Genesis 6–8

Name _____

> a. God
> b. Noah
> c. Noah's sons
> d. The ark
> e. The people of the earth
>
> f. The animals
> g. The rainbow
> h. A mountain
> i. An altar
> j. Rain

Complete each sentence by writing in the blank the letter of the correct answer from the rainbow.

1. __b__ did exactly what God said to do.
2. __c__ and their wives also went into the ark.
3. __g__ showed God's promise of hope.
4. __a__ told Noah how to keep himself and his family safe.
5. __i__ was built by Noah to praise God after the Flood.
6. __d__ was a home for Noah's family until the waters went down.
7. __e__ became very wicked.
8. __j__ fell on the earth for forty days and nights.
9. __f__ were gathered by Noah and his family into the ark.
10. __h__ was where the ark came to rest.

A Servant's Heart • Lesson 8 9

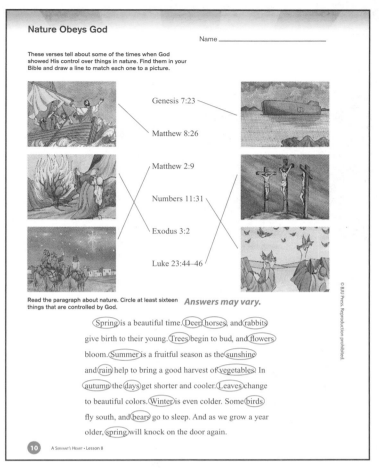

Nature Obeys God

Name _____

These verses tell about some of the times when God showed His control over things in nature. Find them in your Bible and draw a line to match each one to a picture.

Genesis 7:23
Matthew 8:26
Matthew 2:9
Numbers 11:31
Exodus 3:2
Luke 23:44–46

Read the paragraph about nature. Circle at least sixteen things that are controlled by God.   *Answers may vary.*

Spring is a beautiful time. Deer, horses, and rabbits give birth to their young. Trees begin to bud, and flowers bloom. Summer is a fruitful season as the sunshine and rain help to bring a good harvest of vegetables. In autumn the days get shorter and cooler. Leaves change to beautiful colors. Winter is even colder. Some birds fly south, and bears go to sleep. And as we grow a year older, spring will knock on the door again.

10 A Servant's Heart • Lesson 8

Worktext page 9
Recall facts and details. Direct the students' attention to page 9 as you read aloud the words in the rainbow. Direct the students to complete the sentences by writing the letter of the correct answer on the lines.

Worktext page 10
Locate information in the Bible. Direct the students to look up each reference in their Bibles and to match it to the correct picture. If this section cannot be done as an independent activity, choose six volunteers to look up and read aloud the Bible verses as the students match the reference to the correct picture.

Circle elements of nature that God controls. Read the story at the bottom of the page to the students. Then explain that they are to circle things in nature that God controls.

Hymn: "Praise Ye the Lord, the Almighty"
Sing verses one and two of the hymn (Worktext page 212).

Art Connection (optional)
Guide a drawing activity. Ask the students to name some things in nature that God controls. (*rain, wind, earthquakes, volcano eruptions, tornados, etc.*) Remind them that they do not need to worry during storms. Ask the students to look at page A73 ("God Is in Control") and draw something in nature

that God controls. After the drawings are complete, allow the students to place them on the Unit 1 bulletin board.

▶ Going Beyond

Reinforcement
Guide a writing activity. Ask the students to write in their own words the meaning of **Genesis 6:8** and **Genesis 6:22** or ask them to make a list of things they learned from the account of the Flood.

Enrichment
Apply Bible knowledge to everyday life. Review the story of Noah. Mention the following ways Noah was an example of trusting God and doing right. Read aloud the New Testament verse for each.
- The wickedness of the people was throughout the earth, but Noah loved and worshiped God (**1 John 2:15**).
- Noah obeyed God and built an ark (**Acts 5:29**).
- Noah believed God and took his family and the animals into the ark (**Mark 11:22**).
- Noah waited for the water to go down so they could leave the ark (**Romans 8:25**).
- Noah thanked God for His protection (**Ephesians 5:20**).

Ask students how they can follow Noah's example of trusting God and doing what's right. (*Many answers are acceptable.*)

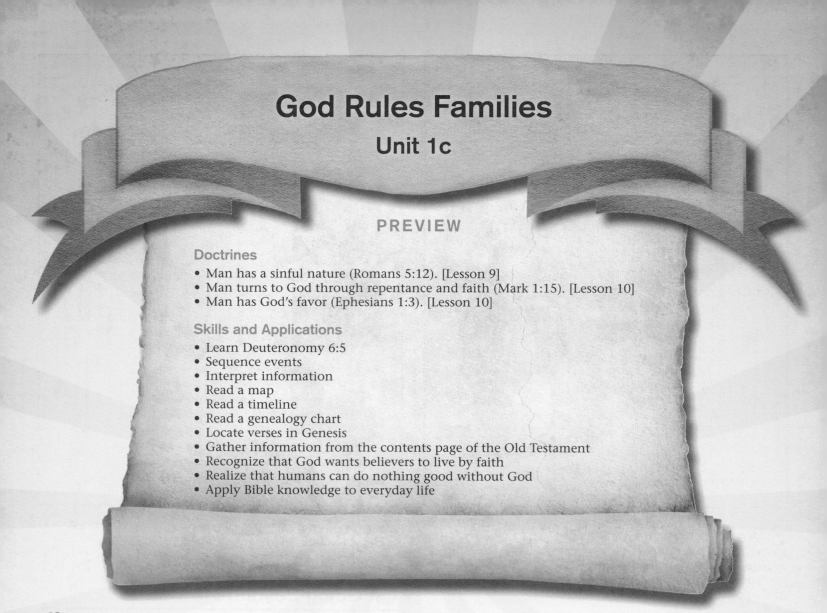

God Rules Families
Unit 1c

Doctrines

- Man has a sinful nature (Romans 5:12). [Lesson 9]
- Man turns to God through repentance and faith (Mark 1:15). [Lesson 10]
- Man has God's favor (Ephesians 1:3). [Lesson 10]

Skills and Applications

- Learn Deuteronomy 6:5
- Sequence events
- Interpret information
- Read a map
- Read a timeline
- Read a genealogy chart
- Locate verses in Genesis
- Gather information from the contents page of the Old Testament
- Recognize that God wants believers to live by faith
- Realize that humans can do nothing good without God
- Apply Bible knowledge to everyday life

LESSON 9 — The Tower of Babel Fails

Materials

- Chart 32, "Ancient Middle East"
- Unit 1 Bookmark for each student
- Highlighter for each student (optional)

Background Information

Ziggurat—*The tower of Babel probably was a ziggurat, a type of building common in Babylon at that time. People gathered at the ziggurat for religious ceremonies and worship of false gods. Most ziggurats were four to seven stories high. Each successive story was smaller than the one below it and made the ziggurat look like a set of giant steps. Some had ramps or stairs that wound around the tower leading to the top. Ziggurats were constructed of mud and straw or clay, and each level usually was painted a different color. Archaeologists have uncovered ruins of over two dozen ziggurats in ancient Babylon.*

The Tower of Babel—*Noah's descendants all spoke one language (**Genesis 11:1**). They journeyed southeast from Mount Ararat to settle in the plains of Shinar or what came to be called Babylon (between the Tigris and the Euphrates rivers). They developed a civilization and started to build a city and tower that would reach "unto heaven" (**Genesis 11:4**). Their pride ("make us a name") and their rebellion ("lest we be scattered") showed that they did not fear God. To prevent further rebellion, God confused their languages: thus the name* Babel (**Genesis 11:9**). *As a result, the nations with their different languages moved and settled in different places throughout the world.*

Introducing the Bible Account

Guide a discussion. Tell your students to look at the picture on Worktext page 11. Explain that this is similar to what the tower of Babel might have looked like. Use the background information and Chart 32, "Ancient Middle East," to show the students where the tower of Babel is thought to have been located. Then explain to them that towers built by ancient Babylonians were called *ziggurats*. The tower of Babel is thought to have been a ziggurat-type structure. Each level of a ziggurat was usually a different color. Tell the students that they will work with Worktext page 11 after the Bible account.

Bible Account

Read Genesis 11:1–9 or use the following retelling of the passage. Listening question: **What displeased God?** *(God was displeased because the people were trying to be as powerful as God.)*

The Tower of Babel Fails

After the Flood, Noah's sons and daughters-in-law had children, and their children had children, and those children had children, and so on. The number of families grew and moved apart, but they still spoke the same language.

After Noah and his sons died, people continued to rebel against God. People began to do that which they, and not God, thought was right.

The more that sin ruled the earth, the more people began to be very proud; and the prouder they became, the more they thought they could rule themselves. One day, someone suggested that they build a tower that would reach to heaven and make a name for themselves.

People came from near and far to help with the project. They began to work on the tower, and they worked very hard. The tower got taller and taller. We do not know how long God let this go on. But we do know that God was displeased with the people.

God decided to "confound" their languages, to make them have many different languages. All at once, there was so much confusion when they talked that the people became discouraged and stopped working.

God knew they would never reach heaven, and He also knew their hearts. He knew that their reason for wanting to build was selfish. They wanted to display their own power rather than God's. But God is the only Creator and the only all-powerful being. God is the One in authority over all. He directs the events in our lives although we may choose to go our own way or God's way. These people tried to be like God rather than letting Him control them.

Discussion Questions

▶ **Why did the people want to build a tower?** *(to reach heaven)*

💡 **Could they have ever reached heaven?** *(No. They understood their limitations, but they did want to build something very high that they could be proud of.)*

▶ **How do we know that their desire to make a name for themselves was wrong?** *(God kept them from succeeding in their building project by confounding their languages and dividing them.)*

Give the background information about the meaning of the word *babel*.

▶ **How did God bring an end to the building of the tower?** *(He confused the people's language so that they could not understand one another.)*

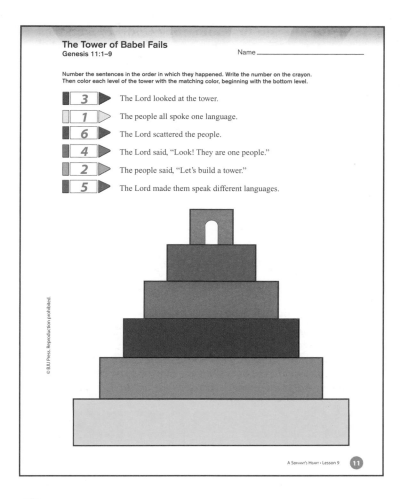

🖊 Worktext page 11

Teach the skill of finding information. Direct the students to find Genesis 11 in their Bibles. Explain the directions on Worktext page 11. Read **Genesis 11:1–9** to the students as they read the verses silently; then ask the students what happened first. *(The people all spoke one language.)* Direct them to color the bottom level of the tower *yellow*. Provide help as needed.

♥ Memory Verse—Deuteronomy 6:5

Principle: God wants each person to love Him with his whole heart.

Tell the students that Moses wrote Deuteronomy to remind the Israelites, God's chosen people, about the laws of God. Assist the students in highlighting the verse (optional) and marking the location with the Unit 1 Bookmark.

Practice the memory verse. Consult the list of ideas and methods (page xii) for practicing the memory verses as necessary. Memorization is an important key to understanding biblical truths and applying them to our lives. Encourage the students to be able to recite the verses from memory at the end of each subunit.

Discussion Questions

💡 **What is another way of saying how much we should love God?** *(Answers will vary. We should love God with our whole being—all that we are and have.)*

Why should you love and obey God? *(He created me. He commands me to love Him, and He is worthy of my whole life.)*

LESSON

10 God Chooses Abram

Materials

- TimeLine and picture: Abram
- Chart 32, "Ancient Middle East"
- Hymn: "Praise Ye the Lord, the Almighty"
- A sheet of sturdy paper for each student (light construction paper or copier paper)
- A container of sand or sugar

Memory Verse—Deuteronomy 6:5

Review the memory verse.

Background Information

Ur—*The city of Ur was located on the banks of the Euphrates River in the land of Sumer. Abram lived in Ur until God told him to leave and go to Canaan. He took his wife Sarai, his father Terah, and his nephew Lot with him. On the way, they stayed in Haran for a short time, where Abram's father died. Then Abram, Sarai, and Lot moved to Canaan.*

Canaan—*This land was between the Jordan River and the Mediterranean Sea. Canaan comes from an old word meaning "belonging to the red-purple." Canaanite or Phoenician merchants traded a red-purple dye made from the murex shells found along the Mediterranean coast. The name* Palestine *comes from a late Greek term for Philistine, after the people who lived along the southwestern coast of Canaan.*

Egypt—*When a famine came to Canaan, Abram moved still farther south to Egypt, which is located in northern Africa. Abram must have seen the pyramids when he went into Egypt. They had been built hundreds of years before Abram's visit. The great Pyramid of Khufu, one of the seven wonders of the ancient world, is the largest pyramid. Each block of the pyramid weighs about two and one-half tons. There are more than two million blocks in it. The pyramids were built to show the glory of the kings who built them. The pharaoh's mummified body was placed in his pyramid after he died.*

Introducing the Bible Account

Introduce the geography of Abram's travels. Use Chart 32, "Ancient Middle East," and the map on Worktext page 12 to show the students Abram's travels. Trace with your finger the path beginning in Ur and going to Haran, to Canaan, and then to Egypt.

Introduce God's blessing on Abram. Gather the students around the container of sand or sugar. Pour some sand or sugar out across a flat surface and let two volunteers begin counting the grains. After a few minutes, ask how many grains they have counted. Tell them that all the grains of sand on a beach would be too numerous to count. Explain that in the Bible account, God promises one man, Abram, that he will have a big family. God describes Abram's large family as the dust of the earth. Later God describes it as hav-ing more family members than the number of stars in the sky or grains of sand on the seashore.

Bible Account

Read Genesis 12:1–13:18 or use the following retelling of the passage. Listening question: **Who was the ruler or leader in Abram's family?** *(God)* Remind students of the title of Unit 1c—God Rules Families.

God Chooses Abram

A long time after the people of the earth tried to build a tower to heaven, there was a man named Abram living in the land of Ur. One day God spoke to Abram, telling him to leave his home and go to a land that He, God, would show him. God also said that He would make a great nation from Abram's son, grandsons, great-grandsons, and so on.

God told Abram something else too: He said that He would bless the people who blessed Abram's family and curse the people who cursed Abram's family. But the best promise God gave Abram was that through Abram's family all the nations of the earth would be blessed.

Abram did not understand all this, but he knew it was God Who had said it, so he did as God instructed him. Abram took his wife, his father, his nephew Lot, his workers, and all his possessions and moved. He did not know where God was taking him, but he trusted in God.

After Abram reached Canaan, God said that He would give this great land to Abram's family. So Abram built an altar to the Lord on a mountain near Bethel, and he worshiped God there with those who traveled with him.

However, when a famine came to Canaan, Abram moved everybody to Egypt. There Abram lied about his wife because he was not trusting God for protection. God used the pagan king there to rebuke him, and then Abram moved his family back to Canaan, the land God had promised him.

Lot, Abram's nephew, was still with Abram, and the two men had become very rich in cattle and also in gold and silver. When their herdsmen (those taking care of the cattle) began arguing about pasture land, Abram suggested that he and Lot separate.

Abram let Lot choose where he wanted to go, and Lot chose Jordan, which had rich soil but was also home to some evil people. Lot pitched his tent not far from Sodom, a very wicked city.

One day God told Abram to look in all directions, and that He would give Abram all the land within sight.

God also said that Abram would be the patriarch of a great family with as many members as the dust of the earth. Abram's descendants would face battles to keep this land, but God would be faithful to His promise to Abram, so that the land would be theirs in the end.

God Chooses Abram
Genesis 12–15

Name _____

Follow the directions to complete the map.

Find **Ur.** Draw and color a purple to show where Abram lived with his family.
Find **Haran.** Draw and color a red to show where Abram moved with his family.
Find **Canaan.** Draw and color a blue to show where God told Abram to go.
Find **Egypt.** Draw and color a green to show where Abram went to escape the famine in Canaan. After the famine, God brought Abram back to Canaan.

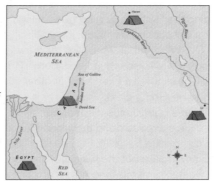

Abram pleased God by obeying and going where God told him to go. As Abram stood in the land of Canaan, God told him to look north, south, east, and west. God promised to give Abram and his family who came after him all the land that he could see. God promised him a large family. God described the size of Abram's family as the dust of the earth. Later God described it as the number of stars in the sky and sand on the seashore.

In this space draw and color a picture of the seashore or the night sky.

As you draw, think of the way God kept His promise to Abram and of how He still keeps His promises to His people. You can trust His promises too!

(12) A SERVANT'S HEART • Lesson 10

Discussion Questions

💡 **Did Abram deserve God's blessing?** *(No, nobody deserves to receive God's goodness. God is good to us because He loves us.)*

▶ **Where did God tell Abram to go when He told him to leave Ur?** *(God did not say where; He said that He would guide Abram as he went.)*

▶ **What did Abram do when he settled in Bethel of Canaan?** *(He built an altar and called upon God.)*

💡 **Why do you think God was pleased every time Abram built an altar and called upon Him?** *(God is pleased when people love Him, call upon Him, and spend time with Him.)*

▶ **Who was Lot?** *(Lot was Abram's nephew.)*

▶ **Why did Lot and Abram separate?** *(There was not enough land for everybody living with them and all their cattle.)*

▶ **What did God tell Abram about the land of Canaan?** *(that God was going to give it to Abram and his family)*

💡 **Can you think of someone in your family who encourages you to follow God and do right?** *(Answers will vary, but remind the students to be thankful for family members who love God, such as siblings, parents, grandparents, aunts, and great-grandparents.)*

💡 **Will you be saved because your parents have faith in God?** *(No. Each person must repent and be saved through faith.)*

Worktext page 12

Guide a map reading activity. Direct the students' attention to the map on page 12. Help the students locate the listed cities and draw the correct colored tent.

Read God's promise to Abram. Tell the students to draw and color a picture of the seashore or the night sky.

🎵 Hymn: "Praise Ye the Lord, the Almighty"

Sing the third verse (Worktext page 212). Consult the list of ideas and methods for practicing the hymn (page xii) as necessary. Help the students to understand the hymn and apply its truths to their lives.

🕐 TimeLine

Add Abram to the TimeLine. Choose a student to place the picture of Abram on the TimeLine (2165 BC), pointing out that more than three hundred fifty years passed from Noah's time to Abram's time. Guide the students as they glue their pictures of Abram (from the Student Materials section of the CD ToolKit) onto their TimeLines.

LESSON
11 Trust Obeys and Waits

Materials
- Hymn: "Praise Ye the Lord, the Almighty"
- Transparent tape for each student
- Copy of page A74 ("God Rules Families") for each student (optional)

🎵 Hymn: "Praise Ye the Lord, the Almighty"

Sing the third verse (Worktext page 212). Consult the list of ideas and methods for practicing the hymn (page xii) as necessary. Help the students to understand the hymn and apply its truths to their lives.

❤ Memory Verse — Deuteronomy 6:5

Practice the verse. Use the paper visual that was made in Lesson 2 to study the verse.

Introducing the Application Story

Guide a discussion about growing plants. Ask the students whether they have ever grown a plant from a seed. Let them share some of their experiences.

Application Story

Read or tell the following story. Listening question: **Who is responsible for making things grow?** *(God)*

Emily Tries Too Hard

Emily and Anna carried their paper cups outside to the back porch. Emily stared down into hers. "It looks like just a bunch of dirt," she said.

"I know, but remember what the Sunday school teacher said. The seeds are planted in there, and all we have to do is water them and wait for them to start growing."

Anna placed her cup on the rail of the porch.

Emily frowned. "Are you going to leave yours there? I would rather keep mine in my room."

"But it needs sunlight," said Anna. "That's what Mrs. Andrews said."

Emily sighed and placed her cup beside Anna's.

The next morning Emily rushed out to the porch to look in her cup. "Still just a bunch of dirt," she said. She looked in Anna's cup. "Same thing."

Then she remembered. Water! That's what Mrs. Andrews had said. She ran to the kitchen, got Mom's water bucket, and filled it to the top. She carefully poured a little water into the cup and watched it sink into the dirt. She poured a little more. Then a little more. Still nothing. "If only a little green shoot or something would pop out," she said.

Anna came up behind her. "Emily, stop pouring water in there!"

Anna put her hand over the top of the cup, turned it upside down, and let the extra water drip out through her fingers. "There," she said. "Emily, you can't make it grow faster by watering it more."

That afternoon the sun warmed the porch, and Emily sat in the big swing, swaying back and forth. She squinted her eyes and looked at the paper cups. What if they were getting too much sun? "I know how to solve that," she said.

Anna walked out onto the porch a few minutes later. "Emily, what are you doing up there?" she asked.

Emily looked down at Anna from her perch on the porch rail. "I'm trying to hang this blanket from those hooks," she said, pointing to the porch roof. "I thought our plants needed some shade."

She reached her arms up again. Suddenly she teetered, and her foot slipped off the rail. "Help!" But it was too late. Emily crashed into the bushes below.

She groaned and tried to sit up. All around her, leaves and twigs scratched her face and arms. The blanket was caught around her head, so she couldn't even see her way out of the bush.

Then she felt arms lifting her. She heard Mom's voice. "Come inside, Emily."

Emily wiped tears away while Mom put lotion on her scratches. "You know what I've told you girls about climbing on that porch rail," Mom said.

"I know." Then Emily told Mom the whole story about Mrs. Andrews and the plant that wouldn't grow.

"I just wanted to make the plant grow, Mom," she said.

Mom put the lotion bottle down and looked straight into Emily's eyes. "Emily, you can't make the plant grow," she said. "Only God can do that."

"But Mrs. Andrews said I should water it and give it sunlight."

"That's right," said Mom. "But God is the only One Who can take a seed and make new life—a green, growing thing—come out of it. You can try as hard as you want, but God has to do that part of the work."

Emily rubbed a sore spot on her elbow. "It hurts to try so hard."

Mom smiled. "It's the same with people," she said. "We can try to make our lives new and good by going to church and reading the Bible and doing good things. But if we think those things will change us inside, we'll fail."

"Oh, I remember what Mrs. Andrews said in Sunday school. It's just like when I was born in the hospital. I need to trust Christ now so I can have another kind of birth—a spiritual birth to be God's child."

"That's right. Jesus died for our sins and rose from the dead. He's already done the work. He's the only One Who can give us new life."

Emily looked out the window. She thought about the last few weeks, remembering how many times she had tried to obey, how many times she had tried not to sin, and how many times she had tried to be kind. But no matter how good she tried to be, she knew she couldn't change herself. Then her mother's words came back to her: "You must repent of trusting in anything but Jesus to save you, and you must put your trust in Christ alone. Only the blood of Christ can save you and give you a new birth." Emily bowed her head and prayed, putting her trust in Jesus.

Just a couple of days later, Anna rushed into the house yelling, "Emily, hurry! Come out to the porch!" They ran outside, and Emily looked into her cup. And there it was, a tiny green sprout poking up out of the dirt. Emily was so excited. "I can hardly wait for Sunday school!" she said.

That week in Sunday school, she showed the other children her new plant and told how she had tried to make it grow, and how that didn't work—just like when she tried to change herself. Then with a big smile, she announced that she had put her trust in Christ alone for salvation.

Discussion Questions

▶ **Who could make Emily's plant grow?** (*God*)

▶ **What did Emily do to try to make her plant grow?** (*She drowned it with water and tried to shade it with a blanket.*)

 What happened when Emily waited for God to make the plant grow? (*The plant sprouted.*)

▶ **What did Emily do to try to make herself good?** (*She tried to do good, to be kind, and not to sin.*)

▶ **Who told Emily how to be saved?** (*her mother and Mrs. Andrews*)

▶ **What did Emily do when she went to Sunday school after she had trusted Christ as her Savior?** (*She told her class.*)

Present your salvation testimony, describing how and when you trusted Christ as Savior.

⊙ Worktext pages 13–14

Teach the skill of sequencing. Direct the students' attention to page 13, telling them to study each picture. Direct them to cut out and tape the pictures together in three rows with two pictures in each row. After they have completed taping the pictures together, direct the students to turn

Trust Obeys and Waits

Name _____

Cut out the pictures and put them in the order that they happened.
Tape the pictures together in order like the diagram at right. Turn
the page over to find the father of the nation of Israel.

1	2
3	4
5	6

5 Genesis 13:9

4 Genesis 12:20

3 Genesis 12:8

1 Genesis 11:31

2 Genesis 12:4

6 Genesis 13:12

A Servant's Heart • Lesson 11   **13**

Father of a Nation
Genesis 11–13

14   A Servant's Heart • Lesson 11

Hero of the Faith

Read or tell the following narrative based on the life of John Bunyan.

John Bunyan

John grew up in a peasant family in England. His father was a tinker (someone who repaired pots and pans) and worked out of a shed at the back of his house. John became his father's apprentice and trained to have the same job.

When John was young, a strange sickness killed many people in his village. John's mother and sister were killed by this disease.

Many people in England in the 1630s were angry with the king who ruled over them. The king even decided what religion the people should follow. Because the king had too much power, the people of England started a civil war.

John's grandfather also believed that people should have the freedom to worship God as they wished, not as the king said. Although John was not a Christian, he agreed with his grandfather. When John was sixteen, he joined the army in fighting against the king. One night a friend took John's place as watchman. That night his friend was killed. This bothered John. He felt his friend had died in his place. When John mentioned this to his commander, the officer reminded John that Jesus Christ took his place when He died on the cross for our sins.

them over to see who is considered the father of the nation of Israel. *(Abram)*

Art Connection (optional)

Guide an activity to relate Bible knowledge to everyday life. Explain the directions for Activity page A74, "God Rules Families," to the students; then let them work on their pictures. After the drawings are complete, allow the students to place them on the Unit 1 bulletin board.

LESSON 12 — Hero of the Faith: John Bunyan 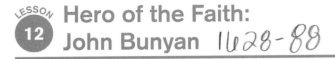 1628-88

Materials
- TimeLine and picture: John Bunyan
- Hymn: "Praise Ye the Lord, the Almighty"
- A copy of the book *Pilgrim's Progress*
- Three names written for display—your paternal great-grandfather, your grandfather, and your father in descending order with a downward arrow from each name to the one below it

Hymn: "Praise Ye the Lord, the Almighty"
Sing the first three verses (Worktext page 212).

♥ Memory Verse—Deuteronomy 6:5
Practice the memory verse.

John began to understand what his grandfather had taught him years before.

After leaving the army, John worked as a tinker. One day he heard a conversation among several women. They were talking about Jesus—the new birth, regeneration, putting off the old man and putting on the new. John asked them so many questions that they sent him to talk to their pastor.

The pastor showed John verses from the Bible about salvation, but John did not believe that God could forgive him. The pastor gave John a book to read. John read the book and studied the Bible. John finally trusted God to save him from his sin.

John and his godly wife Mary had four children, but Mary became sick and died. John was left alone with the four children, including his oldest daughter who was blind. John married Mary's cousin Elizabeth.

John became the pastor of a church in his village. Because he did not have a license to preach, he was arrested and put in prison. God watched over John in prison. A kind jailer tried to make John comfortable and became his friend. John wrote stories while in jail. During a visit with his family, John told them a story about a pilgrim on his way to a heavenly city. John made the story into a book and called it *Pilgrim's Progress.*

John's jailer allowed John to preach in the prison on Sundays. After one of the services, the jailer was saved. John spent twelve years in prison. He made and sold shoelaces to other prisoners to give money to his family. The Lord allowed John Bunyan to write other books even after he was freed from prison. John continued to preach and write until his death. By the time of his death, John had written sixty books—one for each year that he had lived.

Discussion Questions

▶ **Who influenced John Bunyan to believe that each person should have a choice about his own religion?** *(his grandfather)*

▶ **What happened when John was in the army that would affect his life forever?** *(A friend who had taken his place as watchman was killed. He felt his friend had died in his place; an officer told him that, in the same way, Jesus had died in his place.)*

▶ **What two things helped John finally trust Jesus Christ to save him?** *(He read a book and studied the Bible.)*

▶ **What did John become after he was saved?** *(a preacher and a writer)*

▶ **Why was John arrested and put in prison?** *(He did not have a government license to preach.)*

▶ **What great book did John write from his prison cell?** *(Pilgrim's Progress)*

▶ **What was that book about?** *(a pilgrim and his journey to a heavenly city)*

▶ **How many years was John in prison?** *(twelve years)*

▶ **What did John do after he was released from prison?** *(He continued preaching and writing until his death.)*

John Bunyan

Name _____

John Bunyan was born in 1628 in a village in England. He left school when he was sixteen to help his father, who was a tinker (one who repairs pots and pans). He continued to learn by reading and finding out things on his own.

When his country was divided by war, John joined the army. When the war was over, he became a tinker again. One day he heard some village women talking about the peace they had in knowing Jesus Christ. So he began asking questions and studying the Bible. Later, he trusted Christ to save him and became a preacher of the gospel.

In 1659, the king made a law that all preachers had to have a license from the government to preach. John continued to preach without a license until he was arrested and put in prison. While he was there, he wrote his best-known book, *Pilgrim's Progress,* the imaginary adventures of a character named Christian traveling to a beautiful city. It is really a story about how someone is saved and goes through many trials and temptations on the way to heaven. When John Bunyan was released from prison, he continued to preach the gospel. He also wrote many other books.

Fill in the circle next to the correct answer.

1. John Bunyan was a
   ○ trader.
   ● tinker.
   ○ teacher.

2. He heard some women talking about
   ● the peace of Christ.
   ○ the war in Britain.
   ○ the price of wool.

3. He was saved
   ○ by asking questions.
   ○ by becoming a preacher.
   ● by trusting in Christ.

4. He wrote a book called
   ○ *The Heavenly City.*
   ● *Pilgrim's Progress.*
   ○ the Bible.

238 A Servant's Heart • Lesson 12

 Are you letting God control you? Do your thoughts and actions show that God is your king? *(An oral answer is not necessary, but point out that when children yield their lives to God, He can use them to serve Him.)*

TimeLine

Add John Bunyan to the TimeLine. Place the picture of John Bunyan on the TimeLine (AD 1628–88), pointing out the time that has passed from then until today. Guide the students as they glue their pictures of John Bunyan (from the Student Materials section of the Toolkit CD) onto their TimeLines.

Worktext page 238 (optional)

Review the events of John Bunyan's life. Point out that from the time that he was saved, John Bunyan always told others about God, even when he was in prison and had to do it in writing. Direct the students to choose the correct answer to complete each sentence.

Bible Study Skills, Worktext page 15

Teach the skill of using the contents page in a Bible. Direct students' attention to the Old Testament contents box at the top of the Worktext page. Instruct the students to complete the sentences using the information given.

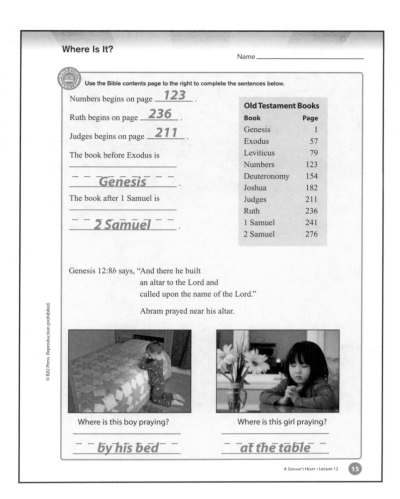

Name _____

Use the Bible contents page to the right to complete the sentences below.

Numbers begins on page __123__.

Ruth begins on page __236__.

Judges begins on page __211__.

The book before Exodus is

__Genesis__.

The book after 1 Samuel is

__2 Samuel__.

Old Testament Books	
Book	**Page**
Genesis	1
Exodus	57
Leviticus	79
Numbers	123
Deuteronomy	154
Joshua	182
Judges	211
Ruth	236
1 Samuel	241
2 Samuel	276

Genesis 12:8b says, "And there he built an altar to the Lord and called upon the name of the Lord."

Abram prayed near his altar.

Where is this boy praying?

__by his bed__

Where is this girl praying?

__at the table__

A SERVANT'S HEART • Lesson 12   15

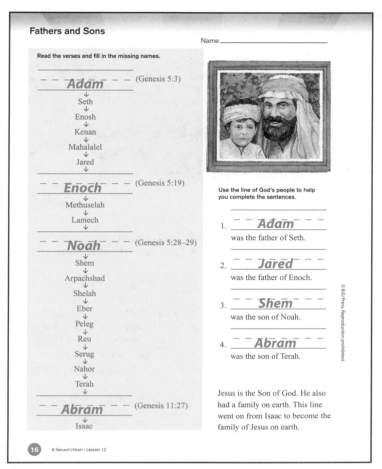

Name _____

Read the verses and fill in the missing names.

__Adam__ (Genesis 5:3)
↓
Seth
↓
Enosh
↓
Kenan
↓
Mahalalel
↓
Jared
↓

__Enoch__ (Genesis 5:19)
↓
Methuselah
↓
Lamech
↓

__Noah__ (Genesis 5:28–29)
↓
Shem
↓
Arpachshad
↓
Shelah
↓
Eber
↓
Peleg
↓
Reu
↓
Serug
↓
Nahor
↓
Terah
↓

__Abram__ (Genesis 11:27)
↓
Isaac

Use the line of God's people to help you complete the sentences.

1. __Adam__ was the father of Seth.

2. __Jared__ was the father of Enoch.

3. __Shem__ was the son of Noah.

4. __Abram__ was the son of Terah.

Jesus is the Son of God. He also had a family on earth. This line went on from Isaac to become the family of Jesus on earth.

16   A SERVANT'S HEART • Lesson 12

Worktext page 16

Introduce a genealogy. Explain that a *genealogy* is a family record used to list ancestors (relatives). Draw attention to the list of names written for display. Write your name below the list. Point out your father's name. Ask the students the names of your great-grandfather and his son.

Teach the skill of reading a genealogy. Direct the students to look on page 16 at the line of God's people starting from Adam. Name each person of importance and ask about the ones they have studied in this unit. Use the following pronunciation guide as needed. Explain the directions on the page and let the students answer the questions independently, giving help when needed. (*Note:* This list uses the modern spellings of these names.)

Arpachshad (är păk shăd)
Eber (ē bər)
Enoch (ē nŭk)
Enosh (ē nŏsh)
Kenan (kĕ năn)
Lamech (lă mĕk)
Mahalalelel (mə hā lă lē lĕl)

Methuselah (mĕ thū zĕ lä)
Nahor (nā hôr)
Peleg (pĕ lĕg)
Reu (rēū)
Serug (sĕ rŭg)
Shelah (shĕ lə)
Terah (tĕ rä)

▶ Going Beyond

Reinforcement

Materials

• A sheet of art paper with Romans 4:3 printed in the center (for each student)

Review God's promise to Abram. Demonstrate on the board how to make looped designs. Show the students how to make each loop into a face by adding features. Direct the students to draw and color a "sea" of faces all around the Bible verse and then to title their drawing "Abram Believed God."

Enrichment

Write a journal entry. Guide students to write a journal from Abram's or Lot's point of view. Encourage them to think about what Abram or Lot might have written. The students may refer to their Bibles or to their Worktext pages to review what they have learned about the lives of Abram and Lot.

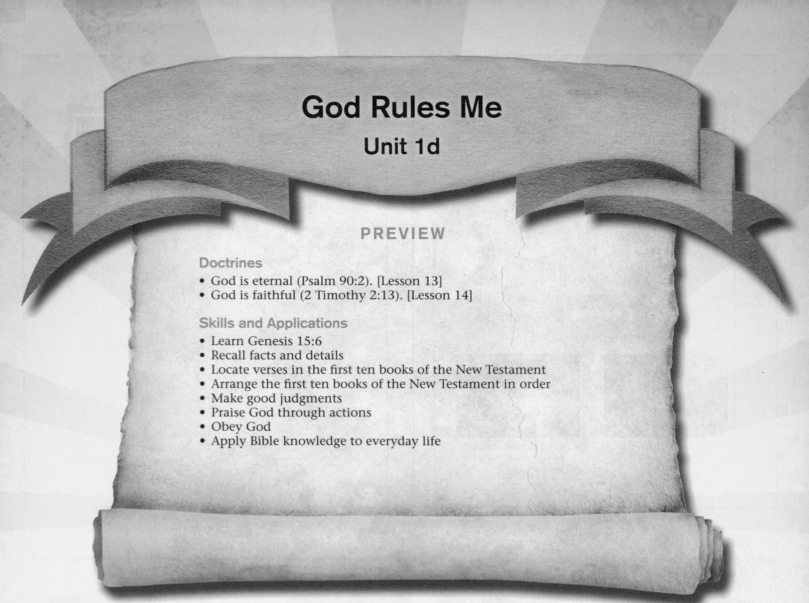

God Rules Me

Unit 1d

PREVIEW

Doctrines

- God is eternal (Psalm 90:2). [Lesson 13]
- God is faithful (2 Timothy 2:13). [Lesson 14]

Skills and Applications

- Learn Genesis 15:6
- Recall facts and details
- Locate verses in the first ten books of the New Testament
- Arrange the first ten books of the New Testament in order
- Make good judgments
- Praise God through actions
- Obey God
- Apply Bible knowledge to everyday life

LESSON

13 God Gives Abraham a Son

Materials

- Chart 31, "World Map"
- TimeLine and picture: Abraham and Sarah
- Hymn: "Praise Ye the Lord, the Almighty"
- Unit 1 Bookmark for each student
- Highlighter for each student (optional)

Background Information

Abraham—*When God changed the name of Abram ("high father") to Abraham ("father of many nations"), He showed Abraham that He planned to bless all nations through the Messiah, Who would come through Abraham's family.*

Sarah—*God changed Sarai's name to Sarah ("princess").*

Isaac—*His name means "laughter." At his birth, Sarah said, "God hath made me to laugh, so that all that hear will laugh with me" (**Genesis 21:6**). Isaac's name reminds us of the joy that the Lord Jesus brings into the world.*

El Shaddai—El *(or Elohim) is translated "God." It is the name used to show God's mighty power at Creation (**Genesis 1:1**).* El Shaddai, *translated "the Almighty God" (**Genesis 17:1**), refers to God's sustaining care for His people.*

Covenant—*A covenant is a solemn promise or agreement made between two or more persons. When God makes a covenant with someone, He always keeps the agreement. Humans, however, often fall short. After God made a covenant with Adam, Adam disobeyed God. God is always faithful.*

🎵 Hymn: "Praise Ye the Lord, the Almighty"

Teach the fourth verse (Worktext page 212). Consult the list of ideas and methods for practicing the hymn (page xii) as necessary. Help the students to understand the hymn and apply its truths to their lives.

Introducing the Bible Account

Discuss the nation of Israel. Write the word *Israel* for display and show the students where the nation of Israel is located on Chart 31, "World Map." Tell them that today they will learn about Abram having a son, Isaac. When Isaac grew up, he had two sons, Jacob and Esau. When Jacob was a grown man,

God changed his name to Israel; and from that time to this, God's people have been the nation of Israel. As a nation, they believed that one day, the Savior of the world would come through Abraham's seed as the fulfillment of God's promise to Abraham. However, the nation's religious leaders did not believe that Jesus was the Messiah and therefore had Him crucified. The Bible tells us that someday the people of Israel will accept Jesus as their promised Deliverer.

Bible Account

Read Genesis 17:1–19 and 21:1–8 or use the following retelling of the passage. Listening question: **What did Abram have that we too must have if we are going to come to God?** *(He had faith because he believed God exists eternally even though he had never seen Him. We can trust God although we cannot see Him.)*

God Gives Abraham a Son

Long after God first told Abram that He would bless him, God visited Abram again. This time, God told Abram another name for Himself. God said, "I am the Almighty God; walk before Me and be perfect." He told Abram that He was making a covenant with him and that he, Abram, would have many descendants.

Abram fell on his face before Almighty God, and God kept talking to Abram. God told him that he would be the father of many nations, and then God changed Abram's name to Abraham. God told Abraham again that the land where Abraham was a stranger would be his someday. He said Abraham's descendants would live in Canaan forever. He also told Abraham that his wife Sarai would be the mother of nations, and God changed her name to Sarah.

Time passed, and Abraham still had no children. No doubt he wondered how he could have many descendants when he did not even have a child. Abraham had more visits with God and more exciting things happened to him, but still he did not have a child. His wife, Sarah, grew very old and was past the time of having children. Abraham did good things and also made mistakes, but he continued to have faith in his God. He believed!

Finally, among all the exciting things that happened to Abraham, the most exciting thing of all happened: Sarah was going to have a child. When it was time, a son was born to Abraham and Sarah in their old age. It was a miracle! Abraham called his son Isaac as God had instructed him. Sarah laughed when she heard she would have a baby boy. And Abraham gave a great feast to honor God and the son that God had sent to him.

❦

Discussion Questions

💡 **Why do you think God kept coming to visit Abram?** *(Answers may vary, but emphasize that it was by grace that God continued to instruct, encourage, and correct Abram about believing and obeying God.)*

God Gives Abraham a Son
Genesis 21   Name _____

God made a covenant with Abraham. God promised him many blessings. Some of them are listed below. Draw a line from each promise to the matching reference on the right.

A covenant is a solemn promise or agreement between two or more persons.

1. All families or nations will be blessed through Abraham.   Genesis 15:4
2. God would bless those who bless Abraham.   Genesis 12:3b
3. Abraham's heir would be his own child.   Genesis 12:3a
4. Abraham would become a great nation.   Genesis 17:16
5. Abraham's wife Sarah would have a son.   Genesis 12:2

Fill in the blanks in the sentences below. If you need help, read the verse given.

1. Even though Abraham and Sarah were too old to have a baby,
   God gave them a ___*son*___ (Genesis 18:10).

2. Abraham received God's promise by ___*faith*___ (Romans 4:20).

When Jesus came, He also promised us blessings through faith. Use the words from the word bank to complete the following sentence.

Word Bank
forgive   eternal   believe

If you ___*believe*___ in the Lord Jesus Christ (Acts 16:31),

He will ___*forgive*___ your sin (Acts 10:43) and give you

___*eternal*___ life (John 6:47).

A SERVANT'S HEART • Lesson 13   17

© BJU Press. Reproduction prohibited.

▶ **Why did God change Abram's name to Abraham?** *(God said it was because He was going to make Abraham the father of many nations.)*

💡 **Explain what God meant when He told Abraham that he would be the father of many nations.** *(People from all nations who trust in Christ for salvation and are united to Him are spiritual descendants of Abraham since Christ is the descendant of Abraham. See Romans 4:16–18; Galatians 3:29.)*

▶ **What did God change Sarai's name to?** *(Sarah)*

⊙ TimeLine

Replace Abram on the TimeLine. Explain that since God changed Abram's name to Abraham, "the father of many nations," we need to change our TimeLine. Choose a student to take down the Abram card and replace it with the covenant names Abraham and Sarah. Read the sentence on the tag. Help students to glue the picture of Abraham and Sarah over the picture of Abram on their TimeLines.

♥ Memory Verse—Genesis 15:6

Principle: God gives us righteousness by faith. Assist in highlighting the verse (optional) and marking the location with the Unit 1 Bookmark.

Consult the list of ideas and methods (page xii) for practicing the memory verses as necessary. Memorization is an important key to understanding biblical truths and applying them to our lives. Encourage the students to be able to recite the verses from memory at the end of each subunit.

Discussion Questions

- 💡 **What is righteousness?** *(that which is right in the sight of God)*
- ▶ **What did Abraham do to be declared righteous?** *(He believed God.)*
- 💡 **Who is it that makes us righteous?** *(God)*
  If God calls us righteous, what do we get? *(Answers may include getting to be a child of God, a home in heaven, eternal life, and joy here on earth.)*
- 💡 **When we trust Jesus Christ as our Savior, what is one thing we receive?** *(the righteousness of Jesus)*
- 💡 **Why is Jesus righteous?** *(because He is God)*

 Worktext page 17

Guide a discussion about God's covenant with Abraham. Direct the students' attention to the top of the worktext page. Read the definition of *covenant* and then read each reference. Help the students to match each reference to its summary statement.

Guide the finding of information in the Bible. Direct students to find the contents page in their Bibles. Read the names of the first five books of the New Testament together. Guide the students as they read the verses at the bottom of Worktext page 17 and choose the missing word from the word bank. Give help as needed.

LESSON 14 — Abraham Gives to God

Background Information

Altar—*The word* altar *comes from the Latin word meaning "high." An altar was a raised place used for worship or sacrifice. People usually built altars by piling earth and stones together. The Israelites sacrificed animals on their altars and burned the meat as an offering to the Lord. Abraham built an altar to worship God. Christians do not need to build altars today because Jesus became the sacrifice "once for all." We can show our love to Him by obeying His Word.*

Mount Moriah—*This is the mountain on which Abraham offered Isaac. Centuries later in the same area, David claimed the city of Jebus, and developed it into Jerusalem. Just north of the city, he purchased a field on which he built an altar to stop a plague that God sent due to David's sin.*

Introducing the Bible Account

Guide a review about Abraham. Ask your students the following questions to review the previous Bible account.

- ▶ **What did God promise Abraham that He would bless him with?** *(Possible answers include a son and a nation of many people from which the Messiah would come.)*
- ▶ **Did that mean Abraham would have to have a child?** *(yes)*
- ▶ **Who was the son that God gave to Abraham?** *(Isaac)*
- ▶ **Was Isaac the link to the many nations that Abraham would father?** *(yes)*

Read Genesis 22 or use the following retelling of the passage. Listening question: **What offering did God provide in place of Isaac?** *(a ram)*

Abraham Gives to God

God spoke to Abraham when his son Isaac was just a young man. God said to take Isaac to Mount Moriah. There Abraham was to offer Isaac as a burnt offering on an altar.

Abraham trusted and obeyed God. He woke up early the next morning and took Isaac to the mountain, along with two young men and wood to burn the offering.

Three days later, Abraham saw the place where he was to offer his son. As they walked, Isaac asked his father, "Where is the lamb for a burnt offering?"

Abraham said, "My son, God will provide Himself a lamb for a burnt offering." When they arrived at the place where God had told them to go, Abraham set up an altar and laid out the wood. He bound Isaac and had him lie down on the altar on top of the wood.

As Abraham took the knife, the Angel of the Lord called down from heaven and stopped him. Abraham had passed the test of obedience. God knew that Abraham trusted Him and was therefore willing to offer his son as a sacrifice to the Lord. Abraham loved God more than anything else, including his family.

God then provided an animal for the sacrifice. Abraham saw "a ram caught in a thicket by his horns." The ram was offered instead of Isaac.

The Angel of the Lord spoke to Abraham again. God promised to bless Abraham and to give him as many children as the stars in the sky and the sand on the shore.

Because Abraham obeyed the Lord, he would be the father of a large family and a great nation.

Discussion Questions

- ▶ **What difficult thing did God ask Abraham to do?** *(to sacrifice his son Isaac as a burnt offering)*
- ▶ **Did Abraham obey God?** *(yes)*
- ▶ **Did Isaac obey his father?** *(yes)*
- 💡 **What kept Abraham from sacrificing Isaac?** *(The Angel of the Lord told Abraham to not sacrifice him.)*
- 💡 **Why do you think God tested Abraham in this way?** *(Answers will vary.)* Discuss God's knowledge that Abraham would pass the test before He gave him the test. God knows everything. Also, God used the story of Abraham's offering up his son as a way to explain how God gave His Son for the sins of the world. God also uses Abraham's faith to obey as an example to all who read the Scriptures. Read **Hebrews 11:8–12** if you would like to continue the discussion about faith.
- 💡 **Would you be willing to obey God in a difficult situation?** *(Make the point that our very lives belong to God; so does everything we own.)*

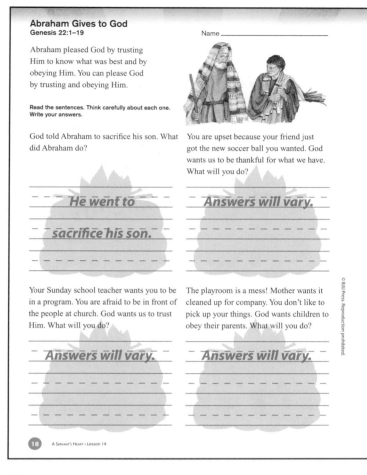

Abraham Gives to God
Genesis 22:1–19

Name _____

Abraham pleased God by trusting Him to know what was best and by obeying Him. You can please God by trusting and obeying Him.

Read the sentences. Think carefully about each one. Write your answers.

God told Abraham to sacrifice his son. What did Abraham do?

He went to sacrifice his son.

You are upset because your friend just got the new soccer ball you wanted. God wants us to be thankful for what we have. What will you do?

Answers will vary.

Your Sunday school teacher wants you to be in a program. You are afraid to be in front of the people at church. God wants us to trust Him. What will you do?

Answers will vary.

The playroom is a mess! Mother wants it cleaned up for company. You don't like to pick up your things. God wants children to obey their parents. What will you do?

Answers will vary.

© BJU Press. Reproduction prohibited.

18 A SERVANT'S HEART • Lesson 14

❤ **Memory Verse—Genesis 15:6**
Practice the verse.

✏ **Worktext page 18**
Teach the skill of applying Bible truth to everyday life. Explain the directions for page 18 to the class. Choose a volunteer to read the group of sentences above the first altar. Discuss what Abraham did. Choose another volunteer to read the second group of sentences. Ask volunteers to share their ideas about what they would do in this situation. Let the students work independently to complete the page, giving help as needed.

LESSON

15 Worthy of Praise

Materials
• Hymn: "Praise Ye the Lord, the Almighty"

🎵 **Hymn: "Praise Ye the Lord, the Almighty"**
Sing the hymn (Worktext page 212).

❤ **Memory Verse—Genesis 15:6**
Practice the verse.

Introducing the Application Story
Ask the following questions about work.

💡 **Do you ever need money to buy something?** (Answers will vary.)

💡 **How do you get the money you need?** (Answers will vary.)

💡 **How does your family get the money the family needs?** (Answers will vary.)

Discuss the importance of working for what they need, not just waiting for someone to give it to them.

Application Story

Read or tell the following story. Listening question: **How was Clay able to earn $10.00?** (dog sitting)

Almost Impossible

Clay and his friend Travis hurried out of church. "Guess what?" said Travis. "My dad said he would give me ten dollars to help that missionary. How about you?"

Clay looked down. He wished he could tell Travis that he was going to help too.

Pastor Davis had said this morning that one of their missionaries, Mr. Wright, needed Bibles for the people in his church in Russia. Ten dollars would buy a Bible for a Russian believer.

"I wish I could give ten dollars for a Bible," Clay thought. Aloud he said, "I'll ask my dad." But he thought he already knew what Dad would say.

He was right. As Dad spooned chicken casserole onto his plate at lunch, he answered Clay's question. "I could just give you the money, Clay," he said. "But then the Bible wouldn't really be from you. It would be from me. I think it would be better if you gave the money yourself."

"Yes, sir," Clay said. But he didn't smile. He stayed quiet through lunch, and he didn't even take seconds on the chicken. How could he come up with ten dollars all by himself?

After lunch, Clay went to his room and opened the canvas pouch he kept in his bottom drawer. He dumped the contents on the floor and counted out two quarters, three dimes, and seven pennies: eighty-seven cents. That was a long way from ten dollars.

The sound of a footstep in the doorway made him look up. Dad was leaning on the door frame. "How much do you have?" he asked.

"Eighty-seven cents," Clay said.

Dad came in and said, "Thought about how you'll get that ten dollars?"

Clay shook his head.

"There's a verse in the Bible that says there is nothing too hard for God," said Dad. "And another one that says if we ask God to do anything that is in line with His will, He will do it."

Clay frowned. "Do you think I should ask God for the money?"

Dad put a hand on his shoulder. "I think that's exactly what you should do," he said. "Let's pray together."

The next morning, Mom got a phone call from one of the neighbors. "Clay," she said, "Mrs. Burton needs someone to

---

feed her dog and water her plants for a few days while her family is out of town. Would you like to do that?"

"Sure!" said Clay. He and the Burtons' golden retriever, Quincy, were good friends.

Early on Tuesday, Clay unlocked the front door of the Burtons' house with the key Mrs. Burton had given him. Quincy ran out of the kitchen, barking and wagging his tail. "Hey, there, pal!" Clay scratched Quincy's favorite spot behind his ears.

Clay followed Mrs. Burton's instructions carefully, pouring food into Quincy's bowl, filling his water dish, and watering the plants on each windowsill. As he backed away from the last plant, he bumped into something and heard a crash.

"Oh no!" Looking down, he saw peppermint candies and pieces of glass all over the floor. The glass candy dish! He had knocked it off the table and broken it.

Clay cleaned up the mess, put the candy on the table, and walked home with his head down. He would have to pay Mrs. Burton for the broken dish. Now it would be impossible to buy the Bible for Mr. Wright.

For the next few days, Clay's stomach hurt when he ate. He had trouble falling asleep at night. And even though he kept feeding Quincy and watering the plants, he didn't enjoy his jobs anymore.

At last Friday came. Clay watched the Burtons' green van pull into their driveway. "You'll have to go over to the Burtons and explain what happened, Clay," said Mom. "Do you want me to come with you?"

Clay shook his head. He could feel Mom watching him as he trudged slowly across the front lawn.

"Clay!" Mrs. Burton said when she answered his knock. "I'm glad to see you. The plants look so nice and green, and Quincy is as healthy and happy as ever. You've done a good job."

Clay felt tears behind his eyes. He blinked and swallowed a few times. "Mrs. Burton, I—I broke your candy dish," he blurted out. "It was an accident. I bumped into the table. I know I'll have to pay for it, and I have eighty-seven cents saved up, but that's all I have right now."

Mrs. Burton frowned. "Which candy dish was that?" she asked.

Clay followed her inside. "The one that was here on the table. With these peppermints in it." He pointed to the spot where the dish had sat.

Mrs. Burton smiled. "Oh, Clay, don't worry about that," she said. "I picked that up at a garage sale for fifty cents."

Clay's head jerked up. "Fifty cents? That's all? I can pay you for it, then!"

She laughed and handed him a peppermint. "You will do no such thing," she said. "I'm the one who owes you money for taking such good care of Quincy and my plants." She reached in her purse, pulled out a folded bill, and handed it to Clay. "Thank you so much."

Clay ran back across the lawn, hardly breathing. He didn't stop till he reached his front porch. Then he opened the bill. It was ten dollars!

"Mom! Dad!" Clay shouted. "Guess what God did!"

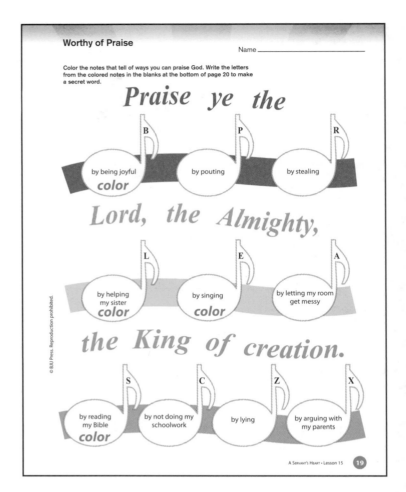

Discussion Questions

▶ **Why did Clay want money?** *(to buy a Bible for the missionary to take to Russia)*

▶ **Why did Clay's dad not want to give him the ten dollars it took to buy a Bible?** *(He thought the Bible would mean more to Clay if he earned the ten dollars.)*

▶ **At first did Clay really believe that God could give him ten dollars?** *(no)*

▶ **What encouraged him by giving him a chance to earn money?** *(when the neighbor offered him a job taking care of the dog and the plants)*

💡 **Why did breaking the candy dish discourage him?** *(He thought he would have to pay for the dish, and he didn't know if he had even made enough to do that by working.)*

▶ **How did God work it out that Clay made enough to buy the Bible?** *(Clay did not have to pay for the candy dish, and Mrs. Burton paid him ten dollars.)*

🖊 Worktext pages 19–20

Guide an activity in making judgments. Choose volunteers to read the words on the notes on pages 19–20. Ask the class whether these words sound familiar to them. *(They are from the hymn.)* Explain the directions on the pages and discuss the first two examples. Allow the students to work independently, giving help to those who need it.

Worthy of Praise (continued) — Name ____

O my soul, praise
(D) by crying to get my way
(H) by wanting the best toys
(J) by playing video games
(S) by talking to God — color

Him, for He is
(Q) by fighting
(I) by sharing — color
(W) by not listening to my teacher
(M) by cheating

thy health and salvation.
(N) by learning God's Word — color
(K) by screaming at my brother
(G) by smiling at someone — color
(V) by being lazy

God gave Abraham a _b_ _l_ _e_ _s_ _s_ _i_ _n_ _g_.

© BJU Press. Reproduction prohibited.

20   A Servant's Heart • Lesson 15

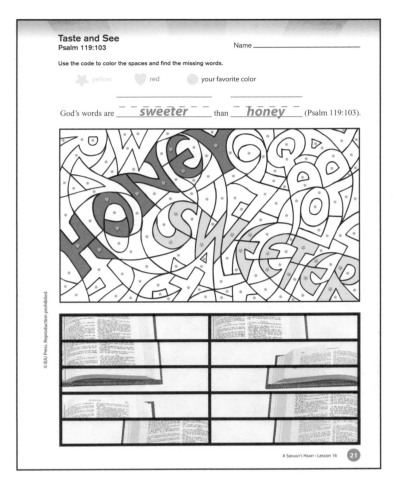

Taste and See
Psalm 119:103   Name ____

Use the code to color the spaces and find the missing words.
⭐ yellow   ❤ red   ● your favorite color

God's words are _sweeter_ than _honey_ (Psalm 119:103).

© BJU Press. Reproduction prohibited.

21   A Servant's Heart • Lesson 16

LESSON 16 — Taste and See

Materials
- Hymn: "Praise Ye the Lord, the Almighty"
- Transparent tape for each student
- Copy of page A75 ("God Rules Me") for each student (optional)

♥ Memory Verse—Genesis 15:6
Suggested memory verse practice: guide a discussion about faith. Write the word *believe* for display and ask the students to read it to you. Ask various students to tell what the word *believe* means. *(to trust, to have faith, to depend on)* Next, write the words *Lord, counted,* and *righteousness* for display. Ask what those words mean. Ask four students to stand at the front of the classroom. Each time the class says Genesis 15:6, one of the four may be seated. Call on volunteers to recite the verse.

♫ Hymn: "Praise Ye the Lord, the Almighty"
Sing the hymn (Worktext page 212).

📖 Bible Study Skills, Worktext page 21
Guide a discussion about obeying God. Ask the students where they learn how to obey God. *(in the Bible)* Point out that God wants us to obey because we love Him. Remind them of the importance of reading and memorizing

God's Word to know how God wants to instruct them. As the students look at Worktext page 21, explain to them the coloring code for the puzzle. Tell them to color the puzzle and complete the verse. After the coloring is completed, call on a volunteer to read the verse.

📖 Bible Study Skills, Worktext page 22
Locate verses and apply them to our lives. Direct the students to find the New Testament books on the contents page in their Bibles. Lead them in reading aloud the names of the first ten books several times. Read aloud the verses listed on Worktext page 22. Guide the students in writing about a time the verses could help them. *(Note: The ability to write sentences varies with second graders. Encourage each student to do his best even if he can write only a word or two.)*

Guide a sequencing activity. Invite the students to refer to the contents page in their Bibles to number the first ten New Testament books in sequence by writing the correct numbers in the blanks. Explain the "Do at Home" activity. They are to cut apart the New Testament book names and place them in correct order. Then they should tape the slips of paper together to form a rectangle. Tell the students that when they sequence the books correctly, they will have a picture of the best book on the back of their rectangles. *(the Bible)*

🔗 Art Connection (optional)
Guide an activity to relate Bible knowledge to daily life. Ask the students Who should be ruling their lives. *(God)*

Help from God's Word

Answers will vary.

Name _____

God gave us His Word to help us live the way that pleases Him. Listen as your teacher reads each verse from the Bible. Think of a time when the verse might help you, and write it on the lines.

Ephesians 6:1   ─ ─ ─ ─ ─ ─ ─ ─ ─ ─ ─ ─ ─
  _____
  _____

Acts 5:29   ─ ─ ─ ─ ─ ─ ─ ─ ─ ─ ─ ─ ─
  _____
  _____

Romans 12:14   ─ ─ ─ ─ ─ ─ ─ ─ ─ ─ ─ ─
  _____
  _____

To do in class: Fill in the missing numbers according to the order the books appear in the Bible. Check your numbers by looking at the contents page in your Bible.
To do at home: Cut the names apart. Put them in order according to the grid above the list of names. Tape the names together. Turn the rectangle over to see what God has given you to help you please Him.

1	2
3	4
5	6
7	8
9	10

__5__ Acts	__3__ Luke
__2__ Mark	__7__ 1 Corinthians
__10__ Ephesians	__9__ Galatians
__8__ 2 Corinthians	__1__ Matthew
__4__ John	__6__ Romans

22   A SERVANT'S HEART • Lesson 16

Unit 1 Review

Name _____

Write a word from the word bank in each blank.

1. God created the world in six _____ *days* _____

2. On the seventh day, God _____ *rested* _____ .

3. God created man in His own _____ *image* _____ .

4. God told Noah to build an _____ *ark* _____ .

Word bank: image, ark, rested, days

Circle the correct word in the parentheses.

5. God spared Noah and his family because they (believed, saw) God.

6. God destroyed the world with a (fire, flood).

7. God promised Abraham a nation of (many, tall) people.

8. Abraham gave his (room, son) to God.

Write your name on the lines.

9. God wants _____ to trust Him.

10. God wants _____ to obey Him.

Unit Reviews   Lessons 1–16 • A55

Explain the directions for page A75, ("God Rules Me"). Invite students to work on their pictures. After the drawings are complete, allow the students to place them on the Unit 1 bulletin board.

▶ Going Beyond

Reinforcement

Materials

• An individual or family photograph from each student

Guide an activity that applies Bible truth to everyday life. Direct the students to exchange photographs. Tell them they may examine only that picture to find a person or object you mention. Instruct them to hold up the pictures and answer the following questions. After each question, remind the students of a Bible truth listed below.

• Find someone wearing glasses. **Who made you?** *(God)* God knows all about you.
• Find a picture taken in winter (or any other specific season). **Name the four seasons.** *(winter, spring, summer, fall)* God made everything and has a plan.
• Find a picture of a family. **Do the people in the photo look happy?** God gives parents to guide and instruct the family.
• Find a family picture with grandparents. **Do your grandparents live nearby or far away?** Be thankful for

parents or grandparents who take you to church and encourage you to follow God.
• Find a picture showing rain. **Is it raining today?** Remember that God sends or withholds the rain.

Enrichment

Materials

• Drawing paper for each student or for each group

Make a picture book. List the different events that took place during the life of Abraham: Abraham built an altar in Bethel; Abraham moved to Egypt; Abraham moved back to Bethel and offered sacrifices on an altar; Abraham and Sarah had no children; Isaac was born; Abraham traveled to Mount Moriah to offer his son Isaac on the altar, but God provided a ram. Assign each student or group of students a picture to draw. After the pictures are complete, put them together to make a picture book about the life of Abraham.

◀◀ Unit Review

Materials

• Copy of page A55 ("Unit 1 Review") for each student

Guide a review of Lessons 1–16. Review the people and events in preparation for the Unit 1 Test (optional).

2

An Obedient Heart

OVERVIEW

Preparing the Teacher

Read **Joshua 24:24**. God's people were willing to serve and obey Him because they were humble. The word *obey* comes from a Latin word meaning "to listen." Many times it may seem that a student doesn't listen to a word you say. How do you know he isn't listening? He is not responding with obedience. Even if he is hearing with his ears, listening in the sense of heeding is obviously not occurring. How are your listening skills? Are you as attentive to God's Word as you expect your students to be? As you make suggestions about how they can incorporate God's wisdom into their lives, are you applying it to your circumstances as well? Ask God to improve your listening skills, as well as those of your students.

Preparing the Materials

17–19—A walking stick to represent Moses's rod; Unit 2 bookmark [E]
19–20—Small beanbag
Unit 2a Going Beyond—Pocket chart; seven sentence strips or large cards
21—Two large pieces of poster board [O]; roll of paper towels (or rolled wrapping paper)
22—Figurine
28—Copy of A76 ("Words of Encouragement") [E, O]
31—Lightweight rubber ball; cookie [E, O]
32—Five pieces of construction paper; copy of page A56 ("Unit 2 Review") [E]

[E] = for each student; [O] = optional

Unit 2   An Obedient Heart

Theme, Memory Verse, and Principle	Lesson Number	TE Page	Worktext Page(s)	Appendix Page(s)	Lesson Title	Scripture or Focus
Unit 2a **Obedient Feet** Exodus 14:31 *God's display of power causes people to fear and believe.*	**17**	36	23–24		God Calls Moses	Exodus 3:1–4:17
	18	39	25–26		God Shows His Power	Exodus 4:29–12:51
	19	41	27		God Shows the Way	Exodus 13:21–14:31
	20	42	28		Called to Witness	Application Story
Unit 2b **Obedient Eyes** Exodus 32:26 *God hates sin. We should stand on God's side.*	**21**	45	29		The Ten Commandments	Exodus 19:1–20:17
	22	47	30		The Golden Calf	Exodus 32–33
	23	48	31		Rules Are for Our Good	Application Story
	24	50	32–34		Prophet Focus: Jonah	Jonah 1–4
Unit 2c **Obedient Speech** John 14:15 *If we love Christ, we will cheerfully obey the Bible.*	**25**	53	35–36		A Message for Balaam	Numbers 22:1–35
	26	55	37		Balaam and His Prophecy	Numbers 22:36–24:17
	27	57			Be Kind to One Another	Application Story
	28	58	38	A76	What Should You Say?	Proverbs 16:24
Unit 2d **Obedient Hands** Micah 6:8b *It is better to obey God than to have an outward appearance of worshiping Him.*	**29**	60	39		Jericho First	Joshua 1–6
	30	62	40		Victory and Defeat	Joshua 7
	31	63	41		Obey All the Way	Application Story
	32	64	42	A56	Who Disobeyed?	Joshua 7

Connections	Bible Doctrines	Skills/Applications
L18—TimeLine: Moses World History **L24**—TimeLine: Jonah **L25**—World History **L28**—Drama Art **L32**—Art	### The Doctrine of God *Attributes of God* God is all-knowing (omniscient) (Job 42:2; Ps. 94:11). God is all-powerful (omnipotent) (Matt. 19:26). God is merciful (Ps. 86:15). God is holy (1 Pet. 1:16). God is righteous (Ps. 116:5). God is unchanging (immutable) (James 1:17). God is faithful (1 Cor. 1:9; 2 Tim. 2:13). God is love (1 John 4:8). ### The Doctrine of Man *Fall of Man* Man is guilty before God (Rom. 3:10–12). Man is in a hopeless condition (Is. 64:6).	### Foundational • Understand that sin must be paid for • Know that God protected His chosen people ### Practical • Locate verses in Genesis–Proverbs • Locate verses in Matthew–2 Thessalonians • Infer cause and effect • Draw conclusions from characters' actions • Recall facts and details • Identify character traits • Infer information • Draw conclusions based on the Bible • Interpret pictures ### Personal • Realize God's faithfulness to answer prayer • Know that God's laws are for our benefit • Understand that God wants total obedience • Know that God wants the saved to witness to the unsaved • Understand and apply Bible knowledge to everyday life

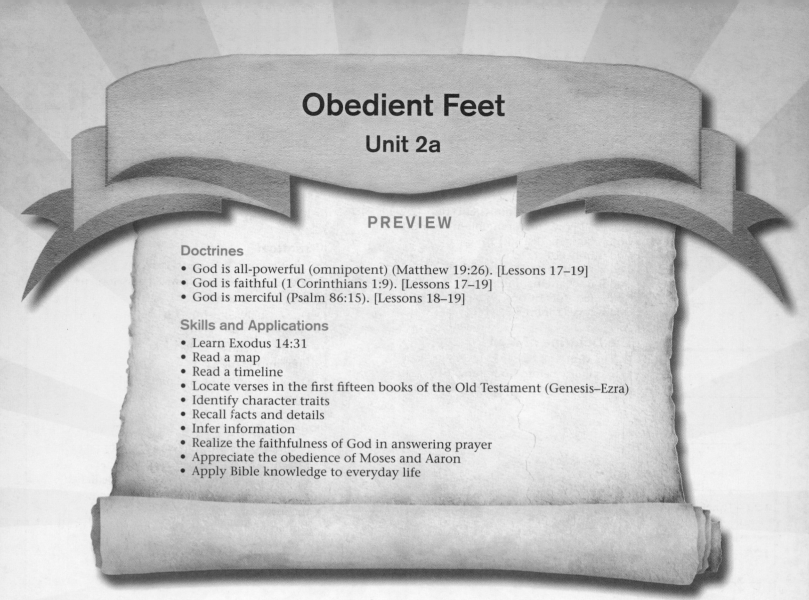

Obedient Feet

Unit 2a

PREVIEW

Doctrines

- God is all-powerful (omnipotent) (Matthew 19:26). [Lessons 17–19]
- God is faithful (1 Corinthians 1:9). [Lessons 17–19]
- God is merciful (Psalm 86:15). [Lessons 18–19]

Skills and Applications

- Learn Exodus 14:31
- Read a map
- Read a timeline
- Locate verses in the first fifteen books of the Old Testament (Genesis–Ezra)
- Identify character traits
- Recall facts and details
- Infer information
- Realize the faithfulness of God in answering prayer
- Appreciate the obedience of Moses and Aaron
- Apply Bible knowledge to everyday life

LESSON 17

God Calls Moses

Materials

Material	Location
Charts Maps InfoScenes TimeLine and pictures	Visual Packet (or the Visuals section of the Toolkit CD)
Student Bookmarks Student TimeLine and pictures	Student Materials section of the Toolkit CD
Music for teaching the unit hymns is found in the appendix of both this Teacher's Edition and the Student Worktext. A recording of children singing these hymns is available on CD. Included in the appendix of this Teacher's Edition are two additional hymns or songs for each unit. See listing on page A1.	

- Chart 6, "God Calls Moses"
- Hymn: "Lead On, O King Eternal"

- Unit 2 Bookmark for each student
- Highlighter for each student (optional)
- Walking stick to represent the rod of Moses

♥ Memory Verse—Exodus 14:31

Principle: God's display of power causes people to fear and believe. Explain that this verse goes with the next Bible story (Lesson 18) about all the miracles God did to convince Pharaoh to let His people go. Direct the students to highlight the verse (optional). Distribute the Unit 2 Bookmark and advise them to mark the location of the verse.

Consult the list of ideas and methods (page xii) for practicing the memory verses as necessary. Memorization is an important key to understanding biblical truths and applying them to our lives. Encourage the students to be able to recite the verses from memory at the end of each subunit.

Background Information

Moses—*Threatened by the increasing Israelite population in the land, the new Egyptian ruler decreed that all Hebrew male children were to be killed at birth. God had other plans for one Hebrew boy. Left by his mother in the river to avoid the decree, he*

God Calls Moses
Exodus 3:1–4:17

Mount Horeb (Sinai) where God spoke to Moses is mostly barren rock. Here and there grass, trees, and shrubs grow at oases. Even today it is a wilderness where few people and animals live.

© BJU Press. Reproduction prohibited.

A Servant's Heart • Lesson 17   23

was found by Pharaoh's own daughter, who drew him from the water and took him with her to be her own child. She named him Moses, which means "to draw from the water" (Exodus 2:10). Moses grew up in Pharaoh's palace. When he became an adult, he gave up all the privileges and wealth that could have been his in order to identify himself with his God and his people. After he got in trouble with Pharaoh for killing an Egyptian, Moses ran away to the land of Midian, where he married a woman named Zipporah and tended sheep for his father-in-law, Jethro. He stayed there for forty years before God sent him back to Egypt.

"I AM"—*When God told Moses to go in the name of "I AM" (Exodus 3:14), He was assuring Moses that He was the covenant-keeping God. God made a covenant with Abraham, Isaac, and Jacob. God said that He would make of them a great nation. They would be a blessing to the entire world. "I AM" is actually the name Jehovah. In the New Testament, the Lord Jesus Christ is the great I AM.*

Introducing the Bible Account

Guide a discussion about Moses. Examine Worktext page 23 together. Ask the students what they know about the birth, childhood, and marriage of Moses. Share the background information about Moses.

Bible Account

Read Exodus 3:1–4:17 or use the following retelling of the passage. Direct attention to the map on Worktext page 24.

Guide the students as they locate Egypt, Midian (the land where Moses fled when escaping the pharaoh of Egypt), and Mount Sinai (the place where Moses brought the sheep to graze). Listening question: **What did Moses say he could not do well?** *(speak)* Hold the walking stick as you relate the story.

InfoScene: "God Calls Moses"
Display Chart 6 from the Visual Packet for the students to refer to throughout this unit.

God Calls Moses

Moses was watching the sheep of Jethro, his father-in-law. Suddenly, he saw fire! A bush was on fire! When Moses went closer to see the fire, he noticed that the bush was not burning up. The bush just kept burning! Did he see something in that bush? Did it look like an angel? As he studied the bush, a voice coming out of the bush startled him, and he stepped back in amazement. The voice said, "Moses, Moses."

Moses answered, "Here am I."

Then the voice of God told Moses not to come any closer and to take off his shoes because the ground he was standing on was holy ground. God said that He had heard the crying prayers of the Hebrews in Egypt and that He had seen how badly they were being treated by the Egyptians. Because of this, God was going to bring His people out of Egypt. God told Moses that He was the God of Moses's ancestors: Abraham, Isaac, and Jacob. Then he said something that really shocked Moses. God told Moses that He was going to send Moses to tell Pharaoh to let His people go.

Moses protested and said to God, "Who am I, that I should go before Pharaoh, and that I should bring the children of Israel out of Egypt?"

God said that He would be with Moses and promised him that after leading the people out of Egypt, Moses would come to that mountain again and serve God.

Moses still argued with God. "When I speak to the people of Israel and tell them that the God of their fathers has sent me, they will ask me what His name is. What do I say to them?"

God answered, "I AM WHO I AM." Then He told Moses to gather the elders of Israel together and tell them the Lord God of their fathers, the God of Abraham, Isaac, and Jacob, had seen their suffering and had sent Moses to them. He said to tell them that their God would lead them out of Egypt into the lands of other peoples. After a three-day journey, they should build altars and sacrifice to Him. And God told Moses that they would come to a wonderful land that flowed with milk and honey, and He would give them that land. God said to tell them that when they left Egypt, they would take with them gold, silver, and jewels from Egypt.

Moses still told God that he was not the one to do this thing. God asked Moses what was in his hand.

Moses said, "A rod."

God told Moses to throw the rod on the ground. When Moses did this *[throw your stick down]*, the rod turned into a snake. Then God told Moses to pick it up again *[pick up the stick]*. When Moses did so, the snake turned back into a rod.

Moses kept saying he couldn't do what God wanted him to do, and God showed Moses another miracle. Then Moses said that he could not speak to Pharaoh because he was not a good speaker. Moses asked God to send someone else. Then God was angry and told Moses that his own brother, Aaron, would come out to meet him and be the speaker. Moses would say the words to Aaron, and Aaron would say them to others. God told Moses to take the rod with him because he would be doing miracles with it.

Finally, Moses obeyed God, went back to Midian, got his family, and started out for Egypt. And, just as God had said, Aaron came to the mountain of God, met Moses, and was told how God planned to use them both in Egypt.

Discussion Questions

▶ **When Moses came to the mountain of God, what did he see?** *(a bush on fire)*

▶ **What was the unusual thing about this bush?** *(The bush did not burn up.)*

▶ **What startled Moses as he watched the bush?** *(A voice spoke out of the bush.)*

▶ **What did the voice say?** *("Take off your shoes because the ground you are standing on is holy ground.")*

▶ **Whose voice was it?** *(God's)*

▶ **How do we know it was God's voice?** *(The voice said He was the God of Abraham, Isaac, and Jacob.)*

▶ **What did God tell Moses?** *(God said that He had seen the suffering of His people, had heard their prayers, and was going to bring them out of Egypt.)*

💡 **What does this tell us about God?** *(Elicit that God watches over His children and hears their prayers and that God is faithful to those who love Him.* **Romans 8:28***)*

▶ **What did God say that frightened Moses?** *(that He wanted Moses to be the one to lead His people out of Egypt)*

▶ **Did Moses agree right away to do what God wanted?** *(No. Moses did not think he could do it.)*

▶ **When Moses asked God for His name, what did God say?** *("I AM WHO I AM.")*

▶ **Who did God say would do the speaking for Moses?** *(his brother Aaron)*

▶ **What reason did God give Moses for his being able to do this big job?** *(He said that He would go with Moses.)*

💡 **Do you think Moses got the idea that God could do anything, that God was that powerful?** *(Many answers are acceptable; discuss as many as time allows.)*

🎵 Hymn: "Lead On, O King Eternal"

Introduce the hymn (Worktext page 213). Read **2 Timothy 2:1–3** to the students. Explain that this hymn is based on Paul's warning to Timothy. Ask the students to look at this hymn. Tell them that in this unit they are going to study how Moses went into Egypt and told Pharaoh to let God's people, the Jews, leave and go to their own country. Emphasize the attitudes of self-denial, dedication to God, dependence on God, and readiness to follow and serve God, all of which are evidenced in this song. All who serve God need

---

God Calls Moses (continued)
Exodus 2–4   Name _____

Follow the directions to complete the map. You may use your Bible to help you.

Put a 👑 on the place where Moses was born and grew up as the adopted son of Pharaoh's daughter (Exodus 3:7).

Put a ⟋ on the place where Moses became a shepherd after he fled from Pharaoh (Exodus 2:15).

Color red the mountain where God spoke to Moses from the burning bush (Exodus 3:1).

Draw a green star by the name of the good land that God promised to give His people (Exodus 3:8).

Moses had many questions and excuses when God explained the task He wanted him to do. God patiently answered his questions until Moses asked Him to send someone else (Exodus 4:13–14).

Draw a line to match what Moses said with God's replies.

Moses said	God's replies
Who am I that I should stand before Pharaoh?	Show them the signs with the rod, the hand, and the river water.
What should I tell the children of Israel when they ask Your name?	I will certainly be with you.
Suppose the children of Israel will not believe me.	I AM WHO I AM.
I am not a good speaker.	Who has made man's mouth? Have not I, the Lord?

(24) A Servant's Heart • Lesson 17

---

to have the kind of heart this song displays. The students need God's power in everything they do. Point out that God's grace is always sufficient for every need in their lives. Ask them how God has helped them be obedient for His glory.

Teach the first verse. Consult the list of ideas and methods for practicing the hymn (page xii) as necessary. Help the students understand the hymn and apply its truths to their lives.

Discussion Questions

💡 **Who do you think will see God's great work?** *(Israel)*

💡 **When the people see God's power, what do you think they will do?** *(They will realize how powerful He is and fear Him.)*

💡 **Whom will the people believe?** *(They will believe the Lord and His servant Moses.)*

✏️ Worktext page 24

Guide the reading of a map. Choose volunteers to look up the Bible verses in Exodus. Take turns letting each volunteer tell the class what place to locate and to mark on the map.

Recall facts and details. Direct attention to the bottom part of page 24. Point out God's questions and statements and Moses's questions and statements. Instruct the students to read and follow the directions on the page. Give help as needed.

18 God Shows His Power

Materials
- Hymn: "Lead On, O King Eternal"
- TimeLine and picture: Moses
- Walking stick from the previous lesson

🎵 Hymn: "Lead On, O King Eternal"
Sing the first verse (Worktext page 213; music CD track 5).

Background Information
Egypt and Pharaoh—*Even though Israel was a slave nation under Pharaoh, they saw God's power on their behalf. Likewise today, a Christian, no matter how insignificant his position is in the family or world, may also see God work in his life for God's glory.*

The Passover—*The Jewish Passover commemorates the last plague God visited on Egypt. The Passover pictures our Redemption in Christ and the new life that He gives us when we are born again. The lamb, slain to provide blood for the doorpost and meat for the meal, portrays Christ's death on Calvary. The unleavened bread shows that we are to be separated from evil. Leaven in the Bible is often considered a symbol of sin and wickedness. The bitter herbs show the bitterness of slavery. Since the firstborn was saved from the death angel through the application of the lamb's blood, we learn that putting faith in Christ's death for us, as the sacrificial Lamb, is the only way we can escape eternal death. Those whom the Lord redeems He calls to live holy and separated lives for Him.*

Introducing the Bible Account
Review the previous account of Moses. Let individual students tell parts of the account about Moses being called by God. Tell them that Moses and Aaron met by the mountain to plan their trip to Egypt.

Bible Account

Read Exodus 4:29–12:51 or use the following retelling of the passage. Listening question: **What did God tell Moses and Aaron that the Egyptians would do when they left Egypt?** *(The Egyptians would force them out and give them their gold, silver, and jewels.)* Hold the walking stick as you tell the account.

Moses Before Pharaoh

Moses and Aaron first went to the children of Israel. Aaron spoke to them with the words God gave to Moses. The Israelites believed what Aaron said, and they worshiped the Lord for hearing their cries for help.

Moses and Aaron went to Pharaoh and told him what the Lord wanted: "Let My people go so that they can hold a feast for Me in the wilderness."

Pharaoh answered, "Who is the Lord that I should obey His voice and let Israel go?" That day, Pharaoh commanded that the Israelites be given more work as slaves to make them work even harder.

God told Moses that He would free the Israelites. Although Pharaoh would not let the Israelites go now, God said that soon the Egyptians would beg the Israelites to leave. Moses told the Israelites this, but they would not listen to him anymore.

Pharaoh's heart was hard, and he would not listen to Moses and Aaron, who were speaking God's Word. God sent ten plagues (troubles or suffering) to Egypt so they would know that God is the Lord. The first plague happened the next day. Moses and Aaron met Pharaoh by the Nile River. There, Aaron stretched out his rod, and all *the water in Egypt turned to blood*. Everything living in the river died, and no one had fresh water for a week. Pharaoh still refused to let the Israelites go because he hardened his heart just as the Lord had said.

Next, God sent *frogs* to Egypt. They came out of the water and covered the land. Pharaoh said that if God took away the frogs, the Israelites could go. Moses and Aaron prayed to God, and the frogs were gone, but Pharaoh changed his mind because he hardened his heart just as the Lord had said. Third, God sent *lice* to crawl all over the Egyptian people and animals. Fourth, God sent *flies* all over Egypt. Fifth, *all the cattle of the Egyptians died*. Sixth, God sent *boils* to cover the skin of all the Egyptians. Seventh, He sent *thunder, fire, and hail* so strong that it killed all the animals and food the Egyptians grew in the fields. Eighth, God sent *locusts* to the Egyptians; and ninth, He sent *darkness*.

During these plagues, God protected the Israelites. They were living in the land of Goshen, where the plagues did not come. For the tenth and last plague, Moses gave the Israelites two special instructions. That night, each Israelite family had to sacrifice a lamb and put the blood of the lamb on their doorposts. The other instruction was to prepare to leave Egypt.

At midnight, *every first-born son and every first-born male animal was killed* by the death angel. This was the tenth plague. Only those families who had sprinkled lamb's blood on their doorposts were spared.

Pharaoh and the Egyptians could not disobey God any longer. They begged the Israelites to leave and gave them gold, silver, jewels, and other gifts so that they would leave. The Israelites were free from their slavery and went out to sacrifice and to worship the God of their salvation.

Discussion Questions
▶ **Name the plagues God sent on Egypt.** *(water turned to blood, frogs, lice, flies, killed cattle, boils, hail and fire, locusts, darkness, and death to first-born sons and first-born male animals)*

💡 **Do you think it was hard for Moses to obey God and go back to Pharaoh many times?** *(Accept any answer.)*

▶ **Which of the plagues convinced Pharaoh to let the Israelites go?** *(the killing of his first-born son)*

Name _____

The ten plagues are found in this puzzle. Complete the puzzle using the words in the word bank.

Word Bank

blood	boils
hail	firstborn
flies	locusts
cattle	lice
frogs	darkness

ACROSS

1. The **seventh** plague rained _____ on the land of Egypt.

3. The **third** plague made the dust become _____.

5. The **tenth** plague killed all the _____ in the land except where there was blood on the doorposts.

6. The **first** plague turned the water to _____, and all the fish died.

8. The **ninth** plague brought _____ over all the land, even during the day.

9. The **fourth** plague caused swarms of _____ to be in all the houses of Egypt.

Pharaoh would not let God's people leave Egypt. God used His power over all things to bring **plagues** on Egypt. A plague is something that causes great trouble and suffering.

DOWN

2. The **eighth** plague was _____ brought by the east wind.

4. The **sixth** plague caused the skin of the Egyptians to break out in _____.

5. The **second** plague was _____ that hopped everywhere.

7. The **fifth** plague caused the _____ to become sick and die.

Crossword solution:
- 1 ACROSS / 1 DOWN: HAIL / LOUSTS (LOCUSTS)
- LICE
- FIRSTBORN / BOILS
- BLOOD / FROG
- DARKNESS / CATTLE
- FLIES

Moses's Character

Name _____

Place the letter of one of Moses's character traits beside the sentence that tells about a time when it was shown. You may use the Bible verses to help you.

1. __A__ God told Moses, "I AM the Lord" (Exodus 6:8).

2. __C__ Moses and Aaron told Pharaoh that the Lord God of Israel said, "Let my people go" (Exodus 5:1).

3. __D__ Moses asked the Lord why He had treated His people badly (Exodus 5:22).

4. __B__ Moses did as the Lord had commanded (Exodus 7:6).

A person's **character** is shown by the way he **thinks**, **speaks**, and **acts**. Each of these ways can be called a trait. (Moses showed both good and bad **character traits**.) Read some of them here.

A. Moses listened to God.
B. Moses obeyed God.
C. Moses told others what God said.
D. Moses complained to God in disbelief.

God can help you have the good character traits of Moses. Use these questions to help you think of some ways.

God speaks through His Word. How can you listen?

_____
Answers will vary but should include reading His Word.

We are to obey God in all things. What is one way that you need to be especially careful to obey today?

_____
Answers will vary.

Who is one person with whom you need to share what God says?

_____
Answers will vary.

What prayer requests of others do you need to pray about?

_____
Answers will vary.

▶ **How did the children of Israel escape having their first-born children killed?** *(Each family had to kill a lamb and put the lamb's blood on their doorpost. Discuss how the decision of whether to obey always yields a consequence in our lives.)*

💡 **How was the killing of the lamb and the blood on the doorposts a picture of how we are saved today?** *(Elicit that Jesus, the Lamb of God, shed His blood so that we would not have to suffer the punishment of death for our sins. Just as the Israelites had to believe God and sacrifice an animal in the place of the firstborn son, today people must trust that God will save them from eternal death in the lake of fire on the basis of their faith in the sacrifice of Jesus on the cross.)*

🕐 **TimeLine**

Add Moses to the TimeLine. Place the picture of Moses on the TimeLine (1525–1405 BC), pointing out that Moses lived about six hundred years after Abraham. Guide the students as they glue the picture of Moses (from the Student Materials section of the Toolkit CD) onto their TimeLines.

❤ **Memory Verse—Exodus 14:31**

Practice the memory verse.

📝 **Worktext page 25**

Recall facts and details. Read the clue and give the missing word for 1-Across of the puzzle. Show the students where

to write the word *hail*. Tell them to complete the crossword puzzle using the words from the word bank.

📝 **Worktext page 26**

Identify character traits. Read the directions to the students. Discuss the character traits of Moses. Guide the students in matching the character traits of Moses.

Apply character traits. Explain the second part of the page and let the students work independently, giving help to the individuals who need it. After the students have completed the page, call on students to share their prayer requests. Conclude with prayer time.

🔗 **World History Connection (optional)**

Discuss the Israelite slaves. Explain to the students that the Israelite slaves had to work hard under the leadership of cruel taskmasters. One of their projects may have been building the royal storehouse cities for keeping the provisions and armaments. One city may have been Pithom, modern-day Tell er-Retabeh, and another may have been Qantir, which was later renamed Rameses after a later pharaoh, Rameses II. The slaves made the bricks used in building. The bricks were made from mud mixed with straw, palm fiber, shell, or charcoal. The slaves were also forced to work at hauling huge blocks of stone to the building site.

💡 **What do you think it may have been like to be an Israelite slave?** *(Accept any answer that conveys a negative aspect.)*

▶ **What did the slaves make the bricks out of?** *(a mixture of mud with straw, palm fiber, shell, or charcoal)*

Discuss living in tents. Tell the students that the Bedouins, a group of Arab nomads, live in tents today. Ask whether anyone knows what nomads are. *(people who move from place to place)* Explain that their tents are like the tents in which the Israelites lived. Allow the students to guess what the tents are made of. *(fabric woven from goat hair)* Explain that it is the women who put up these tents. Allow the students to share their experiences with putting up tents.

LESSON 19 God Shows the Way

Materials
- Hymn: "Lead On, O King Eternal"
- Walking stick from Lesson 17
- Beanbag

♫ Hymn: "Lead On, O King Eternal"
Sing the first verse (Worktext page 213).

♥ Memory Verse—Exodus 14:31
Practice the memory verse.

Background Information

Chariots—*Chariots were two-wheeled carts pulled by horses and used for fighting as well as for transportation. Early chariots were heavy and awkward, and they were pulled by donkeys. Later Egyptian chariots were light and close to the ground, and they were pulled by fast horses.*

The Red Sea—*Israel's deliverance at the Red Sea is the most dramatic and memorable event in that people's history. The event symbolizes the message of the book of Exodus—Redemption.*

Introducing the Bible Account

Guide a review about the Israelites. Remind the students that the Israelites camped on the edge of the wilderness and praised God for His faithfulness. Allow them to describe what they think life there would have been like for the Israelites. Explain that the journey was just beginning.

Bible Account

Read Exodus 13:21–14:31 or use the following retelling of the passage. Listening question: **What happened to the Egyptians?** *(The Lord overthrew them in the middle of the sea.)*

Lead the class in reciting **Exodus 14:31.** Tell the class that Moses and the children of Israel sang a wonderful song of praise to God after this miraculous deliverance. And as they continued on their journey, God went before them in a pillar of cloud by day and a pillar of fire by night. They were redeemed, and God was with them.

God Shows the Way

To help the Israelites know where to go, God went before them in a cloud that looked like a pillar. As long as they followed that cloud, they were protected by God. At night, God watched over them from a pillar of fire. Just imagine seeing that cloud in front of you during the day and that pillar of fire protecting you at night.

God spoke to Moses and told him to lead the children of Israel to a place near the sea to spend the next night. He even told Moses His reason. He said that He would again harden Pharaoh's heart and Pharaoh would come after the Israelites to destroy them. Surely the Israelites had thought they were through with the Egyptians.

As the Israelites were camped by the sea, the army of Egypt in their chariots came after them. The people immediately came to Moses, telling him that he should have left them in Egypt instead of bringing them out to die at the hands of the Egyptians.

Moses told the people, "Don't be afraid. Just stand still, and you will see the salvation of the Lord. He will show it to you today. The Egyptians you have seen today are about to be destroyed. The Lord Himself will fight for you." God, in the pillar of cloud, went behind them and came between them and the Egyptians. The cloud gave light to the Israelites ahead of it and darkness or fog to the Egyptians behind it. God told Moses to stretch his rod *[demonstrate, using the walking stick]* over the sea that was before them. Moses did that and when he did, the sea rose up on two sides! God divided the waters, like two walls. And in the middle of the walls of water was dry ground! Imagine walking between two giant walls of water. That is what the Israelites did. The people walked right into the middle of the sea on dry ground.

But the Egyptians kept coming, right into the sea. The Bible says that God looked at the Egyptians through the cloud and the fire, and He caused them to panic. The wheels fell off the chariots, and all was confusion. Most of the Egyptians were crying out that they should flee. They were turning back to get out of the sea, but God was not going to let them do that.

As soon as all the Israelites were on the other side, God told Moses to stretch out his rod again *[demonstrate, using the walking stick]*. As he did, the waters started coming back over the dry ground. The Bible tells us that the sea returned to its place. The Egyptians tried to get away from it, but the Lord overthrew them in the middle of the sea. The Lord saved Israel that day.

⚜

Discussion Questions
▶ **How did God lead His children after they left Egypt?** *(He led them in a pillar of cloud by day and a pillar of fire by night.)*
▶ **Where did God tell Moses to camp?** *(by the sea)*
💡 **Why do you think God had the Israelites camp there?** *(Explain that God knew what He was going to do and was setting up the destruction of the Egyptians.)*

God Shows the Way

Name _____

C

B

D

A

E

God guided the Israelites with a pillar of cloud by day and a pillar of fire by night. Today God guides us too. He has given us the Bible.

Look at the pictures. Match them with the correct Bible verse.

A. They went to church and told what God had done (Acts 14:27).

B. Honor your father and your mother (Ephesians 6:2).

C. You are wise if you win souls (Proverbs 11:30).

D. Sing a new song unto the Lord (Psalm 96:1).

E. Do good and be willing to share (1 Timothy 6:18).

© BJU Press. Reproduction prohibited.

A Servant's Heart • Lesson 19   27

▸ **Had the Israelites doubted God?** *(Yes. They told Moses that he should have left them in Egypt.)*

▸ **Where did the Israelites go when the Egyptians started chasing them?** *(into the sea because God had parted the waters and made a path of dry land for the Israelites to walk on)*

▸ **Did the Egyptians cross on that same path?** *(They tried, but God allowed the water to flow over the Egyptians, and they all died.)*

▸ **Who was it that fought the battle for the Israelites?** *(God)*

💡 **Do you think the Israelites would trust God on the rest of their trip and not complain or doubt God?** *(Accept any answer, but tell the students that three days after they praised God for saving them, they were complaining to Moses again because there was no water. And God did another miracle for them. This pattern would continue throughout their trip to the land God promised them.)*

💡 **Do Christians doubt God and complain although they know God is all-powerful and know that they should trust in Him?** *(Discuss how Christians can do what is asked, but with grumbling and complaining. As Christians surrender to God, they can obey and be happy.)*

✍ Worktext page 27

Infer meaning and apply Bible verses. As the students turn to the Worktext page, emphasize that God's Word, the Bible, has instructions from God and leads a Christian in God's way. Choose volunteers to read the verses; then direct

the students to match the picture with the correct Bible verse.

LESSON 20 Called to Witness

Materials
- Hymn: "Lead On, O King Eternal"
- Beanbag
- Chart 3, "Books of the Bible: Old Testament" (optional)

🎵 Hymn: "Lead On, O King Eternal"
Sing the first verse (Worktext page 213).

♥ Memory Verse—Exodus 14:31
Practice the memory verse.

Introduce the Application Story
Discuss sharing the gospel with relatives. Ask volunteers to tell of circumstances in which they have witnessed to a relative.

Application Story

Read or tell the following story. Listening question: **What does Nathaniel do when he is called to witness?** *(He makes excuses.)*

Called to Witness

Nathaniel squirmed on the hard wooden pew. He glanced at his watch: 12:15. He groaned inside. When was Pastor White ever going to stop talking?

"Every day, people are dying and going to hell," Pastor White was saying. "Probably nearly every one of us here knows someone who is unsaved. The question is, have you witnessed to that person?"

Nathaniel thought of his grandfather. He was a good man, always kind, and he had given Nathaniel some of the best gifts. But Nathaniel knew his grandfather was not a Christian. He never went to church, and when someone tried to talk to him about Christ, he would say, "I live a good, clean life. I don't need any of that religious stuff."

Pastor White was concluding, "If you know someone who is unsaved, why not decide today that you will talk to that person? If this is your decision, please come forward during this invitation, and someone here will be happy to pray with you."

The pianist played softly. Nathaniel knew he should go forward to pray for his grandfather. He just could not leave his seat, though. "I'm no good at talking about serious things like that," he argued to himself. "Besides, Grandpa might get angry, and what will my friends think?" The music stopped, and Pastor White prayed. Church was over, but Nathaniel felt miserable—he knew he should trust God for strength to obey.

The next day, Nathaniel's friend David came over to play baseball. They practiced pitching and hitting the ball.

"Nate," his mom called from the back door, "Come in, Nate." He shrugged at David and went in. His mother looked sad. "Grandfather Stone has had a heart attack. He's in the hospital. Dad's already gone to see him," his mother said. "Hurry now, and get into the car."

Nathaniel was silent all the way to the hospital. He wondered whether his grandfather would be all right. He knew people sometimes died from heart attacks.

Nathaniel's father was sitting in the waiting room at the hospital. He stood up when Nathaniel and his mother arrived. "He's going to be okay," he said. "He's resting right now. The doctors said that Grandpa will have to lose some weight and watch what he eats from now on."

Nathaniel was thoughtful. "Dad," he said, "did Grandpa nearly die?"

"Well, son, the heart attack wasn't so bad that it would have killed him. It could have been, though. Thankfully, the Lord spared his life."

Nathaniel walked over to a chair and sat down. He bowed his head. "I'm sorry, Lord," he prayed, "that I haven't witnessed to Grandpa as I should have. Please help me to talk to him. You know that I have trouble talking to grownups about things like that. Please help me know what to say. Thank you for giving me more time. In Jesus' name, Amen."

Discussion Questions

▶ **Whom did Nathaniel think of when the pastor was preaching?** *(his grandfather)*

▶ **Why did Grandfather Stone think he didn't need the Lord?** *(He thought he lived a good life. He was depending on his works.)*

▶ **Why did Nathaniel not want to make a commitment to witness to his grandfather?** *(He didn't think he was any good at telling people about the Lord. He also thought Grandfather might get angry. He was worried what his friends would think.)*

 Do you ever have the same thoughts that Nathaniel had?

▶ **What happened that caused Nathaniel to decide he must witness to Grandfather?** *(Grandfather had a heart attack.)*

▶ **How did Nathaniel get the courage to witness to him?** *(He confessed to God that he was afraid and asked God to help him. Point out that it is impossible to please God when we are selfish or fearful. Remind the students to trust God and ask Him for help to obey.)*

📖 Bible Study Skills, Worktext page 28

Study the books of the Old Testament. Ask the students to open their Bibles to the Old Testament contents page, or display Chart 3, "Books of the Bible: Old Testament." Direct the class to read together the names of the first fifteen books of the Old Testament (Genesis–Ezra). Read the list several times. Choose fifteen students to stand at the front of the classroom. Ask the first student to name the first book of the Bible (Genesis); then have each student in turn name the next book of the Old Testament.

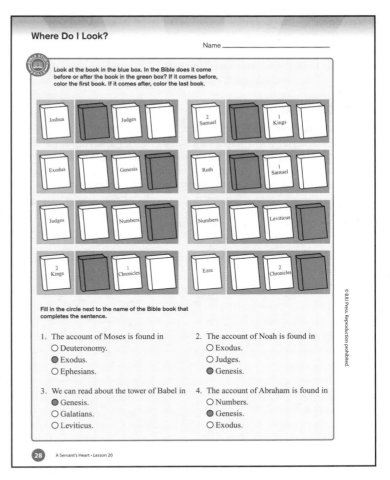

Locate verses. Guide the students in locating and reading the following verses with a partner: **2 Chronicles 9:7**, **1 Samuel 12:24**, and **Genesis 45:7**. As the students turn to Worktext page 28, explain that they are to color the book in the green box that indicates whether the book in the blue box comes *before* or *after*. Do several examples with the students.

Locate Bible accounts. Read the directions for the bottom of the page and let the students work independently.

▶ Going Beyond

Reinforcement

Materials

- Pocket chart (optional)
- Sentence strips or large cards with one sentence on each strip (without the sequence number):

(1) Moses told God he could not speak well.
(2) God sent Moses and Aaron to Pharaoh.
(3) Moses showed God's signs to Pharaoh.
(4) The Israelites put blood on their doorposts.
(5) Pharaoh told Moses to take the Israelites and go.
(6) God led Israel with a pillar of cloud/pillar of fire.
(7) The Israelites walked through the sea.

Sequence events. Display the sentences in random order in a pocket chart or on the board. Choose a student to arrange the sentences in the order that the events took place. Rescramble the sentences and repeat the activity. Place the sentences in a learning center for individual review if desired.

Enrichment

Guide a rhyme-writing activity. Encourage students to write a rhyme for a song or chorus, using **Exodus 14:31** as its text. The rhyme might be only two lines. Then you or someone you know can put the rhyme to music for all the students to sing. Consider the following example:

They believed what God could do
Because they saw that He was true.

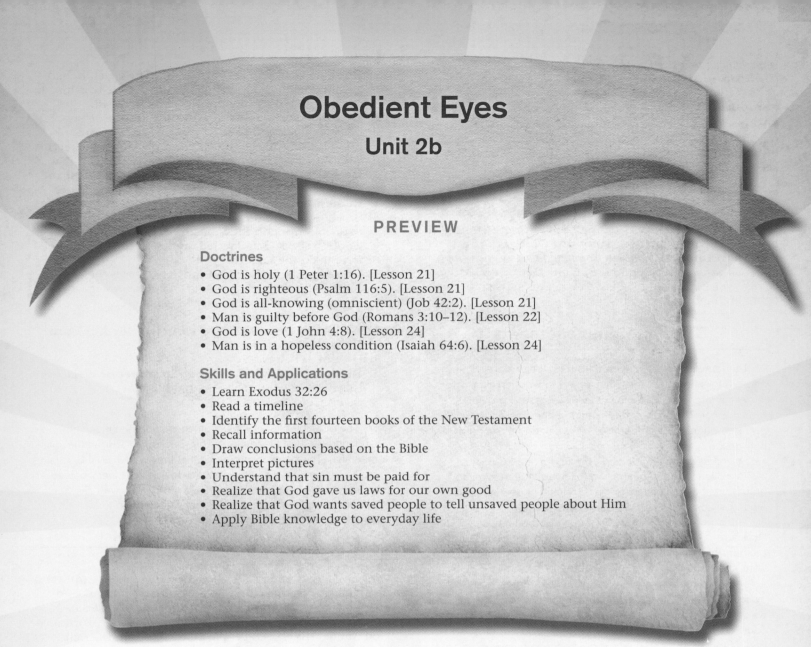

Obedient Eyes
Unit 2b

PREVIEW

Doctrines

- God is holy (1 Peter 1:16). [Lesson 21]
- God is righteous (Psalm 116:5). [Lesson 21]
- God is all-knowing (omniscient) (Job 42:2). [Lesson 21]
- Man is guilty before God (Romans 3:10–12). [Lesson 22]
- God is love (1 John 4:8). [Lesson 24]
- Man is in a hopeless condition (Isaiah 64:6). [Lesson 24]

Skills and Applications

- Learn Exodus 32:26
- Read a timeline
- Identify the first fourteen books of the New Testament
- Recall information
- Draw conclusions based on the Bible
- Interpret pictures
- Understand that sin must be paid for
- Realize that God gave us laws for our own good
- Realize that God wants saved people to tell unsaved people about Him
- Apply Bible knowledge to everyday life

LESSON **21** The Ten Commandments

Materials

- Hymn: "Lead On, O King Eternal"
- Unit 2 Bookmark for each student
- Highlighter for each student (optional)
- Roll of paper towels: On the paper towels (or rolled wrapping paper), write using a marker the phrases of the memory verse with the reference. As you unroll the paper towels, the parts of the verse are revealed.
- Two pieces of poster board: Prepare two large tablets to resemble those on Worktext page 29. Write the Ten Commandments on the tablets (optional).

♫ Hymn: "Lead On, O King Eternal"

Teach the second verse (Worktext page 213). The hymnwriter is asking God to lead us until we are no longer fighting sin in our lives and in our surroundings. He says that when we are in heaven and we sin no more, we will be holy and peaceful. He knows God's spiritual kingdom comes through His love and mercy toward us (that He sent His Son to die and pay for our sins). Consult the list of ideas and methods for practicing the hymn (page xii) as necessary. Help the students to understand the hymn and apply its truths to their lives.

Background Information

Commandments—*God gave many commandments in the Bible. The summary of the Old Testament law is the Ten Commandments. Our word* commandment *comes from the late Latin word* commandare, *meaning "to give someone a responsibility." God gave Israel the responsibility of keeping all His commandments. God gave the law to show that no one can be good or holy*

*enough to get to heaven. The law shows us our need of Christ (**Galatians 3:24–25**).*

Introducing the Bible Account

Discuss the focus of our eyes. Read **Psalm 101:3**. Point out that we must be careful what we allow into our minds by guarding what we see. Emphasize the importance of keeping our eyes focused on things that please God.

Bible Account

Read Exodus 19:1–20:17 or use the following retelling of the passage. Listening question: **Why did God give the Ten Commandments?** *(The Ten Commandments were a group of laws God gave to the people to live by, and they were a basis for all other laws.)* Show the tablets as you present each of the commandments (optional).

The Ten Commandments

The Israelites were now free from Egyptian slavery. God had brought them into the Sinai desert to worship Him. The Israelites pitched their tents in the wilderness and camped at Mount Sinai. There, God told them that they were a special group of people to Him and that He wanted to make them His holy nation.

"You have seen what I did to the Egyptians," God said to the Israelites. The Egyptians had followed the Israelites to bring them back into slavery, but God had caused their chariots to collapse and the Red Sea to drown them.

The Lord said that He wanted to make the Israelites a "treasure . . . above all people." Moses told the people all that the Lord had said. They answered, "We will do everything the Lord says to do."

The Lord told Moses that everyone had to get ready because in three days He would come to them. The Israelites washed their clothes and cleaned themselves. None of them could climb Mount Sinai or even touch the border of it and live. Whoever touched it would die because this was the holy place where the Lord God would come to them in three days.

In the morning on the third day, there was thunder and lightning. A thick cloud formed on top of the mountain, and there was a voice like a trumpet, so loud that all the people in the camp trembled.

The Lord descended on the mountain in fire, and the mountain was surrounded with smoke as if the whole thing were on fire. The whole mountain shook with the presence of the Lord.

Moses brought the people out of the camp, and they stood around the mountain, being careful not to touch it. God called Moses up to the top of the mountain and told him to remind the people not to come up the mountain. If any of them tried to see the Lord, they would die.

Moses said, "The people cannot come up to Mount Sinai." They knew what would happen and did not dare disobey the Lord.

The Lord told Moses and Aaron to come to the top of the mountain. Then God gave Moses the Ten Commandments:

1. **Have no other gods before me.** The Israelites had been living in Egypt where many gods were worshiped. God wanted them to know that this was a sin.
2. **Do not worship any man-made image.** The Israelites were not to make or worship any statues of anything in heaven, the earth, or the sea. God is jealous of anything that takes worship away from Him.
3. **Do not take the name of the Lord your God in vain.**
4. **Remember the Sabbath day to keep it holy.** The Israelites were to do all their work in six days but not to do any work on the Sabbath. Just as God created the world in six days and rested on the seventh, His people were to do the same.
5. **Honor your father and mother.** This is the first commandment with a promise. A child who obeys this commandment is promised a long life.
6. **Do not kill** *(murder)*.
7. **Do not be unfaithful to your wife or husband.**
8. **Do not steal.**
9. **Do not tell lies.**
10. **Do not want what belongs to someone else.** The Israelites were not to want anything that belonged to their neighbors.

The people of Israel were frightened at the thunder, lightning, and noise of the trumpet. They backed away from the mountain. The people were afraid that they would die if God spoke to them, so they asked Moses to speak to them instead.

Moses told them not to be afraid. God had given His people these laws to test them. He wanted them to fear Him out of respect for His holiness and not to sin.

God gave Moses other rules about offerings, about eating and drinking, about what things were clean and unclean, and about what was appropriate in worship. The Israelites had spent a long time in Egypt, where other gods were worshiped. God wanted His chosen people to worship Him the right way.

Discussion Questions

💡 **What are some things in your life that are so important that they are like other gods you put before the living God?** *(Accept any answer, but let the students discuss the false gods they worship and sometimes put before God.)*

💡 **What are some examples of things a second grader might steal?** *(Let the students discuss this, but remind them that taking anything, such as a pencil or a cookie, that belongs to someone else, even members of one's own family, is stealing.)*

💡 **What is wrong with wanting something that belongs to someone else?** *(Let the students discuss that even though you may not steal something, when you want it badly enough to steal it if you could, you are coveting. Coveting is sin. Encourage the students to be thankful and content.)*

▶ **What did God want people to do on the Sabbath?** *(keep it holy, rest)*

💡 **Why do you think God gave His people all the laws that He gave them?** *(Let the students discuss this, and then tell them that all of God's laws help us. None of them*

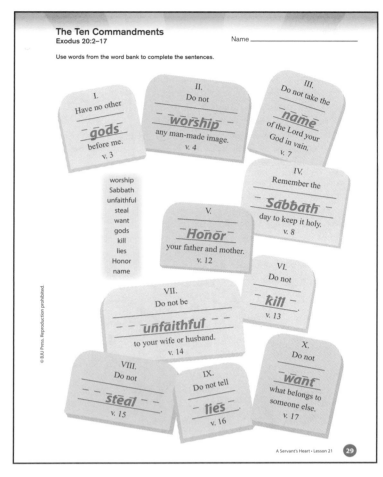

hurts us. You might compare this to the instructions given in the box with a toy to help the owner keep the toy undamaged and to protect the owner from possible injury.)

✍ Worktext page 29

Recall facts and details. Review the list of commandments from the lesson. Tell the students to use the words from the word bank to complete each commandment. Give help as needed.

♥ Memory Verse—Exodus 32:26

Practice the memory verse. Consult the list of ideas and methods (page xii) for practicing the memory verses as necessary. Memorization is an important key to understanding biblical truths and applying them to our lives. Encourage the students to be able to recite the verses at the end of each subunit.

LESSON
22 The Golden Calf

Materials
• Hymn: "Lead On, O King Eternal"
• A figurine

♫ Hymn: "Lead On, O King Eternal"

Sing the second verse (Worktext page 213; music CD track 6).

Introducing the Bible Account

Show the figurine. Ask the students whether the figurine can hear (*no*), see (*no*), or talk (*no*). Read **Psalm 115:2–8** and **Psalm 135:15–18**. Point out that while we cannot see God, He always sees us.

Bible Account

Read Exodus 32–33 or use the following retelling of the passage. Listening question: **Why did Moses throw down the tablets made of stone?** *(He was angry when he saw the people worshiping the golden calf.)* Show the figurine as you read.

The Golden Calf

Moses had been up on the mountain with God for a long time. The Israelites who waited for him at the foot of the mountain got worried. What could be taking him so long? The people's strong leader was gone, and they began to complain to Aaron. They complained that they didn't know what had happened to Moses.

They wanted a god that they could look at and touch. They asked Aaron to make a golden calf so they could gather and worship. They gave Aaron their golden earrings that they had brought with them out of Egypt. He melted the gold and made a golden calf. Aaron did what they wanted. He built an altar and made a proclamation, "Tomorrow is a feast to the Lord."

Early the next day the people came. They brought offerings, and then they ate and drank and began to do wicked things.

One of the laws God gave Moses on the mountain said God's people were not to worship any graven image (anything man had made). As God finished writing the laws on two large tablets of stone, He told Moses to go back down to the people because they were doing something they shouldn't. They were going astray by worshiping the statue of a calf. God called the people proud, and He was angry.

For a time, Moses pleaded for the people; then he started down the mountain. As he came near the bottom with God's laws written on the two tablets, he heard the people below. They were singing, dancing, and yelling. In his anger, Moses threw down the stone tablets and broke them!

He went into the middle of the people, took the golden calf, and put it in the fire. He ground the gold into powder, threw it into the water, and made the people drink the water. Moses went to Aaron and asked why he had made this idol. Aaron made excuses, but Moses did not listen.

Then Moses went and stood in the gate of the camp and said, "Whoever is on the Lord's side should come over to me." Many of the people came to him. Then he told the people that were on the Lord's side to go throughout the camp and kill those people who were sinning against God. God's people did what Moses had said, and about three thousand of the people whom Moses had led out of Egypt died that day!

Moses told all the people who were left that they had sinned in making a golden calf and worshiping it. Moses talked to God and asked God to put the sins of the people on

---

him, but God said that He would punish the people who had sinned. The Bible says God sent plagues (maybe like some of the plagues He had sent to the Egyptians) to the people who had worshiped the golden calf.

God then spoke through Moses to the people and told them an angel would go before them and kill their enemies, but that He, God, would not go with them to the land He had promised them. He said they were proud and stubborn, or "stiff-necked." Only after Moses begged God did God say He would stay with the people. He told Moses to set up a tent and to make it a place where the people could worship God. Now the people who wanted to worship God went outside the camp to the tent-tabernacle to worship.

＊

Discussion Questions

▶ **Where was Moses when the Bible account begins?** *(at the top of Mount Sinai)*

▶ **What was he doing?** *(getting the law from God)*

▶ **Did God want the people to worship man-made things?** *(No. God said they were not to worship images; they were to worship only the living God.)*

▶ **What did Aaron make?** *(a golden calf that the people could worship)*

💡 **Why do you think Aaron did what the people wanted?** *(Accept any answer, but discuss how Aaron might have justified such a thing.)*

💡 **Why do you think the people thought they needed a golden image to worship?** *(Accept any answer, but discuss the fear and insecurity of the people and their memory of the bulls that the Egyptians worshiped.)*

💡 **Do you think Moses was right to be angry with the people?** *(yes)*

▶ **What does God hate?** *(sin)*

▶ **What is sin?** *(Sin is not obeying God's commandments; sin is doing anything that God does not want you to do.)*

❤ Memory Verse—Exodus 32:26

Principle: God hates sin. We should stand on God's side.

▶ **What question did Moses ask?** *(Who is on the Lord's side?)*

▶ **Why did Moses have to ask the people this question?** *(They had sinned by worshiping the golden calf.)*

▶ **Did all the people come to Moses to indicate they were on the Lord's side?** *(no)*

✍ Worktext page 30

Interpret pictures. Direct the students' attention to the account on Worktext page 30. Read the account to them, pausing for the students to identify and say what each drawing represents. Direct the students to locate and color each hidden item in the picture.

Explain to the students that God is asking us the same question today. He wants us to make a decision. God wants us to do right. Lead the students in reading the verse several times. Discuss with them how they can be on the Lord's side.

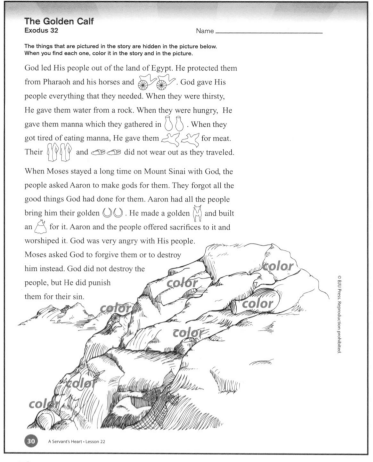

The Golden Calf
Exodus 32   Name _____

The things that are pictured in the story are hidden in the picture below. When you find each one, color it in the story and in the picture.

God led His people out of the land of Egypt. He protected them from Pharaoh and his horses and 🐎. God gave His people everything that they needed. When they were thirsty, He gave them water from a rock. When they were hungry, He gave them manna which they gathered in 🏺. When they got tired of eating manna, He gave them 🦅 for meat. Their 👡 and 👕 did not wear out as they traveled.

When Moses stayed a long time on Mount Sinai with God, the people asked Aaron to make gods for them. They forgot all the good things God had done for them. Aaron had all the people bring him their golden ⭕. He made a golden 🐂 and built an ⛪ for it. Aaron and the people offered sacrifices to it and worshiped it. God was very angry with His people. Moses asked God to forgive them or to destroy him instead. God did not destroy the people, but He did punish them for their sin.

color *color* *color* *color* *color* *color* *color*

30   A Servant's Heart • Lesson 22

LESSON 23 — Rules Are for Our Good

Materials

• Hymn: "Lead On, O King Eternal"
• Tablets prepared for Lesson 21 (optional)

🎵 Hymn: "Lead On, O King Eternal"

Sing the first and second verses (Worktext page 213).

❤ Memory Verse—Exodus 32:26

Review the memory verse. Remind the students that when Moses saw the sin of the people, he wanted those who truly feared God to come away from the others. Ask the students what they should do if a friend asks them to help steal something. Ask them to tell of times when they have had to do what was right even though it was difficult.

Introducing the Application Story

Guide a discussion about God's laws. Review the Ten Commandments on Worktext page 29 or on the tablets prepared for Lesson 21. Tell the students that the God Who made man would naturally know what would make man happy. Remind them that God gave these rules for our own good. Read each commandment again, calling on students to comment on how each rule helps not God, but man.

Read or tell the following story. Listening question: **What is the purpose of rules?** *(Rules protect us.)*

A Rule for a Reason

Jamie brought his bike to a skidding halt in the gravel. "Hey, Kev. Let's go fishing."

"I can't; my bike is broken." Kevin indicated the bits and pieces around where he sat with the bike upside down on its seat and handlebars.

"How 'bout Maloney's pond? We can walk down there."

Kevin squinted through the trees toward Mr. Maloney's pond. At the dead-end road was a tall board fence with a sign. From where he sat by his bike, Kevin could see only the tops of the letters on the sign, but he knew it said "No Trespassing."

"Mr. Maloney's car isn't in the driveway, so he's probably not home," Jamie urged. "And there's a ladder over there under your mom's apple trees."

Kevin paused for a moment. He had a funny feeling in his stomach. Then Jamie called him a chicken.

"I'm not a chicken," Kevin declared. "You get the ladder and find a good place to climb the fence, and I'll get the fishing poles."

They reached Mr. Maloney's fence with the ladder and fishing poles at the same time.

Kevin carefully climbed the ladder, balancing with one hand and keeping the poles clear with the other. He peered over the top of the fence.

"What do you see?" Jamie asked.

Kevin stared around at the well-kept lawn which sloped down into the woods toward the pond. "Just looks like anybody's backyard," he said. "Nothing special."

Kevin and Jamie scrambled over the fence and dropped down into Mr. Maloney's backyard. Kevin landed on top of a plant, and he grabbed its leaves to steady himself.

"Wonder whether he's home," he whispered. Kevin bent to pick up the poles he had tossed over the fence.

"Let's walk around the edge of the yard till we get to those woods down there," said Jamie, pointing to a path at the bottom of the yard.

As Kevin and Jamie walked, the leaves of the vines around the trees brushed against their arms. Kevin wiped the sweat off his face with his forearms. "I hope it's cooler down by the pond."

As the boys fished, Kevin's face started to feel warm and itchy. He scooped up some water and splashed his face and arms. After a couple of hours of catching tiny bluegills, the boys got bored and figured Maloney's pond must be too small for "keepers."

They wrapped the lines around the poles and headed back to Mr. Maloney's backyard. Jamie was scratching his arms, and Kevin was scratching his face. Jamie looked down at his arms and saw that three little red bumps had appeared in the crook of one arm. On the other arm a rash covered the whole back of his wrist and hand.

He glanced up quickly and noticed Kevin scratching his red face. Red bumps covered Kevin's forehead and eyelids. The boys made their way through Mr. Maloney's backyard, slapping the leaves of the vines out of their way. "Hey, Kevin!" he said, just above a whisper. "Do you think these plants are . . ."

"Morning, boys," a cheerful voice said suddenly.

Kevin and Jamie whirled around. Mr. Maloney had come silently up behind them, wearing gloves and carrying an enormous pair of hedge clippers.

Jamie eyed the clippers and said in a shaky voice, "Morning, sir."

Mr. Maloney laughed. "I see you found my poison ivy plants," he said. "Been meaning to get rid of them for a long time. Was just coming out here to do it, in fact."

Kevin leaped away from the nearest plant as though it had come alive. He scratched his arms and inspected them. More bumps had appeared.

"You must be allergic to poison ivy," Mr. Maloney said. "Come on inside, boys, and I'll get you some lotion to rub on those bumps. You know, those bumps remind me that sin always costs us something. You disobeyed my sign, and now you're suffering for it. God tells us there's a far greater eternal punishment for sin. You need to trust Christ for salvation to escape that punishment."

"We're sorry, Mr. Maloney," both boys spoke at the same time. Then Kevin said, "We were wrong, Mr. Maloney. We should not have come fishing at your pond without your permission."

Mr. Maloney folded his arms and smiled. "I would have been glad to let you fish there if you'd come around to my front door and asked me," he said. "I'd have warned you that there aren't any 'keepers' down there, and I'd have warned you about the poison ivy around the fence too." His face grew serious. "Rules are made for a reason. I guess you boys can see that now. And by the looks of you, you'll remember this lesson for a while to come."

Kevin looked at Jamie. The boys nodded. Then at the same time, they both winced. Kevin scratched his face while Jamie scratched his arms.

Discussion Questions

▶ **How did the boys know they should not have gone into Mr. Maloney's yard?** *(The sign said, "No Trespassing.")*

▶ **How did Jamie get Kevin to go with him into the yard?** *(He called him a "chicken.")*

 Have you ever had an experience like this?

▶ **What happened soon after they got into the yard?** *(They started itching and developed red spots.)*

▶ **What makes you think they suspected poison ivy?** *(One of them said, "Do you think these plants are. . .")*

▶ **What was Mr. Maloney about to do?** *(get rid of the poison ivy)*

 How do you think they felt about the "No Trespassing" sign after their trouble? *(They realized that the sign was there for their own protection.)*

Worktext page 31

Interpret pictures. Read **Psalm 1** to the students. Direct them to color the picture of the tree that is described in Psalm 1.

Identify obedient actions. Tell the students to look at the pictures on the tree and decide which ones show obedience to God. Explain to the students that they are to color each picture or circle containing a picture that shows people obeying God's laws. (Students may prefer to use colored pencils on this page.)

24 Prophet Focus: Jonah

Materials
- Hymn: "Lead On, O King Eternal"
- Chart 32, "Ancient Middle East"
- TimeLine and picture: Jonah
- Roll of paper towels from Lesson 21
- Chart 2, "Books of the Bible: New Testament" (optional)

🎵 Hymn: "Lead On, O King Eternal"
Sing the first and second verses (Worktext page 213).

❤ Memory Verse—Exodus 32:26
Practice the memory verse.

Background Information

Prophets—*God raised up men from among the Jewish people to be prophets. God gave each prophet the words He wanted him to speak. Some of these words have already been fulfilled, and others will be fulfilled in the future. Their teachings agreed with the doctrine of the law concerning God and His attributes. The word* prophet *comes from a Greek word that means "one who speaks for another" and "one who speaks beforehand; a predictor." The last seventeen books of the Old Testament are major and minor prophets (Isaiah–Malachi). The prophets brought warnings to the people, called for the people to repent before God's judgment fell, and told the people about God's continuing love for them. Their words often began with "God says" or "God spoke."*

What the Prophets Wore—*At different times the Bible describes prophets' clothes as being made of sheepskins, goatskins, or camel's hair. They wore garments like these as a symbol of their mourning for the people's sin.*

Jonah—*The Lord Jesus said that Jonah was an important picture of His death and Resurrection (**Matthew 12:40**). God wanted Jonah's experience to picture His mercy toward sinful people. God commanded Jonah (meaning "dove") to preach to the wicked city of Nineveh.*

Nineveh—*Described as "that great city," Nineveh was the capital of the prosperous Assyrian nation, which reached its zenith under Sennacherib. The city measured thirty miles long and ten miles wide. Five walls and three moats fortified the city. The walls were one hundred feet high and wide enough at the top for four chariots to be driven side-by-side. Fifteen gates decorated by large lions and bulls opened into the city. But the city was as great in wickedness as it was in power and wealth. God determined to judge the city but would first give the people an opportunity to repent. God sent Jonah to Nineveh to preach to them.*

"God repented"—*God is sinless and does not need to repent of sin. This word* repented *is used in the Old Testament to show His decision to change His method of dealing with someone. In Nineveh's case, God promised judgment because of their wickedness (**Jonah 1:2**). But when they turned to God, the Lord "repented of the evil, that he had said that he would do unto them" (**Jonah 3:10**). As we look at God's actions, it would appear that He had changed His mind, but God knows everything that He is going to do. He knew that He would withhold judgment from Nineveh when the people obeyed His message.*

Introducing the Prophet Focus

Explain the role of a prophet. Share as much as you would like of the background information on prophets. Explain that the account today is about the prophet Jonah and comes from the Bible book named Jonah.

Prophet Focus

Read Jonah 1–4 or use the following retelling of the passage. Show Chart 32, "Ancient Middle East." Locate the cities of Nineveh, Tarshish, and Joppa. Point out that the account begins with Jonah near Joppa.

Jonah

Jonah was a prophet, and God wanted him to preach to the wicked city of Nineveh. Instead of obeying God, the prophet tried to flee "from the presence of the Lord." He got on a ship and headed in the opposite direction.

Soon after the ship set sail, God sent a great storm, and the ship and its passengers were in danger. Jonah confessed to the other men on the boat that he was the cause of the storm and told the men to throw him overboard. When they did, the storm stopped.

God had prepared a giant fish to swallow Jonah and take him to land. After three days and nights in the belly of the fish, Jonah prayed to the Lord. The fish spit Jonah out onto dry ground. God gave Jonah a second chance, telling him again to go to Nineveh and preach to the Ninevites. This time he obeyed.

Jonah went to Nineveh and spoke God's words: "In forty days, Nineveh will be overthrown." God warned them that judgment was coming because of their wickedness. God loved the people but hated their sin. The people repented when they heard Jonah's message. They believed God and humbled themselves. The Lord heard their cries of repentance and had mercy on them.

Jonah knew that if the people of Nineveh repented of their sin, God would not judge them, but Jonah wanted them to be judged. When Nineveh repented, Jonah was disappointed. In fact, he was very angry. Jonah waited outside the city to see what would happen.

God prepared a large, fast-growing plant to shade the prophet from the heat. Jonah was glad about the gourd plant, but the next night the Lord sent a worm to devour it. Jonah was angry when the gourd was gone. God told Jonah that He wanted him to learn a lesson from the gourd. Jonah was concerned about a plant that gave him coolness for a little while. How much more concern God shows about sinners who turn away from sin and turn to Him for salvation.

Discussion Questions

▶ **What did God want Jonah to tell the people of Nineveh?** *(that God was going to judge Nineveh)*

▶ **How did Jonah try to escape from God?** *(by taking a ship in the opposite direction)*

 Why could he not get away from God? *(God is everywhere.)*

 What does this account teach you about God? *(God loves all people and commands His people to go everywhere, telling the message of salvation from sin and hell to the unsaved. However, God does leave it up to people to decide whether or not they will obey Him.)*

 God wanted Jonah to tell the people about God. Do you think God wants you to tell people about Him too? *(Make certain the students know that God does want them to take His message to others.)*

 Read John 4:35 to the students. According to this verse, what should we see? *(others and their need for salvation)*

⏱ TimeLine

Add Jonah to the TimeLine. As you place the picture of Jonah on the TimeLine (765 BC), point out again that Jonah lived about seven hundred years before Christ came to earth. Guide the students as they glue the picture of Jonah (from the Student Materials section of the Toolkit CD) onto their TimeLines.

📖 Bible Study Skills, Worktext page 32

Study the books of the New Testament. Instruct the students to find the contents page in their Bibles, or show Chart 2, "Books of the Bible: New Testament." Direct them to read together the names of the first fourteen books of the New Testament (Matthew–2 Thessalonians). Call on volunteers to each name one of the first fourteen books of the New Testament and then to stand at the front of the classroom in sequence. Ask the students which book comes before Romans. *(Acts)* Guide the class in saying these books of the New Testament as the students are seated. Direct the students to stand by their desks when you say the name of a book from the New Testament. Call out the books of the Bible in no particular order. (Exodus, Mark, Joshua, Romans, John, Ruth, Ephesians) Tell the students to complete the worktext page by coloring black any space containing the name of an Old Testament book and coloring yellow any space containing a New Testament book.

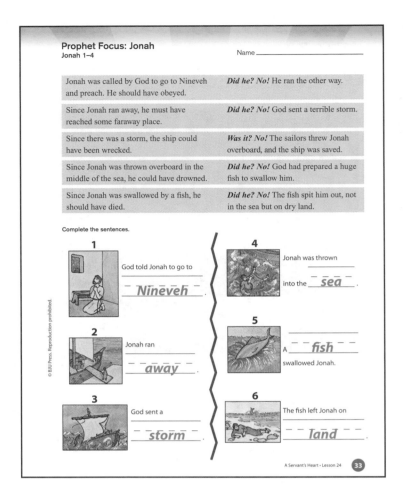

Jonah was called by God to go to Nineveh and preach. He should have obeyed.	*Did he? No!* He ran the other way.
Since Jonah ran away, he must have reached some faraway place.	*Did he? No!* God sent a terrible storm.
Since there was a storm, the ship could have been wrecked.	*Was it? No!* The sailors threw Jonah overboard, and the ship was saved.
Since Jonah was thrown overboard in the middle of the sea, he could have drowned.	*Did he? No!* God had prepared a huge fish to swallow him.
Since Jonah was swallowed by a fish, he should have died.	*Did he? No!* The fish spit him out, not in the sea but on dry land.

Complete the sentences.

1 God told Jonah to go to __Nineveh__

2 Jonah ran __away__.

3 God sent a __storm__.

4 Jonah was thrown into the __sea__.

5 A __fish__ swallowed Jonah.

6 The fish left Jonah on __land__.

A Servant's Heart • Lesson 24   33

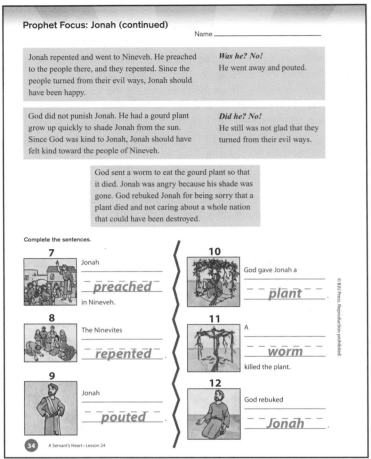

| Jonah repented and went to Nineveh. He preached to the people there, and they repented. Since the people turned from their evil ways, Jonah should have been happy. | *Was he? No!* He went away and pouted. |
| God did not punish Jonah. He had a gourd plant grow up quickly to shade Jonah from the sun. Since God was kind to Jonah, Jonah should have felt kind toward the people of Nineveh. | *Did he? No!* He still was not glad that they turned from their evil ways. |

God sent a worm to eat the gourd plant so that it died. Jonah was angry because his shade was gone. God rebuked Jonah for being sorry that a plant died and not caring about a whole nation that could have been destroyed.

Complete the sentences.

7 Jonah __preached__ in Nineveh.

8 The Ninevites __repented__.

9 Jonah __pouted__.

10 God gave Jonah a __plant__.

11 A __worm__ killed the plant.

12 God rebuked __Jonah__.

34   A Servant's Heart • Lesson 24

Guide the finding of information in the Bible. Direct the students to find **Exodus 3:14** and **John 8:58** in their Bibles. Call on volunteers to read the verses and identify the name God calls Himself.

Worktext pages 33–34

Recall facts and details. Read the summary of events on Worktext pages 33 and 34. Direct the students to complete the twelve sentences using the information provided at the top of each page.

▶ Going Beyond

Reinforcement

Guide a pantomiming activity. Divide the class into groups. Allow each group to present a pantomime of one scene depicted in the Bible accounts of Moses or Jonah. List some scenes they can choose from:

• The Israelites leaving Egypt
• The Israelites crossing the Red Sea
• The people making the golden calf
• Moses coming down from the mountain and finding the people sinning
• Jonah preaching in Nineveh

Enrichment

Guide an activity in the skill of paraphrasing. Challenge the students to make a list of the Ten Commandments, writing each one in their own words.

Assign an art project. After a student has listed the Ten Commandments in his own words and it is in his best writing, encourage him to decorate his list so it can be posted.

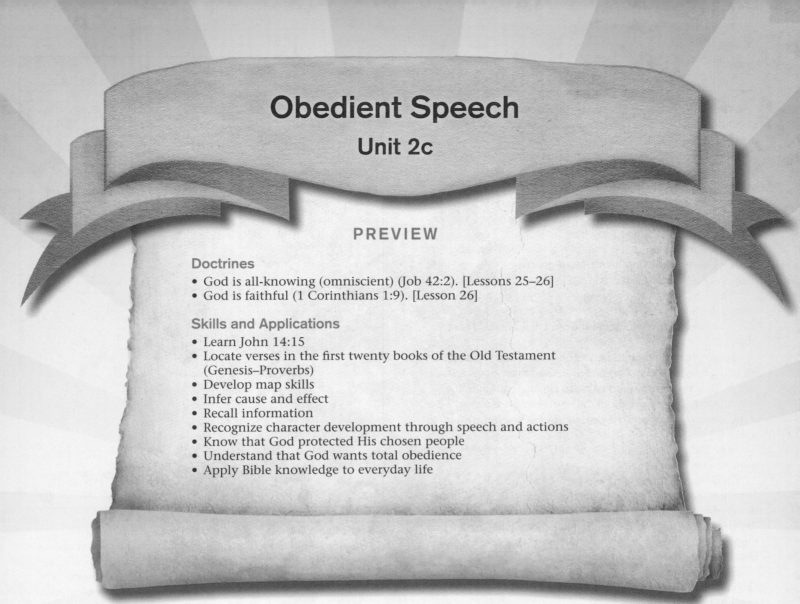

Obedient Speech

Unit 2c

PREVIEW

Doctrines

- God is all-knowing (omniscient) (Job 42:2). [Lessons 25–26]
- God is faithful (1 Corinthians 1:9). [Lesson 26]

Skills and Applications

- Learn John 14:15
- Locate verses in the first twenty books of the Old Testament (Genesis–Proverbs)
- Develop map skills
- Infer cause and effect
- Recall information
- Recognize character development through speech and actions
- Know that God protected His chosen people
- Understand that God wants total obedience
- Apply Bible knowledge to everyday life

LESSON 25

A Message for Balaam

Materials

- Hymn: "Lead On, O King Eternal"
- Unit 2 Bookmark for each student
- Highlighter for each student (optional)

♬ Hymn: "Lead On, O King Eternal"

Teach the third verse (Worktext page 213; music CD track 7).

Background Information

The Israelites—*When Israel arrived at Kadesh, they sent spies into Canaan to determine their enemy's military strength, their wealth, and the condition of their cities and crops. When the people asked for this mission (**Deuteronomy 1:22–23**), Moses gave it his blessing. Only Caleb and Joshua returned with a report of faith. But the unbelieving spies swayed the people in the opposite direction (**Numbers 13:31**). Those who responded in unbelief died in the wilderness.*

Kadesh to Moab—*Thirty-eight years of wandering occurred between the last verse of **Numbers 19** and the first verse of the next chapter. Scripture passes over these years of judgment with silence. The old generation had died. Israel was now about to enter the Promised Land. As they moved toward Canaan, Esau's descendants, the Edomites, refused entry to their land. Taking the long route around Edom, Israel passed through the land of Moab.*

Introducing the Bible Account

Describe the setting. Use the background information *Kadesh to Moab* to update the students on where the children of Israel were at the time of this account. Then tell them that this account is about a prophet named Balaam and a donkey that God used.

Bible Account

Read Numbers 22:1–35 or use the following retelling of the passage. Listening question: **What two ways or things did God use to get Balaam's attention?** *(God used an angel and a donkey to speak to Balaam.)*

A Message for Balaam

When the people of Israel were about to enter the Promised Land, they camped on the plains of Moab on the east side of the Jordan River.

Someone was watching as the great number of Israelites set up their tents on his land. That person was Balak, the king of Moab. He was afraid. The Israelites were being led by God and Moses. They didn't want to fight or take over the land of Moab; they just needed to camp there as they passed through the land. But Balak didn't know that.

Balak wanted to put a curse on the Israelites, so he gave some of his high ranking men a lot of gold and silver and sent them to hire Balaam to curse Israel.

When this group came to Balaam, they told him about the many people camped near Jericho. They explained that King Balak wanted Balaam to curse the Israelites so that Moab could defeat them.

Balaam told the men to stay at his house that night so that he could talk to God to find out what God thought about a curse. That very night, God came to Balaam (not the other way around) and asked about the men who were at his house. (God already knew who they were, but He wanted Balaam to tell Him.)

After Balaam answered, God said, "Don't curse My people; they are blessed."

So Balaam told the men that he couldn't go against God and that he wouldn't go with them to Balak. But Balak didn't give up easily; he sent another group to Balaam, more important than the first group. This time they told Balaam that the king would give him great honors and whatever payment Balaam wanted if he would come.

Balaam told the men to stay the night and he would ask God again. Why did Balaam do that? Because he wanted to go to Moab for the power and money. That night God told Balaam he could go with them, but he should do only what God would tell him. But God was not pleased.

The Bible tells us that Balaam got on his donkey and started out for Moab the next morning. But as he and his donkey were going down the road, the Angel of the Lord stopped the donkey by standing in front of it. The donkey could see that the Angel was mighty and had a sword in His hand. But Balaam couldn't see the Angel at all. The donkey turned aside from the Angel and went into a field. Balaam got angry and hit the donkey.

In the field, the Angel stood in front of the donkey again, and the donkey crashed into a wall, hurting Balaam's foot. Balaam hit the donkey again. When the Angel stopped the donkey the third time, the donkey fell down with Balaam on it, and Balaam beat the donkey again.

This time the donkey spoke to Balaam and asked Balaam why he had hit him three times. Balaam answered the donkey.

Finally, God opened Balaam's eyes so he could see the Angel of the Lord standing there holding a sword. The Angel rebuked Balaam for hitting the donkey. It was really Balaam who was acting stubborn like a donkey; the donkey had been used by God.

Balaam was shocked at what he saw. Here before him was the Angel of the Lord. Balaam told the Angel that he had sinned; he didn't know it was the Angel standing in his way. He said he would go back if God wanted him to. The Angel repeated God's message that Balaam could go to Moab but he must say only what God would tell him to say. Balaam continued on his way.

▶ **What made the king of Moab afraid?** (*There were many Israelites in his land.*)

▶ **What did the king want from Balaam?** (*He wanted Balaam to come and curse the people so his army could defeat them and drive them out.*)

▶ **What did Balaam tell the men from Moab when they requested a curse?** (*that he would have to ask God*)

▶ **What did God tell Balaam about cursing God's own people?** (*not to curse them*)

▶ **When a group came the second time for a curse on God's people, what did Balaam say to them?** (*He again said that he would have to ask God.*)

💡 **What should Balaam have told the second group?** (*God had already said not to curse His people the first time, and that was final.*)

▶ **Why did Balaam ask God again?** (*because he wanted the honors and the gold and silver*)

💡 **Do you think Balaam really thought that God might have changed His mind?** (*Accept any answer,*

God Led His People

Name _____

God led His people and took care of them all the way from Egypt to Canaan.

Follow the directions to complete the map.
You may use your Bible to help you.

1. The dotted line shows the way God led His people from Egypt to Moab. Trace it with purple.

2. Put an orange *X* on the place where God gave Moses laws to give to His people (Exodus 19:20).

3. Draw a brown box around the name of the country where Balak was king (Numbers 22:10).

4. God opened up the waters of the Red Sea for His people to escape from the Egyptians. Make a red circle around the place where this happened (Exodus 15:4).

5. God promised to give His people all of Canaan. Draw a green box around its name (Numbers 13:2).

6. God had Joshua lead His people across the Jordan River into Canaan. Draw a blue triangle on the river (Joshua 3:17).

7. God's people obeyed Him and won the battle of Jericho. Put a yellow star on it (Joshua 6:2).

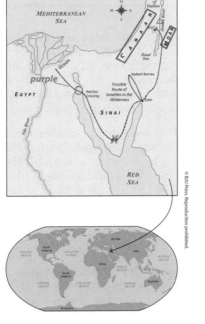

36 A Servant's Heart • Lesson 25

---

but point out that if Balaam had known God at all, he would have known that God would not curse His own people.)

▶ **What did God tell Balaam?** *(that he could go to Moab but he was to say only what God would tell him)*

💡 **What does God's Word say about our speech?** *(Answers may vary, but point out that our words should be honest, truthful, and kind.)* Read **Psalm 19:14** to the students. Remind them that our words should be pleasing to God.

♥ Memory Verse—John 14:15

Principle: If we love Christ, we will cheerfully obey the Bible. Explain that when Jesus mentioned "my commandments," He wasn't talking about only the things He told His followers to do, but also about the Word of God—the whole Bible. Explain that love for Christ cannot exist apart from obedience to what He said.

Practice the verse. The following suggested way of studying this verse may be helpful since it uses the word *if*.

Explain that even though the word *then* does not appear in this verse, it is an *if-then* statement. Give some simple examples of a condition followed by an instruction that students can do, e.g., *If you like bananas, then raise your hand.* Point out that students for whom the condition (*if*) isn't true should not follow the instruction.

Divide the students into an *if* group and a *then* group. When you say *if*, the first group should say the first part of the verse: "If ye love me." When you say *then*, the second group

should say the rest of the verse: "keep my commandments." When you say a different word, they should remain silent. Say *if* and *then* in random order, interspersing other words such as *when, because, whether,* and *as*.

Give a series of *if-then* instructions to which students can respond individually or as a group.
　　　If you have a brother, stand up.
　　　If you can ride a bike, raise your right hand.
　　　If you are happy, clap your hands once.
　　　If you like to play outdoors, look out the window.
　　　If you know John 14:15, say it together.
　　　If you love Jesus, keep His commandments!

Guide a discussion about Balaam. Lead students to see that since Balaam didn't want to obey God, he didn't really love God.

✎ Worktext page 35

Develop the recognition of characters through speech. Choose a volunteer to read the first box on Worktext page 35 and tell who could have said it. Direct the students to draw a line from each statement to the one who spoke it or did it and then color the pictures. Provide help as needed.

✎ Worktext page 36

Locate places on a map. As your students look at the map on Worktext page 36, point out that the dotted line indicates a path the Israelites and Moses may have taken from Egypt. Discuss the background information, *The Israelites.* Talk about the city of Jericho, which was the biggest city in the Eshcol region of Canaan. Use the map to show how close the Israelites were to the Promised Land when they were in Moab, but they did not know it because of all the mountains. Choose volunteers to read the Bible verses as you help the students complete the map.

🗺 World History Connections

Discuss an ancient custom. Explain that in Bible times, people believed very strongly in curses. Ask the class whether a curse is a good thing or bad thing. *(bad thing)* When a curse was pronounced, people believed that a supernatural power would carry it out. A common custom in the ancient East was to curse a man's mother. For example, if a man made a poor product, his mother, wives, sisters, and daughters were cursed (not the man himself).

Discuss a method of travel. Aside from walking, people used donkeys as their main mode of travel in the days of Moses and during the Israelites' wanderings. Donkeys were also used for grinding grain, plowing, and carrying baggage. The donkey was a symbol of peace and a sign of prosperity. Ask whether anyone has ever ridden a donkey.

LESSON
26 **Balaam and His Prophecy**

Materials
• Hymn: "Lead On, O King Eternal"

♫ Hymn: "Lead On, O King Eternal"

Sing the hymn (Worktext page 213).

Introducing the Bible Account

Use role-playing to review the previous account.
Allow a student to pretend to be the donkey. The child who pretends to be Balaam can just stand beside him. Choose a student to be the Angel. Allow the students to act out this part of the account. Tell them today's account begins with Balak coming out of his home to meet Balaam in a town on the border.

Bible Account

Read Numbers 22:36–24:17a or use the following retelling of the passage. Listening question: **Who would not let Balaam put a curse on Israel?** *(God)*

Balaam and His Prophecy

When King Balak heard that Balaam was near, he came out to meet him in a town on the edge of Moab. Balak asked Balaam why he had waited so long when Balak wanted to honor him.

Balaam replied that he didn't have permission from God to curse Israel, but that he would be able to speak only what God ordered. In spite of that, Balak gave Balaam gifts to persuade him to make the curse. The next day Balak took Balaam to the high places of Baal. He took Balaam up there, not to worship Balak's god, Baal, but to show him the encampment of Israel.

Balaam could see how badly Balak wanted the curse on Israel, and even though he knew he couldn't curse Israel, he told Balak to build seven altars. When this was done, Balaam offered a bull and a ram on each of them.

When the sacrifices had been made, Balaam told Balak to stand by his offerings. Balaam went to talk to God, and God told Balaam what to say. Balaam went back to Balak and said he could not curse those whom God had not cursed. Then Balaam praised Israel because of God's love for them.

King Balak was very angry, as you can imagine. He had asked for a curse, but Balaam had given a blessing!

Balaam answered, "Shouldn't I say what the Lord has put in my mouth?"

So Balak took Balaam to another mountain where they could see the whole camp of Israel. When Balaam saw this great camp of people, he again built seven altars and offered sacrifices on them. He again told Balak to stay there while he talked to God. When he came back to Balak, he said he had another command to bless Israel, not to curse Israel.

Balak tried a third time. This time he took Balaam to the highest mountain of all and asked him to curse the great encampment of Israelites. They built the altars again and offered sacrifices. This time when Balaam looked out, he realized what big plans God had for Israel. This time Balaam gave a greater speech about Israel. Part of the speech was a prophecy about the Star (Jesus) that was to come out of Judah and the Scepter (Jesus) that was to come out of Israel.

He also told Balak how Israel would destroy Balak's nation. (See Numbers 24:17.)

Balak got very angry, and he smacked his hands together in anger. Balaam repeated that he couldn't go against God. So Balaam went home, and Balak went home because all the offering of sacrifices hadn't changed God's mind.

It would be fourteen hundred years before God would send the Savior of Israel as a little baby in a manger. Even after God's Son came, most of Israel didn't accept Him as their King. But today God still has plans to save His people, Israel. Jesus will come again, and then He will draw them to Him, and they will worship Him as their King.

From this account we can learn that God is more interested in our loving Him and obeying Him than our putting on a show like Balaam did with all the sacrificing. God wants obedience. We might say the right words, but God sees our hearts. We should be willing to say and do what pleases God. We can also learn that God is faithful to His Word. He made a promise to Abraham, Isaac, Jacob (Israel), and Moses; God was keeping His promise. God's Word has many promises for us also.

▸ **How many times did Balak take Balaam up high to see the encampment of Israel?** *(three)*
▸ **How many times were altars built and sacrifices made to God?** *(three)*
▸ **Did any of that do any good? Did Balak get the curse he wanted?** *(no)*
💡 **To whom was God being faithful?** *(the people of Israel)*
▸ **Why would God not let Balaam curse Israel?** *(because He had promised to bless Israel)*
▸ **To whom had God first made the promise to bless his descendants and make them as many as the sand of the seashore?** *(Abraham: Lesson 14)*
▸ **Whom else in this unit did God tell that He would keep His promise?** *(Moses)*
▸ **In Numbers 24:17, Whom does God promise to send through Judah and Israel?** *(the Messiah, Jesus Christ, the king of Israel)*
💡 **Has Jesus come yet?** *(Yes. Jesus came to earth, was killed, and rose from the dead.)*
💡 **Who benefits from the coming of Israel's King?** *(All those who trust in Him, asking Him to save them from their sin.)*

✏ Worktext page 37

Recall facts and details. Tell the students to use the words given to complete each sentence on the worktext page. Give help as needed.

♥ Memory Verse—John 14:15

Practice the memory verse.

Balaam and His Prophecy
Numbers 22:36–24:17

Name _____

Balaam did not speak to Balak without asking God what he should say. God wants us to ask Him for the wisdom we need, and He never scolds us for asking (James 1:5).

Complete the sentences with a word from one of the altars.

1. Balaam told Balak that he could speak only the _____ **word** _____ that God gave him (Numbers 22:38).

2. Balaam had Balak build _____ **seven** _____ altars (Numbers 23:1).

3. Balaam offered a _____ **bull** _____ and a _____ **ram** _____ on each altar (Numbers 23:2).

4. Balak wanted Balaam to _____ **curse** _____ Israel (Numbers 23:11).

5. Balaam told Balak that God does not _____ **lie** _____ .
God does what He _____ **says** _____ He will do (Numbers 23:19).

6. Balaam _____ **blessed** _____ the Israelites instead of cursing them (Numbers 24:5–9).

7. Balaam said that the Lord Jesus would come. He called Him a _____ **Star** _____ and a _____ **Scepter** _____ (Numbers 24:17a).

Altars (word bank): says, ram, Star, word, curse, Scepter, bull, lie, blessed, seven

© BJU Press. Reproduction prohibited.

A Servant's Heart • Lesson 26   **37**

Be Kind to One Another

Materials
- Hymn: "Lead On, O King Eternal"
- Chart 3, "Books of the Bible: Old Testament" (optional)

♫ Hymn: "Lead On, O King Eternal"
Sing the hymn (Worktext page 213). Use rows of students to practice the hymn. Let the whole class start the verse, and then point to a row and let them continue, pointing at another row and another, as each takes up the singing and the other drops off. Do the verse several times. Practice all three verses.

♥ Memory Verse—John 14:15
Practice the verse.

Introducing the Application Story
Discuss how to treat others. Allow students to share experiences about how they treat or are treated by others. Encourage stories about correct behavior. Read **Psalm 141:3** aloud. Discuss how our words reflect what we think in our hearts.

Read or tell the following story. Listening question: **Why should we memorize Bible verses?** *(to know what God wants us to do, to strengthen ourselves with Scripture in trials, to fight sin, to reflect on God and His character, to allow God to direct our thoughts and our ways through His Word)*

Be Kind to One Another

Andrea ran to catch up with her friends as they left the Sunday school room. "I got three stars for saying all my verses," she said.

Melody looked down. "I got only one."

"How many stars did you get, Jason?" Andrea asked.

"Didn't get any. I kind of forgot about the verses."

Andrea twirled the end of her ponytail around her finger and smiled to herself. She always said her verses.

Andrea reached into her coin purse and pulled out her dimes for the offering. She clinked them together in her cupped hands so that they jingled. As she and her friends walked past the glass doors in the lobby of the church, she turned and glanced at her reflection. Her mom had tied her new yellow hair bow onto her ponytail. Andrea held her head up a little higher.

Andrea, Melody, and Jason stopped beside the coat rack to wait for their mothers. "I'm meeting a friend here," said Melody. "My next-door neighbor and her mom are coming this morning."

"What's her name?" asked Andrea.

"Liz. She goes to our school."

At that moment, a little girl in a faded blue denim dress walked over to them. "Hi, Melody."

"Hi, Liz."

Andrea's mouth dropped open. Liz Grover! Or Liz *Grosser*, as Andrea and her friend Jenny called her. They thought Liz was grosser than gross. Her hair always looked as though it hadn't been combed in weeks, and she wore the ugliest, plainest-looking clothes. Andrea backed up a little.

"Hi, Liz," said Jason. "I'm glad you came to our church."

Liz glanced at Andrea and then looked quickly away.

Andrea suddenly felt as though someone had dropped a big rock into her stomach. She had just remembered something she had said to Liz on Friday. Jenny had dared her to say it. "Did your mom get your dress out of the rag bag, or did the cat drag it in?" The words echoed through Andrea's mind. She wished the floor would open and swallow her up.

"Liz, you know Andrea, don't you?" said Melody. "She goes to our school too."

Liz raised her eyes to Andrea's face. Andrea bit her lip. Would Liz say something in front of Melody and Jason about Andrea's unkindness at school?

Liz nodded. "I didn't know you came to church, Andrea," she said quietly.

Andrea's face felt hot. Her heart beat quickly. "My dad's a Sunday school teacher here," she said. "And my mom's in charge of the nursery."

Liz didn't answer. She just looked down at her shoes.

"Come on, Liz," said Melody. "I see your mom talking to my mom."

Melody, Liz, and Jason walked away. Andrea looked down at the Sunday school paper she still held in her hand. "Be ye kind one to another," it said. She had just received a star on her chart for memorizing that verse. But now she didn't feel very happy about that. She had been feeling so good and clean on the way out of Sunday school. But now she felt like . . . well, like something the cat had dragged in. Grosser than gross.

"Dear Jesus," she prayed silently, "please forgive me. I've been so mean. Help me to tell Liz I'm sorry even though I'm scared she'll hate me now."

❖

 How did Andrea feel about her memory verse stars? *(She was very proud.)*

▶ **What were some other things she was proud of?** *(her yellow bow, her dimes for the offering)*

▶ Read Proverbs 6:16–19. **What is the first thing mentioned in these verses that God hates?** *(a proud look)*

 Do you think Andrea had a proud look? *(Yes. Point out the importance God also places on our words. God hates a lying tongue and mean words.)*

 What do you think Andrea meant by the word *gross*? *(Accept any answer.)*

▶ **Who obeyed God in the way they treated Liz?** *(Melody and Jason)*

▶ **Which verse did Andrea see on her paper?** *("Be kind one to another.")*

 Why do Christians read and memorize Bible verses? *(to know what God wants them to do, to strengthen them with Scripture in trials, to fight sin, to reflect on God and His character, to allow God to direct their thoughts and their ways through His Word)*

📖 Bible Study Skills

Study the books of the Old Testament. Tell the students to find the Old Testament portion of the contents page in their Bibles. Direct the class to read together the names of the first twenty books (Genesis–Proverbs). Read the list several times or show Chart 3, "Books of the Bible: Old Testament"; then choose individual students or small groups to close their Bibles and say the books together. Ask questions to identify the book that comes before or after a given book. The following are some suggestions:

▶ **Which book comes before Psalms?** *(Job)*

▶ **Which book comes after Deuteronomy?** *(Joshua)*

LESSON

28 **What Should You Say?**

Materials
- Hymn: "Lead On, O King Eternal"
- Copy of page A76 ("Words of Encouragement") for each student (optional)

What Should You Say?

Name _____

God wants you to speak wisely. Write what you think He would want you to say in each speech bubble. The Bible verses will help you. *Answers will vary.*

One of your classmates is very good at games and makes fun of you if you make a mistake. In a game of kick ball, she kicks and misses completely and falls down.
Proverbs 24:17

Your teacher thinks that one of your classmates did something wrong, but you were the one who did it.
Proverbs 25:18

Your friend failed a test and feels really bad about it.
Proverbs 16:24

A classmate is angry with you and shouts at you. You get angry, too, and want to say even worse things.
Proverbs 15:1 and
Proverbs 17:14

You and a friend are nice to one of your classmates when he is with you, but as soon as he goes away, your friend says bad things about him.
Proverbs 10:18

38   A Servant's Heart • Lesson 28

🎵 Hymn: "Lead On, O King Eternal"
Sing the hymn (Worktext page 213).

❤ Memory Verse—John 14:15
Practice the verse. Here is an exercise using sign language to accompany the verse.
- *If ye* (point to another person)
- *love* (place both hands over your heart)
- *me* (point to yourself)
- *keep* (tap fist gently on open palm twice)
- *my* (point to yourself)
- *commandments* (put index finger on lips and move it away from your mouth to represent words beings said)

✍ Worktext page 38
Apply Bible knowledge to everyday life. Call on a volunteer to read the first example on Worktext page 38. Instruct the students to locate and read **Proverbs 24:17**. Ask them what they would write. Direct the students to read each situation and the verse from Proverbs and then write what God would want them to say. Let the students complete the page independently, giving help as needed. After the students complete the page, discuss the situations and let students share what they wrote. Reread the verses aloud and discuss their meanings.

Drama Connection

Apply Bible knowledge to everyday life. Guide the students in role-playing some real-life situations. Use some from Worktext page 38 or use the following situations. Point out that they should learn to speak God's way all the time. God's way is always the best way.

- Your best friend forgot to take his book home to study for a test. He wants you to share your test answers with him. What will you say?
- Your friend hurt himself at recess, and your best friend took him to the office. You went to the lunchroom to save seats for the three of you. You could only find two seats together. What will you tell your friends when they arrive?

Art Connection (optional)

Create an encouraging card. Explain the directions for page A76 ("Words of Encouragement") and demonstrate how to fold the paper. Direct students to follow the instructions to prepare their cards. You may also want to provide felt-tip pens, stencils, or stickers.

Going Beyond

Reinforcement

Guide a storytelling activity. Assign several students to be the following characters: Balak, Balaam, the donkey, and the Angel. Direct each student to stand in front of the class and tell about his character in first person. The following is an example of what the student might say: *I am Balaam. I am a prophet. King Balak wanted me to curse the people. I asked God, and He said no. King Balak offered me many rewards, so I asked God again.* You could stop the student at this point and call on another student to continue the story from his point of view. Allow time for each character (Balaam, King Balak, donkey, Angel) to make a presentation.

Enrichment

Challenge the students to write a journal entry. Provide a blank composition book. Allow volunteers to record a segment in the journal. Tell them to pretend they are children in an Israelite family. Explain that they may each write a part of the journal, starting the journal from the first day Moses goes before Pharaoh to ask him to let God's people go from Egypt. Instruct the students to select one of the events given below and to write their entry in the journal. For more details, the students can find information in the passages given.

- the plagues God sent to Egypt (Exodus 5–11)
- leaving Egypt (Exodus 11–13)
- crossing the Red Sea (Exodus 14)
- making the golden calf (Exodus 32)
- getting the Ten Commandments (Exodus 20:1–17 and 34:1–8)

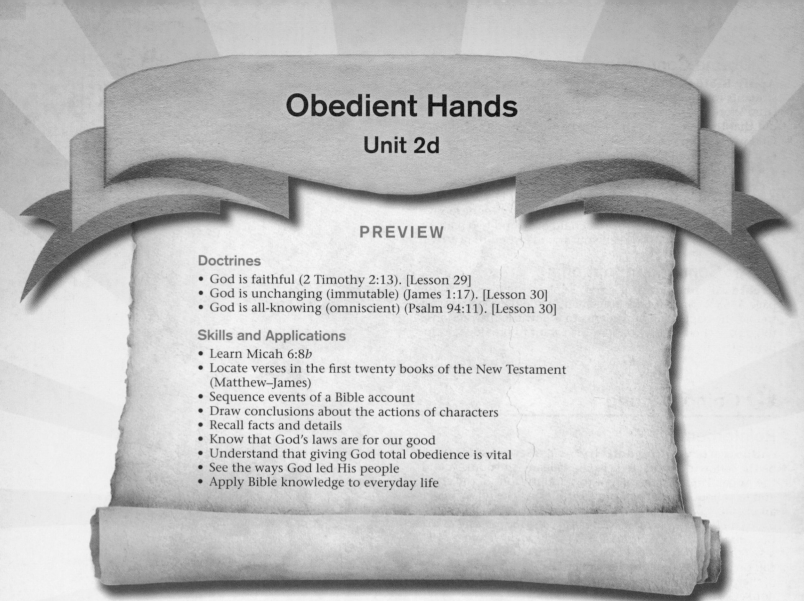

Obedient Hands
Unit 2d

PREVIEW

Doctrines

- God is faithful (2 Timothy 2:13). [Lesson 29]
- God is unchanging (immutable) (James 1:17). [Lesson 30]
- God is all-knowing (omniscient) (Psalm 94:11). [Lesson 30]

Skills and Applications

- Learn Micah 6:8*b*
- Locate verses in the first twenty books of the New Testament (Matthew–James)
- Sequence events of a Bible account
- Draw conclusions about the actions of characters
- Recall facts and details
- Know that God's laws are for our good
- Understand that giving God total obedience is vital
- See the ways God led His people
- Apply Bible knowledge to everyday life

LESSON 29 Jericho First

Materials

- Chart 7, "Jericho First"
- Chart 33, "The Journey"
- Hymn: "Lead On, O King Eternal"
- Unit 2 Bookmark for each student
- Highlighter for each student (optional)

Background Information

Joshua—*God buried Moses in Moab, but Israel still had work to do. They had to cross the Jordan River, enter the land of Canaan, drive out the enemy, and take possession of the land. Joshua, who for many years was Moses's "minister" (**Joshua 1:1**), had to lead the people forward. Joshua means "Jehovah is salvation" and is the Old Testament name for "Jesus."*

Jericho—*Jericho existed as a fortified city as early as 3000 BC. Situated at the southern end of the Jordan Valley eight hundred feet below sea level, it is warm and pleasant during winter months. Although not a large city in Joshua's day, Jericho was important since it lay at a popular entrance into Canaan across the Jordan River. Jericho had been destroyed and rebuilt many times. The people of Jericho built massive walls to protect against invaders, but Jericho's walls were not strong enough to hold back God's power. After Jericho's defeat, God, speaking through Joshua, pronounced a curse on anyone who would rebuild it. This curse was fulfilled when Hiel rebuilt the city many years later (**1 Kings 16:34**). Centuries after that, Herod built his winter palace there.*

Introducing the Bible Account

Guide a discussion. Use Chart 33, "The Journey," to review the journey the Israelites have taken so far. Locate the Jordan River and the city of Jericho. Let the students name things that they think the Israelites had to prepare to take on their journey into Canaan, the Promised Land.

Bible Account

Read Joshua 1–6 or use the following retelling of the passage. Listening question: **What did Rahab hang out her window?** *(a red cord or ribbon)* Direct the students to look at Worktext page 39 as they listen to the Bible account.

Jericho First

Joshua became God's chosen leader of Israel after Moses died. Joshua led God's people to the banks of the Jordan River. Across the river lay the wicked city of Jericho. Joshua sent two spies ahead to discover what they could about the situation in the city.

The spies soon realized that the people there had already heard about the Israelites being camped across the river. In danger, these spies went to the home of Rahab, a Canaanite woman. While they were there, some officers of Jericho came looking for them.

Rahab, led by God, hid the spies. She then helped them escape from the city. She told the spies that she had heard of their great God. They promised her that when the armies of God came to destroy the city, she would be spared. To ensure this, Rahab hung a scarlet ribbon or cord from the window of her house, which was on an outside wall of the city.

Rahab then let the spies down from her second-story window by a rope, and the spies escaped back to the Israelite camp. When they returned to Joshua, the two spies told him all the things that had happened to them, including how Rahab had helped them escape. They also assured Joshua that Israel could conquer the city of Jericho.

Joshua and all the people of Israel got up early the next morning and went to the Jordan River and set up their tents to stay there. After three days, the officers of Israel went through all the camp and instructed the people that priests carrying the ark of the covenant (which contained the Ten Commandment tablets and was the symbol of God's promise to them) would go first and that the people were to keep their distance from it. They were also told to make themselves clean because God was about to do one of His great miracles.

The next morning, following the priests who carried the ark of the covenant, two million or so of God's people walked through the river on dry ground as God parted the waters for them. When the kings of the land of Canaan heard that God had dried up the Jordan so the Israelites could pass through, they became weak with awe at such a miracle. As the Bible says, "Their heart melted."

Joshua went outside the camp to view the walled city and was met by the Angel of the Lord, dressed for battle and carrying a sword. God told Joshua to have seven priests, blowing rams' horns, follow the armed men. The other priests, carrying the ark of God, would go next, and then the people would follow and surround the city. So this happened: with the priests blowing their horns, the soldiers walked silently around the city each day for six days. At the end of every day, they walked quietly back to their camp and then reappeared to do the same thing the next day. Finally on the seventh day, they walked around the city seven times, with the priests continuing to blow their horns.

At the end of the seven times of marching around the city, the priests blew loudly on the horns, the armies gave a loud shout, and the walls of this wicked city just fell flat. The only part of the wall that remained standing was the part with

Name _____

Jericho First
Joshua 2:1–2

The first wall had gone up around Jericho thousands of years before the Israelites entered Canaan.

Jericho was rebuilt hundreds of years after Joshua conquered it, but not on the same spot. It is one and a half miles from the Jericho that was destroyed.

Jericho's walls were very thick. There were towers on top of the walls. Strong gates could shut out enemies.

A spring at Jericho gave water for people, animals, and crops.

The wall had been repaired and made stronger many times.

Rahab helped Israel's spies escape.

© BJU Press. Reproduction prohibited.

A Servant's Heart • Lesson 29   39

Rahab's house on it (with the scarlet cord hanging from the window).

The Israelites killed every person in the city except Rahab and her family. The soldiers knew that God had commanded that all the treasures from the city were to go into the treasury of God. God had commanded the Israelites to take nothing for themselves.

It had been forty years since the first twelve spies had gone into the land of Canaan to bring back a report. Only two of those first twelve spies had believed that they could conquer the people of Canaan. The other ten had been afraid and had reported men like giants living there. The Israelites, lacking faith in God, had agreed with the ten and not the two.

The day Jericho's walls fell, the armies of God did what God said to do; with the trumpets and the shout, God rewarded them with a victory over Jericho. God's people were finally in their Promised Land. They would have to fight every army they met, but they now had the faith to do it. As a result of this great victory, Joshua's name was respected by all the people of Canaan.

❦

💡 **Why do you think there happened to be a woman in Jericho who was willing to help?** *(Explain that God was working in her heart and she responded in faith to what she knew about Him.)*

💡 **Does God still prepare people who will help and guide Christians in doing His will?** *(Answers will*

vary, but make certain the students realize that God still goes ahead of us to prepare our way and often uses people in doing this. Read Romans 8:28 and explain.)

▶ **Where did Joshua get the unusual plan for the battle of Jericho?** *(from God)*

▶ **What was the battle plan?** *(Let several students describe the unusual plan: Once a day for six days the priests, soldiers, and people marched around Jericho. On the seventh day they marched around the city seven times; then the priests blew their horns loudly, the people shouted, and the walls fell.)*

▶ **What is the name of the Promised Land, where Jericho was located?** *(Canaan)*

💡 **The Bible calls Canaan a "land that flows with milk and honey." How different do you think Canaan was from Egypt, where the Israelites had been slaves?** *(Let the students discuss this and then explain the differences between Canaan and Egypt.)* Canaan is made up of rocky hills and sandy places where not much grows. Among the rock and sand, however, Canaan has fertile plains and green valleys. Egypt, on the other hand, is a desert; only near the Nile River is there good soil and enough water to grow crops and raise cattle. In contrast to Egypt and the wilderness through which the Israelites wandered for forty years, Canaan was a land where crops can grow and cattle can graze. Egypt was like a desert, and Canaan was like an oasis in the desert.

▶ **What were the people of Israel to do with any riches they found in Jericho?** *(They were to put all treasures into the treasury of God. Point out that obedience brings victory.)*

InfoScene: "Jericho First"
Display Chart 7 from the Visual Packet for the students to refer to throughout this unit.

🎵 **Hymn: "Lead On, O King Eternal"**
Sing all three verses (Worktext page 213).

♥ **Memory Verse—Micah 6:8*b***
Principle: It is better to obey God than to have an outward appearance of worshiping Him.

Practice the verse. Direct the students to highlight the verse (optional) and mark the location with the Unit 2 Bookmark.

Discuss the meaning of the verse. In the verses that precede this verse, God reminds Israel of His goodness to them. Because of His goodness, it is asked if their response should be to offer great sacrifices to God. In His answer, God tells us that He wants our hearts. We should not make a show of outward devotion but rather offer to God our hearts, resulting in living a life of justice, kindness, and humility before God. The greatest thing we can give to God is ourselves. An obedient Christian life is a great honor to God.

Victory and Defeat

Materials
• Chart 33, "The Journey"
• Hymn: "Lead On, O King Eternal"

🎵 **Hymn: "Lead On, O King Eternal"**
Sing the hymn again (Worktext page 213).

Introducing the Bible Account

Guide a discussion. Ask the students whether they remember what was to happen to the treasures taken in the defeat of Jericho. *(They were to go into God's treasury, not into any individual Israelite's possession.)* Point out the cities of Jericho and Ai on Chart 33, "The Journey."

Bible Account

Read Joshua 7 or use the following retelling of the passage. Listening question: **How did Achan disobey?** *(He took things from Jericho that the people of Israel were told not to take.)*

Victory and Defeat

When Joshua and the Israelites defeated Jericho, God told them not to take anything from the city but to put everything in the treasury of the Lord. One man disobeyed. Achan had taken things for himself, causing God to be displeased with the Israelites.

Joshua, who didn't know of Achan's sin, prepared for his next battle. He sent men from Jericho to Ai to spy out the land. They returned and said to Joshua, "Do not send all the soldiers into this battle. Send only about two or three thousand." Joshua sent about three thousand men into battle, and they returned in defeat. Thirty-six of his men were killed at Ai.

Joshua ripped his clothes in sadness. He prayed to the Lord and asked why this had happened. The Lord gave Him the answer: "Israel has sinned." God told Joshua that He would show who the sinner was the next day.

Joshua woke up early the next morning and organized the Israelites by their tribes and families. God chose the tribe of Judah, which Achan was in; then He chose Achan's family and finally Achan himself.

Joshua urged Achan to admit what he had done. Achan confessed, "I saw some silver and gold, and I wanted it. So I took it and hid it in my tent." Joshua sent some men to bring the stolen goods. Then Joshua took those things along with Achan, his family, and all their possessions out of the camp.

Joshua said to him, "Why have you troubled us? The Lord shall trouble you this day." The Israelites killed Achan by stoning him. This was God's punishment for his sin. Then they burned all of his possessions. Achan's sin wasn't hidden from God. It affected his relationship with God and his relationship with others. Only when Achan's sin was paid for did the Lord's anger against the Israelites end.

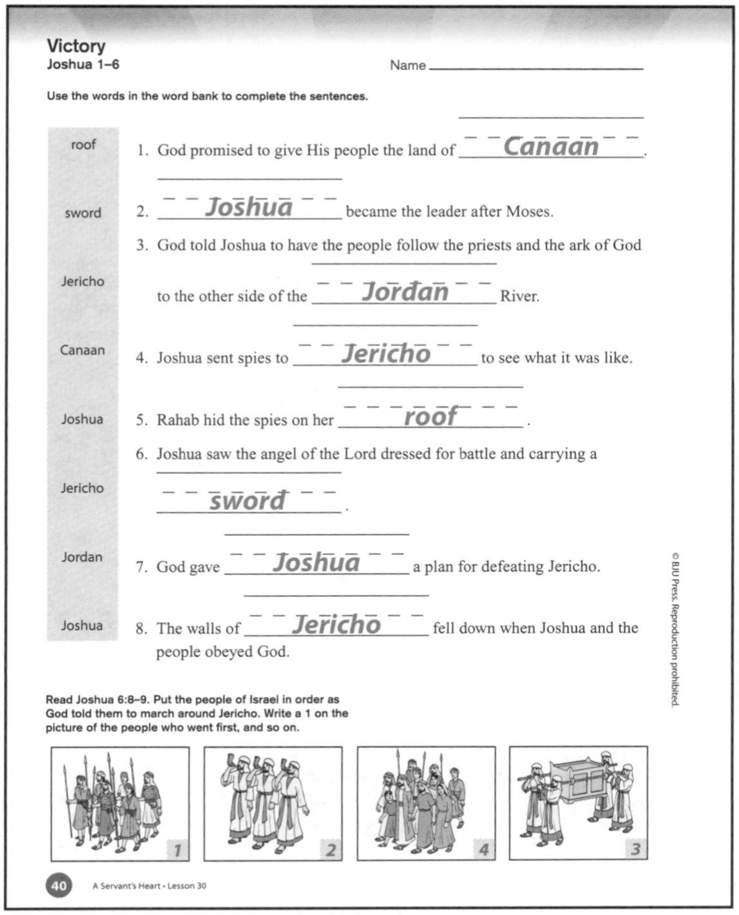

Worktext page (reproduced)

Victory
Joshua 1–6

Name _____

Use the words in the word bank to complete the sentences.

Word Bank
roof
sword
Jericho
Canaan
Joshua
Jericho
Jordan
Joshua

1. God promised to give His people the land of __Canaan__.

2. __Joshua__ became the leader after Moses.

3. God told Joshua to have the people follow the priests and the ark of God to the other side of the __Jordan__ River.

4. Joshua sent spies to __Jericho__ to see what it was like.

5. Rahab hid the spies on her __roof__.

6. Joshua saw the angel of the Lord dressed for battle and carrying a __sword__.

7. God gave __Joshua__ a plan for defeating Jericho.

8. The walls of __Jericho__ fell down when Joshua and the people obeyed God.

Read Joshua 6:8–9. Put the people of Israel in order as God told them to march around Jericho. Write a 1 on the picture of the people who went first, and so on.

40 A Servant's Heart • Lesson 30

▶ **What was the real cause of the defeat at Ai?** *(The sin among the people had not been confessed and forsaken.)*

▶ **How did Joshua find the sin that was hidden among the people in Israel's camp?** *(by bringing every tribe before him so God could show him)*

▶ **Where did Achan hide the items?** *(in his tent)* Read **Proverbs 28:13** and **Jeremiah 23:24** to the students. Remind them that sin affects every person. Unbelievers are slaves to sin, but believers can experience daily victory over sin.

♥ Memory Verse—Micah 6:8*b*
Practice the memory verse.

✎ Worktext page 40
Recall facts and details. As the students look at Worktext page 40, read aloud the names and words in the word bank. Ask the students which names are mentioned more than once. *(Jericho, Joshua)* Direct the students to use words in the word bank to complete each sentence. Give help as needed.

Sequence events. Ask the students to find **Joshua 6:8–9** in their Bibles. As they read silently, read the verses aloud to them. Discuss the order of the people; then tell the students to number the pictures in order.

---

31 Obey all the Way

Materials
- Hymn: "Lead On, O King Eternal"
- Lightweight rubber ball
- A cookie for each student (optional)

♫ Hymn: "Lead On, O King Eternal"
Practice the hymn.

♥ Memory Verse—Micah 6:8*b*
Practice the memory verse.

Introducing the Application Story
Provide cookies (optional). Allow the students to eat the cookies as you tell the story.

Application Story

Read or tell the following story. Listening question: **What is better than helping your mother?** *(obeying)*

Better Than Helping

"Mmmmmmm," said Rebecca. Ginger cookies in all different shapes—hearts, circles, teddy bears, ducks, and rabbits. Mom had rolled the dough thin, and Rebecca had cut out the shapes with the cookie cutters.

"They smell pretty good, don't they?" said Mom. "When they cool, you may have one."

"Can I have two?" asked Rebecca.

Mom shook her head. "Just one, honey. It's only half an hour till supper time. And after that, we'll decorate the cookies with icing. Why don't you set the table now."

Rebecca began setting the table. She kept glancing over at the cookies as she set five places at the table.

"Okay, Rebecca, I think they're cool enough now," said Mom as Rebecca put down the last plate.

Rebecca bit into a spicy, crumbly ginger duck. "Oh, Mom, they're so good!" she said. "We're good cooks."

The phone rang, and Mom left the kitchen to answer it. "Hi, Mother!" Rebecca heard her say. She was talking to Grandma—that meant she would be on the phone for a long time. Rebecca swallowed the last bite of her cookie and looked at the others cooling on the rack.

"Mom would never know if I ate one more cookie," she thought. "One more won't spoil my supper." Rebecca picked up a heart. She had just bitten off the tip when she heard Mom say, "Yes, she's out in the kitchen. Let me get her."

Rebecca quickly dropped the rest of the heart cookie into the pocket of her apron.

Mom poked her head around the doorway. She smiled. "You finished with that cookie? Your grandma wants to talk to you."

Rebecca took the phone. "Hi, Grandma."

"Hi, Sweetie! I heard you were helping bake cookies."

"Yes. They're all baked now. Mom and I still have to put icing on them."

"Well, that sure was nice of you to help Mom, Rebecca."

Rebecca couldn't think of anything to say. What would Grandma think if she knew about the cookie in her apron pocket? She probably wouldn't say that she was quite so nice then.

After Grandma had said good-bye, Rebecca sat and thought for a moment. She took the cookie out of her pocket and looked at it. Mom didn't know about it. Grandma didn't know about it. They both thought she was good and helpful. But God knew.

"Rebecca?" Mom called from the kitchen.

Rebecca felt her eyes getting all prickly like they did when she was going to cry. She walked into the kitchen. "Mom," she said softly. "I took another cookie." A tear dripped on her hand, and she brushed it away. "I was going to eat it, but then Grandma told me how nice I was to help you; I knew I wasn't as nice as she thought. I'm sorry, Mom, that I didn't obey you." She handed the cookie to her mother.

Mom laid the cookie aside and put her arms around Rebecca. "I forgive you, Rebecca. And remember, you need to ask Jesus to forgive you too. I really appreciate your help with the cookies."

She pulled back and looked Rebecca right in the eyes. "But," she said, "I would rather have you obey me than help me bake all the cookies in the world. Obeying is even better than helping. That's why it pleases me so much that you told me what you did." Rebecca smiled.

"And now," said Mom, "why don't you help me by finding your brothers and telling them to get cleaned up for supper? They're going to love those delicious cookies we made."

▶ **Why did Rebecca feel guilty after talking to her grandma?** *(because her grandma had praised her for helping her mother)*

💡 **Do you think Rebecca deserved to have a second cookie?** *(Answers will vary.)*

💡 **Should she have taken another cookie after her mom said "only one"?** *(No. She needed to obey her mom.)*

💡 **Why do you think her mom said "only one"?** *(She didn't want her to eat too many before supper.)*

💡 **Did Rebecca's mom really know what was best for Rebecca?** *(yes)*

💡 **Does God always know what's best for us, and is that a good reason to obey Him?** *(Yes. God made us, and He knows what will be good for us and what will be bad for us.)*

💡 **Can you tell of a time when you disobeyed and what you did that was not good for you?** *(Allow several students to answer.)*

Tell the students about a time when you disobeyed, then confessed it and received forgiveness. Allow time for them to share their own experiences of disobedience and confession.

Obey All the Way
Micah 6:8*b*

Name _____

Color the cookie above the word that best fits each situation.

Jed's mother told him to leave his pet lizard in the garage. After Jed explained that the lizard needed to be kept warm, she allowed him to keep it in his room.

Jed
obeyed   disobeyed

Amanda's father told her to turn off the television and do her homework. She turned the sound down low and did her homework.

Amanda
obeyed   disobeyed

Jamal and his friends were playing soccer against the third graders. They couldn't ever seem to get the ball. Jamal got more and more upset when he kept getting tripped. But the verses he had learned at Bible club helped him to remember what God says about controlling anger. God helped him not to be bitter. He finished the game without saying or doing anything mean.

Jamal
obeyed   disobeyed

No one wanted to be friends with Matthew. He wasn't very nice to anyone, and he didn't want to play anything the other boys wanted to play. The teacher asked Ernest to try to include Matthew in some of the games. Ernest tried and tried to be friendly to Matthew and play with him, but Matthew kept on being unfriendly to Ernest and everyone else.

Ernest
obeyed   disobeyed

The second-grade class was choosing partners for a spelling game. The teacher said not to choose the same partner as last week. Cathy and Monica are best friends. They wanted to be together again. They chose each other, and the teacher didn't notice.

Cathy and Monica
obeyed   disobeyed

A Servant's Heart • Lesson 31   41

🖊 **Worktext page 41**

Draw conclusions about the actions of characters. Lead the class in reciting **Micah 6:8***b*. Read the first example to the students. Tell them to color the shape that shows whether Jed obeyed or disobeyed. Choose a volunteer to tell the answer. Instruct the students to decide whether or not the characters in the remaining stories obeyed. Call on students to tell their answers. Point out that sin always has a consequence. Read **Ecclesiastes 9:10***a* and **1 Corinthians 10:31** to the students. Remind them to work hard and to do their best for God.

LESSON
32 ## Who Disobeyed?

Materials

- Hymn: "Lead On, O King Eternal"
- Chart 2, "Books of the Bible: New Testament" (optional)
- Suggested memory verse aid: Staple together five sheets or half-sheets of construction paper to make a booklet. On the cover print *Micah 6:8*b. On the first page, write *What?* On the second page, put *to do.* The third page should contain the word *mercy.* The word *humbly* goes on the last page.

Who Disobeyed?
Joshua 7

Name _____

Fill in the circle next to the correct answer for each question.

1. The spies told Joshua to
   ○ send all the men against Ai.
   ● send only two or three thousand men against Ai.
   ○ send only the women and children against Ai.

2. The men of Israel
   ○ won the battle and took the city of Ai.
   ○ went to war against Jerusalem instead.
   ● lost the battle and ran away.

3. Joshua asked God
   ○ why He had told him to send only a few men.
   ● why He had brought them across the Jordan River.
   ○ why He had let them take the city of Jericho.

4. God told Joshua that
   ○ the people had sinned by taking treasures from Ai.
   ○ the people had sinned by taking treasures from Egypt.
   ● the people had sinned by taking treasures from Jericho.

5. Joshua learned that
   ○ Ai had sinned.
   ○ Abiram had sinned.
   ● Achan had sinned.

6. The stolen treasures included
   ○ trumpets and rams' horns.
   ● silver coins and a gold bar.
   ○ vessels of brass and iron.

7. Because of his sin, Achan and his family
   ● were stoned.
   ○ had to leave the camp.
   ○ were sent back to Egypt.

42   A Servant's Heart • Lesson 32

---

the book that comes *before* or *after* a given book. The following are some suggestions.

▶ **Which book comes before Galatians?** *(2 Corinthians)*
▶ **Which book comes after Hebrews?** *(James)*

🎵 Hymn: "Lead On, O King Eternal"
Sing the hymn.

❤ Memory Verse—Micah 6:8*b*
Practice the verse. Show the cover of the construction-paper booklet to the first row of students, asking them to read the reference. Then show the first page to the next row, asking them to say the first phrase of the verse, and so on until each row has said one part of the verse. Let individuals try to recite the verse.

✍ Worktext page 42
Recall facts and details. Read the first statement and the answer selections from Worktext page 42. Call on a student to tell the answer. Direct the students to fill in the circle next to the correct answer. Remind the students that if they do not remember an answer they can refer to the Bible account in **Joshua 7** for help.

📖 Bible Study Skills
Study the books of the New Testament. Tell the students to find the New Testament contents page in their Bibles. Direct the class to read together the names of the first twenty books (Matthew–James). Read the list several times or show Chart 2, "Books of the Bible: New Testament." Then choose individual students or small groups to close their Bibles and say the books together. Ask questions to identify

---

Unit Review

Materials

• Copy of page A56 ("Unit 2 Review") for each student

Guide a review of Lessons 17–32. Review the people and events in Unit 2 Test (optional).

 Going Beyond

Reinforcement

Play a review game. Choose a student to be one of the characters from the Bible accounts studied in this unit. *(Moses, Pharaoh, Aaron, Jonah, Balaam, Joshua,* or *Achan)* Whisper to him the character you want him to be. The student should then give a clue to the class about himself (e.g., Achan might say, "I tried to hide my sin"). Then that student should call on a student to guess who he is. Repeat this procedure until all the main characters of the account have been covered.

Enrichment

Encourage a drawing activity. Suggest that the students draw a picture story of the Jericho battle. Tell them to make a cover and then put a different scene on each page until they have told about the battle in pictures. Then each student can staple all his pages and the cover together to form a booklet. Explain that there are to be no words in this book except on the cover, which will have a title and the artist's name on it.

3

A Humble Heart

OVERVIEW

Preparing the Teacher

Read **Philippians 2:2–8.** The word *humility* causes some people to picture a poor soul with downcast eyes, slumped shoulders, and wringing hands, but that's not a biblical picture of true humility. Note in Jesus Christ the total lack of selfish ambition, conceit, and arrogance. He willingly humbled Himself and obeyed the Father, dying on the cross for all people. Jesus Christ relinquished His reputation, position, and life. Keep His example in mind as you share with your students these lessons about humility. Ask for His help to model true humility before your students.

Preparing the Materials

33—Unit 3 bookmark [E]

34—Items for optional Science Connection experiment [O]: Hot plate and pan (or hot pot); cotton balls (or piece of wool); tray; small cake pan; ice

36—Copy of page A77 ("Humble Obedience") [E, O]

Unit 3a Going Beyond—Box containing wheat kernels, a stone, a stick, a closed container of water, plastic animals (bull, sheep, camel), and a toy trumpet; construction-paper heart; two large "wiggle" eyes [E]

37—Small tags, each with the name and address of an elementary-aged missionary child or a famous missionary from the past such as Jonathan and Rosalind Goforth (China), Jim Elliot (Ecuador), Count Nikolaus von Zinzendorf (Austria), William Carey (India), John Hyde (India), and Mary Slessor (Africa) [E, O]

39—Transparent tape [E]

40—Copy of page A78 ("Humble Prayer") [E, O]

Unit 3b Going Beyond—prepared pie-visual attached to the board; ten 3" × 5" cards with the name and address or email address of a missionary child from Lesson 37

41—Four sentence-strips

43—Copy of page A79 ("Humble Service") [E, O]

Unit 3c Going Beyond—Construction paper; magazine pictures

45—Copy of page A80 ("Walk Like Samuel") [E, O]

46—Small and large flashlight; poster or a sheet of art paper with the memory verse written on it

48—Copy of page A57 ("Unit 3 Review") [E]

Unit 3d Going Beyond—Stuffed animal; best listener award ribbon

Unit 3   A Humble Heart

Theme, Memory Verse, and Principle	Lesson Number	TE Page	Worktext Page(s)	Appendix Page(s)	Lesson Title	Scripture or Focus
Unit 3a **There Is Only One God** Isaiah 45:22 *There is only one God.*	33	70	43–44		God Calls Gideon	Judges 6:1–32
	34	72	45		Gideon's Assurance	Judges 6:33–7:14
	35	74	46–47		Gideon Serves the Lord	Judges 7:15–8:33
	36	75	48	A77	Obedience Is the Best Way	Application Story
Unit 3b **Humble Yourself Before God** 2 Chronicles 7:14 *The Lord calls us to humble ourselves before Him.*	37	78	49		Humbling Yourself	Application Story
	38	80	50		Samson Needs Humility	Judges 13–14
	39	81	51–53		Samson Reaps the Results of Pride	Judges 15–16
	40	84	54	A78	A Humble Spirit	Application Story
Unit 3c **Humble Yourself Before Others** Galatians 6:10 *Serve others, doing good to them.*	41	86	55–56		Ruth Has a Servant's Heart	Ruth 1–4
	42	89	57–58		Hannah Gives Her Gift	1 Samuel 1
	43	90	59, 249	A79	Hero of the Faith: Richard Allen	Biography
	44	92	60		A Heart for Serving	Application Story
Unit 3d **Walk in a Spirit of Humility** 1 John 1:7 *Christians have fellowship and forgiveness when they live God's way.*	45	95	61	A80	God Speaks to Samuel	1 Samuel 2–3
	46	97	62–63		Samuel Speaks to the People	1 Samuel 12 Picture the Point
	47	99	64		God Can Change Sinful Attitudes	Application Story
	48	100		A57	Walking in Humility	Application Story

Connections	Bible Doctrines	Skills/Applications
	### The Doctrine of God	### Foundational
	Attributes of God	• Realize that God commands us to worship only Him
L34—Science	God is all-knowing (omniscient) (Ps. 94:11).	• Realize that we are an example of God's work
	God is all-powerful (omnipotent) (Jer. 32:27).	
	God is unchanging (immutable) (Mal. 3:6).	
	God is faithful (1 Cor. 1:9).	### Practical
	God is merciful (Ps. 86:15).	• Classify verses into Old and New Testaments
		• Locate verses in the first thirty books of the Old Testament (Genesis–Amos)
L36—Art	*Nature of God*	• Locate verses in the New Testament
	God's being is not multiple: God is the only one (no other gods) (Isa. 44:6; 45:22).	• Identify content in a book of the Bible
		• Read a timeline
L37—Geography	### The Doctrine of Man	• Sequence events
	Original State of Man	• Identify characters
	God created man for His glory (Rev. 4:11).	• Recall facts and details
		• Identify causes of anger and infer proper responses
	Fall of Man	
	Man has a sinful nature; he lost communion with God (Rom. 5:12, 19).	### Personal
		• Praise God
	### The Doctrine of Salvation	• Love one another
L40—Art	*Elements of Salvation*	• Humble yourself before God
	God calls men through men (Rom. 10:14–15).	• Understand that serving others is serving God
	God, working through the Holy Spirit, makes the believer holy in heart and behavior (sanctification) (2 Cor. 3:18).	• Choose to serve others
L41—TimeLine: Ruth		• Understand that God works in the lives of Christians
		• Realize that God knows best
	### The Doctrine of the Church	• Realize that God can solve attitude problems
	Functions of the Local Church	• Understand that Christians choose to walk in God's light
	Care for those having special needs (Acts 6:1–3; Rom. 12:13).	• Understand and apply Bible knowledge to everyday life
L43—TimeLine: Richard Allen, Art, History.	Evangelize the lost (Matt. 28:19–20).	
	### The Doctrine of Angels and Satan	
	Organization	
	Angels were used to reveal God's will to man (Gen. 19:12–13).	
L45—TimeLine: Samuel Art		
L46—Writing		

There Is Only One God
Unit 3a

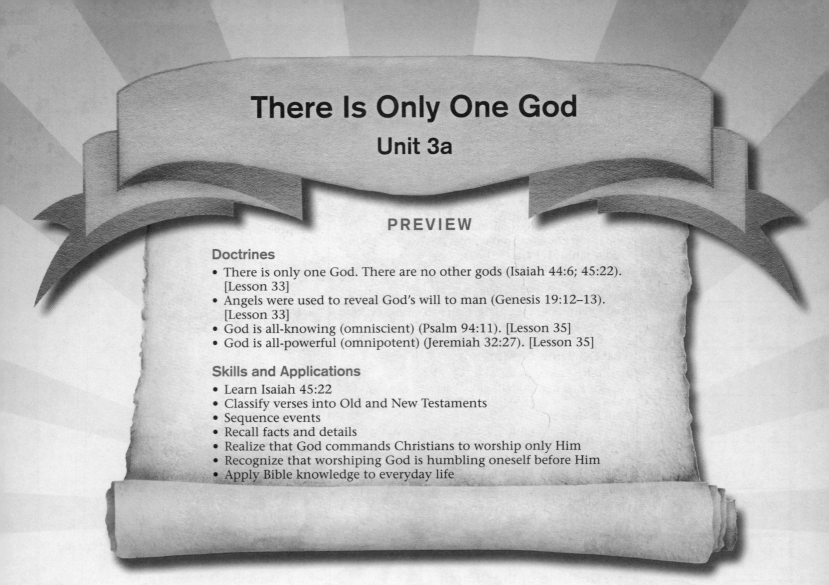

PREVIEW

Doctrines

- There is only one God. There are no other gods (Isaiah 44:6; 45:22). [Lesson 33]
- Angels were used to reveal God's will to man (Genesis 19:12–13). [Lesson 33]
- God is all-knowing (omniscient) (Psalm 94:11). [Lesson 35]
- God is all-powerful (omnipotent) (Jeremiah 32:27). [Lesson 35]

Skills and Applications

- Learn Isaiah 45:22
- Classify verses into Old and New Testaments
- Sequence events
- Recall facts and details
- Realize that God commands Christians to worship only Him
- Recognize that worshiping God is humbling oneself before Him
- Apply Bible knowledge to everyday life

LESSON 33

God Calls Gideon

Materials

- Chart 34, "The Israelites"
- Unit 3 Bookmark for each student
- Highlighter for each student (optional)
- Stapler (optional)

Background Information

Midianites—*Midian was one of the six sons born to Abraham and his second wife, Keturah. He and his brothers were sent away with gifts during Abraham's life in order not to interfere with Isaac, who was Abraham's only child from his first wife, Sarah. The Midianites were joined with the Ishmaelites and the Amalekites dwelling in the Aramean Desert (modern-day Jordan). Most were nomadic herdsmen who, by the time of Gideon, were neither an organized army of warriors nor a nation powerful enough to conquer Israel. They united with the other tribes and swelled into what the Bible describes as an innumerable host of locusts. The Midianites oppressed the Israelites. Each year for seven years, just at harvest time, they came with a mob of hungry people and animals to steal and destroy the crops of the Israelites.*

Camels—*Camels were commonly used for hundreds of years prior to the era of the judges. Abraham had quite a number of camels. They are well suited for travel in the desert. They have long, strong legs and powerful muscles and typically can carry more than 330 pounds. They can go for long periods of time without water. They are also a source of meat and milk as well as wool and leather for clothing and shelter.*

Baal—*Baal is the common Canaanite word for* master *or* lord. *One of the highest of the false gods of the Canaanites, Baal was associated with agriculture and was said to increase family, crops, flocks, and herds. He was also associated with the rain necessary for crops. These worshipers used animal sacrifices, ritualistic meals, and dancing in an effort to bring rain or increase their crops and herds. The Israelites whose crops and herds were being stolen were enticed to worship Baal by the false promises of increase.*

Introducing the Bible Account

Locate places on a map. Share the background information about camels and how they made the Midianites effective in the desert. Display Chart 34, "The Israelites." Point out the desert features of the Aramean areas. Point to the Israelite tribes that were being attacked: *Asher, Zebulun, Manasseh,* and *Naphtali.* Explain that the Israelites and Canaan-

ites still lived in the land of Canaan because the Israelites had not obeyed God completely.

Bible Account

Read Judges 6:1–32 or use the following retelling of the passage. Listening question: **Why were the Midianites able to invade the land that the Lord had given to the Israelites?** *(The Israelites were worshiping Baal.)*

God Calls Gideon

The Israelites had trouble remembering the lessons God had taught them in the past. Many times the people stopped worshiping the Lord, and the Lord allowed them to be captured, punished, or defeated by an enemy. One time when the Israelites were worshiping Baal—a false god of the Canaanites—the Lord allowed the Midianites to come in and steal the Israelites' food just at harvest time. The Midianites came year after year, stealing and causing the Israelites to hide in the mountains and to live in caves. So many Midianites came into Israel with their camels that the Israelites finally called on the Lord for help. The Lord sent a prophet to remind them how He had saved them many times. The prophet told them that God said, "I brought you out of Egypt, from the house of bondage; and I delivered you out of the hand of the Egyptians, and out of the hand of all that oppressed you, and drove them out from before you, and gave you their land. I said I am the Lord your God; don't be afraid of the gods of the Amorites, in whose land you dwell: but you have not obeyed my voice."

The Lord loved His people and came to Gideon in the appearance of an Angel. While hiding from the Midianites by a winepress, Gideon threshed wheat *(beat the kernels off the stalks)*. He said to Gideon, "The Lord is with you, you man of courage." But Gideon had a hard time believing this promise since the Midianites had stolen everything. He asked the Angel why such terrible things had happened. He wanted to know where the miracles were that God had done before. He wondered why the Lord had left his people and allowed the Midianites to take the Israelites' harvest. But the Lord told Gideon that He was going to send him to save Israel from the Midianites.

Gideon said he didn't think he was a very good choice, being the youngest son of a poor man. God promised Gideon that He would be with him and Gideon would conquer the Midianites. But Gideon was still unsure that this was really a divine message, so he asked God for a test. Gideon went to cook meat, bread, and broth and brought them to the Angel. The Angel told him to put the meat and bread on a stone and to pour the broth over them. Then the Angel touched the end of His staff to the food, and fire came out of the rock and burned up the food. Then the Angel disappeared. Now Gideon knew for sure that the traveler was the Angel of the Lord, and Gideon was very frightened. But God spoke to Gideon and told him not to be afraid. Gideon built an altar to the Lord on the very spot the Lord had stood at Ophrah and called it Jehovah-shalom *(God of peace)*.

What did God want the Israelites to do? *(worship Him and Him alone)*

💡 **What does God want us to do?** *(realize that He is the only true God and worship only Him)*

Why did Gideon think he was not a good choice for God's work? *(He thought he was too poor and unimportant.)*

💡 **Did Gideon's weakness prevent him from being used by God?** *(No. God can enable weak people to do His will.)*

💡 **Can God use anyone?** *(Yes. God can enable anyone to do His will.)*

That night the Lord told Gideon to take two of his father's oxen and to do three things. First, he was to pull down the altar to Baal and cut down the grove of trees that surrounded the false god's altar. Then he was to build an altar to the Lord in its place. Finally, he was to sacrifice a young ox on that altar. So in the middle of the night, Gideon took ten servants and did as the Lord had said.

The next morning when the worshipers of Baal came, they found their altar destroyed and an altar of the Lord in its place, and they were very angry. They asked who had done this. They were told that this was the work of Gideon.

The angry men went to Gideon's father, Joash, and demanded that he give them Gideon so that they could kill him. Joash said that if Baal was angry with Gideon, Baal would have to punish him. Of course, Baal was no god at all, so he couldn't kill Gideon.

How did the worshipers of Baal respond when Gideon obeyed God? *(They were angry and wanted to kill Gideon.)*

💡 **When Christians obey God, Who is pleased?** *(God)*

Why was punishment from Baal not possible? *(Baal never existed.)*

❤ Memory Verse—Isaiah 45:22

Principle: There is only one God. Practice the memory verse with open Bibles. Instruct the students to read silently as you read aloud.

What are the two commands that God gives in this verse? *("Look unto me" and "be saved.")*

Explain that when the Bible says "look," it does not always mean with the eyes; often it means to give attention with the mind and heart. Christians are to think about God and His way, not their own way. They are to trust Him.

Who is included in these commands? *(all the ends of the earth; everyone)*

Explain that in the second part of the verse the Lord tells Christians why they are to do what He has commanded: "I am God, and there is none else."

Practice the memory verse. Direct the students to highlight the verse (optional) and mark the location with the Unit 3 Bookmark.

Worktext pages 43–44

Make Memory Verse Glasses. Direct the students to page 43. Tell them to write the two commands in **Isaiah 45:22** across the lenses. Direct the students to page 44. Instruct them to write the reason on the first line of the glasses (*for I am God*) and God's explanation on the second line (*there is none else*). Tell the students to cut out the parts of the glasses. Attach (staple or glue) the arms of the glasses to the frames. Instruct the students to keep the glasses at school since they will be used in future lessons.

💡 **What does God want us to learn about Him from this verse?** (*He is the true God Whom we are to trust. He alone can save us.*)

💡 **What sin does He want us to avoid?** (*He does not want us to think that there are any other gods.*)

Because He is the only God, what must we do? (*Look to Him [trust Him] and be saved.*)

How did Gideon show that he knew there was only one God? (*Gideon pulled down the altar of Baal.*)

💡 **How can Christians show that they know the Lord is the only God?** (*Answers will vary. Guide the students to understand that how they act and what they say also show whether they believe there is only one God.*)

LESSON 34 Gideon's Assurance

Materials

- Memory Verse Glasses from the previous lesson
- For the Science Connection experiment (optional): hot plate and pan for boiling water (or hot pot); cotton balls (or piece of wool); tray; small cake pan; ice

Background Information

The Well of Harod—*Strategically Gideon's plan was brilliant. By placing his army around the well of Harod, he blocked the herdsmen of Midian from any local source of water.*

Introducing the Bible Account

Explain *assurance*. Write the word *assurance* for display. Read the word aloud and tell the students that the base word is *assure*. Write the word *assure* for display and underline *sure*. Explain that it means to be certain or confident of something. Review the previous Bible account about Gideon and the Angel. Explain that Gideon had wanted *assurance* that the Angel was from God.

Bible Account

Read Judges 6:33–7:14 or use the following retelling of the passage. Listening question: **How did Gideon know for sure he was to fight the Midianites?** (*He put out the lamb's fleece and prayed. First, the fleece was wet and the ground was dry. The second time, the fleece was dry and the ground was wet.*)

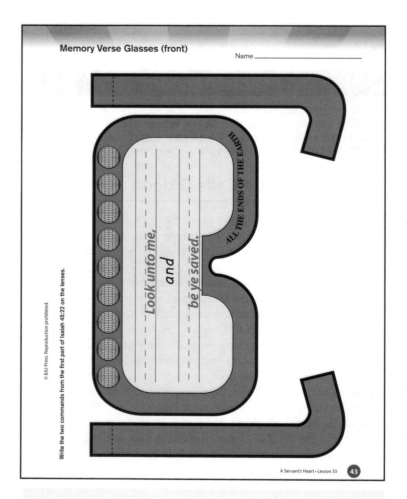

Memory Verse Glasses (front)   Name _____

Look unto me, and be ye saved.

ALL THE ENDS OF THE EARTH

Write the two commands from the first part of Isaiah 45:22 on the lenses.

© BJU Press. Reproduction prohibited.

A Servant's Heart • Lesson 33   **43**

Gideon's Assurance

Gideon had done the first part of what the Lord had asked, but tearing down the altar of Baal was easy compared to conquering all the Midianites. Gideon was afraid to go against them by himself, so he sent messengers to some of the leaders of the other tribes to ask for help. When the leaders gathered at Ophrah, Gideon still wanted more assurance that he was doing what the Lord wanted him to do. He prayed and told God that he would put a lamb's wool fleece (skin) on the ground, and if the night dew settled only on the wool and not on the ground around it, then he would know that the Lord had promised to save Israel by Gideon's hand. In the morning Gideon picked up the lamb fleece and wrung a whole bowl of water from it, but the ground around the fleece wasn't even damp. God had sent His sign of assurance to Gideon.

Gideon was still afraid. That night he prayed and asked the Lord to give him assurance one more time that he was doing what God wanted him to do. He asked that the fleece be dry but the ground around it be wet with dew. The next morning Gideon picked up the dry lamb's wool from the wet ground. With that, Gideon was sure that he was supposed to fight the Midianites.

Gideon told the thirty-two thousand Israelite soldiers who had come to help him to pitch their tents by the well of Harod. But the Lord told Gideon that too many people were with him.

Memory Verse Glasses (back)

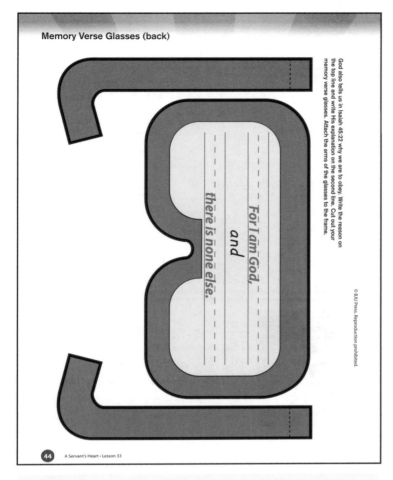

For I am God, and there is none else.

God also tells us in Isaiah 45:22 why we are to obey. Write the reason on the top line and write His explanation on the second line. Cut out your memory verse glasses. Attach the arms of the glasses to the frame.

44 A Servant's Heart • Lesson 33

"strengthened" to lead the soldiers against the Midianites.

Gideon did go down to the valley of Jezreel with Purah, and he listened outside a tent. Gideon overheard a man telling his dream to a wise man. In his dream he saw a large loaf of barley bread come tumbling into camp and knock down the Midianites' tents. Then the wise man in the tent told what the dream meant; he said, "This is the sword of Gideon, the son of an Israelite named Joash. God has delivered Midian into Gideon's hands." As Gideon listened, his fear left him because he knew God's promises were true.

⚜

Why did Gideon pray for the lamb's wool to be wet one night and dry the next? *(Gideon wanted assurance of what God wanted.)* Explain that lamb's wool would naturally repel and not absorb the moisture.

Which men were chosen to fight? *(those who drank the water from their hands)*

Why did God tell Gideon not to use many soldiers? *(The Israelites would have thought their power and great number had won the battle, not God.)*

💡 **Why would God not want the Israelites to think they had conquered the Midianites?** *(He wanted them to rely on Him.)*

💡 **What can Christians do when they are afraid?** *(They should pray and trust God.)*

💡 **How does the Lord give Christians assurance?** *(through prayer, reading the Bible, and conviction by the Holy Spirit [**John 14:26**])*

⊘ Science Connection (optional)

Experiment with dew. Tell the students that science can show us God's wonderful provisions for the world. One way He provides the earth with the necessary moisture for plants is with dew. Ask whether students have walked in the wet grass early in the morning. Tell them that the wetness is caused by dew. Dew is drops of water formed from the air that settle on the leaves, grass, and the ground. *(Note: The time needed to complete this experiment may vary by location. You may want to time this experiment beforehand.)*

- Collect moisture on the cake pan by holding it over boiling water. Explain that this is similar to water evaporating from the oceans, rivers, and lakes and being collected in the clouds.
- Place ice cubes in the cake pan. Hold the cake pan above a tray containing the cotton balls (or piece of wool). Ask the students to predict what will happen to the cotton balls.
- Pass the tray containing the cotton balls (or piece of wool) around the class, allowing the students to feel the wet cotton balls. Explain that at night the air cools and the water droplets in the air collect on the ground. This is called condensation.

Where is the water (moisture) that was on the cake pan? *(It is on the tray and on the cotton balls.)*

If we repeated the experiment, would the water ever form just on the cotton balls and not on the tray? *(no)*

If we repeated the experiment, would the water ever form just on the tray and not on the cotton

If Gideon led that many troops against the Midianites, they might believe that they had conquered the Midianites by their own power. God told him to go and tell the people, "Whoever is fearful and afraid, let him depart early from Mount Gilead." So Gideon did as the Lord had said, and twenty-two thousand men left Mount Gilead, leaving Gideon with only ten thousand men.

Then God told Gideon that there were still too many people. He directed Gideon to take them down to get a drink of water.

God said to put the ones who cupped their hands in the water and drank from their hands into one group; God said to put the ones who bent down on all fours and drank from the water into another group. Only three hundred soldiers drank from their hands; the rest got down on their knees to drink the water. And the Lord said that by the three hundred men who drank from their hands He would save Gideon and the Israelites and give them victory over the Midianites.

Gideon kept the three hundred and sent the others home as the Lord had instructed. Then he looked north at the many Midianites in the valley of Jezreel, and he was afraid. That same night the Lord told Gideon to go down to the host of the Midianites and fight because He would deliver them into his hands. But the Lord knew that Gideon was afraid, so He gave Gideon more assurance. God told Gideon that if he was afraid to go down with his soldiers, he should go with his servant Purah down to the Midianite camp and listen to what the Midianites said. God promised that then Gideon would be

balls? *(no)*

What miracle did God do for Gideon? *(God had the dew form on the fleece but not the ground and then form on the ground but not the fleece. Both should have been wet.)*

♥ Memory Verse—Isaiah 45:22

Practice the memory verse. Call on several volunteers to read the verse aloud as the others read silently. Tell the students to take out the verse glasses they made in the previous lesson.

Who is to look unto God and be saved? *(everyone)*

How can people everywhere know what God has commanded? *(They can read the Bible, and Christians should tell them.)*

Tell the students to look on the back of the glasses as you lead the class in saying the verse.

According to the verse, what should Christians tell people around the world about God? *(There is only one God; there are no other gods.)*

✍ Worktext page 45

Guide a review of characters. Call attention to the top part of the page. Read the directions with the students. Write the first four problems on the board as examples, and model finding the solution by writing and crossing out the appropriate letters. Direct the students to copy your work on their pages. Allow them to do the last two themselves and then use all six names to match with the clues in the bottom exercise. Review the events of Gideon's victory.

35 Gideon Serves the Lord

Materials
- Chart 34, "The Israelites"
- Charts 2–3, "Books of the Bible: Old Testament, New Testament"

♥ Memory Verse—Isaiah 45:22

Practice the memory verse. Read the verse aloud as a class. Write it for display. Tell the students that you will erase one or more words each time they read the verse, so they will have to remember the erased words. Continue the activity until there are no words left and the students are reciting the entire verse.

Introducing the Bible Account

Guide a review about Gideon. Call attention to Chart 34, "The Israelites." Review the account, pointing out on the map where the Angel met Gideon *(Ophrah, where Gideon built the altar)* and where Gideon led his army *(by the well of Harod)* with the Midianites in the valley of Jezreel.

Bible Account

Read Judges 7:15–8:33 or use the following retelling of the passage. Direct the students to look at Worktext page 46.

Gideon's Assurance
Judges 6:11–7:14

Name _____

Solve each puzzle to find a Bible name. When you see + , add (or keep) the letters. When you see – , subtract (or cross out) the letters. Check your answers by finding and reading the verses.

a. Glide – l + on =   _ _ _ _ _ _ **Gideon**   Judges 6:11

b. Bad – d + all – l =   _ _ _ _ **Baal**   Judges 6:25

c. Mind – n + i + granite – gr – s =   _ _ _ _ _ _ _ _ _ **Midianites**   Judges 7:1

d. Is + race – c + look – ook =   _ _ _ _ _ _ **Israel**   Judges 6:14

e. Job – b + dash – d =   _ _ _ _ _ **Joash**   Judges 6:11

f. Rang – R + elk – k =   _ _ _ _ _ **angel**   Judges 6:11

Match one of the names above with each of these statements by writing the letter of the name you choose in the blank. The first one is done for you.

F the one who gave God's message to Gideon

E the father of Gideon

B a false god of the Canaanites

A the man chosen by God to destroy the Midianites

C desert people who raided the land of Israel

D God's chosen nation

A Servant's Heart • Lesson 34 **45**

Gideon Serves the Lord

Gideon knew the Lord was with him because the Lord had shown Gideon that even the Midianites were having dreams about God's blessings on Gideon. Gideon went back to his waiting men. Each man took a trumpet in one hand and a lighted torch hidden under a pitcher in the other hand. Gideon divided the three hundred men into three groups to surround the Midianite camp and told them to look at him and do what he did. They were to blow their trumpets when he did, then say, "The sword of the Lord, and of Gideon."

The men crept down the valley and surrounded the camp. Everyone was asleep in the Midianite camp except the watchman, whom the Israelites carefully avoided. At midnight Gideon gave a long, loud blast on his trumpet, and his men joined in. They shouted, "The sword of the Lord, and of Gideon!" Then Gideon broke the pitcher over his torch, and all his men did the same. The Midianites awoke to loud sounds and bright lights surrounding them. Believing that Gideon had brought a huge army, all the Midianites ran. The Lord made the Midianites so confused that they raised their swords against each other, killing 120,000 of their own men.

Fifteen thousand Midianites escaped, but Gideon and his men chased them. Gideon and his three hundred soldiers crossed the Jordan River to follow the kings of Midian and the remaining fifteen thousand men to Karkor. Gideon was clever and took his three hundred soldiers by the route of

Gideon Serves the Lord
Judges 7:15–8:33

Name _____

As you listen to your teacher read the Bible account, decide which picture shows what happened first, second, and so on. Write a number in the box to show the order in which the events happened.

1   4

6   2

3   5

46   A Servant's Heart • Lesson 35

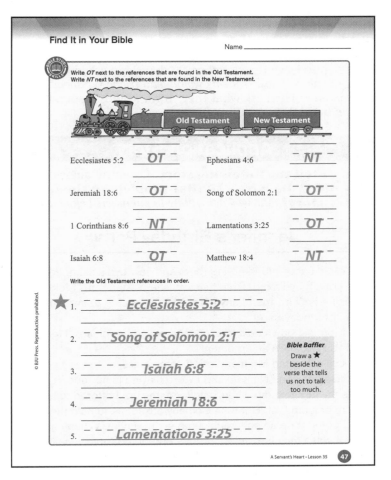

Find It in Your Bible

Name _____

Write *OT* next to the references that are found in the Old Testament.
Write *NT* next to the references that are found in the New Testament.

Old Testament   New Testament

Ecclesiastes 5:2   **OT**   Ephesians 4:6   **NT**

Jeremiah 18:6   **OT**   Song of Solomon 2:1   **OT**

1 Corinthians 8:6   **NT**   Lamentations 3:25   **OT**

Isaiah 6:8   **OT**   Matthew 18:4   **NT**

Write the Old Testament references in order.

 1. *Ecclesiastes 5:2*

2. *Song of Solomon 2:1*

3. *Isaiah 6:8*

4. *Jeremiah 18:6*

5. *Lamentations 3:25*

Bible Baffler
Draw a ★ beside the verse that tells us not to talk too much.

A Servant's Heart • Lesson 35   47

---

the nomads. The enemy soldiers in Karkor weren't expecting him and were killed. With no army left to protect them, two Midianite kings tried to run away, but Gideon went after them and captured them.

God won the victory for Gideon and his three hundred men. For forty years the Israelites followed the Lord, but after Gideon died, they forgot what the Lord had done through Gideon.

❦

Why did the Midianites use their swords against each other? *(They were confused by the lights and the noise. They thought Gideon had brought a large army.)* Explain that it was God's power that won the battle, not Gideon's strategy.

✍ Worktext page 46

Sequence events. Direct the students' attention to Worktext page 46 as you review the Bible account with them. Instruct them to write a number in the box of each picture to show the order of the events.

📖 Bible Study Skills, Worktext page 47

Classify verses as belonging to the Old or New Testament. Read the directions from the top of the page with the students. Remind them to use the contents page in their Bibles or Charts 2–3, "Books of the Bible: Old Testament, New Testament," if needed. Check the answers with the students before they complete the bottom of the page.

Study the books of the Old Testament. Tell the students to turn to the Old Testament contents page in their Bibles or display Chart 3, "Books of the Bible: Old Testament." Direct the class to read together the names of the first twenty-five books of the Old Testament *(Genesis–Lamentations)*. Point out that the books of *Job, Psalms, Proverbs, Ecclesiastes,* and the *Song of Solomon* are called the Books of Poetry. *Isaiah, Jeremiah,* and *Lamentations* are three of the Prophets. Remind the students that *a prophet* was chosen by God to tell the words God wanted him to speak. Direct the students to write the Old Testament verses from the top of the page in order.

Locate verses. Read the directions for the *Bible Baffler* exercise. Guide the students in locating and reading each Old Testament verse. Let the students work independently to decide which verse gets the star.

LESSON 36   Obedience Is the Best Way

Materials
• Hymn: "Be Thou Exalted"
• Memory Verse Glasses from Lesson 33
• Copy of page A77 ("Humble Obedience") for each student (optional)

♥ Memory Verse—Isaiah 45:22
Review the memory verse.

Introducing the Application Story

Guide a discussion about predicting effects. Ask students to tell what they think would happen if they were lining up to leave the classroom and a friend asked to get in front of them. *(Most students would let a friend get ahead of them in line.)* Then ask what they think would happen if the person behind them complained.

Application Story

Read or tell the following story. Listening question: **Why did Lydia have a similar problem in the following story?** *(She was not willing to put others before herself.)*

Jennifer's Birthday Party

Mom came into the living room and saw Lydia slumped on the couch. Lydia burst into tears as she blurted out, "Mom, Jennifer isn't my friend anymore. She isn't going to invite me to her birthday party."

Mom sat down next to Lydia and pulled her close. "Honey, did you two have an argument?"

Lydia hugged Mom and cried some more.

"Bethany and Nichole and I were playing jump rope. It was my turn to jump when Jennifer came up. I offered to let Jennifer jump first. But then Bethany asked me to hold the end of the rope so she could jump with Jennifer. When I told her it wasn't my turn yet to turn the end of the rope, Jennifer got mad and said I wasn't her friend anymore. And she said I wouldn't be invited to her birthday party."

Mom stroked Lydia's hair. "Lydia, you need to forgive the girls for hurting your feelings and try to put it behind you."

"But Mom, you don't understand; all the girls will be invited except me. Jennifer's mom always gives bags of prizes."

"Lydia," Mom said quietly, "birthday parties are to honor the person having the party and to thank God for creating that person."

"But Mom, I was going to wear my new dress."

"Lydia, you'll be able to wear your new dress another time, won't you?"

"Well, y—yes, but . . ."

"Lydia, you're sitting here upset because you won't get to wear your new dress to the party and get prizes for yourself. How would you feel if your friends came to your birthday party not to honor you but just to get prizes and be able to wear their new clothes?"

"I would think they were being selfish."

Lydia did feel hurt, but she knew her mom was right. "Lydia, I'm not saying you shouldn't feel bad about having a broken friendship," Mom continued, "but God wants you to put Him first and others before yourself. What can you do to put God first, Lydia?"

"I guess I need to pray and ask for God to forgive me."

"That would be a good start, Honey, but what about the girls? Did you put others before yourself?"

"No, Mom, I didn't. If I had put others before myself, I would have taken Bethany's end of the rope and let her and Jennifer jump together. I need to ask their forgiveness. And I want Jennifer to have a nice birthday party!"

Why was Lydia upset? *(Jennifer was not going to invite her to her birthday party.)*

Why did Lydia want to go to the party? *(She wanted to win prizes and wear her new dress. All the other girls were invited.)*

After talking with her mom, what was Lydia willing to do that pleases God? *(She was willing to put others before herself and to put God first.)*

💡 **How do you know that Lydia's attitude changed?** *(She planned to ask God to forgive her, and she was willing to forgive Jennifer.)*

Read Philippians 2:3. What should you do when others treat you unfairly? *(Direct a conversation that focuses on Christ's response to us—the ways He loves us, forgives us, befriends us, and so on.)*

✍ Worktext page 48

Recall facts and details. Direct attention to the words and pictures across the top of the page. Indicate to the students that an object is missing in each picture. Read the directions with them. Tell them to use their pencils to draw

the missing objects and write in the words. Allow them to color the pictures with colored pencils or a felt-tip marker if they choose. Point out that each character first humbled himself and then obeyed God.

🎵 Hymn: "Be Thou Exalted"

Introduce the hymn. The words of this hymn are taken from a poem that Fanny Crosby sent to someone in a letter. Over seventy years later, the poem was revised and put to music by the famous hymnologist and gospel song writer Alfred B. Smith.

As an infant, Fanny was blinded when the wrong medication was applied to her eyes. Her Christian grandmother decided to take care of Fanny. In a way, her grandmother became her eyes, describing what she could not see. Fanny learned the Bible so well that she could quote much of it. Out of her love for the Lord and God's Word, she wrote more than eight thousand songs and hymns.

Teach the first verse (Worktext pages 214–15).
Explain the following words as necessary: *exalt* (to speak highly of), *eternity* (time without end or beginning), *Ancient of Days* (God), *majestic* (like a king), *holiness* (purity from sin), *seraph* (angel), *anthem* (song of praise), *rapture* (feeling of joy), *adore* (love or worship). Sing the verse again.

> **Why should God be exalted?** *(He is the wise, eternal, holy, all-powerful ruler of all. He is worthy of praise.)*
> **How can Christians show God that they love Him?** *(with harp and with song, with their voices, and with musical instruments)*

✏️ Art Connection (optional)

Illustrate the Bible account. Read the directions for page A77 ("Humble Obedience"). Instruct the students to draw their pictures. They may use their Bibles to recall the account from **Judges 6–8** and to complete the sentence on the page. After the students complete their drawings, direct them to post the drawings on the Unit 3 bulletin board.

Going Beyond

Reinforcement

Materials
- A sturdy box containing wheat kernels, a stone, a stick, a closed container of water, a pitcher, a small plastic sword, small plastic animals (bull, sheep, and camel), and a toy trumpet

Reinforcement

Review the Bible account of Gideon. Assign each student to a partner. Instruct each student to choose an item from the box and show it to his partner. Explain that the partner is to identify the item and tell the significance as it relates to the Bible account about Gideon's victory.

- **Wheat kernels**—Gideon was threshing wheat when the Angel appeared to him.
- **Stone**—Gideon placed his offering of meat and bread on a stone.
- **Stick**—The Angel touched the offering with His staff, and it immediately went up in flames.
- **Bull**—Gideon sacrificed his father's bull as a burnt offering to the Lord on the altar he built.
- **Sheep**—Gideon used a fleece (sheepskin) as a test to see if God had really called him to fight the Midianites.
- **Water**—God used the ways the men drank water to separate out the three hundred He wanted to accompany Gideon.
- **Camel**—The Midianites had a very large army and many camels.
- **Pitcher and trumpet**—When Gideon led his three hundred men into battle, each one carried a pitcher (with a torch inside) and a trumpet.
- **Sword**—The Midianite soldiers were so scared they used their swords against each other.

Enrichment

Materials
- Two large "wiggle eyes" for each student
- A red construction-paper heart for each student

Apply Bible knowledge to everyday life. Direct the students to glue two "wiggle" eyes on their paper hearts. Guide them as they write, "Look with your heart" on their hearts. Discuss the necessity for God's people to look with their hearts at God's way. Discuss how God looked at the incidents in Gideon's life.

Humble Yourself Before God
Unit 3b

PREVIEW

Doctrines

- Evangelize the lost (Matthew 28:19–20). [Lesson 37]
- God calls men through men (Romans 10:14–15). [Lesson 37]
- Man has a sinful nature: he lost communion with God (Romans 5:12, 19). [Lesson 38]

Skills and Applications

- Learn 2 Chronicles 7:14
- Sequence events
- Recall facts and details
- Identify causes of anger and infer proper responses
- Praise God
- Humble yourself before God
- Love one another
- Apply Bible knowledge to everyday life

LESSON 37 Humbling Yourself

Materials

- Chart 31, "World Map"
- Hymn: "Be Thou Exalted"
- Unit 3 Bookmark for each student
- Highlighter for each student (optional)
- A missionary name tag for each student: Adhesive notes can be used. On each tag write a missionary child's name and the country or continent where that child serves, or the name and country of a famous missionary of the past from the list on page 67. (optional)

Introducing the Application Story

Guide a discussion about giving to God. Encourage the students to mention what people can give to God. Elicit that they can also give intangible gifts. *(cleaning the church or grounds, helping parents, praying, praising, and so on)* Point out that being willing to serve God and others shows a humble heart.

Application Story

Read or tell the following story. Listening question: **Who in the story shows a humble heart?** *(Answers may vary but could include Grandma, Vanessa, and the missionaries.)*

Vanessa's Dollar

"Grandma, Grandma," called Vanessa as she came running in from school, "Look what I earned!"

Vanessa walked to her grandma's every day after school and stayed until her mom came home from work. "Grandma, Mr. Green asked me to sweep his walk, and he gave me a dollar. Will you take me to buy a candy bar?"

"Vanessa," Grandma said, "did you forget? Today we're going to church to meet the new missionaries, the Blakes."

"Oh, I forgot. How many kids do they have?"

"One daughter, Debbie, who is your age, and twin sons, Matthew and Michael, who are a year younger," Grandma said with a smile.

"I suppose my dollar isn't enough to get candy bars for all of us," said Vanessa.

"No, it's not, dear, but it was a nice thought." Grandma took two pies out of the oven and packed them in warmers. Vanessa thought about how much work Grandma had done to make the pies. Vanessa had helped make pies before, and Grandma was always tired afterward; but as Vanessa looked from the pies to Grandma, she saw that Grandma didn't look tired at all.

Vanessa held the door open for her grandmother.

"Grandma, how did you remember last week to get everything for the pies for the Blakes?"

"Well, I pray for them every week, and I read the letters they send to the church," Grandma said, as she turned the car toward the church.

"They said in one letter that they missed blueberry pie. I couldn't send them blueberry pie in the mail, so when they came home last month, I thought I'd make them a blueberry pie."

"I wish I had thought about what the children would want." Vanessa thought about the yo-yo she had bought with her allowance. She realized that if she had saved her allowance from last Saturday she would have had enough to get something for each of the Blake kids.

Vanessa and Grandma arrived at church and helped decorate the tables with streamers.

Many families arrived with casseroles, brownies, chips, vegetables, and cakes. Then everyone joined the Blakes for the service. The Blakes told about how God had given them the desire to share His Word and about the people who had been saved.

As Vanessa watched the DVD, she saw Debbie and her brothers giving other children booklets. After everyone went down to dinner, Vanessa asked Debbie about the booklets.

"They tell about Jesus in pictures and in their own language," Debbie explained, "but we gave them all away. Dad said we are going to have to get some more donations before we can order more booklets."

"How much do the booklets cost?" Vanessa asked.

Debbie thought for a moment and said, "They cost about fifty cents each."

Vanessa thought about what she had planned to buy with her dollar. Then she took her money to the pastor and told him that she wanted to give it as a donation for the missionaries to buy booklets so that children in the Blakes' city could learn about Jesus. "It will buy only two booklets," Vanessa said. "But that will help."

"Yes, Vanessa," the pastor said, "every gift helps. Thank you. As each person in the church does his part, we'll be able to help spread the gospel in other countries."

Right then Vanessa determined to give part of her next allowance too.

What did Vanessa give? *(She gave what she earned to buy two missionary booklets.)*

 If two children each received a booklet, what could God do with Vanessa's gift? *(God could bring those two children, and possibly more people to Himself. Each*

Humbling Yourself
2 Chronicles 7:14

Name _____

Find 2 Chronicles 7:14 in your Bible. Read it carefully. In the space below write *God's people* beside each thing that they should do. Write *God* beside each thing that He has promised to do.

pray	*God's people*
forgive sins	*God*
hear from heaven	*God*
turn from wicked ways	*God's people*
humble themselves	*God's people*
seek God's face	*God's people*
heal the land	*God*

A Servant's Heart • Lesson 37 **49**

---

child might share with his or her family what God did. God might save many people through that small gift.) Make sure the students understand it is Vanessa's willingness to give that God blesses.

♥ Memory Verse—2 Chronicles 7:14

Principle: The Lord calls us to humble ourselves before Him.

Practice the memory verse. Explain that we must respond to God in humility.

What are four things God wants us to do? *(humble ourselves, [not be proud, but modest or meek]; pray; seek God; and turn from our wicked ways)*

Instruct the students to highlight the verse (optional) and mark the location with the Unit 3 Bookmark.

💡 **How did Vanessa show humility?** *(She put God's work before her desire for candy. She prayed for God to bless her gift.)*

💡 **How can Christians show humility?** *(Possible answers include worshiping God, doing what He commands, praying, seeking God, and realizing and turning from our wicked ways.)*

♫ Hymn: "Be Thou Exalted"

Review and sing the first verse (Worktext pages 214–15). Point out that Fanny Crosby wrote this hymn. Remind the students that Fanny was blind from infancy, yet she wrote more than eight thousand gospel hymns.

- **Why should God be exalted or honored?** *(Elicit that God is the wise, eternal, holy, and all-powerful ruler: God has no beginning and no end.)*
- **How can Christians exalt (honor) God?** *(Possible answers include songs of praise, prayers of thanksgiving, and service for others.)*

Divide the class into four groups and assign a part of the first verse to each group. While playing the recording, each group should sing the assigned part and all groups sing the chorus together. Change the parts until each group has sung each of the parts. Then guide the students as they sing the first verse of the hymn together.

Worktext page 49
Guide an activity to review 2 Chronicles 7:14. Read aloud the directions for Worktext page 49. Explain that the verse tells what God's people should do and it tells what God has promised to do for His people. Instruct the students to complete the page independently.

Geography Connection (optional)
Identify countries (continents). Give each student one of the tags you prepared. Guide each student in attaching his tag to Chart 31, "World Map," at the correct location.

LESSON 38 Samson Needs Humility

Materials
- Chart 2, "Books of the Bible: New Testament"

Background Information
Nazirite—*Nazirite means "separated" or "dedicated." A Nazirite vows to be separated for the service of God. The individual may not cut his hair or eat anything unclean or of the vine: grapes, raisins, wine, grape juice, or anything made with grape seeds or skins. The Nazirite must not go near a dead body (**Numbers 6:1–21**). If someone died in the presence of a Nazirite, the Nazirite would be required to shave his head and begin the vow again. None of the time prior to the death would count as part of the term of service. Samson did not choose to make himself a Nazirite—God chose him before his birth (**Judges 13:5**), and there was no end to the term of his service. Only two other people mentioned by name in the Bible were Nazirites—Samuel (**1 Samuel 1:11**) and John the Baptist (**Luke 1:15**).*

Deliverance from the Philistines—*God created Samson for His service to begin the deliverance of Israel from the Philistines. The deliverance was continued in the time of Samuel (**1 Samuel 7:10–14**) and completed under the reign of David (**2 Samuel 5:17–25; 8:1**).*

Introducing the Bible Account
Discuss how a Nazirite must act. Share the background information, explaining that God has instructed Christians through His Word. However, He gave special rules that a Nazirite must follow when taking the vow to separate himself or herself for God's use.

Read Judges 13–14 or use the following retelling of the passage. Listening question: **What rules did this Nazirite disobey?** *(Samson ate unclean food and touched a dead lion.)*

Samson Needs Humility

Many of the Israelites were doing evil again in the sight of the Lord, so the Lord let the Philistines rule over them for forty years. Some of God's people, such as Manoah and his wife, remained faithful to Him. Manoah's wife hadn't given birth to any children yet.

The Angel of the Lord appeared to her and told her she would have a son. But He told her that because God was blessing her this way she must not drink wine or eat any unclean thing, and she must not let her son's hair be cut. Then the Angel told her that her son was to be a Nazirite because God would use him to begin to free the Israelites from the Philistines. The woman gave birth to the son that God had promised. She named him Samson, which means "like the sun," because she was so happy. Samson grew up, and the Lord blessed him.

One time Samson went down to Timnath and saw a Philistine woman whom he wanted for his wife. When Samson told his father and mother, they were upset because the Lord had commanded that no Israelite was to marry outside the tribes of Israel. His father said, "Why don't you find a wife from among our own people?" But Samson wouldn't listen to his father's wisdom and told his father to make arrangements for him to marry the Philistine woman.

The family went to Timnath and on the way a lion roared at Samson. The Lord's strength came upon Samson, and he tore the lion in pieces.

Some time later, Samson went back to Timnath to marry the woman, and he passed the dead body of the lion. He found that bees had made a beehive in the lion's carcass. Samson took the honey and began eating it, and when he came to his parents, he gave it to them and they ate it too. But Samson didn't tell them that the honey was unclean food because it had come from the dead body of the lion.

As Samson's father went to make the arrangements for the wedding, Samson had the bridegroom's feast. Thirty men of the bride's village came to celebrate with him, and Samson made a bet with them that they couldn't answer his riddle (a question or problem that is hard to figure out). Samson said that if they could answer the riddle by the end of the seven-day feast he would give each of them a new set of clothes, but that if they couldn't, they would each owe him one set of clothing. Since there were thirty of them, Samson would either give away thirty sets of clothing or he would receive thirty sets of clothing. They agreed to the terms, so Samson told them the riddle; however, after three days of thinking they still couldn't solve the riddle.

Finally, they went to Samson's bride and demanded the answer, threatening her and her father's household. Samson's bride was very worried about her family so she cried and

Samson Needs Humility

Name _____

Samson wasn't humble. God's people always need to have humility. Read 2 Chronicles 7:14 in your Bible. Fingerspell the word *humble* when you come to it.

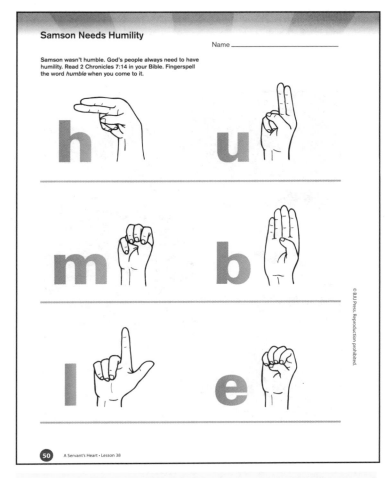

© BJU Press. Reproduction prohibited.

---

pleaded with Samson. By the seventh day he couldn't stand it anymore. He told her the answer to the riddle. She told the men, and they gave the right answer to Samson. Then Samson knew that his bride had tricked him.

The strength of the Lord came to Samson, and he went to Ashkelon and killed thirty Philistines. He took their clothes and gave them to the villagers who had answered the riddle. Samson was still angry so he left without his bride and went back to his father's house.

How did Samson use his mighty strength? (*Samson killed a lion, and he killed thirty Philistines.*)

 Why did Samson make a riddle? (*He made a riddle so that he could trick others to give him suits of clothes. Samson was greedy and proud.*)

What Nazirite rules did Samson break? (*Samson ate unclean food, and he touched the dead lion. The Nazirite law said not to touch or even be near a dead body.*)

 Did Samson glorify God with the strength God gave him? Whom did Samson glorify? (*No. Samson used his great strength to make himself look and feel good.*)

 How are Christians to use the gifts (talents) God has given them? (*Christians are to use all their gifts for the glory of God.*)

Worktext page 50

Review 2 Chronicles 7:14 and fingerspell the word humble. Teach the students to fingerspell the word *humble* using American Sign Language. Tell the students that *humble* means modest and meek, not proud or boastful. Direct attention to the fingerspelling signs on Worktext page 50. As you say the verse, have the students fingerspell rather than say the word *humble*. Guide the class in saying the verse several times, asking different students to lead the fingerspelling of *humble*.

Bible Study Skills

Study the last seven books of the New Testament (1 Peter–Revelation). Tell the students to locate the last book in the Bible, Revelation. Guide them as they continue to locate the books discussed.

> **What book of the Bible is before Revelation?** (*Jude*)
>
> **What are the three letters written by John, which come just before Jude?** (*1 John, 2 John, and 3 John. John also wrote the Gospel of John.*)
>
> **What are the two books written by Peter, which come before 1, 2, and 3 John?** (*1 and 2 Peter*)

Display Chart 2, "Books of the Bible: New Testament." Call on volunteers to name the last seven books of the New Testament. (*1 and 2 Peter; 1, 2, and 3 John; Jude; and Revelation*)

LESSON 39 Samson Reaps the Results of Pride

Materials
• Hymn: "Be Thou Exalted"
• Transparent tape for each student

Background Information

Delilah's Silver—*Delilah was probably a Philistine woman. She was willing to give Samson over to the Philistine leaders for fifty-five hundred pieces of silver. In Bible times this money represented a fortune, even to the very rich. Therefore, the Philistine leaders were extremely serious about capturing Samson.*

Grinding Grain—*Grinding wheat for flour was traditionally women's work. Therefore, not only were Samson's blindness and imprisonment degrading, but the work he was forced to do was also belittling for a man.*

Introducing the Bible Account

Guide a review about Samson. Call on students to recall the major events of the Bible account in the previous lesson. (*Samson killed a lion, ate honey from the body of the dead lion, married an unbeliever, told a riddle, had to pay the Philistines thirty suits of clothing, and then abandoned his wife.*)

Bible Account

Read Judges 15–16 or use the following retelling of the passage. Listening question: **How was Samson humbled?**

(The Philistines captured Samson, blinded him, and made him grind grain.)

Samson Reaps the Results of Pride

When Samson went back to his wife, he found that she had married his friend. This made Samson even angrier with the Philistines, so he decided to harm all the people of the village. Samson caught three hundred foxes and tied them in pairs tail to tail. In each pair of tails he tied a flaming torch and let the foxes loose in the fields that were ripe for harvest. The fields, vineyards, and olive orchards all burned.

When the Philistines found out that Samson had done this, they took revenge on the household of his wife and her father. Even though Samson was angry with his wife and her family, he was angrier with the Philistines for having harmed the family. He promised to take revenge on the Philistines and killed many of them. Then he went and lived in a cave at the top of a mountain called Etam.

The Philistines became even angrier, and they went into Judah, looking for Samson. The men of Judah wanted to know why the Philistines had come to their land. The Philistines explained that they were coming to capture Samson and do to him what he had done to them. Then three thousand men of Judah went to the top of Etam. They told Samson that the Philistines were the rulers over Judah, and that he was making life hard for Judah by being at Etam. Then they told Samson they had come to tie him up and take him to the Philistines.

Samson made the men of Judah promise that they would not try to harm him while he was tied, so they bound him with two new ropes and took him to the Philistines. When they reached the Philistines, the angry people shouted at Samson, and the Spirit of the Lord came upon Samson. The ropes broke as easily as pieces of thread burn in a flame. Samson found a jawbone of a donkey and used it to kill one thousand Philistines.

Why was Samson angry? *(The woman Samson married was now married to his friend; later she and her family were harmed because the Philistines were angry with Samson.)*

💡 **How did Samson's anger get him into trouble?** *(Samson acted in anger and punished the Philistines, which made them angrier with him.)*

But the Philistines were not defeated, and when Samson went to Gaza, the Philistines surrounded the town, locked the gate, and planned to capture Samson in the morning. At midnight, however, Samson decided to leave. He broke the whole gate out of the city wall and carried it thirty miles to the top of a hill near Hebron.

Later Samson fell in love with a woman named Delilah. The Philistine leaders promised her fifty-five hundred pieces of silver if she would find out the secret to Samson's mighty strength. Delilah tried to get Samson to tell her the secret to his strength. First, he told her that if he were tied up with seven new bow strings, then he would be as weak as other men. Samson was tied up with the bow strings while he slept.

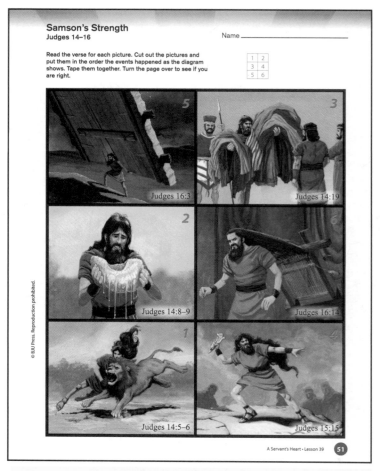

Samson's Strength
Judges 14–16

Name _____

Read the verse for each picture. Cut out the pictures and put them in the order the events happened as the diagram shows. Tape them together. Turn the page over to see if you are right.

1	2
3	4
5	6

Judges 16:3 — Judges 14:19

Judges 14:8–9 — Judges 16:14

Judges 14:5–6 — Judges 15:15

A Servant's Heart · Lesson 39   51

Then Delilah called, "The Philistines are going to get you, Samson," but he broke the bow strings easily.

Next, he told her that if he were tied up with brand new ropes that had never been used, then he would be weak like other men. But when Samson was tied up with the ropes, Delilah called, "The Philistines are going to get you, Samson," and he broke the ropes like threads. The third time Samson told Delilah that if his hair were woven on a loom (a machine used for weaving threads to make cloth), he would be weak. Delilah did this and when Samson woke up, he got up with the whole loom hanging from his hair.

Later, Delilah told Samson that he must not love her because he had lied to her three times and would not tell her how he could be made like other men. She nagged him daily. Finally, he told her the secret: "My hair has never been cut because I have been a Nazirite since before I was born. If my head is shaved, then I will lose my strength and be like any other man."

Now that was what Delilah had wanted to know, and she was certain he had told the truth this time.

When Samson fell asleep, the Philistine men shaved his head and tied him up. When Delilah called, "The Philistines are going to get you, Samson," he thought that he could just shake himself as before and be free, but the Lord's strength had departed from him.

The Philistines took Samson to Gaza and put out his eyes. They made him grind wheat into flour in the prison house.

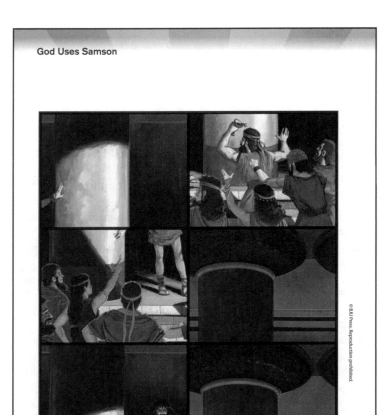

52 A Servant's Heart • Lesson 39

Samson Reaps the Results of Pride
Judges 13–16

Name _____

Choose a word from the word bank to complete each sentence.

Word Bank

ropes	pillars	razor	humble	eyes
gate	thread	silver	hair	boy

1. Samson broke the _____ __gate__ of Gaza and carried it away.

2. The Philistines promised _____ __silver__ to Delilah if she would find out Samson's secret.

3. Delilah tied Samson up with new _____ __ropes__ .

4. Samson was able to break the ropes like __thread__ .

5. Delilah wove Samson's __hair__ on a loom.

6. Samson was a Nazirite dedicated to God, and a __razor__ had never been used on his head.

7. The Philistines cut Samson's hair and put out his __eyes__ .

8. Samson was so helpless that he had to be led by a small __boy__ .

9. God strengthened Samson to pull down the __pillars__ .

10. All Christians need to pray, turn from sin, __humble__ themselves, and seek God.

A Servant's Heart • Lesson 39 53

While he worked, the hair on his head began to grow back. Sometime later the Philistines had a great festival to their false god, Dagon. They gathered together to rejoice because they thought that their false god had given Samson into their hand. They called for Samson to be brought out. A small boy led the blind Samson from the prison so that the Philistines could make fun of him.

Samson asked the boy to help him find the pillars that held up the temple so that he could lean on them. The temple was full of Philistine people, and about three thousand Philistines stood on the roof. Samson prayed, "Oh Lord God, please remember me and strengthen me one more time so that I may get revenge against the Philistines because of my two eyes." Samson got in position between the two middle pillars and said, "Let me die with the Philistines." He pushed with all his might, and the temple came crashing down on the rulers and all the people. More people died at Samson's death than he had killed in his lifetime.

💡 **Was God's purpose for Samson fulfilled in spite of his disobedience?** *(yes)*

💡 **What was the final result of Samson's disobedience?** *(He died.)*

💡 **Does God want Christians to take revenge on people who hurt them?** *(No. God will bring vengeance on those who try to hurt Christians if the Christians humble themselves before God.)*

💡 **How can Christians exalt God?** *(Answers may vary, but lead the students to the answers in **2 Chronicles 7:14**: we can turn from sin, humble ourselves, pray, and seek God's will for our lives.)*

Read and discuss Proverbs 14:29.

🎵 **Hymn: "Be Thou Exalted"**
Teach the second verse (Worktext pages 214–15).
Help the students understand the following words: *redeemer* (one who saves, Jesus Christ), *co-equal* (same rank or level), and *homage* (to give honor or respect).

Whom are Christians to honor in the second verse? *(Jesus, the Son of God)*

Why are they to honor Him? *(He is their Savior. Only the sinless Son of God can save sinful people. To realize one's sinful condition and then turn to Christ requires humility.)*

✍️ **Worktext pages 51–52**

Sequence events. Tell the students to cut the pictures apart from Worktext page 51 and place them in chronological order. Check their work before allowing them to tape the pictures together. A picture of God using Samson to accomplish His purpose will be on page 52 if the events on page 51 are arranged correctly.

✍️ **Worktext page 53**

Recall facts and details. As the students turn to Work-

text page 53, emphasize that we ought to be humble when we think about Who God is. Remind them that God created and controls everything, that He gives us every breath, and that He is holy. Direct the students' attention to the word bank at the top of the page. Read the directions with them. Instruct the students to complete the page.

LESSON 40 A Humble Spirit

Materials

- Copy of page A78 ("Humble Prayer") for each student (optional)

❤ Memory Verse—2 Chronicles 7:14

Practice the memory verse.

Introducing the Application Story

Guide a discussion about arguments. Ask the students if they have ever quarreled with someone while playing a game. Choose several volunteers to share with the class what they quarreled about. Point out that quarreling shows selfishness and pride rather than humility.

Application Story

Read or tell the following story. Listening question: **Who settled the quarrel?** *(Dad)*

Stopping a Fight

Derek kicked the ball around, practicing the moves his soccer coach had taught him. His older sister Nichole came out and asked if she could practice with him. They started doing passing drills. Then Derek said, "How about if we practice passing the ball back and forth with our heads; the first one to make a wild pass has—"

Nichole interrupted him, "That's silly. Why would you try to hit the ball to the same player by bouncing it off your head?"

Derek said, "I'm *not* silly; only *girls* are *silly*."

Nichole yelled at Derek, "You're just a baby. You can't admit it when you're wrong."

"Can too," cried Derek. "Girls don't know anything about sports."

"I know soccer players don't pass the ball back and forth with their heads," she said.

"Well, Coach said it's good for learning to control the pass," he said angrily.

"Hey, you two," Dad called over their bickering voices, "Quiet down and come over here."

"It's your fault," Derek said to Nichole. "I just made a suggestion."

"What's the trouble?" Dad asked.

"She called me 'silly' and 'baby'," said Derek.

Dad looked at Nichole. "Did you call your brother names?"

"No, sir, . . . at least not at first."

"Yes, you did!" Derek said.

Dad held up his hand to quiet Derek. "You'll get your turn,

young man. Nichole, Derek said you called him 'silly' and 'baby.'"

"I only said his *idea* was silly because soccer players don't pass the ball back to the same player with their heads. After he said girls were always wrong about sports, I said he was a baby."

Dad looked at Derek. "All right. Derek?"

Derek said, "Coach said we should do head passes for practice. She doesn't know more than Coach."

"Did you say girls are always wrong about sports?"

"Yes."

Their father said, "It seems you two have missed the point. Both of you were wrong. Derek, girls are not always wrong about sports. Nichole, you shouldn't have called Derek a baby just because he disagreed with you."

Derek and Nichole both stared at the ground, embarrassed.

Their father went on, "The point here is that instead of thinking you were right, you both should've been trying to understand the other's point of view. The Bible says that wherever there is pride, there will be bickering and fighting. But God also says He will help the humble."

Dad looked at Nicole and Derek. "Now toss me that ball. I want to see if I can pass the ball with my head."

Nichole and Derek looked at each other and then burst out laughing.

💡 **What could Derek have done when he thought Nichole called him 'silly'?** *(Possible answers include that Derek could have asked her whether she did not understand or whether she just did not want to do that drill; he could have explained his idea.)*

Read aloud and discuss **John 13:34**, **15:12**, and **15:17**. Remind the students that God says it is important to love others.

💡 **How should we act when someone does something to us that seems mean?** *(Elicit the following options from the students:*

- *Check out the situation. If you misunderstood, apologize. If someone is being mean, be nice to him.*
- *Tell him you forgive him, or tell him you want to be his friend and not fight.*
- *If he is still mean, walk away. In **James 1:20** we are told that our anger never brings about a godly solution.)*

✍ Worktext page 54

Infer proper responses. Direct the students to turn to page 54 and read the sentence in the circle under the picture. Tell the students that it is possible to have a humble spirit toward others.

💡 **How do we know how to respond to others?** *(Answers may include that God teaches us in His Word how we should act toward others, Jesus showed us how we should answer others, and God gives us the help we need to get along with others.)*

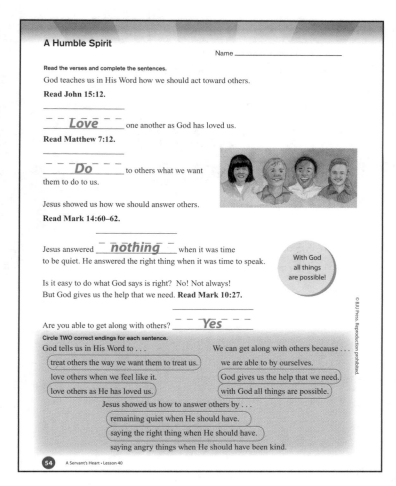

A Humble Spirit

Name _____

Read the verses and complete the sentences.

God teaches us in His Word how we should act toward others.

Read John 15:12.

_____ **Love** _____ one another as God has loved us.

Read Matthew 7:12.

_____ **Do** _____ to others what we want them to do to us.

Jesus showed us how we should answer others.

Read Mark 14:60–62.

Jesus answered _____ **nothing** _____ when it was time to be quiet. He answered the right thing when it was time to speak.

With God all things are possible!

Is it easy to do what God says is right? No! Not always! But God gives us the help that we need. **Read Mark 10:27.**

Are you able to get along with others? _____ **Yes** _____

Circle TWO correct endings for each sentence.

God tells us in His Word to . . .

(treat others the way we want them to treat us.)

love others when we feel like it.

(love others as He has loved us.)

We can get along with others because . . .

we are able to by ourselves.

(God gives us the help that we need.)

(with God all things are possible.)

Jesus showed us how to answer others by . . .

(remaining quiet when He should have.)

(saying the right thing when He should have.)

saying angry things when He should have been kind.

54   A Servant's Heart · Lesson 40

Guide the students as they find and read each verse to complete the sentences or choose volunteers to look up and read the verses aloud. For the exercise at the bottom of the page, tell them to circle two correct endings for each sentence. After students complete the page independently, call on volunteers to read the sentences aloud.

Art Connections (optional)

Illustrate the Bible account. Explain the directions for page A78 ("Trusting God"). Instruct the students to work on their pictures and complete the sentence on the page. After the drawings are complete, direct the students to post their drawings on the Unit 3 bulletin board.

Going Beyond

Reinforcement

Materials

Draw, color, and cut out a pie visual aid. Cut into four or eight slices to attach to the board.

Guide an activity to recognize humility. Remind the students that humility is shown by obedience and by thinking of others first. By attaching to the board or wall a piece of the pie, recognize throughout the day or week those students who show thoughtfulness and humility. After the pie shape is completed, you may want to bring and share a pie or a different treat with the class.

Enrichment

Materials

Prepare ten 3" × 5" cards with the name and address or e-mail address of a missionary child; use the names that you put on the map in Lesson 37. Place the cards in alphabetical order in a file box.

Write a letter to a missionary child. Tell the students to choose one of the missionary children from the map and write him a letter or an e-mail. Encourage them to tell about their own lives and then ask the missionary child to write back, telling about his daily activities and giving some prayer requests. You may wish to have students contact their pastors to obtain the name and address of a missionary child. If the students receive replies, you may attach them to Chart 31, "World Map," or display them on a bulletin board. If you used famous missionaries of the past instead, students can practice writing letters, but you will not need to mail them.

Humble Yourself Before Others
Unit 3c

PREVIEW

Doctrines

- Care for those having special needs (Acts 6:1–7; Romans 12:13). [Lesson 41]
- God is merciful (Psalm 86:15). [Lesson 42]

Skills and Applications

- Learn Galatians 6:10
- Read a timeline
- Identify characters
- Identify content in a book of the Bible
- Understand that serving others is serving God
- Choose to serve others
- Apply Bible knowledge to everyday life

LESSON 41 Ruth Has a Servant's Heart

Materials

- Charts 8–9, "Ruth and the Barley Harvest"
- Chart 34, "The Israelites"
- Hymn: "Be Thou Exalted"
- TimeLine and picture: Ruth
- Unit 3 Bookmark for each student
- Highlighter for each student (optional)
- Four sentence strips, three each containing a phrase from Galatians 6:10, the fourth containing the reference

🎵 Hymn: "Be Thou Exalted"

Sing the first and second verses (Worktext pages 214–15). Listen to the recording and then sing verses one and two several times, dividing the hymn with girls singing one verse, boys singing the other, and all singing the chorus. Direct the students to sing the last phrase of the chorus softly.

Background Information

Kinsman-Redeemer—*In Bible times it was the custom that when a man died without children, his unmarried brother would marry the man's wife and provide her with a child. That way the deceased's inheritance would be given to the nearest male relative. The wife did not inherit her husband's property because if she remarried and had children, the property would leave the first husband's family. Since she did not have an inheritance, the law of the kinsman-redeemer (nearest male blood relation) required her husband's family to take care of her. If a man had no brothers, then another male relative (his father, an uncle, or a cousin) could be the redeemer. Boaz became the kinsman-redeemer of Elimelech's (Naomi's husband's) estate when he married Ruth.*

The Transaction—*Boaz was not the nearest blood relative. However, the nearer kinsman chose to transfer the inheritance to Boaz. Boaz showed the transfer to be complete by taking off his sandal (Ruth 4:7–8).*

Our Redeemer—*Ruth was the great-grandmother of King David. God chose Boaz and Ruth to be the family through whom He would send us our Redeemer, the Lord Jesus Christ.*

Introducing the Bible Account

Introduce the account. Point to Moab and Bethlehem on Chart 34, "The Israelites." Tell the students that today's account begins in Bethlehem. The family moved from Bethlehem to Moab and later moved back to Bethlehem.

Bible Account

Read Ruth 1–4 or use the following retelling of the passage. Listening question: **How was Ruth humble and helpful?** *(She was willing to go to a strange country, she worked hard, and she helped provide for Naomi.)*

Ruth Has a Servant's Heart

During the days when the judges ruled Israel, there was a famine, or a lack of food to eat. Naomi, her husband, and their two sons moved to Moab. After several years Naomi's husband died, and her sons married Moabite women, Orpah and Ruth. After about ten more years Naomi's sons both died, and she was left without any family except her daughters-in-law.

Naomi decided to return to Israel because the famine was over and there were now plenty of crops. But she didn't want to force her daughters-in-law to leave their homeland. She told them to return to their mothers' homes, desiring the Lord to be kind to them just as they had shown kindness to their husbands and to her. They both cried and wanted to go with her. However, Orpah kissed Naomi goodbye; only Ruth stayed with Naomi.

Naomi told Ruth again that she should go like Orpah to her own people and her own gods, but Ruth said that she didn't want to leave Naomi or stop following her. She wanted to go where Naomi went and live where Naomi lived. She wanted to be a part of Naomi's family and have the same God as Naomi. She wanted to live and be buried where Naomi was. She didn't want anything to separate them.

Why was Naomi leaving? *(Naomi's husband and sons had died, the famine in Israel was over, and she decided to go home to be with her people.)*

Who decided to stay in Moab? *(Orpah decided to stay with her own people.)*

💡 **Why do you think Ruth decided to go with Naomi?** *(Ruth loved Naomi.)*

Tell the students to look at Worktext pages 55–56 as you continue the account.

Ruth and Naomi returned to Bethlehem at the beginning of the barley harvest. Because they had nothing to eat, Ruth asked Naomi whether she would go to the fields to pick up the stalks of barley that the harvesters left behind. This is called gleaning. Naomi agreed. God directed Ruth to the fields owned by Boaz, who was a relative of her deceased husband. After getting permission, Ruth gleaned in his fields.

When Boaz came out to his fields, he asked his servant about the woman who was gleaning. His servant told him that Ruth was the Moabite woman who had come back with Naomi. He explained that Ruth had asked his permission to

Ruth and the Barley Harvest
Ruth 2–3

Water and food were brought to the field for the workers. *Boaz told Ruth to help herself to it.*

The stalks of grain were gathered into a bundle as large as a worker could hold in his arms. The stalks were bound to form a **sheaf**.

Grain was cut with a **sickle**, which had a long, curved blade made of flint or iron attached to a short wooden handle.

The law of Moses said that not all the grain was to be gathered. Some was to be left in the corners of the field for the poor and strangers to gather. *Boaz told his workers to let Ruth gather grain in the middle of the field and to let some grain fall on purpose so that she could pick it up.*

© BJU Press. Reproduction prohibited.

A Servant's Heart • Lesson 41   55

glean in the field and that she had worked very hard. Boaz called Ruth and told her to stay in his fields and work with his servants. Ruth fell on her knees and asked Boaz why he had noticed her, a foreigner. Boaz said that he had heard what Ruth had done for Naomi and how she had left her homeland and parents to serve Naomi. Then Boaz told her to drink the water and to eat the food provided for his servants. He also told her to stay only in his fields gleaning after his servants until the end of the harvest.

After Ruth went back to work, Boaz told his servants to leave handfuls of barley stalks for Ruth to glean but not to embarrass her. At the end of the day Ruth separated the barley and took it to Naomi. Naomi was surprised by how much Ruth had gathered. Naomi asked Ruth where she had gleaned. Naomi told Ruth that Boaz was a relative of her husband's family. Then Naomi told Ruth that she should stay with the servants of Boaz until the harvest was over since she might be in danger somewhere else. So Ruth gleaned with Boaz's servants until both the barley and the wheat harvests were complete.

Naomi was determined to provide a proper marriage for Ruth. Naomi advised Ruth to ask Boaz to care for her needs all the time. Ruth did so. Boaz knew Ruth was a virtuous woman, and he married her. Boaz and Ruth's great-grandson was King David.

Where did Ruth go to glean barley? *(into Boaz's fields)*

💡 **How did God show His love to Ruth?** *(He directed Ruth to Boaz's field.)*

💡 **Why was Boaz kind to Ruth?** *(He heard that Ruth had been kind to Naomi.)*

💡 **What kind of man was Boaz?** *(He was kind, humble, and generous.)*

💡 **How did Ruth show she was humble?** *(She was helpful to her mother-in-law. She was thankful to Boaz. She chose to serve God and follow Naomi.)*

What did Ruth give to Naomi? *(Ruth gave of herself—her time, energy, and loyalty.)*

💡 **How can we help others?** *(We can give our time, money, loyalty, friendship, and talents.)*

InfoScene: "The Barley Harvest"
Display Charts 8–9 from the Visual Packet for the students to refer to throughout this unit.

🕐 **TimeLine**

Add Ruth to the TimeLine. Place the picture of Ruth on the TimeLine (1125 BC), pointing out that she lived about a thousand years before the birth of Jesus. Guide the students as they glue the picture of Ruth (from the Student Materials section of the ToolKit CD) onto their TimeLines.

♥ **Memory Verse—Galatians 6:10**

Principle: Serve others, doing good to them. Explain that *reap* means "to cut or harvest the crop that has been planted." We are not to become weary *(tired)* or faint *(lack courage)* in doing good. Elicit that the result of Christians' efforts may include seeing others come to Christ because of their kindness or seeing other Christians strengthened and encouraged to follow the Lord.

Tell the students that God says Christians should do good to all people as they have the opportunity. Boaz showed this kind of goodness to Ruth.

To whom does the verse say to be specifically helpful? *(the household of faith, Christians, believers)*
Tell the students to highlight the verse (optional) and mark the location in their Bibles with the Unit 3 Bookmark.

Practice the memory verse. Utilize the sentence strips.

💡 **What good did Ruth do by gleaning barley?** *(Ruth was gathering food for Naomi.)* Point out that in doing good for others, Christians are serving the Lord.

💡 **What were some of the results of Ruth's gleaning?** *(Naomi and Ruth had food to eat. Boaz saw Ruth's faithfulness to Naomi and provided her with a home and family.)*

💡 **What are some ways that you can do good?** *(Many answers are acceptable such as helping a parent, friend, or neighbor; doing chores cheerfully; and being kind to your classmates. Lead the students to understand that they should do good things for others not to receive a reward or payment, but because that is what God requires of them.)*

Ruth and the Barley Harvest (continued)

The grain was **threshed** by hitting the stalks with a **flail** to separate the grain. *Ruth beat out the grain that she had gathered.* Sometimes the oxen trampled on the stalks or dragged boards covered with sharp stones over them.

The grain was **winnowed** by throwing it against the wind. The grain was heaviest, so it fell to the ground. The straw (stalks without grain) was thrown to the side to be used for animal food. The chaff (the dusty waste part of the grain) was blown farther away by the wind. It was gathered later and burned. Winnowing usually took place in the evening when the wind was stronger. *Naomi told Ruth to go to the threshing floor where Boaz was winnowing barley at night.*

The grain was carried by camels or donkeys to the **threshing floor**, which was a large circle of hard-packed earth.

Small amounts of grain were stored in earthenware jars. Large amounts were stored in round storehouses or barns, many of which were underground.

The grain was sifted through a **sieve** to remove small stones and leftover chaff.

© BJU Press. Reproduction prohibited.

56   A Servant's Heart · Lesson 41

Game: Who Am I? (optional)

Identify people in a Bible account. Display the following four names: *Ruth, Orpah, Naomi,* and *Boaz.* Read the following clues and let the class identify the Bible people. (Scripture references are from the book of Ruth.)

• Both my sons and my husband died, so I wanted to go back to my own people in Bethlehem. Who am I? *(Naomi; 1:3)*

• My husband died. I didn't want to leave my people and the gods of my childhood. Who am I? *(Orpah; Ruth 1:14–15)*

• I owned many fields, but I had no son to own them after me. Who am I? *(Boaz; 2:1)*

• My husband died. I went with my mother-in-law back to her homeland. I wanted to continue worshiping the one true God. Who am I? *(Ruth; 1:22)*

• I loved my mother-in-law and wept when she left, but I stayed in my homeland of Moab. Who am I? *(Orpah; 1:14–15)*

• The Lord gave me a kind husband to look after my mother-in-law and me. He was called my kinsman-redeemer. Who am I? *(Ruth; 3:7–12; 4:13)*

• My daughter-in-law went with me back to my homeland to serve the one true God with me. Who am I? *(Naomi; 1:22)*

• I told my workers to be kind to Ruth and to leave some extra grain for her to find. Who am I? *(Boaz; 2:15)*

Hannah Gives Her Gift

Materials

- Hymn: "Be Thou Exalted"
- Sentence strips prepared for the previous lesson
- Stapler

♫ Hymn: "Be Thou Exalted"

Teach the third verse (Worktext pages 214–15). Tell the students to read silently the words of the third verse as you play the recording. Sing or read the third verse, explaining that *Spirit of Power* is another name for the Holy Spirit. Point out that the Holy Spirit lives in us when we ask Jesus to save us from our sins.

> **What three names for God are mentioned in the verse and what does each name mean?** *(God of the ages means "always present." Lord of Salvation means "our Savior." Ruler of heaven and earth means "all-powerful.")*

We praise God because He is all-powerful, ever-present, and offers salvation to everybody. Repeat the singing of the third verse several times; then sing the entire hymn.

Background Information

Festivals—*Three times each year all the men of Israel were required to be at the central or most important place of worship. They offered sacrifices in observation of the main religious festivals: Passover, Pentecost, and the Feast of Tabernacles. In 1 Samuel, Hannah was probably participating in the Feast of Tabernacles. This feast was celebrated on the fifteenth day of the seventh month and lasted for seven days. It honored the period when the Israelites wandered in the wilderness and lived in tents called tabernacles.*

Introducing the Bible Account

Lead a discussion about humility. Ask volunteers to name something they asked their parents for recently. Discuss whether this item was something they could use to help others. Point out that a humble Christian submits to God and is willing to help others.

Bible Account

Read 1 Samuel 1 or use the following retelling of the passage. Listening question: **What gift is requested and what promise is made?** *(Hannah asked God for a son. She promised that her son would serve the Lord.)*

Hannah Gives Her Gift

In the time of the judges over Israel, a man named Elkanah had two wives: Hannah and Peninnah. Peninnah had several children, but Hannah had none. Every year they went to worship the Lord at the tabernacle in Shiloh. When Elkanah made his sacrificial offering, he gave portions to Peninnah and all her children. Because Elkanah loved Hannah more, he gave her a double portion. But still Hannah had no children.

Year after year they went to the feast. Peninnah continually made fun of Hannah because Hannah had no children.

Hannah cried and couldn't eat. Elkanah asked why she was unhappy even though he loved her very much.

Hannah got up and went to the tabernacle. She knew she was unhappy about the life the Lord had chosen for her, and she wept and prayed to the Lord. Then Hannah made a promise to God that if the Lord gave her a son, she would give him back to the Lord. Hannah prayed in her heart, but her lips moved; no sound came out. Eli, the priest, watched from where he sat by the door. He thought Hannah had been drinking alcohol. He told her to stop drinking.

Hannah replied, "I am full of sorrow. I have not been drinking wine or strong drink, but I have poured out my soul before the Lord." Then Eli told her, "Go in peace: and the God of Israel will give you what you asked Him for." Hannah was happy as she went out of the tabernacle.

The Lord answered Hannah and soon gave her a child. She named her son Samuel, which means "asked of God."

When Samuel was still a young child, Hannah took him to worship the Lord at the tabernacle. She brought Samuel to Eli. Hannah reminded Eli of her prayer for a son; now she was giving back to the Lord what the Lord had given to her. Samuel would stay and serve the Lord at the tabernacle.

---❦---

Why was Hannah sad? *(She did not have any children.)*
What did Hannah ask God for? *(a son)*

What did Hannah promise God? *(She would give her child back to God.)*

What did Hannah name her son? *(Samuel)*

What does *Samuel* mean? *("asked of God")*

How did Hannah keep her promise? *(Hannah took Samuel to live at the tabernacle with Eli, the priest.)*

💡 **How did Hannah show humility?** *(She trained Samuel to serve God and gave him to God.)*

✍️ Worktext pages 57–58

Make a take-home booklet. Direct the students to look at Worktext page 57 and read together the title of their booklet. Guide them as they cut and fold the pages according to the directions. Staple each student booklet. Direct the students to read the account and complete each sentence. Encourage the students to use the booklet to retell the Bible account to a family member, neighbor, or friend.

❤️ Memory Verse—Galatians 6:10

Practice the memory verse using the sentence strips.

LESSON 43 — Hero of the Faith: Richard Allen

Materials

- TimeLine and picture: Richard Allen
- Copy of page A79 ("Humble Service") for each student (optional)

❤️ Memory Verse—Galatians 6:10

Practice the memory verse.

Hero of the Faith

Read the following narrative based on the life of Richard Allen. Listening question: **Why do we still remember Richard Allen?** *(Richard Allen founded the African Methodist Episcopal Church.)*

Richard Allen

Young Richard Allen stood close to his brother in front of the Delaware farmhouse. He waved to his parents as they rode away in their new master's wagon. Master Stokely, standing nearby, waved as the wagon passed him.

Richard's throat felt tight. His brother looked up at him.

"Will Mama and Papa ever be back?"

"This is just the way it is," Richard told his brother. "Master just can't afford to keep all of us anymore."

Richard and his brother were young boys, but they understood. He and his family were slaves, and slaves worked wherever the master decided.

Richard and his brother stayed with Master Stokely for many years. One day, when Richard was a teenager, a preacher visited their farm. The preacher gathered all of

Hannah Gives Her Gift (continued)
1 Samuel 1

(Panel 1) It is time to go to Shiloh.

Hannah went with her husband, ___Elkanah___, every year to worship the Lord. 2

(Panel 2) I prayed for this child, and God gave him to me.

Hannah gave ___Samuel___ to God. 7

(Panel 3) How long will you be drunk?

No, I am not drunk. I am very sad.

___Eli___ did not understand. 4

(Panel 4) Go in peace. God will give you what you ask.

Please think well of me.

Eli spoke kindly to ___Hannah___. 5

© BJU Press. Reproduction prohibited.

58 A Servant's Heart • Lesson 42

Master Stokely's slaves together. "The only way to have forgiveness for the wrong we have done," said the preacher, "is through Jesus Christ. Everyone has to answer to God for his own sins."

Richard and his brother both knelt that day and prayed for Jesus to save them from their sins. Other slaves became Christians that day too.

"I must tell others about my dear Savior," Richard said. "They must know of God's mercy through the blood of Jesus." Richard began preaching on evenings and Sundays.

The neighbors feared that the Christian slaves might turn against their masters. They asked Mr. Stokely to forbid the slaves from listening to preachers. Richard Allen challenged the Christian slaves to do their best work because now they were working to please God. Within a few weeks Master Stokely's land and house were in better condition than his neighbors'.

Master Stokely noticed the change in his slaves. He was greatly impressed by their hard work and change of attitude. Master Stokely also trusted Christ. "If you can pay me two thousand dollars," he told his slaves, "I will give you your freedom." Richard and his brother worked hard and saved their money. Three years later, they bought their freedom.

Now Richard Allen could travel from city to city to preach. He stopped to work as he had need. Everywhere he went, he told others about Jesus Christ.

After the Revolutionary War, Richard moved to Philadelphia. He now had a wife and family to support, and work

Richard Allen

Name _____

Richard Allen was born a slave in the city of Philadelphia, Pennsylvania. He grew up with his older brother on the farm of a man named Stokely.

One day when Richard was in his teens, a preacher came to the farm and gathered all the slaves together. He told them they needed to trust Jesus Christ for forgiveness of their sins. Richard, his brother, and many of the other slaves were saved that day. Right away he wanted to tell others about his wonderful Savior, so he began preaching in the evenings and on Sundays.

Richard and his brother at last bought their freedom from Master Stokely. Then Richard was able to go from place to place preaching. A church in Philadelphia asked him to preach to a group of African Americans who came to the services. When this group went down to the main floor of the church to join in prayer, they were turned away. Richard started a church for them, the Bethel African Methodist Episcopal Church. God also used him to help other preachers start churches in many parts of the world. He is known as the founder of the African Methodist Episcopal Church.

Write a word from the word bank to complete each sentence.

Word Bank	
churches	pray
preached	slave

1. Richard Allen was born a

   _ _ _ _ _ slave _ _ _ _ _ .

2. He bought his freedom and

   _ _ _ preached _ _ _

   about his wonderful Savior.

3. He started a church because he and other African Americans were not allowed to

   _ _ _ _ pray _ _ _ _ with

   white people.

4. He helped many other preachers start

   _ _ _ churches _ _ _ .

was hard to find. He met many other African Americans in Philadelphia. Many of his new friends were freed slaves like himself, and they had trouble getting good jobs.

One church asked Richard to preach to the group of black people that came to its services. Richard agreed.

His little congregation continued to meet, although not welcomed by all. But one day, Richard and his friends went to the main floor to join in prayer. They were turned away. "We will start our own church," Richard told his friends.

The new church was called the Bethel African Methodist Episcopal Church. In a few years, Richard's congregation built their own church building. Richard and his wife led the church for many years.

Richard always tried to help others. During a sickness that swept through the city of Philadelphia, he cared for many people when it was difficult to get others to assist. Later, the Allens even started a school for the city's African American children.

By the time of Pastor Allen's death, he was known around the world. God used Richard Allen to help other black preachers start churches like his in places as far away as Haiti, Canada, and West Africa.

Why did Richard and the other Christian slaves work so hard to do their best for Master Stokely?
(Lead students to understand that the slaves wanted to do their best for the Lord.)

How did Mr. Allen and his family serve others?
(They started a new church and helped people during sickness.)

How did Richard Allen show that he was humble?
(He was willing to help others.)

TimeLine

Add Richard Allen to the TimeLine. Place the picture of Richard Allen on the TimeLine (AD 1760–1831), pointing out that he acted on his faith. He served the Lord humbly throughout his life even in difficult circumstances. Guide the students in gluing their pictures of Richard Allen (from the Student Materials section of the ToolKit CD) onto their TimeLines.

Worktext page 239 (optional)

Recall facts and details. Review the events in Richard Allen's life. Point out that because he had been a slave, Richard was able to understand the problems of others who were mistreated. Direct the students to choose the correct words to complete the sentences.

History Connection (optional)

Guide a discussion about slavery. Ask the students whether they know how many slaves first came to America. Explain that between 1500 and the mid-1800s (over three hundred fifty years) more than twelve million slaves were brought from Africa. Nearly two million died on the way to North and South America. In 1807, the United States passed a law against bringing more slaves into the country. By the mid-1830s all of the northern states had abolished or stopped slavery, but it was still legal until 1863.

Call on volunteers to tell why they think many slaves tried to run away to be free. Explain that thousands succeeded, including those who followed the runaway slave Harriet Tubman using an escape system called the Underground Railroad. It was not under the ground nor was it a railroad, but the term *underground railroad* and the code words used were taken from railroad jargon. The runaway slaves traveled by night and hid by day at "stations." "Conductors" hid the runaway slaves and provided them with food, clothing, and directions to the next hiding place or station.

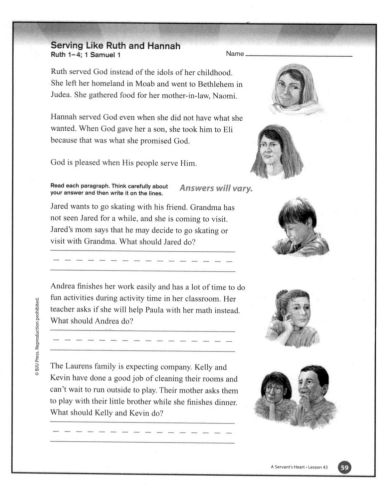

Serving Like Ruth and Hannah
Ruth 1–4; 1 Samuel 1

Name _____

Ruth served God instead of the idols of her childhood. She left her homeland in Moab and went to Bethlehem in Judea. She gathered food for her mother-in-law, Naomi.

Hannah served God even when she did not have what she wanted. When God gave her a son, she took him to Eli because that was what she promised God.

God is pleased when His people serve Him.

Read each paragraph. Think carefully about your answer and then write it on the lines. *Answers will vary.*

Jared wants to go skating with his friend. Grandma has not seen Jared for a while, and she is coming to visit. Jared's mom says that he may decide to go skating or visit with Grandma. What should Jared do?

_____

Andrea finishes her work easily and has a lot of time to do fun activities during activity time in her classroom. Her teacher asks if she will help Paula with her math instead. What should Andrea do?

_____

The Laurens family is expecting company. Kelly and Kevin have done a good job of cleaning their rooms and can't wait to run outside to play. Their mother asks them to play with their little brother while she finishes dinner. What should Kelly and Kevin do?

_____

A Servant's Heart • Lesson 43   **59**

Where Is It?

Name _____

Write the name of the book in the Bible where the account is located. You may look at the contents page in your Bible to spell the books correctly. One answer is used two times.

"God Created the Heavens and the Earth"   *Genesis*

"The Answer to Hannah's Prayer"   *1 Samuel*

"Naomi's Faithful Daughter-in-law"   *Ruth*

"God Gives Gideon a Battle Plan"   *Judges*

"Moses Leads God's People Out"   *Exodus*

"God Gives Samson Special Strength"   *Judges*

Put these books of the prophets in order. You may use the contents page in your Bible.

Word Bank
Amos   Joel   Hosea
Daniel   Ezekiel

1. *Ezekiel*

2. *Daniel*

3. *Hosea*

4. *Joel*

5. *Amos*

60   A Servant's Heart • Lesson 44

 Worktext page 59

Apply Bible knowledge to everyday life. Read the sentences about Ruth at the top of the page. Instruct the students to read each paragraph and decide the appropriate action. Direct them to complete the page independently. Allow time for the students to share their answers. Remind them that God is pleased when Christians serve others. Point out that God helps Christians to do right.

Art Connection (optional)

Illustrate serving others. Read the directions for page A79 ("Humble Service"). Instruct the students to work on their pictures and complete the sentence on the page. After the drawings are complete, allow the students to display them on the Unit 3 bulletin board.

LESSON
44   **A Heart for Serving**

Materials
• Chart 3, "Books of the Bible: Old Testament" (optional)

Bible Study Skills, Worktext page 60

Study the books in the Old Testament. Direct the students to turn to the contents page in their Bibles, or display Chart 3, "Books of the Bible: Old Testament." Direct the

students to read together the names of the first thirty books of the Old Testament (Genesis–Amos). Guide the students as they say from memory the names of these Old Testament books in order. Direct attention to Worktext page 60. Guide the students as they write the names of the books in which the people and accounts appear. Read aloud the directions for the second exercise. Instruct the students to use their Bibles to put the books of the Prophets in order.

Introducing the Application Story

Guide a discussion about friends. Call on students to tell what they like best about their friends. Write their answers for display. Elicit from the students that a person's physical appearance, abilities, or popularity may not make a person a good friend. Lead them to understand that they should include others in their activities, even those who may not have a lot of friends. Point out that a friend should also encourage them to do right and follow God.

Read or tell the following story. Listening question: **Why does Jesse not have many friends?** *(Jesse does not play much with the other boys. He goes home to take care of his grandfather after school each day.)*

Jesse's Gift

Jesse wanted to do the same things other boys liked to do. He liked to go bullfrog hunting by the creek and fishing out by the bluffs, and he liked to help the teacher with the science experiments. But the other boys didn't ask Jesse to join them anymore because many times he turned them down.

When the new P.E. coach asked Jesse to join the summer little league, Jesse said that he couldn't join. The boys called him a sissy and other mean names, but Jesse didn't answer back. When school got out, Jesse went home to Grandma and Grandpa Riley's as usual.

Grandma Riley was still at work, and Jesse let himself in. Grandpa Riley called from his chair by the window, "Jesse, my boy, is that you?"

"Hi, Grandpa, it's me. Do you want some juice?" Jesse went to the kitchen and poured two glasses of apple juice as he always did and grabbed some grapes.

"Grandpa, are you hungry?" Jesse asked as he came into the living room balancing a plate on top of each glass of juice. "Let's go out on the back porch."

Grandpa struggled to his feet and reached for his cane. Jesse moved in front of Grandpa, and Grandpa placed his other shaking hand on Jesse's shoulder. As Jesse led the way to the porch, he told Grandpa that the new P.E. coach had asked him to play in the little league. "That sounds like a fine idea," Grandpa Riley said.

Jesse said, "I couldn't leave you here all summer by yourself. It's bad enough I can't get home for lunch during the school year. This is the third time this week you haven't eaten lunch because it spilled." Jesse led Grandpa to his chair on the porch and set the glasses down carefully. As Jesse gave Grandpa a bunch of grapes, he watched closely to make sure Grandpa did not drop any. He guided Grandpa's hand to his mouth. When Grandpa needed a drink, Jesse held the glass for him. When he was finished, Jesse helped Grandpa clean his beard.

"Never you mind about being home for me," Grandpa said. "I'm seeing better every day."

Jesse didn't say anything to that, but Grandma had explained that Grandpa was very ill and that the blindness and shaking hands weren't going to get better. Jesse got out Grandpa's Bible and asked, "Gramps, what passage do you want me to read today?"

On Monday, Jesse did his usual morning chores and went to school. He ate lunch at a table by himself because no one would sit next to him. Jesse prayed over his lunch and asked God to help Grandpa eat. When the end-of-lunch bell rang, Jesse hurried back to class. After school he headed home to help Grandpa.

Today two boys followed him. Jesse looked back, wishing they would go away.

"Hey, Jesse, is this where you live?" questioned one. Jesse said, "Yes."

"Who's that?" said the other boy, pointing to the man on the front porch.

Jesse's grandfather suddenly spoke. "Just an old railroad man."

All three boys looked at him in surprise.

"When I was Jesse's age, I loved the trains. I would go to the train yard and watch the men change the cars from one train to another and hook and unhook the cars. When I was older," the old man added, "I became a switchman on the Burlington Western. Now being a switchman back then was a job for the biggest, strongest men—real muscle work. We had to go out and reset the tracks so that trains wouldn't collide."

The boys stared at the blind man with the shaking hands. "Back in the old days before automated switches and computerized everything, men had to do back-breaking work," the man went on.

"In some places the same track was used for trains both a-comin' and a-goin', so we had some side trackers at important stations. We would switch a train to a small piece of track that was only the length of the train, and that train would wait there while the train going the other way passed. That stopped train was doing important work even when it wasn't going anywhere. It's kind of like my grandson Jesse: he doesn't go all the places you boys can go because he's busy taking care of me."

"It's okay, Grandpa," Jesse interrupted.

"Hey Jesse," said the first boy, "you come home every day after school?"

Jesse nodded.

"Well," said the boy, "maybe we could come hear more stories sometime, OK?"

"I don't see why not," Grandpa said, smiling.

❦

Why did the other boys tease Jesse? *(because Jesse did not go places or do things like they did)*

How does Jesse serve his grandfather? *(Jesse makes sure Grandpa gets the food he needs and reads what Grandpa likes to hear.)*

What job did Grandpa have years ago? *(He was a switchman for the railroad.)*

 Why did Grandpa Riley tell the boys his story? *(He wanted the boys to see that what Jesse was doing was important.)*

When Grandpa said he was seeing better every day, what was he seeing? *(Guide the students to understand that Grandpa saw that Jesse was not doing things that he might like to be doing because he was loyal.)*

What gift did Grandpa give Jesse? *(Grandpa helped Jesse make friends.)*

If we learn more about people, what we give can be multiplied, just as Hannah's gift gave a good leader to the people of Israel. What can you give to people? *(We can give our friendship, caring, and encouragement to others. When we get to know people, we can learn what they need and how we can help them. Remind the students to use their time and talents from the Lord to serve others.)*

Memory Verse—Galatians 6:10
Practice the memory verse.

💡 **Christians are able to give because God gave to them first. How can Christians give to others what God has given them?** *(Christians can think about what others need and put those needs ahead of their own wants; Christians can tell them about God's love.)*

▶ Going Beyond

Reinforcement

Keep a journal. Tell your students to write the names of their family members on a sheet of paper. Instruct them to write beside each name what they plan to do for, give to, or help each family member with.

Enrichment

Materials

- Construction paper
- Magazine pictures

Make cards for retirement-home residents. Instruct the students to create friendship cards for the residents of a local nursing home. Remind them to think of what the residents might like to receive. Guide the students as they write encouraging messages: *The Lord Is with You, Happy Is the Day with God, Given with Care, Jesus Loves You,* or *Have a Happy Day.* The students may deliver the cards to the nursing home or retirement center as a field trip activity. (Refer to the field trip idea in the Unit 3d Enrichment on page 100.)

Walk in a Spirit of Humility
Unit 3d

PREVIEW

Doctrines
- God makes the believer holy in heart and in behavior (Hebrews 13:21). [Lesson 45]
- God is unchanging (immutable) (Malachi 3:6). [Lesson 46]
- God is faithful (1 Corinthians 1:9). [Lesson 46]

Skills and Applications
- Learn 1 John 1:7
- Read a timeline
- Recall facts and details
- Sequence the last seven books of the Bible (1 Peter–Revelation)
- Understand that God works in the lives of Christians
- Realize that God knows best
- Realize that God can solve attitude problems
- Understand that Christians should always walk in God's light
- Apply Bible knowledge to everyday life

LESSON 45 God Speaks to Samuel

Material
- TimeLine and picture: Samuel
- Hymn: "Be Thou Exalted"
- Unit 3 Bookmark for each student
- Highlighter for each student (optional)
- A copy of page A80 ("Walk Like Samuel") for each student (optional)

♫ Hymn: "Be Thou Exalted"

Sing the hymn (Worktext pages 214–15). Remind the students that how Christians act determines whether or not others see God in them. They can either be good examples of how God is working in their lives or poor examples of what it means to be saved.

Introducing the Bible Account

Review Hannah's gift. Discuss the following questions.

What did Hannah pray for, and what promise did she make to the Lord in return? (*Hannah asked for a boy, and she promised to give Samuel to the Lord.*)

What does the name *Samuel* mean? (*"asked of God"*)

Bible Account

Read 1 Samuel 2–3 or use the following retelling of the passage. Listening question: **Why did God choose Samuel as a prophet?** (*He was willing to listen and to obey God.*)

God Speaks to Samuel

Samuel served in the tabernacle under the guidance of Eli. Hannah made a coat and brought it to Samuel each year. Eli thanked the Lord and praised Him for Hannah's gift to the Lord. Eli said that the Lord would give her more children because she had faithfully kept her promise. Hannah had three more sons and two daughters.

Samuel grew and served the Lord with Eli, but Eli was very unhappy because his own sons were not faithfully serving the

Lord. When a person brought a sacrifice to Eli's sons, Hophni and Phinehas demanded the best portions before it was sacrificed. If the person refused and asked for the sacrifice to be made according to God's law, the priests would take the meat anyway and deprive the person of his proper sacrifice. Eli was very angry and said to them, "Why do you do such things? The people tell me about all the evil you do. It's not a good report that I hear. You cause the Lord's people to sin." Eli's sons wouldn't listen to their father. But Samuel listened and grew in favor both with the Lord and with men.

Then a prophet came and told Eli what God planned to do to Eli's wicked family. He said the Lord had promised not to allow Eli and his sons to be priests anymore, and that there would not be any old men in the family. The Lord also said that Eli would see a time when the enemies of Israel would be in God's place and take all the wealth that the Lord would give to Israel. It would be a sign to Eli that both of his sons would die on that same day.

Now the Lord didn't speak directly to people very often in those days. But one night while Eli and Samuel slept, Samuel was awakened by Someone calling his name. Samuel ran to Eli and asked him what he needed. Eli told Samuel to go back to bed; he had not called him. A second time Samuel woke up when he heard Someone call his name. Samuel went to help Eli, but Eli told him to go back to bed. Eli hadn't called Samuel. A third time Samuel heard his name and went to Eli. This time Eli told Samuel, "Go and lie down. If He calls you again, you should say, 'Speak, Lord. I'm Your servant, and I'm ready to listen.'" So the boy went back and lay down.

Once again, he heard a voice calling, "Samuel, Samuel." But this time, he answered just as Eli had told him to. The Lord told Samuel that He would do something that would make everyone in Israel listen and that He would do to Eli's family what the man of God had said. Samuel lay awake until morning, but he was afraid to tell Eli about the message from the Lord.

Soon Eli called Samuel and told Samuel to tell him everything that the Lord had said. Eli said if Samuel didn't tell him, God would punish Samuel. Samuel told Eli every word, and Eli said, "It is the Lord: let Him do what seems good to Him."

As Samuel grew up, the Lord was with him. Samuel would hear many other messages from God, and every prophecy he gave to the people came true. That's how everybody in Israel knew that Samuel was really God's prophet.

❧

Why did God tell Eli that his sons would die and his family could no longer be the high priests of Israel? (Eli's sons had been rebellious and sinful.)

How was Samuel different from Eli's sons? (Samuel served faithfully and did not cause the people to sin.)

💡 **How did God show that He was not pleased with Eli but pleased with Samuel?** (God spoke to Samuel.)

How did the Israelites know that God had chosen Samuel to be His prophet? (When Samuel gave a prophecy, everything happened just as the Lord said it would.)

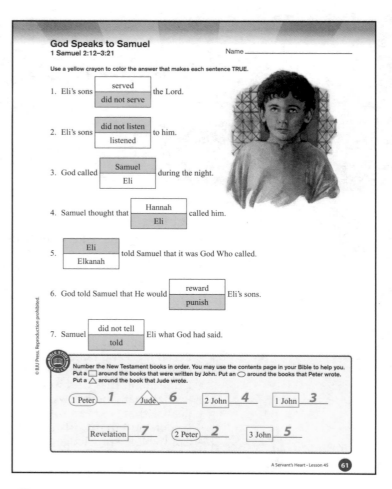

⏱ Timeline

Add Samuel to the TimeLine. Place the picture of Samuel on the TimeLine (1100–1015 BC), counting the centuries between the time of Moses and Samuel. *(four centuries)* Guide the students as they glue the picture of Samuel (from the Student Materials section of the ToolKit CD) onto their TimeLines.

✏ Worktext page 61

Recall facts and details. Read the directions at the top of the page. Model the reading of the sentence with each choice *before* instructing the students to color the correct answer with a yellow crayon or highlighter. Direct the students to complete the sentences independently.

📖 Bible Study Skills

Sequencing the last books of the Bible. Direct the students' attention to the bottom of Worktext page 61. Instruct them to sequence these seven books by numbering them in order (1–7). If necessary, students may use the contents page in their Bibles. Read each instruction, pausing as the students complete that operation.

❤ Memory Verse—1 John 1:7

Principle: Christians have fellowship and forgiveness when they live God's way (in a spirit of humility). Tell the students to find the verse in their Bibles and to read silently as you read it aloud.

What makes light good? *(Answers will vary. Elicit that light gives guidance in the dark; without it plants would die, and then we wouldn't have food.)*

God tells us light is good and that He is light. God says that Christians have fellowship with one another when they walk in His way in a spirit of humility (not proud or boastful in their own ways). Christians have fellowship with God when they come to Him in humility and confess sin. Direct the students to highlight the verse (optional) and mark its location in their Bibles with the Unit 3 Bookmark.

Practice the verse.

 What does "walk in the light" mean? *(It means knowing what God says and obeying Him.)*

 Since God does not speak aloud to Christians today as He did to Samuel, how can they know God's directions? *(They can read their Bibles daily and follow what they learn from God's Word.)*

 How does a Christian become clean after he sins? *(The blood of Christ cleanses us from all sin.)*

Art Connection (optional)

Illustrate the Bible account. Read the directions for page A80 ("Walk Like Samuel"). Instruct the students to work on their pictures and complete the sentence on the page. After the drawings are complete, direct the students to place them on the Unit 3 bulletin board.

LESSON 46 Samuel Speaks to the People

Materials
- Chart 10, "God is King"
- Hymn: "Be Thou Exalted"
- Two flashlights: one small and one large
- A poster or a sheet of art paper with the memory verse written on it

♫ Hymn: "Be Thou Exalted"

Sing the hymn (Worktext pages 214–15). Play the recording and sing the hymn together. Since all the verses have been taught, you may want to practice for the optional Enrichment Activity in Unit 3d (field trip).

Background Information

Anointer of Kings—*When the Israelites asked for a king to lead their army, it was because they wanted to be like the nations around them. They thought that if they had a king, he could deliver them from their enemies. They were forgetting that the invasions they kept experiencing were the result of their own sin. God, Who is perfectly capable of defeating any enemy, wanted His people to change their sinful ways. The people didn't want to deal with their sin, so they rejected God as their King. They ignored the fact that the Lord's kingship cannot be set aside easily. The Lord gave Samuel permission to anoint a man named Saul as their king. Samuel walked humbly before the Lord and did as the Lord commanded him. He privately anointed Saul as the king of*

Samuel called all the people to Mizpeh (Mizpah). Mizpeh means *watch-tower.* It was a regular stop on Samuel's circuit as judge (1 Samuel 10:17).

Samuel promised to continue praying for Israel.

Samuel spoke of the history of the Israelites.

Samuel Speaks to the People
1 Samuel 12

It was the time of wheat harvest when thunder and lightning were as rare as snow in summer but a big storm came.

He told of the many victories God had given them.

Saul was not difficult to point out. He was head and shoulders taller than anyone else (1 Samuel 9:2).

© BJU Press. Reproduction prohibited.

62 A Servant's Heart • Lesson 46

Israel. Then when the people chose a king by lottery, the Lord gave the lot to Saul.

Saul did not become king immediately. The people of Jabesh Gilead were threatened by Nahash the Ammonite, and Saul gathered an army and led Israel to victory. This showed Israel how to serve both the Lord and a human king. By the Lord's leading, Samuel was able to bring Israel together to establish Saul's kingship and renew God's covenant. King Saul would be accountable to God. The king of Israel was not to be like the kings of other countries who did as they pleased. Israel's king was to be a servant of God and His laws, a channel through whom God would rule His people.

Introducing the Bible Account

Share the background information. Explain Israel's rejection of God and how Samuel was used to keep the human king under the authority of God's law and the word of the prophet.

Bible Account

Read 1 Samuel 12 or use the following retelling of the passage. Listening question: **What words of advice did Samuel give to the people of Israel?** *(Fear God, serve Him, and remember what great things He has done.)* Direct attention to the illustration on Worktext page 62.

Samuel Speaks to the People

After Samuel had been judge over Israel many years, the Israelites wanted a king to rule over them just as all the other nations had. Samuel told the Israelites that their king would take their money in taxes and take their sons, husbands, and fathers for an army. But they still called for a king, and the Lord told Samuel to anoint Saul. After Saul had led the Israelites against the Ammonites, Samuel called all of the people to Gilgal to renew the kingdom under King Saul.

On that day Samuel told the people that he had listened to them and had given them what they wanted. Then he called them to witness against him before the Lord and before their new king. Samuel asked them whose ox or donkey he had taken or whom he had cheated or misused. He promised to make any wrong things right.

The people answered that Samuel had not cheated or misused or stolen from anyone. They didn't have any reason to hold anything against Samuel.

After Samuel had established his worthiness, he rebuked the people for their sins. He reminded them that the Lord had been righteous with all the ancestors of Israel. The Lord had used Moses and Aaron to lead the people out of Egypt and had given them the land they now lived in, but the people forgot to serve God. Then God punished them until the people cried out for the Lord and promised to serve the Lord. So God gave them Gideon and others, including Samuel. However, each time God delivered the Israelites, they turn away from Him, and then when trouble came, they called on Him again. And again God would deliver them from the enemies and give them safety.

Now they had forgotten again that God was their King. They asked for an earthly king to rule over them even though they already had the King of Kings as their ruler. Samuel said, "Here's the king you've chosen, the king you wanted! He's the one the Lord has put over you."

Samuel reminded them that if they would fear the Lord, serve Him, obey His voice, and not rebel against His commandments, then the people and the king would continue in God's favor. However, if they didn't fear, serve, and obey, but instead rebelled, the Lord would be against them as He was when He punished their forefathers.

As a final reminder, Samuel said that he would call on God to make it rain and thunder that day in the dry season so that the people would understand the great wickedness that they had done against God in asking for a king. Samuel prayed, and the Lord sent thunder and rain that day, and all the people greatly feared the Lord and Samuel. Then the people asked Samuel to pray for them because they understood that they had added to their sins by asking for a king other than the Lord.

But Samuel told them not to fear, that even though they had done this, the Lord would keep His promises to them if they would serve the Lord with all their hearts.

Samuel said, "Fear the Lord and serve Him with all your heart. Don't forget what great things He's done for you. But if you continue to sin, God will wipe out both you and your king."

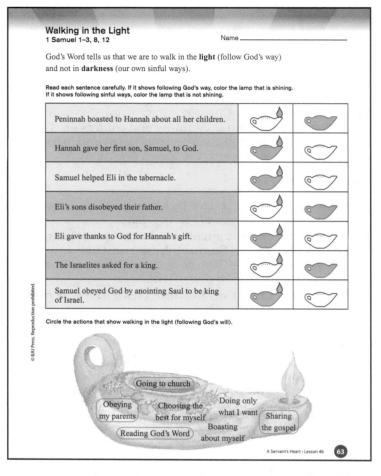

Why did Samuel anoint Saul the king of Israel? *(The people asked for an earthly king; God told Samuel to anoint Saul.)*

Why was it a sin for Israel to ask for a king? *(Israel's desire to be like the other nations rather than depending on the Lord was a rejection of God.)*

Why were the Israelites to really serve God with all their hearts? *(because of the great things God had done for them)*

How are Christians supposed to be like Israel? *(Christians should live according to God's Word.)*

What warning did Samuel give the people? *(God will punish sin.)*

InfoScene: "God Is King"
Display Chart 10 from the Visual Packet for the students to refer to throughout this unit.

Writing Connection (optional)
Write the story. Write the following word bank for display: *thunder, lightning, Israelites, Samuel, Saul, Moses, Aaron,* and *enemies*. Direct the students' attention to the pictures on Worktext page 62. Instruct them to write the account in their own words.

Memory Verse—1 John 1:7
Practice the memory verse.

Picture the Point

Demonstrate walking in God's light. Display the poster on which the memory verse is written. Darken the classroom. Instruct the class to read the verse from the poster. Discuss the difficulty they have in reading the verse without much light. Shine the light of the small flashlight onto the memory verse. Tell the students to read the verse again. Point out that they can see it a little better this time. Shine the large flashlight on the verse and read it. Finally, turn the classroom lights on to read the verse again.

Explain that the different amounts of light and what they were able to see is like the understanding that the Lord gives us. Before salvation a person cannot understand God's Word: it is as if he is in a darkened room. After a person is saved, he begins to understand God's Word a little at a time like a little light on the words. Just as more light makes the words clearer, so God gives a Christian more and more light of understanding as he reads God's Word and learns to obey Him.

✏ Worktext page 63

Recall facts and details. Read the directions aloud. Call on a volunteer to read each of the sentences in the first part. Guide the students in deciding whether it represents walking in light *(lamp is lit)* or darkness *(lamp is not lit)* and instruct them to color accordingly.

Apply Bible knowledge to everyday life. Read the directions for the bottom of the page. Instruct the students to circle the actions Christians can do to walk in the light.

LESSON 47 · God Can Change Sinful Attitudes

Materials
- Hymn: "Be Thou Exalted"
- Memory verse poster from the previous lesson

🎵 Hymn: "Be Thou Exalted"
Sing the hymn (Worktext pages 214–15).

♥ Memory Verse—1 John 1:7
Practice the memory verse.

What does it mean to "walk in the light"? *(to obey and serve God)*

💡 **How can a Christian walk in the light?** *(Read God's Word and obey it. Walk humbly before the Lord and not in a proud way.)*

Elicit from the students that they need to hide God's Word in their hearts *(memorize it)* so that they will always have it with them even when they do not have their Bibles. Display the memory verse poster. Direct the students to read each line. Then take the poster away and recite the verse.

Introducing the Application Story
Guide a discussion about anger. Tell the students that everything a Christian says and does is a reflection of his walk with Jesus. Other people notice how we act and talk.

💡 **Have you ever become angry and lost your temper?** *(Answers will vary.)*

Did this show that you were letting God take care of the situation? *(no)*

Application Story

Read or tell the following story. Listening question: **What happened when Hal did not control his temper?** *(He could not be on the baseball team.)*

Hotheaded Hal

Hal felt the blood rush to his face. "What a stupid, wild pitch!" he exploded.

Jeff glared at him. "Hey! Nobody asked you for your opinion." Hal moved toward the pitcher.

The coach stepped over to them, "Relax, guys. Tempers ruin sportsmanship. Behave yourselves and get back in the game. Hal, I've warned you before."

"Sorry, coach," Jeff said as he picked up his glove. But Hal stomped away from the pitcher's mound without a word.

After practice, Hal walked off the field. Jeff ran up beside Hal. "Seems like you Christians have worse tempers than we sinners."

Hal said quickly, "Oh, in our family we get angry fast and get over it just as fast. And you know me, I was angry at you earlier, but I'm not angry now."

Jeff said slowly, "I call that a funny way to be a Christian."

"Hey, my temper's really no big deal. So did you ask—are you coming to church with me on the bus Sunday?"

Jeff turned away, shrugging his shoulders. "I really can't. I've gotta go. See ya."

The next night at practice Hal hit a homer in the first inning. The coach said, "Nice work, Hal." But the last inning wasn't good. The coach called his players in for review. "Hal, wild throws to home will cost us a game if you play that way again." Hal swallowed, clenching his fists. "Don't let your temper get the best of your throwing arm, okay?"

"I didn't do anything wrong. It wasn't my fault Brian couldn't catch it. I threw it fine."

The coach said, "Sit on the bench, Hal. You need to pay attention to rules next time, and do it right." Hal marched off and plopped down on the bench.

At the showers, Hal overheard Jeff say, "I'm surprised the coach didn't kick him off the team."

"I wonder how long the coach will put up with it," said Brian. "Hal should've been kicked off a long time ago, but he's a good player."

Hal thought to himself, "I won't be kicked off. I've batted in more runs for the team than anyone else this season."

Hal waited for Brian outside. "So you think I should be kicked off the team, do you?"

Brian looked at him a minute and then said, "I just think you have a bad temper."

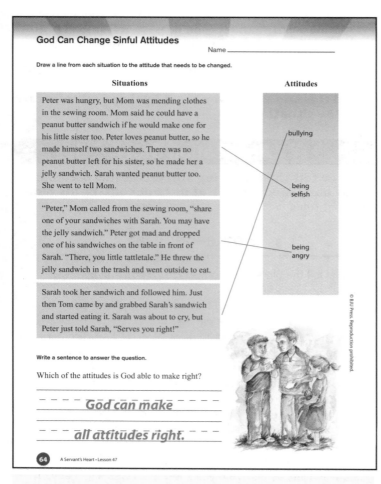

God Can Change Sinful Attitudes

Name_____

Draw a line from each situation to the attitude that needs to be changed.

Situations	Attitudes

Peter was hungry, but Mom was mending clothes in the sewing room. Mom said he could have a peanut butter sandwich if he would make one for his little sister too. Peter loves peanut butter, so he made himself two sandwiches. There was no peanut butter left for his sister, so he made her a jelly sandwich. Sarah wanted peanut butter too. She went to tell Mom.

bullying

"Peter," Mom called from the sewing room, "share one of your sandwiches with Sarah. You may have the jelly sandwich." Peter got mad and dropped one of his sandwiches on the table in front of Sarah. "There, you little tattletale." He threw the jelly sandwich in the trash and went outside to eat.

being selfish

Sarah took her sandwich and followed him. Just then Tom came by and grabbed Sarah's sandwich and started eating it. Sarah was about to cry, but Peter just told Sarah, "Serves you right!"

being angry

Write a sentence to answer the question.

Which of the attitudes is God able to make right?

God can make

all attitudes right.

64   A Servant's Heart • Lesson 47

Hal shoved him. Brian tried to get by. Hal stepped in front of him and put his hand on Brian's chest. Brian swatted the hand off. Hal shoved Brian, harder this time. And suddenly the coach was there, pulling Hal away. Brian straightened his shirt.

The coach gave Hal a grim look. "Well, that does it! You might think your fireworks are impressive, but that is one display I can do without. You're off the team, Hal!"

Hal's anger drained away. "You're joking, Coach," he said hoarsely.

"No, I'm not, Hal. I've given you plenty of chances, and I can't give you any more."

Hal stared at the coach and then walked slowly off the field. They wouldn't win without him. They'd lose every game. Then Coach would be sorry.

He went to the game the next night. At the end of the ninth inning, the scoreboard showed a tie. Hal sat on the edge of the bench. Brian was pitching. "He'll save the game," Hal thought. With two outs and the bases loaded, Brian had to get this player out or they would lose. Brian raised his arm to throw the ball. The ball rose. The Lincoln player pulled back his bat. There was a crack of wood against the ball. It was a home run!

(Note: This story is continued in Lesson 48.)

(by Margaret N. Freeman, adapted from "Courage," copyright Regular Baptist Press, used by permission.)

Why was Jeff surprised that Hal's temper was so short? *(Jeff thought that Hal was a Christian because Hal was always inviting Jeff to church.)*

💡 **Should Christians be expected to have their tempers under control?** *(Yes. Christians have a loving God who will help them be like Jesus if they ask Him, so they do not have to be angry at others.)*

What does God tell Christians their attitude toward neighbors should be? *(They should love their neighbors as themselves.)*

Whom did Hal blame for his problem? *(He said his family was just like that, or he blamed the coach or the other boys or anyone else who did something Hal did not like.)*

✎ Worktext page 64

Apply knowledge to everyday life. Tell the students that each of the children in the situations on the page displays an ungodly attitude. Guide the students as they read each situation and then match the situation with the attitude that needs changing. Instruct them to answer the question at the bottom of the page. Discuss the following questions.

Why should Peter have made his sister a peanut butter sandwich? *(He should have obeyed his mother.)*

💡 **How could Peter handle the "bully" in the future?** *(Answers may vary.)*

Why was Sarah whining to her mother? *(She didn't get what she wanted. Remind the students that it is not necessary for us to get everything we want.)*

LESSON 48   # Walking in Humility

Materials
• Hymn: "Be Thou Exalted"

♫ Hymn: "Be Thou Exalted"

Sing the hymn (Worktext pages 214–15). Play the recording and sing the hymn. Sing the hymn several times to practice for the Enrichment activity in Going Beyond (optional).

♥ Memory Verse—1 John 1:7

Practice the memory verse.

Introducing the Application Story

Review the first part of the story. Remind the students that Hal learned how his temper affected his testimony.

Why was Hal kicked off the baseball team? *(He lost his temper, and he started a fight with his friend Brian.)*

Read or tell the following story. Listening question:
What did Hal do about the sin of losing his temper?
(He prayed and asked the Lord to help him control it.)

Hal Learns Humility

One night not long after the big game, there was a special youth meeting at church. Hal tried to get his unsaved parents to go, but they wouldn't and suggested he ask Jeff or Brian. "Maybe if you try, you can all be friends again," his dad said. But Hal couldn't bring himself to ask. He was sure they wouldn't go. Besides, they were probably practicing baseball somewhere.

Hal went alone and listened closely to the message. "If you have a problem," the preacher said, "turn it over to the Lord. Let Him handle it for you."

"Have I got a problem!" Hal thought.

"It's not too late," the preacher said. "The Lord is kind and willing to forgive. Like Paul, you can do all things through Christ Who will strengthen you."

"Could He?" Hal wondered. He realized now his temper *was* a problem. Could the Lord really help him overcome his terrible temper problem—this sin that caused him so much trouble and heartache? Hal decided to pray about it daily.

The next day Hal made himself watch the other guys practice. Every night that week Hal watched the boys play. He prayed that the coach wouldn't throw him out. At first the boys were so cool that Hal almost expected to see icicles forming on the walls. After that week, the coach took him aside. "Hal, why are you coming here every night? You're not part of the team anymore and can't be."

"Please, Coach, give me another chance," Hal begged.

The coach shook his head. "I really can't take you back, Hal."

"I've changed, Coach."

"I don't like to withhold giving you another chance if you've changed, but how do I know?"

"Coach, I'm a Christian. I've turned my temper problem over to the Lord."

The coach was unsure. "Well, I'll take you back on a trial basis only."

Hal grinned. He was thanking God for another chance. Sometimes the boys teased Hal, tempting him to lose his temper. But Hal prayed desperately and trusted God. The Lord always gave him strength and victory to do and say things without getting angry.

After a few weeks, the coach said with a friendly smile, "You *have* changed, Hal. You've become one of the most stable players on this team. I never thought you could do it."

"I couldn't do it alone," Hal said softly.

"Well," the coach said kindly, "I'm ready to believe that too. You were such a hothead, I don't think you could've changed that much by yourself."

One day Jeff and Brian surprised Hal by accepting his invitation to church. After that they kept on coming.

"What gives, Son?" Hal's dad asked one day. "Mother and I don't understand the change in you!"

Hal told them how he had turned his temper problem over to the Lord.

"You know," his dad said, "your mother and I need to know more about this God Who can make such a wonderful change in a person."

Hal was a radiant boy that Sunday morning as he walked into church beside his parents. He had a faith that worked. It would work for them too!

(by Margaret N. Freeman, adapted from "Courage," copyright Regular Baptist Press, used by permission.)

When the coach finally took Hal aside, what did Hal do? *(He humbled himself, told the coach he had changed, and asked for another chance.)*

 Did Hal ever lose his temper? *(Discuss that he probably did but not as much as he had before.)*

How did Hal's change help others? *(Hal's mom and dad wanted to find out more about the God Who could make those changes, and Hal's friends wanted to go to church with him too.)*

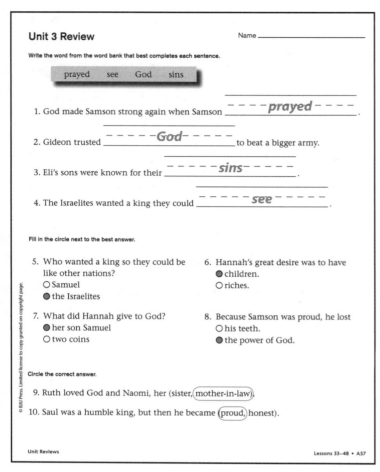

Unit 3 Review   Name _____

Write the word from the word bank that best completes each sentence.

| prayed | see | God | sins |

1. God made Samson strong again when Samson _____ _ _ _ _ _ _ _*prayed*_ _ _ _ _ .

2. Gideon trusted _ _ _ _ _ _ *God* _ _ _ _ _ _ to beat a bigger army.

3. Eli's sons were known for their _ _ _ _ _ _ _*sins*_ _ _ _ _ .

4. The Israelites wanted a king they could _ _ _ _ _ _ *see* _ _ _ _ _ .

Fill in the circle next to the best answer.

5. Who wanted a king so they could be like other nations?
   ○ Samuel
   ● the Israelites

6. Hannah's great desire was to have
   ● children.
   ○ riches.

7. What did Hannah give to God?
   ● her son Samuel
   ○ two coins

8. Because Samson was proud, he lost
   ○ his teeth.
   ● the power of God.

Circle the correct answer.

9. Ruth loved God and Naomi, her (sister, (mother-in-law)).

10. Saul was a humble king, but then he became ((proud,) honest).

Unit Reviews   Lessons 33–48 • A57

Unit Review

Materials
• Copy of page A57 ("Unit 3 Review") for each student

Guide a review of Lessons 33–48. Review the people and events in preparation for the Unit 3 test (optional).

Going Beyond

Reinforcement

Materials
• A toy/stuffed animal to be placed on students' desks

Guide an activity to recognize those students who listen and obey. Remind the students that Samuel was willing to listen and to obey God. Recognize those students who listen and obey by placing the stuffed animal on various desks throughout the day. You may also prepare a ribbon with a gold seal as the Best Listener Award to be worn by the student(s).

Enrichment

Take a field trip to a retirement center (or nursing home). Contact a nearby retirement center and ask permission to bring your class to sing a hymn and distribute friendship cards (made in the Unit 3c Going Beyond Enrichment activity.) If this is not possible, you may be able to mail the cards or take them yourself.

4

Christmas: Birth of the Savior

OVERVIEW

Preparing the Teacher

Read **John 1:1–18.** As you read these familiar verses, think about the areas of your life on which the light of Christ has shone. What is different about your thoughts, habits, relationships, and pursuits because He is your Savior? Are there other areas that need to be subjected to the light? Ask God to illuminate your life and the lives of your students, even if the revealing light shows the need for change.

Preparing the Materials

49—Unit 4 bookmark [E]; art paper [E]
50—Recording of Handel's *Messiah* [O]
50—Picture of an animal to be placed on a 3" × 5" card
51—Transparency of page A81 ("The Genealogy of Jesus, from Adam to Isaac"); recording of sounds [O]: running water, singing, animal noises, and children; verse visual: two paper circles with approximately a seven-inch diameter
Unit 4a Going Beyond—Book of *Aesop's Fables*
53—Recording of Handel's *Messiah* [O]
55—Paper crown made of yellow construction paper for the teacher
56—One 7" × 9" piece of construction paper [E]; copy of page A82 ("Good News") [E, O]; completed card from page A82 ("Good News") to show students; Christmas ornament wrapped in a gift box; copy of page A58 ("Unit 4 Review") [E]
Unit 4b Going Beyond—Items needed for a birthday party to celebrate Christ's birth [O]

Unit 4   Christmas: Birth of the Savior   Hymn: "Joy to the World"

Theme, Memory Verse, and Principle	Lesson Number	TE Page	Worktext Page(s)	Appendix Page(s)	Lesson Title	Scripture or Focus
Unit 4a Foretelling Christ's Birth Isaiah 9:6 *Christ's birth was foretold.*	**49**	106	65–66		We Need a Savior	Genesis 2:15–3:24
	50	108	67		Isaiah Prophesies About Chist	Isaiah 7:14–16
	51	109	68, 240	A81	Hero of the Faith: John Calvin	Biography
	52	112	69–70		Who Knew?	Application Story
Unit 4b Christ's Birth Luke 2:11 *God sent us a Savior.*	**53**	114	71–72		The Shepherds Seek Jesus	Luke 2:1–20
	54	116			The Gift	Application Story
	55	117	73–75		The Wise Men Seek Jesus	Matthew 2:1–13
	56	119	76	A82, A58	Giving Gifts	Picture the Point

Connections	Bible Doctrines	Skills/Applications
L50—TimeLine: Isaiah Music **L51**—TimeLine: John Calvin **L53**—TimeLine: Birth of Christ Music **L56**—Art	**The Doctrine of God** *Existence of God* God has shown Himself in the Bible (John 5:39). *Attributes of God* God is love (1 John 4:8). **The Doctrine of Man** *Redemption of Man* Man has hope (Phil. 3:20–21). **The Doctrine of Salvation** *Provision of God* Christ became man (incarnation) (John 1:14; Phil. 2:5–8). **The Doctrine of Angels and Satan** *Organization* Angels worship God (Rev. 5:11–12). *Satan* Satan is the Father of Lies (John 8:44).	**Foundational** • Realize that God is everlasting • Realize that man has been guilty of sin since Adam and Eve • Realize that the Lord is coming again **Practical** • Read a map • Read and complete a genealogy chart • Read a timeline • Locate information in the Bible • Identify characters and their words • Recall facts and details **Personal** • Realize that in Genesis 3 God promised His Son to us • Realize the need to receive the gift of God's Son • Understand and apply Bible knowledge to everyday life

Foretelling Christ's Birth
Unit 4a

PREVIEW

Doctrines

- Christ became human (Philippians 2:5–8). [Lesson 49]
- Man has hope (Philippians 3:20–21). [Lesson 49]
- Satan is the Father of Lies (John 8:44). [Lesson 49]
- God is love (1 John 4:8). [Lesson 50]

Skills and Applications

- Learn Isaiah 9:6
- Read a timeline
- Recall facts and details
- Locate information in the Bible
- Read and complete a genealogy chart
- Develop an understanding of foreknowledge
- Realize that people have been guilty of sin since Adam and Eve
- Realize that God is everlasting
- Realize that in Genesis 3 God promised His Son to us
- Apply Bible knowledge to everyday life

LESSON 49 We Need a Savior

Materials

- Chart 11, "We Need a Savior"
- Hymn: "Joy to the World"
- Unit 4 Bookmark for each student
- Art paper for each student
- Highlighter for each student (optional)

Background Information

Garden of Eden—*Refer to Lesson 2.*

Introducing the Bible Account

Guide a discussion about the Garden of Eden. Remind the students that the Garden of Eden, where Adam and Eve lived at first, was perfect. Call on volunteers to describe the Garden of Eden. *(Many answers are acceptable. Elicit that the garden had everything Adam and Eve needed. In the garden they were not sad, angry, or hurt. There was no death.)*

Bible Account

Read Genesis 2:15–3:24 or use the following retelling of the passage. Listening question: **What happened that changed Adam and Eve and their perfect home?** *(Adam and Eve chose to sin.)* Direct attention to Worktext page 65.

We Need a Savior

God made the earth, sky, water, animals, and plants all for man. Adam and Eve could have anything they wanted in the garden except for fruit from one special tree. God told Adam they were allowed to eat the fruit from every tree in the garden except the tree of the knowledge of good and evil. They weren't to eat from that tree or else they would die. Adam and Eve knew only good, and they had no need to know evil.

God gave them enjoyment, responsibilities, and work. Nothing bad or wrong ever happened to Adam and Eve until one sad day.

We Need a Savior

No one knows exactly where the Garden of Eden was.

No one knows exactly what kind of creature Satan used when he tempted Eve. Bible scholars and scientists who study snakes cannot determine the specific species of serpents or snakes mentioned in the Scriptures.

We know that God's promise of a Savior is true.

Jesus Christ paid for the sin of man when He died on the cross.

Jesus Christ triumphed over death when He rose from the dead.

© BJU Press. Reproduction prohibited.

A Servant's Heart • Lesson 49 65

S Is for Savior

Name _____

Read Isaiah 9:6 in your Bible. Use the words in the word bank to complete the sentences.

Word bank: us, Counselor, Peace, son, shoulder

1. God told Isaiah to say that a child would be born to _____ _____us_____ .

2. He said that a _____son_____ would be given to us.

3. The government would be on His _____shoulder_____ .

4. His name would be Wonderful and _____Counselor_____ .

5. He would also be named Mighty God, Everlasting Father, and Prince of _____Peace_____ .

Choose the correct ending for each sentence and color the star next to it.

1. God told Adam and Eve
☆ not to eat any fruit.
★ not to eat fruit from one tree.
☆ not to talk to the serpent.

2. The serpent told Eve that
★ she and Adam would not die.
☆ she and Adam would die.
☆ she and Adam would become foolish.

3. After Adam and Eve sinned, they were
★ ashamed.
☆ puzzled.
☆ hungry.

4. After Adam and Eve sinned, God
☆ never spoke to them again.
☆ said it did not matter.
★ still loved them.

5. God promised that
☆ they could come back to the garden.
★ He would provide a Savior for them.
☆ they would never have to work.

© BJU Press. Reproduction prohibited.

66 A Servant's Heart • Lesson 49

The serpent came to Eve and asked her if God had really said that they weren't allowed to eat from any tree in the garden.

Eve told the serpent that God had given them permission to eat from all the trees in the garden except the one in the middle of the garden. Eve then added that they couldn't even touch its fruit or they would die.

The serpent told Eve that God was wrong. "You won't die," he told her. Eve looked at the fruit on the tree and believed it would make her wise. She ate some and gave some to Adam. He ate it too.

Adam and Eve knew it was wrong to eat the fruit, and now they were ashamed of their sin. They were also afraid of God. This separation from God was part of the death that God said would happen to them if they ate from the tree.

Later they heard God coming and tried to hide among the trees. But God sees everything and knew right where they were.

"Have you eaten of the tree that I commanded you not to eat from?" asked God. Adam blamed Eve for giving him the fruit. When God asked Eve what she had done, she blamed it on the serpent (Satan).

God punished the serpent by cursing it to slither on its belly. God told Adam and Eve their punishment was pain and eventual death. They even had to leave the garden. But God promised them a Savior Who would conquer Satan and death.

💡 **What did Eve add to God's words?** *(She said that they would die if they even touched the forbidden fruit.)*

💡 **What happened that changed Adam and Eve and their perfect home?** *(Adam and Eve chose to sin.)*

▶ **What was Adam and Eve's punishment for eating the fruit that they were told not to eat?** *(They would die.)*

▶ **Why did Adam and Eve try to hide?** *(They knew they had done wrong.)*

▶ **Could Adam and Eve hide from God?** *(No. God sees everything.)*

▶ **What did God promise Adam and Eve so they could escape eternal death?** *(a Savior to die for them)*

💡 **How did God's Son come to earth?** *(as a baby)*

InfoScene: "We Need a Savior"
Display Chart 11 from the Visual Packet for the students to refer to throughout this unit.

💟 Memory Verse—Isaiah 9:6

Principle: Christ's birth was foretold. Direct the students to draw a picture on their art paper of someone or something they think is wonderful. Tell them to write down or explain why it is wonderful. Explain that all of the names given to Christ describe something about Him.

Explain the meaning of the verse. Read the verse to the class again and ask the following questions.

► **Who is this Child?** *(Jesus, God's Son)* Explain that God told Adam and Eve that He would send His Son, but now God describes His Son to us. Tell them that Christ is more wonderful than anyone or anything we can draw on paper or describe.

💡 **What makes Christ wonderful?** *(Many answers are acceptable, but emphasize the fact that He is God.)*

💡 **What is a counselor?** *(someone who gives help or advice)*

💡 **Have you ever needed help with something?** *(Accept any answer. Discuss how God can help with any need.)*

Practice the memory verse. Assist the students in highlighting the verse (optional) and marking the location in their Bibles with the Unit 4 Bookmark.

⊘ Worktext page 66

Locate information in the Bible. Direct the students to look up **Isaiah 9:6** in their Bibles and read the verse together. Instruct them to complete the missing word in each sentence using the words in the word bank.

Recall facts and details. Direct the students' attention to the bottom of the page. Read the first sentence with each of the choices. Call on a volunteer to read the sentence with the correct ending. You may need to draw a star for display and demonstrate how to fill it in. Instruct the students to complete the page. Provide help as needed.

🎵 Hymn: "Joy to the World"

Introduce the hymn. Isaac Watts was born in England in 1674 as the oldest of nine brothers and sisters. At thirteen years of age, he was learning his fifth language. Isaac Watts often used the book of Psalms as a basis for his hymns. "Joy to the World" was the result of his studying **Psalm 98:4–9**. The first verse of the hymn talks about the past coming of Christ to earth as a baby. The second verse talks about Jesus's future reign as King. The third verse focuses on the fact that there will be no sin or sadness in the future. The fourth verse tells of the future coming of Christ.

Sing the first verse (Worktext page 216). Utilize the recording as necessary throughout the unit.

► **Why should the world rejoice?** *(The Lord is come.)*

► **What does the hymn say the Lord has come as?** *(a King)*

💡 **How can we "prepare Him room"?** *(by repenting of our sins and asking Jesus to save us)*

LESSON 50 Isaiah Prophesies About Christ

Materials
• TimeLine and pictures: Isaiah and The Birth of Christ
• Recording of Handel's *Messiah* (optional)
• Animal card: Put the picture and name of one animal on a 3" × 5" card.

♥ Memory Verse—Isaiah 9:6

Play the recording of "For Unto Us a Child Is Born" from Handel's *Messiah* [Part I, Section 12] (optional). Tell the students that this is a way that we can sing our joy to God—putting His words to music. Practice the memory verse.

💡 **What does the word *mighty* mean?** *(powerful, strong)*

💡 **What are some things that God can do that humans cannot?** *(Answers will vary, but lead the students to see that God is all-powerful, everywhere, all-knowing, unchanging, perfect, and He alone can forgive sin.)*

Background Information

Isaiah—*Isaiah made his prophecy around 701 BC. Christ was born approximately seven hundred years after Isaiah's prophecy. Isaiah's prophecy revealed how God would save Israel. See also Lesson 124.*

Introducing the Bible Account

Discuss prophecy. Tell the students to pretend they are making plans for a picnic for a certain Saturday afternoon next spring. Discuss food, items, games, and other activities they would like to have at the picnic.

💡 **What would happen to our plans if it rained on the Saturday we had scheduled the picnic?** *(Plans would have to be changed.)*

💡 **Is there any way we could know right now what the weather will be like on a day next spring?** *(no)*

💡 **When God makes plans for the future, does anything ever happen to upset or change them?** *(no)*

Explain that when God promises to do something, it will always happen. He can promise something thousands of years ahead of time, and there is no doubt that He will do what He said He would do. He is almighty, and He knows everything about the past, present, and future. In the Old Testament, God would sometimes tell people what was going to happen in the future.

💡 **Why would God tell people the future?** *(Possible answers include that God wanted to show His power; He is the only true God; He wanted to warn His people so that they would turn from their evil ways and avoid being punished.)*

Bible Account

Read or tell the following Bible account, which is a retelling of prophecies from the book of Isaiah. Listening question: **What event did the prophet Isaiah prophesy before it happened?** *(the birth of Jesus Christ)*

Isaiah Prophesies About Christ

Isaiah was a prophet, a man to whom God told a little bit of the future. God gave Isaiah a message for people who lived in the land of Israel. God told them He would send a Child to save them.

How could a child save a whole nation? This was a special Child. He was God's Son. Isaiah told the people who lived in

Worksheet (Worktext page 67)

Isaiah Prophesies About Christ

Name _____

Because God told him what to say, Isaiah was able to tell many things about the Savior Who was to come. People in Isaiah's time did not have the New Testament. None of the things written in it had happened yet. Some believed the prophecies, and some did not. But Isaiah's words were true because they had come from God. In the New Testament, we can now read how these prophecies came true in the life of Jesus Christ.

Here are some of the things that God told Isaiah to say. He said many other things about Jesus. Read the New Testament verses that show that the prophecies came true and write the answers on the lines.

Isaiah said that a great light would shine in Galilee beyond the Jordan (Isaiah 9:1–2).	Where does **Mark 1:14** say Jesus was preaching the good news of the kingdom of God? __ __ __ __ __ __ __ **Galilee** .
Isaiah said that the blind, the deaf, the disabled, and the mute would be healed (Isaiah 35:5–6).	**Mark 7:32–35:** Jesus healed a man who could not __ __ **hear** __ or __ __ **speak** __ . **Mark 8:22–25:** Jesus healed a man who was __ __ __ __ **blind** __ __ . **Luke 6:6–10:** Jesus healed a man who had a withered __ __ __ **hand** __ .
Isaiah said that the Savior would suffer for our sins (Isaiah 53:5).	**John 19:1–3** and **17–18** tell of how Jesus was beaten, had a crown of thorns put on His head, and was finally **crucified (or killed)** .

© BJU Press. Reproduction prohibited.

A Servant's Heart • Lesson 50   **67**

Israel many things about this Child. Isaiah knew God's Son would come to take away the sins of the world. Isaiah knew these things because God told him.

Christ's birth was foretold by other prophets. Christ wasn't born until seven hundred years after Isaiah wrote down the words God had given him. Those who heard the prophecy didn't live long enough to see Christ come, but Isaiah and the other prophets believed what God had spoken.

⚜

► **Who were the first people God told about the birth of a Savior?** *(Adam and Eve)*

💡 **Why did God give His Son?** *(He loved us, and He wanted to provide a way of salvation.)*

► **Who told others that God would send His Son?** *(Isaiah and other prophets)*

► **How did Isaiah know?** *(God told him.)*

✎ Worktext page 67

Find verses to prove the fulfillment of prophecy. Read aloud the paragraph at the top of the page. Remind the students that the prophecy Isaiah gave was not fulfilled until centuries later, but Jesus *was* born as Isaiah had said. Assign each student a partner to work with. Direct one student in each pair to read the prophecy in the box on the left and then to find and read the Old Testament verses. Tell the other student in each pair to read the corresponding box on the right and then to find and read the New

Testament verses. Instruct the students to complete the page. Provide help as needed.

🕐 TimeLine

Add Isaiah to the TimeLine. Place the picture of Isaiah on the TimeLine (740–700 BC), explaining that he lived over seven hundred years before the birth of Jesus Christ. Guide the students as they glue their picture of Isaiah (from the Student Materials section of the ToolKit CD) onto their TimeLines.

Place the Birth of Christ card on the large TimeLine from the Visual Packet at the change from BC to AD, pointing out the span of time from Christ's birth until the Present Day (today's date). Write the present year, preceded by AD, for display. *(Note: Do not have students glue their picture of the Birth of Christ on their individual TimeLines at this time.)*

Explain the meaning of *BC* and *AD*. Call on a student to write today's date for display. Explain that we recognize the fact of Christ's birth each time we write the date. Discuss the following details.

For events that happened before Christ's birth, we use the abbreviation BC for *before Christ*.

We use the abbreviation AD (short for *anno Domini,* the Latin words for "in the year of the Lord") for the years after Christ's birth.

The abbreviation BC is written *after* the year, while AD is written *before* the year.

We usually do not use the abbreviation AD unless we think there may be some confusion.

🎵 Hymn: "Joy to the World"
Sing the first verse (Worktext page 216).

🔵 LESSON 51 John Calvin

Materials
- Hymn: "Joy to the World"
- TimeLine and picture: John Calvin
- A transparency of page A81 ("The Genealogy of Jesus, from Adam to Isaac")
- Recording of sounds: running water, singing, animal noises, and children (optional)
- Verse visual: Cut out two paper circles with approximately a seven-inch diameter. Divide both circles into six equal sections like pieces of a pie. Write each of the five names of Christ (in the order they appear in Isaiah 9:6) on a different section of one of the circles. In the sixth section write the verse reference. Cut out one section from the second circle for a window. Attach the second circle over the first circle with a brass fastener in the center.

♥ Memory Verse—Isaiah 9:6
Practice the memory verse. Explain the meaning of *everlasting*. Write the word for display, drawing a line to divide it into *ever* and *lasting*. Explain to the students that

even though Jesus had a birthday here on earth because He took on the form of a human, He lived before the days of Creation when there was nothing but God. Review day 1 on the TimeLine.

Illustrate that God is everlasting. Draw a circle for display.

💡 **Where is the beginning and the end of the circle?** (*Elicit that there is no beginning or end to the circle.*)

Explain that the circle can remind us of God because neither has a beginning or an end. Lead the class in saying the verse together using the verse visual. Point to the circle as a signal to say the verse throughout the day.

📖 Worktext page 68

Read a genealogy. Display the transparency of page A81 ("The Genealogy of Jesus, from Adam to Isaac.") Remind the students that a genealogy is a family record listing ancestors or relatives. Review the genealogy of Jesus from Adam to Isaac. (*Note:* This list uses the modern spellings of the names, e.g., *Kenan* instead of *Cainan.* Pronunciations are given in Lesson 12.) Point out that Jacob is Isaac's son. Explain that the genealogy on page 68 continues from Jacob to the birth of the Savior.

▶ **Who was the father of Enosh?** (*Seth*)

▶ **Who was the son of Enoch and the grandfather of Noah?** (*Methuselah*)

▶ **Who was the son of Terah and the father of Isaac?** (*Abraham*)

▶ **Who was Isaac's grandfather?** (*Terah*)

Direct the students' attention to Worktext page 68. Explain that the names listed represent some of Jesus's human ancestors. Point out that some of these men reigned as kings, but some did not. Direct the students to write in the names that have been left out, providing help if necessary. Use the following pronunciation guide as needed. (*Note:* The names on this page use modern spellings, which in some cases are different from those used in the KJV [e.g., *Nahshon* instead of *Naasson, Abijah* rather than *Abia, Hezekiah* rather than *Ezekias* and so on]. The only case where this involves a student answer is Josiah [vs. KJV Josias].)

Jacob (*jā′ kəb*)	**Ahaz** (*ā′ hăz*)
Judah (*joo′ dä*)	**Hezekiah** (*hĕz ə kī′ ä*)
Perez (*pĕ′ rez*)	**Manasseh** (*mən ăs′ ə*)
Hezron (*hĕz′ rŏn*)	**Amon** (*ā′ mŏn*)
Ram (*räm*)	**Josiah** (*jōs ī′ ə*)
Aminadab (*ə mĭn′ ə dăb*)	**Jeconiah** (*jĕ kō nī′ ə*)
Nahshon (*nä′ shon*)	**Shealtiel** (*shēl′ tī′ əl*)
Salmon (*săl′ mŏn*)	**Zerubbabel** (*zə rub′ ə bəl*)
Boaz (*bō′ ăz*)	**Abiud** (*ä bī′ ŭd*)
Obed (*ō′ bĕd*)	**Eliakim** (*ĕ lī′ ä kĭm*)
Jesse (*jĕs′ ē*)	**Azor** (*ā′ zŏr*)
David (*dā′ vĭd*)	**Zadok** (*zā′ dŏk*)
Solomon (*sŏl′ ə mŏn*)	**Achim** (*ā′ kĭm*)
Rehoboam (*rā hə bō′ ăm*)	**Eliud** (*ĕ lī′ ud*)
Abijah (*ä bī′ jə*)	**Eleazar** (*ĕl ē ā′ zär*)
Asa (*ā′ sə*)	**Matthan** (*măt′ thăn*)
Jehoshaphat (*jə hŏsh′ ə făt*)	**Jacob** (*jā′ kəb*)

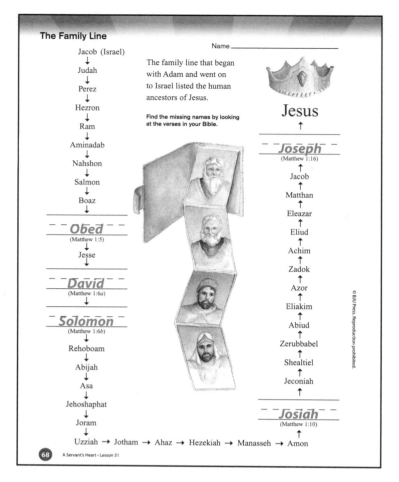

Joram (*jō′ răm*)
Uzziah (*yoo zī′ ə*)
Jotham (*jō′ thăm*)

Joseph (*jō′ sĕf*)
Jesus (*jē′ zŭs*)

🎵 Hymn: "Joy to the World"

Sing the second verse (Worktext page 216). Direct a guessing activity (optional). Play the recording you made of various sounds. Pause after each sound and call on students to guess what it is. Remind them that God made all things.

Hero of the Faith

Read or tell the following narrative based on the life of John Calvin. Listening question: **Why did John Calvin have to leave France?** (*He was disliked because of his beliefs.*)

John Calvin

Moonlight shone on the empty Paris street. At a second-story window, the dark form of a man appeared, holding a bundle. He looked up the street one way and down it the other. Then he tossed something out the window—something long and trailing, like a rope.

The rope was made of bed sheets tied together. The man, John Calvin, climbed onto the windowsill and pulled on the rope, testing it and making certain it would hold him. Then, quickly and silently, he slid down to the ground.

John Calvin was fleeing for his safety—not because he had stolen or murdered, but because of what he believed. He believed what the Bible said—that salvation is through faith in Jesus Christ alone and not through works. People who held this belief in the 1500s were called Protestants, and Protestants were not welcome in France.

John left Paris in disguise. He put on the clothes of a poor gardener (vinedresser) and carried a hoe over his shoulder. He sighed with relief as he left the city behind.

But once out of the city, he was a man on the run. He traveled from city to city and stayed with Protestant friends, preaching and writing. Everywhere he went, the authorities looked for him. He finally left France altogether and spent time in Germany and Switzerland, where Protestants were safe.

John traveled to Italy. During his stay there, he lived in a castle. His friend, Princess Renée, was married to the castle's owner, the duke of Italy. Although the duke was a Catholic, Princess Renée was a Protestant like John. She used her home as a shelter and hiding place for other Protestants. John was safe for a while. But when the duke began banishing Protestants from his court, John knew he had to flee again.

John Calvin became a pastor in Geneva, Switzerland. But now he faced a new problem. A group of people in Geneva believed they should be able to do as they pleased. They didn't like John's preaching. They did all they could to anger and frighten him. They named their dogs "Calvin." They fired guns outside the church during his meetings. One time a large mob surrounded him, threatening his life. "If you want blood," said John, pointing to his chest, "there are still a few drops here. Strike, then!" The shocked mob only stared at him. They left without harming him.

God protected John. And He gave him a wife, Idelette, whom John called "the excellent companion of my life." God used John to write an important book called *Institutes of the Christian Religion*, which is still read today. John also wrote many other books, commentaries, and sermons. He even helped publish one of the first hymnbooks. He also started the first organization for sending out Protestant missionaries.

▶ **Why did John Calvin have to escape from Paris at night?** (*The authorities were after him because he was a Protestant.*)

▶ **What did he believe that was different from the religious leaders of his day?** (*He believed that Christ is the only way of salvation; works cannot save anyone.*)

▶ **According to the Bible, how is a person saved?** (*by faith in Jesus Christ alone*) Read **Ephesians 2:8–9** and **Romans 6:23** to the students.

▶ **How did the enemies in Switzerland try to anger and frighten John Calvin?** (*They named their dogs "Calvin," fired guns outside the church during meetings, and threatened his life.*)

▶ **How did John Calvin serve the Lord?** (*Possible answers include that he wrote books, preached, started a Protestant missionary agency, and helped publish a hymnal.*)

John Calvin

John Calvin was born in 1509 in France. He believed and taught that salvation is through faith in Christ alone. People who believed as he did were called Protestants because they protested against the idea that salvation could be earned by doing good deeds. Protestants were in danger of being sent to prison or killed. John secretly left his home city of Paris, dressed as a gardener.

After traveling from city to city in France, John had to leave for a safer place. He spent some time in Germany and Italy. He then became a pastor in Switzerland.

Protestants were welcome there, but John ran into another problem. A group of people did not like his preaching. They did not want to be reminded that some of the things they did were wrong. They tried many ways to frighten him and make him angry, but he kept preaching.

God protected John Calvin and used him as a powerful witness to the truth. He helped publish one of the first hymn books. His books and sermons are still studied by some Christians today. He is remembered for his faith in Christ and his willingness to speak for God.

Name _____

Put an *X* beside TRUE or FALSE for each sentence.

1. John Calvin had to leave France because he stole money.
   ——— TRUE   _X_ FALSE

2. John Calvin taught that salvation is through Christ alone.
   _X_ TRUE   ——— FALSE

3. John Calvin became the pastor of a church in America.
   ——— TRUE   _X_ FALSE

4. John Calvin was too afraid to speak the truth.
   ——— TRUE   _X_ FALSE

5. John Calvin and others like him were called Protestants.
   _X_ TRUE   ——— FALSE

© BJU Press. Reproduction prohibited.

(240) A Servant's Heart · Lesson 51

TimeLine

Add John Calvin to the TimeLine. Place the picture of John Calvin on the TimeLine (AD 1509–1564), counting the span of years in centuries from then to today's date. Guide the students as they glue their picture of John Calvin (from the Student Materials section of the CD) onto their TimeLines. Tell the students that John Calvin also founded the first Protestant university in Europe, called the Geneva Academy. He continued ministering until his death at age fifty-five.

Worktext page 240 (optional)

Hero of the Faith: John Calvin. Review the events in John Calvin's life. Point out that John Calvin risked his life to express his beliefs as we do freely today. We should thank God that we can read our Bibles, listen to preaching, and attend church without danger. Direct the students to read each sentence and mark whether it is true or false.

Who Knew?

Materials
- Hymn: "Joy to the World"

✍ Worktext page 69

Recall facts and details. Read the directions for the top of the page. Instruct the students to read each sentence and decide whether it is true (circle *yes*) or not true (circle *no*).

Find information in the Bible. Direct the students to locate each verse at the bottom of the page and to match the first part to the second part of the names for Jesus Christ our Savior.

♥ Memory Verse—Isaiah 9:6

Practice the memory verse. Explain *Prince of Peace*.

▶ **What is a king?** *(a ruler)*

The word *prince* here has the idea of a captain, chief, or leader who rules over a land or a people. Remind students that Christ is all-knowing and all-powerful. He is peaceful Himself and will therefore reign in peace when He rules over the whole world. He is the Prince of Peace because He will stop all evil and make everything on earth right. Remind the students that all these things about Christ were said of Him before He was born. Direct small groups to stand and say the verse from memory.

🎵 Hymn: "Joy to the World"

Sing the first two verses (Worktext page 216).

Introducing the Application Story

Guide a discussion about barns. Call on students to tell who lives in a barn, who takes care of a barn, whether they have ever been in a barn, and so on. Let students who have been in a barn tell what it was like.

Application Story

Read or tell the following story. Listening question:
What happens to Mark? *(He falls.)*

"Don't Go Up There"

Mark followed his dad through the barn door.

Dad said, "This is where I grew up, you know—me and good ol' Ginger." Dad walked over to a brown cow and rubbed her head.

"And all her friends," said Mark. Grandpa's farm was different from what he had imagined. "This place is huge," he said.

"Animals need a lot of room," said Dad. "Even cats."

"Oh, who needs cats, anyway?" said Mark. He looked over at an orange cat curled up in a ball on the windowsill. "They don't do *any*thing."

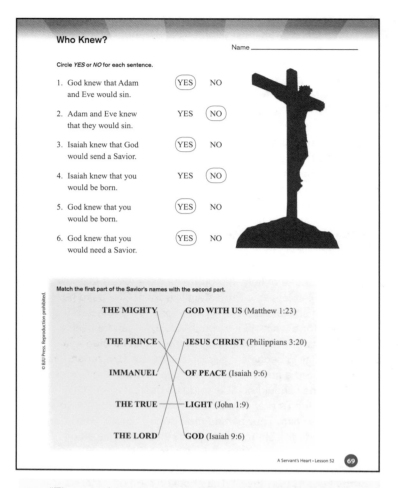

Who Knew? Name _____

Circle *YES* or *NO* for each sentence.

1. God knew that Adam and Eve would sin. (YES) NO
2. Adam and Eve knew that they would sin. YES (NO)
3. Isaiah knew that God would send a Savior. (YES) NO
4. Isaiah knew that you would be born. YES (NO)
5. God knew that you would be born. (YES) NO
6. God knew that you would need a Savior. (YES) NO

Match the first part of the Savior's names with the second part.

THE MIGHTY — GOD WITH US (Matthew 1:23)
THE PRINCE — JESUS CHRIST (Philippians 3:20)
IMMANUEL — OF PEACE (Isaiah 9:6)
THE TRUE — LIGHT (John 1:9)
THE LORD — GOD (Isaiah 9:6)

A Servant's Heart • Lesson 52 **69**

"They get rid of pests," said his dad. "Say, look at the swallows. Those birds build their nests on the beams and rafters." He pointed up to the high timbers that held up the roof.

"Neat," said Mark. "How do you get up there?"

"*You* don't." said Dad. "It's too high and too dangerous. Don't go up there." Mark nodded.

After they had looked around in the calf pens, the loft, and the milkhouse, Dad said, "I think I'll see whether Grandma has that pie ready."

Mark said, "I'll be along. I just want to look around some more."

Dad said, "Okay. You'll be all right out here?"

"Dad, I'm seven." Dad kept looking at Mark. "Yes, I'll behave."

Dad left the barn, and Mark looked at the cat on the windowsill. "How do you get up there?" he thought. He spotted hay bales stacked to the ceiling. "I just want to see if they lead to the rafters," he thought.

He climbed the hay. Although it wasn't hard to climb, it was prickly and itchy. Mark was a good climber and reached the top in no time.

Once there, he saw how close the beams were. He stepped out onto the beam and stood up straight. "Plenty of room," he thought. "Just the right size for me." The rafters had looked a lot wider from the ground.

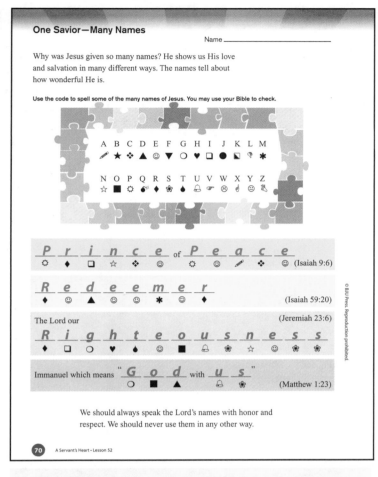

One Savior—Many Names

Name _____

Why was Jesus given so many names? He shows us His love and salvation in many different ways. The names tell about how wonderful He is.

Use the code to spell some of the many names of Jesus. You may use your Bible to check.

A B C D E F G H I J K L M

N O P Q R S T U V W X Y Z

P r i n c e of P e a c e
(Isaiah 9:6)

R e d e e m e r
(Isaiah 59:20)

The Lord our (Jeremiah 23:6)
R i g h t e o u s n e s s

Immanuel which means " G o d with u s "
(Matthew 1:23)

We should always speak the Lord's names with honor and respect. We should never use them in any other way.

70 A Servant's Heart • Lesson 52

Mark was halfway across the rafter when he saw that there was nothing on the other side to climb down. He would have to turn around. He twisted his back foot around to face the other way and then followed with his other foot. "Piece of cake," he thought. A barn swallow swooped right past his head. Mark tottered on the beam.

He couldn't think fast enough. He felt himself falling as if in slow motion. "Grab the beam," he thought. But it was too late.

Mark hit something hard, but he could hear his dad's voice. He opened his eyes. "I'm not dead?" he thought. He had landed in a net made of rope that hung under the rafters. He hadn't noticed the net before. He was saved! And in big trouble.

Dad told Mark not to move. He brought a ladder and helped Mark get out. Dad waited until they were safely on the ground before scolding him.

"How did the net get there?" asked Mark.

"Grandpa put that net up a long time ago when I was little because he was concerned that someone might climb up there and fall. In this case, that net probably saved your life. But we need to have a little talk about your disobedience." Mark looked up at the net and breathed a big sigh of relief. He was just glad to still be alive.

▶ **Why did Mark climb the hay bales?** *(He wanted to see where they led.)*

▶ **Why did Grandpa hang up the net?** *(in case someone fell)*

💡 **What did Adam and Eve do that they were told not to do?** *(They ate the forbidden fruit.)*

💡 **Who saved Adam and Eve from spending eternity apart from God (spiritual death)?** *(God)*

💡 **What did God do to save them from death?** *(He sent the Savior, His Son.)*

Worktext page 70

Locate verses in the Bible. Explain to the students that they will use the code to find each letter for four names of Jesus. Direct attention to the first symbol in the first name. Demonstrate how to find the symbol and the corresponding letter in the box above. Complete the first name together. Instruct the students to locate the verse in their Bibles and check the answer. Direct them to complete the page independently.

▶ Going Beyond

Materials

• *Aesop's Fables*

Reinforcement

Read a few stories from *Aesop's Fables*. Stop before the end of each story and let the students predict what will happen. Explain to the students that only the author of the story knows what will happen because he is in control. Point out that the Lord is the Author and Controller of our lives in a similar way.

Enrichment

Role-play the account of Adam and Eve. Choose two students to act out the account of Adam and Eve. Switch characters between "scenes" of the play. Explain to the students that because Adam and Eve sinned, all of us were born sinners and need to be saved.

Christ's Birth
Unit 4b

PREVIEW

Doctrines
- Christ became a man (John 1:14). [Lesson 53]
- Angels worship God (Revelation 5:11–12). [Lesson 53]
- God has shown Himself in the Bible (John 5:39). [Lesson 55]

Skills and Applications
- Learn Luke 2:11
- Identify characters and their words
- Read a map
- Read a timeline
- Realize the need to receive the gift of God's Son
- Realize the significance of the shepherds and wise men
- Realize the Lord is coming again
- Apply Bible knowledge to everyday life

LESSON 53 The Shepherds Seek Jesus

Materials
- Chart 12, "The Shepherds Seek Jesus"
- Chart 35, "Christ's Birth"
- Hymn: "Joy to the World"
- TimeLine and picture: Birth of Christ
- Unit 4 Bookmark for each student
- Highlighter for each student (optional)
- Recording of Handel's *Messiah* (optional)

Background Information

Shepherds—*Sheep were used for food (milk, cheese, and meat), clothing, and sacrifices. Therefore, shepherds had an important job. Shepherds were responsible for the welfare of their sheep. This included leading them (because sheep only follow) to water for drink, to shelter for protection, and to pasture for food. A shepherd carried a staff and a sling to protect his fold from wild animals. Since he spent so much time with the sheep, a shepherd would become as attached to the sheep as they were to him. This attachment would motivate a shepherd to even risk his life for one of his sheep. The shepherd's job was not one that many people wanted since the men had to stay outside with the sheep for weeks at a time. Shepherds were neither rich nor powerful, but God chose these men to be the first Israelites after Mary and Joseph to see His own Son.*

Swaddling Clothes—*Newborns were wrapped in a square piece of cloth with the corners tucked under the head and feet and over the midsection. Then the baby was wrapped tightly in long strips of cloth. This covering kept the child warm and protected.*

Manger—*Mangers were boxes (often made out of stone) used for feeding cattle.*

Introducing the Bible Account

Discuss the meaning of Christmas. Write the word *Christmas* for display. Call on students to tell a word or phrase that comes to their minds. Underline *Christ* within the word *Christmas*. Elicit from the students that Christmas is a celebration of the birth of Christ. Review the account of Isaiah who prophesied the birth of Christ to the people of Israel.

Bible Account

Read Luke 2:1–20 or use the following retelling of the passage. Listening question: **Who were the first people in Israel that God told about the birth of His Son?** *(the shepherds)* Display Chart 35, "Christ's Birth." Point to Galilee, Nazareth, and Bethlehem.

The Shepherds Seek Jesus

About the time Jesus was to be born, Joseph and Mary left Galilee *[point to Galilee]* and went to Bethlehem, also called the city of David. *[Show the route from Nazareth to Bethlehem.]* While they were in Bethlehem, Jesus was born. Mary wrapped Jesus in swaddling clothes and laid Him in a manger. *[Use the background information to explain swaddling clothes and a manger.]*

[Direct the students' attention to the picture on Worktext page 71 as you continue to tell the account.]

After God's Son was born, the Bible tells us that the angel of the Lord came to some shepherds. The sight of the angel was so magnificent that they were afraid.

The angel told them to not be afraid because he had some joyful news for them. He said the good news was for everyone. Isaiah's prophecy from the Old Testament was well known. *[Point to the picture of Isaiah on the TimeLine.]* But now it had happened after seven hundred years. *[Point to the picture of the birth of Christ on the TimeLine.]*

The angel told them that they would find the baby wrapped in swaddling clothes and lying in a manger.

After the shepherds heard about the baby, they saw a group of angels in the sky all saying, "Glory to God in the highest, and on earth peace, good will toward men." When the angels were gone, the shepherds hurried to Bethlehem to find Jesus.

They found the baby just as the angel had said. Then they went out and told everyone they saw what had happened to them. They praised God for bringing a Savior to Israel, just as He promised He would.

⚜

▶ **What was the name of the town where Jesus was born?** *(Bethlehem)*

▶ **How did the angel describe Jesus to the shepherds?** *(as a baby wrapped in swaddling clothes, lying in a manger)* Share the background information about swaddling clothes and the manger if desired.

▶ **How long did the shepherds wait before going to find Jesus?** *(They started looking right away.)*

▶ **What did the shepherds do after finding the baby?** *(They went out and told people.)* Share the background information about shepherds if desired.

 Does God send angels to tell people things now? *(Elicit from the students that God tells us things through His Word and no longer sends angels as messengers the way He did back then [**Hebrews 1:1–2**].)*

InfoScene: "The Shepherds Seek Jesus"
Display Chart 12 from the Visual Packet for the students to refer to throughout this unit.

TimeLine
Add Christ's birth to the TimeLine. Guide the students as they glue the picture of the birth of Christ (from the Student Materials section of the ToolKit CD) onto their TimeLines. Point to the pictures of Isaiah and the Present Day card on the TimeLine. Remind the students that Isaiah foretold Christ's birth almost seven hundred years before it happened.

Music Connection (optional)
Play the recording of "Glory to God" from Handel's *Messiah* [Part I, Sections 16–17] (optional). Explain to the students that Handel wrote this song based on the angels' words to the shepherds in **Luke 2:13–14**.

Hymn: "Joy to the World"
Sing the third verse (Worktext page 216). As a point of interest, call attention to the references to a garden.

▶ **What Bible account tells about a garden?** *(Adam and Eve)*

▶ **What was the result of the sin in the Garden of Eden?** *(Man would die and, without salvation, be separated from God.)*

 Where is the Curse found? *(throughout the entire world [**Romans 8:22**])*

▶ **Who makes blessings grow?** *(Christ)*

Explain that this verse could also be describing heaven.

♥ Memory Verse—Luke 2:11

Principle: God sent us a Savior.

Explain and practice the memory verse. Discuss who spoke these words and to whom they were spoken. *(An angel of the Lord spoke them to the shepherds.)* Explain that although the shepherds received the announcement, the message of salvation through Christ is for the whole world (**John 3:16**).

Explain that everyone has a sinful nature and must trust only Christ for salvation. One day Jesus Christ the Savior will return for those in His family. To be a child of God, a person must repent of sin and turn by faith to God. Let the students read Luke 2:11 together several times. Instruct them to highlight the verse (optional) and mark the location in their Bibles with the Unit 4 Bookmark.

✎ Worktext page 72

Apply Bible knowledge to everyday life. Instruct the students to answer the questions on the page. Call on volunteers to share the name of someone who has not heard the good news of the Savior. Allow the students to work with partners as they use Worktext page 72 to explain why Jesus came to earth. Conclude with a time of prayer.

LESSON 54 The Gift

Materials
- Hymn: "Joy to the World"
- Chart 35, "Christ's Birth" (optional)

♥ Memory Verse—Luke 2:11

Guide a discussion about David. Tell the students that the "city of David" is Bethlehem. Explain that David was the famous Israelite king who came from Bethlehem and fought for the Israelites against the Philistines. The shepherds knew where Jesus was because they knew where King David came from.

Practice the memory verse. Point to Bethlehem on Chart 35, "Christ's Birth," during the day as a signal to say the verse (optional).

Introducing the Application Story

Guide a discussion about Christmas presents. Call on volunteers to tell about their favorite Christmas present. Point out that God gave us a Christmas present too—the same one He gave to Adam and Eve: God gave us a Savior!

Application Story

Read or tell the following story. Listening question: **What is J.D.'s favorite Christmas present?** *(a coloring book)*

Can't Reach

The book seemed to stare down at J.D. from the top shelf of the closet. Dad had given the book to him a few weeks before as a Christmas present. It was a coloring book, but not like any other. It was gigantic, almost the size of J.D. The book was so big it had to be kept on the top shelf of the closet.

He took the chair from his desk and dragged it to the closet. He put his left foot on top of the chair and followed with his right one. He slowly stood up straight and reached up. Still he was too short. He leaned forward and stood on his tiptoes. He slid his fingers toward the book and touched it. He accidentally pushed it away.

J.D. stretched himself all that he could stretch, but it was not enough. He jumped off the chair and landed with a thud. "J.D.?" his mother called from the kitchen, "Everything okay?"

"I'm fine," he called back. He looked around the room for something that would reach farther. A hanger, he thought. He took down one of his wire hangers and bent it from its original shape and then returned to the chair.

He held onto the doorway with one hand and reached the hook of the hanger out with the other. He took his hand from the doorway and pushed with both hands down on the hanger. The book moved an inch toward him.

The book stopped moving and the hanger came toward him, scratching the book on the way. Without a hand on the doorway for balance, he wobbled on the chair. He grabbed his shoe bag to catch himself, but it just fell with him.

J.D. landed on his back with the hanger, shoe bag, and chair on top of him. His mother came running into the room. She pulled him out and put him on his bed. "J.D.," she asked, "what were you doing?"

Go and Tell!
Luke 2:1–17   Name _____

The shepherds heard some very good news from the angels.

Write a short answer to each question.

Who was born? _____ *Jesus* _____

Where was He born? _ *the city of David (Bethlehem)* _

Why was He important enough for the shepherds to hurry to Bethlehem to see Him?

_____ *He is the Savior (Son of God).* _____

Many people have heard about the birth of Jesus, but they do not know that He could be their Savior. Whom do you know who has not heard this good news?

_____ *Answers will vary.* _____

Pray for the person you named. Use the pictures on page 71 to help you share the good news of the Savior that God gave to everyone.

72   A Servant's Heart • Lesson 53

J.D.'s mind raced with ideas, but he knew that telling the truth was the right thing to do. He told her what he had done. "Why didn't you just ask for the book? You know I would have given it to you."

"Oh, Mom," said J.D., "I wanted to do it myself."

▶ **What did J.D. want?** *(the coloring book)*
▶ **Who gave J.D. the coloring book for Christmas?** *(Dad)*
▶ **How did J.D. try to get his book off the shelf?** *(standing on the chair and trying to reach it with a hanger)*
▶ **Why could J.D. not get the book?** *(He was too short to reach it.)*
▶ **Who could have reached the book?** *(Mom)*
💡 **When J. D. could not reach the book on his own, he should have asked his mother. Since we cannot reach heaven on our own, how can we be saved from our sins?** *(Elicit from the students that the Bible tells us that we must ask God in order to accept the gift He has prepared. Explain that our hearts are sinful and we are not able to be good enough. Through Christ, God gives us something we could never deserve.)*

🎵 **Hymn: "Joy to the World"**

Sing the first three verses (Worktext page 216). Review the meaning as the students sing each verse.

LESSON 55 The Wise Men Seek Jesus

Materials

- Chart 13, "Bethlehem: Birthplace of a Savior King"
- Chart 35, "Christ's Birth"
- Hymn: "Joy to the World"
- A yellow construction-paper crown for the teacher

🎵 **Hymn: "Joy to the World"**

Teach the fourth verse (Worktext page 216). Play the recording for the fourth verse of the hymn. Sing the verse once as a class. Define any words the students may not know. Explain that the third and fourth verses describe events that have not yet happened. Someday Christians will live in a place as described in the third verse. Christ will come again to rule as in the fourth verse. Explain that just as nature sings God's praises (in the second verse), the nations (all different lands and places) will prove (show) how wonderful God is. Sing the verse several times and then sing the entire hymn.

❤️ **Memory Verse—Luke 2:11**

Practice the memory verse. Define the word *Lord*. Read the verse together. Place the paper crown on your head. Call on volunteers to give ideas of what a lord or king is. Explain to the students that although Christ rules over us as a king, He is loving, kind, and perfectly just, which means He will not allow anything, except what is for our good, to happen to us. Allow individuals to say the verse every time

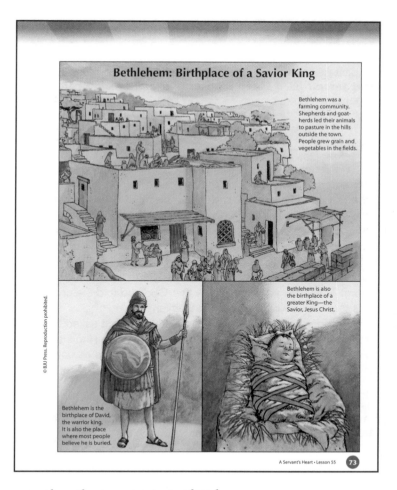

Bethlehem: Birthplace of a Savior King

Bethlehem was a farming community. Shepherds and goat-herds led their animals to pasture in the hills outside the town. People grew grain and vegetables in the fields.

Bethlehem is the birthplace of David, the warrior king. It is also the place where most people believe he is buried.

Bethlehem is also the birthplace of a greater King—the Savior, Jesus Christ.

A Servant's Heart • Lesson 55   **73**

you place the crown on your head.

Background Information

The Wise Men—*The wise men (sometimes called the* Magi) *were men who studied the stars (astronomers), so it is fitting that they recognized a special star. No one knows how many of them there were or exactly what age Christ was when they found Him, although He may have been one or two years old. They brought gifts worthy of a king, and these gifts provided the money Joseph needed to travel and to live in Egypt. It is significant that these men were Gentiles, signifying that Christ came to save the whole world, not only Jews.*

Herod—*Herod the Great was not in the line of David and, therefore, not the true king of Israel. Abraham and Sarah gave birth to Isaac. Isaac married Rebekah, who gave birth to twins, Esau and Jacob. Each brother represented a nation: Jacob, an ancestor of David and the Israelites, and Esau, an ancestor of the Edomites. Herod was from the line of Esau. The Jews hated Herod because they knew he was not their true king.*

Introducing the Bible Account

Guide a discussion about stars. The Bible tells us that God placed the sun, moon, and stars in the sky. Explain that this means He spoke them into being. Discuss what students like about stars and their beauty.

Read Matthew 2:1–13 or use the following retelling of the passage. Listening question: **How did the wise men find Jesus?** (*God used a special star to guide them.*) Direct the students to look at page 73 as you speak.

The Wise Men Seek Jesus

While Jesus was still young, a group of men came to Jerusalem looking for Him. The men asked where the king of the Jews had been born, saying that they had seen His star in the east and had come to worship Him. Herod, the king over Israel, was upset by this because he was the king, and these men came asking for another king.

Herod gathered all of the religious experts together (the priests and scribes), wanting to know where Christ would be born. These religious men knew that God had told the prophets that Christ would be born in Bethlehem.

Herod sent the wise men on to Bethlehem but asked them to report back to him so he could go and worship Him also. Herod didn't really want to worship Jesus because he considered himself to be the only king of the Jews.

Display Chart 35, "Christ's Birth." Trace the general path from the east to Bethlehem. Show the trip south from Jerusalem to Bethlehem on the map.

As the wise men traveled the five miles to Bethlehem, the star appeared to them again. They followed the star to the home of Jesus. They went in and worshiped Christ and gave Him expensive gifts of gold, which is very valuable; frankincense, which smells good when burned; and myrrh, which is used for perfume. These gifts seem strange to give to such a small child, but the wise men knew that this child was going to be their Savior and King. God also warned the wise men *not* to return to Herod.

▸ **Where did the wise men come from?** (*the east*)
▸ **What did God utilize to lead the wise men to Jerusalem?** (*a star*)
▸ **Who were the wise men looking for?** (*Christ, the King of the Jews*)
▸ **Where did Herod send the wise men to look for Christ?** (*Bethlehem*)
▸ **What gifts did they bring Jesus?** (*gold, frankincense, and myrrh*)

InfoScene: "Bethlehem: Birthplace of a Savior King"
Display Chart 13 from the Visual Packet for the students to refer to throughout this unit.

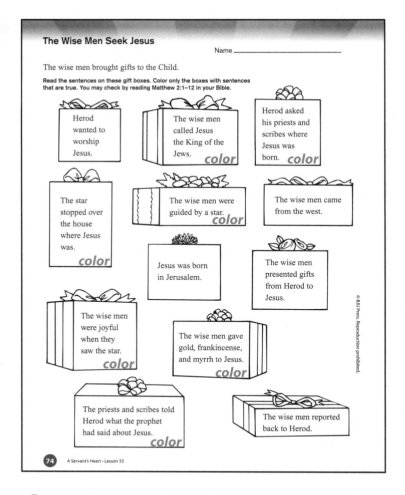

The Wise Men Seek Jesus

Name _____

The wise men brought gifts to the Child.

Read the sentences on these gift boxes. Color only the boxes with sentences that are true. You may check by reading Matthew 2:1–12 in your Bible.

Herod wanted to worship Jesus.

The wise men called Jesus the King of the Jews. *color*

Herod asked his priests and scribes where Jesus was born. *color*

The star stopped over the house where Jesus was. *color*

The wise men were guided by a star. *color*

The wise men came from the west.

Jesus was born in Jerusalem.

The wise men presented gifts from Herod to Jesus.

The wise men were joyful when they saw the star. *color*

The wise men gave gold, frankincense, and myrrh to Jesus. *color*

The priests and scribes told Herod what the prophet had said about Jesus. *color*

The wise men reported back to Herod.

74 A Servant's Heart • Lesson 55

© BJU Press. Reproduction prohibited.

Worktext page 74

Recall facts and details. Instruct the students to read each sentence, decide whether it is true, and then color the gifts that display true sentences.

Palestine in Christ's Time

Name _____

Follow the directions to complete the map.

1. Put a green *X* on Nazareth, where Mary and Joseph lived.

2. Trace in green the way they probably traveled to Bethlehem to be taxed.

3. Draw a blue circle around Bethlehem, where Jesus was born.

4. Draw a purple crown on Jerusalem, where Herod lived.

5. Trace in brown the way the wise men probably came to Jerusalem.

6. Draw a yellow star near Bethlehem, where the star stopped and the wise men found Jesus.

7. Trace in brown the way the wise men went from Jerusalem to Bethlehem.

8. The wise men did not return to Herod. Trace in blue the way they probably went home.

The rectangle on the world map shows where Israel is.

© BJU Press. Reproduction prohibited.

A Servant's Heart • Lesson 55   **75**

✍ Worktext page 75

Guide a map-reading activity. Direct the students' attention to the map on the page. Instruct them to complete each step as you read the directions. Provide assistance as needed. Remind them that travel during Bible times was often done on foot or by riding a donkey.

Materials

- Hymn: "Joy to the World"
- A 7" × 9" piece of construction paper for each student
- A copy of page A82 ("Good News") for each student (optional)
- A completed card from page A82 ("Good News") to show students
- A Christmas ornament wrapped in a gift box

♫ Hymn: "Joy to the World"

Sing the hymn (Worktext page 216). Sing all four verses, choosing girls and boys to sing different verses.

Picture the Point

Illustrate the giving and receiving of gifts. Display the wrapped gift.

💡 **Why do we give gifts?** *(Accept any answer, but remind the students about the wise men who brought gifts and about the gift of salvation through Jesus.)*

💡 **What do you like about gifts?** *(Accept any answer. Point out that a gift can be special to you because it comes from someone special, is expensive, is something you wanted or needed, or shows someone's love for you.)*

Choose a volunteer to help picture the point. Hand the gift to the student and allow him to open it. Lead a discussion of the steps in the process of gift-giving. Write for display the steps the students identify. The list may include things like the following.

> *The teacher buys the gift.*
> *The teacher wraps the gift.*
> *The teacher chooses someone to give it to.*
> *The teacher hands the gift to the student.*
> *The student unwraps the gift.*
> *The student takes the gift out of the box.*
> *The student says "thank you" to the teacher.*

Unless prompted, the students will probably omit the step of the student taking or receiving the gift. Ask students if the list leaves out any step. Explain that the step of receiving could be added to the list.

> *The student takes (receives) the gift.*

Explain that most people leave out this step in salvation. God has given us all a gift *(His Son)*, but we must receive this gift. Encourage the students to ask people this Christmas if they have received God's gift.

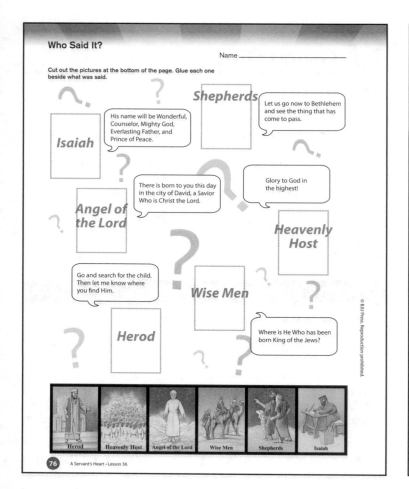

Who Said It?

Name _____

Cut out the pictures at the bottom of the page. Glue each one beside what was said.

Shepherds — Let us go now to Bethlehem and see the thing that has come to pass.

Isaiah — His name will be Wonderful, Counselor, Mighty God, Everlasting Father, and Prince of Peace.

Angel of the Lord — There is born to you this day in the city of David, a Savior Who is Christ the Lord.

Heavenly Host — Glory to God in the highest!

Go and search for the child. Then let me know where you find Him.

Wise Men

Herod — Where is He Who has been born King of the Jews?

Herod | Heavenly Host | Angel of the Lord | Wise Men | Shepherds | Isaiah

76   A Servant's Heart • Lesson 56

Unit 4 Review

Name _____

Circle *True* or *False* for each sentence.

1. God promised Adam and Eve a Savior.   (True)   False
2. God stopped loving Adam and Eve after they sinned.   True   (False)
3. The angels told the news of John's birth to the wise men.   True   (False)
4. King David was related to Jesus.   (True)   False
5. Immanuel means "God with us."   (True)   False
6. The wise men called Herod the "King of the Jews."   True   (False)
7. Herod wanted to worship Jesus.   True   (False)
8. Only some of the prophecies about Christ's birth came true.   True   (False)

Fill in the circle next to the correct answer.

9. Isaiah told what the name of _____ would be.
   ○ every king
   ● Jesus

10. Isaiah lived _____ Christ's lifetime.
    ● before
    ○ during

11. The shepherds praised God and then
    ● told others.
    ○ went to sleep.

12. The wise men gave gifts to
    ○ Herod.
    ● Jesus.

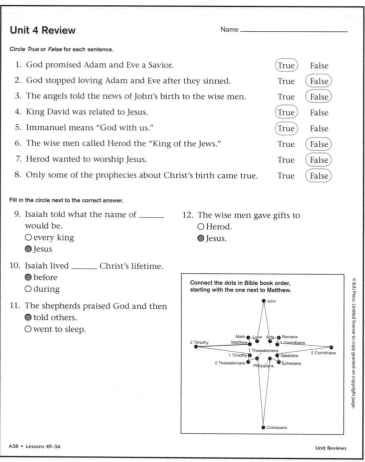

Connect the dots in Bible book order, starting with the one next to Matthew.

A58 • Lessons 49–56   Unit Reviews

♥ Memory Verse—Luke 2:11

Practice the memory verse. Discuss the following.

▶ **Who is the Savior?** (*Christ the Lord*)

💡 **Why do people need a Savior?** (*God is holy and must punish sin. Only the perfect Son of God could die on the cross to pay the penalty for sin. People must repent and turn to God, accepting by faith God's gift of salvation.*)

💡 **Have you asked Jesus Christ to be your Savior?** (*Remind the students that Jesus is coming again one day.*)

Choose individuals by handing the ornament to them to recite the verse. Hang the ornament in the classroom and point to it as a signal for the class to say the verse throughout the day.

✎ Worktext page 76

Identify characters by their words. Call on students to identify each picture at the bottom of the page. Instruct the students to cut apart the pictures. Tell them to glue each picture beside the matching words.

✐ Art Connection (optional)

Share the good news. Instruct the students to follow the directions on page A82 ("Good News") to make a greeting card. Demonstrate how to fold and cut the angel wings. You may also want to display a completed card.

▶ Going Beyond

Reinforcement

Role-play the visit of the wise men. Choose several students to act out the visit of the wise men. Switch characters between scenes of the play. Review what gifts were brought. (*gold, frankincense, and myrrh*) Remind the students that God's gift of salvation is available for all people. Read and discuss **John 3:16**.

Enrichment

Add a verse. Write a fifth verse to "Joy to the World." Sing the verse together in class.

Celebrate the birth of Christ. Have a birthday party to celebrate Christ's birth. Guide the students in listing gifts they can give Christ.

◀◀ Unit Review

Materials

• A copy of page A58 ("Unit 4 Review") for each student

Guide a review of Lessons 49–56. Review the people and events in preparation for the Unit 4 Test (optional).

5

A Serving Heart

OVERVIEW

Preparing the Teacher

Know has several meanings, including (1) to be acquainted or familiar with and (2) to be certain or sure of. God's Word records the marvelous works of God in the lives of Jonathan, David, Jeremiah, and others. These accounts are familiar to you and to the students. Pause to realize that while these men may not have fully comprehended what God would do, they were certain that they should be devoted to Him and act for Him. You may not know what God will do in the life of each student, but you can be certain that He has chosen you to be a part of it. Read **Psalm 78:4**, thanking God for allowing you to participate in telling future generations of His strength and wonderful works.

Preparing the Materials

57—Unit 5 bookmark [E]

58—Tape measure (10'); memory verse visual; five pieces of brown poster board

60—Vase, flowers, a cloth; drawing of dot-to-dot crown (see diagram)

Unit 5a Going Beyond—Joy jar; stickers or small treats; two craft sticks (long and short) [E]; three sheets of 9" × 12" construction paper [E]; felt-tip pens

61—Copy of page A83 ("Serving One Another") [E, O]; five small hearts drawn for display; verse visual: red construction paper

62—Pictures of people with special needs [O]

Unit 5b Going Beyond—Heavy paper or oak tag; two large paper clips [E]; glitter [O]

66—Cake mix or recipe; one square of construction paper [E, O]

67—Squares of construction paper from Lesson 66; crown from a piece of 9" × 12" gold (or yellow) construction paper; glitter [O]

68—Various tools (kitchen, carpentry, or gardening)

Unit 5c Going Beyond—Construction paper; art paper

69—Map markers [E]; copy of page A84 [E, O]; verse visual (12" × 18" piece of construction paper); transparency or PowerPoint slide of page A86

70–71—Small stone

71—Bell or picture of a large bell; transparent tape [E]; small stone

72—Copy of page A59 ("Unit 5 Review") [E]

Unit 5d Going Beyond—Shoe box; blue, red, and brown construction paper; Operation Cooperation: a place that needs some clean-up; parent volunteers to help oversee the project

Unit 5   A Serving Heart

Hymn: "Joy in Serving Jesus"

Theme, Memory Verse, and Principle	Lesson Number	TE Page	Worktext Page(s)	Appendix Page(s)	Lesson Title	Scripture or Focus
Unit 5a **God's Servants Know God** Mark 10:45 *We must serve God and minister to others.*	57	124	77–78		Jonathan Knew God	1 Samuel 12:14–14:23
	58	126	79		David Puts God First	1 Samuel 16–17
	59	128	81		Prophet Focus: Jeremiah	Jeremiah 18:1–10
	60	129	82		Putting God and Others First	Picture the Point Application Activity
Unit 5b **God's Servants Serve in Love** 1 Samuel 12:24 *Serve God from the heart.*	61	132	83–84	A83	A Prince and a Shepherd Serve Together	1 Samuel 18:1–11; 20:1–12
	62	135	85–86		King David Serves	1 Samuel 13:1–4; 2 Samuel 4:4; 9:1–13
	63	137	87–90		In Love Serve One Another	Galatians 5:13
	64	139			Thinking of Others	Application Story
Unit 5c **God Can Use Me** 1 Chronicles 28:20a *God will help me serve Him.*	65	141	91		God Uses a Servant Girl	2 Kings 5:1–4
	66	143	92–94		A Captain Becomes a Servant	2 Kings 5:5–16
	67	146	95–96		A Servant's Crown	Application Story
	68	148	97–98		God's People Serve Him	Romans 6:13
Unit 5d **God Wants Us to Work Together** Psalm 133:1 *God's servants should live together in peace.*	69	151	99–100	A84–86	Nehemiah Wants to Rebuild	Nehemiah 1:1–2:8
	70	154	101–2		Rebuilding Together	Nehemiah 2:9–6:19
	71	156	103–4		Helping Hands?	Application Story
	72	158	105–6	A59	Who Will Do God's Work?	One-Act Play

Connections	Bible Doctrines	Skills/Applications
L58—TimeLine: David **L59**—TimeLine: Jeremiah	**The Doctrine of the Bible** *Details of Inspiration* God's Word is eternal (Ps. 119:89). **The Doctrine of God** *Attributes of God* God is all-powerful (omnipotent) (Jer. 32:27). God is everywhere (omnipresent) (Ps. 139:7–10). God is faithful (1 Cor. 1:9; 2 Tim. 2:13). **The Doctrine of Man** *Redemption of Man* Man has hope (Phil. 3:20–21). **The Doctrine of Salvation** *Elements of Salvation* Christ died for man (1 Cor. 15:3) God calls men through men (Rom. 10:14–15) **The Doctrine of the Church** *Functions of the Local Church* Care for those having special needs (Acts 6:1–7; Rom. 12:13).	**Foundational** • Realize that serving God begins in the heart • Identify the Bible as the source of knowing God • Recognize that all believers can and should serve God • Recognize that God wants Christians to work together **Practical** • Read a map • Read a timeline • Locate verses in the Old Testament from Genesis to Malachi • Order books of the Old Testament • Sequence events • Recall facts and details • Identify character traits of Nehemiah **Personal** • Demonstrate serving God from the heart (focus on attitudes) • Demonstrate serving God by serving others (focus on actions) • Realize that believers are God's servants • Realize that there is joy in service • Recognize that God's servants can know God's way and live according to it • Understand and apply Bible knowledge to everyday life
L69—History **L70**—TimeLine: Nehemiah		

God's Servants Know God

Unit 5a

PREVIEW

Doctrines

- God is all-powerful (omnipotent) (Jeremiah 32:27). [Lessons 57–58]
- Christ died for man (1 Corinthians 15:3). [Lesson 57]
- God's Word is eternal (Psalm 119:89). [Lesson 59]

Skills and Applications

- Learn Mark 10:45
- Read a timeline
- Recall facts and details
- Locate places on a map
- Identify the Bible as the source of knowing God
- Realize that believers are God's servants
- Realize that there is joy in service
- Apply Bible knowledge to everyday life

LESSON 57

Jonathan Knew God

Materials

- Chart 14, "Jonathan Knew God"
- Chart 36, "Kingdom of Saul"
- Hymn: "Joy in Serving Jesus"
- Unit 5 Bookmark for each student
- Highlighter for each student (optional)

Memory Verse—Mark 10:45

Principle: We must serve God and minister to others. Direct the students to highlight the verse (optional) and mark the location with the Unit 5 Bookmark.

Background Information

Philistine Iron—*During the time of Saul, the Philistines controlled the making of iron and did not let the Israelites melt it to make their own tools or weapons. Anyone who wanted something made from iron had to buy it from a Philistine ironsmith. The Israelites also had to pay the Philistines a high price to get their farming tools sharpened. These farming tools were the only items that most Israelites had to use in battle.*

Garrison—*A garrison is a group of soldiers. The group was commanded to defend a fortress or an area of land. The Philistines placed garrisons in Israel to try to control the land.*

Introducing the Bible Account

Use the background information to explain *garrison*. Call a student to the front of the room. Direct eight more to stand together in another area of the room. Explain that the two groups represent garrisons and that each student in the group represents one hundred men.

💡 **Which garrison do you think would win in a war?** *(Point out that often the army with more soldiers has the advantage.)* Tell the students that today's Bible account will show that this is not always true.

Bible Account

Read 1 Samuel 12:14–14:23 or use the following retelling of the passage. Listening question: **What was Saul's punishment for his sin?** *(Saul's punishment was the loss of the kingdom. God would choose another king.)* Direct attention to Chart 36, "Kingdom of Saul," as you point to the locations mentioned.

Jonathan Knew God

The people of Israel wanted a king so that they could be like other nations. God chose a tall, handsome man whose name was Saul.

Samuel anointed Saul as king and told the people that they should continue to fear, serve, and obey the Lord. If the people continued to disobey, then they and Saul, their king, would be overthrown.

Jonathan was one of Saul's sons. King Saul gave Jonathan a very important job to do. King Saul made Jonathan a leader over one thousand soldiers. Jonathan and his army helped Saul get rid of the Israelites' enemies, especially the mighty Philistines.

The Philistines were a strong people. They were gathering together to fight against Israel. They were angry because Jonathan and his army had attacked a Philistine garrison at Geba. The Philistines had gathered thirty thousand chariots, six thousand horsemen, and as many soldiers as sand on the seashore. Poor Israel! No one except Saul and Jonathan had swords. The Israelites had only their farming tools as weapons. The men of Israel were afraid. They went to hide in caves, under thickets, between rocks, and in pits.

To make matters worse, King Saul disobeyed God. Saul was told that the prophet Samuel would come to make a burnt offering. He would ask God what they should do. But Saul didn't wait for Samuel. Saul decided to make the burnt offering himself. When Samuel finally did come, he told Saul that he had disobeyed the Lord's command and that he would be punished for his disobedience. Saul's punishment would be the loss of the kingdom. God would choose another king. Samuel left without telling Saul what God wanted him to do about the Philistines.

Saul didn't know what to do. He went back to his home in Gibeah with his six hundred soldiers and sat under a tree.

▶ **Why were the Philistines angry?** *(Jonathan and his army had attacked a Philistine garrison.)*

▶ **Who had more troops, the Israelites or the Philistines?** *(Philistines)*

💡 **Why do you think the Israelites used farming tools for weapons?** *(Answers will vary.)* Share the background information about Philistine iron.

▶ **Why did Israel not know what God wanted them to do about the Philistines?** *(Saul had disobeyed God.)*

Direct the students' attention to Worktext page 77. Call on students to describe the soldiers' weapons and attire. Choose a volunteer to read why the Philistines were an army to fear. Instruct the students to look at the page as you finish telling the Bible account.

Saul sat under a tree. Perhaps he was thinking about the loss of his kingdom. Perhaps he was trying to think of a plan to attack the Philistines.

Jonathan was thinking too. He could sit no longer. He told his armor-bearer that they should go over to the Philistine

garrison at Michmash. Jonathan didn't tell anyone where they were going. He didn't even take his army of one thousand soldiers.

The two men traveled until they got to a place near the garrison. Jonathan said to his armor-bearer, "Come on, and let's go over to the Philistines." Jonathan thought the Lord might help them even though there were only two of them. He was not afraid to serve God. Jonathan told his armor-bearer that if the Philistines saw them and came to them, Jonathan and his servant would not attack the garrison. But if the Philistines saw them and told Jonathan to come closer, then that would be a sign that God would defeat them.

The two men went up to the garrison. The Philistines called for them to come up because the Philistines had something to show them. That was the sign that God was with them! Jonathan and his armor-bearer went up to the garrison and killed twenty men. Then the earth began to shake, and there was a great trembling. The Philistine troops were confused.

In the meantime, Saul's watchmen reported to him that the Philistines were running in all directions.

Saul wondered whether some of his army was missing. The soldiers counted and found that Jonathan and his armor-bearer were missing. Saul assembled his army and went to join his son. By the time Saul and his army arrived, the Philistines had turned on each other and were fighting among themselves. All the men of Israel came out of hiding, and the

Israelites who had been with the Philistines helped push the Philistine army out of Israel. Shouts of victory rang throughout all of Israel.

———————————⚜———————————

▶ **How many men did Jonathan take with him?** *(one, his armor-bearer)*

💡 **What did Jonathan know about God?** *(God is all powerful; God can save by many or by few.)*

Point out that in the demonstration earlier they may have thought the eight hundred men would defeat the one hundred, but with God's help, one hundred men could defeat eight hundred men. Remind the students about Gideon and his army of three hundred men defeating the thousands of Midianites. Stress that we have a God Who can do anything.

▶ **How did God defeat the Philistines?** *(He sent an earthquake and helped Jonathan and his armor-bearer to win even though they were outnumbered.)*

💡 **Is any problem, whether big or small, too hard for God?** *(No. God can help us have the victory over any problem.)*

💡 **What should you do if you have a problem?** *(Search for the answer in God's Word and trust Him to help you solve it. Ask your parents or a teacher to help you.)*

InfoScene: "Jonathan Knew God"
Display Chart 14 from the Visual Packet for the students to refer to throughout this unit.

🎵 Hymn: "Joy in Serving Jesus"

Teach the first verse (Worktext page 217). Utilize the recording as necessary throughout the unit. Ask students to tell what it means to serve Jesus.

⦿ Worktext page 78

Recalling facts and details. Guide the students as they write the correct name from the word bank in each sentence.

LESSON 58 David Puts God First

Materials

- Chart 36, "Kingdom of Saul"
- Hymn: "Joy in Serving Jesus"
- TimeLine and picture: David
- A measuring tape at least ten feet long
- A memory verse visual made from five pieces of brown poster board taped together in the shape of a cross. Use three squares (9" × 9") and two rectangles (9" × 12") as shown in the diagram. Write in the verse and reference.

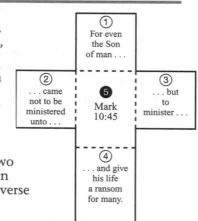

① For even the Son of man . . .
② . . . came not to be ministered unto . . .
⑤ Mark 10:45
③ . . . but to minister . . .
④ . . . and give his life a ransom for many.

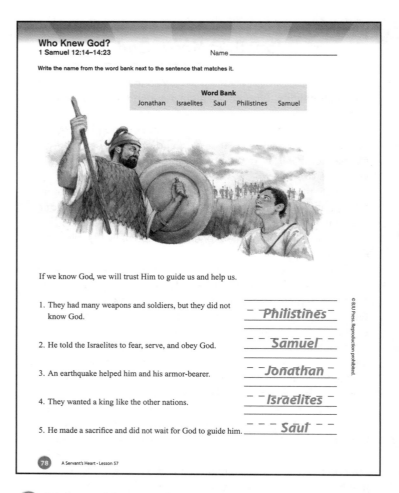

🎵 Hymn: "Joy in Serving Jesus"

Sing the first verse (Worktext page 217). Write the word *JOY* vertically for display. Write *Jesus, Others,* and *You* using the letters already written as the first letter of each word. *(Note:* This is taken from the chorus "J-O-Y.") After answering the following questions, lead the students in singing the first verse of the song with the recording.

▶ **Whom are you to serve first?** *(Jesus)* **Next?** *(others)* **Last?** *(you, yourself)*

💡 **Can Christians have joy if they sin against God?** *(No. When Christians sin, they cannot have joy.)*

Background Information

The Country of Philistia and Its People—*The Philistines, who were a people of war, wanted to conquer the countries around them. They were also a sea-going people. They traded with others around the Mediterranean Sea. Because of this, the Philistines had a far more advanced culture than nearby inland countries. Even though Philistia was advanced in many ways, God gave Israel many victories over Philistia when Israel obeyed God's commands.*

Introducing the Bible Account

Guide a discussion about choices. Allow the students to share any experiences they have had telling others about Jesus. Discuss that sometimes it is difficult to make choices. They need to pray and ask God to help them make the right choice. Tell the students that in today's Bible account a young man had two choices.

Bible Account

Read 1 Samuel 16–17 or use the following retelling of the passage. Listening question: **Whom did God choose to be the next king and why?** *(God chose David to be the next king. God knew David's heart. David loved God and others.)* Direct attention to Chart 36, "Kingdom of Saul," as you point to the locations mentioned.

David Puts God First

Who would be the next king of Israel? Saul couldn't be the king anymore because he didn't wait for the prophet Samuel to come make a sacrifice. Instead, Saul disobeyed God's command and made the sacrifice himself at Gilgal. Usually the king's first-born son was the next in line for the throne. But God had a different plan. He told Samuel to fill his horn with oil and go to Bethlehem. God told Samuel that He would make one of Jesse's eight sons the next king.

Samuel obeyed God and went to Bethlehem. He told Jesse to bring his sons and come make a sacrifice. When they came, Samuel looked on Jesse's oldest son. He thought surely God would make this oldest son the next king. Eliab was tall and handsome. But God told Samuel, "The Lord does not see as man sees; for man looks on the outward appearance, but the Lord looks on the heart."

💡 **What did God mean?** *(God would not choose a king based on his physical appearance. God would choose a king based on his heart, a heart that loves and serves God and others.)*

As each of Jesse's sons passed before Samuel, Samuel told Jesse that that one wasn't God's choice. Samuel asked Jesse whether he had any other sons. Jesse said that his youngest son was tending the sheep. Samuel told Jesse to send for him.

When David, Jesse's youngest son, stood in front of Samuel, God said, "Get up and anoint him. He's the one."

Samuel took his horn of oil and anointed the shepherd boy as the next king of Israel. The Spirit of the Lord came on David. God would help David. God wanted David to be a king who served God first.

💡 **Do you think David went to sit on the king's throne right away?** *(No. David went back to tend the sheep.)*

After tending the sheep, this newly anointed king's next opportunity for service was to play his harp for King Saul because Saul was frequently troubled by God.

Later, David again returned to his sheep. And the mighty Philistines came back again to fight Israel in the Valley of Elah. David's brothers were in Saul's army. Jesse told David to leave his sheep and take food to his brothers. When David arrived, he heard how one Philistine who was almost ten feet tall hated God. That was David's God! The giant Philistine challenged

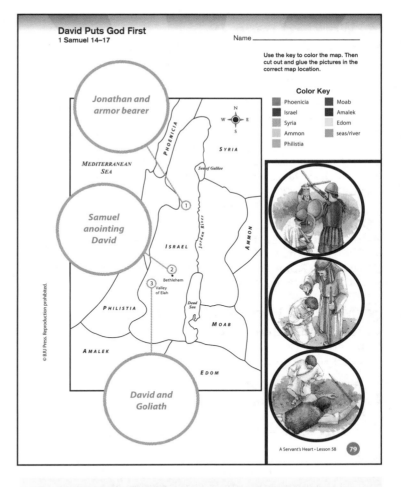

any Israelite soldier to come and fight against him. To the amazement of both the Philistines and the Israelites, David the shepherd volunteered to go against the mighty Goliath.

David went closer to the giant and told him that God would give him the victory. David told the giant that all the people would know that the Lord doesn't save with sword and spear but that the battle was His and He would defeat the giant.

The mighty Goliath died that day because a young shepherd put God first. David could have delivered the food to his brothers and then gone back to the safety of tending the sheep. But David decided to put God first. He stood against an evil giant, and God gave David the victory.

⚜

💡 **How do you know that David put God first in his life?** *(David took a stand for God and went up against the giant, risking his life for God's glory.)*

💡 **How can you put God first in your life?** *(Answers may vary.)*

▶ **How tall was Goliath?** *(He was almost ten feet tall.)*

Measure ten feet along the wall using the tape measure.

💡 **How could David ever think that he could win?** *(David was confident because he knew and trusted God.)*

Worktext page 79

Guide a map activity. Display Chart 36, "Kingdom of Saul." Point out Israel and the surrounding countries. Explain to the students that the countries shown were often at war with Israel. Direct attention to the color key on Worktext page 79. Instruct the students to color each country as shown in the color key. Tell the students to cut the picture circles from the side of page 79. Review the events from each picture. Guide the students as they glue the pictures to the correct map locations. Remind the students that Jonathan, Samuel, and David were serving God. Their actions showed their love for God.

TimeLine

Add David to the TimeLine. Place the picture of David on the TimeLine (1040–970 BC), pointing out the time that passed from Abraham to David. Guide the students as they glue the picture of David onto their TimeLines.

Memory Verse—Mark 10:45

Practice the memory verse. Direct the students' attention to the cross visual. Lead them in reading Mark 10:45 together several times.

💡 **Who is the Son of Man?** *(Jesus Christ)*
💡 **Why did He come (two reasons)?** *(to minister and to give His life)*
💡 **In this verse, what does *to minister* mean?** *(to serve)*

Fold the visual where the sections are taped together. Fold section 4 in first, then 3, then 2, and then 1. Allow a student to hold the visual and unfold it one section at a time as the rest of the class recites the verse. Repeat as desired, giving different students the opportunity to hold the visual.

59 Prophet Focus: Jeremiah

Materials

- Hymn: "Joy in Serving Jesus"
- TimeLine and picture: Jeremiah
- Verse visual from Lesson 58 (cross)

Hymn: "Joy in Serving Jesus"

Sing the first verse (Worktext page 217). Discuss the phrase "joy that fills the heart with praises." Tell the students that someone who has a heart filled with praises is someone who is thankful all the time. Call on students to tell what they can be thankful for on rainy days or when they are sick. Tell the students that they can be thankful even when sad things happen in their lives. Christians can be thankful for their salvation. Rainy days will not wash their joy away, and sickness will not take it from them (**Hebrews 13:5**). Lead the students in singing the first verse several times.

Memory Verse—Mark 10:45

Practice the memory verse. Choose a student to hold the verse visual. Say the verse together. Instruct the stu-

dent holding the cross to fold in one of the flaps. Direct the students to repeat the memory verse again with this part hidden. Tell the student with the visual to fold in another flap. Continue saying the verse until all the flaps have been folded in, and then have volunteers recite it.

Background Information

Prophets—*(Review the information given about prophets in Lesson 24.)*

Prophet Focus

Read or tell the following narrative about Jeremiah. Jeremiah allowed himself to be used by God and served Him through many difficulties. He lived near Jerusalem, and though some of the prophets of God were married, Jeremiah was not. Listening question: **What did the clay represent in the object lesson God showed Jeremiah in the potter's house?** *(the people of Israel)*

Jeremiah

God chose Jeremiah to be a prophet to the Israelites. He obeyed God even though he thought that he was too young for the job.

"I am a child," Jeremiah told God. "I cannot speak."

But God said, "Don't say that you're a child." God had chosen Jeremiah for this job even before he was born. God wanted Jeremiah to be a prophet to Israel. He would go to the Israelites and say everything that God told him to say. "Don't be afraid of them," God said. He promised to be with Jeremiah, and God would give Jeremiah His words.

God showed Jeremiah many signs. These signs were a warning to the Israelites. One of the signs God used was a branch from an almond tree. In Israel, the almond tree was the first to bloom in the spring. People would watch it to see when spring was coming. The almond branch was a symbol to Jeremiah that God watches over His word, causing it to come to pass.

Another sign was a potter and his clay. God told Jeremiah to go down to the potter's house.

Jeremiah obeyed, and there the potter was forming a piece of pottery on the wheel. But it had a defect and wasn't good. So the potter started over.

The people of Israel were like the clay in God's hands. He could do whatever He wanted with them. God is powerful. He could destroy them, but He wanted to take their sin away and make them useful. If a piece of pottery with a defect dries, it is good for nothing and has to be broken.

The Israelites didn't love and obey God anymore. They made and worshiped idols, but their idols would not be able to help them when God punished them. God took care of them for so many years. He loved them and would have to punish them.

God also gave them hope. He is merciful. "Return," God said. He wanted the Israelites to obey Him and love Him with all of their hearts. God promised to forgive them if they would admit that they had sinned and if they would obey Him again.

Jeremiah prophesied God's words to many people. He even told kings about the punishment God would send. But the Israelites didn't like what Jeremiah said even though they were God's words. Sometimes, they wouldn't listen; other times they hurt Jeremiah and even put him in prison.

Jeremiah is called the weeping prophet because the Israelites' sinfulness made Jeremiah sad. But Jeremiah obeyed God even when he was discouraged. God used Jeremiah to write two books in the Bible. He wrote Jeremiah and Lamentations. God wants His children to obey Him even though the job may seem to be too hard.

❧

💡 **How old do you think Jeremiah was when God called him to be a prophet?** *(He was a young man; he may have been about twenty.)*

▶ **Why did Jeremiah not think he could be a prophet?** *(Jeremiah told God he could not speak.)*

▶ **What did God tell Jeremiah He would do?** *(give Jeremiah the words to speak)*

▶ **What did Jeremiah need to do?** *(trust that God would help him)*

💡 **What do Christians need to do when they think they cannot do something?** *(ask God to help them, trust that He will, and obey Him)*

Tell the students that Jeremiah did trust God and went about preaching God's Word and warning the people that God wanted them to turn from their sins. He told the people that if they would turn from their sins, then God would save them from their enemy, Babylon.

▶ **Did the people listen to Jeremiah?** *(No. Explain that the people did not listen to God's warnings that Jeremiah gave. Point out that Jeremiah continued to preach God's Word even though the people continued in their sins and wouldn't listen.)*

💡 **How do you think Jeremiah was treated by the people who would not listen to him?** *(Answers will vary but explain to the students that Jeremiah was ridiculed and mocked, put into jail, and accused of being a traitor.)*

💡 **How should we respond when people who we talk to do not believe God's Word?** *(pray for them, love them, keep believing and speaking God's Word, and trust God to do His work in them)*

▶ **What book(s) of the Bible did Jeremiah write?** *(Jeremiah and Lamentations)*

Explain to the class that Jeremiah had his scribe, Baruch, write down God's words. Then a king burned the scroll, and Jeremiah had to write down God's words again.

💡 **Could God's Word ever be completely destroyed?** *(Answers will vary. Elicit from the students that people sometimes destroy Bibles, but God tells us that His Word will never be destroyed. It will last forever.)*

⏱ TimeLine

Add Jeremiah to the TimeLine. Place the picture of Jeremiah on the TimeLine (627–570 BC), pointing out that Jeremiah lived about seventy years after the prophet Isaiah

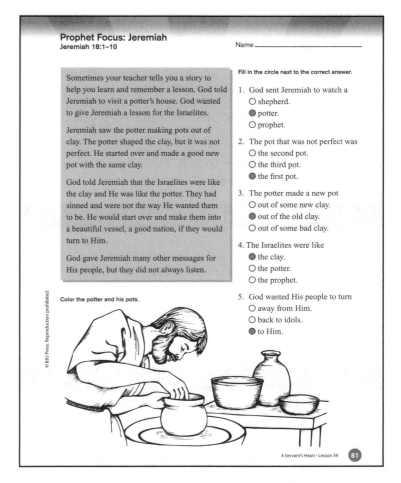

and about four hundred years after David. Guide the students as they glue the picture of Jeremiah onto their TimeLines.

✏ Prophet Focus: Worktext page 81

Recall facts and details. Review Jeremiah by reading the paragraphs to the students. Guide the students as they complete the sentences on the page. Allow time for them to color the picture.

LESSON 60 Putting God and Others First

Materials
• Hymn: "Joy in Serving Jesus"
• A vase, flowers (real or artificial), and a cloth
• A dot-to-dot crown drawn for display (with the dots not connected but numbered from 1 to 7 as shown below)

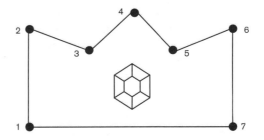

♫ Hymn: "Joy in Serving Jesus"

Sing the first verse (Worktext page 217). Emphasize that we "draw upon His power." Explain that having joy is different than just being happy. True joy for the Christian comes from knowing that we will be with the Lord in the new Jerusalem forever; this life on earth is only temporary. No matter what happens, Christians can have joy. Sing the first verse again.

♥ Memory Verse—Mark 10:45

Practice the memory verse.

Picture the Point

Illustrate usefulness. Display the vase. Discuss with the students the usefulness of a vase. Elicit from them that the vase is not useful unless it is used for the purpose for which it was made. Place a cloth over the vase and ask whether the vase is useful now. (no) Remove the cloth and place flowers in the vase. Ask whether the vase is useful now. *(yes)* Tell the students that today they will be thinking about how children can be useful to God.

Application Activity

Apply Bible knowledge to everyday life. Direct attention to the set of dots you drew. Explain that when a student gives a correct answer, he may connect two dots. If an answer is incorrect, call on another student for the answer. Read each situation listed below; then make up other situations until the crown is complete. In each situation the students must decide what the person would do if God is put first in his life. Accept any answer as long as God and others are placed before self.

Putting God and Others First

1. Amanda's mom is sick today. Her little sister Kristi keeps asking Mom to play with her. Kristi is too little to understand how sick Mom is. Amanda looks toward her room. She has a new doll. She looks at her little sister tugging on Mom's arm.
What should Amanda choose to do?

2. Derick's friend Bill comes over to play. Bill shows Derick a special coin. Later, when it's time to go, Bill notices that his coin is missing. It's lost somewhere in the back yard. Derick looks at his watch; it's time for his favorite TV program.
What should Derick choose to do?

3. Dad calls to his boys. It's time for church. Tom, Brian, and Sam run to the door. Tom, the oldest, gets there first. He almost always arrives at the door before his brother Brian and always arrives before little Sam. Tom looks at Sam. He thinks about who should go first.
What should Tom choose to do?

4. Mom asks Katie to clean up her toys from the den. Katie picks up all her toys. She goes back into the den to make sure she didn't forget any. The only things left are baby Mark's toys scattered throughout the room. Mom didn't tell her to pick up Mark's toys. Katie looks at the baby's toys.
What should Katie choose to do?

5. It's time for recess in Stephen's second-grade class. The children are lining up at the classroom door. Bob accidentally knocks a box off the shelf. The contents of the box scatter on the floor. The teacher tells Bob that as soon as he finishes putting the items back into the box, he can come out to play. Stephen looks at Bob. He looks out the window at the children already on the playground.
What should Stephen choose to do?

6. Ben's neighbor, Mrs. Smith, sweeps the leaves from her front walk every morning. Ben rides his bike and waves to Mrs. Smith every morning. Today while riding his bike, Ben notices that Mrs. Smith's front walk is full of leaves. Mother told Ben that Mrs. Smith was ill today. Ben looks at his bike, then at the leaves on Mrs. Smith's front walk.
What should Ben choose to do?

7. Esther's family has a missionary family coming to stay with them. Mother gives each of her four children a list of chores to help get the house ready for the visitors. Esther finishes her list. She had planned to go finish reading a book she had started earlier. Her younger sister Elizabeth has four more jobs on her list. Esther thinks about the book she wanted to finish reading. She looks at her sister Elizabeth.
What should Esther choose to do?

When all the dots have been connected, ask the students what they have drawn. *(a crown)* Write the word *JOY* across the front of the crown using the jewel to represent the letter *O*. Ask what putting God and others first will bring us. *(joy)*

Worktext page 82

Guide a review about Samuel and the Israelites. Read the title on the page together. Identify Samuel and God's people, the Israelites. Direct the students to read silently the speech bubbles at the top of the page.

▸ **What did Samuel say would happen if God's people and their king would fear, serve, and obey God?** *(They would continue following God.)*

▸ **What did he say would happen if they did not fear, serve, and obey God?** *(The Lord's hand would be against them.)*

▸ **What sin did God's people say they had added?** *(They had asked for a king.)*

▸ **What did they want Samuel to do for them?** *(pray so that they would not die)*

Guide the students as they complete the sentence. Continue with the following questions as they complete the bottom of the page.

Putting God First
1 Samuel 12:14–25; 13:5–14

Name _____

Read each speech bubble and complete the sentences.

> If you fear, serve, and obey God and do not go against His commandment, you and your king will continue following God. If you do not, the hand of the Lord will be against you.

> Pray for your servants so that we will not die. We have added to our sins by asking for a king.

Samuel told God's people they should

__ __ __ fear __ __ __ , __ __ serve __ __ , and __ __ obey __ __ God.

> My people were scattered. The Philistines were ready to fight us. You didn't come, so I made an offering to God before you came.

> You have done a foolish thing. You have disobeyed God. He would have set up your kingdom forever if you had obeyed, but now you will be replaced.

Saul did a __ __ foolish __ __ thing. He __ disobeyed __ God.

© BJU Press. Reproduction prohibited.

82 A Servant's Heart • Lesson 60

💡 **Did Saul fear God?** *(No. Saul rebelled against God by making the offering that God's priest should have made.)*

Guide the students as they complete the sentences.

▶ Going Beyond

Reinforcement

Materials

- A container
- Stickers or treats

Reward students with a Joy Jar. Label the container *Joy Jar* and fill it with stickers or treats. Throughout the day reward the students who show joy in their lives by what they say, by how they act, and by the attitude they show.

Enrichment

Materials

- Two craft sticks (one long, one short) for each student
- Three sheets of 9" × 12" construction paper for each student
- Felt-tip pens

Guide the production of a play with puppets. Direct the students to make stick puppets of David and Goliath, using the construction paper and craft sticks. Demonstrate how to represent the armies with construction paper. Fold two pieces of construction paper lengthwise. Explain that each fold represents the top of a mountain. Draw the Israelite army on one sheet and the Philistine army on the other sheet. Stand the mountains up with the armies facing each other and a valley between them. Each student may tell the Bible account of David and Goliath to a partner using his stick puppets.

God's Servants Serve in Love

Unit 5b

PREVIEW

Doctrines

- God is everywhere (omnipresent) (Psalm 139:7–10). [Lesson 61]
- Care for those having special needs (Acts 6:1–7; Romans 12:13). [Lesson 62]

Skills and Applications

- Learn 1 Samuel 12:24
- Read a map
- Locate verses in the Old Testament (Genesis–Habakkuk)
- Realize that serving God begins in the heart
- Demonstrate serving God from the heart (focus on attitudes)
- Demonstrate serving God by serving others (focus on actions)
- Apply Bible knowledge to everyday life

A Prince and a Shepherd Serve Together

LESSON 61

Materials

- Chart 4, "Bible Garments"
- Chart 15, "A Story of Two Friends"
- Hymn: "Joy in Serving Jesus"
- Unit 5 Bookmark for each student
- Copy of page A83 ("Serving One Another") for each student (optional)
- Highlighter for each student (optional)
- Five small hearts drawn for display
- A verse visual of four large hearts made of red construction paper with one phrase of the verse written on each

♫ Hymn: "Joy in Serving Jesus"

Teach the second verse (Worktext page 217). Read the words of the second verse. Discuss the phrase "joy that triumphs over pain." *(Lead the students in understanding that God is in control of their lives. When Christians serve God, they can have joy knowing God is with them even in a sad time [e.g., if*

they get sick or break an arm]. Maybe someone in the hospital bed beside them needs to be saved. They can have joy because they have led someone to the Lord.) Discuss the phrase "fills my soul with heaven's music." (Elicit from the students that to fill their souls with heaven's music means to fill their minds with God's Word.) Sing the second verse of the hymn.*

♥ Memory Verse—1 Samuel 12:24

Principle: Serve God from the heart. Allow the students to highlight the verse (optional) and to mark the location with the Unit 5 Bookmark.

▶ **What does God reveal about Himself in 1 Samuel 12:24?** *(God is to be feared, God is to be served, and God has done great things.)*

💡 **What does it mean for a Christian to serve God with all his heart?** *(When a Christian is given a job to do, he should do it to the best of his ability and with the right attitude because of his love for God.)*

💡 **What has God done for you?** *(Many answers are acceptable. Include in your discussion that God sent His Son to pay the penalty for our sins so that we can spend eternity with Him.)*

💡 **How can you serve God today?** *(Many answers are acceptable, but lead the students to understand that Christians are to do every task (no matter how small it seems) to the best of their ability, with the right attitude and a love for those they serve.)*

Practice the verse with a countdown activity. Choose students to hold the verse visuals. When you tap a student on the shoulder, the class will read the words on the visual held by that student. After the verse has been said, erase one of the small hearts on the board to indicate that the verse is to be recited four more times. Remember to erase one of the small hearts each time the class reads the verse. Repeat as desired during the Bible lesson or extend the repetitions throughout the day.

Background Information

Covenant—*A covenant is a solemn promise or agreement between two or more persons. Two items often seal the promise. First, a gift is given to symbolize the sincerity of the promise. Second, a witness testifies (or announces) that a promise has been made. It is a sin to break a promise. Therefore, promises are to be seriously considered before they are made. Jonathan and David sealed their promise with a gift, and though there was not a human witness in this case, God was their witness, as He is for every promise that we make* (**1 Samuel 18:1–4; 20:15–17**).

Bible Garments—*A tunic is like a big, loose undershirt. Poor people had sleeveless tunics that reached to the knees and sometimes the ankles. The rich had ankle-length tunics with sleeves. The girdle was a type of wide belt. It held the tunic at the waist. This belt was made of leather or cloth. The rich often had belts that were decorated with embroidery. The belt had a pouch in which money was kept. The belt could also hold a warrior's sword. The robe was worn by the rich. It was worn over the tunic. The robe was usually very elegant in texture, color, and style.* (See Chart 4 from the Visual Packet.)

Javelin—*The javelin is a kind of spear. It has a metal head mounted on a long wooden shaft.*

Introducing the Bible Account

Discuss what motivates our actions. Allow the students to share ways they show their parents that they love them. Elicit from the students that we show others our love by our actions. Tell the students that when Christians show love to others, they are showing God how much they love Him (see **Hebrews 6:10**).

Bible Account

Read 1 Samuel 18:1–11 and 20:1–42 or use the following retelling of those passages. Listening question: **What was the item of highest honor for a prince?** *(his sword)* Direct attention to Worktext page 83 as you speak.

A Prince and a Shepherd Serve Together

After David's victory over the Philistine giant Goliath, King Saul told David to come live in the palace. Saul gave David jobs to do, and David was an obedient servant to the king.

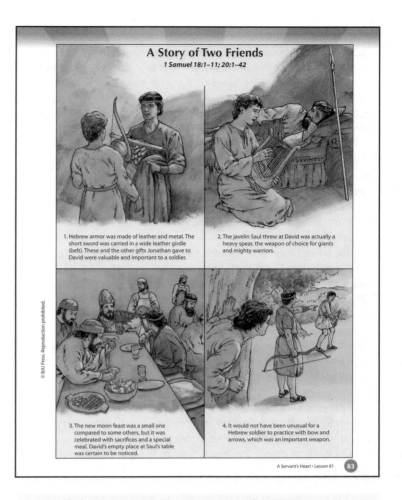

A Story of Two Friends
1 Samuel 18:1–11; 20:1–42

1. Hebrew armor was made of leather and metal. The short sword was carried in a wide leather girdle (belt). These and the other gifts Jonathan gave to David were valuable and important to a soldier.

2. The javelin Saul threw at David was actually a heavy spear, the weapon of choice for giants and mighty warriors.

3. The new moon feast was a small one compared to some others, but it was celebrated with sacrifices and a special meal. David's empty place at Saul's table was certain to be noticed.

4. It would not have been unusual for a Hebrew soldier to practice with bow and arrows, which was an important weapon.

A Servant's Heart • Lesson 61 **83**

© BJU Press. Reproduction prohibited.

David was such a faithful servant that Saul made David a leader over a part of the army.

All the people loved David. Jonathan, King Saul's son, loved David too. Jonathan wanted to make a covenant of friendship with David. To seal the covenant, Jonathan took off his princely robe and gave it to David. He gave David other royal clothing. Jonathan pulled out his warrior's sword. He handed David this item of highest honor. He also gave David his bow and his belt. What special gifts! Jonathan, without his elegant robe and expensive belt, looked more like a shepherd boy, and David looked more like a prince. Would you be willing to give up your most loved and valuable possessions for someone you love?

💡 **How did Jonathan show David his love?** *(Jonathan gave David his sword, robe, armor, bow, and belt.)*

Display Chart 4, "Bible Dress," from the Visual Packet. Point out the tunic, belt, and robe on the chart. Explain the significance of each item as described in the Background Information.

What is a covenant? *(A covenant is a solemn promise or agreement between two or more persons.)* Include in your discussion the background information concerning a covenant.

As time went on, King Saul grew jealous of David. Saul and David returned from a victorious battle against the Philistines.

The people met the army with singing. The people sang, "Saul has killed his thousands, and David his ten thousands." Saul was angry that they praised David more than they praised him.

The next day David played his harp for King Saul. Saul was still angry with David and threw a javelin at him to kill him. David quickly ran from the king's presence. In the days to come, Saul tried other ways to kill David. Saul wouldn't give up.

David went to speak to Jonathan. He wanted to know why Saul was trying to kill him. Jonathan said that David wouldn't die. Jonathan said his father had told him of all his plans. David didn't think Saul would have told Jonathan of his plan. David thought he was one step away from death. Jonathan's love for David stirred in his heart. He would do whatever he could to help David.

Together David and Jonathan planned what they would do. The next day was the beginning of a special three-day feast. David would be expected to sit at the king's table each day. But instead, David would go and hide in the field. If Saul got angry about David's absence, then he surely meant evil against David. If Saul spoke well of David, then it would be safe for David to return. Jonathan would let David know the outcome. He would come to the field with a servant boy and shoot some arrows. If he shot arrows on the near side of a rock, he would tell the boy to come back and David would know it was safe to return. If the arrows were shot beyond the rock, Jonathan would tell the boy to go get them, and then David would know he needed to flee for his life.

On the first day of the feast, Saul didn't ask Jonathan about David's absence. On the second day of the feast, Saul became angry. He asked Jonathan whether he realized that he wouldn't be the next king if David lived. Saul wanted Jonathan to bring David to him so that he could kill him.

Jonathan asked what David had done to deserve death. Saul didn't speak but threw his javelin at his son. Jonathan knew it wasn't safe for David to return: he was in grave danger. Jonathan left the room and ate nothing because of his great sadness.

The next morning, Jonathan took a boy with him to the field where David was hiding. He told the boy to run and find the arrows that he was going to shoot. Jonathan must have been sad as he loaded an arrow onto his bow. He raised his bow and let the arrow go. The boy was already running. Jonathan had shot the arrow beyond the rock. He called out to the boy that the arrow was beyond him. The boy didn't know that the message was meant for David. The boy returned the arrows to Jonathan, and Jonathan told him to return to the city.

David now came out of hiding to say goodbye to his dear friend. Tears streamed down the faces of both young men. Jonathan told David to go in peace. He knew he might not see David for a long time. He spoke with David about their promise to be kind to each other's children in the generations to come. David left to find a place of safety, and Jonathan returned to the city.

⚜

▶ **Why did Saul want to kill David?** *(He was jealous. Explain to the students that Saul wanted to kill David to get what David had: the love of the people.)*

▶ **If David lived, Jonathan would not be the next king. Why did Jonathan choose to warn David?** *(He loved David. Help the students understand that godly love is stronger than the desire for material possessions or royal positions.)*

▶ **What promise did David and Jonathan make to each other?** *(They promised to be kind to each other's children for generations to come.)*

💡 **Why should you want to help others?** *(God commands it and has helped us so much. We should help others as we have been helped. Help the students to understand that love should motivate them.)*

InfoScene: "A Story of Two Friends"

Display Chart 15 from the Visual Packet for the students to refer to throughout this unit.

📝 Worktext page 84

Apply Bible knowledge to everyday life. Guide the students as they decide which child was serving in love. You may want to discuss what the child who was *not* serving in love should have done. Guide the students in completing the page. Conclude by asking a student to read the two sentences that tell about a person with a servant's heart.

Home Assignment (optional)

Demonstrate serving others in love. Give a copy of page A83 ("Serving One Another") to each student and

read the Parent Letter aloud. Instruct a student to read the sentence in each of the boxes. Elicit ideas of what the students can do at home to serve others without being told. Explain that these are to be deeds done beyond assigned daily chores. Tell the students to take the sheet home. After they do a good deed, they are to write what they did and ask a parent to sign that section. Guide the students as they write a return date on the parent note. When the sheets are returned, allow the students to tell about their deeds of love.

LESSON
62 King David Serves

Materials
- Chart 36, "The Kingdom of Saul"
- Chart 3, "Books of the Bible: Old Testament" (optional)
- Hymn: "Joy in Serving Jesus"
- Verse visual (hearts) prepared in the previous lesson
- Pictures of people with special needs (optional)

🎵 Hymn: "Joy in Serving Jesus"
Sing the first two verses (Worktext page 217).
Choose about five volunteers to sing the word *joy* in the chorus. Tell this "Joy Choir" to stand at the front of the room. Point to them when they are to sing the word *joy*. Play the recording as you direct the entire class in singing the first two verses and the other words in the chorus.

Background Information
Saul's Palace—*The king's palace was simple. His throne room was about fifteen by twenty-four feet. Saul's home was also a fortress. It was enclosed by strong walls because Israel was often at war. The fortress enclosure was about forty by sixty yards (approximately the size of half of a football field).*

David's Palace—*King David had a lovely home. He overthrew the Jebusites that lived in Jerusalem and made this city his home. He called Jerusalem "the city of David" (**2 Samuel 5:9**). David made an alliance with Hiram, the king of Tyre. Hiram gave David the materials and craftsmen needed to build the first royal palace.*

Introducing the Bible Account
Discuss people with special needs. Show pictures of people with special needs (optional). Discuss how the people are the same and how they are different. Ask the students to close their eyes and pretend that they cannot get out of their chairs. Tell them that they would be able to walk only if they had crutches, or if they are unable to walk at all, they would need to use a wheelchair. Discuss other limitations as time allows.

💡 **Does God have a plan for the lives of people with limitations?** *(yes)*

💡 **Why did God make you?** *(God made each person for His own glory.)*

Explain that *all* God has made is for His own glory. You do not need to have special talents to serve God, only a willing heart.

Read 1 Samuel 31:1–4, 2 Samuel 4:4, and 9:1–13 or use the following retelling of the passages. Listening question: **Who had a willing heart to serve God?** *(David)* Direct attention to Chart 36, "Kingdom of Saul," as you point to the italicized locations while speaking.

King David Serves

The Philistines had come again. This time the Israelites battled against the Philistines at Mount Gilboa. The battle didn't go well. Many Israelites were killed that day, and many others ran away. David's beloved friend Jonathan was among the dead. King Saul was badly wounded by Philistine archers and, not wanting to be found by the enemy, chose to fall on his own sword. What a sad day for Israel!

The bad news that Saul and Jonathan were killed in battle reached Gibeah, Saul's home. A little prince only five years old heard the news too. He was the son of Jonathan, and his name was Mephibosheth (mə fĭb' ə shĕth). He felt sad that his father and grandfather were dead. All of the people of Saul's house ran for fear that the Philistines might attack them too. A nurse was taking care of Mephibosheth, and on hearing the bad news she quickly picked up the little prince and ran. She wanted to get them both to a place of safety. She ran so fast that she let the little prince fall. Mephibosheth's feet were hurt so badly that he became lame. The prince went to live with a very kind man. He stayed with that man for many years.

▶ **What happened at Mount Gilboa?** *(Many Israelites, including Saul and Jonathan, died in a battle against the Philistines.)*
▶ **What was the name of Jonathan's son?** *(Mephibosheth)*
▶ **What happened when the nurse fled Gibeah with Mephibosheth?** *(He fell and hurt his feet so badly that he became lame.)*

It had been many years since Samuel had anointed David as king. God let David know that it was time for him to sit on the throne. David had been serving God for many years. Now he was to serve God as king, and he asked his heavenly King for help many times.

Miles away from Mephibosheth in the royal city, Jerusalem, King David was thinking about Jonathan. Perhaps David remembered his promise to be kind to Jonathan's children. David spoke to a servant named Ziba (zē' ba), who had served in the house of Saul many years before. David asked Ziba whether anyone of Saul's family was still alive. If so, David wanted to do something kind for him.

Ziba told King David that Jonathan's son, Mephibosheth, was still living but lame in the feet. David must have been very excited to hear the news that his beloved friend Jonathan's son was still alive. David found out where Mephibosheth lived and told some men to bring him to the palace.

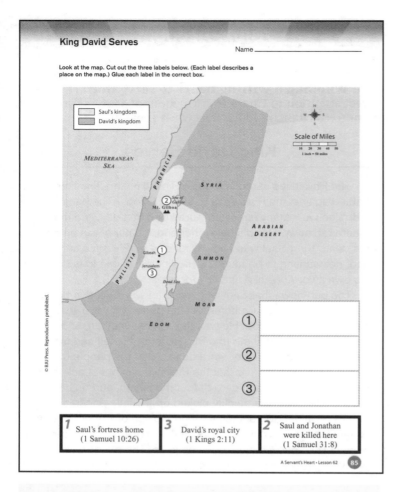

Look at the map. Cut out the three labels below. (Each label describes a place on the map.) Glue each label in the correct box.

Saul's kingdom
David's kingdom

Scale of Miles

MEDITERRANEAN SEA

PHOENICIA

SYRIA

Sea of Galilee
② Mt. Gilboa

ARABIAN DESERT

Jordan River

Gibeah ①
Jerusalem ③
PHILISTIA
AMMON

Dead Sea

MOAB

EDOM

①
②
③

1	Saul's fortress home (1 Samuel 10:26)
3	David's royal city (1 Kings 2:11)
2	Saul and Jonathan were killed here (1 Samuel 31:8)

A Servant's Heart • Lesson 62 85

© BJU Press. Reproduction prohibited.

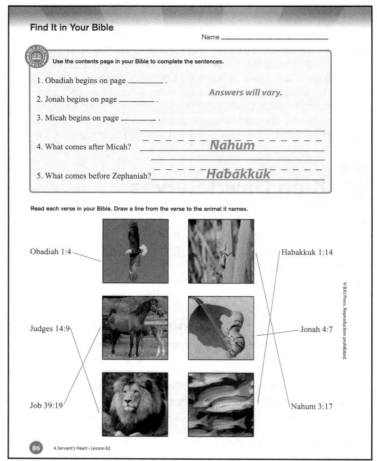

Use the contents page in your Bible to complete the sentences.

1. Obadiah begins on page _____ .

2. Jonah begins on page _____ .

3. Micah begins on page _____ .

Answers will vary.

4. What comes after Micah? _____ Nahum _____

5. What comes before Zephaniah? _____ Habakkuk _____

Read each verse in your Bible. Draw a line from the verse to the animal it names.

Obadiah 1:4

Habakkuk 1:14

Judges 14:9

Jonah 4:7

Job 39:19

Nahum 3:17

A Servant's Heart • Lesson 62 86

© BJU Press. Reproduction prohibited.

The king's men went to Mephibosheth and asked him to go to the palace. Perhaps Mephibosheth was afraid, wondering what the king of Israel wanted with him. Because Mephibosheth was the only living son of Jonathan the son of Saul, he had had a claim to the kingship of the land. Some kings in David's position would have killed any heirs (family who had claims to the throne), but David's promise to his friend Jonathan guided him.

When Mephibosheth was brought before David, he knelt in front of the king. He told David that he would be David's servant even though he was lame. Mephibosheth knew that he couldn't serve the king as other men could, but he would do his best in the ways he was able.

David was very happy to see Mephibosheth. Because Jonathan had been David's friend, he told Mephibosheth that he would be kind to him and his family. He told him that he would give him the land that had belonged to his grandfather, Saul. David invited Mephibosheth to eat at his table and offered to give him servants to help him. David appointed Ziba to help Mephibosheth take care of the land.

Mephibosheth could hardly believe what David had said. He was surprised that the king wanted to give him land, servants, and even a place at the royal table. Mephibosheth's heart rejoiced with gladness over the kindness of the king. Mephibosheth was ready to be a servant of the king, but the king of Israel was being a servant to him.

▶ **What promise had David made to Jonathan?** (*David had promised to be kind to Jonathan's children.*)

▶ **What did Mephibosheth first say to the king?** (*He would be David's servant.*) Remind the students that a person who is humble is willing to serve others.

💡 **How did David show a servant's heart toward Mephibosheth?** (*David gave him land, servants, and permission to eat at the king's table.*)

▶ **Who had a willing heart to serve God?** (*both David and Mephibosheth*)

💡 **How can Christians show a servant's heart to others?** (*Many answers are acceptable. Elicit that if they obey and serve with the right attitude, they show a servant's heart.*)

✎ Worktext page 85

Guide a map activity. Choose students to read what is in the boxes at the bottom of the page. Display Chart 36, "The Kingdom of Saul." Point to the places on the chart as the students locate the places on the map in their Worktexts. Discuss the mileage scale and talk about the approximate distances between the places. Remind the students that most of the people walked from place to place in those days. (Try to relate these distances with distances with which the students may be familiar.) Direct the students to cut the boxes from the bottom of the page and glue them in the correct places.

♥ Memory Verse—1 Samuel 12:24

Practice the memory verse. Read the verse aloud as the students read silently. Direct four students to stand at the front of the classroom. Distribute the heart verse visuals to students who are sitting at their desks. Tell the students who are sitting that when you say the word *serve*, they are to give their visuals to a student standing in the front of the room so that the verse is in the correct order. Lead the class in saying the verse. If you choose to repeat the activity, tell the students standing with the verse visuals to serve their visual to a student who is sitting. Choose another group of students to come to the front of the room and repeat the activity as time allows.

✎ Bible Study Skills, Worktext page 86

Locate the books of the Old Testament. Direct the students to open their Bibles to the contents page of the Old Testament or display Chart 3, "Books of the Bible: Old Testament." Read the list of Old Testament books, Genesis through Habakkuk, together. Guide the students as they answer the questions on Worktext page 86.

Locate Bible verses. Direct the students to use the contents page to locate each book. Guide the students in locating the verses listed at the bottom of page 86. Instruct the students to read the verse and match it to the correct animal. You may choose to let the students work together in pairs to complete the page.

LESSON 63

In Love Serve One Another

Materials
- Hymn: "Joy in Serving Jesus"
- Verse visual (hearts) from Lesson 61
- A stapler (optional)

♫ Hymn: "Joy in Serving Jesus"

Sing the first two verses (Worktext page 217). Form a double choir by dividing the class into two groups. Tell the class that each choir will sing a phrase of the first verse. Lead each choir by pointing to the group when it is its turn to sing. Direct both choirs to sing the chorus. Repeat the procedure for the second verse.

Choir 1—"There is joy in serving Jesus
Choir 2—As I journey on my way,
Choir 1—Joy that fills my heart with praises
Choir 2—Every hour and every day."
All—Chorus

♥ Memory Verse—1 Samuel 12:24

Practice the memory verse. Review the verse together. Direct the students to put their heads down and close their eyes. Explain that you will distribute the heart verse visuals to those who are quiet. Tell them to open their eyes when you say the word *love*. Say the word *love*. Direct students

with the visuals to come to the front of the classroom and arrange themselves in order. Lead the class in reciting the verse. Repeat as time allows.

✏ Worktext pages 87–90

Discuss choices in serving. Ask the students what would come to mind first if their mothers asked them to clean their rooms. Explain to the students that when God gives them an opportunity for service they have two choices. Elicit that the two choices are serving God or not serving God. Tell the students that they are going to assemble a booklet today that will help them learn more about these choices.

Assemble the booklet. Instruct the students to cut on the solid lines. Demonstrate how the pages are to be ordered. Staple the booklet on the left side.

Introduce the booklet by discussing the cover. Direct a student to read the question. Allow the students to tell what they think love for others is. Point out that love for others is more than just a feeling.

Guide the reading of page 1. Direct the class to read the words in the heart and one student to read the verse. Lead the class in discussing the following:

💡 **What does God want Christians to fill their minds with?** *(God wants Christians to fill their minds with His Word. If they think the way God thinks, then they will know how to love others.)*

💡 **Whom should you think about first, yourself or others?** *(Christians are not serving God unless they first have a love for others as Christ did when He died for the sins of the world.)*

Guide the reading of page 2. Direct one student to read the thought in the caption on the left and another student to read the caption on the right. Discuss the pictures.

💡 **If the boy thinks about only himself, what will he probably do?** *(not share the bat and ball)*

💡 **If the boy thinks about what God says about serving others, what will he likely do?** *(share)*

💡 **Why should you share your toys?** *(You share because it is the right thing to do; it is a way to show that you love others.)*

Guide the reading of page 3. Direct the class to read the words in the heart and one student to read the verse. Lead the class in discussing the following:

💡 **How often do you tell your friends about God?** *(Answers will vary.)*

💡 **What should we tell our friends about God?** *(that God loves them, cares and provides for them, that He died for their sins and will save them if they trust in Him)*

Guide the reading of page 4. Direct one student to read the caption on the left and another student to read the caption on the right. Discuss the pictures.

- **If the girl speaks in an angry voice to her friend, is she speaking in love?** (*No. Perhaps she is thinking that the mess is an inconvenience to her.*)
- **The girl has another choice. What should she think about first?** (*She should think about how God wants her to respond. Elicit that if the students think of a biblical example, it will help them make the right choice.*)
- **If the girl has a godly response, what will she do?** (*She will help her friend and not make her feel bad about the accident.*)

Guide the reading of page 5. Direct the class to read the words in the heart and one student to read the verse. Lead the class in discussing the following:

- **What does the word *act* mean?** (*To act means "to take action, do something."*)
- ▶ **What does 1 Samuel 12:24 say about serving God?** (*We are to serve God in truth and with all our hearts. We are to remember all the things that God has done for us.*) Point out that we will become humble when we focus on Who God is and what He has done for us.
- **What has God done for us?** (*Many answers are acceptable. Include in the discussion that God gave His Son to die on the cross in our place so that we may have eternal life by trusting Christ.*)

Guide the reading of page 6. Direct one student to read the caption on the left and another student to read the caption on the right. Discuss the pictures.

- **If the boy thinks only about himself, will he sweep the walk?** (*no*)
- **If the boy thinks about what God says about serving others, what will he do?** (*He will sweep the walk.*)
- **Why should you do things for others?** (*God commands us to.*)
- **How do others feel when you do something for them?** (*They feel happy and thankful. Point out that sometimes others may not thank us. Remind them that God will reward us for our loving deeds in other ways.*)
- **How do you feel when you do something for others?** (*Many answers are acceptable. Point out that when we do things for others, it gives us joy too.*)

Guide the reading of page 7. Direct the students to read the three phrases that remind them about the meaning of love. Discuss the picture.

Direct the students to take the booklets home and share them with their families.

Thinking of Others

Materials
- Hymn: "Joy in Serving Jesus"

🎵 Hymn: "Joy in Serving Jesus"
Sing the first two verses (Worktext page 217).

❤ Memory Verse—1 Samuel 12:24
Practice the memory verse.

Introducing the Application Story
Guide a discussion about winning. Discuss the following questions. (*Answers will vary.*)

- **Have you ever won anything?**
- **How does it feel to win?**
- **How does it feel to lose?**

Application Story

Read or tell the following story. Listening question: **Does Stephen win a prize?** (*Yes, he wins a sword.*)

The Winning Event

"Is it time to go yet?" Stephen asked his parents. Stephen's school was having a field day. He was going to compete against other boys in the soccer kick and the softball throw. There were going to be races and a carnival too. Stephen's whole family would go. There would be things for Stephen's brothers to do too. Caleb was six, and Michael was three.

Finally Dad spoke the words Stephen had been waiting for: "Line up at the door."

Stephen and his brothers scrambled for the door. The day had started out rather gloomy; Mother came at the back of the line, carrying raincoats just in case there was a downpour.

Mother handed each of the boys a little bag. "This is for the prizes you win at the carnival," she said.

Dad motioned for everyone to go to the van. On the way to the field, Stephen thought about the ribbons he had won last year. He got one ribbon for first place and one for second place. He hoped to win some ribbons again this year.

The family arrived at the field. Stephen went to find his class, and the rest of the family went to sit in the stands for the opening ceremonies. All the classes paraded around the track. One student in each class carried a flag, and another student carried a bunch of green and white balloons. Stephen didn't get to hold the flag. He didn't get to hold the bunch of green and white balloons. But he didn't mind because he looked forward to winning some ribbons. After the prayer, Stephen went to find his parents. Stephen's events weren't scheduled until later in the morning, so his family went to the carnival. The family went from booth to booth. Stephen and Caleb won many prizes and put their treasures into the little bags Mother had given to them. But Michael didn't win many prizes.

"I want a sword," Michael said, pulling on Mother's arm.

Stephen and Caleb had each won a sword. Michael looked longingly at the little plastic swords. "Mom, could I try to win a sword for Michael?" Stephen asked.

"That would be nice," said Mother. "Which booth has swords as prizes?"

Stephen pointed to a booth where two swords were left. The game had three hoops placed on the grass. There were three lawn darts. Stephen would have to get at least one dart in one of the circles to win the sword. The girl at the booth handed him three darts. He was just about to toss the first dart when the girl stopped him.

"What grade are you in?" asked the girl.

"I'm in second grade," said Stephen.

The girl backed Stephen up farther from the hoops. He glanced at Mother and Dad. "Just try your best," said Dad.

Stephen tossed the first lawn dart. It went in the circle and then bounced out. That was the problem with lawn darts. If they were tossed too hard, they bounced.

The girl tried to encourage him. "Toss it gently," she said.

Stephen tossed the second lawn dart. But it too went into the circle and bounced out again. Only one dart was left. He tossed it slowly. Plop! It came down on the grass with only a little bounce. But this time it stayed in the circle! Cheers went up. Michael clapped his hands. The girl handed Stephen a sword. He handed it to Michael.

Michael beamed with delight. "Thank you," he said.

The weather got colder, and Mother took the two younger boys home. Stephen and his Dad stayed for the events. When Dad and Stephen returned home, Stephen's head drooped as he walked in the door.

"No ribbons?" asked Mother.

"No," replied Stephen.

"Well, you know," said Dad, "you did win in a very important way today."

"What do you mean?" Stephen asked as he looked up.

"Do you remember what you did for Michael this morning?" said Dad. "That was better than any ribbon you could have won in any event. You won the event of helping someone you love. Jesus said that we're to love others as we love ourselves. That means we'll do things that are kind. You were right on target with that one today!" Michael came bounding into the kitchen with his treasured sword.

Stephen smiled and took his own sword out of his bag. "Want to play with me?" he asked Michael.

Michael ran toward his big brother. "On guard," said Stephen and raised his sword, ready for battle.

▸ **What did Stephen think he would win?** *(ribbons)*

▸ **Did he win any ribbons?** *(no)*

▸ **What did Stephen do for Michael?** *(won a sword for him)*

 Why do you think Stephen won the sword for his brother? *(Many answers may be acceptable, but elicit that Stephen did it because he loved his brother.)*

▸ **What was the best reward Stephen won at field day?** *(Stephen's reward was not only winning the sword for Michael but also seeing the delight on his younger brother's face. Point out that when we serve others, the intangible rewards can give as much joy as those that are tangible.)*

 Why should you help other people? *(God commands it, and it shows you love them.)*

▶ Going Beyond

Reinforcement

Create situations for service. Think of some situations that you can create in your classroom for service besides the regular classroom jobs. Do not let the students know what you are doing ahead of time, but you may choose to explain later. These situations would cause the students to make a choice to serve or not to serve. Some of these situations happen naturally in the classroom. Some suggestions are given below. When a student comes to help, say to him, "Thank you for serving." Ask him why he helped you. When situations arise where one student helps another student without being asked, thank the student for serving.

> Drop a book, pencil, or piece of chalk.
> After sitting down, say, "I left my _____ on my desk."
> Leave an object on a shelf or table easily seen. Say, "Does anyone see my _____?"
> Say, "I need a pencil." (or crayon, scissors, paper towel, and so on)

Enrichment

Materials

- Heavy paper or oak tag
- Two large paper clips for each student
- Colored markers (optional)
- Glitter (optional)

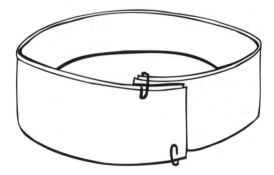

Guide the construction of a Jonathan belt. Cut six-inch-wide strips from heavy paper, such as oak tag. Cut the strips long enough to fit around the students' waists and to overlap about four inches. Distribute the strips to the students and direct them to fold the strips in half lengthwise. Explain that the open side is the top. Tell them that people in Bible times would have places in the belt to hold items and put their money. Direct the students to decorate one side of the belt. You may want to provide colorful markers or glitter. Hold the belts in place around the students' waists with two large paper clips.

God Can Use Me

Unit 5c

PREVIEW

Doctrines

• Man has hope (Philippians 3:20–21). [Lesson 65]
• God calls men through men (Romans 10:14–15). [Lesson 66]

Skills and Applications

• Learn 1 Chronicles 28:20*a*
• Recall facts and details
• Identify and locate the last four books of the Old Testament
• Sequence events
• Recognize that all believers can serve God
• Recognize that God's servants can know and live God's way
• Apply Bible knowledge to everyday life

LESSON 65   God Uses a Servant Girl

Materials

• Chart 37, "Divided Kingdom"
• Hymn: "Joy in Serving Jesus"
• Unit 5 Bookmark
• Highlighter for each student (optional)
• Verse visual of 1 Chronicles 28:20*a* using five different colors of 12" × 18" construction paper with each part of the verse on a different color of paper:
  "And David said to Solomon his son"
  "Be strong and of good courage, and do it"
  "fear not, nor be dismayed"
  "for the Lord God, even my God, will be with thee"
  "he will not fail thee, nor forsake thee."

♫ Hymn: "Joy in Serving Jesus"

Teach the third verse (Worktext page 217). Read and discuss the phrase "As I walk alone with God." Explain that to walk with God conveys the ideas of wanting to please God alone, knowing Him better than you do your best friend, and obeying Him in every area of your life. Point out that Christians can have joy in finding things out about Who God is by reading their Bibles. Remind students that human friends may fail them, but joy can always be found in knowing our loving God.

Background Information

Solomon—*King David's son Solomon became the third king of Israel. Solomon built a beautiful temple for God. God granted Solomon more wisdom than any other king that was before or after him. This wisdom was a gracious gift to a man who was sometimes obedient and sometimes disobedient. God is always ready to show Christians what He wants them to do in any situation. All they need to do is ask, just as Solomon did. When they search God's Word, He will show them the answer.*

After Solomon died, Israel returned to its sinful ways. Because of Solomon's sin, Israel was divided into two nations. The northern nation was Israel, and the southern nation was Judah. Each nation had its own king. Over the next eighty years, there were nine different kings in Israel. None of them obeyed God. They refused to submit to the King of Kings.

Introducing the Bible Account

Review the kings of Israel. Display Chart 37, "The Divided Kingdom," and locate Israel, Judah, and Syria.

▶ **Who were the first two kings of Israel?** *(Saul, David)*

Bible Account

Read 2 Kings 5:1–4 or use the following retelling of the passage. Listening question: **What is the name of the prophet that Naaman was told could make him well?** *(Elisha)*

God Uses a Servant Girl

Jehoram was king of Israel. God sent the prophet Elisha to be God's messenger during the reign of Jehoram. You would think that Jehoram and Elisha would have worked closely together. But Jehoram, like many of the kings before him, did not obey God.

During the reign of Jehoram, the nation of Syria caused a great deal of trouble for Israel. Sometimes Syria sent armies into the Israelite villages that were near the Syrian border. The Syrians often took some of the Israelites, especially women and children, back to Syria. These women and children became slaves to the Syrians. One day a little girl was taken from her home in Israel. The soldiers took this little girl and other captives to Syria.

The captain of the Syrian army was Naaman. He was an important man. Naaman was given a lot of responsibility by the king of Syria. Naaman must have won many victories for the king. The king was proud to have such a mighty man of valor heading up his armies. Naaman was also a rich man. He probably had a big house with many servants. Naaman chose a girl from the captives to be a servant for his wife. That was how this little girl found herself living and serving in the house of this important man.

Naaman might have been a great man, but all those that looked at him were saddened by what they saw. Naaman had a terrible disease. He had leprosy. The little maid probably knew there was no cure for leprosy. Those that had the dreadful disease saw their fingers and toes rot away and fall off. The disease spread throughout the whole body and brought death.

The little maid must have felt sad when she looked at Naaman. Perhaps as she waited on Naaman's wife she saw sadness in her eyes also. It was probably through her parents that she had learned about God and about His prophet Elisha. God gave Elisha power to heal others. If the little girl would share this good news, her master could be healed.

The little maid went to her mistress and told her that she wished that Naaman would go to the prophet who lived in Samaria.

If Naaman would go, Elisha would cure him of his leprosy. This news must have given hope to Naaman's wife. She sent word of this hope to Naaman. He had a chance to be healed! God had sent a little maid away from her family to give this family hope. Naaman could be cured if he would listen to the voice of God given through this little maid. In the next lesson we will find out what Naaman did.

God Uses A Servant Girl
2 Kings 5:1–4

Name _____

Number the sentences to show the order in which the events happened.

1. __3__ An Israelite girl was a servant of Naaman's wife.
2. __4__ The girl wanted her master to go to the prophet of God.
3. __2__ Naaman brought Israelite captives to Syria.
4. __5__ Naaman was told what the girl said about the prophet.
5. __1__ The Syrians defeated the Israelites.

Serve God Now

You do not have to wait until you are grown up to serve God. Read each of these verses to discover the name of a child who served God. Write each name on the lines.

1. 1 Samuel 3:1 ___ *Samuel*
2. 1 Samuel 17:49 ___ *David*
3. 2 Kings 11:21; 12:2 ___ *Jehoash*
4. 2 Chronicles 34:1, 3 ___ *Josiah*

Think of one thing you can do to serve God today. Write it here.

_____
Answers will vary.
_____

© BJU Press. Reproduction prohibited.

A Servant's Heart • Lesson 65 **91**

💡 **Did all the kings who lived after Solomon serve God?** *(No, most of them did not.)* **Why not?** *(Answers will vary. Explain that there are only two choices in service. One is serving God, and the other is serving self. Those kings chose to serve self.)*

▶ **How did the country of Syria trouble Israel?** *(Syria raided the Israelite villages and took people captive.)*

💡 **Why didn't the little girl need to be afraid when she was taken captive?** *(God was in control. He was with her even in Syria.)*

▶ **How did the little maid serve God in Syria?** *(She told her mistress about God's man who had power to heal. Point out that this maid did not need special abilities to give hope to this family. She pointed this family to her God, Who had power to meet their needs. She also lived in such a way that caused people to believe what she said.)*

💡 **How can you serve God today?** *(Answers will vary. Point out that service does not require special abilities. Sharing the good news of salvation is serving God. Helping someone who has a need and giving a word of encouragement to those who are sad are ways to serve God.)*

🖊 Worktext page 91

Sequence events. Review the Bible account. Explain the directions for the top of the page. **Apply Bible knowledge to everyday life.** Explain the directions for the two sections at the bottom of the page. Direct the students to complete the page independently. Read the student's service suggestions and provide guidance as needed.

❤ Memory Verse—1 Chronicles 28:20a

Principle: God will help me serve Him. Explain that David is speaking to his son Solomon about building the temple. Direct the students to highlight the verse (optional) and to mark the location with the Unit 5 Bookmark.

▶ **Who would be with Solomon as he built the temple?** *(God)*

💡 **Is serving God always easy?** *(No. Sometimes things can be very hard and may not work out just the way we want them to.)*

💡 **Will God ever stop helping you if you are serving Him?** *(no)*

💡 **As God helped Solomon, what should Solomon have been thinking and doing?** *(Tell the students that there are five commands given in the verse. List the key words for display as you elicit the following from the students: "Be strong," "Be courageous," "Do it," "Don't be afraid," "Don't be dismayed.")*

Practice the memory verse. Write seven blanks for display. Each blank represents a letter in the word *servant*. Write the *e* and the *a* in their places (_ e _ _ a _ _). Choose five students to hold the verse visuals at the front of the classroom. Direct them to take one step forward each time their phrase is read. Lead the class in saying the verse together.

Direct attention to the blanks you wrote. Tell students they will recite the verse again, pausing after each phrase to allow two students to guess a missing letter for the word. Choose two students to guess a letter: one student from the group holding the visuals and one student at his desk. Explain that if the letter guessed is part of the word, you will write it in the blank. Write the letter of any incorrect guesses for display so that they will not be repeated. Tell the students to raise their hands whenever they know the secret word. Allow a different group of students to hold the visuals for each recitation. Continue reciting the verse until the secret word is completed.

LESSON 66 A Captain Becomes a Servant

Materials
- Hymn: "Joy in Serving Jesus"
- A cake mix or recipe
- One small square of construction paper for each student: Use the same five colors used for the verse visual in the previous lesson. Prepare the same number of squares for each of the five colors. *(Note: These squares will be used again in the next lesson.)*

Background Information

Weights Used in the Old Testament—*Naaman took ten talents of silver with him to give Elisha for the healing of his leprosy (**2 Kings 5:5**). A talent is not a coin but a unit of weight. A talent weighed between 75 and 160 pounds and was the largest unit of weight measurement among the Hebrews. The Bible says Naaman took ten talents of silver with him, but in colloquial English we might say he took a "ton of money" with him—a sum large enough to buy a big house, several cars, or thousands of computers.*

The Tearing of Clothes—*In Bible times, people tore their clothing as an outward sign of great inner grief.*

Introducing the Bible Account

Discuss following directions. Read the directions on the cake mix or the recipe to the students. Ask them whether they think it matters if you decide to leave the eggs out and use chocolate milk or orange juice instead of the liquid ingredient called for. Point out that if you want to have the cake turn out right you need to follow the directions. In today's Bible account, we will learn about one man who learned to follow God's directions.

Bible Account

Read 2 Kings 5:5–16 or use the following retelling of the passage. Remind the students that they learned about a young maid who was serving God in faraway Syria. She served the wife of the mighty Captain Naaman of the Syrian army. She had told her mistress that Naaman could be healed of his leprosy if he would go to see the prophet in Samaria. Listening question: **Who had to learn to humble himself?** *(Naaman)*

A Captain Becomes a Servant

Naaman went to tell the king of Syria this good news. The king, however, didn't want to send Naaman to the prophet. He sent Naaman to King Jehoram of Israel. In those days people thought that the king was the most powerful man in the land. Those earthly kings had forgotten about a king greater than they were. So the king of Syria sent Naaman to the king of Israel. But Naaman didn't go emptyhanded. The king of Syria sent a letter to be given to the king of Israel. Naaman took ten talents of silver and six thousand pieces of gold. He also took ten different changes of clothing. These were probably made from the finest materials. It was clothing fit for a king!

Naaman finally arrived at the palace of Jehoram, the king of Israel. His chariot and horses were laden with treasures to be given to the one who would free him of his disease. Naaman presented the letter to King Jehoram of Israel. Jehoram must have been very suspicious of this Syrian. Remember that the countries of Syria and Israel weren't friends. Syria often raided the Israelite villages.

Jehoram read the letter. The letter said that Naaman was a servant of the king of Syria. It asked the king of Israel to cure Naaman of his leprosy. After reading the letter, Jehoram tore his clothes! He asked if the king of Syria thought that the king of Israel was God. Only God could kill and make alive again. He thought that the king of Syria was trying to start an argument. Maybe the king of Syria wanted to start a war with Israel. Jehoram didn't know what to do.

Elisha heard that Naaman had come to the king to be cured of leprosy and that the king tore his clothes because he didn't know what to do. Elisha told the king to send Naaman to him. Naaman would soon know that there was a prophet in Israel.

Soon Naaman came to Elisha. Along with him came a parade of servants, horses, and fine gifts. To Naaman's surprise, Elisha's servant answered the door. The servant told Naaman

to go wash in the Jordan River seven times and he would be cured. However Naaman turned and walked away. He was angry!

Naaman thought that Elisha himself should have come out to meet him. Naaman wanted Elisha to come out and call on his God, wave his hand over Naaman, and cure him of his disease. Naaman expected a great display to be made in curing him. God knew that Naaman had to learn an important lesson first.

Naaman didn't want to wash in the dirty Jordan River. In spite of his rage, Naaman's servants came and spoke quietly and respectfully to him. The prophet had given Naaman such a simple assignment: wash and be healed. Finally, they convinced him, and he humbled himself.

Naaman went to the Jordan River and dipped himself one time, two times, three, four, five, six times! No change came until he obeyed and dipped seven times. When Naaman came up the seventh time, his skin was healthy like that of a little child, and he was cured. Naaman was filled with joy and so were his servants who saw the miracle.

Naaman and his company returned to the home of the prophet. Naaman stood before Elisha himself this time. Naaman was not only healed from a physical disease, he was also healed from something worse than leprosy. Naaman told Elisha, "Behold, now I know that there is no God in all the earth, but in Israel." Something very important had just happened. Naaman had acknowledged the God of Israel as the only God.

Naaman wanted to show his gratitude. He wanted to give Elisha all the wonderful gifts he had brought with him. Elisha declined, saying he wouldn't take anything.

Naaman came to Israel as a master and mighty warrior. He returned to Syria a humble servant of the living God.

▶ **Why would Elisha not take anything?** *(Elisha wanted Naaman to know that God's healing is a gift from God. It cannot be bought with silver or gold.)*

▶ **What gifts did Naaman take to give to the king of Israel?** *(He took ten talents of silver, six thousand pieces of gold, and ten changes of fine clothing.)* Discuss the background information concerning a talent.

💡 **Do you think that if King Jehoram had known God he would have torn his clothes?** *(No. He would have known right away that Elisha could have helped.)* Discuss the background information concerning the meaning of tearing of clothing.

💡 **Why was Naaman angry?** *(He wanted to be healed his own way. But this was not God's way. Point out that Naaman would not have been cured by only partly obeying God.)*

▶ **Whom did God use to calm Naaman's anger and help him obey?** *(Naaman's own servants)*

▶ **What was the most important thing that happened to Naaman that day?** *(He acknowledged the God of Israel as the only God. He had to learn to humble himself so that God could work in his life and use him. He had to become a servant instead of a master.)*

A Captain Becomes a Servant
2 Kings 5:1–16   Name _____

Write the letter of the correct person next to each sentence. (Answers can be used more than one time.)

a. Elisha   b. servant girl   c. Naaman   d. King Jehoram

1. __b__ I told Naaman's wife that the prophet in Israel could heal Naaman.

2. __c__ I had leprosy.

3. __d__ I tore my clothes when I read a letter from the king of Syria.

4. __c__ I obeyed God by washing in the Jordan River seven times.

5. __a__ I wanted Naaman to know that there was a God in Israel.

6. __c__ I went home to Syria a humble servant of the living God.

Color the pot of silver if the answer is *YES*.
Color the parchment if the answer is *NO*.   YES   NO

1. Israel was divided into two nations. One was Israel and the other was Judah.

2. Jehoram was the king of Israel.

3. Samuel was the prophet during the reign of Jehoram.

4. The country of Syria was very kind to the people of Israel.

5. An Israelite girl was a servant of the wife of the captain of the Syrian army.

92   A Servant's Heart • Lesson 66

💡 **For God to use you, Who must be master of your life?** *(God)*

💡 **How do Christians learn how to serve God?** *(Many answers may be acceptable. Elicit that they must first fill their minds with God's Word by reading it and memorizing it. If their minds are filled with God's Word, the words that come out of their mouths will be what God wants. They will do things that please God. In other words, they must think "not my will but Thine be done." Remind them that humility yields service and gratitude.)*

🔲 Worktext page 92

Recall facts and details. Read the directions at the top of the page and the name choices. Guide the students as they match the name to the correct person described. Read the directions at the bottom of the page to the students. Guide the students as they determine the correct answers. For sentences 3 and 4, ask a student to give the correct information.

🎵 Hymn: "Joy in Serving Jesus"

Sing the third verse (Worktext page 217). Read and explain the phrase " 'Tis the joy of Christ, my Savior, / Who the path of suffering trod."

💡 **What was Christ's path of suffering?** *(the cross)*

💡 **Why did Christ choose this path?** *(He loved us. We are sinners, and only His blood sacrifice could open the way for us to get to heaven.)*

Joy in Serving Jesus (verse 3)

Practice the words using American Sign Language.
Sing the third verse of the hymn using the signs.

There is joy in serving Jesus,

As I walk alone with God;

'Tis the joy of Christ my Savior

Who the path of suffering trod.

A Servant's Heart • Lesson 66   93

Joy in Serving Jesus (chorus)

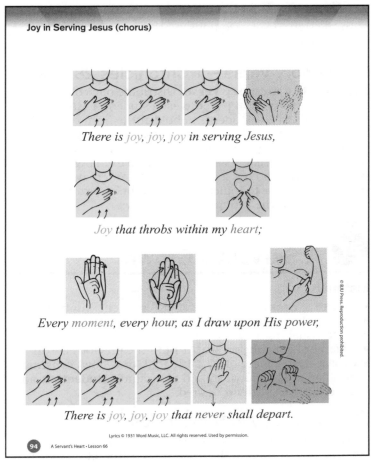

There is joy, joy, joy in serving Jesus,

Joy that throbs within my heart;

Every moment, every hour, as I draw upon His power,

There is joy, joy, joy that never shall depart.

94   A Servant's Heart • Lesson 66

💡 **How could Christ have joy in suffering for sinners?** *(He loved us, and it was His Father's will.)*

🔊 **Worktext pages 93–94**

Sing the third verse of the hymn in sign language.
Direct the students' attention to Worktext page 93. Tell them that they will use American Sign Language for some of the key words in the third verse of the hymn. Read the verse and demonstrate the following signs, pausing for the students to make each sign with you.

- **joy**—open right hand; pat the chest with an upward motion
- **Jesus**—touch the end of the middle finger on the right hand to the left palm; then touch the left middle finger to the right palm [represents nailprints]
- **walk**—open hands, palm downward; move hands forward and downward alternately
- **God**—hand closed, pointing to the sky with index finger; bring hand down while opening hand; touch thumb to chest [shows that God comes to dwell in man]
- **Savior**—begin with the letter S, shown by both hands (closed) with wrists crossed and facing yourself; move hands to the sides and facing outward [represents being bound and then free]; then bring hands down with palms facing inward to add the "person" ending
- **path**—move both hands forward with a zigzag motion
- **trod**—same as **walk** above

Sing the third verse with the signs. You may want to sing without the recording, singing slowly enough to help the students learn the signs. Direct attention to Worktext page 94. Repeat the signs for *joy* and *Jesus* from above.

Demonstrate the following signs for the chorus.

- **heart**—move index fingers (or middle fingers) to trace a heart shape on the chest
- **moment**—left hand open and pointing up with palm facing right; close the right hand except for the thumb and index finger; place the right thumb and index finger against the left palm; move the index finger clockwise slightly [similar to one tick of the second hand of a clock]
- **hour**—left hand open and pointing up with palm facing right; close the right hand except for the thumb and index finger; place the right thumb and index finger against the left palm; move the index finger clockwise and rotate the wrist to make a circle [represents the hour hand of a clock]
- **power**—touch shoulders with hands (right to right and left to left); pull hands away; make the letter S shown by both hands [Note: The illustration in Worktext is not the ASL sign for this word.]
- **never**—open right hand with palm down; move the hand clockwise (up, right, down, left); then abruptly down
- **depart**—begin with open hands in front of you and to the left; palms downward; and fingertips forward; move both hands back toward yourself and up into the letter A position (closed hands facing outward)

Lead the students as they practice each sign. Sing the chorus with the signs. (*Note:* Do not send these pages home until the end of Unit 5.)

❤ Memory Verse—1 Chronicles 28:20*a*

Practice the memory verse. Distribute one colored square of construction paper to each student. Distribute the verse visuals to five students to hold at the front of the classroom. As you point to each verse visual, direct the students with the matching color square at their desks to say the phrase. Tell the students at their desks to exchange squares with someone who has a different color. You may want to use the word *serve* to indicate that it is time to exchange squares. Repeat the activity as time allows.

67 A Servant's Crown

Materials
- Chart 3, "Books of the Bible: Old Testament" (optional)
- Hymn: "Joy in Serving Jesus"
- Verse visual from Lesson 65
- Squares of construction paper from the previous lesson
- Crown from a piece of 9" × 12" gold (or yellow) construction paper: The crown should fit around a student's head. Decorate with glitter if desired.

🎵 Hymn: "Joy in Serving Jesus"

Sing the first three verses (Worktext page 217). Lead the students in singing the third verse using sign language.

❤ Memory Verse—1 Chronicles 28:20*a*

Practice the memory verse. Read the verse together. Distribute the colored squares used in the previous lesson. Choose five students to hold the verse visuals at the front of the classroom. Instruct the students to push back their chairs from their desks so that they can stand quickly and quietly when it is their turn. Repeat the activity from the previous lesson. Tell the students you will indicate when they are to stand (point up) and to sit (point down). Stand behind the student with the first visual (point up). Direct the students with the same color construction paper as the visual to stand and say the phrase. Point down when they are finished and continue with the next verse visual phrase. Lead the class in saying the verse. Allow the students to exchange squares and repeat the activity as time allows.

Introducing the Application Story

Guide a discussion about crowns. Place the paper crown on a student's head. Call on students to tell what they know about different crowns.

💡 **Do all crowns look the same?** *(no)*
💡 **May just anyone wear a real crown?** *(No. Elicit that usually only members of royalty wear crowns.)*

Remove the crown from the student's head.

Read or tell the following story. Listening question: **What type of people get to wear a crown?** *(Those who help others.)*

A Servant's Crown

There once was a boy who lived in a fine house. He had two servants to help him. Each servant had a golden crown, but the little boy had no crown. The servants were very kind to the little boy. They loved him very much. The three had many happy times together.

Each morning the little boy would wake up and lie in his bed. He could hear one servant humming a happy tune as he worked outside the boy's bedroom door. He could smell the pancakes that the other servant was cooking on the griddle in the kitchen. The little boy's tummy rumbled. He always was eager to eat the pancakes being prepared for him.

As soon as the boy hopped out of bed, the servant who was working in the hall opened the bedroom door. He greeted the little boy with a happy smile and kind words. The servant's crown shone in the morning sunlight as he raised the window shades. The little boy often wondered why he didn't have a crown too, but he never asked.

The little boy dressed and went to the kitchen for breakfast. The servant there placed big, fluffy pancakes in front of him. The boy ate and ate until he could hold no more. The servant smiled at the little boy and swept the crumbs from the floor. The little boy got out of his chair and went to the door. The servant smiled and opened the door for him. With the door open, the kitchen was flooded with the morning sun. The little boy looked up at the servant and smiled. The boy noticed again the loveliness of the crown on the servant's head. Again he wondered why he didn't have a crown too. He went out to play and had a wonderful day. But sometimes he would stop and touch his head and wonder why he had no crown.

▶ **Who waited on the little boy?** *(two servants)*
▶ **What did the little boy do all day?** *(play)*
▶ **What did the little boy wonder about?** *(why he had no crown)*
💡 **Why do you think the servants had crowns but the boy had no crown?** *(Any answer is acceptable at this point.)*
💡 **Do you think the servants liked their jobs?** *(yes)*
💡 **How do you know that the servants were happy with their work?** *(They loved the boy and were kind to him; they had many happy times together; one servant hummed happy tunes as he worked; they spoke kindly and smiled at the boy.)*

One morning the little boy woke up earlier than usual. He lay in bed for a minute, but he didn't hear the servant humming a happy tune. He didn't smell the pancakes cooking on the griddle in the kitchen. The little boy's tummy rumbled. He jumped out of bed, dressed, and went to the kitchen. On

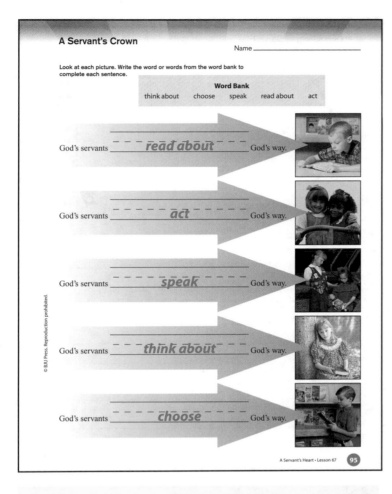

A Servant's Crown

Name_____

Look at each picture. Write the word or words from the word bank to complete each sentence.

Word Bank

think about   choose   speak   read about   act

God's servants ___*read about*___ God's way.

God's servants ___*act*___ God's way.

God's servants ___*speak*___ God's way.

God's servants ___*think about*___ God's way.

God's servants ___*choose*___ God's way.

© BJU Press. Reproduction prohibited.

A Servant's Heart · Lesson 67 **95**

---

the table was a bowl of cereal and a note saying that one of the servants was sick in bed and the other servant had to help the sick servant. The little boy ran to the servant's room and lightly knocked on the door. The door was opened, and the little boy walked quietly to the bedside and held the sick servant's hand. The boy noticed the other servant sitting in a chair making a list. The little boy walked over and looked over the servant's shoulder to read the list. It was a list of things to do. The little boy smiled as he saw some things on the list that he could do. One item read, "Get clean bed sheets." The boy quietly left the room. He returned a few minutes later with clean bedding. The servant smiled. He took the clean sheets from the little boy and crossed off "Get clean bed sheets" from the list.

The little boy worked all day. He helped take care of the sick servant, and he helped take care of the house. When the little boy climbed into bed that night, he was very tired. *[Place the crown on the same student's head.]* He went to scratch his head, but something more than just hair was there. Gently he removed the item from his head and brought it down before his eyes. *[Remove the crown as the boy in the story did.]* His eyes widened, and he smiled big. The gold glistened in the moonlight shining in through the window. He placed it back on his head again and lay down on his pillow. *[Place the crown on the same student's head again.]* The little boy thought about all the things he had done that day. It was

---

such an enjoyable, satisfying day. He now understood about a servant's crown.

❧

▸ **What happened to one of the servants?** *(She was sick.)*
▸ **Did the boy go out to play this time?** *(no)* **Why not?** *(He chose to go and help care for the sick servant.)*
▸ **What did the boy notice at bedtime?** *(He had a crown on his head.)*
▸ **How did the boy get his crown?** *(He earned it by helping others. He took care of the needs of others instead of his own desires.)*
💡 **Do you have two servants like the boy in the story?** *(Accept any answer, but elicit that the two servants could represent the boy's parents. Lead students to see that even though their parents are the authorities over them, they also serve in many ways.)*

Write the letters *J*, *O*, and *Y* aligned vertically. As you complete the words *Jesus*, *Others*, and *You*, say something like this: "These letters will help you remember that you should put Jesus and others ahead of yourself. Living for Jesus in an unselfish way will bring us joy."

✏ **Worktext page 95**

Develop the meaning of servanthood. Discuss each picture and point out that students must choose many times each day whether to follow God's way. Read the words *God's servants* and call on volunteers to finish each sentence orally before writing the word to complete the sentence. Tell the students that God wants His servants to take time to know their Master every day.

Worktext page 96

Name _____

Use the contents page in your Bible to write the names of the last four books found in the Old Testament. Write the page number on which each book begins in your Bible.

Answers will vary.

Page

Zephaniah _____

Haggai _____

Zechariah _____

Malachi _____

One or two Bible books are missing from each group below. Write a letter on each blank book cover to show which book name from the word bank belongs there.

A. Zechariah

B. Jeremiah

C. Micah

D. Ezra

E. Ecclesiastes

F. Ezekiel

1. **C** | Nahum | Habakkuk | Zephaniah | Haggai | **A**

2. 2 Kings | 1 Chronicles | 2 Chronicles | **D** | Nehemiah | Esther

3. Isaiah | **B** | Lamentations | **F** | Daniel | Hosea

4. Psalms | Proverbs | **E** | Song of Solomon | Isaiah | Jeremiah

© BJU Press. Reproduction prohibited.

96   A Servant's Heart • Lesson 67

Worktext page 97

Name _____

Draw and color a picture of a tool that you have used.

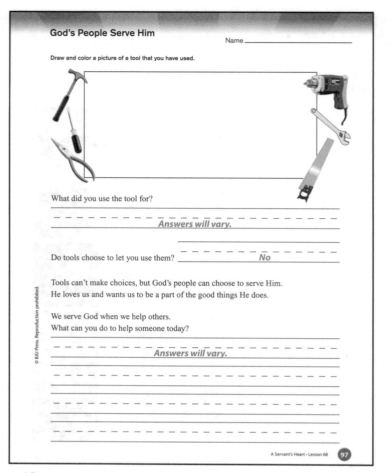

What did you use the tool for?

_____
Answers will vary.
_____

Do tools choose to let you use them? _____ *No*

Tools can't make choices, but God's people can choose to serve Him. He loves us and wants us to be a part of the good things He does.

We serve God when we help others. What can you do to help someone today?

_____
Answers will vary.
_____
_____
_____
_____
_____

© BJU Press. Reproduction prohibited.

A Servant's Heart • Lesson 68   97

Bible Study Skills, Worktext page 96

Locate the last four books in the Old Testament. Direct the students to find the contents page in their Bibles, or display Chart 3, "Books of the Bible: Old Testament." Guide the class in reading together the names of all the books of the Old Testament. Call on volunteers to name the last four books of the Old Testament. (*Zephaniah, Haggai, Zechariah, Malachi*) Direct the students to complete Worktext page 96 by writing the page number on which each of these books begins in their Bibles.

Lead the class in counting the number of books in the Old Testament. (*thirty-nine*) Instruct the students to complete the page by putting the letters of the missing Bible books in the correct locations. Ask the following questions to review the books of the Old Testament.

▸ **Where in the Old Testament is the account of Creation given?** (*Genesis*)
▸ **What book gives the Ten Commandments?** (*Exodus*)
▸ **Which book comes before Jeremiah?** (*Isaiah*)
▸ **Which book comes after the book of Psalms?** (*Proverbs*)

LESSON 68 God's People Serve Him

Materials
- Hymn: "Joy in Serving Jesus"
- Several tools (kitchen items, carpentry tools, gardening tools)
- Write a story on chart paper or for display about one of your tools. Use the following sample.
  I have a garden spade. (*name of tool*)
  I use it to dig holes in the soil. (*tool's use*)
  I can use my spade to help my neighbor.
  I can help my neighbor put flowers in her garden.
  (*how to use the tool to help others*)

♫ Hymn: "Joy in Serving Jesus"
Sing the first three verses (Worktext page 217). Direct the students to sing the third verse using sign language.

♥ Memory Verse—1 Chronicles 28:20a
Practice the memory verse. Practice the verse using the activity with colored construction-paper squares if desired (as in Lessons 66 and 67).

✎ Worktext page 97
Apply Bible knowledge to everyday life. Display the tools. Discuss how they are used. Read the story about how your tool can be used to help others. Call on volunteers to

share how they could use tools to help someone. *(Answers will vary but may include a broom to sweep the floor, a hose to wash the car, and so on.)*

Tell the students to think of a tool they could use to help someone and then draw a picture of it on page 97. Call on volunteers to name their tools and explain how they can use their tools to help others. Direct the students to answer the remaining questions. Provide help as needed. When the students are finished, allow them to share with the class what they wrote.

Application Activity

Apply Bible knowledge to everyday life. Hold up a tool. Remind the students that we can use tools to help others. Point out that God can also use us to help others. We can be God's tools. If we obey God, He will use us as tools to help others. Explain that you are going to read some situations to them. At the end of each situation you will ask whether that person is serving God. Instruct the students to stand if the person is helping someone. If the person is not helping, they are to remain seated. Use the last question in each situation for discussion.

God's People Serve Him

1. Father had to leave for work early this morning. This was trash day. Tom looked at his watch. He had ten minutes before he had to leave for school. He remembered how the apostle Paul talked about the Thessalonians laboring in love. Tom went outside and rolled the trash can to the curb. He smiled. He thought how pleased Father would be when he came home.

▶ **Was Tom serving God?** *(Students stand.)*
💡 **In what way was Tom serving God?** *(Elicit that when Tom took out the trash for Dad, he thought about someone else before himself. When Christians serve God, they put the needs of others before their own desires.)*

2. Karen's friend Marcy left with her family for the mission field of Africa. A few weeks later Karen received a letter from Marcy in the mail. Marcy was glad God had sent them to teach people in Africa, but she was very lonely. Karen put the letter beside her bed. Days went by. Then Karen's mother suggested that she write Marcy to encourage her. More days and then weeks went by. Karen kept saying to herself that she would write, but she kept forgetting.

▶ **Was Karen serving God?** *(Students remain seated.)*
💡 **How could Karen have served God?** *(Karen should have written back right away. Karen could have served God by encouraging Marcy. Point out that Christians don't need to have special talents to serve God. They can serve God even by sending a letter of encouragement to someone.)*

3. Betty's neighbor, Mrs. Nelson, broke her leg. Before this happened, Mrs. Nelson would come over and have lunch with Betty and her mother. It was now lunch time, and Betty's mother called her to the table. The table was lovely. Mother

had cut some flowers from the garden. There were tuna sandwiches, pickles, apple slices, and homemade oatmeal cookies. Betty frowned. Mother asked Betty what was wrong as they sat down to eat. Betty told Mother that this was one of Mrs. Nelson's favorite meals, but she could not come to lunch because of her broken leg. Betty's eyes suddenly lit up. She had a wonderful idea! She shared her idea with her mother. They both went into action and soon arrived at Mrs. Nelson's door. Mother was carrying a large picnic basket, and Betty held a lovely vase of fresh flowers. The lunch was a wonderful surprise for Mrs. Nelson.

▶ **Was Betty serving God?** *(Students stand.)*
💡 **How did Betty serve God?** *(She took lunch to Mrs. Nelson's house because Mrs. Nelson couldn't come to their house. Remind students that it often takes extra work and time to help others.)*

4. Two-year-old Jackie let their big dog Ginger into the house. Mother was in the basement doing laundry. Kevin was reading a book. Kevin suddenly felt wet paws on his legs. He looked over the top of his book. Ginger was covered in mud. There was also a trail of mud leading back to the kitchen door. Jackie ran to tell Mother. Kevin grabbed Ginger by the collar and led her back outside. The kitchen floor was a mess! Mother came into the kitchen and sighed. Kevin explained what had happened. Mother went to get the mop. Kevin looked at the muddy floor. He looked at his book. He had ten more pages and then the book would be finished. Kevin wanted to finish his book. He went to his room to read.

▶ **Was Kevin serving God?** *(Students remain seated.)*
💡 **What do you think Kevin should have done?** *(Kevin should have helped Mother clean the floor. Point out that God will often put us into situations in which someone needs help. Mother didn't ask Kevin to help. Even when nobody asks us, we should learn to ask, "May I help you?" Even if it's not our mess, we can help. God is pleased when Christians are willing to help others without being told.)*

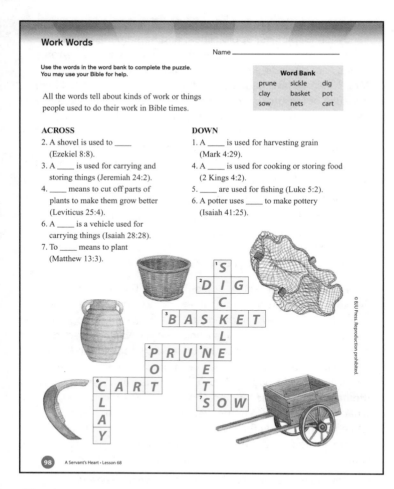

Work Words

Name _____

Use the words in the word bank to complete the puzzle.
You may use your Bible for help.

Word Bank		
prune	sickle	dig
clay	basket	pot
sow	nets	cart

All the words tell about kinds of work or things
people used to do their work in Bible times.

ACROSS

2. A shovel is used to _____
   (Ezekiel 8:8).

3. A _____ is used for carrying and
   storing things (Jeremiah 24:2).

4. _____ means to cut off parts of
   plants to make them grow better
   (Leviticus 25:4).

6. A _____ is a vehicle used for
   carrying things (Isaiah 28:28).

7. To _____ means to plant
   (Matthew 13:3).

DOWN

1. A _____ is used for harvesting grain
   (Mark 4:29).

4. A _____ is used for cooking or storing food
   (2 Kings 4:2).

5. _____ are used for fishing (Luke 5:2).

6. A potter uses _____ to make pottery
   (Isaiah 41:25).

98   A Servant's Heart • Lesson 68

Worktext page 98

Locate information in Bible verses. Tell the students
that they are going to find a word about work in each verse.
Direct attention to the column labeled *Across*. Read the clue
for number 2–Across. Direct the students to find **Ezekiel
8:8** in their Bibles and read it silently. Explain how to write
the word *dig* in the puzzle boxes beside the number 2.
Instruct the students to complete each *Across* word before
continuing with the *Down* words, if possible. Explain that
they can use the letters already in the boxes to help them
figure out each *Down* word. Provide help as needed. *(Note:
Students can use the word bank to find the answers, or you
may choose volunteers to read aloud the verses to the class.)*

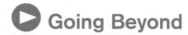 **Going Beyond**

Reinforcement

Materials

• Construction paper

Remind students that God's servants live God's way.
Make arrows out of construction paper. Write one of the
sentences below on each arrow. Display the arrows. As a student needs reminders throughout the day, quietly point to
the one the student needs to remember. The arrows can be a
quiet reminder of how to live God's way at school.

> *God's servants do things God's way.*
> *God's servants choose God's way.*
> *God's servants say things God's way.*

Enrichment

Materials

• Construction paper
• Art paper
• Felt-tip markers

Make a *Serving Others* book to color. Provide dark
markers for the students to draw a picture of themselves
doing something to help someone in their family, neighborhood, church, or school. Explain that they are to draw
outlines only and not to color or fill in the pictures with
markers. Tell them to think of something that needs to be
done, not just to make up a story. Possibilities might include
raking leaves, cleaning a room in the house, remembering
to do a chore without being reminded, or writing a letter to
someone.

Explain that they are making pictures that will be put into
a book to color. Direct each student to write a sentence at
the bottom of his picture that tells what it is about. Remind
them to use their best handwriting. Copy each student's
page so that there is one copy for each child in your class.
Provide each child with a sheet of construction paper for the
cover. Keep the books at school until all of the pages have
been colored.

God Wants Us to Work Together
Unit 5d

PREVIEW

Doctrines
- God is faithful (1 Corinthians 1:9). [Lesson 69]
- God is all-powerful (omnipotent) (Jeremiah 32:27). [Lesson 70]

Skills
- Learn Psalm 133:1
- Order the books of the Old Testament
- Read a map
- Read a timeline
- Recall facts and details
- Identify character traits of Nehemiah
- Recognize that God wants Christians to work together
- Apply Bible knowledge to everyday life

LESSON 69 — Nehemiah Wants to Rebuild

Materials
- Chart 38, "Empires"
- Hymn: "Joy in Serving Jesus"
- Map marker for each student (e.g., button, coin)
- Unit 5 Bookmark for each student
- Highlighter for each student (optional)
- Copy of page A84, "A Faithful Servant" for each student (optional)
- Verse visual for Psalm 133:1: Fold a 12" × 18" piece of construction paper in half. Trace the pattern from page A85, "Verse Visual Outline," onto the construction paper as shown (hand and foot touching fold). Cut out the paper dolls but do *not* cut on the fold. When opened there will be two paper dolls attached. Prepare four of these on which to write the verse.
- Transparency or PowerPoint slide of page A86, "Kings of Persia"
- Five stick figures drawn for display

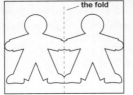

the fold

🎵 Hymn: "Joy in Serving Jesus"

Teach the fourth verse (Worktext page 217). Sing and play the fourth verse of the hymn.

💡 **What might *the darkest night* refer to?** *(This phrase probably means sad times or hard times. The Bible sometimes calls hard times "trials.")* Give examples of trials your students are familiar with.

▶ **What are we to have when God sends us trials?** *(joy)*

Explain the following key phrases.
Read the phrase "For I've learned the wondrous secret."

💡 **What might this secret be?** *(serving Jesus)*

Read the last phrase "And I'm walking in the light."

💡 **Whose light is this?** *(It is God's light. When God sends us trials, the comfort and strength of His Word are always there to see us through.)*

Lead the students as they sing the fourth verse of the hymn several times.

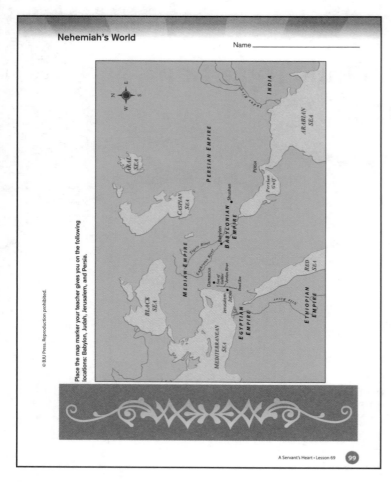

Nehemiah's World

Name _____

Place the map marker your teacher gives you on the following locations: Babylon, Judah, Jerusalem, and Persia.

A Servant's Heart • Lesson 69   99

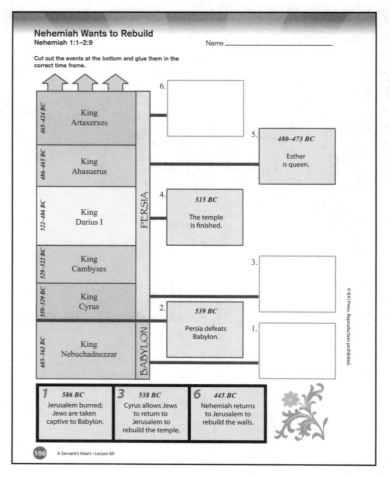

Nehemiah Wants to Rebuild
Nehemiah 1:1–2:9

Name _____

Cut out the events at the bottom and glue them in the correct time frame.

465–424 BC	King Artaxerxes	
486–465 BC	King Ahasuerus	
522–486 BC	King Darius I	
529–522 BC	King Cambyses	
559–529 BC	King Cyrus	
605–562 BC	King Nebuchadnezzar	

6.

5. 480–473 BC Esther is queen.

4. 515 BC The temple is finished.

3.

2. 539 BC Persia defeats Babylon.

1.

PERSIA

BABYLON

1 586 BC Jerusalem burned; Jews are taken captive to Babylon.

3 538 BC Cyrus allows Jews to return to Jerusalem to rebuild the temple.

6 445 BC Nehemiah returns to Jerusalem to rebuild the walls.

100   A Servant's Heart • Lesson 69

Background Information

Persian Empire—*In 549 BC, Cyrus declared himself king of Persia and began leading his army in conquering other lands. He conquered Asia Minor, the Chaldean Empire, Mesopotamia, Syria, Palestine, and Phoenicia. Later, his son conquered Egypt. Cyrus ruled his territories by allowing the people to keep their customs, religions, and governments. He then established a Persian governor over the territory to keep the peace, collect taxes, and control rebellions. The Persian Empire lasted until the middle of the seventh century AD when it was conquered by the Muslims.*

⊘ History Connection, Worktext pages 99–100

Use a map and timeline activity to explain why many Jews (including Nehemiah) were living in Persia. Share the background information about the Persian Empire (optional).

💡 **Do you think Israel won every time they fought against other countries?** *(No. Sometimes they lost.)*

💡 **Do you know why Israel lost sometimes?** *(The outcome often depended on whether they obeyed God.)*

Throughout its history Israel had different enemies. God used Israel's enemies to teach the people about obedience to Him. God wanted Israel to know that He was to be first in their lives.

Direct the students to look at the map on Worktext page 99. Distribute a map marker to each student. Discuss and read the following information to the students. Direct the students' attention to Chart 38, "Empires," as you point to the italicized locations while reading the following paragraphs. Guide the students in placing their map markers on the locations indicated.

Over two hundred years had passed since Naaman the Syrian was healed of his leprosy. Other countries had battled against Israel. One country had become very powerful. It had conquered many of the weaker countries around it and became the *Babylonian Empire.*

King Nebuchadnezzar was king of the Babylonian Empire during a time when Israel was not obeying God. King Nebuchadnezzar sent troops to the country of *Judah.* They marched right up to the capital city, *Jerusalem.* God allowed the Babylonians to destroy the city. They tore down the beautiful temple of God that Solomon had built. The walls of the city were reduced to rubble. The city was then burned. This shows us how God sees sin and how terrible sin is! The Jews were then taken captive and brought back to *Babylon* to be slaves to the Babylonians.

The Israelites were captive in Babylon for seventy years. God used *Persia's* takeover of the Babylonian Empire to bring them back to Jerusalem.

Display the transparency or slide of page A86, "Kings of Persia." Point to the beginning of the timeline on the diagram.

Direct the students to put their map markers at the beginning of their timelines on Worktext page 100. *(King Nebuchadnezzar)* Instruct the students to move their markers along the timeline on their page as you move your finger along the timeline on the display. Discuss the kings that are italicized in the following information.

Other kings reigned after *King Nebuchadnezzar's* reign came to an end, but finally the Babylonians were conquered by the mighty Persians. *King Cyrus* was king over the Persian Empire at the time this happened (539 BC). But God has power over earthly kings. God used Cyrus to set many of the Israelites free. God is always in control. Some went back to the ruined city of Jerusalem (538 BC) and banded together. They worked to rebuild the temple of God for worship. But the walls had yet to be restored.

The Persian Empire had several other kings. Then *Artaxerxes* became king. He lived in the city of *Shushan* and reigned as king from 465 to 424 BC. This king had a very special cupbearer. Some people who did not like the king might try to poison his food or his drink. The king's cupbearer tasted the king's food before the king ate it. This very important job was given to a man named Nehemiah.

Order events on the timeline. Direct the students' attention to their timelines on Worktext page 100. Discuss the events and where they appear in sequence. Direct the students to cut out the boxes at the bottom of Worktext page 100. Guide them as they glue each box in the correct place beside the timeline.

Introducing the Bible Account

Discuss what it means to *long* for something. Tell them that Nehemiah longed to be back in his home country. Explain that if they have *a strong desire* to go somewhere then they *long* to go. Call on students to tell what places they have never been before but would like to visit. Direct the students to turn to the contents page in their Bibles. Write the name *Nehemiah* for display. Instruct the students to find the book of Nehemiah on the contents page. Ask what books come before and after Nehemiah. *(Ezra and Esther)*

Bible Account

Read Nehemiah 1:1–2:8 or use the following retelling of the passage. Listening question: **What did Nehemiah do when he heard some bad news?** *(prayed)* Point to the city of Shushan on Chart 38, "Empires."

Nehemiah Wants to Rebuild

One day Nehemiah's brother, Hanani, came to see him in Shushan. He had just returned from a visit to Jerusalem. He told Nehemiah that the temple had been rebuilt, but the walls of Jerusalem were still broken down and there were no gates. Nehemiah's heart cried for his beloved city. Jerusalem was a special place to the Jews because it was the home of the temple of God. It was the city where the Jews were to worship. Hanani had further news to report. He told Nehemiah

that it wasn't safe to live in Jerusalem. People of neighboring countries mocked and laughed at the ruins. They said that the God of the Hebrews wasn't a strong God.

Nehemiah prayed. He prayed every day for over four months. Sometimes he didn't even stop to eat. Nehemiah knew that someone had to go and rebuild the walls. He was willing to be the one to go. More importantly, he wanted the countries around Jerusalem to know that there was an all-powerful God. But how could he go? He was a servant to the king of Persia.

One day as Nehemiah served the king, his heart was very sad. It was dangerous for a servant not to be cheerful while serving the king because a servant could be punished. He liked serving the king and tried to serve cheerfully because God had given him this work. The king inquired about Nehemiah's sadness. Nehemiah told the king the bad news. The king asked what Nehemiah wanted to do about the city without walls or gates.

Nehemiah prayed and took some time to think about what he would need. He would need timber from the king's forest for building. He would need letters to give to the countries so he could safely pass through on his journey. Nehemiah told the king his plans. The king didn't want Nehemiah to be gone too long because he liked his cupbearer. But the king granted Nehemiah all that he asked.

▶ **How did Nehemiah find out about the walls of Jerusalem?** *(His brother, Hanani, had just returned from Jerusalem and told Nehemiah.)*

▶ **What did Nehemiah do when he heard the bad news?** *(He prayed for over four months.)*

▶ **What did Nehemiah ask God?** *(He asked that the king let him go rebuild the walls.)*

💡 **What should Christians do when they hear bad news?** *(pray)* **Why?** *(God is always in control.)* Sometimes God allows hard things to happen to people. When He does this, they still need to remember that He is in control and trust and praise Him, knowing He has a good reason for it.

💡 **What kind of servant was Nehemiah?** *(Elicit some of the following possible answers: cheerful, faithful, willing, loving toward God, loving toward others, hard working, prayerful, obedient.)*

💡 **What kind of servant should you be?** *(Many answers are acceptable.)*

♥ Memory Verse—Psalm 133:1
Principle: God's servants should live together in peace. Direct the students to highlight the verse (optional) and mark the location with the Unit 5 Bookmark.

▶ **How are people to dwell or live?** *(in unity)*

💡 **What is unity?** *(Unity is living at peace with others.)* While the true meaning of unity is oneness, the definition given includes the idea of oneness on a level that a second grader will understand.

▶ **What words does the psalmist use to describe living in unity?** *(good, pleasant)*

 Are you living in unity with others when you work together? *(yes)*

 What are some other things that you can do to live in unity with others? *(Answers will vary but may include speaking kindly to others and taking turns in games.)*

Practice the memory verse with a countdown activity. Direct four students to hold the verse visuals at the front of the classroom. Erase one of the stick figures drawn for display each time the class recites the verse. Allow different students to hold the visuals each time the verse is recited. The goal is five recitations. You may choose to have the students say the verse five times now or throughout the school day.

Home Assignment, page A84 (optional)

Practice being a faithful servant at home. Distribute a copy of page A84, "A Faithful Servant," to each student. Read the parent letter to the students. Instruct them to write a due date on the blank where indicated. Challenge the students to return the sheets with all the bricks colored.

LESSON 70 Rebuilding Together

Materials

- Chart 16, "Rebuilding Together"
- Chart 38, "Empires"
- Hymn: "Joy in Serving Jesus"
- TimeLine and picture: Nehemiah
- A small stone

♫ Hymn: "Joy in Serving Jesus"

Sing all four verses (Worktext page 217).

Introducing the Bible Account

Review the account from the previous lesson. Discuss the following questions.

▶ **How did Nehemiah feel about the ruined walls of Jerusalem?** *(He was very sad.)*

▶ **Why did he feel this way?** *(This was the place where the Jews worshiped God.)*

▶ **What did Nehemiah want to do about the ruined city of Jerusalem?** *(He prayed for the king to let him go to rebuild the city walls.)*

 What does it mean to take initiative? *(to do something without being told)*

 When you see a job that needs to be done, do you hope someone else will do it or do you take the initiative to do it yourself? *(Answers will vary.)*

 Did Nehemiah take initiative? *(Yes. He saw that there was a job to do, and he took steps to do the job. He prayed and he planned.)*

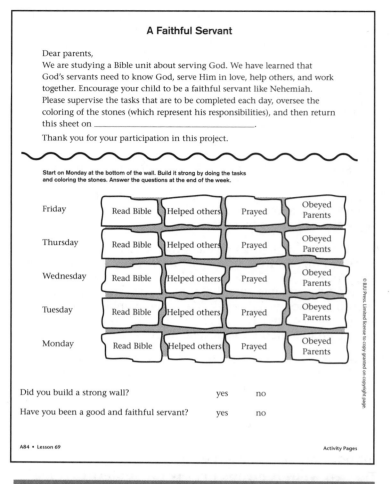

A Faithful Servant

Dear parents,

We are studying a Bible unit about serving God. We have learned that God's servants need to know God, serve Him in love, help others, and work together. Encourage your child to be a faithful servant like Nehemiah. Please supervise the tasks that are to be completed each day, oversee the coloring of the stones (which represent his responsibilities), and then return this sheet on _____.

Thank you for your participation in this project.

Start on Monday at the bottom of the wall. Build it strong by doing the tasks and coloring the stones. Answer the questions at the end of the week.

Friday	Read Bible	Helped others	Prayed	Obeyed Parents
Thursday	Read Bible	Helped others	Prayed	Obeyed Parents
Wednesday	Read Bible	Helped others	Prayed	Obeyed Parents
Tuesday	Read Bible	Helped others	Prayed	Obeyed Parents
Monday	Read Bible	Helped others	Prayed	Obeyed Parents

Did you build a strong wall?   yes   no

Have you been a good and faithful servant?   yes   no

A84 • Lesson 69   Activity Pages

© BJU Press. Limited license to copy granted on copyright page.

Bible Account

Read Nehemiah 2:9–6:19 or use the following retelling of the passage. Listening question: **How long did it take Nehemiah and the people to rebuild the walls?** *(fifty-two days)* Direct attention to Worktext page 101 as you speak. Display Chart 38, "Empires." Trace the journey of Nehemiah as you speak, locating the places that have been italicized.

Rebuilding Together

Nehemiah set out from the city of *Shushan* with a caravan of people and supplies sent by the king. The king also sent some of his soldiers to protect and help Nehemiah. Nehemiah had the letters that the king had given to him. The letters would give them safety in traveling. The six-hundred-mile journey took several months in the heat of summer. When Nehemiah crossed over the wide Euphrates River, he gave letters to the governors of the region. The governors allowed the caravan, or group of people, to continue on their journey because Nehemiah had permission from the king of Persia. Soon the caravan came to the city of Damascus. Nehemiah gave another letter to the keeper of the king's forest to get wood for repairing the walls.

Finally, Nehemiah and his tired travelers reached the place that he longed to see, *Jerusalem*. No one knew why Nehemiah had come to Jerusalem. He kept his plans quiet for the

first three days. He wanted to survey the situation before he told the Jews why God had sent him. One night Nehemiah mounted his horse. He and some of his men went to inspect the gates and wall. All the gates had been burned. At one point Nehemiah couldn't even get his horse through because of the large piles of rubble. Rebuilding was going to be a lot of hard work, but Nehemiah had a plan.

Now it was time to rally the people. Nehemiah told the people that God had sent him to Jerusalem to help rebuild the walls so that the city would be safe. Then their enemies would no longer laugh and say that the God of the Jews wasn't strong. Nehemiah would need many people to help. What do you think the people said? They said they would rebuild the walls.

In the nearby region of Samaria, two men, Tobiah and Sanballat, heard about the Jews getting together in order to rebuild the walls. They didn't want Jerusalem to be strong again. They mocked the Jews to try to stop them.

Nehemiah heard what Tobiah and Sanballat were doing. He prayed that God would deal with Tobiah and Sanballat.

Nehemiah focused on the task God had given him. He set his plan into action. He divided the work among the families. Some families rebuilt the gates and some the watchtowers. Other families were each given a section of wall to rebuild.

Sanballat heard that the Jews had started to rebuild the wall. He spoke to his army, "What are these feeble Jews doing?"

Tobiah was standing by Sanballat. He mocked the Jews. He said that the weight of a little fox would bring down the wall of Jerusalem. He didn't think that the Jews even knew how to build a strong wall.

Again, Nehemiah found out what the Samaritans said about the Jews. Once more Nehemiah prayed. Do you think the mocking made the people stop working? No! In fact, the people worked even faster! Soon the wall was half finished because the people had a mind to work.

Tobiah and Sanballat were very angry when they heard that the wall was half finished. They gathered their army together and planned to attack the Jews. Mocking the Jews hadn't stopped them, but surely an attack would, they thought.

News reached Nehemiah about the Samaritans. What do you think Nehemiah did? Nehemiah's first course of action was always to pray. He made another plan and put it into action. He set up guards to watch for the Samaritan army both day and night. He told the people to arm themselves with swords, spears, and bows. Each worker also wore a sword at his side. Did the work stop? No! The work went on. Half of the Jews held weapons, and the other half continued the work.

Nehemiah encouraged the people. He told them not to be afraid. He reminded the people that the God they served was great and powerful. But how would the Jews know when the Samaritan army arrived? The families were spread apart along the wall. Nehemiah had a plan for this too. He appointed a trumpeter to blow a horn to warn the workers. He also reminded the people that God would fight for His people. How wonderful to know that God is always on the side of His servants, especially when they are obeying and serving Him!

Rebuilding Together
Nehemiah 2:9–Nehemiah 6

For thousands of years all important cities had walls and gates to keep out enemies.

The walls were thick and high with towers and walkways for guards.

The gates were closed at sunset and opened at sunrise.

The Jews who worked with Nehemiah had to remove the ruins of the old walls before they could build the new ones.

1. Remove rubble.
2. Guard against enemies.
3. Rebuild walls.

52 Days

A Servant's Heart · Lesson 70   101

The Samaritan army didn't attack. The Samaritans tried two other ways to get Nehemiah to stop the work. Nehemiah prayed again for God to strengthen the hands of the people to complete the work.

When the last stone was put into place, a cry of joy rang out around the wall. The work was finished! The wall was finished in fifty-two days. Now all the enemies of the Jews looked on in amazement. They now knew that the Jews worshiped a great and powerful God.

Read **Nehemiah 8:9–10**. Explain that these verses record the celebration following the completion of the wall. Explain that Ezra the priest read the book of the law to the people. The people responded with humility, and they worshiped the Lord. Nehemiah was the governor of Judah and continued his responsibilities as a leader. Nehemiah, Ezra, and the other leaders told the people to rejoice.

▶ **Why did Nehemiah tell the people it was important to rebuild the walls?** *(to make the city safe, so that their enemies would know that the God of the Jews is strong)*

▶ **In what ways did the Samaritans try to stop the Jews?** *(They mocked the Jews.)*

▶ **What did Nehemiah do first when there was a problem?** *(pray)* **What did he do next?** *(plan)* **What did he do last?** *(put the plan into action)*

Worktext page 102 (reproduced)

Rebuilding Together: God's Servant

Name _____

Color the bricks that describe Nehemiah.

Do any of these phrases describe *you*?

is giving	easily gives up	is a good leader	is a cheerful worker
	is a prayer warrior	is selfish	is courageous	
is lazy	cooperates with others	loves God and others	laughs at others

Write the letter of the correct answer next to each question.

A. God

B. prayed and set a watch

C. planned

D. how great God is

E. prayed

F. Nehemiah

G. They wanted to stop the work.

H. fifty-two

___C___ What did Nehemiah do for the first three days he was in Jerusalem?

___A___ Who gave Nehemiah the job of building the walls?

___G___ Why did the enemies of Israel laugh at the wall builders?

___B___ What did Nehemiah do when his enemies were making plans to attack Jerusalem?

___D___ What did Nehemiah tell the people to remember so they would not be afraid of their enemies?

___F___ Who was appointed governor of Judah?

___E___ What did Nehemiah always do first?

___H___ How many days did it take to complete the walls?

© BJU Press. Reproduction prohibited.

102   A Servant's Heart • Lesson 70

💡 **How did the wall get done in fifty-two days?** (*The Jews worshiped the great and powerful God. They were unified, and God enabled them to work diligently and effectively in the face of opposition because they trusted in Him.*)

💡 **What jobs get done faster in your home if everyone works together?** (*Answers will vary. Emphasize that unity affects every area of life.*)

Guide a discussion about the importance of gates. Read Worktext page 101 to explain the importance of gates in more detail.

InfoScene: "Rebuilding Together"
Display Chart 16 from the Visual Packet for the students to refer to throughout this unit.

✍ Worktext page 102
Identify the character traits of Nehemiah. Read the phrases on the bricks to the students. Define any terms they do not know. Instruct the students to color the bricks that tell about Nehemiah. Read the directions and the choices at the bottom of the page. Direct the students to complete the page.

🕐 TimeLine
Add Nehemiah to the TimeLine. Place the picture of Nehemiah on the TimeLine (445–410 BC), pointing out that he returned to build the walls in Jerusalem. Remind them that walls were very important to protect cities. Tell them that Nehemiah lived about thirty years after the events in the book of Esther. Point out that over one hundred forty years had passed since the Israelites had been taken to Babylon as captives (586 BC), and about ninety years since some of the Jews had returned and rebuilt the temple (538 BC). Guide the students as they glue the picture of Nehemiah onto their TimeLines.

♥ Memory Verse—Psalm 133:1
Practice the memory verse using a game. Read the verse together several times. Instruct the students to stand in a circle, facing outward. Choose one student to be *it* and stand, with eyes closed, in the center of the circle. Give a student from the circle a small stone. Direct the students to say the verse together slowly, passing the stone around the circle on each word of the verse. When the students finish saying the verse, they all turn around with their hands closed. *It* has three guesses to identify the student with the stone. If he is correct, he exchanges places with the student who had the stone and that student becomes *it*. If the student does not guess correctly, have the student with the stone reveal himself. Choose another student to be *it* and repeat the game several times.

LESSON 71 Helping Hands?

Materials
- Hymn: "Joy in Serving Jesus"
- Transparent tape for each student
- A bell or picture of a large bell
- A small stone from the previous lesson (optional)

🎵 Hymn: "Joy in Serving Jesus"
Sing all four verses (Worktext page 217).

♥ Memory Verse—Psalm 133:1
Practice the memory verse. Read the verse together several times. Repeat the game with the stone as in the previous lesson (optional).

Introducing the Application Story
Discuss different types of bells. Display the bell or picture of a bell. Discuss how people would put large bells in church towers long ago. There would be a day set aside for raising the bell into the tower. A pulley (a grooved wheel) would be put at the top of the tower. A rope would go around the pulley and be tied to the bell. Many people would come and hold the rope. Everyone would work together to hoist (raise) the bell into the tower. After the bell was in place, there was often a picnic or celebration. In today's story some children learn about the importance of working together.

Read or tell the following story. Listening question:
Who was disappointed in the girls' actions? *(Mrs. Joselyn and Jesus)*

Helping Hands?

Ding! Ding! Ding! Ding! Mrs. Joselyn glanced down the stony dirt road, first one way and then the other. From each direction she could see her students heading toward the schoolhouse. At the sound of the bell, all the students looked up and began to walk faster, knowing they had only ten minutes to be in their assigned seats. In no time at all, everyone was in the schoolhouse. Mrs. Joselyn motioned for the students to stand and say the Pledge of Allegiance.

After the pledge, Mrs. Joselyn said, "Good morning, class. Please get out your Bible homework. As Abbey collects it, I will assign the classroom jobs."

Each week a different grade in the one-room schoolhouse helped Mrs. Joselyn wash the chalkboards, sweep the classroom floor, and ring the recess bells. This week it was the second-grade students' turn to help. Jane glanced at her two friends, Diana and Olivia. They were the only second graders in the school. All three girls were hoping for the same job. Each girl wanted to ring the bell.

"Diana," said Mrs. Joselyn, "you will help me sweep the floor this week. Jane, you will be responsible for washing the chalkboards, and Olivia, you will ring the bell after each recess."

Jane and Diana sighed. As the morning went on, they grew tired of seeing Olivia's happy smiles. Why had Mrs. Joselyn decided to let Olivia ring the bell? It wasn't fair. When the three girls opened their tin lunch pails under the shade of the maple tree as they usually did, Jane and Diana didn't say much in response to Olivia's excited chatter. Diana quietly nibbled her lunch; Jane glanced grumpily at the tall bell tower. Soon Olivia sensed the unhappiness of her friends.

"What's wrong? she asked.

Diana frowned. "We just wish you'd stop being so happy about becoming the teacher's pet."

Olivia looked confused. "Teacher's pet? What do you mean?"

"Well," said Jane, "she's letting you ring the bell."

"You're angry at me because Mrs. Joselyn is letting me ring the bell?" said Olivia. "But that was Mrs. Joselyn's decision. There's nothing I can do about it!"

"You could always let me ring the bell," said Diana.

"You!" said Jane, "I want to!"

Olivia said, "It's my job, and I'll ring the bell!"

She started to stand up, ready to go and do just that when Diana leaped to her feet.

"I say that whoever gets there first gets to ring it!" she said.

All three girls rushed up the school steps at the same time. They all grabbed the rope. There was a loud "DING!" and a terrible "THUD!" The weight of the swinging bell pulled the bell rope from the girls' hands and through its hole in the ceiling. Breathless, Olivia, Diana, and Jane looked up in horror. They had turned the bell over! Now it looked like a tea cup without a handle.

Mrs. Joselyn appeared in the doorway. She was not smiling. Suddenly, the girls were ashamed. Their teacher spoke quietly. "Girls," she said, "I'm very disappointed in your actions, and I'm sure that Jesus is too."

That was all Mrs. Joselyn had to say. She had the girls look up Ephesians 4:32 and read it together. They were reminded that God wanted them to be kind and tenderhearted to each other.

During afternoon recess, the three friends sat under the maple tree again, watching Jane's father while he stood on the school roof and tried to fix the bell.

"Olivia," said Jane, "I'm really sorry I was so mean."

"Me too," added Diana. "I should have been happy that you got the bell job. It wasn't right for me to be angry with you." Olivia smiled.

"I forgive you," she said. "I just wish there was a way I could share my job. We're friends, and friends share things."

Suddenly, Olivia had an idea.

"I know!" she shouted, "I'll help you with your after-school chores, and you can help me ring the bell! We can take turns! I'll ring it at morning recess, Diana can ring it at lunch recess, and Jane can ring it at afternoon recess!"

"What a great idea!" said Diana and Jane. They all ran to tell Mrs. Joselyn.

"I'm so glad you've found a way to work together," she said with a smile, "and I know Someone else Who is also very pleased."

▸ **Why were Olivia's friends unhappy with her?** *(She got the job of ringing the bell, and they did not.)*

▸ **What happened when all the girls tried to pull the rope at the same time?** *(The bell turned over.)*

▸ **What did the girls decide to do about ringing the bell?** *(take turns)*

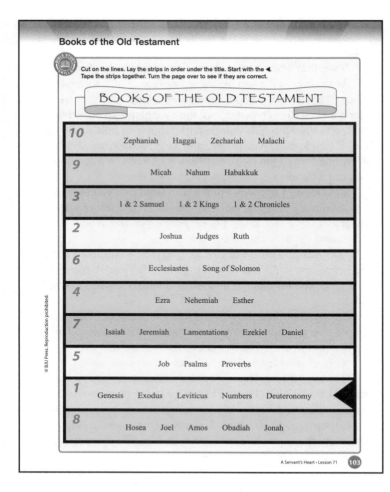

Books of the Old Testament

Cut on the lines. Lay the strips in order under the title. Start with the ◄. Tape the strips together. Turn the page over to see if they are correct.

BOOKS OF THE OLD TESTAMENT

10	Zephaniah Haggai Zechariah Malachi
9	Micah Nahum Habakkuk
3	1 & 2 Samuel 1 & 2 Kings 1 & 2 Chronicles
2	Joshua Judges Ruth
6	Ecclesiastes Song of Solomon
4	Ezra Nehemiah Esther
7	Isaiah Jeremiah Lamentations Ezekiel Daniel
5	Job Psalms Proverbs
1	Genesis Exodus Leviticus Numbers Deuteronomy
8	Hosea Joel Amos Obadiah Jonah

© BJU Press. Reproduction prohibited.

A Servant's Heart • Lesson 71   103

📖 Bible Study Skills, Worktext page 103

Order the books of the Old Testament. Direct the students to cut apart the strips on Worktext page 103. Direct them to use the contents page in their Bibles and put the books in order. Tell them to arrange the strips one below the other. Instruct the students to tape the strips together and turn the list over. As time allows, discuss the photo of the family working together.

Who Will Do God's Work?

Materials

- Hymn: "Joy in Serving Jesus"

🎵 Hymn: "Joy in Serving Jesus"

Sing the hymn (Worktext page 217). Discuss the chorus using these questions.

▶ **Who gives Christians joy?** *(God)*

💡 **How do Christians get joy?** *(Many answers are acceptable. Discuss asking God in prayer; reading the Bible, and confessing sin if they are not mentioned.)*

▶ **If Christians know God is in control, will their joy ever go away** *(depart)***?** *(No. Recite 1 Chronicles 28:20a together. Remind the students that God is with them as they serve Him.)*

❤ Memory Verse—Psalm 133:1

Practice the verse.

Introducing the Play

Discuss the advantages of working together. Ask the following questions.

💡 **How do you feel when you must clean up a messy room by yourself?** *(Answers may vary.)*

💡 **What would make the job easier?** *(Guide the students to realize that when other people help clean up, the job is accomplished faster, one person is not worn out, and God is pleased.)*

Tell the students that there are times when we must do a job by ourselves. Point out that God will help them finish the job.

Explain to the students that they will present a minidrama, which is like a short play. Tell them that in this minidrama there has been a terrible storm. Challenge the students to listen to find out what happens.

Who Will Do God's Work?
A Play

Choose students to read each of these parts.

Narrators 1–6
Pastor Thomas
Matt
Nathan
Caroline

Divide the remainder of the class and assign them to Group 1, 2, or 3.

Narrator 1: Friday morning a bad thunderstorm hit the little town. It rained very hard all day. By evening, the rain stopped, and the sun peeked through the clouds.

Narrator 2: Pastor Thomas looked out the window of his house on Saturday morning. What he saw made him sad. The little church did not look the same. Broken branches lay everywhere. A tree had fallen on the church and had broken some windows. He wondered how the mess could ever be cleaned up in time for Sunday morning.

Narrator 3: Pastor Thomas called all the church members. By the middle of the morning, every family was there to help clean up.

Scene One

Matt: What a mess! It will take a lot of work to clean this up!

Nathan: Oh, let the grownups clean it up. It's not our fault the church is a mess.

Caroline: Nathan, it's not anybody's fault. If we all work together, it won't take as long.

Nathan: It's too much work!

Narrator 4: Pastor Thomas and some of the other men made a list of things to do. Pastor Thomas called all the people together.

Scene Two

Pastor Thomas: (Reads Nehemiah 2:18.) We need to work together as the people did in Nehemiah's time. Each group will have a job to do. Who will clean up the backyard of the church?

Group 1: We will!

Pastor Thomas: Who will clean up the front yard?

Group 2: We will!

Who Will Do God's Work? (continued)
A Play

Pastor Thomas: Who will fix the windows and clean up the glass?

Group 3: We will!

Narrator 5: After prayer, the families all went to work. Pastor Thomas was working too. He let the children take turns riding in the wheelbarrow. Cleaning up the mess was hard work, but it was fun too.

Scene Three

Pastor Thomas: Nathan, why aren't you working today? Do you feel sick?

Nathan: This work is too hard. There is too much to do!

Pastor Thomas: Do you know why Nehemiah rebuilt the wall of Jerusalem?

Nathan: So the city would be safe.

Pastor Thomas: Yes, and there was another reason. Nehemiah wanted his enemies to know that the Jews served a God Who loved them and could keep them safe. By working together, they showed that they loved God and each other.

Nathan: I never thought of that. I want others to see that we work together because we love each other. Maybe when they see that, they will want to come to church and they will be saved.

Narrator 6: The rest of the day Nathan worked with everyone else. By supper time the work was almost done. Pastor Thomas got into his truck and drove away. Everyone was tired and hungry. Just as the work was finished, Pastor Thomas returned. He called everyone over to his truck.

Pastor Thomas: Thank you for working so hard. The church looks wonderful! I have a surprise for all of you hard workers.

All: Pizza! Thank you, Pastor Thomas!

✎ Worktext pages 105–6

Guide the students in presenting a play. Direct the students' attention to Worktext page 105. Assign parts to the students. Direct the students to read their assigned parts silently for practice. Then present the play. Follow up with the discussion questions.

▶ **What damage did the storm cause?** *(A tree fell and broke some windows in the church, and tree branches were everywhere.)*

 **Do you think Pastor Thomas was discouraged about the mess? Why or why not?** *(Any answer is acceptable.)*

▶ **Why do you think Nathan did not want to help clean up at first?** *(He said the mess was not his fault. Guide the students to understand that Nathan needed to remember that God is always in control and He had allowed the damage to be done. God allows trials into Christians' lives to teach them and to show Himself strong.)*

 What lesson do you think God was trying to teach the people of this little church? *(Many answers are acceptable. Elicit that God may also be teaching the people to work together.)*

 What did Pastor Thomas do before the cleanup began? *(He planned the day and took time to pray and read the Bible.)*

▶ **Why did Nathan change his mind and decide to help?** *(Pastor Thomas reminded Nathan about the walls of Jerusalem that Nehemiah and the people built. He told Nathan that when Christians work together to take care of their church building, they show others that they love each other and God.)*

 What should Christians do when they have a problem? *(Many answers are acceptable. Guide the students to understand that Christians should first pray and read God's Word for direction. Then they should plan and take action. People can work together to solve problems.)*

Unit 5 Review

Name _____

Fill in the circle next to the correct answer.

1. Nehemiah helped to
   ○ give manna.
   ● build a city's walls.

2. Samuel told God's people to
   ● obey God.
   ○ please themselves.

3. A servant girl told Naaman's wife about
   ● the prophet of God.
   ○ Noah's ark.

4. David, the shepherd boy, trusted God when he faced
   ○ a snake.
   ● Goliath.

Circle the correct word to complete each sentence.

5. Nehemiah honored God by rebuilding the walls of (Jerusalem, his boss's house).

6. Saul disobeyed God, so God (honored, punished) him.

7. The Philistines had (many, a few) soldiers.

8. Naaman obeyed God's prophet and was (beaten, healed).

Circle *True* or *False* for each sentence.

9. David loved God. — (True) False

10. Jonathan was mean to David. — True (False)

11. Saul's sacrifice honored God. — True (False)

12. Jeremiah learned from a potter. — (True) False

Unit Reviews

Lessons 57–72 • A59

© BJU Press. Limited license to copy granted on copyright page.

---

and give each group a job. Ask for parent volunteers to help oversee the project. Give the project a special name, such as *Operation Cooperation*.

 Unit Review

Materials
- Copy of page A59 ("Unit 5 Review") for each student

Guide a review of Unit 5. Review the people and events in preparation for the Unit 5 Test (optional).

▶ Going Beyond

Reinforcement

Materials
- Construction paper
- Shoe box

Build a Service Wall. Cut rectangles from blue, red, and brown construction paper approximately 3" × 6". Place the "bricks" in a box. On the outside of the box, write the words *In love serve one another*. Provide a place for the wall to be built, such as a door, wall, or bulletin board. When you see a student serving others in some way, hand him a brick. Direct him to put his name on the brick and attach it to the place you have designated for this activity. Set a goal for the students to reach, such as making the wall to the top of the door. Make sure all the students get their names on the wall by allowing various students to help with classroom chores.

Enrichment

Pray, plan, and do a cleanup project. Check with individuals, your church, or your community to find a place that needs some cleanup. Explain the problem to the students. Choose a passage of Scripture to encourage the students and challenge them to do the work. Pray about those involved and for supplies needed to complete the job. Plan what needs to be done. Divide the students into groups

---

Unit 5d • God Wants Us to Work Together

A Courageous Heart

OVERVIEW

Preparing the Teacher

Read **Psalm 121**. Many times there is a gap between theory and practice, knowing and doing. Many people believe that God keeps them safe from harm, that He delivers them from their enemies, and that He can use even bad circumstances for His glory. In practice, however, they may be afraid to trust their lives to God. They may fear what others might say or do, and they may be disturbed by even the minutest adversities. God alone can give His peace, presence, and power to face the day-to-day circumstances.

In this unit, the students explore God-given courage in the lives of some of God's people. Claim the promise in **2 Timothy 1:7** for each student and for yourself. Seek the Lord Jesus in prayer in your regular activities throughout the day.

Preparing the Materials

73—Unit 6 bookmark [E]; copy of page A87 ("News! News!") [E, O]

74—Scepter [O]

75—Fresh sweet potato or yam; toothpicks; glass or jar of water [O]

75–88—Copy of Gloria Repp's *A Question of Yams* [E] or one for the teacher

76—Three or four descriptions of real-life situations on cards or paper

77—Copy of page A87 ("News! News!") [E, O]; transparency or PowerPoint of page A86 ("Kings")

Unit 6b Going Beyond—One 2" × 8" construction paper strip [E]

82—Balance scale or picture of scale; copy of page A87 ("News! News!") [E, O]; large card with the word *Teacher* printed on one side and the word *Students* printed on the other

84—Beanbag

Unit 6c Going Beyond—Guest speaker (missionary or Bible translator) [O]

86—Page A87 ("News! News!") for each student [O]; stick puppet; outline of a human figure on a piece of white construction paper

88—Beanbag; canned yams, yam chips, or items for making yam pudding [O] (a slow cooker, measuring utensils, paper cups and plastic spoons, 1 large can [29 oz.] sweet potatoes, 1 can [12 oz.] evaporated milk, margarine, 2 eggs, cloves, nutmeg, cinnamon, sugar); copy of page A60 ("Unit 6 Review") [E]

Unit 6 　A Courageous Heart

Theme, Memory Verse, and Principle	Lesson Number	TE Page	Worktext Page(s)	Appendix Page(s)	Lesson Title	Scripture or Focus
Unit 6a **Courage to Trust God** Romans 8:28 *If we love God, we will understand that He works out the details of our lives for our good.*	73	164	107–8	A87	Esther Becomes Queen	Esther 1–4
	74	166	109–10		Esther Goes Before the King	Esther 5–10
	75	168	111–12		Character: What Was Mordecai Like?	Missionary Story
	76	170	246		All Things Work Together	Missionary Story
Unit 6b **Courage During Hard Times** Deuteronomy 31:6 *We can be courageous because God is with us.*	77	172	113–14	A87	God Gives Courage to Do Right	Daniel 3:1–30
	78	174	115, 241		Hero of the Faith: Adoniram Judson	Biography
	79	176	116, 247		Strength and Courage	Missionary Story
	80	178	117, 248		Before and After	Missionary Story
Unit 6c **Courage to Speak God's Word** Romans 1:16 *We should not be ashamed to tell others about the gospel of Jesus Christ.*	81	179	119–20		Daniel's Reputation	Daniel 5:1–16
	82	181	121	A87	A Message from God	Daniel 5:17–31
	83	182	122, 249		Whose Way?	Missionary Story
	84	183	250		God's Book	Missionary Story
Unit 6d **Courage to Live a Godly Life** Psalm 56:11 *When we put our trust in God, we do not need to fear what people can do to us.*	85	185	123–24		A Godly Man Keeps Praying	Daniel 6:1–15
	86	186	125–26	A87	God Protects Daniel	Daniel 6:16–28
	87	188	127, 251		Whose Laws?	Missionary Story
	88	190	128, 252	A88–89, A60	Trusting God	Missionary Story

Connections	Bible Doctrines	Skills/Applications
L73—Writing	**The Doctrine of God**	**Foundational**
	Attributes of God	• Understand that God directs the lives of those who love Him
	God is all-powerful (omnipotent) (Jer. 32:27; Matt. 19:26).	• Realize that God's power is limitless
	God is everywhere (omnipresent) (Ps. 139:7–10).	• Realize that man's inclination is to sin, not to obey God
	God is faithful (1 Cor. 1:9).	• Realize that God always gives grace to those who serve Him in humility
L75—Science	**The Doctrine of Man**	
	Fall of Man	**Practical**
	Man is in a hopeless condition (Isa. 64:6).	• Recall facts and details
	Man lives in a corrupted environment (Rom. 8:22).	• Classify books of the Bible into Old and New Testaments
	Man is guilty before God (Rom. 3:10–12).	• Sequence the books of the Bible
L77—Writing	*Redemption of Man*	• Locate verses in the Bible
	Man has God's favor through Christ (Eph. 1:3).	• Identify characters
		• Compare and contrast characters
L78—TimeLine: Adoniram Judson	**The Doctrine of Salvation**	• Find information
	Elements of Salvation	• Read a map
	God calls men through providence (Rom. 2:4).	• Read a timeline
		• Illustrate an incident
		• Identify cause-and-effect relationships
		• Predict outcomes
		• Draw conclusions
		• Sequence events
L82—Writing		• Infer what a character in a story might have said
		Personal
		• Distinguish between God's way and man's way
		• Know that God takes care of Christians
		• Desire to have courage that rests on God's power
		• Recognize the gospel of Jesus Christ and not be ashamed of it
L86—TimeLine: Daniel Writing		• Appreciate the ability to hear and to read God's Word
		• Understand and apply Bible knowledge to everyday life
L88—Math		

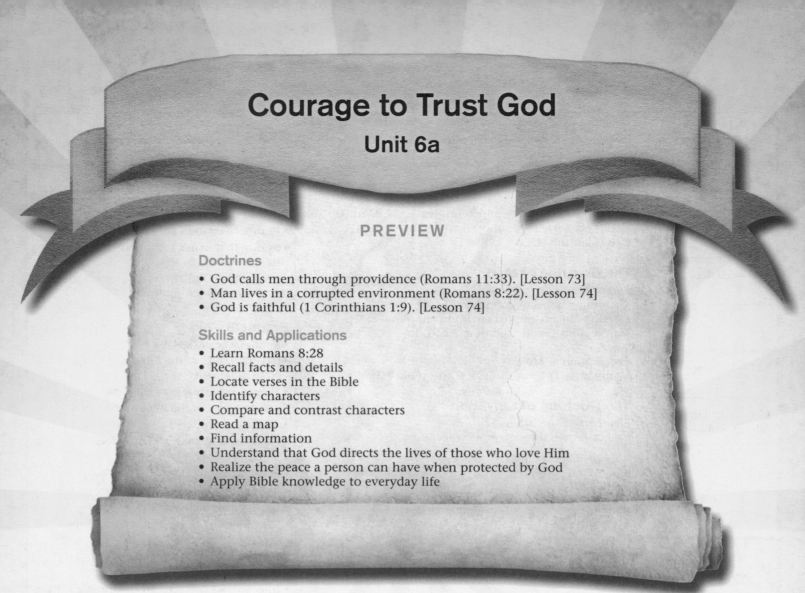

Courage to Trust God
Unit 6a

PREVIEW

Doctrines

- God calls men through providence (Romans 11:33). [Lesson 73]
- Man lives in a corrupted environment (Romans 8:22). [Lesson 74]
- God is faithful (1 Corinthians 1:9). [Lesson 74]

Skills and Applications

- Learn Romans 8:28
- Recall facts and details
- Locate verses in the Bible
- Identify characters
- Compare and contrast characters
- Read a map
- Find information
- Understand that God directs the lives of those who love Him
- Realize the peace a person can have when protected by God
- Apply Bible knowledge to everyday life

LESSON 73 Esther Becomes Queen

Materials

- Unit 6 Bookmark for each student
- Copy of page A87 ("News! News!") for each student (optional)
- Highlighter for each student (optional)

Background Information

The Book of Esther—*The events in the book of Esther took place in the city of Shushan in Persia sometime before Nehemiah rebuilt the walls of Jerusalem. Persia had replaced Babylon as the strongest world power, and many Jews chose to remain there rather than go back to Palestine. Esther and Mordecai were among those who remained, but they trusted in God. God used them to save the Jewish people. The book of Esther teaches that God controls human affairs. Although God's name is not mentioned in this book, God's presence is evident on every page.*

Esther—*Esther came to prominence in the kingdom because she was chosen to replace the deposed queen Vashti, who had refused to obey a wicked command of the king. The selection of Esther*

started a series of events that culminated in Esther's saving the Jewish people from execution.

Mordecai—*Esther's cousin, Mordecai, took care of her like a father (**Esther 2:7**). He continued to advise her even after she was made queen. He and Esther began the Feast of Purim, a time when the Jews celebrate their deliverance from destruction. Eventually this Feast of Purim would include the reading of the book of Esther by the Jews. The congregation would join the reading with shouts or curses at the mention of Haman's name and praises for Esther and Mordecai.*

King Ahasuerus—*King Ahasuerus (or Xerxes I) ruled Persia from 486 BC until 465 BC.*

Haman—*Wicked Haman deceived the king into issuing a decree demanding that all Jews be killed because Haman hated Mordecai. But before the order could be carried out, Haman proved disloyal to the king and was hanged on the gallows he had prepared for Mordecai.*

Introducing the Bible Account

Introduce Esther, Mordecai, and King Ahasuerus.
Tell the students to look at the map on Worktext page 107 as you give the background information about the book of

Esther. Make certain that the students understand that there were many Jews in Persia living peaceably with the Persians, and some of them had important jobs working for the king.

Bible Account

Read Esther 1–4 or use the following retelling of the passage. Listening question: **Why did Esther have courage?** *(because she trusted God)*

Esther Becomes Queen

Mordecai was living in Jerusalem at the time it was conquered by the Persians, and he was taken captive along with many other Jews. Mordecai now lived in Shushan. He had raised his orphaned cousin, Esther, like his own child since she was very young.

Esther was very beautiful. King Ahasuerus married Esther and made her queen. He didn't know that she was a Jew, one of God's chosen people. Mordecai had told her not to tell anyone.

One day as Mordecai sat at the gate of the city, he heard two men plotting to kill the king. He told Esther about the plot, and she told the king. The king's men put these men to death, and the king was grateful to Esther. He also had his men write down the name of Mordecai in the history records kept in the palace.

Haman was the head of all the princes in the kingdom. He had been given the top position in the king's service. When Haman rode through the city, the people were to bow down to him. One day, he noticed that one Jew sitting at the city gate didn't bow down. It was Mordecai. His refusal to bow made Haman very angry.

So Haman made a plan. He went to the king and told the king that there was a group of people that didn't obey the king's laws. He explained that these people had their own laws, and he got the king to sign a law that all these people should be put to death on a certain day. These people were the Jews, God's chosen people. Haman even offered to pay the men who would kill them.

The new law caused all the Jews to be afraid. Mordecai dressed in rags, covered himself with ashes, and no longer sat at the city gate but fasted (did not eat) and prayed.

When Esther heard that Mordecai was fasting and wearing rags, she sent good clothes to him and told him to come and eat with her. But Mordecai sent a message back to Esther about Haman's wicked plan to kill the Jews and told her he had to fast and pray. He also advised her to go to the king and tell him that she too was a Jew and that her life was in danger from Haman's new law.

When Queen Esther received Mordecai's request, she became afraid. Everyone knew that if someone went into the king's throne room without an invitation, that person could be killed, no matter who he was. Only if the king held out his scepter to the person would he be spared from death. Esther sent a message back to her cousin saying she was afraid to go before the king unless he sent for her.

Mordecai replied to Esther that God had probably put her in her position as the queen so that she could save her people. He told her that if she didn't speak up, God would save His people another way. Esther decided to take Mordecai's advice and prepared to enter the king's throne room without an invitation. She also sent back a message for Mordecai to tell all the Jews to fast and pray for her. She would fast and pray too.

───── ❧ ─────

▶ **Both Mordecai and Esther were Jews who lived in Persia. Why were they there?** *(The Jews had been taken captive in a war between their countries.)*

▶ **How was Haman offended by Mordecai?** *(Mordecai would not bow down to Haman.)*

▶ **What wicked plan did Haman devise?** *(He got the king to make a law that the Jews would be put to death.)*

💡 **How did this law affect Mordecai and Esther?** *(Since they were both Jews, they would be put to death.)*

▶ **What did Mordecai do, and what did he suggest that Esther do?** *(He dressed in rags, covered himself with ashes, and fasted and prayed. He suggested to Esther that she go tell the king she was a Jew and that this new law would mean her death also.)*

▶ **What did Mordecai tell Esther when she said she was afraid to go?** *(that God would save His people some other way if she didn't go)*

💡 **How did Esther show courage?** *(She decided to appear before the king without an invitation.)*

♥ Memory Verse—Romans 8:28

Principle: If we love God, we will understand that He works out the details of our lives for our good. Direct the students to turn in their Bibles to Romans 8:28. Read the verse aloud as the students read it silently. Direct the class to highlight the verse (optional) and mark the location with the Unit 6 Bookmark.

▶ **In a Christian's life, how many things work together for good?** *(all things)*

▶ **Does this include things that we think are not so good?** *(yes)*

▶ **For whom do all things work together for good?** *(those who love God and are the called according to His purpose)*

💡 **Who do you think are the called?** *(All those who have trusted Christ to save them from their sins are the called.)*

💡 **How can even bad things work together for good?** *(God uses even bad things for His purposes. Explain that the very next verse [Romans 8:29] gives God's purpose for both the good things and the bad things He allows in our lives—to make us more like Christ.)*

This would be a good time to present the gospel and to encourage all students to be sure they are saved. Also emphasize that they should view everything in their lives as God's goodness to accomplish *His* purpose in their lives.

Practice the memory verse. Divide the class into two groups. Direct one group to read the first part of the verse and the second group to read the last part of the verse.

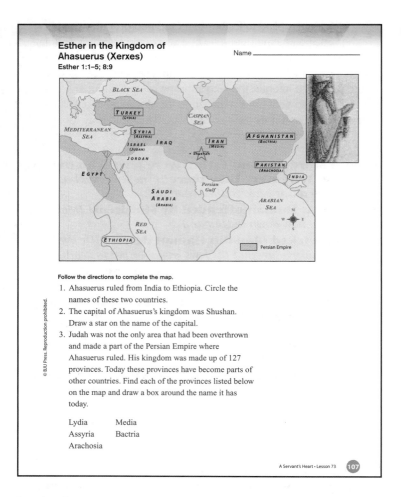

Esther in the Kingdom of
Ahasuerus (Xerxes)
Esther 1:1–5; 8:9

Name _____

Follow the directions to complete the map.

1. Ahasuerus ruled from India to Ethiopia. Circle the names of these two countries.

2. The capital of Ahasuerus's kingdom was Shushan. Draw a star on the name of the capital.

3. Judah was not the only area that had been overthrown and made a part of the Persian Empire where Ahasuerus ruled. His kingdom was made up of 127 provinces. Today these provinces have become parts of other countries. Find each of the provinces listed below on the map and draw a box around the name it has today.

Lydia   Media
Assyria   Bactria
Arachosia

A Servant's Heart • Lesson 73 107

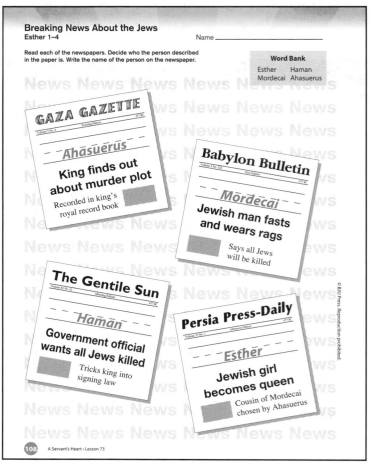

Breaking News About the Jews
Esther 1–4

Name _____

Read each of the newspapers. Decide who the person described in the paper is. Write the name of the person on the newspaper.

Word Bank
Esther   Haman
Mordecai Ahasuerus

108 A Servant's Heart • Lesson 73

Repeat this several times and then exchange the parts each group reads.

Worktext page 107

Read a map. Read **Esther 1:1** aloud to the students. Guide the class in locating India and Ethiopia on the map at the top of the page. Instruct them to circle the names of these countries on the map.

Read **Esther 1:5** aloud. Guide the students as they locate Shushan on the map and draw a star.

Read aloud the paragraph in number 3. Read each province listed at the bottom of the Worktext page and guide the students as they locate the province (names in parentheses) on the map. Direct the students to draw a box around the modern name for each area.

Worktext page 108

Identify characters. Ask the students where they can look for answers to problems they will have throughout their lives. *(in the Bible)* Direct their attention to Worktext page 108. Call on a student to read the headline and sentences on the first newspaper. Choose a volunteer to read the choices from the word bank and then tell who the person described is before they write the answer. Guide the students as they complete the page.

Writing Connection (optional)

Guide the writing of a newspaper story. Direct the students' attention to the top of the page A87 ("News! News!"). Explain that the headlines of a newspaper are short and capture the attention of the reader. Write the name *Mordecai* for display. Instruct the students to write the name *Mordecai* on the big lines on their page. Tell them to write a few sentences describing a situation in the Bible account about Mordecai. Remind the students to draw a picture about their sentences. Display the completed articles on the Unit 6 bulletin board (see the Toolkit CD).

LESSON
74 Esther Goes Before the King

Materials
- Hymn: "Am I a Soldier of the Cross?"
- Scepter (or something that represents a scepter)

Introducing the Bible Account
Guide a role-playing activity. Pretend that you are the king. Tell the students that you are thinking kindly of a student in the room and if that student is the one who comes up to you, you will hold out the scepter, and that student will be accepted and can touch the scepter. If someone other than that student comes up, he will be turned away. Ask for a volunteer to come to you; as he approaches, hold out the scepter to him and let him touch it. When this activity is

over, tell them that you were thinking kindly toward all of them, so anyone would have been accepted and allowed to touch the scepter.

Bible Account

Read Esther 5–10 or use the following retelling of the passage. Listening question: **What is the name of the man that the king wanted to honor?** *(Mordecai)* Hold the scepter as you speak.

Esther Goes Before the King

As Esther approached the king, he looked up, surprised to see her, but he immediately held out his scepter for her to touch. He told her that whatever her request was, he would grant it. But all Esther asked was that the king and Haman attend a banquet that would be given in the king's honor. The king readily accepted the invitation for himself and Haman. Esther then left the king's presence, praising God for working everything together for good.

In the meantime, Haman proceeded in his plan to kill the Jews. He went to the queen's banquet and was asked to go with the king to a second banquet the next day.

He had a huge gallows (a stand for hanging people) built because he planned to first hang Mordecai and then all the Jews he could find. He was thrilled about this plan.

The night after the first banquet, God caused the king to be unable to sleep. To pass the time, he had the history records read to him. In one of the records, he heard about the time when Mordecai had told Esther of the plot the two men had made to kill the king and how Mordecai had saved the king's life.

Haman went the next day intending to ask the king's permission to kill Mordecai. Before Haman could ask his question, the king asked Haman to advise him about how he should honor a man who had done a great deed for the king. Haman thought he was the one to be honored, so he said such a hero should be given a kingly robe and should ride on a kingly horse. The royal emblem should be placed on the horse's head. He should ride through the streets being proclaimed a hero. The king then told Haman to do all these things for Mordecai the Jew.

Haman was very unhappy about having to honor Mordecai and was downhearted that night when he attended the queen's banquet. When Esther revealed to the king that the law Haman had persuaded him to make was against her people, the king became very angry.

The king sentenced Haman to be hanged on the gallows that Haman had ordered to be built. Then the king wrote another law. This law said that the Jews could defend themselves against anyone who would try to kill them. God's people were saved from destruction. Mordecai was given the king's ring and Haman's job. God had used Esther to save His people.

💡 **How did Esther trust God throughout the story?** *(Answers will vary, but direct the students to the fact that she went before the king, something she could have been killed for doing, and pleaded for the lives of her people, the Jews.)*

▶ **Did the king hold out his scepter to Esther?** *(Yes. He even told her he would grant any request she had. Remind the students that God gives courage when we trust Him.)*

💡 **After the king went to Esther's first banquet, he could not sleep that night. Why do you think this happened?** *(Answers may vary, but elicit that God caused it.)*

▶ **Whom did the king decide to honor after he heard the court records?** *(Mordecai)*

💡 **Was the news that he must honor Mordecai the worst news Haman received?** *(No. When the king discovered that Haman's plans to kill the Jews included Queen Esther, the king sentenced Haman to death.)*

💡 **Is it ever a good idea to plan and purpose to hurt someone else just because of our own pride?** *(No. God hates pride. Wicked planning always hurts the one who does it.)*

▶ **What does God do with everything that happens in the life of the believer, according to Romans 8:28?** *(He works everything out for good.)*

💡 **Can you tell about a time in your life when God worked everything for good?**

💗 **Memory Verse—Romans 8:28**
Review the verse.

▶ **Who does the expression "the called" refer to?** *(all people who have believed the gospel and experienced new birth)*

🎵 **Hymn: "Am I a Soldier of the Cross?"**
Introduce the hymn. At age eighteen, Isaac Watts told his father that the church songs could be better. His father answered him by saying that he should write something better. For the next two years, Isaac wrote the text of one new hymn each week. By the time he died in 1748, he had written more than six hundred hymns. "Am I a Soldier of the Cross?" was read as a poem at the end of a sermon when Isaac Watts was a pastor in Scotland. The original name of the hymn was "Holy Fortitude" because that was the title of the sermon. The text is based on **1 Corinthians 16:13**.

Teach the first verse (Worktext page 218). Utilize the recording as necessary throughout the unit.
Direct the students to read silently the first verse as you play the recording. Explain that God often uses examples from wars and armies to show us how we are to act as Christians in God's army.

Explain that the first verse is a series of four questions that help us to think about being the right kind of soldier for God. Read the first verse aloud and explain the following: *soldier of the cross* (Christ's disciple), *Lamb* (Jesus), and *blush* (being ashamed of Jesus).

▶ **What are the first two questions asked?** *(Am I a soldier of the cross? A follower of the Lamb?)*

💡 **What answer does God want from us for those questions?** *(yes)*

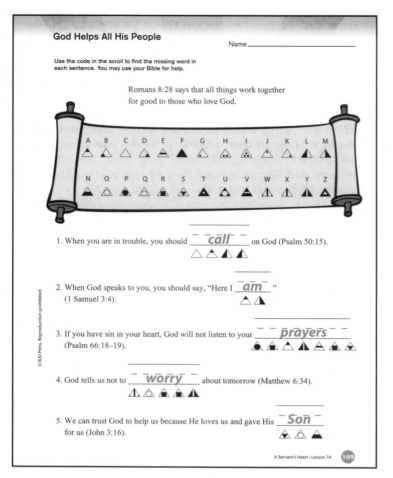

God Helps All His People

Name_____

Use the code in the scroll to find the missing word in each sentence. You may use your Bible for help.

Romans 8:28 says that all things work together for good to those who love God.

[scroll with code A through Z with triangle symbols]

1. When you are in trouble, you should __call__ on God (Psalm 50:15).

2. When God speaks to you, you should say, "Here I __am__" (1 Samuel 3:4).

3. If you have sin in your heart, God will not listen to your __prayers__ (Psalm 66:18–19).

4. God tells us not to __worry__ about tomorrow (Matthew 6:34).

5. We can trust God to help us because He loves us and gave His __Son__ for us (John 3:16).

A Servant's Heart • Lesson 74   109

© BJU Press. Reproduction prohibited.

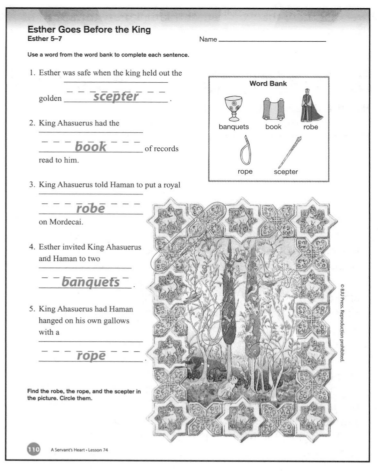

Esther Goes Before the King
Esther 5–7

Name_____

Use a word from the word bank to complete each sentence.

1. Esther was safe when the king held out the golden __scepter__.

2. King Ahasuerus had the __book__ of records read to him.

3. King Ahasuerus told Haman to put a royal __robe__ on Mordecai.

4. Esther invited King Ahasuerus and Haman to two __banquets__.

5. King Ahasuerus had Haman hanged on his own gallows with a __rope__.

Word Bank

banquets   book   robe

rope   scepter

Find the robe, the rope, and the scepter in the picture. Circle them.

110   A Servant's Heart • Lesson 74

© BJU Press. Reproduction prohibited.

💡 **How can Christians show others that they are followers of Jesus?** *(by their love for Jesus and others)*

Play and sing the first verse of the hymn together several times.

✍ Worktext page 109

Apply Romans 8:28 to everyday life. Read the directions and demonstrate how to find the word in the first sentence. Choose a student to find and read aloud the Bible verse. You may choose to use the page as a class activity or an independent activity.

✍ Worktext page 110

Recall facts and details. Read the directions and the word bank choices to the students. Direct the students to complete the sentences. Tell them to find the three items from the word bank that are hidden in the picture. Provide help as needed.

LESSON 75 Character: What Was Mordecai Like?

Materials

- Chart 31, "World Map," or a globe
- Hymn: "Am I a Soldier of the Cross?"
- Copy of *A Question of Yams* for each student or one for the teacher
- A fresh sweet potato or yam (optional)
- Toothpicks (optional)
- Glass or jar of water (optional)

🎵 Hymn: "Am I a Soldier of the Cross?"

Sing the first verse (Worktext page 218). Lead the class in singing the first verse.

❤ Memory Verse—Romans 8:28

Practice the memory verse.

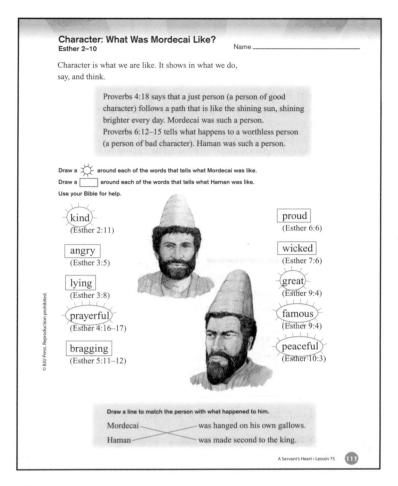

Worktext page 111

Examine the character of Mordecai. Tell the students that *character* is what a person is like. Explain that faithfulness, determination, and honesty are some examples of character qualities that might be used to describe people. Examples of bad character can include dishonesty and laziness. Call on students to tell what words could be used to describe Esther. (*Answers could include courageous and loyal.*) Read aloud the two paragraphs at the top of the page. Explain the directions and instruct the students to complete the page.

Introducing the Missionary Story

Setting—*The story told in* A Question of Yams *is based on the experience of a Christian man who lived in a village in Papua New Guinea.*

Plot—*The people in the village believe they need to pray to their gods or else their gardens will not produce. The Word of God is translated into the language of the village people, and one man comes to know the true God. He and his family endure opposition and ridicule from the village leaders. Despite their difficult circumstances, God blesses the man and his family in many ways.*

Yams—*Yams are a major food crop in many tropical countries. Some weigh as much as one hundred pounds and are as long as six feet. About twenty-one million tons are grown each year. Western Africa produces a large amount of this crop, as do India and countries of Southeast Asia and the Caribbean Sea. The* climate of the United States is too cold and the growing season too short to produce many yams.

Generate interest in the story. Display a yam (optional). Call on a student to tell what this food is called. Allow students to share their experiences with planting gardens. Tell them they are going to read the book called *A Question of Yams.* Distribute a copy of the book to each student. Direct their attention to the picture of Kuri on the cover and the picture on page 1. Ask them where they think this story takes place. Read about the author, Gloria Repp, from the back of the book. Read the publisher's note to them (from page vii) or share the background information. Using Chart 31, "World Map," or the globe, point to the place where you live and then to Papua New Guinea. Explain to the class that this book will be used throughout this unit.

Missionary Story

Read Chapter 1 of *A Question of Yams.* Direct each student to read Chapter 1 silently. If each student does not have a copy of the book, read the chapter aloud. Comprehension question: **How were the Head Men acting toward Kuri's father?** *(angrily)*

▶ **Where was Kuri's favorite rock?** *(just a few steps into the jungle)*

💡 **Why did Kuri like that rock?** *(He was hidden there.)*

▶ **To what did Kuri compare how well he was hidden on his favorite rock?** *(to how well a possum is hidden in the treetops)*

▶ **Whom was Kuri waiting for?** *(his father)*

▶ **What was Kuri afraid his father would do?** *(plant the garden without praying to the spirits)*

▶ **Who did Kuri think had influenced his father?** *(the missionaries)*

▶ **Who was following Kuri's father to his garden?** *(the Head Men)*

💡 **Who do you think the Head Men were?** *(Any response is acceptable.)*

▶ **What were the Head Men angry about?** *(They were angry because Kuri's father wasn't going to pray to the spirits before he planted his garden.)*

▶ **Was Kuri's father afraid of their anger?** *(no)*

▶ **To whom did he pray about his garden?** *(He prayed to God in the name of Jesus Christ. Point out that a Christian finds courage through talking to God in prayer.)*

💡 **What words make you think Kuri was not so sure about his father's mighty God?** *(He wondered how strong his father's God was.)*

Worktext page 112

Relate Bible knowledge to everyday life. Read **Deuteronomy 31:6** to the class and explain the directions. Choose a student to read aloud the first situation. Discuss possible ideas about what could be done. Direct the students to write a sentence or several words for each of the three situations explaining what they would do. Provide help as needed. Choose volunteers to read what they have written.

✍ Science Connection (optional)

Discuss the yam. Display the yam and explain that it is the part of the plant that grows underground. It stores food for the plant. Tell the students that some wild yams produce special chemicals that can be used to make medicines. Share the background information about yams.

Sprout a yam. Place three or four toothpicks around the midline of a yam or sweet potato to support it on the rim of a glass or jar. Add water to the glass or jar until the bottom half of the potato is in the water. Within a few weeks the potato should grow roots and can then be planted in soil.

Materials

- Hymn: "Am I a Soldier of the Cross?"
- A copy of *A Question of Yams* for each student or one for the teacher
- Three or four descriptions of real-life situations on cards or paper (for students to read). The following is an example.

  "My grandma is sick, and that worries me. Why would God let my grandma get sick? What if she can't go on long walks with me anymore or take me to the store with her? I need my grandma, and I don't understand why she got sick."

🎵 Hymn: "Am I a Soldier of the Cross?"

Sing the first verse (Worktext page 218). Play the recording of the first verse. Ask a student to explain the verse in his own words. *(Answers will vary but should include the idea of being a Christian who is not ashamed of Christ.)*

♥ Memory Verse—Romans 8:28

Practice the memory verse. Call on a volunteer to read one of the real-life situations that you prepared. Lead the class in responding to it by saying Romans 8:28 together. Repeat this several times to help students understand how God's Word can help us in our everyday lives.

Missionary Story

Read Chapter 2 of *A Question of Yams*. Call on students to review what they read about Kuri and his father in Chapter 1. Direct the students to read Chapter 2 silently or read it to them. Comprehension question: **Did the Christians' yams sprout?** *(yes)*

- 💡 **What was Kuri's father referring to when he spoke of God's Carving?** *(the Bible)*
- ▶ **How had Kuri's father come to read God's Carving?** *(He had helped the missionaries translate the Bible into his language.)*
- ▶ **Was Kuri sure the yams would grow if only God took care of them?** *(no)*
- ▶ **Was Kuri's father afraid when he was threatened by the Head Men?** *(no)*
- ▶ **What did he do after he was threatened?** *(He prayed to God to open the eyes of the Head Men.)* Explain that when trusting God you should pray for others, including your enemies.

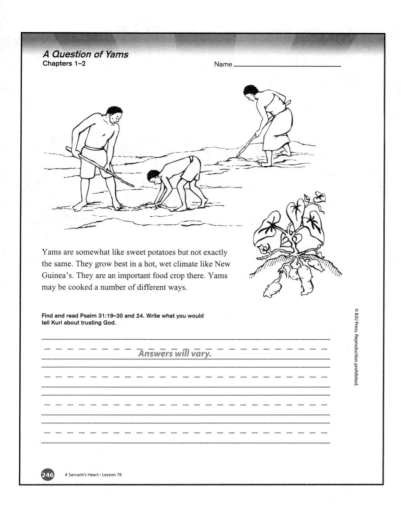

A Question of Yams
Chapters 1–2

Name _____

Yams are somewhat like sweet potatoes but not exactly the same. They grow best in a hot, wet climate like New Guinea's. They are an important food crop there. Yams may be cooked a number of different ways.

Find and read Psalm 31:19–20 and 24. Write what you would tell Kuri about trusting God.

_ _
_____
_ _ _ _ _ _ _ _ _ _ _ _ *Answers will vary.* _ _ _ _ _ _ _ _ _
_____
_ _
_____
_ _
_____
_ _

246 A Servant's Heart • Lesson 76

 **Worktext page 246**

***A Question of Yams:* Chapters 1–2.** Read the information about yams from the page. Remind the students that yams were an important source of food for these people. Direct the students to find **Psalm 31:19–20, 24** in their Bibles and follow along as you read the passage aloud. Instruct the students to answer the question in the Worktext; then call on volunteers to read their answers.

▶ Going Beyond

Reinforcement

Apply Bible knowledge to everyday life. Direct each student to write about an everyday situation (such as those you used in reviewing Romans 8:28). Let volunteers choose a partner and role-play their situations in front of the class.

Enrichment

Draw a map. After hearing or reading the first two chapters of *A Question of Yams,* direct the students to draw a simple map of Kuri's surroundings: his home, his father's garden, his favorite rock, and so on.

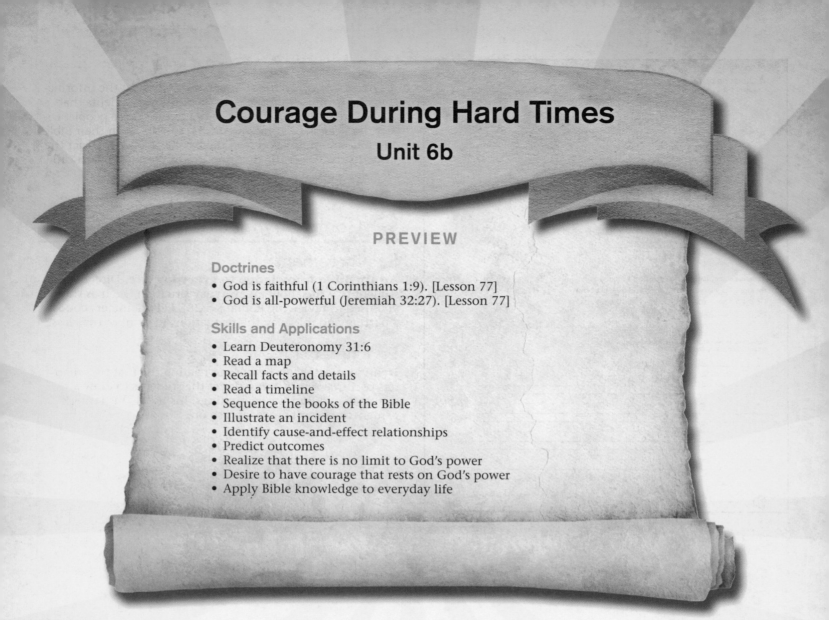

Courage During Hard Times
Unit 6b

PREVIEW

Doctrines

- God is faithful (1 Corinthians 1:9). [Lesson 77]
- God is all-powerful (Jeremiah 32:27). [Lesson 77]

Skills and Applications

- Learn Deuteronomy 31:6
- Read a map
- Recall facts and details
- Read a timeline
- Sequence the books of the Bible
- Illustrate an incident
- Identify cause-and-effect relationships
- Predict outcomes
- Realize that there is no limit to God's power
- Desire to have courage that rests on God's power
- Apply Bible knowledge to everyday life

LESSON 77 God Gives Courage to Do Right

Materials

- Chart 17, "God Gives Courage to Do Right"
- Chart 38, "Empires"
- Unit 6 Bookmark for each student
- Copy of page A87 ("News! News!") for each student (optional)
- Transparency or PowerPoint of page A86 ("Kings") used for Lesson 69
- Highlighter for each student (optional)

Background Information

City of Babylon—*Excavations at the site of ancient Babylon have unearthed ruins of the splendid city made famous by Nebuchadnezzar's hanging gardens, one of the seven wonders of the ancient world. Thousands of clay tiles have been found bearing the inscription of Nebuchadnezzar. Ruins include the Temple of Ishtar, the royal palace, and a ziggurat (a rectangular, multistoried temple). The Ishtar Gate and the royal palace were covered with colored, enameled brick. The historian Herodotus says that the city was square, with each side more than thirteen miles long. The Euphrates River ran through the city, providing water.*

Daniel and His Friends—*After Nebuchadnezzar brought Daniel, Hananiah, Mishael, and Azariah from Palestine as captives, he included them in a group of Jewish youths who were to receive training in Chaldean culture. They were given names honoring Babylonian gods. That's why we know three of these young men better by the names Shadrach, Meshach, and Abednego. The pagan king could change their names, but he could not alter their godly character—they stayed true to their God even in a foreign country. They refused to disobey God and bow down to the image the king had erected. God honored them for their faithfulness and courage.*

The Fiery Furnace—*King Nebuchadnezzar's fiery furnace was more like a giant kiln. Such ovens were used to bake bricks and melt metal.*

Introducing the Bible Account

Introduce Daniel and his friends. Display Chart 38, "Empires," as you relay the background information. Display the PowerPoint or transparency of page A86 ("Kings") as you discuss the time period for the following account.

Read Daniel 3:1–30 or use the following retelling of the passage. Listening question: **Why would Shadrach, Meshach, and Abednego not bow down to the golden image?** *(God's law says not to worship images.)* Direct the students to look at Worktext page 113 as you speak.

God Gives Courage
to Do Right
Daniel 3:1–30

90 feet tall

Music was a prominent art in ancient times. It was often a part of worship. Instruments included percussion (drums, tambourines, cymbals), strings (psaltery or harp, zither, sackbut), horns (both animal and metal), and woodwinds (flutes of reeds and clay).

A Servant's Heart • Lesson 77 113

God Gives Courage to Do Right

Four particular young men were among those taken from Judah by the armies of the Babylonian empire. They were taken to the king's court to be servants of King Nebuchadnezzar. These men had been chosen to be servants of the king because they were wise and healthy. They were given the names of Belteshazzar (his Hebrew name was Daniel), Shadrach, Meshach, and Abednego.

These four Jewish young men living in the court of King Nebuchadnezzar, the ruler of Babylon, faced some problems. The true God was not recognized and certainly not worshiped there.

Nebuchadnezzar had ordered a huge golden image to be built. At the dedication of the image, all Babylonian officials were to line up, bow with their faces to the ground, and worship the image. When all the other people bowed down, Shadrach, Meshach, and Abednego didn't bow. God's law says not to worship images.

When the king heard that these men wouldn't bow down to the golden image, he became furious. He had the men brought before him and told them that they must bow. If they refused, he would have them thrown into his furnace burning with fire. The king ordered the furnace to be heated to seven times its normal temperature. Shadrach, Meshach, and Abednego told the king that they served a God Who could deliver them from the fiery furnace but that even if He didn't, they would never worship false gods or bow down to the golden statue.

▶ **Why were Shadrach, Meshach, and Abednego in Babylon?** *(They had been taken captive.)*
▶ **Why were they chosen to live in the court of Nebuchadnezzar?** *(They were wise and healthy.)*
▶ **What happened that made these three be especially noticed by the head of the king's servants?** *(They would not bow down to the golden image that had been set up.)*
▶ **What did the king threaten to do to these young men?** *(have them thrown into the furnace of fire)*
▶ **How did the three young men respond to the king?** *(They said that their God could save them, but even if He didn't, they would not bow down to any god made with hands. They worshiped the true God.)*

King Nebuchadnezzar commanded his guards to tie up the three men and throw them into the furnace. The fire was so hot that the guards were killed while throwing Shadrach, Meshach, and Abednego onto the floor of the furnace. The king looked into the furnace and asked his servants, "Didn't we tie up three men and throw them into the fire?"

They answered, "That's right, Your Majesty."

Then the king replied that he saw four men walking in the fire, untied, without being hurt at all by the fire! The king said that one of them looked godlike.

The king came closer to the furnace and called Shadrach, Meshach, and Abednego and told them to come out of the fire. Then the three young men walked out of the furnace and stood before the king; not even a hair of their heads was singed. The king said to them, "Blessed be the God of Shadrach, Meshach, and Abednego, Who has rescued His servants who trusted in Him."

Then King Nebuchadnezzar commanded that anyone who spoke against their God would be cut into pieces. Nebuchadnezzar knew that no other god could save men as God had done.

▶ **What did the king do after the three young men told him why they would not bow to an idol?** *(He became very angry and demanded that they be thrown into the fiery furnace.)*
▶ **What happened to the guards who threw Shadrach, Meshach, and Abednego into the furnace?** *(They were killed by the heat of the fire.)*
▶ **When the king looked into the furnace, what did he see?** *(four men walking around untied)*

▶ **What did the king say about the fourth man?** *(He looked godlike.)*

💡 **Who do you think the fourth man was?** *(Accept any answer; but inform them that some Bible scholars think it was Jesus Christ.)*

💡 **What did the king decree after he had called Shadrach, Meshach, and Abednego out of the furnace?** *(They were to be allowed to worship their powerful God and anyone who spoke against their God would be cut into pieces.)*

InfoScene: "God Gives Courage to Do Right"
Display Chart 17 for the students to refer to throughout this unit.

💗 Memory Verse—Deuteronomy 31:6

Principle: We can be courageous because God is with us. Direct the students to open their Bibles to the memory verse. Read the verse aloud as they read it silently.

💡 **The verse says that the Lord your God goes with you. Is God your Lord? How can you make God your Lord?** *(You can make God your Lord by believing that Jesus is God, that He died on the cross to pay for your sins, and that He rose again, and by asking Him to be your Savior.)*

▶ **Since the Lord God is with Christians, what are they not to do, according to the verse?** *(They are not to fear.)*

▶ **What are Christians supposed to do according to the verse?** *(Be strong and courageous.)*

▶ **What does the verse say God will do?** *(He will be with His people wherever they go.)*

💡 **Are there any places you go that you think God would not want to go?** *(Answers may vary.)*

Read **1 Corinthians 6:19–20** aloud with open Bibles. Remind the students that we know God is with us everywhere we go. Point out that a Christian should not bring shame to the name of Christ by going places where he ought not to go. Direct the students to highlight the memory verse (optional) and mark the location with the Unit 6 Bookmark.

✍️ Worktext page 114

Recall facts and details. Direct the students' attention to the word bank. Explain to the students that they are to read each question, find the correct answer from the word bank, and write it in the space provided.

Read the directions for the word search exercise at the bottom of the page. Ask a volunteer to name the three Hebrew men. *(Shadrach, Meshach, and Abednego)* Direct the students' attention to the names at the top of the page for the correct spellings. Provide help as needed. Continue the directions to find the words *courage* and *trust.* Remind the students that they too can have courage to do what is right.

✏️ Writing Connection (optional)

Guide the writing of a newspaper story. Write for display the names *Shadrach, Meshach,* and *Abednego.* Direct the students' attention to the top of page A87 ("News! News!"). Review the headlines of a newspaper with the class. Direct

God Gives Courage: Alive in the Fire
Daniel 3:1–30   Name _____

Read each question about Shadrach, Meshach, and Abednego. Find the answer in the word bank and write it on the line.

Word Bank
very hot · fire · God · three · the king

1. How many men would not bow down when the music sounded? *three*

2. What was to kill these Hebrew men if they disobeyed the king again? *fire*

3. Whom did they say they trusted in to let them live or die? *God*

4. How would you describe the fire that killed the men in the king's army? *very hot*

5. Who was very surprised to see four men walking instead of three? *the king*

Find the names of the three Hebrew young men and circle them with red. Find the word *courage* and draw an orange box around it. Find the word *trust* and color it blue.

114   A Servant's Heart · Lesson 78

the students to choose one of the main characters from the list you wrote and write the name on the top lines of their page. Tell them to write a few sentences describing a situation in the Bible account about that person. Remind the students to draw a picture about their sentences. Display the completed articles on the Unit 6 bulletin board.

LESSON 78 — Hero of the Faith: Adoniram Judson

Materials

- Chart 31, "World Map"
- Hymn: "Am I a Soldier of the Cross?"
- TimeLine and picture: Adoniram Judson

🎵 Hymn: "Am I a Soldier of the Cross?"

Teach the second verse (Worktext page 218). Direct the students to find the hymn in their Worktexts. Sing or play the recording of the second verse for the students. Explain that the verse is talking about two different kinds of Christians. One has an easy life (maybe because he does not work for the Lord and take a stand when he should). This is a person who wants to be taken to heaven on "flow'ry beds of ease." The other kind of Christian is determined to do right and is rewarded. Point out that some Christians have even given their lives for Christ. They are represented by the

phrase "And sailed thru bloody seas." Challenge the students to be the kind of Christian who pleases God. Lead the students in singing the second verse of the hymn with the recording.

Introduction to the Hero of the Faith

Introduce the setting. Locate Myanmar (formerly Burma) on Chart 31, "World Map." Point out India (to the west), the Bay of Bengal, and China. Tell the students that Adoniram Judson went to the country of Burma as a missionary in the 1800s. Point out that he was willing to suffer hardship for God, just like Shadrach, Meshach, and Abednego were willing to take a stand for the Lord.

Hero of the Faith

Read or tell the following narrative based on the life of Adoniram Judson. Listening question: **What event led to Adoniram Judson's salvation?** *(the death of his friend in the next room)*

Adoniram Judson

Adoniram Judson was the first American missionary to a foreign country. He also encouraged other Americans to become missionaries.

Adoniram grew up in Massachusetts as the son of a pastor. He loved to read—no matter what kind of book.

At age 16, Adoniram began college. Here he became friends with a student who did not believe that the Bible was true, that Jesus Christ was God, or that He could save people from their sins. Adoniram began to doubt the Bible and believe the false ideas of his friend instead.

Adoniram finished college and began traveling around the country. One night in a country inn, he heard a man groaning in the room next to his. The man seemed to be in such horrible pain that Adoniram thought he must be dying. This made Adoniram think about what would happen if he died himself. He was afraid. He thought about his college friend. Adoniram knew this friend would laugh at him if he discovered how fearful he was about death.

The next day Adoniram found out that the man in the next room had died. He also found out who the man was—his friend from college! Where was his friend now? This made Adoniram start to think about his own sin. He knew now that he needed to be saved from his sin, but he was still not sure he believed the Bible.

Adoniram decided he needed to go back to college and study more about the Bible. As he studied, he came to believe that the Bible is God's Word. He also believed that Jesus is God and that He died to save people from their sin. In December 1808, Adoniram trusted Christ as his Savior.

About a year after he was saved, Adoniram read about a pastor who was telling people in India about the Lord Jesus Christ. Adoniram decided he too wanted to be a missionary.

Adoniram married a woman named Ann, and the two of them went to serve the Lord in India. After less than a year they went to Burma, where they worked translating the Bible into the Burmese language. They printed tracts that told

the people there how to be saved. After Judson had been witnessing for seven years, only three people had accepted Jesus as their Savior and been baptized.

Both Adoniram and Ann got sick from living in Burma. Their first son died. When war broke out between Burma and Britain, Adoniram was put into prison. Ann went many times to the governor to plead for her husband's release. The governor wouldn't release Adoniram, but he promised to spare his life.

The Burmese king ordered his men to search all foreigners' homes. Ann Judson knew that the portions of the Bible she and her husband had translated were in danger. She carefully sewed them into a pillow and took the pillow to her husband in prison. For many nights Adoniram slept with the Bible hidden beneath his head.

Shortly after Adoniram was released from prison in 1826, Ann died. Adoniram spent most of his time working on the translation.

Adoniram married a woman named Sarah a few years later. Sarah helped Adoniram with his ministry in Burma until she died. Adoniram returned to the United States for a visit. He worked with an author named Emily to write a book about Sarah's life. A year later, Adoniram and Emily were married. Together they went to Burma. Adoniram finished the Burmese Bible and an English-Burmese dictionary before he died.

Worksheet

Adoniram Judson

Name _____

Adoniram Judson grew up in Massachusetts, where his father was a pastor. Judson went to Providence College when he was sixteen. There he made a friend who caused him to doubt the Bible. Before long he had turned away from God.

After college, Adoniram traveled with a group of actors. One night when he was staying in an inn, he heard terrible groans from the next room. He was frightened as he lay awake thinking about dying. The next morning he heard that the man who had died next door was his friend from college. He knew that the man had died without Christ. Judson then decided to study the Bible. In December, 1808, he trusted Christ to save him.

Soon, Adoniram knew that God wanted him to be a missionary. He and his wife Ann went to the country of Burma, where they translated the Bible into the Burmese language. When war started between Burma and Britain, he was put in prison. The Burmese soldiers searched their home, but Ann hid the Bible translations in a pillow, which she carried to her husband in prison. He slept for many nights with his head on the safely hidden Word of God. Judson was released from prison in 1826 and lived to finish translating the whole Bible into Burmese. As a result, many thousands of Burmese trusted Jesus Christ as Savior. God used Adoniram Judson, the man who had rejected Him in his youth, to take the gospel to Burma.

Put an *X* beside each thing that Adoniram Judson did *after* he trusted Christ to save him.

_____ Went to Providence College

_X_ Became a missionary

_X_ Translated the Bible

_____ Traveled as an actor

_X_ Slept on the Word of God

_X_ Took the gospel to Burma

_____ Was afraid of dying

_____ Doubted what the Bible says

_X_ Was a hero of the faith

A Servant's Heart • Lesson 78　**241**

God Gives Help Every Day

Name _____

Draw a line from the Bible truth to the picture that illustrates it. (You may use your Bible.)

When something seems too hard for us, we can ask God for courage and help (Philippians 4:13).

We can ask God to help us control our tongues (Psalm 141:3).

When others do wrong, God can help us do right (Romans 12:21).

God can help us not to want or take things that belong to others (Ephesians 4:28).

Whenever we are disappointed, we can ask God to help us be joyful in Him (Psalm 16:11).

We can give thanks even when things do not go our way (Ephesians 5:20).

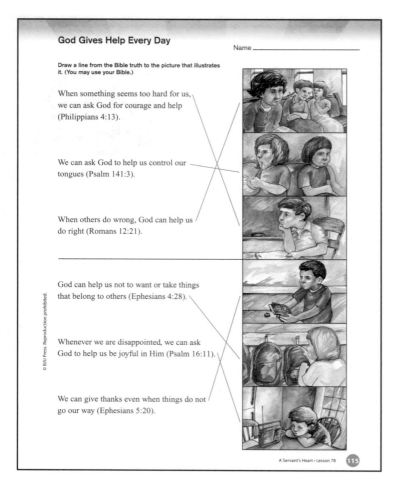

A Servant's Heart • Lesson 78 **115**

Strength and Courage
Deuteronomy 31:6

Name _____

Draw a picture of a time when you needed courage.

Read Luke 8:22–24 and then answer the questions.

1. Who was afraid? **disciples**

2. What were they afraid of? **storm**

3. Who helped them? **Jesus**

Write a sentence that tells what you should do when you need courage. *Answers will vary.*

116 A Servant's Heart • Lesson 79

▶ **To what country did Mr. Judson become a missionary?** *(Burma, today called Myanmar)*

💡 **Why do you think Mr. Judson was a hero?** *(Adoniram Judson suffered many difficulties and could easily have become discouraged. Emphasize that Adoniram's willingness to go to Burma and print tracts and translate the Bible allowed those people to have the Word of God in their own language.)*

🖊 Worktext page 241 (optional)

Hero of the Faith: Adoniram Judson. Review the events in Adoniram Judson's life. Point out that he risked his life to give the people of Burma a translation of the Bible that they could read. We should thank God that we have Bibles that we can read. Direct the students to mark the phrases as indicated on the page.

🕐 TimeLine

Add Adoniram Judson to the TimeLine. Place the picture of Adoniram Judson on the TimeLine (1788–1850), reminding the students that the Judsons were America's first foreign missionaries. Encourage the students that they too can have courage in the midst of hard times when they trust God. Guide the students as they glue their pictures of Adoniram Judson onto their TimeLines.

🖊 Worktext page 115

Apply Bible knowledge to everyday life. Direct the students to examine the pictures. Explain the directions and

allow the students to complete the page independently. Call on volunteers to tell which Bible truth is most helpful to them.

❤ Memory Verse: Deuteronomy 31:6

Practice the memory verse. Ask the following questions and let the class answer only with a line from the verse. When the students have the idea, repeat the questions several times to give them practice saying the verse.

▶ **What does the verse tell believers to be?** *(strong and brave)*

▶ **What are believers not to do?** *(be afraid)*

▶ **Who is it that goes with believers?** *(the Lord our God)*

▶ **Who will not fail believers?** *(the Lord our God)*

▶ **Who will not leave or forsake believers?** *(the Lord our God)*

LESSON
79 Strength and Courage

Materials
• Hymn: "Am I a Soldier of the Cross?"
• A copy of *A Question of Yams* for each student or one for the teacher

🎵 Hymn: "Am I a Soldier of the Cross?"
Sing the first two verses (Worktext page 218).

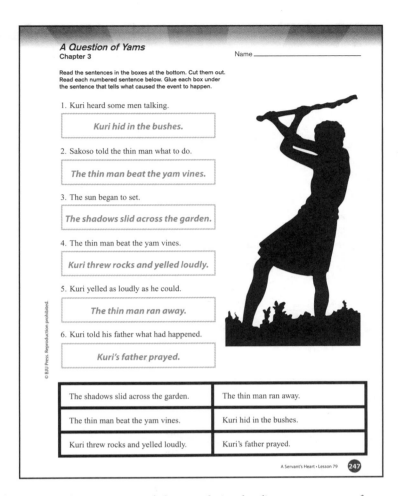

A Question of Yams
Chapter 3

Name _____

Read the sentences in the boxes at the bottom. Cut them out.
Read each numbered sentence below. Glue each box under
the sentence that tells what caused the event to happen.

1. Kuri heard some men talking.

Kuri hid in the bushes.

2. Sakoso told the thin man what to do.

The thin man beat the yam vines.

3. The sun began to set.

The shadows slid across the garden.

4. The thin man beat the yam vines.

Kuri threw rocks and yelled loudly.

5. Kuri yelled as loudly as he could.

The thin man ran away.

6. Kuri told his father what had happened.

Kuri's father prayed.

The shadows slid across the garden.	The thin man ran away.
The thin man beat the yam vines.	Kuri hid in the bushes.
Kuri threw rocks and yelled loudly.	Kuri's father prayed.

A Servant's Heart • Lesson 79 **247**

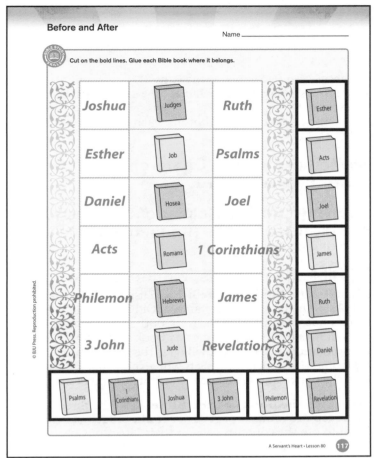

Before and After

Name _____

Cut on the bold lines. Glue each Bible book where it belongs.

Joshua	Judges	Ruth		Esther
Esther	Job	Psalms		Acts
Daniel	Hosea	Joel		Joel
Acts	Romans	1 Corinthians		James
Philemon	Hebrews	James		Ruth
3 John	Jude	Revelation		Daniel

| Psalms | 1 Corinthians | Joshua | 3 John | Philemon | Revelation |

A Servant's Heart • Lesson 80 **117**

Review the meaning of the words in the first two verses of the hymn.

❤ Memory Verse—Deuteronomy 31:6

Practice the memory verse.

✎ Worktext page 116

Apply Bible knowledge to everyday life. Lead the class as they recite **Deuteronomy 31:6** before they start their drawing at the top of the page. Before the students complete the bottom half of the page, instruct them to find **Luke 8:22–24** in their Bibles and read the verses aloud together.

Missionary Story

Read Chapter 3 of *A Question of Yams*. Review what has taken place in the story. Lead a discussion about shadows and then tell the students that the chapter they will read today is Chapter 3, "The Shadow." Direct the students to read the chapter silently (if they have the book) or read it aloud to them. Comprehension question: **What did Kuri's father do after he prayed?** (*He smiled at Kuri and said he was glad Kuri was there when the man tried to spoil the plants.*)

▶ **What was the shadow of that Kuri saw in his father's garden?** (*the thin man who had been talking to Sakoso*)

▶ **What was the thin man doing?** (*beating on Kuri's father's plants*)

▶ **What did Kuri do?** (*He screamed for his father and threw stones.*)

▶ **Did the thin man keep beating on the plants?** (*No. He ran away.*)

▶ **When Kuri told his father what the man had been doing, how did Kuri's father respond?** (*He bowed his head and prayed for the men who wanted to destroy the plants. Point out that Kuri's father showed he trusted God even when the situation did not go as he planned.*)

▶ **What was different about how his father prayed?** (*He prayed loudly to God.*)

💡 **Why do you think he prayed loudly?** (*Any answer is acceptable.*)

✎ Worktext page 247

***A Question of Yams*: Chapter 3.** Choose volunteers to read the sentences at the bottom of the page. Tell the students to think about *why* each event happened. Example: *Why* did the shadows slide across the garden? Model other examples as needed. Instruct the students to cut apart the sentences at the bottom and place them below the appropriate numbered sentence before gluing.

Before and After

Materials

- Hymn: "Am I a Soldier of the Cross?"
- Charts 2–3, "Books of the Bible: New Testament, Old Testament"
- A copy of *A Question of Yams* for each student or one for the teacher

♥ Memory Verse—Deuteronomy 31:6

Review the memory verse.

♫ Hymn: "Am I a Soldier of the Cross?"

Sing the first two verses (Worktext page 218). Use the recording if desired.

📖 Bible Study Skills, Worktext page 117

Identify the books of the Bible. Display Charts 2–3, "Books of the Bible: New Testament, Old Testament." Choose three students to stand at the front of the classroom. Tell the student in the middle to name any book of the Bible. Explain that the student to his right will give the book that comes *before* and the student to his left will give the book that comes *after* the book named. Repeat the activity as you desire.

Sequence the books of the Bible. Read the directions at the top of Worktext page 117 with the students. Remind them to use the contents page in their Bibles or Charts 2–3, "Books of the Bible: New Testament, Old Testament." Point out that they should cut apart the boxes and place them on the page before gluing. Check the answers with the students.

Missionary Story

Read Chapter 4 of *A Question of Yams*. After reviewing the story, direct the students to look at the title of Chapter 4 and the picture on page 27. Comprehension question: **What do you think will happen in this chapter?** Tell them to read the chapter silently to see whether they are correct or to listen while you read it to them.

▶ **What was Kuri thinking about as he cut the firewood?** *(He was wondering about his father's God and the spirits that the other villagers worshiped.)*

▶ **What happened to Kuri next?** *(He was bitten by a snake.)*

▶ **What did Kuri think would be the result of the snake bite?** *(He would die.)*

▶ **How did his father respond when Kuri was bitten?** *(He was calm.)*

💡 **Why was he so calm?** *(Answers may vary.)*

▶ **Who came to help Kuri?** *(the missionary)*

▶ **How did Kuri's legs feel to him?** *(They had no feeling.)*

▶ **What was Kuri thinking as he lay on the mat?** *(about the Head Men, their wicked plans, and that he was glad his father worshiped such a mighty God)*

✍ Worktext page 248

***A Question of Yams*: Chapter 4.** Instruct the students to mark the correct answers by filling in the circles.

A Question of Yams
Chapter 4

Name _____

Fill in the circle beside the correct answer.

1. How did Kuri feel after the snake bit him?
   - ○ glad
   - ○ lazy
   - ● ill

2. Whom did Kuri's father ask to help?
   - ● Joyce
   - ○ Sakoso
   - ○ Kuri

3. Who ran to tell the village?
   - ○ the thin man
   - ● a small boy
   - ○ Kuri

4. How did Kuri feel about the tall missionary?
   - ○ afraid
   - ● not afraid
   - ○ sad

5. How will the doctor get to Kuri's village?
   - ○ airplane
   - ○ Jeep
   - ● helicopter

6. What did Kuri's father get some men to do?
   - ○ sing
   - ● pray
   - ○ plant yams

7. Why did the unsaved people think the snake bit Kuri?
   - ○ He listened to Sakoso and the thin man.
   - ○ His mother sent him into the jungle.
   - ● His father planted yams the Christian way.

8. What did Kuri's mother do to try to help him?
   - ○ boiled tea for him to drink
   - ● rubbed his feet with stinging nettles
   - ○ looked for the snake to see what kind it was

9. Why did Kuri not ask whether he was going to die?
   - ● He was too tired.
   - ○ He didn't want to know.
   - ○ He didn't want to worry his mother.

10. What did Kuri tell himself?
    - ○ Father is foolish to trust God.
    - ○ Father doesn't love me.
    - ● Father is wise to trust God.

(248) A Servant's Heart • Lesson 80

▶ Going Beyond

Reinforcement

Materials

- One 2" × 8" construction-paper strip for each student

Discuss courage in obedience. Call on students to tell what it means to be *courageous*. Write for display the names *Shadrach, Meshach, Abednego,* and *Adoniram Judson.* Remind the students that these men obeyed God. Choose volunteers to tell about people who have shown courage. Encourage them to think about people in their community who have shown courage. Distribute the construction paper strips. Instruct the students to write the name of one courageous person on each strip and to glue the ends together. Demonstrate how to connect the second strip to make a paper chain. Display the chains in the classroom and add more names as desired.

Enrichment

Guide a writing and drawing activity. Assign an activity of drawing a large fiery furnace. You may want to use paper or an old white sheet. Choose four students to represent the men walking around in the fire. Instruct the students to write a few sentences from the point of view of Shadrach, Meshach, or Abednego. Encourage them to tell how it might have felt to have met the fourth man and to have stood before the king untouched by the fire.

Courage to Speak God's Word
Unit 6c

PREVIEW

Doctrines

- Man has God's favor through Christ (Ephesians 1:3). [Lesson 81]
- Man is guilty before God (Romans 3:10–12). [Lesson 82]
- Man is in a hopeless condition (Isaiah 64:6). [Lesson 82]

Skills and Applications

- Learn Romans 1:16
- Recall facts and details
- Draw conclusions
- Sequence events
- Classify books of the Bible into Old and New Testaments
- Distinguish between God's way and man's way
- Recognize the gospel of Jesus Christ and not be ashamed of Him
- Realize that man's inclination is to sin, not to obey God
- Appreciate the ability to hear God's Word and to read it
- Apply Bible knowledge to everyday life

LESSON 81 — Daniel's Reputation

Materials

- Chart 18, "Some Strange Handwriting"
- Hymn: "Am I a Soldier of the Cross?"
- Unit 6 Bookmark for each student
- Highlighter for each student (optional)

Hymn: "Am I a Soldier of the Cross?"

Teach the third verse (Worktext page 218). Sing or play the recording of the third verse. Explain that the hymnwriter is still asking questions such as, "Are there foes (enemies) to fight?" or "Should I be trying to stop the flood of evil in this world?" A Christian must realize that there will be hard times in the Christian life, especially when he takes a stand for what is right and for the Lord. Explain that the hymnwriter knows the answer to the last question, "Is this world my friend, and will it help me to live for God?" Ask the students what the answer is. *(no)* Play and sing the third verse of the hymn together several times.

Background Information

Daniel—*Apparently a member of a high-ranking Jewish family in Israel, Daniel was among the captives taken to Babylon by Nebuchadnezzar. Arriving in Babylon as a youth, Daniel lived until he was almost ninety and became prime minister of the land. During his lifetime he saw the Babylonian empire fall and the Medo-Persian kingdom rise. He lived during the reigns of Nebuchadnezzar, Belshazzar, Darius, and Cyrus. Ezekiel and Jeremiah prophesied during the same time. Daniel lived to see the beginning of Ezra's ministry.*

King Belshazzar—*Belshazzar was a descendant of Nebuchadnezzar. Although Nebuchadnezzar is called his "father" in **Daniel 5:2**, the word father is often used in Scripture to mean "ancestor." Jeremiah prophesied that Nebuchadnezzar would reign and all nations would serve him, his son, and his son's son (**Jeremiah 27:7**).*

Introducing the Bible Account

Guide a review about Daniel. Share the background information about Daniel and King Belshazzar as you introduce the account. Point out that Daniel had good character and that this made it possible for him to be used by God (**2 Timothy 2:21**).

Read Daniel 5:1–16 or use the following retelling of the passage. Listening question: **Who told the king to ask Daniel what the words meant?** *(the queen)* Direct attention to the picture on Worktext page 119.

Daniel's Reputation

King Nebuchadnezzar, ruler of Babylon, had conquered the land of Judah. He went to the temple in Jerusalem and took many treasures from the house of the Lord.

Many years later, Belshazzar took over as ruler of Babylon. One night he was having a great feast. He invited a thousand people to the feast. When they had begun drinking wine, Belshazzar asked for the gold and silver vessels that his grandfather had taken from the temple in Jerusalem. The people at the feast drank from these vessels of the Lord's house while they worshiped false gods.

While they were praising idols, the fingers of a man's hand appeared and wrote on the wall of the king's palace. When the king saw the fingers, he got scared—so scared that his knees knocked against each other.

The king called for his astrologers, magicians, soothsayers, and men who were thought to be wise. He wanted to know what the handwriting meant. He promised to reward anyone who could explain it.

The queen told the king about a man who could help him—a man, she said, who had true wisdom. King Nebuchadnezzar had used this man to interpret dreams and had made him a leader in the kingdom. The man's name was Daniel.

King Belshazzar called for Daniel to tell him what the handwriting on the wall meant. He told Daniel that his wise men couldn't explain it. But Daniel was different; he had the wisdom of God. The king promised to make Daniel the third ruler in the kingdom if he could read the writing.

❦

▶ **What upset King Belshazzar so much that he stopped praising the manmade gods?** *(The fingers of a hand appeared and wrote words on the wall.)*

▶ **Did the king know what the words meant?** *(no)*

▶ **What did the king want to know?** *(the meaning of the words)*

▶ **Whom did the king first call for help?** *(his astrologers, magicians, soothsayers, and wise men)*

▶ **Could any of these men interpret the words?** *(no)*

▶ **Whom did the queen suggest the king bring in to interpret the words?** *(Daniel)*

▶ **Why did she suggest Daniel?** *(She had heard he was wise.)*

💡 **How had Daniel developed good character?** *(Various answers may be acceptable, but elicit that Daniel had purposed not to defile himself [**Daniel 1:8**] and God had given him wisdom not only in his schooling but in other matters also [**1:17**].)*

💡 **Do you think Daniel had been telling the people around him about God or keeping quiet about God?** *(Allow time for discussion.)*

Some Strange Handwriting
Daniel 5:1–16

Belshazzar reigned from about 550 to 539 BC.

Belshazzar's name means "may Bel protect the king." Bel was the god worshiped in Babylon.

MENE MENE TEKEL UPHARSIN

© BJU Press. Reproduction prohibited.

The temple vessels Belshazzar sent for had been brought from the temple in Jerusalem. They were made of solid gold and silver and had been dedicated to the worship of God. For the last forty years they had been stored in Babylon.

A Servant's Heart • Lesson 81 119

💡 **Does God want Christians to tell others about Him?** *(Allow time for discussion.)*

InfoScene: "Some Strange Handwriting"
Display Chart 18 from the Visual Packet for the students to refer to throughout this unit.

💙 **Memory Verse—Romans 1:16**

Principle: We should not be ashamed to tell others about the gospel of Jesus Christ. Jesus is God; Jesus died to pay for our sins; Jesus arose from the dead; Jesus lives today.

Read the verse aloud. Call on volunteers to tell what the gospel of Jesus Christ is. After they have given their answers, direct them to look up **1 Corinthians 15:1–4**. Read the verses aloud as they follow along. Point out that the gospel is that by which we are saved. Read verses 3 and 4 aloud again. Write the following parts of verses 3 and 4 for display: *Christ died for our sins. He was buried. He rose again the third day. He was seen alive by many people.* Explain that this is the gospel of Jesus Christ and if one of them ever wants to help someone trust Jesus as Savior, he can turn to these two verses and show that person the gospel. Turn to Romans 1:16 again and read the verse together several times.

💡 **What did Paul mean when he said, "I am not ashamed of the gospel of Christ"?** *(that he was not afraid or embarrassed to tell others about the Lord)*

Daniel Reads the Writing
Daniel 5:1–16

Name _____

Look at this "newsletter." Use information from the Bible to complete the caption for each picture.

Babylon Bulletin
Volume 10, Number 21

Handwriting on Wall Puzzles Wise Men

__The__ __king__ gave a feast for 1,000 guests.

They were drinking wine when __fingers__ wrote on the wall.

The king called his __wise men__.

None of them could tell what the __words__ meant.

MENE
MENE
TEKEL
UPHARSIN

The __queen__ said to call for the man who had helped King Nebuchadnezzar.

__Daniel__ had told King Nebuchadnezzar about his dream.

King Belshazzar told Daniel that he would make him the third highest in the kingdom if he could tell what the writing meant.

© BJU Press. Reproduction prohibited.

120 A Servant's Heart • Lesson 81

▶ **Why was Paul bold in telling the gospel?** *(He knew its power to save sinners.)*

 Worktext page 120

Recall facts and details. Direct attention to the newspaper headline. Explain that the story on the newspaper page represents what the news about the "handwriting on the wall" might have been if newspapers had been published in King Belshazzar's days. Explain the directions and let the students work independently, giving help if needed.

LESSON
82 A Message from God

Materials
- Hymn: "Am I a Soldier of the Cross?"
- Copy of page A87 ("News! News!") for each student (optional)
- Balance scale or picture of one (optional)
- A large card with the word *Teacher* printed on one side and the word *Students* printed on the other

🎵 **Hymn: "Am I a Soldier of the Cross?"**

Practice the third verse (Worktextpage 218). Sing the third verse together several times. Choose a group to sing the first line and another group to sing the second line, repeating this to the end of the third verse.

Background Information

Daniel's Interpretation—*When Daniel defines the words on the wall, he lists* MENE *just once since one explanation suffices for both occurrences. He defines the word* PERES *instead of the word* UPHARSIN *because* PERES *is the root of the verb* UPHARSIN.

Introducing the Bible Account

Review the Bible account from the previous lesson. Discuss what happened in the first part of the account and how it ended with Daniel's being offered a reward if he could interpret the writing. Display the balance scale or show a picture of one. If neither is available, make a simple drawing for display.

Bible Account

Read Daniel 5:17–31 or use the following retelling of the passage. Listening question: **Was Daniel able to tell the king what the words meant?** *(yes)* A review of Worktext page 119 may by helpful to the students.

Daniel's Interpretation

Daniel told the king that he would read the handwriting on the wall, but not for a reward. The king could keep his gifts.

Before reading the handwriting, Daniel reminded King Belshazzar about King Nebuchadnezzar. Nebuchadnezzar was a king who refused to give God the glory for all that he did. God had to humble Nebuchadnezzar by making him look and act like an animal. Nebuchadnezzar grew long hair and nails and ate grass like an animal. Seven years later, Nebuchadnezzar realized he needed to give praise to God, the King of heaven. Belshazzar knew what had happened to his grandfather, but he had not learned anything from it. He didn't have a humble heart.

Belshazzar's feast showed that he was proud too. He asked for the temple cups to be brought so he could have wine served in them at his proud feast. These cups were from God's holy house, and they were being used to worship idols. Then God caused fingers to appear and write the words *MENE MENE TEKEL UPHARSIN* on the wall.

Daniel was able to tell King Belshazzar what the words meant. *MENE* meant that God had numbered the days left in Belshazzar's kingdom. It would soon come to an end. *TEKEL* meant that Belshazzar's life was put on a scale, and it didn't weigh enough. Belshazzar's life wasn't what it should be. *UPHARSIN* meant that Belshazzar would lose his kingdom to two other groups of people named the Medes and the Persians.

When Daniel finished explaining the meaning of the handwriting, King Belshazzar rewarded him. Daniel was given a scarlet robe and a gold chain, and he was made third highest ruler of Babylon.

That night, King Belshazzar was killed. A man named Darius, who was king of the Medes, took over the kingdom. Daniel lived to serve under this new king.

- ▶ **Did Daniel want the gifts the king offered him?** *(no)*
- ▶ **Did Daniel agree to read the words and interpret them?** *(yes)*
- 💡 **What did Daniel do before he interpreted the words?** *(He recounted the history of King Nebuchadnezzar and Belshazzar as seen from God's eyes.)*
- ▶ **According to Daniel, Who caused the fingers to write on the wall?** *(God)*
- 💡 **How did Daniel show courage?** *(He was willing to speak God's words even though he knew others might not like the message.)*
- ▶ **What was the message of the words on the wall?** *(The words told the king that he had not pleased God and his kingdom would be taken away.)*
- 💡 **What lesson had Belshazzar failed to learn?** *(He had not learned humility.)*
- ▶ **What happened to King Belshazzar?** *(He was killed that night.)*

♥ Memory Verse—Romans 1:16

Practice the memory verse. Hold the *Teacher/Students* card so that the *Teacher* side is toward the students. Explain that you will give the reference and then turn the card. Let the class read (or recite) the first phrase of the verse. Turn the card and recite the next phrase; keep turning the card until the entire verse is repeated. Repeat the activity several times, alternating who says which phrase. Ask the students to recite the verse.

✏ Worktext page 121

Distinguish between God's way and man's way. Read aloud the explanation at the top of the page. Instruct the students to open their Bibles to **Romans 3:23–24**. Read the verses together. Point out that God says that sin keeps everyone from Him, but that He offers forgiveness. When a person trusts Jesus Christ as Savior, he is set free from the penalty of sin.

Direct attention to the balance scale. Point out that if God really weighed our good and bad deeds and attitudes on a scale, we would have no hope. Even our "good works" are mixed up with sinful motives and desires and would have to be placed on the "bad works" side of the scale. Our only hope is that Jesus took the punishment for our bad deeds and is willing to give us His righteousness. Explain that they will mark the balance pans to show whether the phrase tells about God's way (pleasing God) or Belshazzar's way (pleasing self). Choose a volunteer to read the first phrase on the left and tell whose way it describes. *(God's way)* Instruct the students to trace the balance pan with a red crayon. Guide them as they complete the page.

✐ Writing Connection (optional)

Guide the writing of a newspaper story. Write for display the names *Daniel, King Nebuchadnezzar,* and *the queen.* Direct attention to the top of page A87 ("News! News!"). Review the headlines of a newspaper. Tell the students to choose one of the characters from the list on display and write a few sentences describing a situation about that character in the Bible account. Remind them to draw a picture about their sentences. Display the completed articles on the Unit 6 Bulletin Board.

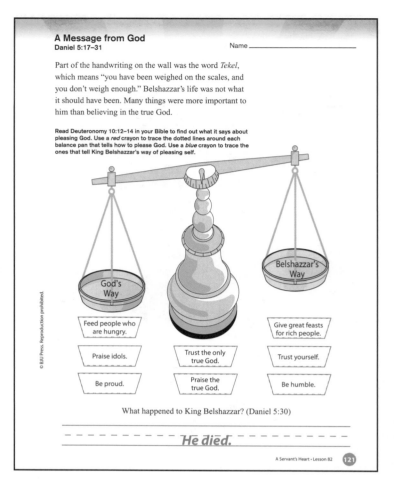

A Message from God
Daniel 5:17–31   Name _____

Part of the handwriting on the wall was the word *Tekel,* which means "you have been weighed on the scales, and you don't weigh enough." Belshazzar's life was not what it should have been. Many things were more important to him than believing in the true God.

Read Deuteronomy 10:12–14 in your Bible to find out what it says about pleasing God. Use a *red* crayon to trace the dotted lines around each balance pan that tells how to please God. Use a *blue* crayon to trace the ones that tell King Belshazzar's way of pleasing self.

God's Way — Belshazzar's Way

Feed people who are hungry.		Give great feasts for rich people.
Praise idols.	Trust the only true God.	Trust yourself.
Be proud.	Praise the true God.	Be humble.

What happened to King Belshazzar? (Daniel 5:30)

 He died.

A Servant's Heart · Lesson 82 **121**

LESSON 83 — Whose Way?

Materials
- Hymn: "Am I a Soldier of the Cross?"
- A copy of *A Question of Yams* for each student or one for the teacher

♥ Memory Verse—Romans 1:16
Practice the memory verse.

♫ Hymn: "Am I a Soldier of the Cross?"
Sing the first three verses (Worktext page 218).

✏ Worktext page 122
Apply Bible knowledge to everyday life. Discuss whose way is best—Daniel's way to be humble and follow God or Belshazzar's way to be proud and please self. Choose a student to read the first example and ask him which picture to circle. *(Belshazzar)* Instruct the students to circle the appropriate picture for each of the other five situations.

Find information. Direct attention to the bottom of the page. Tell the students to use the code to find the name of the next king. Instruct them to read **Daniel 5:31** to check their answer.

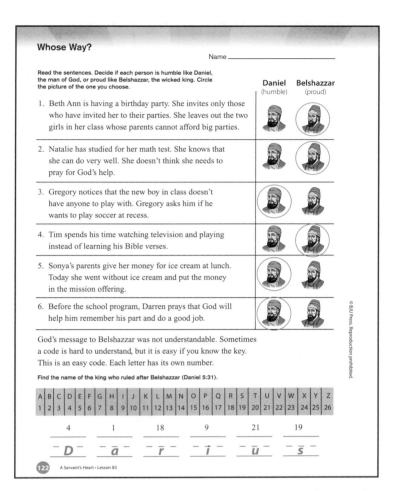

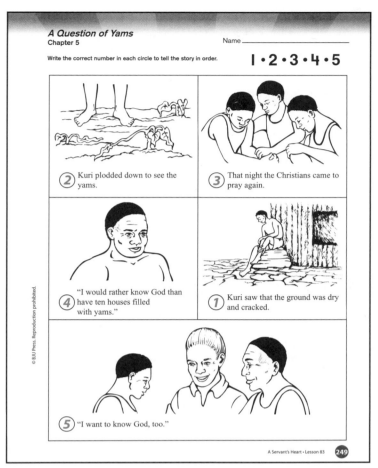

Missionary Story

Read Chapter 5 of *A Question of Yams*. Guide a discussion about the first four chapters. You may use the discussion questions from previous lessons. Direct the students to read Chapter 5 silently or to listen as you read aloud. Comprehension question: **What worried Kuri after he was able to sit outside?** *(the lack of rain)*

▶ **What did Kuri hear when he awoke with a jerk?** *(something as loud as thunder)*

▶ **What had he actually heard?** *(the roar of a helicopter)*

▶ **What did this mean to Kuri?** *(that the doctor had arrived; Kuri could start to get well now)*

▶ **What did the doctor do?** *(gave Kuri a shot)*

 Had the doctor helped Kuri? How do you know? *(Yes. The next time Kuri woke up, he felt better.)*

▶ **How did Kuri's father reassure him that the plants would be fine?** *(He told him that the Christians had been praying for him to get well, and he did. He told him that his mighty God would take care of the plants.)*

▶ **When Kuri's father said that he would rather know God than have ten houses filled with yams, what happened to Kuri?** *(He felt something move in his own heart.)*

 What do you think the moving in Kuri's heart was? *(Accept any answer, but discuss that the Holy Spirit was causing Kuri to understand his need for God's salvation.)*

▶ **What did Kuri tell his father?** *(that he would like to know God)*

Worktext page 249

***A Question of Yams*: Chapter 5.** Direct the students to read each sentence before deciding the order of events. Remind them that Kuri saw his father's faith in God. Point out that their decision to follow God today may encourage others to be obedient to God too.

LESSON 84 God's Book

Materials
- Hymn: "Am I a Soldier of the Cross?"
- Charts 2–3, "Books of the Bible: New Testament, Old Testament"
- A copy of *A Question of Yams* for each student or one for the teacher
- Beanbag

Hymn: "Am I a Soldier of the Cross?"
Sing the third verse.

📖 Bible Study Skills

Review books of the Old and New Testaments. Display Chart 3, "Books of the Bible: Old Testament." Read aloud the books of the Old Testament together. Lead in reciting the books without the chart. Repeat the procedure for the New Testament books with Chart 2, "Books of the Bible: New Testament."

Classify books of the Bible into the Old or the New Testament. Explain that when you call on a student to name a book of the Bible, the class will stand if it is a book from the Old Testament. Tell them to remain seated if the book is from the New Testament. Continue the activity as time allows.

❤ Memory Verse—Romans 1:16

Practice the memory verse.

Missionary Story

Read Chapter 6 of *A Question of Yams*. After reviewing Chapter 5, tell the students to read Chapter 6 or listen as you read aloud. Comprehension question: **What did Kuri think God's Word was written on?** (*something that looked like dried banana leaves*)

▶ **When Kuri went to the missionaries, what did they show him?** (*They showed him God's Word.*)

💡 **Do you think Kuri had ever seen a book?** (*Accept any answer, but point out that Kuri didn't know that God's Word was written on paper. He described the paper as dried banana leaves.*)

▶ **Why did the words not say anything to Kuri when he looked at them?** (*He couldn't read them.*)

▶ **Could Kuri's father read?** (*no*)

💡 **How did Kuri respond to the Word of God when the missionary spoke it to him?** (*He received it. We know this because he felt like singing, he prayed, he looked forward to reading it for himself, he thought about the words as he worked, he said he understood with his heart, and he told others.*)

▶ **To whom did Kuri talk about God?** (*his mother*)

▶ **What did the Christians do to keep their yams growing?** (*carried buckets of water to their gardens*)

💡 **Do you think they stopped praying?** (*Answers may vary.*)

📝 Worktext page 250

***A Question of Yams*: Chapter 6.** Read and discuss briefly the questions on the page. Ask the students to think silently about how many Bibles their families own. Remind them to treasure God's Word. Point out that it is a privilege to hear and to read from the Bible in our own language. Ask them whether they can read the Bible verse at the bottom of the page. (*probably not*) Instruct the students to complete the page. Provide help as needed.

A Question of Yams
Chapter 6
Name _____

Answer the questions.

How do we know what God is like?

— — — — — — — *The Bible tells us.* — — — —

How do we know what Jesus has done for us?

— — — — — — — *The Bible tells us.* — — — —

Can you remember learning to read? Write about it.

— — — — — — *Answers will vary.* — — — — —

Can you remember getting your first Bible? Write about it.

— — — — — — *Answers will vary.* — — — — —

Some missionaries work for many years so that people may read the Bible in their own languages. Languages look very different, but God's Word remains the same.

John 3:16 in Dutch: Want God heeft zoveel liefde voor de wereld, dat Hij Zijn enige Zoon heeft gegeven; zodat ieder die in Hem gelooft, niet verloren gaat maar eeuwig leven heeft.

John 3:16 in Modern Greek: Διότι τόσον ἠγάπησεν ὁ Θεὸς τὸν κόσμον, ὥστε ἔδωκε τὸν Υἱὸν αὐτοῦ τὸν μονογενῆ, διὰ νὰ μὴ ἀπολεσθῇ πᾶς ὁ πιστεύων εἰς αὐτόν, ἀλλὰ νὰ ἔχῃ ζωὴν αἰώνιον.

John 3:16 in Portuguese: Porque assim amou Deus ao mundo, que lhe deu seu Filho unigénito, para que todo o que crê nêle não pereça, mas tenha a vida eterna.

(250) A Servant's Heart • Lesson 84

▶ Going Beyond

Reinforcement

Guide a role-playing activity. Discuss the Bible account of Daniel and the handwriting on the wall. Divide the students into groups. Explain that you want each group to role-play what happened in Belshazzar's court. When all the groups are ready, let each group perform for the class.

Enrichment

Introduce the students to a missionary. Invite a missionary to speak to the class, perhaps a missionary who is translating the Bible into a different language. If this is not possible, write letters to a missionary.

Courage to Live a Godly Life
Unit 6d

PREVIEW

Doctrines

- Man lives in a corrupted environment (Romans 8:22). [Lesson 85]
- Man is in a hopeless condition (Isaiah 64:6). [Lesson 85]
- God is everywhere (omnipresent) (Psalm 139:7–10). [Lesson 86]
- God is all-powerful (omnipotent) (Matthew 19:26). [Lesson 86]

Skills and Applications

- Learn Psalm 56:11
- Identify Bible characters
- Write a summary
- Read a timeline
- Recall facts and details
- Sequence story events
- Infer what a character in a story might have said
- Know that God takes care of His children
- Understand that God can do anything
- Realize that God gives grace to those who serve Him in humility
- Draw conclusions
- Apply Bible knowledge to everyday life

LESSON 85 — A Godly Man Keeps Praying

Materials

- Hymn: "Am I a Soldier of the Cross?"
- Unit 6 Bookmark for each student
- Highlighter for each student (optional)

Introducing the Bible Account

Guide a discussion about Daniel. Review with the students the account of Daniel interpreting the handwriting on the wall for King Belshazzar. Tell them that Daniel was about seventy years old when that happened. That night, King Belshazzar died, and Darius the Mede became ruler in his place. Under King Darius, Daniel had such a high position as one of the presidents in Babylon that the other presidents got jealous and devised a plan to get rid of Daniel.

Bible Account

Read Daniel 6:1–15 or use the following retelling of the passage. Listening question: **How many times did Daniel pray each day?** *(three)*

A Godly Man Keeps Praying

When Darius took over Babylon, he set up a government of 120 princes and three presidents over those princes. The first president he chose was Daniel. King Darius put Daniel over all the other presidents and princes because of Daniel's "excellent spirit."

The other presidents and princes were jealous of Daniel. They wanted to make him look bad, but they couldn't catch Daniel doing anything wrong; he was faithful in everything. The men who wanted to find fault with Daniel tried to find a way to destroy him through Daniel's obedience to God.

These evil men came before the king. They said that they wanted a law to be made that for thirty days, King Darius would be the only one people could come to with their requests. Anyone who asked things of gods or other men would be thrown into the lions' den.

These men made the law sound so good that the king signed it.

Daniel knew about the law, but he continued to pray to God. He opened the windows of his room, looked toward Jerusalem, and prayed three times a day just as he always had.

Daniel's enemies watched him, hoping he would respond to the proclamation in this way. They reported Daniel's actions to the king.

King Darius was very upset by what these men said. He tried to find a way to save Daniel, but since his decree was a law of the Medes and the Persians, it could never be changed.

▶ **Why were the other presidents and princes so jealous of Daniel?** *(The king had given Daniel a position above them.)*

▶ **When Daniel heard about the law, did he stop praying to the only true God?** *(No. He had courage to do what was right because he trusted God.)*

▶ **Why couldn't the king do anything?** *(The law of the Medes and the Persians could never be changed.)*

💡 **Do you think the king was sorry for signing the law?** *(yes)* **How do you know?** *(because he tried to change it)*

💡 **How important was it for Daniel to keep praying?** *(It was very important. We are commanded to pray at all times. It is important to tell God how much we love Him and to thank Him for all He does for us. We also need to ask for wisdom and His strength to live for His glory.)*

❤ Memory Verse—Psalm 56:11

Principle: When we put our trust in God, we do not need to fear what people can do to us.

💡 **What is the most important thing we need to put our trust in God for?** *(Salvation. We receive God's salvation by trusting Jesus to save us from our sin. He is able to forgive us because He died on the cross so that we would not be punished for our sins, and He rose from the dead so that we would one day rise from the dead too.)* Read **Romans 10:9–10** to the students.

▶ **What does Psalm 56:11 say about God's children when they have trusted in God?** *(They will not be afraid of what other people can do to them.)*

Practice the verse. Demonstrate how to divide the verse in two. Read it together several times, pausing between the two parts. Direct the students to highlight the verse (optional) and to mark the location with the Unit 6 Bookmark.

🎵 Hymn: "Am I a Soldier of the Cross?"

Sing the first three verses (Worktext page 218). Review the meanings of key words and phrases in the first three verses of the hymn. Lead in singing the first three verses of the hymn.

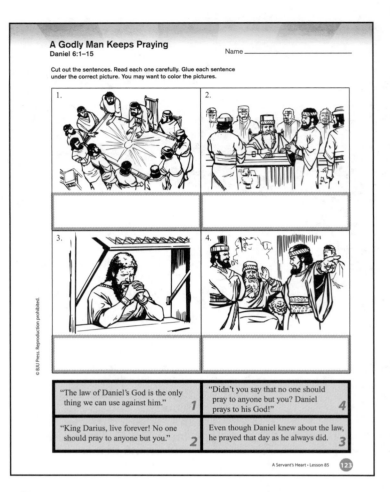

A Godly Man Keeps Praying
Daniel 6:1–15

Name _____

Cut out the sentences. Read each one carefully. Glue each sentence under the correct picture. You may want to color the pictures.

| "The law of Daniel's God is the only thing we can use against him." | **1** | "Didn't you say that no one should pray to anyone but you? Daniel prays to his God!" | **4** |
| "King Darius, live forever! No one should pray to anyone but you." | **2** | Even though Daniel knew about the law, he prayed that day as he always did. | **3** |

A Servant's Heart · Lesson 85   123

✍ Worktext page 123

Guide a sequencing activity. Direct the students' attention to the pictures on the page as you review the Bible account. Instruct them to cut apart the sentences and to match the sentences with the pictures before gluing them in place. Allow time to color the pictures with markers or colored pencils if possible.

✍ Worktext page 124

Apply Bible knowledge to everyday life. Read aloud the sentences at the top of the page. Guide the students in locating and reading each of the verses. Invite them to complete the missing words in the sentences that tell about being wise. Check the answers with the students before completing the word at the bottom of the page.

LESSON
86 **God Protects Daniel**

Materials

- Chart 19, "God Protects Daniel"
- Hymn: "Am I a Soldier of the Cross?"
- TimeLine and picture: Daniel
- Copy of Page A87 ("News! News!") for each student (optional)
- Stick puppet: Prepare a simple drawing of the outline of a human figure on a piece of white construction paper. (You may use page A85 to make a pattern.) Cut out the figure and glue it to a craft stick.

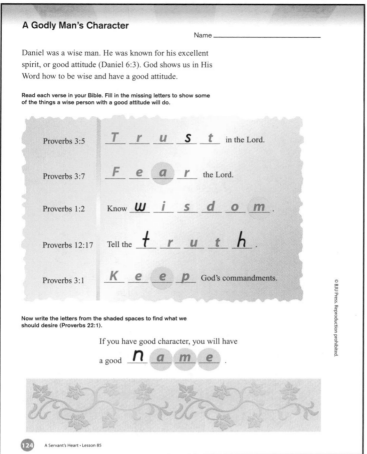

A Godly Man's Character

Name _____

Daniel was a wise man. He was known for his excellent spirit, or good attitude (Daniel 6:3). God shows us in His Word how to be wise and have a good attitude.

Read each verse in your Bible. Fill in the missing letters to show some of the things a wise person with a good attitude will do.

Proverbs 3:5	**T r u s t** in the Lord.
Proverbs 3:7	**F e a r** the Lord.
Proverbs 1:2	Know **w i s d o m**.
Proverbs 12:17	Tell the **t r u t h**.
Proverbs 3:1	**K e e p** God's commandments.

Now write the letters from the shaded spaces to find what we should desire (Proverbs 22:1).

If you have good character, you will have

a good **n a m e**.

124 A Servant's Heart • Lesson 85

God Protects Daniel
Daniel 6:16–28

Some kings kept hungry lions to kill anyone who displeased them.

Bible writers describe the lion as a mighty warrior or a cruel enemy.

Lion-hunting was a sport for kings. They killed hundreds of lions from their chariots.

A Servant's Heart • Lesson 86 125

♪ Hymn: "Am I a Soldier of the Cross?"

Teach the fourth verse (Worktext page 218). Play the recording of the fourth verse and explain each line. Explain that the hymnwriter is telling how he will live for the Lord. He asks the Lord to give him more courage. As God does this through the Bible, the hymnwriter will work and be willing to suffer for God. Elicit from the students that this should be our attitude. Lead in singing the fourth verse of the hymn with the recording. Then direct the girls to sing the first line and the boys to sing the second line. Reverse the parts and sing the verse again.

Background Information

Seal—*When a king made an impression on wax with his signet ring, it had the same authority as his signature. On documents, the seal acted as security.*

Lions' Den—*King Darius's captured lions were kept in a walled space. The top was open, and there was a small opening on the side. This was where the stone was placed and where Darius placed his seal.*

Introducing the Bible Account

Review the account from the previous lesson. Guide a discussion about Daniel's courage. Invite students to predict what might happen to Daniel now that he broke the law of the Medes and Persians. Share the background information.

Bible Account

Read Daniel 6:16–28 or use the following retelling of the passage. Listening question: **What new announcement did the king make?** *(that all people should fear and tremble before the living God of Daniel)* Direct attention to Worktext page 125.

God Protects Daniel

When the king was convinced that he couldn't save Daniel from the lions' den, he called Daniel in and told him, "Your God, the One you're always worshiping, will rescue you." And with that, Daniel was put in the den with the lions, and a stone was put in front of the opening. The king used his signet ring to put a seal on the stone.

The king then went to his bedroom, but he didn't eat or sleep. He was thinking about Daniel, his trusted president, who had been thrown to the lions.

When daylight came, the king went directly to the den of lions. He called out to Daniel and asked if the living God he served had been able to deliver him from the lions.

To the king's amazement, a voice came back saying, "O king, live forever. My God has shut the lions' mouths, and they have not hurt me." Daniel said that the lions didn't hurt him because in God's eyes he was innocent and had done no harm to the king.

The king was glad that Daniel was unhurt, and he had Daniel brought out of the den. Daniel showed the king that he had not been touched.

Then the king commanded that the men who had plotted against Daniel be thrown into the lions' den. These men were killed by the lions within a few seconds.

King Darius sent out an announcement to all the land that the people should fear and tremble before the living God of Daniel. He told all the people of the surrounding lands that Daniel's God would have a kingdom that would never end. He said that Daniel's living God delivers, rescues, shows signs and wonders, and had enough power to save Daniel from a den of lions. Daniel returned to his post in the kingdom and served well during the reign of Darius.

▶ **What did the king say to Daniel before Daniel was led away to the lions' den?** *(that Daniel's God would deliver him)*

▶ **Why did the king not eat or sleep that night?** *(He was worried about Daniel.)*

▶ **What happened when the king spoke to Daniel from outside the lions' den?** *(Daniel answered.)*

▶ **Was the king happy that Daniel was still alive?** *(Yes, he was thrilled.)*

💡 **Had the law of the Medes and Persians been kept?** *(Yes. Daniel was thrown into the den; the law didn't say he had to die.)*

💡 **Do you think the king believed that Daniel's God was the only living God?** *(Accept any answer, but discuss the king's new announcement to all the people.)*

Discuss that because Daniel obeyed, God was able to show His power. When we suffer because of our obedience, God's power is seen through His helping us to love Him and trust Him.

💡 **Is there a specific action of obedience you need to trust God to help you with?** *(Answers will vary. Direct the students to understand that God's word is more important than what we think or feel about something.)*

InfoScene: "God Protects Daniel"
Display Chart 19 from the Visual Packet for the students to refer to throughout this unit.

🕐 TimeLine

▶ **Add Daniel to the TimeLine.** Place the picture of Daniel on the TimeLine (605–540 BC), pointing out that he lived about 150 years before Nehemiah. Guide the students in gluing their pictures of Daniel onto their TimeLines.

❤ Memory Verse—Psalm 56:11

Practice the verse with the stick puppet. Direct the students to open their Bibles and to read the verse together. Now guide a practice of the verse, using the stick puppet. Explain that you will start the verse, then pass the puppet to a student who must continue the verse until he gives the puppet to another student sitting near him, and so on.

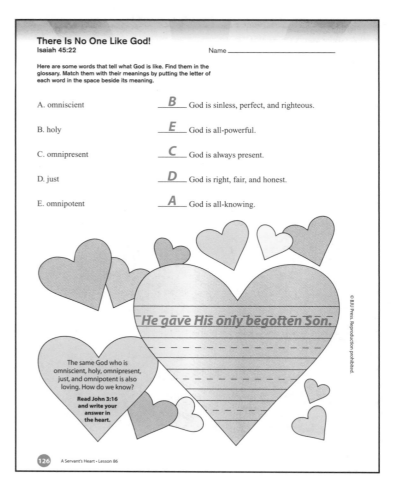

📖 Study Skills, Worktext page 126

Discuss the attributes (descriptions) of God. Read aloud **Isaiah 45:22**. Direct the students to turn to the glossary in their Worktexts. Guide them in locating and reading the meanings of the attributes from the glossary. Choose volunteers to read each statement and tell the attribute or character quality of God described. Read or say **John 3:16** together. Remind the students that God is also loving. Guide them as they answer the question at the bottom of the page.

✏ Writing Connection (optional)

Guide the writing of a newspaper story. Review the events in the Bible account about Daniel and the lions' den. Direct the students to write the name *Daniel* on the headline of page A87 ("News! News!"). Tell them to write a few sentences about Daniel's time in the lions' den. Remind them to draw a picture about their sentences. Display some of their completed articles on the Unit 6 Bulletin Board.

87 Whose Laws?

Materials
- Hymn: "Am I a Soldier of the Cross?"
- A copy of *A Question of Yams* for each student or one for the teacher
- Stick puppet from the previous lesson

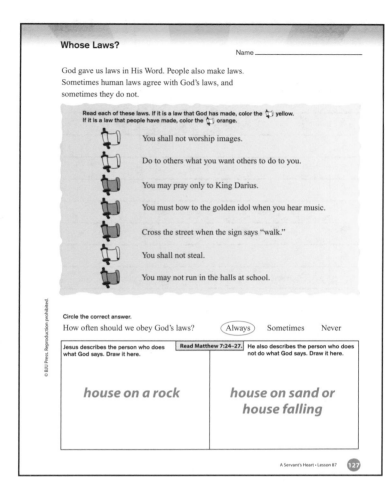

Whose Laws?

Name _____

God gave us laws in His Word. People also make laws. Sometimes human laws agree with God's laws, and sometimes they do not.

Read each of these laws. If it is a law that God has made, color the 📜 yellow. If it is a law that people have made, color the 📜 orange.

You shall not worship images.

Do to others what you want others to do to you.

You may pray only to King Darius.

You must bow to the golden idol when you hear music.

Cross the street when the sign says "walk."

You shall not steal.

You may not run in the halls at school.

Circle the correct answer.

How often should we obey God's laws? (Always) Sometimes Never

Jesus describes the person who does what God says. Draw it here.	Read Matthew 7:24–27. He also describes the person who does not do what God says. Draw it here.
house on a rock	*house on sand or house falling*

A Servant's Heart • Lesson 87 **127**

🎵 **Hymn: "Am I a Soldier of the Cross?"**

Sing all the verses (Worktext page 218). Review the questions and answers in the hymn.

✍ **Worktext page 127**

Apply Bible knowledge to everyday life. Explain to the students that they will be deciding whether the laws listed are made by God or people. Read the directions and let the students complete the top of the page independently. Guide them as they find and read **Matthew 7:24–27**. Direct them to draw the pictures indicated, showing the difference between a person who *does* what God says and a person who does *not*.

❤ **Memory Verse—Psalm 56:11**

Practice the memory verse. Keeping his Bible closed, each student should recite Psalm 56:11 as the stick puppet is passed to him.

Missionary Story

Read Chapter 7 of *A Question of Yams*. Review the events from Chapter 6 and allow students to predict what will happen in Chapter 7.

💡 **Do you think rain will come?**

💡 **Do you think the water that has been put on the plants will save them?**

💡 **What do you think the Head Men will do?**

Tell the students to read Chapter 7 (or to listen as you read it aloud) to find out the answers.

▶ **Did the Christians' yams die because the rains didn't come?** *(no)*

▶ **Why did the yams not die?** *(The Christians kept praying and watering their gardens.)*

💡 **Do you think that the Christians asked God to help their yams grow?** *(Accept any answer, but remind students that we are to pray about everything as Philippians 4:6 says.)*

▶ **What did Sakoso say to Kuri's father about the spirits?** *(They would still be angry even if the yams did not die.)*

▶ **Was Kuri finally able to understand why his father had remained so calm?** *(yes)*

▶ **What was the reason?** *(He knew that the living God was stronger than the evil spirits.)*

▶ **What part of God's Carving did the missionaries want to translate into Kuri's language first?** *(the part that told about Jesus Christ)*

💡 **Why do you suppose they wanted to finish that part first?** *(They wanted the people to read about the gospel so they could get saved: Jesus came as God; Jesus died to pay for their sins; Jesus arose from the dead.)*

▶ **What were the Head Men still saying about the yams?** *(They would be bitter.)*

▶ **Why do you think they were saying that?** *(Answers will vary, but emphasize that the Head Men could not know the future and that they were trying to scare the Christians so that they would stop obeying God.)*

▶ **Should we be afraid of what people say?** *(No. Obeying God is the most important thing.)*

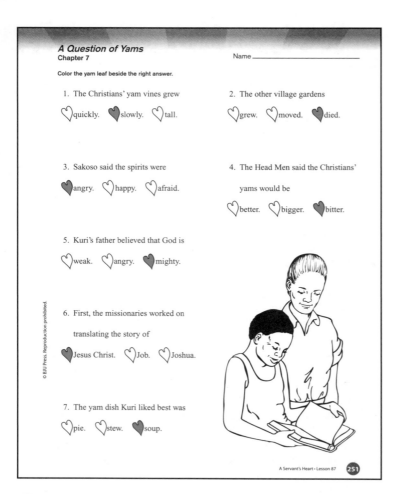

 Worktext page 251

***A Question of Yams:* Chapter 7.** Direct the students to color the leaf next to the word that will correctly complete each sentence. Read aloud **Psalm 21:13**. Discuss how God shows His power. *(Answers may include that God heals sicknesses, He provides for our needs, and He controls weather and events.)* Explain that Christians can face difficulties with calmness and courage because God is in control. He alone is holy, just, loving, all-knowing, and always in control. Lead in prayer thanking God.

LESSON

88 **Trusting God**

Materials

- Hymn: "Am I a Soldier of the Cross?"
- A copy of *A Question of Yams* for each student or one for the teacher
- Beanbag
- Chart 3, "Books of the Bible: Old Testament" (optional)
- Canned yams, yam chips, or the ingredients for the yam pudding recipe given in the Math Connection (optional)

♩ Hymn: "Am I a Soldier of the Cross?"

Sing all four verses of the hymn (Worktext page 218).

Bible Study Skills, Worktext page 128

Review the books of the Old Testament. Direct the students to the contents page in their Bibles or display Chart 3, "Books of the Bible: Old Testament." Read the names of the books of the Old Testament together. Call on students to tell which book comes *after* the book you name.

Proverbs (*Ecclesiastes*)
Jonah (*Micah*)
2 Kings (*1 Chronicles*)
Ezra (*Nehemiah*)
Jeremiah (*Lamentations*)

Read the directions at the top of Worktext page 128. After the students have arranged the Old Testament books in order, explain how to check their answers by solving the math problems at the bottom of the page.

♥ Memory Verse—Psalm 56:11

Practice the memory verse.

A Question of Yams
Chapter 8 and Review

Name _____

Chapter 8
Color the correct answers.

The women and children used these for digging the yams.

The women put the yams in these.

Kuri's mother made soup in this.

Kuri's mother put these in the soup.

tomato   ham bone   water

salt   green onion   ginger   yams   broccoli

Review Chapters 1–8.
Circle the correct answer.

Kuri was bitten by this.

The doctor came in this.

The Christians carried water from this.

Kuri learned to read from this.

© BJU Press. Reproduction prohibited.

252   A Servant's Heart · Lesson 88

Worktext page 252

A Question of Yams: Chapter 8. Review the events from Chapter 8. Discuss how the people gathered and prepared the yams. Direct the students to color the correct answers. Explain that the section at the bottom of the page is a review of the entire book. Tell them to circle the correct answers. Ask which part of the story was their favorite. Point out how others saw the power of God shown by the lives of faithful Christians.

Math Connection (optional)

Make yam pudding or eat canned yams or yam chips. Provide a paper cup and a spoon for each student when the pudding is ready. Measure the ingredients according to the type of measurement you are learning in math class.

Yam Pudding

Metric	Customary	Ingredient
700g	3 cups	sweet potatoes, drained
350ml	1½ cups	evaporated milk
56g	4 tablespoons	margarine
2	2	eggs
0.5g	¼ teaspoon	ground cloves
0.5g	¼ teaspoon	ground nutmeg
0.5g	¼ teaspoon	ground cinnamon
210g	1 cup	sugar

Mash the sweet potatoes and blend with butter and sugar. Add eggs, spices, and milk. Cook in a slow cooker on high for three hours with the lid on.

Missionary Story

Read Chapter 8 of *A Question of Yams*. Guide a discussion of Chapters 7 and 8.

▶ **How did Chapter 7 end?** *(Kuri was thinking about the new part of Mark he had read that day and thought he might read it to his mother.)*

💡 **The title of Chapter 8 is "Bitter Yams?" Do you think the yams will be bitter?** *(Accept any answer)*

Call on a volunteer to name things he has eaten that were bitter. Tell the students that they will find out whether the yams were bitter when they read the conclusion of the story. Direct them to read Chapter 8 silently or read it aloud to them.

▶ **What did the Christians find when they dug up the yams?** *(The yams were not very big, but there were plenty of them.)*

▶ **What did Kuri's father pray before they ate?** *(He thanked God for His care, for his family, the crop of yams, and for Sakoso's asking about God's Word.)*

▶ **As Kuri ate the soup, what was he thinking?** *(It was God that had given him words to read and yam soup to eat!)*

💡 **What do you think Kuri could be the most thankful for?** *(Accept any answer, but discuss with the students that Kuri had come to know the Lord as his Savior, and that was the best part.)*

💡 **What can you be thankful for?** *(Remind the students to thank God and tell others about God's blessings.)*

Going Beyond

Reinforcement

Teach about God's use of lions. Tell the students that the Bible speaks of lions. Read the first reference listed below. Direct them to repeat the reference, find the verse in their Bibles, and then stand. Call on two students: one to read the verse and the other to explain what the verse says about lions. Continue with the remaining verses listed. Share background information as needed.

Judges 14:9 *(Samson broke his vow to the Lord. Samson was to separate himself from wine and strong drink, not let his hair get cut, and touch no dead body (see Numbers 6:1–21). Samson broke his vow by taking honey out of the carcass of a lion.)*

1 Samuel 17:34–35 *(David killed a lion to protect his sheep, and he rescued the sheep from its mouth.)*

2 Samuel 1:23 *(God used a lion to show the strength of Saul and Jonathan.)*

1 Kings 20:36 *(God used a lion to kill a man who was disobedient.)*

Proverbs 28:1 *(God compares the righteous to a bold lion.)*

Proverbs 28:15 *(God compares the wicked ruler to a roaring lion.)*

Isaiah 65:25 *(God tells us that after Christ's Second Coming a lion will eat straw instead of meat. There will be no killing.)*

1 Peter 5:8 *(Satan is compared to a roaring lion that wants to conquer and destroy us.)*

Revelation 5:5 *(Jesus is compared to a lion, symbolizing His power.)*

Enrichment

Perform a miniplay. From Worktext pages 253–54, assign parts to students. Allow them to read or memorize the parts. Encourage the students to use props if practical. You may want to perform this play in your classroom or for another class. (*Note:* The teacher's copy of the miniplay is on pages A88–89.)

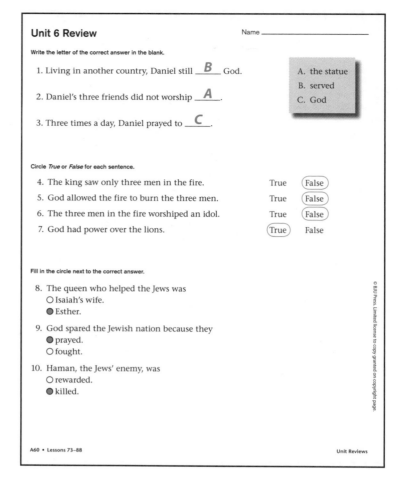

Unit 6 Review   Name _____

Write the letter of the correct answer in the blank.

1. Living in another country, Daniel still __B__ God.
2. Daniel's three friends did not worship __A__.
3. Three times a day, Daniel prayed to __C__.

> A. the statue
> B. served
> C. God

Circle *True* or *False* for each sentence.

4. The king saw only three men in the fire.   True   (False)
5. God allowed the fire to burn the three men.   True   (False)
6. The three men in the fire worshiped an idol.   True   (False)
7. God had power over the lions.   (True)   False

Fill in the circle next to the correct answer.

8. The queen who helped the Jews was
   ○ Isaiah's wife.
   ● Esther.
9. God spared the Jewish nation because they
   ● prayed.
   ○ fought.
10. Haman, the Jews' enemy, was
    ○ rewarded.
    ● killed.

A60 • Lessons 73–88   Unit Reviews

◀◀ Unit Review

Materials

• Copy of page A60 ("Unit 6 Review") for each student

Guide a review of Unit 6. Review the people and events in preparation for the Unit 6 test (optional).

7

A Forgiving Heart

OVERVIEW

Preparing the Teacher

Children are often prompted, "Tell so-and-so you're sorry." But how often do Christians need to confess sin to God and ask His forgiveness? Unit 7 deals with forgiving others as well as asking God's forgiveness. Think back over the past month. Have you wronged anyone? Have you talked to that person and asked forgiveness? Have you asked God to forgive you? God says that He will forgive when confession is made for sin. Read **Colossians 1:14**. Pray that God would help you to ask His forgiveness for your sins, and to be ready to forgive others.

Preparing the Materials

89—Unit 7 bookmark [E]

Unit 7a Going Beyond—Law enforcement officer: copy of page A90 ("Forgiveness Booklet") [E]; five pieces of 3" × 4½" paper [E]

94—Microscope or magnifying glass; two visuals [O]

96—Three name tags; small pieces of wrapped candy (twenty for the story and enough additional for one for each student [O]; copy of page A93 ("Create a Mobile") [E, O]

Unit 7b Going Beyond—adding machine tape (or 2.5" × 22" strip of paper) [E]; transparent tape; string, yarn, or ribbon

98—Four dominoes

Unit 7c Going Beyond—Pocket compass; large letters N, S, E, and W cut out from construction paper

101–3—Pocket chart [O]; memory verse word cards

103—Copy of pages A61–62 ("Unit 7 Review") [E]

Unit 7d Going Beyond—Team markers (three magnets or buttons); piece of thin plastic, such as a transparency [E]

Unit 7   A Forgiving Heart

Theme, Memory Verse, and Principle	Lesson Number	TE Page	Worktext Page(s)	Appendix Page(s)	Lesson Title	Scripture or Focus
Unit 7a **I Need Forgiveness** Romans 3:10–11 *I am sinful. I need God's forgiveness.*	**89**	196	129		Trapped by Sin	Application Story
	90	197	130		The Freedom of Forgiveness	Application Story
	91	199	131–32		Two Short Prayers	Luke 18:9–14
	92	200	133–34	A90	Forgiven but Unforgiving	Matthew 18:21–35
Unit 7b **God Forgives Me** Ephesians 1:7 *God forgives me through Christ's sacrifice.*	**93**	203	135–36	A91–92	Jesus Forgives and Heals	Mark 2:1–12
	94	205	137–38		A New Person	Application Story
	95	207	139–40		Forgiveness and Love	Luke 7:36–50
	96	208		A93	Giving	Picture the Point
Unit 7c **I Accept God's Forgiveness** Psalm 103:12 *God's forgiveness is forever.*	**97**	210	141–42, 242		Hero of the Faith: Abraham Kuyper	Biography
	98	213	143–44		A Whole Family Is Saved	Acts 16:9–34
	99	214	145		Trust God's Word	Application Story
	100	215	146		Thankful for God's Goodness	Picture the Point Luke 17:11–19
Unit 7d **I Forgive Others** Matthew 6:14–15 *Forgive others as God forgives you.*	**101**	218	147–48		Forgiven	Philemon 1:8–21
	102	220	149–50		Two Sons, Two Sins	Luke 15:11–32
	103	222	151		Jesus Forgives the Most	Matthew 27:27–35
	104	223	152	A61–62	Learning to Forgive	Application Story

Connections	Bible Doctrines	Skills/Applications
	The Doctrine of God *Nature of God* The Father, Son, and Spirit are recognized as God (Matt. 28:19). God is righteous (Rev. 16:7). God is love (1 John 4:8). **The Doctrine of Man** *Fall of Man* Man is guilty before God (Rom. 3:10–12). *Redemption of Man* Man in Christ stands perfect before God (Heb. 10:10). **The Doctrine of Salvation** *Elements of Salvation* God calls men through providence (Rom. 2:4). God forgives the believer's sins (Eph. 1:7). God restores the believering sinner to His favor (adoption) (Rom. 5:1–2).	**Foundational** • Understand that the debt of sin must be paid • Understand that Jesus paid my debt for me **Practical** • Recall facts and details • Follow directions • Read a map • Read a compass rose • Read a timeline • Sequence events • Distinguish between books in the Old Testament and New Testament • Locate all the books in the Bible • Match characters and actions • Match content to the correct book in the Bible • Identify cause and effect **Personal** • Distinguish between proud and humble prayer • Understand steps to forgiveness • Understand that we must accept God's forgiveness • Show forgiveness when appropriate • Understand and apply Bible knowledge to everyday life
L93—Drama		
L96—Art		
L97—TimeLine: Abraham Kuyper		
L104—Writing		

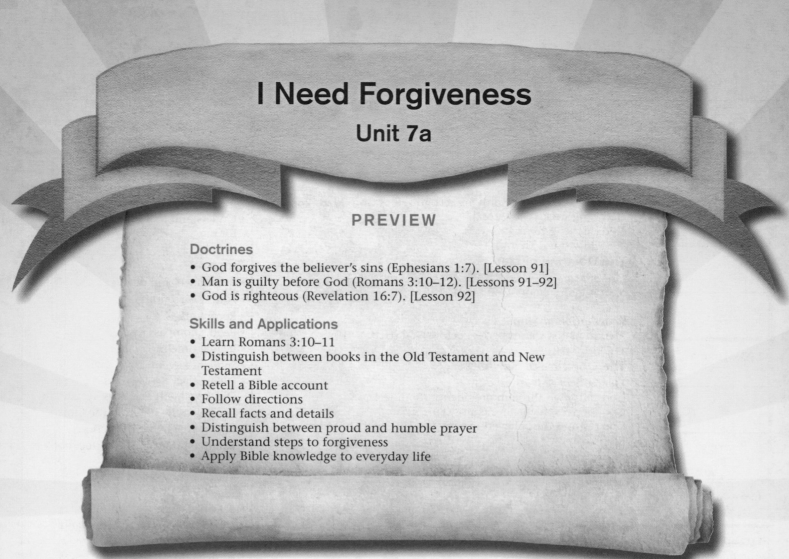

I Need Forgiveness
Unit 7a

PREVIEW

Doctrines

- God forgives the believer's sins (Ephesians 1:7). [Lesson 91]
- Man is guilty before God (Romans 3:10–12). [Lessons 91–92]
- God is righteous (Revelation 16:7). [Lesson 92]

Skills and Applications

- Learn Romans 3:10–11
- Distinguish between books in the Old Testament and New Testament
- Retell a Bible account
- Follow directions
- Recall facts and details
- Distinguish between proud and humble prayer
- Understand steps to forgiveness
- Apply Bible knowledge to everyday life

LESSON
89 Trapped by Sin

Materials

- Hymn: "Cleanse Me"
- Unit 7 Bookmark for each student
- Highlighter for each student (optional)
- Charts 2–3, "Books of the Bible: New Testament, Old Testament" (optional)

 Memory Verses—Romans 3:10–11

Principle: I am sinful. I need God's forgiveness. Direct the students to open their Bibles. Read the verses aloud while the students read silently. Teach that to be *righteous* is to be without sin. God is righteous. All people are guilty of sinning and deserve punishment. The penalty for sin is death and separation from God forever. Christ paid the penalty for sin by His death on the cross. For the person who trusts Christ as Savior, God accepts Christ's death as the payment for his sin, thus declaring him righteous in Christ.

Practice the memory verse. Direct the students to highlight the verses (optional) and mark the location with the Unit 7 Bookmark.

▶ **How many people are righteous without God?**

(none, not even one)

▶ **Can you understand God or seek Him without first having His help?** *(no)*

💡 **How can we become righteous?** *(by asking God's forgiveness for our sins and trusting Christ)*

💡 **What allows God to take away our sins?** *(trusting that Christ's death paid for our sins)*

Introducing the Application Story

Guide a discussion about guilt. Explain that the story is about a boy who is guilty.

💡 **How do you feel when you know you have done wrong?** *(Answers will vary but should include sorry, guilty, and sad.)*

💡 **What causes guilt?** *(Accept any answer at this point.)*

Application Story

Read or tell the following story. Listening question: **Why does Jack feel guilty?** *(He stole his grandfather's quarters and then lied about how he got money to spend.)*

Pop's Quarters

"Hey, Pop, what are all these black books?"

"Just a minute, Jack. I'll be right there," Pop answered.

Pop couldn't walk as fast as Jack's dad. He came slowly into the room, leaning on his cane.

"Let's see—oh, you mean those? That's my coin collection." Pop slowly lifted one book and put it on the table. He opened it, and there inside were all kinds of quarters—some very old and some bright and new. Under each one was a label telling what year it was made. Jack and Pop spent a long time looking at them.

When Pop went outside to work in the garden for a while, Jack stayed behind to look at the black books. Soon he noticed a jar on the shelf. It was full of more coins.

Jack raced out to the kitchen where Grandmother was drying dishes. "What is that big jar of money doing on the shelf?" he asked.

"Those are more quarters. Pop doesn't have a book to put them in yet. I don't think you should play with them."

"All right, Grandmother, I won't." But when he went back into the room, his eyes seemed to be drawn to the jar.

"Well, I'll just look at them," he said to himself.

He tiptoed over to the shelf. It was too high. He quietly put a chair by the shelf.

"Jack, will you help me move this table?" Grandmother called from the kitchen. Jack quietly put the chair back and ran out to the kitchen, his heart pounding. Grandmother had almost caught him!

As soon as the table was moved, Grandmother went to help Pop in the garden. Jack tiptoed quietly back to the jar with the quarters in it. He put the chair in place again and lifted the jar down. He opened the lid and looked inside.

"Wow! Look at all those quarters! I wonder how much money is in here. Must be hundreds of dollars." He put the jar on the table and took some of the quarters out. "I think I'll count them." But when he got to fifty, he realized he would never have time to count them all. Grandmother and Pop would be coming back inside. He put the quarters back into the jar. Oh, how they clinked! He was afraid that Pop might hear. When he had put all but five back in the jar, he stopped.

"I wonder if Pop would miss just five." But five was too many, he decided, so he put them all back except one. Pop could not possibly miss just one. He put the jar back on the shelf, slid the chair into place, and slipped the quarter into his pocket.

Later Jack spent the quarter on some candy. When he got home, his mother wondered how he had the money to buy candy.

"Didn't you spend all your allowance yesterday?"

"Yes, well—I mean—no." Jack didn't know what to say.

The next time he went to Pop's, he had the chance to get out some more quarters. He took two of them.

He spent the money on more candy. Again his mother wondered where he got the money.

"I earned it from Mr. Manley down the street. He asked me to help him clean his yard," Jack said. He knew he was lying, and he felt terrible inside. [to be continued]

▶ **Should Jack have opened the jar to look at the quarters?** *(No. Grandmother told Jack not to play with them.)*

💡 **As soon as Jack felt the need to tiptoe and be sneaky, what should he have known?** *(Jack should have known he was doing wrong. The Holy Spirit helps us know right from wrong.)*

💡 **Whom did Jack hurt by his sin?** *(Pop, Grandmother, himself, his parents, and Jesus)*

💡 **What should Christians do when they feel their conscience bothering them?** *(Stop whatever they are doing and repent, pray for forgiveness, and remove themselves from the place or opportunity of temptation, if possible.)*

💡 **If Christians ignore their consciences over and over, what will happen to them?** *(Their hearts will become hardened toward the Lord, sin will bother them less and less, and they will stop asking for forgiveness.)*

🎵 Hymn: "Cleanse Me"

Introduce the hymn. The words of the first verse of this song are based on **Psalm 139:23–24**. Read aloud the passage. Write the words *search*, *know*, and *try* for display.

Teach the first verse (Worktext page 219). Sing or play the recording of the first verse. Discuss the meanings of the three key words in their context.

search—examine
know—understand without any doubt
try—test

Call on volunteers to read the first verse, using the definitions in place of the words if possible. Lead in singing the first verse several times.

📖 Bible Study Skills, Worktext page 129

Review the books of the Bible. Direct the students to the contents page in their Bibles, or display Charts 2–3, "Books of the Bible: New Testament, Old Testament," from the Visual Packet. Read the books of the Bible aloud together. Direct the students to turn to Worktext page 129. Read the directions to the students. Instruct them to use their contents pages to solve the puzzle.

LESSON

90 The Freedom of Forgiveness

Materials
• Hymn: "Cleanse Me"

❤ Memory Verses—Romans 3:10–11

Practice the memory verses.

💡 **Why can't we understand or seek God?** *(We're sinners. Sinners reject God and don't want to know Him or find Him.)*

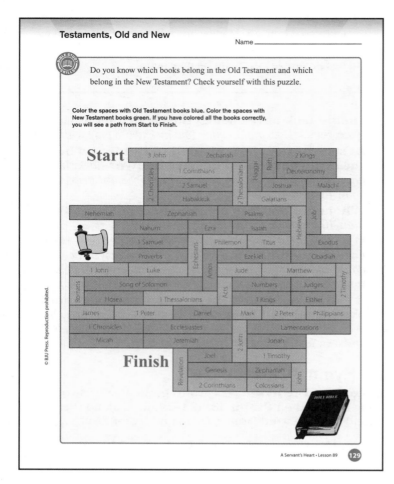

Testaments, Old and New

Name _____

Do you know which books belong in the Old Testament and which belong in the New Testament? Check yourself with this puzzle.

Color the spaces with Old Testament books blue. Color the spaces with New Testament books green. If you have colored all the books correctly, you will see a path from Start to Finish.

Start

Finish

A Servant's Heart • Lesson 89   129

Choose a volunteer to read each verse, pausing for the class to join in saying the word *none* each time it appears. Read the verses together.

🎵 Hymn: "Cleanse Me"

Sing the first verse (Worktext page 219). Play the recording of the first verse while the students silently read the verse.

Introducing the Application Story

Review the first part of "Pop's Quarters."

▶ **What did Jack do wrong in the story in the previous lesson?** (*He stole three of his grandfather's quarters and lied to his mother.*)

Application Story

Read or tell the following story. Listening question: **How did Jack's guilt make him feel?** (*He was miserable.*)

Pop's Quarters (continued)

The next week Jack went to Pop's again. He was very restless all during dinner. He wanted to get to the jar and see whether there were still lots of quarters left. Sure enough, there seemed to be just as many as before. Jack quickly put a handful of quarters in his pocket.

That evening, Pop discovered that a lot of quarters were missing. He asked Grandmother about them.

"I don't know what could have become of them," Grandmother said. "Ask Jack. Maybe he knows."

"Jack, I'm missing quite a few quarters from my big jar. Do you know what happened to them?"

"No, Pop. I don't have any idea."

The next day, Jack's parents questioned him. "No, Dad. How could I know anything about Pop's quarters?"

"Well, those quarters in the jar were special to Pop. He has spent years collecting them. They're not just ordinary quarters, you know. They are very old and rare editions. Only a few coins were made at the time, and hardly any of them are left. Not many coin collectors have anything that rare. Pop was planning to display those in a museum. They were worth a lot of money—a lot more than twenty-five cents apiece. There were a few in the jar that were worth fifty dollars each," Jack's father said.

Jack went to his room and closed the door. He sat down and stared out the window. He felt sick. What should he do?

"If I tell that I took the quarters, everyone will think I'm awful. But if I spend those quarters, it could be . . ." He got a pencil and a piece of paper and figured it up. He gasped. "Eight hundred dollars! Oh no!"

"What am I going to do?" he asked himself over and over. "I know! I'll wait until I go back to Pop's, and I'll just sneak them back into the jar."

But Jack didn't get a chance to go back to Pop's that week—or the next. And he was getting more and more miserable.

When he finally did go, he was horrified when he glanced up at the shelf and saw that the jar was gone.

"Grandma, what did Pop do with his jar of quarters?"

"Well, since someone has been taking them, Pop had to put the rest in the bank. He couldn't take any chances on losing more of them." Jack almost started to cry.

"How will I give the quarters back?" he thought frantically. When Dad came to take him home in the car, Jack decided to confess.

"I took Pop's quarters," he said and then began to cry.

Jack had a hard time telling Pop, but he did. And he gave back the sixteen quarters he had in his pocket. Pop said he would gladly forgive him, but he thought Jack should work to replace the money that the first three quarters were worth. When he and Dad turned to go back out to the car, he felt the heavy burden lift. His dad said, "Jack, who did your dishonesty hurt?"

"Well, it hurt Pop. He lost the money."

"That's right. Who else did it hurt?"

"It hurt me. I felt terrible, and now I have to work all summer."

"OK. Now who else was hurt?"

"Who else? I don't know."

"Think about it."

Jack thought a minute. "Well, I guess it hurt you and Mom."

"You're right. It sure did. How do you think that made us feel?"

"Terrible, I guess."

"Who is the most important person that you hurt?"

"I hurt God."

"That's right. When we do wrong, we're serving His enemy. God loves us and wants us to do right. He hates sin."

"Dad, I hate sin too," said Jack. "Now I need to pray and ask God to forgive me."

 Why did Jack feel so bad? *(Stealing and lying are sins, and he knew it. God was convicting Jack, and his conscience bothered him.)*

 Why did Jack need forgiveness? *(He had broken God's commandments.)*

 What steps do you think Jack should take to be forgiven? *(Jack should ask for God's forgiveness; he should ask for Pop's forgiveness; he should work to pay back the amount that the coins were worth.)*

 Who sins and needs forgiveness? *(everyone)*

When we sin, we sin against God. David said in his confession of sin that his sin was against God. In Christ's parable in **Luke 15:21,** the son who wasted his inheritance realized he had sinned against God. Even when sin is done in secret, it still hurts a lot of people. God hates sin.

Worktext page 130

Review repentance. Read and discuss the Worktext page with the class. Instruct the students to read each verse aloud. Direct them to answer the questions, giving assistance as needed. Read aloud **1 John 1:9**. Point out that asking forgiveness requires humility and confession of sin.

LESSON 91 Two Short Prayers

Materials
- Chart 20, "A Humble Prayer"
- Hymn: "Cleanse Me"

Hymn: "Cleanse Me"

Sing the first verse (Worktext page 219). Utilize the recording as necessary throughout the unit. Lead in singing the first verse with the recording. Discuss the meaning of the verse; then sing the verse again.

▶ **Who can cleanse us?** *(Only the Savior, Jesus Christ, can take away sins.)*

▶ **How was Jesus victorious over death?** *(Though He died on the cross, He rose again.)*

Memory Verses—Romans 3:10–11

Practice the memory verses.

 Who is the only person these verses do not describe? *(Jesus Christ)*

Background Information

Publicans—*Jewish tax collectors were hated by their own people because they worked for the Roman rulers. They also often*

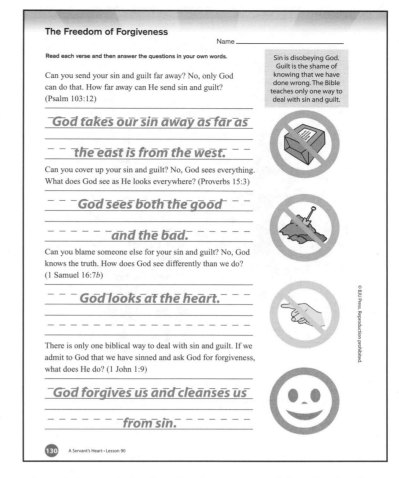

The Freedom of Forgiveness

Name _____

Read each verse and then answer the questions in your own words.

Can you send your sin and guilt far away? No, only God can do that. How far away can He send sin and guilt? (Psalm 103:12)

God takes our sin away as far as the east is from the west.

Can you cover up your sin and guilt? No, God sees everything. What does God see as He looks everywhere? (Proverbs 15:3)

God sees both the good and the bad.

Can you blame someone else for your sin and guilt? No, God knows the truth. How does God see differently than we do? (1 Samuel 16:7b)

God looks at the heart.

There is only one biblical way to deal with sin and guilt. If we admit to God that we have sinned and ask God for forgiveness, what does He do? (1 John 1:9)

God forgives us and cleanses us from sin.

Sin is disobeying God. Guilt is the shame of knowing that we have done wrong. The Bible teaches only one way to deal with sin and guilt.

130 A Servant's Heart • Lesson 90

---

cheated the people by charging them extra and then keeping the money for themselves.

Pharisees—*This sect of Israelite men believed in strictly adhering to the laws of Moses and to the traditions rather than applying the spirit of the laws in obedience to the Lord. Both Jesus and John the Baptist condemned the Pharisees for their attitude of self-righteousness. Religious strictness doesn't make anyone righteous.*

Introducing the Bible Account

Describe publicans and Pharisees. Share the background information as desired. Explain that both the publicans and Pharisees were sinners in the eyes of God. The Bible account gives the Lord's view of each group.

Bible Account

Read Luke 18:9–14 or use the following retelling of the passage. Listening question: **Which man was humble?** *(the publican)* Direct attention to the picture of the publican listening to the proud prayer of the Pharisee (Worktext page 131).

Two Short Prayers

Jesus was talking to some people who thought they could earn salvation by obeying the law. They thought they could please God by their own deeds. They looked down on other Jews who didn't keep the traditional laws as closely as they did.

A Humble Prayer
Luke 18:9–14

Humble

Proud

Publicans collected taxes for the government. Many of them were dishonest. They were not very well liked.

Pharisees were very religious men. They took pride in following every tiny bit of the law. They wanted to be honored and respected for trying so hard to be good.

© BJU Press. Reproduction prohibited.

A Servant's Heart • Lesson 91   **131**

Christ told them about two men who went to the temple to pray.

One of the men thought that he kept all the laws and assumed that he was better than other people. He was a Pharisee.

The Pharisee prayed, thanking God that he was not as sinful as other men . . . or even like this publican. He told God that he fasted twice a week and gave tithes of all that he had.

The other man was a tax collector—a publican. People didn't like tax collectors because sometimes they cheated people, but this tax collector was sorry for his sin.

When the publican prayed, he wouldn't even lift his eyes up to heaven. He hit himself on the chest and said, "God, be merciful to me a sinner."

Jesus told this story to people who believed that they could please God by their own work. The Pharisees looked down on other Jews who weren't as religiously strict as they were.

When Jesus was done, he explained His story. He said that the publican went home with his sins forgiven, but the Pharisee didn't. The publican was humble and asked God's forgiveness. But the Pharisee was proud and thought he was accepted by God because of his own goodness.

❖

 Why were the Pharisees not as good as they thought they were? *(They thought they could get to heaven by their good works. But they deserved judgment because of their sin—just like all other sinners.)*

 Why did the publican look down when he prayed? *(The publican knew he was a sinner and was ashamed. Bowing the head shows humility and is a form of worship.)*

💡 **Which attitude should Christians have?** *(the publican's)*

InfoScene: "A Humble Prayer"

Display Chart 20 from the Visual Packet to refer to throughout this unit.

Worktext page 132

Guide a discussion about humble prayer and proud prayer. Direct attention to the first sentence. Discuss whether the sentence describes the *publican*, the *Pharisee*, or *both*. Instruct the students to put an *X* in the correct columns. Allow the students to complete the page independently. Instruct the students to take the paper home so that they can retell the story to a parent or friend.

LESSON 92 Forgiven but Unforgiving

Materials
- Chart 21, "Forgiven but Unforgiving"
- Hymn: "Cleanse Me"

❤ Memory Verses—Romans 3:10–11

Practice the memory verses. After students have had a good practice time, read aloud **Psalm 14:1–3** and compare the verses to Romans 3:10–11.

🎵 Hymn: "Cleanse Me"

Sing the first verse (Worktext page 219). Play the recording and sing the first verse together. Choose volunteers to sing the verse as a solo or as a duet. Discuss the title of the hymn.

Background Information

Talents and Pence—*The difference in value between these two measurements of money is even more than between a dollar and a penny or between one dollar and a million dollars. A talent was a Hebrew measure of both weight and money. Ten thousand talents would be more money than the average person would make in a lifetime. So Jesus was talking about an enormous amount of money. In the King James Version, pence is the translation of the Greek denarii (plural). A denarius (singular) was a Greek coin that was worth about one day's pay for the average worker in biblical times. That means one hundred pence would have been about three month's wages.*

Introducing the Bible Account

Guide a discussion about debts. Call on volunteers to tell what they have borrowed from a friend or neighbor. List all the items for display. *(Include going next door for Mom or Dad to borrow sugar, milk, a lawn mower, or a wheelbarrow as well as borrowing lunch money from the school office.)* Explain that while they have the borrowed item, they are in *debt*.

Prayer: Humility Is the Key
Luke 18:9–14

Name _____

Put an X under the picture that matches the sentence. If the sentence is true for both men, put an X under both pictures.

	Publican	Pharisee
1. His heart was proud.		X
2. He prayed to God.	X	X
3. He thought he was righteous.		X
4. His heart was humble.	X	
5. He went to the temple to pray.	X	X
6. He knew he was a sinner.	X	
7. He prayed and thanked God that he was not like other men.		X
8. He thought about what others thought of him.		X
9. He prayed that God would be merciful to him.	X	
10. He thought about what God thought of him.	X	
11. God forgave him.	X	

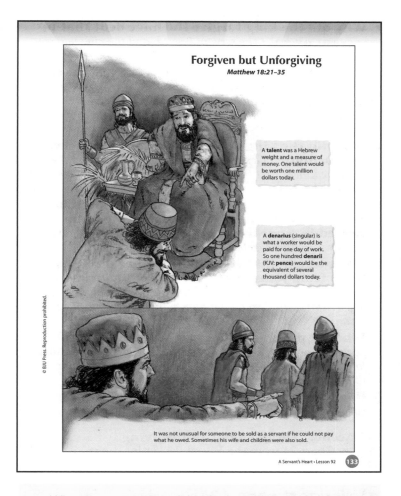

Forgiven but Unforgiving
Matthew 18:21–35

A **talent** was a Hebrew weight and a measure of money. One talent would be worth one million dollars today.

A **denarius** (singular) is what a worker would be paid for one day of work. So one hundred **denarii** (KJV: **pence**) would be the equivalent of several thousand dollars today.

It was not unusual for someone to be sold as a servant if he could not pay what he owed. Sometimes his wife and children were also sold.

💡 **How can a debt be paid back?** *(return the item, replace the item, or pay back the money)*

💡 **How can the debt of sin be paid back to God?** *(Accept any answer that leads to an understanding that we cannot give anything to God that is acceptable payment; we can only ask for forgiveness on the basis of Christ's death being the satisfactory payment of our sin.)*

Bible Account

Read Matthew 18:21–35 or use the following retelling of the passage. Listening question: **Which man was forgiving?** *(the king)* Share the background information. Explain that the account is a *parable* (a short story that teaches a lesson). Direct attention to the picture on Worktext page 133.

Forgiven but Unforgiving

One day Peter asked Jesus how often he should forgive someone who sinned against him. To answer his question, Jesus told Peter this story.

Once there was a king who found that one of his servants owed him ten thousand talents (millions of dollars). The king brought the servant in and told him to pay the debt. The servant cried and told the king that he was unable to pay the money.

The king told the servant that he, his wife, and their children would be sold into slavery to pay the debt.

When the servant heard this, he bowed down to the floor. He begged the king, "Please have patience with me, and I will pay you everything I owe."

The king saw the misery of his servant. He had compassion on the man. The king told the servant that his debt was forgiven.

Then this servant who had been forgiven of so much left the palace. He met another servant, a man who owed him one hundred denarii (about three months' wages). He grabbed the other servant by the throat and demanded, "Pay me what you owe me!" But the man was unable to repay the money. He begged for mercy, but the king's servant didn't listen.

The king's servant wouldn't give the other servant any more time to pay his debt and sent him to prison because he couldn't pay.

Soon the king heard what had happened. He became very angry, and he called his servant in.

"You wicked servant!" he said. "I forgave your entire debt because you wanted me to. Shouldn't you have compassion on your fellow servant just as I did on you?"

The king turned from the servant and signaled his guards. They took the servant and threw him into prison until he could repay all ten thousand talents.

After finishing the story, Jesus told Peter and the rest of the disciples that the heavenly Father would treat them the same way if they didn't forgive others.

▶ **Why did the king forgive the huge debt that his servant owed?** *(The servant begged, and the king had compassion on the servant.)*

💡 **Why did that servant demand a much smaller amount of money from the other servant?** *(Accept any answer that leads the discussion to the unforgiving servant's lack of appreciation for the forgiveness he had been given.)*

▶ **Why did the king throw the unforgiving servant into prison?** *(The king gave the unforgiving servant the same treatment that the servant had given the man who owed him much less.)*

▶ **When Peter asked Jesus the question about how often he should forgive his brother, Jesus answered in a parable. What is a parable?** *(A parable is a short story that teaches a lesson.)*

💡 **What lesson did Peter and the other disciples learn from Jesus's parable?** *(God the Father would treat them the same way the king treated the ungrateful, unforgiving servant if they would not forgive those who sinned against them.)*

💡 **What lesson should Christians learn from the instruction that Jesus gave Peter?** *(Christians too should forgive others because Jesus has forgiven them of much more than they could ever repay.)*

💡 **How can you apply this lesson today?** *(Answers will vary).*

InfoScene: "Forgiven but Unforgiving"
Display Chart 21 from the Visual Packet for the students to refer to throughout this unit.

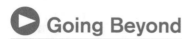 **Worktext page 134**

Recall facts and details. Direct the students to open their Bibles to **Leviticus 5:6** and read the verse together. Direct their attention to Worktext page 134. Read the first question aloud. Tell them to circle the picture that answers the question. Read the verses aloud or choose a volunteer to read the verse before the students choose the correct answer.

⏵ Going Beyond

Reinforcement

Invite a law enforcement officer to talk about the penalty for stealing. Point out the importance of following the laws we have in our communities. Continue the discussion contrasting our sinful human condition and God's grace. Point out that no one can keep God's law and therefore everybody deserves punishment. All people need God's grace.

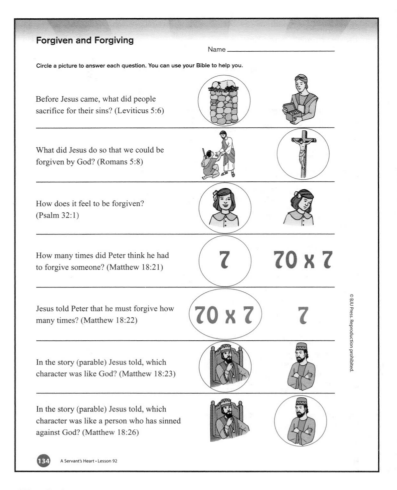

Enrichment

Materials

- A copy of page A90 ("Forgiveness Booklet") for each student
- Enough sheets of student-lined paper cut into 3" × 4½" pieces, for every student to have five or six pieces

Create a handbook about forgiveness. Instruct the students to cut out both sets of praying hands from page A90 ("Forgiveness Booklet"). The one with the title will be the front cover. Tell them to put the five or six pieces of paper between the hands to be the pages of the booklet. Staple each booklet. Instruct the students to find the glossary page listing *forgiveness*. Direct them to write the word and definition on the first page of their booklets. Explain that they are to choose a verse, read it, and write the reference on each of the following pages of their booklet. Choose five or six verses from the following list of verses on forgiveness.

Psalm 32:1; 86:5; 130:4
Daniel 9:9
Matthew 18:21
Luke 7:41–42*a*
Acts 5:31; 13:38; 26:18
Ephesians 1:7; 4:32
Colossians 1:14; 3:13

God Forgives Me
Unit 7b

Doctrines

- Man is guilty before God (Romans 3:10–12). [Lesson 93]
- The Father, Son, and Spirit are recognized as God (Matthew 28:19). [Lesson 93]
- God restores the believing sinner to His favor (adoption) (Romans 5:1–2). [Lesson 95]

Skills and Applications

- Learn Ephesians 1:7
- Recall facts and details
- Match characters and actions
- Understand that the debt of sin must be paid
- Understand that Jesus paid my debt for me
- Ask for forgiveness when appropriate
- Apply Bible knowledge to everyday life

LESSON
93 Jesus Forgives and Heals

Materials

- Chart 39, "Christ's Ministry"
- Hymn: "Cleanse Me"
- Copy of pages A91–92 ("Forgiven and Healed") for the teacher
- Unit 7 Bookmark for each student
- Highlighter for each student (optional)

♩ Hymn: "Cleanse Me"

Teach the second verse (Worktext page 219). Sing the first verse as a review. Review the requests in the first verse: *search me, try me, cleanse me,* and *set me free.* Read the second verse together. Play the recording of the second verse and explain each phrase.

▶ **What does the hymnwriter praise God for in the first phrase?** *(for cleansing him from sin)*

💡 **What does the writer mean by "fulfill Thy Word" in the second phrase?** *(God's promise to forgive us and make us holy)*

💡 **What kind of fire did the writer mean in the third phrase?** *(The Holy Spirit is sometimes referred to as a purifying fire.)*

▶ **What is the desire of the writer in the fourth phrase?** *(to magnify the Lord)*

Background Information

Houses—*The materials that desert-area houses are made from today are much different from the materials used to build desert houses in biblical times. The mud and straw mixtures used back then were baked, but the mixture was not very solid. Too much rain would cause it to wash out and crumble away.*

Palsy—*An old word for paralysis, palsy can refer to a permanent inability to feel or move. It can also mean a temporary condition, such as when someone says his foot has "fallen asleep." In the time of Christ, paralysis was often considered to be a punishment for sin.*

Scribes—*The scribes of the New Testament were experts in biblical law. As scholars and teachers in the synagogues, they*

interpreted the law and emphasized traditions. Often they were Pharisees or Sadducees. These groups did not recognize Jesus as God. Their emphasis on traditions turned the focus away from God and to man.

Introducing the Bible Account

Guide a discussion about friendship. Ask several volunteers how they would be willing to help a friend. *(Encourage answers that are service-oriented rather than materialistic.)* Explain that the four friends in this Bible account believed in Jesus and were therefore willing to do something unusual to get their sick friend to the Lord.

Bible Account

Read Mark 2:1–12 or use the following retelling of the passage. Listening question: **What did Jesus do to heal the man who was paralyzed?** *(He spoke to him.)* Display Chart 39, "Christ's Ministry," showing the location of Capernaum.

Jesus Forgives and Heals

Wherever Jesus went, many people gathered around Him and brought the sick and lame to Him for healing. One time in Capernaum, four men had a friend who was unable to move. The man was paralyzed and couldn't walk. How could he get to Jesus?

His four friends decided they would carry him. They tied ropes to their friend's bed mat and carried him to the house where Jesus was staying. But when they arrived, the house was so full of people they couldn't get inside. They couldn't even get near the door or any windows.

The men carried their sick friend up the stairs on the outside of the house to the flat roof. Then his friends began taking apart a section of the roof. They were going to lower him through the opening right to the feet of Jesus.

That is just what they did. At last the sick man lay on the floor in front of the Lord.

"Son, your sins are forgiven," said Jesus.

Murmurs filled the house. The scribes knew that no one but God could forgive sins. They thought that Jesus was speaking against God.

Jesus knew what was in their hearts. He faced the crowded room and said, "Why are these things in your hearts? Would it be easier to say to this man, 'Your sins are forgiven,' or to say, 'Get up, pick up your mat, and walk'? I want you to know that the Son of Man has the power to forgive sins."

Turning to the man, Jesus went on, "So I'm telling you to get up, pick up your mat, and walk to your own house!"

Would the man be healed? The man believed in Jesus. As soon as Jesus spoke, the man got up, rolled up his bed mat, and walked joyfully out of the crowded room.

The people were amazed! They praised God because they had never seen anything like it.

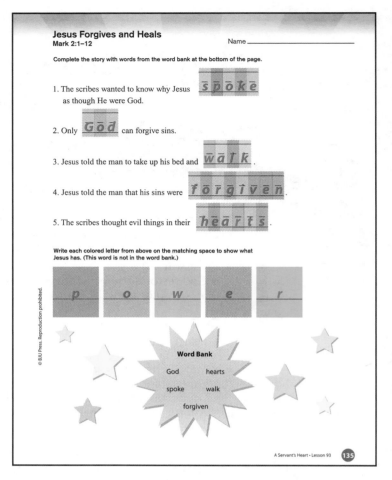

▶ **Why did the men want to get their paralyzed friend to Jesus?** *(They believed Jesus would heal him.)*

💡 **When the four friends saw that they could not get near Jesus, why didn't they give up?** *(They had compassion on their friend and believed that he could be healed.)*

▶ **Why were the scribes upset that Jesus said the paralyzed man's sins were forgiven?** *(They didn't understand that Jesus is God.)*

▶ **How did Jesus prove that He is God just as the Father and the Holy Spirit are God?** *(Jesus healed the paralyzed man.)*

💡 **Have you asked Jesus to forgive you of your sin?** *(Tell students to talk to you individually if they would like to know how.)*

💡 **How can you help others to trust Christ as their Savior?** *(Pray for them, ask them to go to church and Sunday school with you, and tell them what the Bible says about Christ and the forgiveness He offers to all.)*

⊙ Worktext page 135

Recall facts and details. Read the words in the word bank at the bottom of the page. Direct the students to choose one of these words to complete each sentence. Explain that the colored letter from each answer is used in sequence to spell out the missing word.

🎭 Drama Connection (optional)

Direct an echo play. Tell the students that they will use actions to recall the Bible account. Explain that they are to repeat your words and mimic your actions. Read the play on pages A91–92 ("Forgiven and Healed"), demonstrating each action and pausing after each line.

❤️ Memory Verse—Ephesians 1:7

Principle: God forgives me through Christ's sacrifice. Review the definition of *Redemption* in the glossary (Worktext page 283), explaining that it means being freed because someone has paid the price for another.

💡 **Who paid for our Redemption?** *(Christ)*

▶ **Why can we be redeemed?** *(Christ paid the penalty of our sin with His blood.)*

▶ **What happens to our sins when we are redeemed?** *(They are forgiven.)*

💡 **Are people's sins forgiven if they don't trust Christ as Savior?** *(no)*

Briefly review the account of Adam and Eve. Explain that Jesus died to make salvation possible for people who lived even before Christ died. Direct the students to highlight the verse (optional) and mark the location with the Unit 7 Bookmark.

✍️ Worktext page 136

Match characters and dialogue. Call on students to identify the people shown on the page. *(Jesus, the scribes, and the crowd)* Instruct them to cut apart the speech bubbles at the bottom. They should read each speech bubble and place it beside the character who spoke the words. After they have found the right person for each speech bubble, they can glue them in place.

LESSON 94 A New Person

Materials

- Hymn: "Cleanse Me"
- Microscope or magnifying glass
- Two visuals: Choose two bright colors of construction paper. Cut out large circles, one of each color. On one print for display the words *the forgiveness of sins* and on the other *the riches of his grace.*

❤️ Memory Verse—Ephesians 1:7

Practice the memory verse. Ask what the first half of the verse says we receive as a result of Redemption through Christ's blood. *(the forgiveness of sins)* Show the first circle. Read the words together. Read the last half of the verse together and ask why we get Redemption through Christ's blood. *(because of the riches of His grace)* Show the second circle. Read the phrase together. Lead in reading the entire verse aloud together. As you read, display the two circles.

Introducing the Application Story

Guide a discussion of character and reputation. Ask volunteers to define the terms, and write the definitions for display.

💡 **What is character?** *(what a person is really like)*

💡 **What is a reputation?** *(what people think and say about a person)*

💡 **Which is more important to God and why?** *(our character—because a reputation can be pretend, but character always represents our real relationship with God)*

Application Story

Read or tell the following story. Listening question: **How was Sid's character different from his reputation?** *(His character had changed. He was determined to do what was right though he had a reputation of being a troublemaker.)*

No More Lizards

The bus hit a bump, and all the children cheered. "That was the bump," said Will. "We're almost there." He began the Camp Shadybrook cheer, and the others joined in.

Mel sat quietly in his seat. Since this was the first time he had been to summer camp, he didn't know the cheer. The cheer ended, and Will leaned forward to talk to him. "You're going to love camp, Mel," said Will. "I can't wait for you to meet Sid."

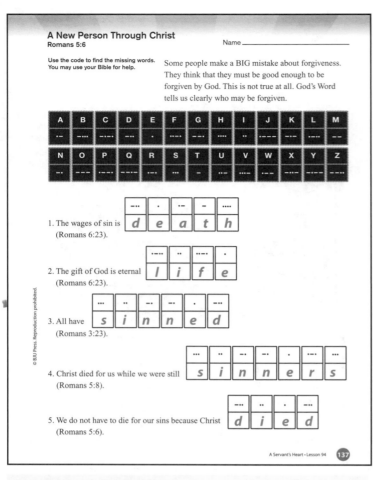

A New Person Through Christ
Romans 5:6

Name _____

Use the code to find the missing words.
You may use your Bible for help.

Some people make a BIG mistake about forgiveness. They think that they must be good enough to be forgiven by God. This is not true at all. God's Word tells us clearly who may be forgiven.

A	B	C	D	E	F	G	H	I	J	K	L	M
N	O	P	Q	R	S	T	U	V	W	X	Y	Z

1. The wages of sin is **d e a t h** (Romans 6:23).

2. The gift of God is eternal **l i f e** (Romans 6:23).

3. All have **s i n n e d** (Romans 3:23).

4. Christ died for us while we were still **s i n n e r s** (Romans 5:8).

5. We do not have to die for our sins because Christ **d i e d** (Romans 5:6).

© BJU Press. Reproduction prohibited.

A Servant's Heart • Lesson 94 137

"Who's Sid?" asked Mel.

"Sid the Lizard," said one of the other boys on the bus. "He's the best. He plays the best tricks on people—better than anyone else at camp."

Another boy stuck his head up from his seat. "My mom said that he was bad news and that I'm not allowed to hang out with him this year."

"Why do you call him 'Lizard'?" asked Mel.

Will pretended his hand was a lizard and ran it up Mel's back. Mel jumped. "That's what he does best," said Will. "Lizards in the girls' bunks!" All the boys on the bus laughed, but the girls didn't think it was funny.

The bus pulled into camp and parked. Everybody got out and went to find out their cabin assignments. Mel followed the crowd until somebody grabbed him. It was Will. "There's Lizard," he said. Will brought him over and introduced him.

"Hey," said Sid, "you can call me Sid, but drop 'the Lizard.'"

"Come on," said Will, "you're the master of playing tricks."

"Not any more," said Sid. "I got saved this year. I asked Jesus to take away my sin."

"So we can't have fun anymore?" asked Will.

Sid shook his head. "We can still have fun. But sometimes people got hurt by our tricks. And a lot of times we broke camp rules."

"So that's it?" said Will. "No more lizards? No more pranks? Everyone knows you're the joker. The counselors are already planning to keep an eye on you."

"Jesus has forgiven me for the wrong that I've done," said Sid. "And I'm going to ask forgiveness from all the people I hurt, including you."

"Forget it," said Will. "I'm here to have fun." Will just walked away.

Mel was left standing there with Sid. He thought for a moment before speaking. "I think you did the right thing, Sid," said Mel. "Would you show me where to check in?"

▶ **Where were the students on the bus going?** (to camp)

▶ **What was Sid known for at camp?** (playing tricks on people)

▶ **What was different about Sid this year?** (He was saved, a Christian.)

▶ **Why was Will angry with Sid?** (He thought Sid wouldn't be fun anymore.)

💡 **Why might others not believe that Sid had changed?** (They all knew him for playing tricks.)

💡 **How could Sid prove to others that he had changed?** (They would see it by his actions.)

💡 **Is there anything you need to change in order to be more like Christ?** (Answers will vary.)

🖊 Worktext page 137

Guide an activity to develop the understanding that Jesus paid the debt for our sins. Read the sentences at the top of the page. Direct attention to the missing word in the first example. Demonstrate how to determine each letter of the word using the code. Read the verse to check the answer. Tell the students to complete the missing words by using the code. Read aloud **Isaiah 53:5–6** after the page is completed.

💡 **When it comes to forgiveness, what is the big mistake many people make?** (They think they can do enough good works to deserve forgiveness.)

💡 **According to God's Word, who can be forgiven?** (only those who confess their sin and trust Christ)

Point out that it is only by God's grace that we can come to Him for salvation. Encourage students to be thankful and humble.

🎵 Hymn: "Cleanse Me"

Illustrate magnifying the Lord. Show the magnifying glass and guide a discussion about its use. Place the magnifying glass over your eye to show how it enlarges objects.

💡 **What does it mean to magnify something?** (to make it appear bigger)

💡 **Why do you magnify something?** (to show detail, to make an object easily seen, to create a clear image)

💡 **How can Christians magnify the Lord in their lives?** (tell others about Him, read the Bible to learn details about Him, make Him the most important person in their lives)

Sing the first and second verses (Worktext page 219). Lead in singing the verses with the recording.

Do You Remember?

Name _____

You have learned about many servants of God in Units 1–6.

Starting with the first letter, circle every other letter to make a name. Write the name correctly on the line.

Ⓐ R Ⓑ C Ⓡ T Ⓐ B Ⓗ C Ⓐ N Ⓜ   Ⓜ S Ⓞ R Ⓢ M Ⓔ A Ⓢ   Ⓢ R Ⓐ W Ⓜ J Ⓢ Q Ⓞ R Ⓝ

____ *Abraham* ____   ____ *Moses* ____   ____ *Samson* ____

Ⓖ E Ⓘ P Ⓓ F Ⓔ C Ⓞ M Ⓝ   Ⓝ Q Ⓞ G Ⓐ P Ⓗ   Ⓡ A Ⓤ I Ⓣ K Ⓗ

____ *Gideon* ____   ____ *Noah* ____   ____ *Ruth* ____

Ⓗ O Ⓐ M Ⓝ M Ⓝ S Ⓐ K Ⓗ   Ⓓ G Ⓐ W Ⓥ O Ⓘ P Ⓓ   Ⓔ E Ⓢ I Ⓣ G Ⓗ F Ⓔ P Ⓡ

____ *Hannah* ____   ____ *David* ____   ____ *Esther* ____

138 A Servant's Heart • Lesson 94

✎ Worktext page 138

Review God's servants. Review the themes of Units 1–6: God rules everything, obedience in words and actions, humility before God and others, Christ's birth foretold and fulfilled, serving God, and courage to trust God. Read aloud the directions for the exercise. Allow the students to complete the page independently. Choose volunteers to tell what they remember about each character.

LESSON 95 Forgiveness and Love

Materials
• Verse visuals prepared for the previous lesson

♥ Memory Verse—Ephesians 1:7

Practice the verse. Hold up the first circle. Call on a student to tell what the phrase means. Recite the first part of the verse together. Hold up the other circle. Call on a student to tell what it means. Recite the second part of the verse in unison. If the students cannot remember, they may open their Bibles or look at the visuals. Allow several students to show the verse visuals while the class reads or recites the verse. Say the verse together again.

Background Information

Alabaster Bottle of Ointment—*Ointment made from the root of a particular plant that grows in India was very expensive*

perfume. A bottle contained only enough oil for one use and had to be broken in order for the oil to be used. It was often a girl's only dowry and cost nearly a year's wages.

Hospitality—*In the time of Christ, sandaled feet on dirt roads gathered dust and mud. It was customary to provide a guest with water to clean his feet. Males greeted one another with a kiss on the cheek, and the host would then anoint his guest's head with common oil. Simon failed to perform any of these customs.*

Introducing the Bible Account

Share the information about the alabaster bottle. Explain that today's account is about a woman who asks Jesus's forgiveness in a very special way. She gives her most precious possession to honor Him. Explain the significance of the alabaster container.

Bible Account

Read Luke 7:36–50 or use the following retelling of the passage. Listening question: **How was the sinful woman saved?** *(by her faith)*

Forgiveness and Love

Jesus wanted all the people to know that He would forgive them. A Pharisee named Simon wanted Jesus to eat dinner with him, so Jesus went to his house. Simon served Him a great feast but didn't give Jesus any of the common courtesies.

There was a sinful woman in that town who knew that Jesus was eating at Simon's house, so she went there with her container of precious perfume. She cried and washed Jesus's feet with her tears and wiped them away with her long hair. She kissed His feet and poured the precious ointment from her bottle onto them.

The Pharisee thought to himself, "If Jesus were really a prophet, He would know that this woman is sinful and wouldn't let such a sinner touch Him." Even though Simon didn't say these things out loud, Jesus knew his thoughts and responded to him.

Jesus told Simon a parable about a businessman. Two men owed the businessman money—one owed ten times more than the other. Neither one of them could pay, so the businessman cancelled both debts. Jesus asked Simon which of the two men would love the businessman more.

Simon said he thought it would be the debtor who had been forgiven more. Jesus said, "That's right."

Looking at the woman, Jesus said, "Simon, do you see this woman? When I came into your house, you didn't give me any water to wash my feet, but she has washed them with her tears and wiped them with her hair. You didn't greet me with a kiss, but she has kissed my feet. You didn't anoint my head with oil, but this woman has poured expensive perfume on my feet. She had many sins, but they've all been forgiven. That's why she loves Me so much. A person who hasn't received much forgiveness doesn't love very much."

Jesus told the woman that her sins were forgiven. The other dinner guests thought to themselves, "Who does He think He is—that He can forgive sins?" Jesus knew what they were thinking, but He told the woman that her faith had saved her.

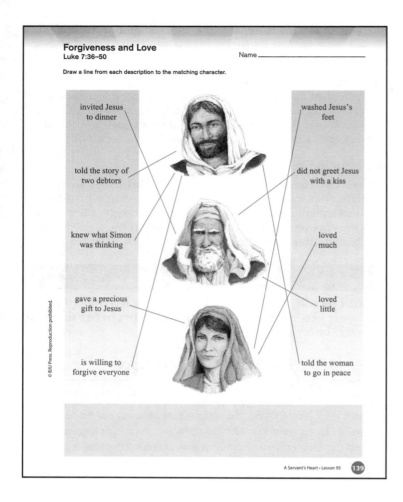

Forgiveness and Love
Luke 7:36–50

Name _____

Draw a line from each description to the matching character.

- invited Jesus to dinner
- told the story of two debtors
- knew what Simon was thinking
- gave a precious gift to Jesus
- is willing to forgive everyone

- washed Jesus's feet
- did not greet Jesus with a kiss
- loved much
- loved little
- told the woman to go in peace

A Servant's Heart • Lesson 95   **139**

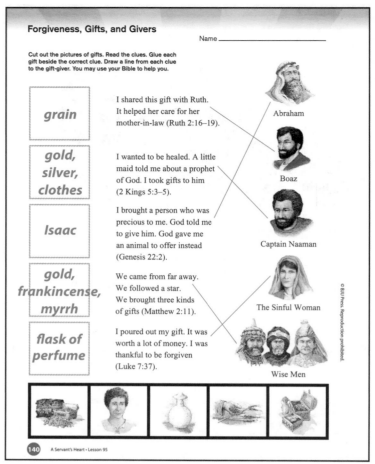

Forgiveness, Gifts, and Givers

Name _____

Cut out the pictures of gifts. Read the clues. Glue each gift beside the correct clue. Draw a line from each clue to the gift-giver. You may use your Bible to help you.

Gift	Clue	Giver
grain	I shared this gift with Ruth. It helped her care for her mother-in-law (Ruth 2:16–19).	Abraham
gold, silver, clothes	I wanted to be healed. A little maid told me about a prophet of God. I took gifts to him (2 Kings 5:3–5).	Boaz
Isaac	I brought a person who was precious to me. God told me to give him. God gave me an animal to offer instead (Genesis 22:2).	Captain Naaman
gold, frankincense, myrrh	We came from far away. We followed a star. We brought three kinds of gifts (Matthew 2:11).	The Sinful Woman
flask of perfume	I poured out my gift. It was worth a lot of money. I was thankful to be forgiven (Luke 7:37).	Wise Men

140   A Servant's Heart • Lesson 95

💡 **Why was Jesus pleased with the woman's offering?** *(It was a sacrificial gift from her heart.)*

💡 **How does Jesus's parable about the two debtors relate to Simon the Pharisee and the woman?** *(Simon is like the man who owed only a little, and the woman owed a lot. Jesus is the creditor Who forgives the amounts owed. The woman is more grateful because she had a better understanding of what a great gift she had been given.)*

💡 **What does Jesus's parable mean to us today?** *(We are all great sinners, and God forgives any sin if we ask Him. We should love God very much.)*

✏️ Worktext page 139

Match characters and actions. Call on volunteers to identify the people shown on the page. *(Jesus, Simon, and the sinful woman)* Direct the students to work independently, reading each sentence and deciding who is described.

✏️ Worktext page 140

Recall facts and details. Instruct the students to cut out the pictures at the bottom of the page. Choose a student to read the first clue. Read the verse aloud to the students. Emphasize that the attitude of the giver is very important. Call on students to identify the gift and the giver before they glue the picture beside the clue.

LESSON **96** Giving

Materials
- Hymn: "Cleanse Me"
- Verse visuals from Lesson 94
- Three name tags, labeled *Malcolm, Peter,* and *Juan*
- Small pieces of wrapped candy, twenty for the story and enough additional for one for each student (optional)
- Copy of page A93 ("Create a Mobile") for each student (optional)
- Items to create a mobile (optional): strips of tagboard, string/yarn, paper clips, and markers

🎵 Hymn: "Cleanse Me"

Sing the first two verses (Worktext page 219). Play the recording and lead in singing both verses.

❤️ Memory Verse—Ephesians 1:7

Practice the memory verse. Show the verse visuals and lead in saying the verse. Choose volunteers to recite the verse.

Picture the Point

Demonstrate giving. Invite volunteers to tell whom they give to. Explain that it is good to give to our friends, to people who are nice to us, and even to strangers who do not have as much as we do. Ask students to listen to the following story and think about who gives more. *(Juan)*

Read or tell the following story as you demonstrate with the candies. Place the three name tags around a table in full view, and place the candy in the middle. As you tell the story, move the candies to the different names. (*Note:* If the class cannot see the demonstration on a table, write the names on a transparency and place the candy on an overhead projector.)

Giving

Malcolm, Peter, and Juan always ate lunch together. One day Malcolm and Juan brought candy, but Peter didn't have any. *[Move all the candy between the tags marked Malcolm and Juan.]*

Juan had five pieces, and Malcolm had a lot more. *[Move five pieces to Juan's name tag and the rest to Malcolm's.]*

When the boys finished their lunch, they pulled out their candy. Peter looked at them, hoping they would offer him a piece. Juan saw that Peter didn't have any, so he gave Peter two pieces. *[Move two of Juan's pieces to Peter's name tag.]*

Malcolm didn't want to be outdone, so he gave Peter three pieces of his candy. *[Move three of Malcolm's candies to Peter's name tag.]*

Now Peter had five pieces and Juan had only three, so Peter gave Juan one of his pieces. Peter and Juan smiled at each other. *[Move one piece from Peter's to Juan's pile.]*

❧

▶ **Who gave more, Malcolm or Juan?** *(Juan's gift was bigger because he gave nearly half of his candy to Peter.)*
💡 **How much did Jesus give to save us?** *(everything)*
💡 **Can we give Jesus a greater gift?** *(No. God's gift is the greatest possible gift.)*
💡 **How can Christians give their lives to God?** *(by daily spending time with Him, making ourselves available to Him, and doing what pleases Him)*

Give each student a piece of candy (optional).

🎨 Art Connection (optional)

Create a mobile. Explain that the mobile on page A93 ("Create a Mobile") will remind the students to ask forgiveness. Distribute the materials needed. Guide them as they follow the directions on the Activity Page. Refer to the illustrations as necessary.

▶ Going Beyond

Reinforcement

Make a forgiveness list. Call on volunteers to name some wrong things that they do for which they need to ask forgiveness of God. Write several of the students' answers for display. *(for example, not sharing, saying unkind words about others, not doing our best work, losing our tempers when playing a game)* Remind them to ask God's forgiveness when needed.

Enrichment

Materials

- For each student, a 2½" × 22" strip of paper or adding-machine tape and a 12" length of string, ribbon, or yarn

Share the story about God's forgiveness using the Salvation Book. Give each student a strip of paper or adding machine tape and a piece of string. Guide them as they follow the directions.

1. Instruct the students to measure 2" from the edge of the strip and make a small mark.
2. Tell the students to fold on the line.
3. Show how to fold the paper back and forth, accordion style.
4. Have each one write "The Salvation Book" on the first panel.
5. Show how to write the Bible reference on the left side and color the right side of each spread. Write the following references and colors for display for the students to refer to.

   Romans 3:23—Dark scribbles (brown, blue, and black) representing the sinner's sin

   Hebrews 9:22—Red to represent Jesus's blood when He died on the cross for our sin

   Isaiah 1:18—White representing sinners washed clean by God's grace

   Revelation 21:21—Gold (or yellow) representing the golden streets in the new Jerusalem where the saved will spend eternity with God

   2 Peter 3:18—Green representing the spiritual growth of the believer while on earth

6. Display how to tape the string in the center on the back of the last panel. Tie the book closed.
7. Read the verses to the students; then give them opportunities to practice explaining the plan of salvation using their books.

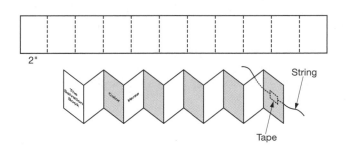

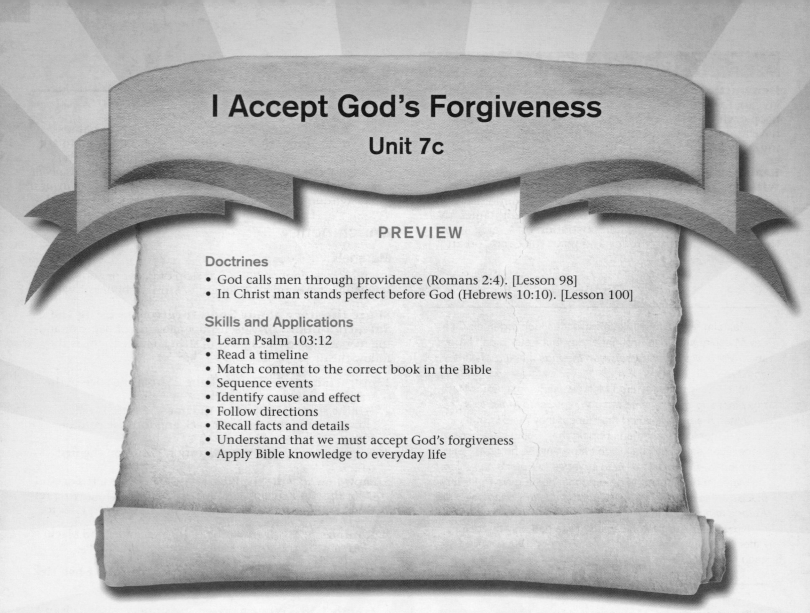

I Accept God's Forgiveness
Unit 7c

PREVIEW

Doctrines

- God calls men through providence (Romans 2:4). [Lesson 98]
- In Christ man stands perfect before God (Hebrews 10:10). [Lesson 100]

Skills and Applications

- Learn Psalm 103:12
- Read a timeline
- Match content to the correct book in the Bible
- Sequence events
- Identify cause and effect
- Follow directions
- Recall facts and details
- Understand that we must accept God's forgiveness
- Apply Bible knowledge to everyday life

LESSON 97 — Hero of the Faith: Abraham Kuyper

Materials

- Hymn: "Cleanse Me"
- Chart 31, "World Map," or a globe
- TimeLine and picture: Abraham Kuyper
- Unit 7 Bookmark for each student
- Highlighter for each student (optional)

♫ Hymn: "Cleanse Me"

Sing the first and second verses (Worktext page 219). Sing both verses of the hymn with the recording. Remind the students that this hymn expresses what a sinner might say in asking God to help him repent of every sin. That includes even the sins he does not remember and the ones he has committed in his heart since the last time he prayed. It is important to know that once God has forgiven a sin, it is gone. We should accept God's forgiveness and stop feeling guilty for that sin.

Background Information

Parliament—*The lawmaking officials in some democratic governments form a* parliament. *The leader of the government is the leader of the country and is called the prime minister.*

Hero of the Faith

Read the following account based on the life of Abraham Kuyper. Explain that Abraham Kuyper (KIGH per) was a great Christian leader in the government of the Netherlands. He became the prime minister. Locate the Netherlands on Chart 31, "World Map," or on the globe for the students. (The country, also known as Holland, is bordered by the North Sea, Belgium, and Germany.)

Read or tell the following short biography. Listening question: **What was the name of the picture Mr. Kuyper bought, and how long did he keep it?** (Christ Crucified; *he kept it until he was an old man.*)

Abraham Kuyper

Abraham Kuyper was born into the home of a pastor in the Netherlands in 1837. "Bram," as his family called him, loved the sea. He often played near the canals or walked down to the harbor to watch the ships sailing away. He dreamed of one day attending the Maritime School to study navigation.

Abraham also loved to read the newspaper. As he grew older, his dream of being a sea captain changed. He began to pay close attention to news reports. He loved to read and hear about politics. He decided to study at Leiden University.

He was a good student. He earned money by tutoring other students. One day he used the money he had saved to buy a picture. The large painting of Christ on the cross was called *Christ Crucified*. Looking at the picture made Abraham feel guilty and sad, but he was not sure why.

He began studying to be a preacher. The university didn't teach the same things that the Bible teaches. Abraham trusted what his teachers said instead of what he had learned as a child. One teacher told his class that he didn't believe Jesus rose from the dead. Abraham and the other students applauded.

Abraham graduated and married a lady named Johanna when he was twenty-five. He was asked to be the minister of a small village church about the same time.

Abraham had many questions in his mind about God. He didn't agree with all of the Bible's teachings about salvation and Jesus Christ. But he still felt that he wanted to preach more than he wanted to do anything else.

A few people in his church weren't happy with his doctrine. As he visited with various families, he began to see that they all believed the Bible. They believed that Jesus Christ is God's Son and that salvation from sin is through Him alone, not through any human effort.

Abraham found himself listening to these people instead of trying to argue with them. "These people know what they believe," he thought, "and they're not ashamed to tell others about their beliefs. I admire that."

One lady refused to attend church because God's Word wasn't being taught there. She read her Bible and studied other books at home. Whenever Abraham went to visit her, she pleaded with him to forget the false teaching and believe what the Bible says. God worked in Abraham's heart, and he soon trusted Jesus Christ as his Savior.

Abraham's habit of reading newspapers as a boy helped him become a good writer of newspaper articles. When he wasn't preaching, he wrote newspaper articles and pamphlets to show that the Bible is true. He also wrote about his ideas for making the Netherlands a better country. He soon became the editor of the newspaper he was writing for.

Abraham found other ways to speak the truth. He served as a member of parliament for three years and later as prime minister of the Netherlands. He wrote books and founded a university that taught students the truth of God's Word.

When he was an old man, sometimes he looked up to the wall above his bed. There hung the picture, *Christ Crucified*,

---

Abraham Kuyper

Abraham Kuyper was born in the Netherlands in 1837. He was a good student who loved to read. He went to Leiden University. He studied to be a minister and graduated with honors. His teachers did not believe all that the Bible teaches. He trusted them instead of what the Bible says. He was asked to pastor a small village church. The people there did not like his preaching because it did not agree with the Bible. They shared with him the truth of what they believed. Soon he began to see that the Bible was right and he was wrong. He trusted Jesus Christ as his Savior and began to preach the truth.

Abraham wrote many newspaper articles about his ideas for making the Netherlands a better country. He was elected a member of parliament, wrote books, and started a university that would teach students the truth of God's Word. He became the prime minister of the Netherlands in the early 1900s. For many years he traveled and wrote and spoke to large crowds. Abraham Kuyper always tried to honor God and to speak for Him.

Name _____

Write a number beside each sentence to show the order in which the events happened.

5 Kuyper became the prime minister of the Netherlands.

4 Kuyper trusted Christ and began to preach the truth.

2 Kuyper believed his teachers instead of the Bible.

3 Kuyper's church members shared the truth from the Bible with him.

1 Kuyper was born in the Netherlands.

© BJU Press. Reproduction prohibited.

(242) A Servant's Heart • Lesson 97

---

to remind Abraham of the One he loved and had lived for—the Savior he would soon see face to face.

❧

▶ **How did Abraham Kuyper come to believe the Bible?** *(One lady from his church believed the Bible and witnessed to him until he was saved.)*

▶ **What did Abraham Kuyper do with this new-found belief?** *(He pastored a church, wrote articles and pamphlets, edited a newspaper, and started a university. He was elected to the parliament, became prime minister, and always spoke out for God.)*

 How can Christians today be like Abraham Kuyper? *(Christians can study hard, believe the Bible, and always speak out for God no matter where the Lord places them.)*

⏱ TimeLine

Add Abraham Kuyper to the TimeLine. Place the picture of Abraham Kuyper on the TimeLine (AD 1837–1920), pointing out that Abraham Kuyper was willing to speak, write, and teach others about God's truth. He also served as prime minister to lead the government of the Netherlands. Guide the students as they glue their pictures of Abraham Kuyper onto their TimeLines.

✎ Worktext page 242 (optional)

Hero of the Faith: Abraham Kuyper. Review the events in Abraham Kuyper's life. Remind the students that after

---

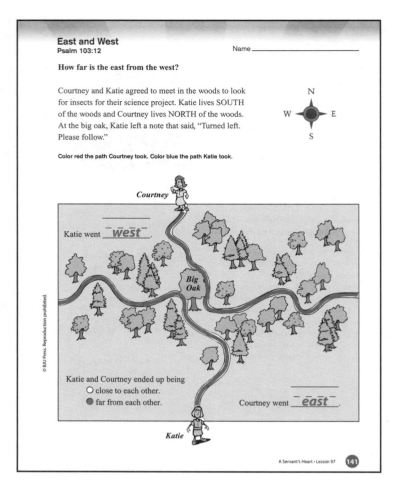

How far is the east from the west?

Courtney and Katie agreed to meet in the woods to look for insects for their science project. Katie lives SOUTH of the woods and Courtney lives NORTH of the woods. At the big oak, Katie left a note that said, "Turned left. Please follow."

Color red the path Courtney took. Color blue the path Katie took.

Courtney

_____
Katie went   *west* .

Big Oak

Katie and Courtney ended up being
○ close to each other.
● far from each other.

Courtney went   *east* .

Katie

Write the letter in the box to match each Bible account with the book in which it is found.

Old Testament

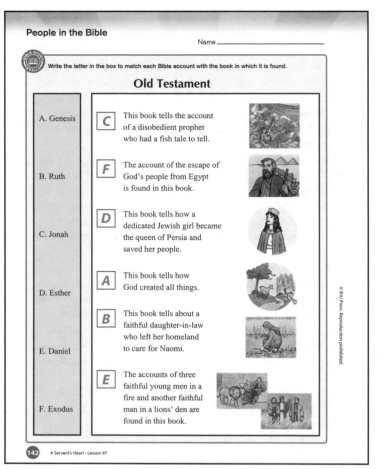

A. Genesis	**C** This book tells the account of a disobedient prophet who had a fish tale to tell.
B. Ruth	**F** The account of the escape of God's people from Egypt is found in this book.
C. Jonah	**D** This book tells how a dedicated Jewish girl became the queen of Persia and saved her people.
D. Esther	**A** This book tells how God created all things.
E. Daniel	**B** This book tells about a faithful daughter-in-law who left her homeland to care for Naomi.
F. Exodus	**E** The accounts of three faithful young men in a fire and another faithful man in a lions' den are found in this book.

---

he was saved, Kuyper always spoke out for God. Direct the students to number the sentences in order.

♥ Memory Verse—Psalm 103:12

Principle: God's forgiveness is forever. Practice the memory verse. Direct the students to highlight the verse (optional) and mark the location with the Unit 7 Bookmark. Students should open their Worktexts to the glossary page listing *transgression*. Choose a volunteer to read the entry. *(sin; act of doing what God forbids)* Explain that the word comes from a Latin word that means "to step over." Call on volunteers to tell what we step over when we sin. *(God's laws)*

💡 **How far is the east from the west?** *(When traveling one direction only, the east and the west never meet.)*

💡 **What does it mean to remove our transgressions?** *(To remove means "to take away.")*

▶ **Who removes sins from Christians?** *(Jesus Christ our Lord)*

💡 **If Christians really believe a sin has been removed, what should they do?** *(thank the Lord for taking it away and never repeat the sin)*

▶ **Do Christians ever have to ask the Lord to forgive that act of sin again?** *(no, unless they do that sin again)*

📖 Worktext page 141

Apply Bible knowledge to everyday life. Read aloud the explanation and the directions at the top of the page. Direct attention to the compass rose. Tell them it shows the

directions north, south, east, and west. Tell them to run their fingers up the arrow pointing to the top of the page. Explain that their fingers are moving north on the map. Continue to point out the directions on the compass.

Help the students think through what compass direction Courtney turns as she turns to her left when coming from the north. Direct the students to turn the map around as if they are Courtney following the path. Guide them as they trace Courtney's path in red.

Tell the students to turn the map around again to trace Katie's path. Tell them to examine the directions indicated by the compass rose and decide the directions Katie and Courtney went. *(Note:* You may call on volunteers to illustrate the paths taken by Courtney and Katie. Choose two students to stand at the front and back of the classroom and then walk toward each other and turn left.)

Read the questions, allowing the students to fill in the blank or choose the correct response. Read aloud **Psalm 103:12** again. Conclude with a discussion that east will never meet west.

📖 Bible Study Skills, Worktext page 142

Match content to the correct book in the Bible. Read the directions at the top of the page. Point out that knowing the content of a book helps you know where to look for specific information when studying the Bible. Allow the students to complete the page independently.

A Whole Family Is Saved

Materials
- Hymn: "Cleanse Me"
- Chart 40, "The Roman Empire in Paul's Day"
- Four dominoes

🎵 Hymn: "Cleanse Me"

Teach the third verse (Worktext page 219). Sing or play the recording of the third verse for the students. Discuss the meaning of the key words, asking volunteers to explain the lines.

💡 **What does *wholly* mean?** *(completely)*
💡 **What does *divine* mean?** *(from God)*
💡 **What does *passion* mean?** *(strong emotions)*
💡 **What does it mean to *abide*?** *(to live in or remain in)*

❤ Memory Verse—Psalm 103:12

Practice the memory verse.

▶ **How far does God remove sins from Christians?** *(completely, as far as the east is from the west)*

Point out that the verse reminds us of God's great forgiveness. Read the verse aloud together. Call on volunteers to read the verse aloud. Allow each student to read the verse aloud with a partner.

Background Information

Roman Guards—*Under Roman law, a guard who allowed his prisoner to escape was liable for the same penalty the prisoner would have suffered.*

Prison—*In Paul's time, prison was not a form of punishment but rather a waiting place until a prisoner was brought to trial. If he was found guilty, he would be beaten with a whip or be executed.*

Introducing the Bible Account

Guide a discussion about influences. Ask volunteers how their behavior influences others. Ask other volunteers to give examples. Explain that the following account discusses how the faith of two of Christ's followers influenced a jailer and his household.

Bible Account

Read Acts 16:9–34 or use the following retelling of the passage. Display Chart 40, "The Roman Empire in Paul's Day." Point to Macedonia. Listening question: **What did the jailer ask the disciples?** *(He asked how he could get saved.)*

A Whole Family Is Saved

When Paul and Silas were traveling, Paul had a vision of a man in his dream. A Macedonian man was standing there saying, "Come over into Macedonia, and help us."

Immediately after Paul saw the vision, they went to Philippi, the main city in Macedonia, because the Lord had made it clear He wanted them to preach the gospel there. They stayed several days until the Sabbath and went down to the riverside, where many women gathered to pray.

On the way to the river they met a slave girl who was possessed with an evil spirit. She brought in a great deal of money for her masters by telling fortunes. She followed Paul and the others around and shouted everywhere they went, "These men are the servants of the most high God, showing us the way of salvation." She did this for many days. This troubled Paul because it was hurting his ministry.

Finally, Paul turned and said to the spirit, "I command you in the name of Jesus Christ to come out of her." At that very moment the evil spirit came out of the young woman.

Direct the students to look at the pictures on Worktext page 143 as you give the rest of the account.

The girl's masters realized that she wouldn't be able to make money for them anymore. They caught Paul and Silas, took them to the marketplace before the city rulers, and said, "These Jews are making trouble in our city and teaching things that we Romans can't receive."

The people in the marketplace turned against Paul and Silas, and the rulers ripped off Paul's and Silas's robes and commanded them to be beaten. After they had been beaten many times, the rulers threw the servants of the Lord into prison and told the jailer to keep them there. So the jailer put them in the inner prison and put their feet in stocks.

Although Paul and Silas were in pain, at midnight they prayed and sang praises to God. Suddenly there was a big earthquake! The foundation of the prison was shaken, all the doors flew open, and the stocks fell off the prisoners' feet.

The shaking woke the jailer up, and when he saw the doors standing open, he thought all the prisoners had escaped. For fear that the authorities would put him to death for allowing the prisoners to get away, he pulled out his sword to kill himself. Paul saw him through the open door and called out, "Don't hurt yourself! We are all still here."

The jailer called for a light and went into the prison trembling. He fell down in front of Paul and Silas. He let them out of their cell and took them to his home. He asked what he needed to do to be saved. They told him, "Believe on the Lord Jesus Christ, and you and your family will be saved." Paul and Silas continued telling them about the Lord as the jailer washed their cuts.

The jailer and his family all trusted Christ as Savior that night and were baptized. Then he fed Paul and Silas, rejoicing in the Lord.

▶ **What did Paul and Silas do that caused them to be put into prison?** *(Paul cast an evil spirit out of a young woman.)*

A Whole Family Is Saved
Acts 16:16–34

Name_____

Write a number in each circle to show the order of the events.

"Believe on the Lord Jesus Christ." 4

"Keep them secure." 2

"These Jews trouble our city." 1

"Don't harm yourself. We are all here." 3

© BJU Press. Reproduction prohibited.

A Servant's Heart • Lesson 98 143

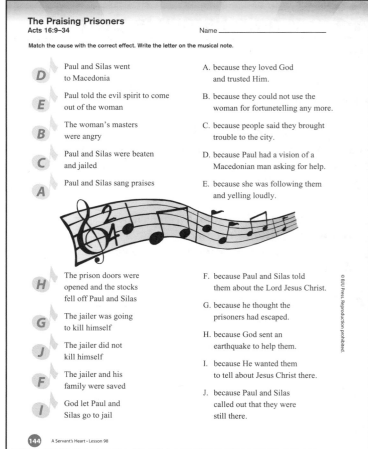

The Praising Prisoners
Acts 16:9–34

Name_____

Match the cause with the correct effect. Write the letter on the musical note.

D Paul and Silas went to Macedonia

E Paul told the evil spirit to come out of the woman

B The woman's masters were angry

C Paul and Silas were beaten and jailed

A Paul and Silas sang praises

A. because they loved God and trusted Him.

B. because they could not use the woman for fortunetelling any more.

C. because people said they brought trouble to the city.

D. because Paul had a vision of a Macedonian man asking for help.

E. because she was following them and yelling loudly.

H The prison doors were opened and the stocks fell off Paul and Silas

G The jailer was going to kill himself

J The jailer did not kill himself

F The jailer and his family were saved

I God let Paul and Silas go to jail

F. because Paul and Silas told them about the Lord Jesus Christ.

G. because he thought the prisoners had escaped.

H. because God sent an earthquake to help them.

I. because He wanted them to tell about Jesus Christ there.

J. because Paul and Silas called out that they were still there.

© BJU Press. Reproduction prohibited.

144 A Servant's Heart • Lesson 98

▶ **Why was the crowd of people mad at Paul and Silas?** *(The masters of the woman lied and told the crowd that Paul and Silas were teaching lies.)*

💡 **What influenced the jailer to trust in Jesus as Savior?** *(He saw that Paul and Silas sang and prayed even though they had been beaten for spreading the gospel. He also saw how the Lord released the prisoners.)*

💡 **How can Christians influence others to accept the Lord's forgiveness?** *(They can always rejoice in the Lord and tell others the gospel, even when the circumstances seem bad.)*

📝 Worktext page 143

Sequence events. Call on volunteers to look at the pictures as they retell the account. Direct the students to number the pictures in the order the events took place.

📝 Worktext page 144

Identify cause and effect. Explain that an attitude or action can cause something else to happen. Line up four dominoes close together and demonstrate how they all fall when the first one is knocked over. Write for display: *Daryl's shoe was untied, which caused him to trip.*

▶ **What happened?** *(Daryl tripped.)* Explain that this was the effect.

▶ **What was the cause?** *(His shoe was untied.)*

Remind the students that attitudes and actions can influence others for good or bad. Read the directions at the top of the Worktext page. Give guidance in completing each sentence. Provide help as needed.

LESSON 99 Trust God's Word

Materials
• Hymn: "Cleanse Me"

🎵 Hymn: "Cleanse Me"

Sing the third verse (Worktext page 219). Read aloud the third verse and then explain that it is about surrendering.

💡 **What does it mean to surrender?** *(give yourself up entirely to someone or something)*

💡 **Name some people who surrender and who they surrender to.** *(criminals to the police, patients to doctors, children to parents)*

💡 **When a person surrenders to God, how much of himself should he surrender?** *(all of himself)*

💡 **How can Christians surrender their lives to God?** *(Christians should do only those things God wants them to do.)*

Sing the third verse of the hymn and then sing all three verses.

♥ Memory Verse—Psalm 103:12

Practice the memory verse. Teach the following hand motions for the verse.

east and west—both hands on the shoulders and gesture with the *right* hand for east, then the *left* hand for west

so far—stretch the arms out to the sides and point

He—hands and arms up

removed—gesture with fingers and hands together then moving apart

our transgressions—both hands over heart

from us—point finger to self

Introducing the Application Story
Guide a discussion about worry.

💡 **What does it mean to worry?** *(to be afraid that God's will is not best for us or that His power is not capable of handling our problems)*

💡 **What are some things you worry about?** *(Accept any answer.)* Discuss whether any of these things should cause them to worry since God is in complete control. *(no)*

Application Story

Read or tell the following story. Listening question: **Why was Nick having a nightmare?** *(He didn't accept forgiveness from others and God. He started worrying.)*

Nick's Nightmare

Nick woke up in tears. He didn't know whether he had screamed aloud or only in his dream. Just then Mom came through the door. The light from the hall glared in Nick's eyes.

"Nicolas, what's the matter?" Mom sat down on the edge of his bed and wiped his tears away, holding his head gently between her warm hands.

"I dreamed Dale was f-falling out of the tr-tree again," Nick said. Mom put her arm around him and hugged him.

"But Nick, Dale forgave you and Jesus forgave you."

"If I-I hadn't called Dale a s-s-sissy and a baby, he wouldn't have gone so high in the tree."

Mom held Nick away from her and said, "Nicolas, we all sin. Your sin was certainly unloving and dangerous, but God can forgive every sin. You prayed for forgiveness with Dale when he forgave you at the hospital. Don't you believe God can forgive you?"

"Well, yes, but . . ."

"Nick, there are no *buts*; when God says He forgives, He does. Your part is to accept God's forgiveness based on His Word and to stop thinking about yourself. That doesn't mean you should forget the lesson you learned about pushing others to do what they don't think they should or about how cruel it is to be unloving. Perhaps God allowed this to happen to Dale

and you so that you can learn to respect others' limits and to love people just the way they are."

"Mom," said Nick, "I don't know how to stop worrying about this."

"How did you accept God's forgiveness for your salvation last year?"

"Well, I believed that Jesus died to pay for my sins and I told God that I was trusting in Jesus," Nick said.

"Nick, if Jesus's death and Resurrection were enough to pay for all your other sins, don't you think that it was enough to pay for this one too?"

"Yes."

"Then you need to trust in His promises. When you think about your past sins, pray and ask Jesus to increase your trust in Him. If you're thinking about Jesus, you won't have time to dwell on yourself."

▶ **How did Nick sin?** *(He made fun of his friend and pressured him to do something dangerous.)*

▶ **Was Nick trusting Jesus when he had the nightmare?** *(no)*

▶ **Could Jesus forgive Nick's sins?** *(yes)*

▶ **How can Christians be forgiven?** *(by repenting and asking God to forgive them)*

▶ **Do Christians have to worry about their sins after they are forgiven?** *(No, worrying is a sin. But Christians should remember the lessons they learned and not repeat the sins.)*

✏ Worktext page 145
Apply Bible knowledge to everyday life. Read aloud the first example. Direct the students to find **Romans 3:23** in their Bibles. Choose a volunteer to read the verse aloud. Call on students to tell what they would say. *(Elicit that all people are sinners.)* Continue with the other two examples. Point out that God forgives sin and expects us to forgive others many times each day.

100 Thankful for God's Goodness

Materials
• Hymn: "Cleanse Me"

🎵 Hymn: "Cleanse Me"
Sing the hymn (Worktext page 219). Sing the hymn several times. You may want to divide the class into three groups allowing each group to sing one verse.

♥ Memory Verse—Psalm 103:12
Practice the memory verse. Incorporate the hand motions taught in the previous lesson.

Background Information
Leprosy—*The Hebrews had no cure for the highly contagious disease of leprosy. Leprosy starts as a discoloration of the skin*

Trust God's Word

Name _____

Read the sentences in each section and the verses that go with them.
Write what you would say.

1. Someone tells you that he doesn't need to ask for forgiveness because he doesn't sin. What would you say? (Romans 3:23)

Answers will vary but should include the
idea that everyone sins.

2. Someone tells you that she has forgiven another person again and again, and the person keeps doing the same thing. She is tired of forgiving over and over. What would you say? (Matthew 18:21–22)

Answers will vary but should include the
idea that Jesus commands us to keep forgiving.

3. Someone tells you that he has asked God for forgiveness, but he keeps worrying that he is not forgiven. What would you say? (1 John 1:9)

Answers will vary but should include the
idea that Jesus promises to forgive our
sins when we confess and repent.

A Servant's Heart • Lesson 99 145

---

and causes the skin, connective tissues, and organs to break down and dissolve. The spongy tumor-like swellings cause the patient to no longer feel heat and pain. Often he was subject to accidental destruction of his limbs before he realized the danger. The Hebrews held to strict isolation laws that caused the lepers to be outcasts from society. There are two types of this disease, which we now call Hansen's disease. Both types of leprosy are caused by a species of bacteria called Mycobacterium lepra. The milder type, left untreated, can heal itself in one to three years. The other is a long, slow disease, causing death in ten to twenty years. Either the disease completely breaks down the organ tissue, or the weakened body is invaded by tuberculosis or some other disease, which causes death.

Samaritans—The Samaritans were related to the Jews in that they were descendants of Israelites from the north. Some say they were people left in the land during the exile who intermarried with foreigners placed in the land by the Assyrian captors. The Samaritans insisted that Mount Gerizim, not Jerusalem, was the place to worship God. This disagreement, which had probably started during the time of the divided kingdoms of Israel and Judah, caused the Jews to reject the Samaritans. When Christ referred to the Samaritan leper who was healed as a "stranger" (Luke 17:18), He meant the Samaritan was of mixed blood and a stranger to worship in Jerusalem.

Introducing the Bible Account

Guide a discussion about asking forgiveness. Tell students that many times people will pray for forgiveness but not accept it from God. Allow students to share examples of

---

this or ask whether they can think of a situation when someone might feel this way. Explain that one of the men in the following account truly accepts Jesus's forgiveness.

Bible Account

Read Luke 17:11–19 or use the following retelling of the passage. Listening question: **How should we respond when God forgives our sins?** *(thank Him)*

Thankful for God's Goodness

When Jesus was traveling to Jerusalem, ten men called to Him from far off because they were lepers and had to stay away from healthy people. They shouted, "Jesus, Master, have mercy on us."

Jesus saw that they were lepers and told them to immediately go and show themselves to the priests.

Because lepers had to obey strict laws and weren't allowed to go to the priests unless their leprosy had been cured, these men knew that Jesus was going to do something for them. So they turned and began to walk toward the temple. As they went, they were healed from their leprosy!

Only one of the ten men, a Samaritan, turned back to Jesus when he saw that he was healed and praised the Lord with a loud voice. When he reached Jesus, he fell down on his face at the Lord's feet, giving thanks.

Jesus was touched by this man's devotion, but He said, "Weren't ten men healed? Where are the other nine?" Jesus was teaching that all who are healed and saved owe thanks to God. Ten men had asked for healing, but only one thanked Him for the answer.

▶ **What did the ten men want from Jesus?** *(to be healed of leprosy)*
▶ **Why did they stay so far away from Him?** *(It was a law, so they would not give others leprosy.)*
▶ **How were the ten men healed?** *(Jesus healed them.)*
▶ **How many men returned to thank Jesus?** *(only one)*
 What should Christians do when the Lord forgives them of their sins? *(They should first thank Him and then tell others about Christ's goodness.)*

Picture the Point

Demonstrate forgiveness. Explain that sometimes when we want to explain things that are hard to understand we use examples to make the idea more clear. Tell the students that we are going to use the board to represent the state of our souls and the eraser to represent the power God has to remove (forgive) our sins.

• Brainstorm with the students and allow them to write a list of sins for display. *(Students will probably mention murder and stealing, but lead them to think about the anger, unloving attitudes, mean words, and disobedience that we all have and display at times.)*

- Discuss the earthly consequences for sins. *(jail, spanking, grounding, losing a friendship, etc.)*
- Write for display the following references: **Isaiah 1:18**, **Isaiah 38:17**, **Isaiah 43:25**, and **Micah 7:19**.

Choose four volunteers to read those verses. Ask the students to tell what happens when God forgives. *(God sees our hearts as white as snow, puts our sins behind Him, blots them out and does not remember them, and throws them into the depths of the sea.)* Explain that these verses use figurative language to teach a spiritual truth.

▶ **How do Christians receive God's forgiveness for their sins?** *(Repent and ask for forgiveness.)*

Erase all the sins previously listed. Explain that all those sins are forgiven when Christians ask forgiveness. God has made them as white as snow, put their sins behind Him, crossed the sins out, not remembered the sins, and thrown the sins into the depths of the sea.

Discussion Questions

 Why don't Christians have to keep asking for forgiveness for the same sin? *(God forgives once and for all and promises not to remember that sin.)*

 If Christians worry about their sins after they have asked God's forgiveness, what have they done? *(They have sinned again by worrying and not trusting in God's promises.)*

 What should Christians do after they pray for forgiveness from God? *(Accept His forgiveness and take the consequences of their actions as a blessing that will remind them of the lessons learned. Thank the Lord that they don't have to pay for the sin with eternal death.)*

Worktext page 146

Recall facts and details. Call on a volunteer to tell where Jesus was going when the lepers saw Him. Tell the students to write *Jerusalem* to complete the sentence at the top of the page. Direct them to draw in the first box the number of lepers that were healed. Tell them to follow the arrow and to write this number. Continue with the remaining two boxes. Call on a student to complete the sentence at the bottom of the page. Read **Luke 17:19** aloud.

Going Beyond

Reinforcement

Writing in a journal. Read aloud **Philippians 4:6**. Tell them to write down some things they worry about. Remind them to pray, trust, and obey God about their worries.

Enrichment

Materials

- A pocket compass
- Large letters N, S, E, and W cut out from construction paper

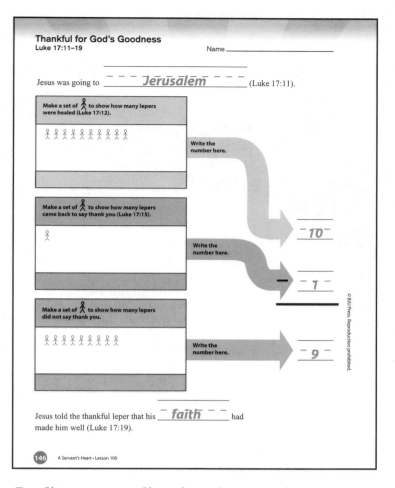

Reading compass directions. Bring a pocket compass to class. Explain that a compass can be used to tell which way you are headed or which way you need to go. Demonstrate how to use the compass.

- Keep the compass level
- Keep the compass away from metal
- Point the directional arrow away from the body

Demonstrate how to find which direction is north. Align the compass needle with the indicator arrow on the face of the dial. Place the letters *N, S, E,* and *W* on the classroom walls to show the directions. Choose a student to stand facing east, at the front of the classroom. Remind them to notice which direction is north. *(The student is facing right. He is headed east.)* Read **Psalm 103:12** together.

Place the compass at the back of the classroom. Challenge the students to find out which direction it is to the clock, to the classroom door, to the window, or to some other location. *(Note: Some students may want to know that north on a map may not always be pointing to true north.)*

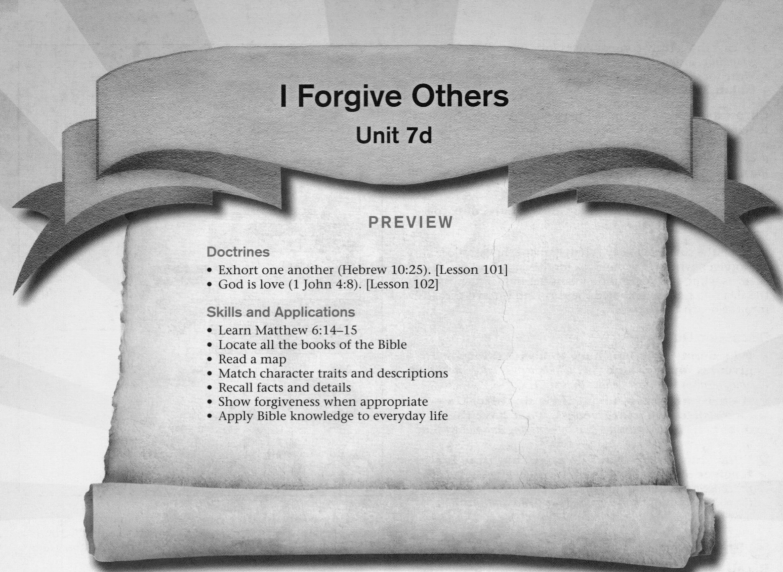

I Forgive Others

Unit 7d

PREVIEW

Doctrines
- Exhort one another (Hebrew 10:25). [Lesson 101]
- God is love (1 John 4:8). [Lesson 102]

Skills and Applications
- Learn Matthew 6:14–15
- Locate all the books of the Bible
- Read a map
- Match character traits and descriptions
- Recall facts and details
- Show forgiveness when appropriate
- Apply Bible knowledge to everyday life

LESSON 101 Forgiven

Materials
- Unit 7 Bookmark for each student
- Pocket chart (optional)
- Highlighter for each student (optional)
- Word cards for the memory verses made from various colors of construction paper: Make sure the word *forgive* is in the same color all four times and the word *trespasses* is in the same contrasting color both times.

Background Information
Servants—*Servants were slaves in biblical times. Running away was often punishable by beatings or death. Even those who aided a runaway slave could be charged as criminals.*

Introducing the Bible Account
Guide a discussion about servants. Call on students to tell how much they think a servant was paid in biblical times. *(nothing)* Explain the difference between *a servant* today and the servitude of *a slave* in biblical times. Share the background information and then tell students that Onesimus was a runaway servant/slave.

Bible Account

Read Philemon 1:8–21 or use the following retelling of the passage. Listening question: **What was different about Onesimus from the last time Philemon had seen him?** *(He had become a Christian.)*

Forgiven

Paul was a prisoner in Rome. He shared the gospel with a slave named Onesimus, who had been the slave of a man named Philemon, who lived in Colosse. He apparently stole from Philemon and then ran away. After Onesimus was saved, the Holy Spirit taught him to make things right with those he had sinned against. Onesimus thought of the wrong he had done to Philemon.

Just before Onesimus returned to his master, Paul wrote to Philemon. In the letter, Paul told Philemon that Onesimus had been saved and that Paul was very grateful for Onesimus's ministry. Paul had confidence that Onesimus would be useful to Philemon now that he was a brother in Christ and a willing servant. He already had a testimony of faithfulness and love for other believers.

Forgiven
Philemon 1:8–21   Name _____

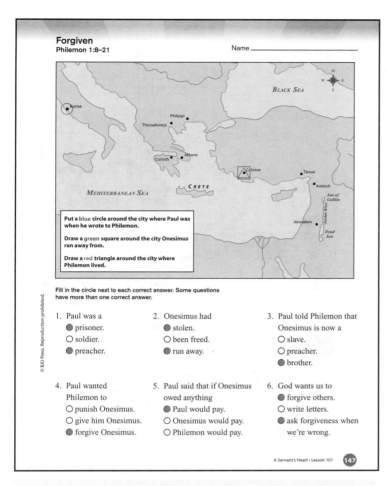

Put a **blue** circle around the city where Paul was when he wrote to Philemon.

Draw a **green** square around the city Onesimus ran away from.

Draw a **red** triangle around the city where Philemon lived.

Fill in the circle next to each correct answer. Some questions have more than one correct answer.

1. Paul was a
   ● prisoner.
   ○ soldier.
   ● preacher.

2. Onesimus had
   ● stolen.
   ○ been freed.
   ● run away.

3. Paul told Philemon that Onesimus is now a
   ○ slave.
   ○ preacher.
   ● brother.

4. Paul wanted Philemon to
   ○ punish Onesimus.
   ○ give him Onesimus.
   ● forgive Onesimus.

5. Paul said that if Onesimus owed anything
   ● Paul would pay.
   ○ Onesimus would pay.
   ○ Philemon would pay.

6. God wants us to
   ● forgive others.
   ○ write letters.
   ● ask forgiveness when we're wrong.

A Servant's Heart • Lesson 101   **147**

Focus on Forgiveness
Ephesians 4:31–32   Name _____

You have learned about forgiveness in your Bible lessons. Read each of the following groups of sentences and answer the questions.

1. Darren is a Christian. He is very thankful that God has forgiven his sin and saved him. He is always watching for others to do wrong things to him. He doesn't get angry and start a fight, but he does look for a way to get even. What would you tell Darren about forgiveness? (Ephesians 4:32)

   *Answers will vary but should include that Christians are not to be*
   *angry toward others or try to get even with them.*

2. Charlie is rough when the second-grade boys play soccer. He runs into the other players and knocks them out of the way. He always acts really sorry, but as soon as the game starts again, he runs into someone else. What would you tell the boys about forgiveness? (Luke 17:3–4)

   *Answers will vary but should include that no matter how many*
   *times someone asks for forgiveness, always forgive.*

3. Beth said something bad about Kim. Their teacher had Beth say she was sorry, but she doesn't act as if she really is. What would you tell Kim about forgiveness? (Ephesians 4:32)

   *Answers will vary but should include that we are to forgive*
   *others as God forgives us.*

148   A Servant's Heart • Lesson 101

Paul felt sure that Philemon wouldn't be angry with Onesimus for running away. Paul told Philemon to accept Onesimus as Philemon would receive Paul himself. Paul added that if Onesimus owed Philemon anything, Paul would pay it back. Finally, Paul said that he had written the letter with confidence in Philemon's obedience. Paul was certain that Philemon would do more than he asked.

❦

▸ **What did Onesimus do that was a sin and hurt Philemon?** (He stole from his master and then ran away.)

💡 **Why did Paul write the letter to Philemon?** (He wanted to encourage Philemon to respond in love toward Onesimus as his brother in Christ, not as his runaway slave.)

💡 **If your friend took something of yours but later asked your forgiveness, what should you do?** (forgive him)

♥ Memory Verses—Matthew 6:14–15
Principle: Forgive others as God forgives you.

▸ **What does *to trespass* mean?** (to disobey, to sin, to cross a line of restriction)

▸ **Why can God not be involved in any sin?** (God is perfect and holy.)

Practice the memory verse. Display the word cards from the verses. Guide the students in reading the verses aloud.

Take away *trespasses* in both verses and direct them to read the verses again. Remove *forgive* from the verses and direct the students to read the verses again.

▸ **What does verse 14 say God will do if we forgive others?** (He will forgive us.)

▸ **What does verse 15 say God will not do if we do not forgive others?** (He will not forgive us.)

💡 **How do these verses teach that Christians can become more like Jesus?** (They should forgive people who sin against them.)

▸ **Read Ephesians 4:29–30 to the students. What happens when Christians choose not to forgive someone?** (They disobey God. They also cause the Holy Spirit to be grieved, sorrowful, or offended.)

Direct the students to highlight Matthew 6:14–15 in their Bibles (optional) and to mark the location with the Unit 7 Bookmark.

✎ Worktext page 147
Locate cities on a map. Paul is writing from prison in Rome to Philemon in Colosse. He sends one letter to Philemon and one letter to the church in Colosse with Onesimus and Tychicus. Direct the students to locate the cities on the map as indicated by the directions.

Recall facts and details. Read aloud the directions for the bottom exercise. Allow independent work, and explain that there may be more than one correct answer.

Worktext page 148

Apply Bible knowledge to everyday life. Read aloud the directions at the top of the page. Choose volunteers to read each of the examples and other volunteers to read the verses. Instruct the students to write how they would respond to each question. Discuss what they have learned about forgiveness. Elicit that God's Word commands us to forgive, even for repeated offenses. Point out that the Bible also says not to be angry and not to try to get even when treated wrongly.

LESSON 102 Two Sons: Two Sins

Materials

- Chart 22, "A Son Returns Home"
- Hymn: "Cleanse Me"
- Word cards for memory verses prepared in previous lesson
- Pocket chart (optional)

♪ Hymn: "Cleanse Me"

Sing the hymn (Worktext page 219). Play the recording of each verse, pausing between verses to review the key ideas and sing the verse.

♥ Memory Verses—Matthew 6:14–15

Practice the memory verses.
Display the word cards except *trespasses* and *forgive*. Say the verse together.

- Remove the *men* cards and say the verse.
- Remove *ye*, *you*, and *your*. Say the verse.
- Choose volunteers to remove the rest of the words one by one, saying the verse each time.

Background Information

Inheritance—*During Old Testament times the firstborn inherited two parts of the father's property. For example, a man with three sons would divide his property into four equal parts, and the younger sons would each get one fourth, while the oldest would get two fourths, or half. It is likely that this tradition was still followed by some Jews in New Testament times. The prodigal son probably received a third of his father's property.*

Introducing the Bible Account

Guide a discussion about doing right. Explain that Jesus told the following story about a man who was angry because his younger brother was not punished for doing wrong.

💡 **Have you ever done something bad and not been punished for it?** *(Any answer is acceptable.)*
💡 **Have you ever done something good and not been rewarded for it?** *(Any answer is acceptable.)*
💡 **Who sees everything we do, whether it is good or bad?** *(God)*
💡 **What will Christians receive from God for doing right for His glory?** *(a reward in heaven)*

Bible Account

Read Luke 15:11–32 or use the following retelling of the

A Son Returns Home
Luke 15:11–32

In the Old Testament, a first-born son received a larger portion of his father's property. At the time of Christ, some still followed this tradition. The younger son in the story probably received one-third of the property.

The **husks** that the son wanted to eat were probably carob pods. These pods were usually food for animals, but poor people sometimes ate them in times of famine.

The **fatted calf** was an animal kept in a stall and overfed to prepare it for slaughter on a special occasion. The arrival of an honored guest would be such an occasion.

© BJU Press. Reproduction prohibited.

A Servant's Heart • Lesson 102 149

passage. Direct the students to look at the pictures on Worktext page 149. Explain that the word *prodigal* means "wasteful." Listening question: **What did the younger son waste?** *(money, good health, time he could have been with his father)*

Two Sons: Two Sins

Jesus told a parable to teach the Pharisees how God deals with sinners. This is the story He told.

There was a man with two sons. The younger son told his father to give him the inheritance that would have been given to him when the father died. So the man divided everything he had and gave the younger son his portion.

Soon the younger son went into a faraway country and wasted everything. A famine came to that country, and he didn't have anything left. He had to work for a foreigner, who sent him into his fields to feed the hogs.

The young man would have gladly eaten the husks that were fed to the hogs. There was no one to give the young man anything to eat.

Then the young man thought about his situation. Here he was starving to death in a foreign country and feeding dirty animals, while even the servants back home had more than enough to eat. The servants were always treated well too.

So the young man said to himself, "I will get up and go back to my father. I will say to him, 'Father, I have sinned against heaven and you. I'm not worthy to be called your son anymore. Treat me like one of your hired servants.'"

So the young man got up and returned to his father's house. When he was still far away, his father saw him, ran to him, and hugged and kissed him.

The son said to his father, "Father, I have sinned against heaven and you. I'm not worthy to be called your son anymore."

But his father told the servants, "Bring some good clothes for him. Bring a ring for his finger and shoes for his feet. Kill the fattened calf, and let's have a big celebration. I thought my son was dead, but he's alive! I thought he was lost, but he's been found!" Then everyone began to celebrate.

But the older son was in the fields and hadn't seen his younger brother come home. When he came in from the fields, he asked one of the servants what was going on.

The servant told him, "Your brother has come home, and your father has invited others to a feast because his son is home safe and sound."

That made the older brother so angry that he wouldn't go into the house. His father came out to plead with him to come in.

The older son told his father that he had worked hard all his life and never disobeyed. The older brother never had a party, but the other son, who wasted all the money that was given to him, received a big party.

But his father reminded him that everything the father owned was the older son's and that it was only proper to make merry and be glad because his brother had returned. His brother had been dead and lost but now he was found and safe.

▶ **How did the father treat his son who had come home?** *(He ran to him and welcomed him home with all the best things: he exchanged the rags for the best robe, gave him the family ring of sonship, and gave him a feast of the best meat in the house.)*

▶ **Who is the Christian's Father in heaven?** *(God)*

💡 **How is the heavenly Father like the father in the story?** *(He loves Christians to return to Him and ask forgiveness when they do wrong so that their fellowship can continue. Though we receive God's forgiveness, we may still have to face the results of our sins here on earth.)*

▶ **Why was the older brother angry?** *(He didn't think it was fair to have a party for his brother who had run away and lived sinfully. He was angry because his father never did anything special to reward his faithfulness to his dad.)*

💡 **Are Christians ever like any of the characters in the parable?** *(Yes. Sometimes Christians are like the prodigal son. They sin and run away from the Father. When they repent, they return to the Father. Sometimes Christians are like the older brother because they are proud of their own righteousness and judgmental of another believer who doesn't have a good testimony.)*

▶ **How many people does God offer salvation to?** *(**First Timothy 2:3–4** reminds us that God is gracious in offering everyone the gift of salvation.)*

InfoScene: "A Son Returns Home"
Display Chart 22 from the Visual Packet for the students to refer to throughout this unit.

✏️ **Worktext page 150**

Match character traits and descriptions. Read the directions and word choices at the top of the page. Direct

---

Two Sons: Two Sins
Luke 15:11–32   Name _____

Jesus told the story of two brothers and their father to the tax collectors, the Pharisees, and other sinners.

Word Bank
humble   proud   loving

Circle the picture of the person the paragraph describes. Write a word from the word bank to describe him.

The character in the story who was like our heavenly Father was ready to forgive and welcome the one who had sinned against him.

He was _____ *loving* _____ .

Father   Older son   Younger son

The character in the story who was like a sinner who realizes he needs forgiveness asked his father for forgiveness.

He was _____ *humble* _____ .

Older son   Father   Younger son

The character in the story who was like a Pharisee did not think he needed to be forgiven because he did not think that he had sinned.

He was _____ *proud* _____ .

Older son   Father   Younger son

(150) A Servant's Heart • Lesson 102

---

the students to read each paragraph and to decide who is described. Remind them to circle the picture and to complete each sentence.

LESSON
103 Jesus Forgives the Most

Materials
- Hymn: "Cleanse Me"
- Pocket chart (optional)

❤ Memory Verses—Matthew 6:14–15
Practice the memory verses. Utilize the word cards for the verses as desired.

🎵 Hymn: "Cleanse Me"
Sing the hymn (Worktext page 219). Lead the students in singing all three verses of the hymn.

Background Information
Christ's Crucifixion—*Christ was crucified at the third hour (9:00 a.m.), and He died at the ninth hour (3:00 p.m.).*

Flogging—*Flogging is beating a person with a leather whip that often has metal or bone embedded in it.*

Introduction to the Bible Account
Guide a discussion to contrast God's holiness and human sinfulness. Tell the students that God is holy,

perfect, and just. Jesus did not deserve the punishment for sin. He Who *never* experienced sin became human to pay sin's penalty (**1 Peter 2:21–24**). Jesus Christ was willing, humble, obedient, and loving (**Philippians 2:5–8**; **John 3:16**). **Romans 5:7–8** tells us that Jesus did not die for good people or righteous people because nobody is good or righteous. We are all sinners.

(*Note:* The telling of this Bible account is not to emphasize the torture of Christ but to show His compassion and forgiveness in the middle of great physical pain.)

Bible Account

Read Matthew 27:27–35, Mark 15:15–25, and Luke 23:34 or use the following retelling of the passages. Listening question: **How did Jesus respond during His sufferings on the cross?** *(He was compassionate and forgiving.)*

Jesus Forgives the Most

Jesus forgave more than anyone else in history. Before Jesus died on the cross, the soldiers beat Him, dressed Him in an officer's scarlet-purple cape, put a crown of thorns on His head, gave Him a staff as a king's rod, and then pretended to worship Him. They said to Him, "Hail, King of the Jews!"

While some of them were making fun of Jesus, others spit on Him. They took the staff and beat Him with it. Then they took off the cape and put His own clothes back on Him.

Jesus was forced to carry His own cross to the place where He would be crucified. He was so weak from being beaten that another man had to help Him. Jesus was stripped and nailed to the cross. People stared at Him as He hung there and made fun of Him. The soldiers gambled to decide who would get Jesus's clothes.

While Jesus was hanging on the cross, near death and in pain, He said, "Father, forgive them." Jesus desired forgiveness for all the people who crucified Him.

Jesus knew that He would die, but He didn't fight against anyone. He suffered in silence and forgives all who trust in Him. Forgiving others is not a sign of weakness but of strength.

Direct a Bible study. Write for display: *Who? What?* Explain that each of the following verses tells about forgiveness. Direct the students to locate **Genesis 50:18–21** in their Bibles. Call on a student to tell who forgives and what he forgives. Write the answers for display before the class finds the next verse.

Genesis 50:18–21—Joseph forgives his brothers for throwing him into a pit, selling him into slavery, and lying to their father about him.
Luke 18:13–14—God forgives the publican for his sins.
Matthew 18:27—A lord forgives his servant for a debt.
Mark 2:5—Jesus forgives the paralyzed man for his sins.
Luke 7:41–42—A creditor forgives the debts of money two men owe him.
Luke 7:48—Jesus forgives a sinful woman.
Luke 23:34—Jesus had a heart of forgiveness for those involved in His Crucifixion.

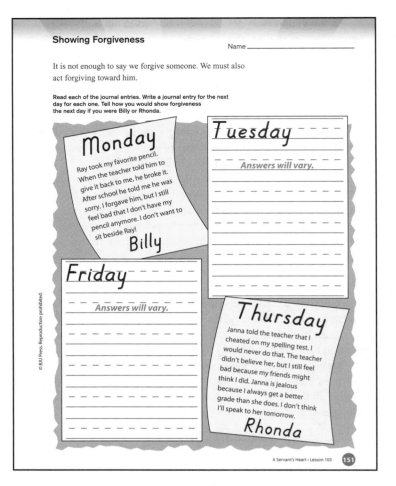

Showing Forgiveness   Name _____

It is not enough to say we forgive someone. We must also act forgiving toward him.

Read each of the journal entries. Write a journal entry for the next day for each one. Tell how you would show forgiveness the next day if you were Billy or Rhonda.

Monday
Ray took my favorite pencil. When the teacher told him to give it back to me, he broke it. After school I forgave him, but I still feel bad that I don't have my pencil anymore. I don't want to sit beside Ray!
Billy

Tuesday
Answers will vary.

Friday
Answers will vary.

Thursday
Janna told the teacher that I cheated on my spelling test. I would never do that. The teacher didn't believe her, but I still feel bad because my friends might think I did. Janna is jealous because I always get a better grade than she does. I don't think I'll speak to her tomorrow.
Rhonda

© BJU Press. Reproduction prohibited.

A Servant's Heart • Lesson 103   151

 Worktext page 151
Apply Bible knowledge to everyday life. Read and discuss each journal entry. Point out that forgiveness is shown by loving, unselfish actions. Allow the students to complete the page independently.

 LESSON
104 Learning to Forgive

Materials
- Charts 2–3, "Books of the Bible: New Testament, Old Testament"
- Hymn: "Cleanse Me"

🎵 Hymn: "Cleanse Me"
Sing the hymn (Worktext page 219). Challenge the students to sing the hymn without the recording.

❤ Memory Verses—Matthew 6:14–15
Practice the memory verses.

Introducing the Application Story
Guide a discussion about anger. Tell students that the following story is about a young girl who learns how God commands us to respond to other people's anger.
💡 **Have you ever had someone angry toward you when it wasn't your fault?** *(Accept any answer.)*

💡 **How did you feel?** *(Accept any answer.)*

Application Story

Read or tell the following story. Listening question: **How should we respond when someone is mean to us?** *(We should forgive him, pray for him, and be kind to him.)*

Linda Learns to Forgive

The smells of tomato soup and grilled cheese wafted up the stairs. Linda sat on her bed and looked down at the kite in her lap. Mom came upstairs. "You're not hungry?" she asked.

"Mattie broke my kite," said Linda.

"Maybe we can fix it," said Mom.

"No, we can't; she broke the sticks and tore the kite too," Linda said. "I'd like to fix Mattie."

"We talked about how things would change when Mattie came," said Mom. "We adopted her into our home, and it's going to take time to adjust."

"You didn't tell me she would break all my stuff," said Linda. "She broke my jewelry box, my video game, my kite, and yesterday she ripped one of my books. Why is she so angry?"

"I don't know," said Mom. "And we can't fix her, but we can pray for her."

"OK." Linda bowed her head and put her hands together. "Dear Lord Jesus, I want to pray for Mattie. She's my foster sister, and I want her to be happy. Please help her to be happy and stop breaking things and being mean. Amen."

Mom prayed, "Lord, thank You for giving Mattie to us so that we can learn about forgiveness. Help us to truly forgive Mattie and love her the way You have forgiven us and loved us. Help us to know just the right words that will show her Your love in us. Amen."

Mom looked up at Linda and said, "Let's get downstairs before the grilled cheese turns cold. Please call Mattie in for lunch."

Mattie climbed down from the tree at the first call. She was quiet, expecting to be scolded for breaking the kite. As soon as she came in, Mom told the girls to wash up for lunch, and the three sat down.

The meal was silent. After lunch, Mom asked Mattie to help her with the dishes and talk to her for a little while. Linda went upstairs and looked at Mattie's half of the room. Mom had told them to clean up because Grandma was coming for dinner, but Mattie's half was still a mess.

After Mom's talk, Mattie went upstairs to clean her half of the room. She stepped through the doorway and looked around. Her dresser was dusted and straightened, her bed was made, all her dirty clothes were put in the hamper, and even her closet was clean.

"Why did you clean *my* half?" asked Mattie.

"So you would know that I'm not angry at you," said Linda, "and because that's what Jesus would do."

⚜

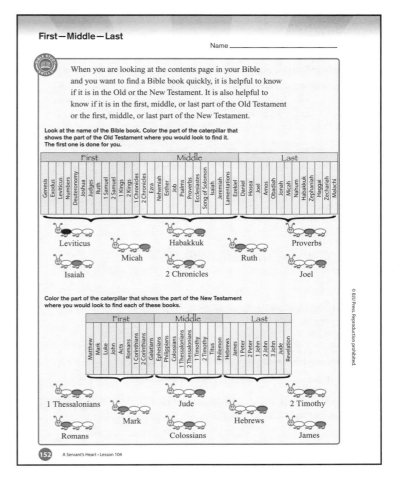

▶ **Why was Linda upset at the beginning of the story?** *(Mattie broke her kite.)*

▶ **How did Linda react?** *(Linda was angry.)*

▶ **How did Linda's mom react?** *(She prayed with Linda.)*

💡 **Why should Christians forgive people who are mean to them?** *(God commands us to forgive others just as He forgave us for Christ's sake.)*

📖 Bible Study Skills, Worktext page 152

Identify books in the first, middle, and last part of the Bible. Tell the students to clap once when you say a book from the Old Testament and to clap twice when it is a New Testament book. Say the following books of the Bible:

Psalms *(one clap)*   **Titus** *(two claps)*
Mark *(two claps)*   **Hebrews** *(two claps)*
Jeremiah *(one clap)*   **Malachi** *(one clap)*

Read the paragraph at the top of Worktext page 152. Display Chart 3, "Books of the Bible: Old Testament." Choose volunteers to point to a Bible book on the chart and tell whether it would be in the first, middle, or last part of the Old Testament. Direct attention to the Worktext page. Allow the students to complete the top of the page independently. Repeat the activity with Chart 2, "Books of the Bible: New Testament," and then complete the bottom of the Worktext page.

Locate verses. Write the reference **Isaiah 53:6** for display. Challenge the students to find the verse in their Bibles.

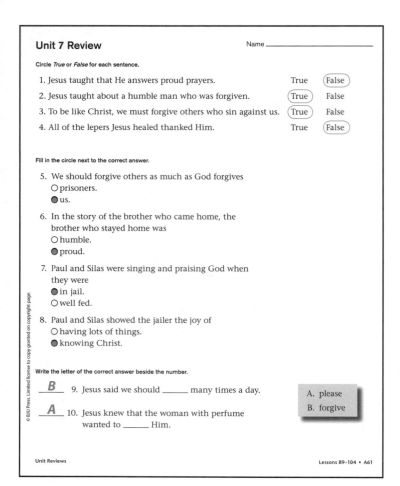

Unit 7 Review   Name _____

Circle True *or* False *for each sentence.*

1. Jesus taught that He answers proud prayers.   True   (False)
2. Jesus taught about a humble man who was forgiven.   (True)   False
3. To be like Christ, we must forgive others who sin against us.   (True)   False
4. All of the lepers Jesus healed thanked Him.   True   (False)

Fill in the circle next to the correct answer.

5. We should forgive others as much as God forgives
   - ○ prisoners.
   - ● us.

6. In the story of the brother who came home, the brother who stayed home was
   - ○ humble.
   - ● proud.

7. Paul and Silas were singing and praising God when they were
   - ● in jail.
   - ○ well fed.

8. Paul and Silas showed the jailer the joy of
   - ○ having lots of things.
   - ● knowing Christ.

Write the letter of the correct answer beside the number.

B   9. Jesus said we should _____ many times a day.

A   10. Jesus knew that the woman with perfume wanted to _____ Him.

     A. please
     B. forgive

Unit Reviews   Lessons 89–104 • A61

Unit 7 Review (continued)   Name _____

Fill in the circle next to the correct answer.

Through the Roof and Healed

11. Jesus said that the lame man's friends were
    - ● kind.
    - ○ forgiven.

12. The Pharisees said that Jesus spoke
    - ● against God.
    - ○ the truth.

A Special Gift

13. The woman
    - ○ sang to Jesus.
    - ● poured perfume on Jesus.

14. Jesus told the woman that
    - ● her sins were forgiven.
    - ○ the perfume was wasted.

Singing in Prison

15. When the earthquake shook the prison,
    - ○ Paul and Silas escaped.
    - ● Paul and Silas stayed.

16. The jailer asked,
    - ● "What must I do to be saved?"
    - ○ "Why are you still here?"

A62 • Lessons 89–104   Unit Reviews

Remind them to think whether it is in the Old or New Testament, then to consider whether it is in the first, middle, or last part. Call on a volunteer to read the verse. Continue with **Luke 19:10**, **1 John 4:9**, and **Micah 7:19**. Encourage the students to be thankful for God's forgiveness.

Writing Connection (optional)

Direct the writing of a letter. Invite the students to imagine that Mattie became a part of their family. Ask them to imagine that Mattie broke one of their favorite things. Instruct the students to write a letter to Mattie explaining why they cleaned her room for her. Encourage them to think about what Linda must have thought after Mom's prayer. Reread Mom's prayer thanking the Lord for Mattie.

▶ Going Beyond

Reinforcement

Materials

- Team markers (three magnets or buttons)

Draw for display a scoreboard with three rows of fourteen boxes in each, allowing spaces between the rows. Write the team titles in the first box at the left of each row. Draw a finish banner at the end of the rows to the right.

Direct a Review Race. Direct attention to the scoreboard. Divide the class into three teams. Ask each team review questions from the lessons in Unit 7. You may also include memory verses. Mark off one space for each correct answer.

Enrichment

Materials

- Transparency for each student
- Markers (black and various colors)

Make a light catcher. Give each student a piece of thin plastic, such as a transparency. Tell the students to draw a picture on a piece of paper, then lay the plastic over the paper and trace over the picture with a black permanent marker. (Picture ideas may include a cross, praying hands, etc.). Allow the students to fill in the outlines with colored markers. Hang the pictures in the windows to create colorful reminders that Jesus paid our debts and forgives us.

◀◀ Unit Review

Materials

- Copy of pages A61–62 ("Unit 7 Review") for each student

Guide a review of Unit 7. Review the people and events in preparation for the Unit 7 Test (optional).

8

Easter: He Lives

OVERVIEW

Preparing the Teacher

Read **1 Corinthians 15:17, 55–58**. Suppose someone asked you, "Was Christ raised from the dead?" You would answer emphatically, "Yes!" Likewise, if someone questioned whether your work was in vain, you would probably reply, "Of course not! I am working for the Lord when I teach these boys and girls." Why then do we sometimes reach the end of a school day feeling as though nothing we do makes a difference? You know that Christ did not die in vain and that your teaching is not in vain; therefore, what do you have? (Reread 15:57.) Victory! What should you be? (Reread 15:58.) Steadfast, unmovable, always abounding in the work of the Lord! Take time to meditate on these verses and to thank God for what He has done in raising Christ from the dead.

Preparing the Materials

105—Unit 8 Bookmark [E]; several puzzle pieces that do not interlock with each other
106—Verse visual (puzzle)
107—Two pieces of poster board; one piece of construction paper
Unit 8a Going Beyond—Approximately ten craft sticks and several newspaper obituaries
109—Newspaper; five sheets of 12" × 18" construction paper
112—Flashlight; bicycle reflector; copy of page A63 ("Unit 9 Review") [E]

Unit 8   Easter: He Lives

Theme, Memory Verse, and Principle	Lesson Number	TE Page	Worktext Page(s)	Appendix Page(s)	Lesson Title	Scripture or Focus
Unit 8a **Christ's Crucifixion** Romans 5:8 *Jesus died for sinners.*	**105**	228	153–54		At the Cross	Matthew 27:32–44; Mark 15:21–32; Luke 23:26–43; John 19:17–27
	106	231	155–56		Jesus's Death and Burial	Matthew 27:45–66; Mark 15:33–47; Luke 23:44–56; John 19:28–42
	107	232	157–58		Reconciliation	Picture the Point
	108	234	159–60, 243		Hero of the Faith: Athanasius	Biography
Unit 8b **Christ's Resurrection** Matthew 28:6 *Christ rose from the dead.*	**109**	237	161–62		He Is Risen	Luke 24:1–12; John 20:1–18
	110	239	163		Jesus Appears to His Followers	Luke 24:13–53; John 21:1–14
	111	240	164		Jesus Christ, Our Mediator	Application Story
	112	242	165–66	A63	Reflecting God's Love	Picture the Point

Connections	Bible Doctrines	Skills/Applications
L105—TimeLine: The Crucifixion World History	**The Doctrine of God** *Provision of God* Christ died for man (1 Cor. 15:3). Christ rose from the dead (Resurrection) (1 Cor. 15:3–8). Christ's Resurrection was followed by His ascension into heaven (Acts 1:9–11).	**Foundational** • Realize that God hates sin • Recognize that man can do nothing good without God • Know that Christ died to pay for man's sin • Believe that Christ rose from the dead
L107— English	*Elements of Salvation* Man turns to God through repentance and faith (2 Cor. 7:9–10).	**Practical** • Recall facts and details • Follow directions • Read a timeline • Identify Bible characters • Read a diagram • Order the books of the New Testament • Use a glossary • Retell a Bible account
L108— TimeLine: Athanasius	**The Doctrine of Man** *Redemption of Man* Man has God's favor (Eph. 1:3).	**Personal** • Understand and apply Bible knowledge to everyday life • Share the plan of salvation

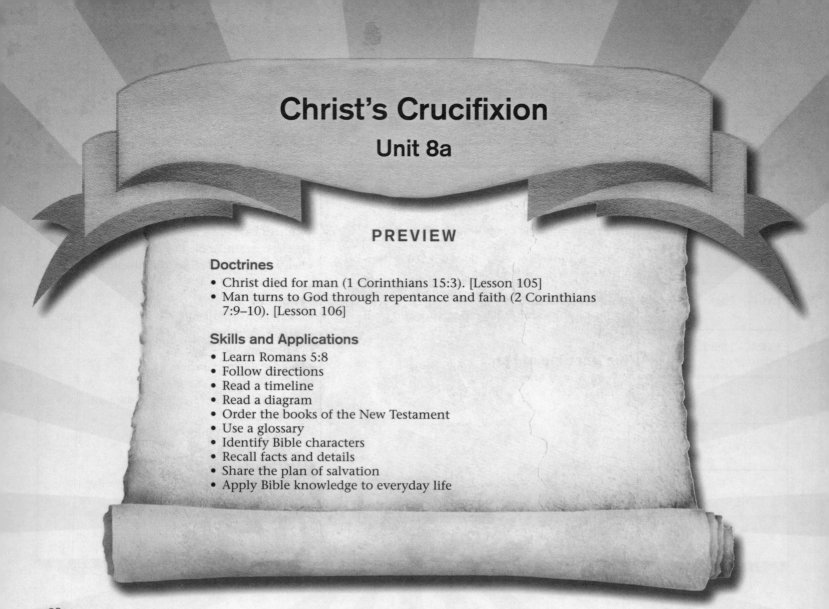

Christ's Crucifixion
Unit 8a

PREVIEW

Doctrines
- Christ died for man (1 Corinthians 15:3). [Lesson 105]
- Man turns to God through repentance and faith (2 Corinthians 7:9–10). [Lesson 106]

Skills and Applications
- Learn Romans 5:8
- Follow directions
- Read a timeline
- Read a diagram
- Order the books of the New Testament
- Use a glossary
- Identify Bible characters
- Recall facts and details
- Share the plan of salvation
- Apply Bible knowledge to everyday life

105 At the Cross

Materials

- Chart 23, "Jesus, Our Savior and King"
- TimeLine and picture: Crucifixion of Christ
- Unit 8 Bookmark for each student
- Several puzzle pieces that do not interlock with each other
- Chart 31, "World Map" (optional)
- Chart 40, "The Roman Empire in Paul's Day" (optional)
- Chart 41, "City of Jerusalem" (optional)
- Highlighter for each student (optional)

Background Information

Golgotha—*The word* Golgotha *means "skull." The Latin word is* Calvary. *Golgotha was a place where criminals were put to death. It was located near a busy road so that all could see what was happening. Death on a cross usually occurred within four to six days, but Jesus died after only six hours. The exact location of Golgotha is unknown. The traditional locations are the Church of the Holy Sepulchre and a location known as Gordon's Calvary (named after the man who discovered it).*

Bible Prophecy—*Many passages in the Old Testament focus on Christ's Crucifixion; the New Testament records their fulfillment. These prophecies were made hundreds of years before the events occurred. They include the following:*

Psalm 41:9 and Mark 14:10—betrayal by one close to Him
Psalm 22:18 and Matthew 27:35—the casting of lots for His clothing
Psalm 22:7–8 and Matthew 27:43—the mocking
Psalm 69:21 and John 19:29—the drink offered
Psalm 34:20 and John 19:36—the unbroken bones
Psalm 22:1 and Matthew 27:46—His cry from the cross
Isaiah 53:9 and Matthew 27:60—His burial with the rich

⏱ TimeLine

Add the Crucifixion card to the TimeLine. Point out Creation on the TimeLine. Explain that God created Adam and Eve sinless and happy. The Bible says that God came daily to talk with them in the garden. Adam and Eve disobeyed God. They chose to sin, and their sin separated them from God. God knew before He created Adam that Adam would sin, and God already had a plan to buy humanity back to Himself.

▶ **What effect did Adam's sin have on all mankind?** *(Because of Adam's sin, every person in the world is born with a nature that wants to do evil and have no fellowship with God.)*

Identify Old Testament events on the TimeLine as you point out that in the Old Testament we see God's plan of a Savior to come. Locate the birth of Christ on the TimeLine. Place the Crucifixion card on the TimeLine (AD 30), pointing out that the Bible prophecies the events of Jesus's birth, life, death, and Resurrection and records their fulfilment. Tell the students we also know that Jesus will return one day and reign forever. Guide them as they glue their pictures of the Crucifixion onto their TimeLines.

Introducing the Bible Account

Show God's plan. Display the puzzle pieces that do not interlock, and call on students to put them together. Elicit that the pieces will not fit. Explain that sometimes we may not understand how everything fits together in our lives. Emphasize that God knows from the beginning how everything fits into His plan because He is *omniscient*.

Write today's date (month, day, and year) for display. Explain that each time the students write the year they can be reminded that Christ died about two thousand years ago.

Bible Account

Read Matthew 27:32–44, Mark 15:21–32, Luke 23:26–43, or John 19:17–27, or use the following retelling of those passages. Listening question: **What crime had been committed by the two men crucified with Jesus?** *(robbery)* Direct the students to look at the picture on Worktext page 153.

At the Cross

Crowds mobbed the streets of Jerusalem. Some people shouted, but others just stared as Roman soldiers led Jesus through the crowd of people toward the gate of the city. Jesus carried a heavy wooden cross, but He was weak and bleeding from having been beaten by the Roman guards. Then one of the guards ordered a bystander named Simon to carry the cross for Jesus.

Once they were outside the city, Jesus, the soldiers, Simon, and the crowd of people came to a hill called Golgotha.

Share the background information about Golgotha, also called "the place of the skull." Point out the possible locations of Golgotha on Chart 41, "City of Jerusalem," if desired.

The soldiers nailed Jesus's hands and feet to the cross and stood the cross up in an upright position so that all could see Jesus. The guards even put a sign above Jesus's head that said in three languages: "This is Jesus the King of the Jews." Then the guards sat down and gambled for Jesus's clothes. As Jesus hung on the cross, He prayed, "Father, forgive them because they don't know what they are doing."

Jesus, Our Savior and King
Matthew 27:32–44; Mark 15:21–32; Luke 23:26–43; John 19:17–27

The first drink offered to Jesus was vinegar and myrrh to deaden the pain. He refused it. He accepted vinegar and water when it was offered to quench His thirst.

The Aramaic word **Golgotha** and the word **Calvary** (from Latin) both mean "skull" or "place of the skull." The hill is shaped somewhat like a skull, and it was a place of punishment by death.

Historical writings tell us that the tenth legion of the Roman army was stationed in Jerusalem at the time of the Crucifixion of Jesus. Roman soldiers were not very well paid, but they were allowed to pick up whatever they could in line with their duties. The clothing of those crucified often went to the soldiers.

© BJU Press. Reproduction prohibited.

A Servant's Heart • Lesson 105 **153**

The soldiers had mocked and hurt Jesus. They offered Him wine mixed with myrrh, but Jesus didn't drink it.

Two robbers were crucified with Jesus, one on His left and the other on His right. The soldiers taunted Him: "If You're the king of the Jews, then save Yourself." One of the robbers said to Jesus, "If You really are the Christ, save Yourself and us!" But the other robber said to the first, "Don't you fear God? We deserve to be punished, but this man hasn't done anything wrong." Then he said to Jesus, "Lord, remember me when You enter into Your kingdom."

Jesus promised him, "Today you will be with Me in paradise."

Several men and women who loved Jesus stood near the cross and cried as they watched Him suffer. One of them was Jesus's mother, Mary. Another was John, one of Jesus's closest friends. Jesus was more concerned for their suffering than His own. "Woman," Jesus said to Mary, "behold your son," Then He said to John, "Behold your mother."

⚜

▶ **Who was crucified with Jesus?** *(two robbers)*

💡 **Did Jesus deserve to die?** *(No. Jesus Christ was holy, sinless, and innocent.)* Explain that God is just. It is only fair, or just, that *we* should be punished for our sins (**2 Corinthians 5:21; Deuteronomy 32:4b**).

💡 **Why did Jesus die?** *(He loves us and wanted to pay the price for our sins so that we could be bought back by God.)*

▶ **Did Jesus die willingly?** *(yes)*

- ▶ **What did Jesus say as He was dying on the cross that showed His forgiving spirit?** *("Father, forgive them; for they know not what they do.")*
- ▶ **What did the two robbers say to Jesus?** *(One robber mocked Jesus. The other robber trusted Christ to save him.)*
- ▶ **What did Jesus promise the robber who asked Jesus to remember him?** *(that he would be with Jesus in heaven that day)*
- 💡 **Why was Jesus concerned about His mother, Mary?** *(Many answers are acceptable, but discuss that Jesus loved Mary as He loves all people, but being her oldest son, He was telling John to take care of her as if she were his own mother.)*

InfoScene: "Jesus, Our Savior and King"
Display Chart 23 for the students to refer to throughout this unit.

♥ Memory Verse—Romans 5:8

Principle: Jesus died for sinners. Discuss the meaning of the verse. Elicit from the students that this verse is telling us that God showed His love to us in a marvelous way.

- ▶ **How did God show His love to us?** *(He sent His only Son to die for us.)*
- 💡 **Would a person be willing to die for someone that was his enemy?** *(no)*
- 💡 **Who are God's enemies?** *(Before a person is saved, he is God's enemy, separated from Him because of sin, serving himself. God is holy, without any sin. See **James 4:4**.)*

Explain that Jesus was willing to come to this earth and die for us so that we could be forgiven of our sin, love and serve God, live joyful lives, and have a home in heaven someday. Lead the students in reading the verse from their Bibles or from the bulletin board several times. Direct the students to highlight the verse (optional) and mark the location with the Unit 8 Bookmark.

✎ Worktext page 154

Match Bible characters with facts. Discuss the pictures on Worktext page 154. Guide the students as they match the statements with the correct Bible characters.

✍ World History Connection (optional)

Discuss the Roman Empire. Ask the following questions to introduce the Roman Empire.

- 💡 **Why was the sign placed above Jesus's head written in three languages?** *(Answers will vary.)*

Explain that the Roman Empire included people who spoke various languages. Writing the sign in Greek, Hebrew, and Latin ensured that most people in Jerusalem would understand.

- 💡 **Why do you think the Romans did not like Jesus's calling Himself a king?** *(They thought He would try to take control of the people and perhaps lead a rebellion against the Roman government.)*

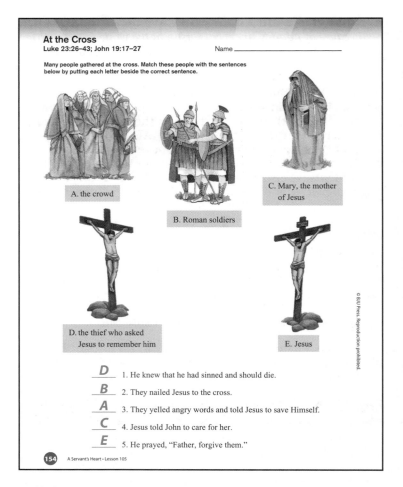

At the Cross
Luke 23:26–43; John 19:17–27   Name _____

Many people gathered at the cross. Match these people with the sentences below by putting each letter beside the correct sentence.

A. the crowd

B. Roman soldiers

C. Mary, the mother of Jesus

D. the thief who asked Jesus to remember him

E. Jesus

- __D__ 1. He knew that he had sinned and should die.
- __B__ 2. They nailed Jesus to the cross.
- __A__ 3. They yelled angry words and told Jesus to save Himself.
- __C__ 4. Jesus told John to care for her.
- __E__ 5. He prayed, "Father, forgive them."

(154)   A Servant's Heart • Lesson 105

Tell the students that the leaders of Rome expected the Jews to be loyal to the Roman government. These leaders became enemies of anyone who threatened the Roman government. Explain that the Jews were eager for someone to rescue them from Roman rule, but the Jewish religious leaders rejected Jesus. They did not believe Jesus was the Son of God, the promised Messiah.

💡 **Do people today reject Jesus?** *(yes)*

The religious leaders wanted to kill Jesus because He said He was God. Although the Jews were looking for a Jewish kingdom on earth, God intended a heavenly kingdom available to all who would believe in Him.

Locate a place on a map. Simon was from the Greek city of Cyrene, along the northern coast of Africa. Call on a student to point to the continent of Africa on Chart 31, "World Map." Locate the northern coast of Africa and tell the students that today this area is in the country of Libya. Display Chart 40, "The Roman Empire in Paul's Day." Compare the views of Africa on Chart 31 and Chart 40. Call on a student to find the city of Cyrene.

LESSON 106 Jesus's Death and Burial

Materials

- Hymn "What a Wonderful Savior!"
- Verse visual: Use sheets of 12" × 18" construction paper to prepare eight puzzle pieces like the one shown below. They should fit together to form a ring as in the center of the bulletin board for Unit 8 (see Toolkit CD). Divide the memory verse into seven phrases and print each phrase on one of seven puzzle pieces. Write the reference (*Romans 5:8*) on the eighth piece.

Background Information

Crucifixion and Burial—*Jesus's execution and burial were done according to the traditions of the day. It was typical for criminals to be crucified if they were slaves or if they were not Roman citizens. Wealthy people were often buried outside the city in tombs carved in the rock. Such a tomb usually had a low entrance that was covered by a stone.*

Joseph of Arimathea—*Joseph of Arimathea was probably a wealthy member of the Sanhedrin, a Jewish court for religious and government cases. He was a secret disciple of Jesus because he feared the religious leaders. He asked Pilate for Jesus's body and placed it in his own new tomb, which was cut out of rock.*

● Memory Verse—Romans 5:8

Practice the memory verse using the verse visuals. Give one of the puzzle pieces to each of eight students in random order. Allow them to work the puzzle by laying the pieces out on the floor or a large table. Read the verse together several times. Explain how the circular form of the puzzle can remind them of the truth of this verse.

▶ **Does a circle have a beginning or an end?** (*No, it just keeps going.*)

💡 **How is God's love like a circle?** (*It never ends.*) God told Jeremiah: "I have loved thee with an everlasting love" (**Jeremiah 31:3**).

💡 **How does God express His love to us?** (*Many answers are acceptable, but elicit that the most important way was sending His Son to die for sinners like us.*)

Bible Account

Read Matthew 27:45–66, Mark 15:33–47, Luke 23:44–56, or John 19:28–42, or use the following retelling of those passages. Listening question: **What happened to the veil (or curtain) in the temple?** (*It was torn.*)

The Death and Burial of Jesus

At noon on the day of Jesus's Crucifixion, a strange thing happened. The sky grew dark, as if it were nighttime. The darkness lasted for three hours. About three o'clock in the afternoon, Jesus cried out in a loud voice, "My God, my God, why have You forsaken me?" In Aramaic it sounded like this: *"Eloi, Eloi, lama sabachthani?"*

Jesus was offered a drink, but He refused to take it. He cried out, "It is finished." Then He bowed His head and gave up His life. At the moment Jesus died, several things happened. The high veil in the temple, the one that separated the holy of holies from the rest of the temple, ripped from top to bottom.

Matthew writes that when Jesus died, the earth shook and rocks split open. It was such a startling day that a Roman centurion (guard) and his soldiers standing with him near the cross were very afraid. The centurion said, "Truly this was the Son of God." The soldiers broke the legs of the two thieves so that the men would die quickly. But when they came to Jesus, He was already dead. The soldiers were surprised. They didn't have to break Jesus's legs. Instead, they pierced His side with a spear, and blood and water poured out.

When evening came, a rich man from Arimathea *(ā ri mə thē´ ə)* named Joseph went to Pilate and asked if he could have the body of Jesus. Pilate agreed and delivered Jesus's body to Joseph. Joseph wrapped the body in a clean linen cloth and laid it in his own new tomb. Then a large stone was rolled in front of the entrance of the tomb.

The next day, the chief priests and Pharisees went to see Pilate. They reminded Pilate that Jesus had said that He would rise in three days. They were worried that the disciples might try to steal Jesus's body to make it look as though Jesus had risen from the tomb. Pilate commanded some guards to watch over the tomb so that the disciples wouldn't come back and steal Jesus's body.

💡 **Why was the darkness so unusual at Jesus's Crucifixion?** (*It was the middle of the day.*)

▶ **What other unusual things happened at Jesus's death?** (*There was an earthquake, the temple veil was ripped from top to bottom, and rocks split open.*)

▶ **Who took Jesus's body to bury it?** (*a rich man named Joseph*)

▶ **Who sent soldiers to guard the tomb?** (*Pilate*)

▶ **Why did he do this?** (*The chief priests and Pharisees thought the disciples might try to steal Christ's body.*)

💡 **What did the darkness for three hours and the earthquake show all people about God?** (*His power; God is omnipotent. He is all-powerful, so He can do anything His holy will desires.*)

▶ **What did Jesus's death show?** (*His love for us*)

💡 **What did the torn veil symbolize?** (*Jesus is the only sacrifice for sin. We can come to God for salvation only through Christ.*)

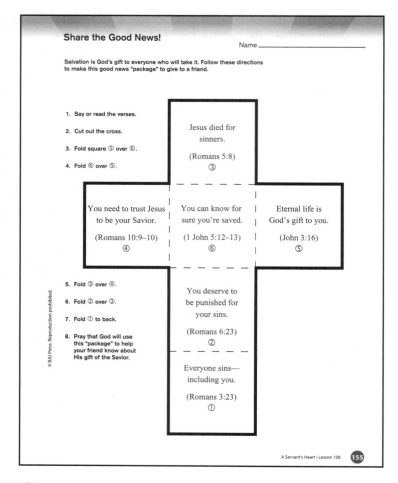

Share the Good News!

Name _____

Salvation is God's gift to everyone who will take it. Follow these directions to make this good news "package" to give to a friend.

1. Say or read the verses.
2. Cut out the cross.
3. Fold square ⑤ over ⑥.
4. Fold ④ over ⑤.

Jesus died for sinners.

(Romans 5:8)
③

You need to trust Jesus to be your Savior.

(Romans 10:9–10)
④

You can know for sure you're saved.

(1 John 5:12–13)
⑥

Eternal life is God's gift to you.

(John 3:16)
⑤

5. Fold ③ over ④.
6. Fold ② over ③.
7. Fold ① to back.
8. Pray that God will use this "package" to help your friend know about His gift of the Savior.

You deserve to be punished for your sins.

(Romans 6:23)
②

Everyone sins— including you.

(Romans 3:23)
①

© BJU Press. Reproduction prohibited.

A Servant's Heart • Lesson 106 155

Worktext pages 155–56

Share the plan of salvation. Guide the students as they follow the directions on the page. Encourage them to use the "gift box" to share the gospel with someone by looking up the references in the Bible and inviting the person to read each verse.

🎵 Hymn: "What a Wonderful Savior!"

Teach the first verse (Worktext page 220). Utilize the recording as necessary throughout the unit. Sing or play the recording of the first verse for the students. Explain the key words or phrases to them and then sing the verse several times.

💡 **What does the word *atonement* mean?** (*Christ took the punishment we deserve for our sin by His sufferings and death.*)

💡 **What does the word *redeem* mean?** (*It means to rescue or buy back; Jesus brings us back to God if we accept Him as our Savior.*)

▶ **Who paid the price for sin?** (*Christ*)

▶ **How did Christ pay?** (*He paid with His blood through the painful and shameful death of the cross.*)

💡 **Why did Jesus die?** (*so that we wouldn't be punished for our sin; because He loved us; so that He could reconcile us [bring us back] to God*)

LESSON 107 Reconciliation

Materials

- Verse visuals (puzzle pieces) from previous lesson
- Hymn: "What a Wonderful Savior!"
- Picture the Point visuals: Write *God* on one large piece of posterboard and write *Man* on another large piece of posterboard. Write *Sin* on a piece of construction paper and draw a cross on a second piece of construction paper. Cut a third piece of construction paper in half and draw an arrow on each half. See diagrams.

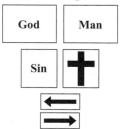

❤ Memory Verse—Romans 5:8

Practice reciting the memory verse. Distribute the memory verse visual puzzle pieces to eight students randomly. Direct them to arrange themselves in the proper word order left to right standing in a row. They should stand in front of the class, each holding his puzzle piece so the rest of the students can see the words. Lead the class in reading the verse and reference several times. Then ask one of the students to turn his puzzle piece around so the words are not visible. Choose a group or row to read the verse again, filling in the missing phrase. Ask another student to turn his puzzle piece around and call on a different group or individual volunteers to read/recite the entire verse. Continue as time allows.

Alternate activity: If you prepared the unit bulletin board suggested on the Toolkit CD, lead the class in reading the verse and reference from the display several times. Then attach a piece of construction paper to the bulletin board to cover one of the puzzle pieces, and choose a group or row to read the verse again, filling in the missing phrase. Cover another phrase and ask a small group or individual volunteers to read/recite the entire verse. Continue as time allows.

🎵 Hymn: "What a Wonderful Savior!"

Teach the second verse (Worktext page 220). Play the recording and sing the first verse together. Say the second verse, and explain that the word *reconcile* means to settle a problem and bring enemies together. Play the recording and sing the second verse several times. A variation you may use is to sing the phrase "What a wonderful Savior!" softly in the verse and then louder in the chorus.

▶ **Who has cleansing blood?** (*Jesus*)

▶ **What is Jesus called?** (*a wonderful Savior*)

▶ **How does Jesus's blood reconcile people to God?** (*It washes away our sin and allows us to be in the presence of our sinless God. Humans are sinful. God is holy—without any sin.*)

Introducing the Lesson

Guide a discussion about reconciliation. Write the word *reconcile* for display. Direct the students to open their Worktexts to the glossary. Tell them to find the word *reconcile* and read the definition silently. Choose a volunteer to it read aloud. *(to bring together again in peace and friendship after being separated)* Allow the students to share how they or someone they know may have settled differences they have had with others.

Jesus Christ is our mediator. He took our place on the cross, bearing our sins that we might be at peace with God. We have been reconciled (brought into fellowship with God) through the work of the Lord Jesus Christ.

Picture the Point

Illustrate reconciliation. Follow the instructions in italics and the diagrams below to show how the students should hold the signs and arrows as you present the lesson.

Display the signs God and Man in front of the classroom. Choose two students to each hold an arrow and stand in front of a sign. Tell them to point the arrows so that they are facing each other.

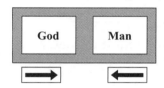

Explain to the class that this shows man's relationship to God before sin came into the world. Man had fellowship with God. God and man were face to face (**Genesis 1:27–28**).

Direct the students to turn the arrows away from one another in opposite directions. Call on a third student to stand between them, holding the sign for sin.

Explain that this picture represents the position of Adam and every person thereafter, having turned from God and having gone his own way (**Romans 3:23; Isaiah 53:6**). Sin has come between man and God (**Romans 5:12; Isaiah 59:2**).

Give the cross to the student holding the sign for sin, telling him to place the cross over the sin sign. Direct the student holding the arrow in front of the sign for God to turn the arrow toward the sign for Man.

Point out to the class that this picture represents God's sending His Son to die for the sins of the world. Christ's death on the cross covers sin and provides a way for us to come back to God (**Romans 5:8**). Now as God seeks man, each person chooses to turn and face God or to keep going his own way. God offers the gift of eternal life through His Son, the Lord Jesus Christ. By His grace we can choose to accept salvation

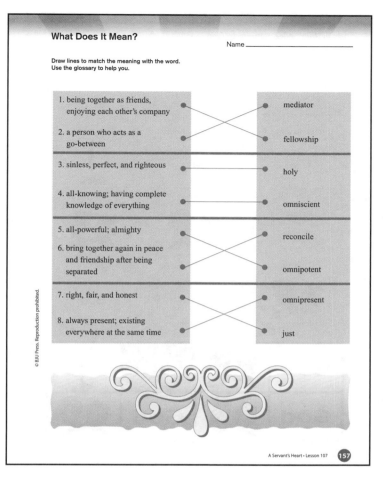

or to reject God's gift. When we accept God's gift of salvation (reconciliation), we become God's children rather than His enemies (**John 1:12**).

Instruct the student in front of the sign for Man to turn his arrow toward the cross.

- ▶ **What relationship did man have with God before sin entered the world?** *(Man had fellowship with God.)*
- ▶ **Why was mankind separated from God?** *(Man chose to sin, but God is holy.)*
- ▶ **How can we be reconciled *(brought back)* to God?** *(We can accept the gift of salvation God has provided through the Lord Jesus Christ.)*

✏ English Connection, Worktext page 157

Guide an activity using the glossary. Write the word *mediator* for display. Direct the students to open their Worktexts to the glossary. Guide the students as they find the word and silently read the definition, referring them to page 281 if needed. Choose a volunteer to read the word and definition aloud. Follow the same steps to find the definition for *fellowship*. Instruct the students to match the first two definitions and words on the Worktext page. Complete the page as a class activity.

Jesus Reconciles Sinners to God

Name _____

▶ Adam and Eve and all people born after them are sinners, separated from God.

▶ Because Jesus took the punishment for sin, all who trust in Him are reconciled to God, and their sins are removed by His blood.

Cut out the boxes at the bottom of the page and glue them in the correct places.

Genesis 1:27	Romans 3:23	Romans 5:8

© BJU Press. Reproduction prohibited.

158   A Servant's Heart · Lesson 107

 ## Worktext page 158

Guide an activity for reading a diagram. Tell the students that they are going to complete and read the diagram. Guide them as they cut out the boxes and glue them in the correct place. Read the completed message and discuss it.

LESSON 108   Hero of the Faith: Athanasius

Materials
- Hymn: "What a Wonderful Savior!"
- TimeLine and picture: Athanasius
- Transparent tape for each student

♥ Memory Verse—Romans 5.8

Review the memory verse. Read the verse aloud together. Display seven of the memory verse puzzle pieces in random order. Instruct students to see if they can determine which phrase is missing. Invite one student to recite the verse filling in the missing phrase. Now alternate reading the verse as a responsive reading, referring to either the bulletin board or the completed puzzle. You say the reference first, the students read the first phrase, and so on around the circle.

♫ Hymn: "What a Wonderful Savior!"

Teach the third verse (Worktext page 220). Explain the phrase "and now He reigns and rules therein," pointing

out that God wants us to let Him rule our lives. Sing the first three verses.

💡 **What is sin?** *(Sin is disobedience to God's Word—failing to do what God commands or doing what God forbids. Our words, thoughts, and actions show whether or not God rules our lives.)*

▶ **What does every sin deserve?** *(Every sin deserves the punishment of God.)*

▶ **What does Jesus's blood cleanse?** *(our sinful hearts)*

▶ **How can Christians make God their King and glorify Him?** *(love Him, say no to self, and do what He commands)*

▶ **Where do Christians learn how to love and obey God?** *(the Bible)*

Background Information

Athanasius—*Athanasius (ăth ə nā´ shəs) was born around AD 295 in Alexandria, Egypt. He grew up during the reign of the evil Roman emperor Diocletian. Athanasius had heard reports about the destruction of churches and Bibles, Christians' being deprived of civil rights and the right to hold public office, and the spread of persecution throughout Europe. Diocletian's persecution of Christians lasted until AD 308.*

Introducing the Hero of Faith

Guide a discussion about heroes. Allow the students to share about individuals they consider heroes. Elicit from the students that a hero may be someone who has shown great courage or has risked his life to defend what he believes. Write the name *Athanasius* for display. Announce that you are going to relate a true account of a man named *Athanasius*.

Hero of the Faith

Read or retell the following account of the life of Athanasius. Listening question: **Based on this account, do you think Athanasius was a hero?** *(Elicit that he was a hero because he stood for the truth of God's Word.)*

Athanasius

Athanasius grew up in Alexandria, a rich, powerful city in Egypt. Many of the people in Alexandria were Greek, and those who weren't Greek by birth followed Greek customs. Like other boys his age, Athanasius learned math, studied music, and read about famous Greek heroes.

Many people in Alexandria were Christians, including Athanasius's parents. He learned very early that Jesus Christ had come to earth, had died for the sins of every person, and had risen from the dead.

But life wasn't easy for Christians. As Athanasius grew up, he often heard of terrible things that happened to Christians in other cities: churches and Bibles were destroyed, and Christians were thrown into arenas to be killed by wild animals. An evil Roman emperor was trying to rid the world of Christians.

When Athanasius was about twelve, he began training for church ministry. Some of his teachers were killed because of their faith in Christ. But nothing changed Athanasius's

mind about what he believed. The bishop of the city's church, Alexander, asked Athanasius to be his personal secretary. Athanasius learned well, and several years later he became a deacon in the church.

Athanasius wanted to teach others what he had learned from the Bible so he wrote some books. These books taught that Christ is God.

Some other Christian leaders disagreed with Athanasius. One important bishop named Arius (ā´ rē əs) taught that Christ was not God, but that He was just a person, and that His death on the cross had not paid for sin. Many people believed Arius because he was an influential leader.

When Alexander died, Alexandria needed a new bishop. The people elected Athanasius. Some in Alexandria thought that he was too young for the position. But Athanasius proved that even a young man could be a good leader. He kept studying the Bible. He kept writing books about the Bible and its teachings. And he kept speaking out against the false teachings of Arius.

Arius had many followers all over Europe. These followers became very angry when Athanasius was elected bishop.

One day Athanasius heard some news from a friend. "The followers of Arius are very angry with you," the friend told him. "I heard some of them planning to kill you."

"God is my refuge," Athanasius reminded his friend. "I can trust Him to do what is best."

Once while Athanasius was preaching, soldiers stormed into his church in the middle of his sermon. Athanasius turned to the song leader. "Begin a hymn," he said, "and tell the people to file out of the building calmly."

The people obeyed, walking quietly around the surprised soldiers. During the confusion, the other church leaders helped Athanasius sneak quietly out of the church. They took him to a place in the desert where he was able to hide in safety.

Athanasius was never safe from his enemies for very long. His friends moved him often from house to house, trying to keep his location a secret. But sometimes Athanasius refused to flee. He spoke to his enemies, answering their questions truthfully and boldly. He lived to be seventy years old. Athanasius made God his refuge, and his strong God protected him.

───────────── ⚜ ─────────────

▶ **Were Athanasius's parents Christians?** *(yes)*
▶ **What did Athanasius do when people were against him?** *(He continued to serve God. He trusted God to protect him and continued to do right.)*
▶ **Why did Athanasius want to write books?** *(He wanted to teach others what he learned from studying the Bible.)*
▶ **What did Athanasius write about in his books?** *(that Jesus is God)*

Athanasius

Name _____

Athanasius was born about 295 in Alexandria, Egypt. His parents were Christians, and he believed in Christ at an early age.

Athanasius became a church leader. He studied the Bible and wrote books about its teachings. He wrote that Jesus Christ is God.

Some disagreed. A church leader named Arius said that Jesus was created by God and was therefore not God. Many people believed Arius. He became Athanasius's enemy. The followers of Arius tried to find Athanasius to kill him. Athanasius trusted God to keep him safe, and God did.

Fill in the circle next to the correct answer.

5. Athanasius was born in
   ○ Jerusalem.
   ● Alexandria.

6. Athanasius became
   ● a church leader.
   ○ a Roman soldier.

7. Athanasius wrote books about
   ○ Arius.
   ● the Bible.

Use a yellow crayon to color only the boxes that are true.

1. Athanasius did not believe in Christ until he was an old man.
2. Athanasius trusted God for safety.
3. Athanasius had an enemy named Arius.
4. Athanasius taught that Jesus was not God.

A Servant's Heart • Lesson 108 243

🕑 TimeLine

Add Athanasius to the TimeLine. Place the picture of Athanasius on the TimeLine (AD 300), pointing out that he lived about three hundred years after Christ. Tell the students that this was during the rule of the Roman emperors. Guide them as they glue the picture of Athanasius onto their TimeLines.

✍ Worktext page 243 (optional)

Hero of the Faith: Athanasius. Review the events in Athanasius's life. Point out that Athanasius stood up for what was right even when others disagreed with him. Read aloud the directions to the students. Provide help as needed.

New Testament—What Next?

Name_____

There are twenty-seven books in the New Testament. Put a number in each box to show the order in which they are found. The first one is done for you.

4	Ephesians Philippians Colossians
6	Titus Philemon Hebrews James
8	Jude Revelation
1	Matthew Mark Luke John
3	1 Corinthians 2 Corinthians Galatians
5	1 Thessalonians 2 Thessalonians 1 Timothy 2 Timothy
7	1 Peter 2 Peter 1 John 2 John 3 John
2	Acts Romans

Now cut out the strips on the bold lines and put them in order by the numbers you wrote. Tape the strips together and turn them over to see a picture of the man God used to write at least thirteen New Testament books.

A Servant's Heart • Lesson 108   159

Bible Study Skills, Worktext pages 159–60

Order the books of the New Testament. Number the students from one to twenty-seven. Call on them in sequence to tell the books of the New Testament. For example, 1–Matthew, 2–Mark. Direct attention to Worktext page 159 and read the directions aloud. Allow the students to complete the page independently. If they tape the strips together in the correct order, they will see a picture of Paul on the back.

▶ Going Beyond

Reinforcement

Materials

• Craft sticks with words written on them (words that relate to the Crucifixion account, such as *tomb, soldiers, robbers, Pilate, earthquake, darkness,* etc.)

Tell me about the story. Direct the students to hold the craft sticks in a bundle above the table and then let them fall. Challenge the students to pick up one craft stick without moving any others, and then tell something about the story, using the word written on the stick.

Enrichment

Materials

• Obituaries from a newspaper

Reading a newspaper obituary. Cut out several newspaper obituaries and prepare a copy for each student. Distribute the copies of the obituaries to the students. Explain that an *obituary* is a report of a person's death. It is a report of such things as the person's age, cause of death, church membership, accomplishments, place of work, and family members as well as funeral service details. Call on students to tell the ages of those people listed on the page. Choose volunteers to tell whether any of the people listed had grandchildren.

Ask the following questions relating to Christ's death.

▶ **About what age was Jesus when He died?** (*around thirty-three years old*)

▶ **Did Jesus have any family members still living?** (*Yes. Jesus's mother was at the cross. His half-brothers James and Jude later wrote books of the New Testament.*)

▶ **How was Jesus's death different from everybody else's death?** (*Many answers are possible, but elicit that He was God; He didn't die as a result of old age, an accident, or a sickness; He was the sin-bearer of the world; numerous aspects of His death were prophesied hundreds of years before; He rose from the dead.*)

Christ's Resurrection
Unit 8b

PREVIEW

Doctrines
- Christ arose from the dead (Resurrection) (1 Corinthians 15:3–8). [Lesson 109]
- Christ's Resurrection was followed by His ascension into heaven (Acts 1:9–11). [Lesson 110]

Skills and Applications
- Learn Matthew 28:6
- Identify Bible characters
- Identify rhyming words
- Recall facts and details
- Draw conclusions
- Retell a Bible account
- Apply Bible knowledge to everyday life

LESSON 109 — He Is Risen

Materials
- Hymn: "What a Wonderful Savior!"
- Unit 8 Bookmark for each student
- A newspaper
- Highlighter for each student (optional)
- Verse visuals: Use sheets of 12" × 18" construction paper to prepare five puzzle pieces like the ones shown below. They should fit together to form a cross as in the center of the bulletin board for Unit 8 (see Toolkit CD). Print a different phrase of Matthew 28:6 on each puzzle piece. On the back of each piece write the first letter of each word on that piece.

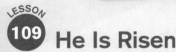

4 pieces   1 piece

♫ Hymn: "What a Wonderful Savior!"
Sing the first three verses (Worktext page 220). Play the recording and sing the first three verses of the hymn together. Review the meanings of the key words *redeem*, *atonement*, and *reconciled*.

Introducing the Bible Account
Discuss good news. Invite the students to share times they have received good news. Display the newspaper.

💡 **What kinds of news can we read about in a newspaper?** (*good news and bad news*)

Explain that someone in the lesson today announces some good news.

Bible Account

Read one of the following passages: Matthew 28:1–15; Mark 16:1–11; Luke 24:1–12; John 20:1–18. Or use the following account, which is a retelling of the Luke and John passages. Listening question: **What did Jesus tell Mary to**

tell the disciples? *(that she had seen Jesus alive)* Direct the students to look at the picture on Worktext page 161.

He Is Risen

Just after sunrise on the first day of the week, some women who loved Jesus came to the garden and approached the tomb where His body had been laid. They brought perfumes and spices to put on the body of Jesus. They wondered how they would move the stone, but when they arrived, they were surprised to see that the huge stone had already been rolled away! They looked into the tomb—it was empty! The women were afraid. Mary Magdalene ran to find Simon Peter and John as the other women stood there perplexed.

Luke writes that two men in shining garments stood in front of the women. They were angels, who said, "Why do you seek the living among the dead? He's not here. He is risen." Then the angels asked the women if they remembered what Jesus had said to them: "The Son of man must be delivered into the hands of sinful men to be crucified and then rise again on the third day." The women remembered that Jesus had said that.

Then Mary Magdalene went and told Simon Peter and John about the empty tomb. Peter and John ran to the garden. John reached the tomb first, but he stopped outside. Peter rushed right in. He found the linen cloth that had covered Jesus's face folded up and set aside from the rest of the grave clothes. When Peter and John saw these things, they were sure that Jesus had risen.

Peter and John left, but Mary Magdalene stood outside the tomb weeping. She bent over to look into the tomb once more and saw two angels inside. They asked her why she was weeping. She said to them, "Because they have taken away my Lord, and I don't know where they have laid him."

She turned around and saw someone but didn't know that He was Jesus. She thought He was the gardener. Jesus asked her, "Why are you crying? Who are you looking for?" Mary asked where Jesus's body was. Then Jesus called her by name, and she immediately recognized Him.

She called Jesus *Rabboni*, which means Master. Jesus told her to go tell the disciples that she had seen Him. Jesus was going back up to heaven to be with His Father, but first He would meet them in Galilee. Mary hurried to tell them the good news.

⚜

▶ **Why were the women going to the tomb early in the morning?** *(to put perfumes and spices on Jesus's body)*

▶ **What did they find when they arrived?** *(The stone had been rolled away, and the tomb was empty.)*

💡 **Why do you think the angels moved the stone from the entrance of the tomb?** *(It wasn't so that Jesus could get out, but so that people could see in.)*

▶ **What did Mary Magdalene do?** *(She ran to tell Peter and John.)*

▶ **What message did the angels give to the other women?** *(Jesus is not here; He is risen.)*

He Is Risen!
Luke 24:1–12

Cut out the figures and the storage pocket below. Glue the storage pocket onto the back of this page. Retell the Bible account, placing the figures on the scene.

© BJU Press. Reproduction prohibited.

angel Jesus John

the women Mary Peter

Storage Pocket

A Servant's Heart • Lesson 109 **161**

▶ **Who arrived at the tomb next?** *(John and then Peter)*

▶ **What did they find?** *(The tomb was empty; the grave clothes were left there; the linen napkin was folded up.)*

▶ **When Mary Magdalene returned, who spoke to her?** *(two angels and Jesus)*

▶ **What did Jesus say to her?** *("Why are you crying? Who are you looking for?")*

▶ **What did Mary call Jesus?** *(Rabboni, which means Master)*

✒ Worktext pages 161–62

Retell the Bible account. Guide the students as they cut out the figures from the bottom of Worktext page 161. Direct them to glue the storage pocket for the figures on the back of the page. Guide the students as they retell the account, using the figures with the scene on the top of page 161. Encourage the students to take the page and figures home and tell the story again. *(Note:* You may reproduce the figures to place in a learning center. Allow the students to use these for storytelling [to another student or to record] or story writing.)

♥ Memory Verse—Matthew 28:6

Principle: Christ rose from the dead. Direct the students to open their Bibles and highlight the verse (optional) and mark the location with the Unit 8 Bookmark.

▶ **What message did the angel give to the women who came to the tomb looking for Jesus?** *(He said Jesus was not there.)*

▶ **Why was Jesus not there?** *(He had risen!)*

💡 **How would you have reacted if you had arrived at the tomb and found that Jesus was not there?** *(Any answer is acceptable and may include surprised, excited, frightened, joyful, puzzled, or believing.)*

Practice the memory verse. Direct attention to the bulletin board or the memory verse visual puzzle pieces. Lead the class in reading the verse. Distribute the verse visual cards to the students. Lead the class in reciting the verse as the person holding the card for the recited words comes to the front of the classroom. Direct them to hold the cards so that the words are showing. Tell the students to reverse the cards, showing only the first letter of each word. Lead the students in saying the verse again, using the first-letter clues.

LESSON 110 Jesus Appears to His Followers

Materials

- Hymn: "What a Wonderful Savior!"
- Verse visual cards from the previous lesson

🎵 Hymn: "What a Wonderful Savior!"

Teach the fourth verse (Worktext page 220). Direct the students to open their Worktexts to the hymn. Read aloud the fourth verse, pausing to explain the phrases "He gives me overcoming pow'r" and "triumph in each trying hour."

💡 **What are some things that make us sad?** *(Answers will vary, but may include disappointments, sickness, family difficulties, or death of a loved one.)*

💡 **What sins can God give Christians the power to overcome?** *(all sins)*

Background Information

Jesus Appears to His Followers—*At first, the disciples were slow to believe that Jesus had risen. When the two people on the Emmaus road told the disciples what they had experienced, the disciples didn't believe them (**Mark 16:12–13**). **Luke 24:11** records that the women's words about the empty tomb seemed to be idle talk, or foolishness, to the disciples. Mary Magdalene thought someone had taken Jesus's body (**John 20:13–14**). Thomas said he personally had to see Jesus to believe (**John 20:25**). There are ten recorded times Christ was seen after His Resurrection. He was seen by small groups of individuals and by as many as five hundred at one time (**1 Corinthians 15:6**).*

Introducing the Bible Account

Discuss the Resurrection. Share the background information with the students before presenting the Bible account. Be sure they realize that the Scriptures give many accounts of people who saw Jesus after He rose from the dead. Read aloud **1 Corinthians 15:6**.

Bible Account

Read one of the following passages: Matthew 28:16–20; Mark 16:12–20; Luke 24:13–53; John 20:19–21:14. Or use the following account, which is a retelling of Luke 24 and John 21. Listening question: **How many of the prophecies about Christ's death, burial, and Resurrection came true?** *(all of them)* Direct attention to the picture on Worktext page 163.

Jesus Appears to His Followers

Two of Jesus's friends walked slowly along a dusty road. They talked about Jesus's death on the cross and the empty tomb. They thought that Jesus was the Son of God, but now He was gone.

Another man came and began to walk along with them. He asked what they were talking about that made them look so sad. One of the men, Cleopas, answered, "Are you a stranger that you don't know what things have happened here?"

"What things?" asked the man. The two men told the stranger about Jesus—about His death on the cross, the empty tomb, and their hopes that He might have been the one to redeem Israel.

The stranger (who was Jesus) listened quietly. Then He explained what the Old Testament writers had said about Jesus Christ and that every prophecy concerning His death, burial, and Resurrection had come true.

When they reached the house, the two men invited the stranger to eat supper with them. The stranger sat at the table, prayed, and ate with them. Then God opened their eyes, and they immediately knew that the stranger was Jesus.

As soon as the men recognized Him, Jesus disappeared. The men returned quickly to Jerusalem to find the eleven disciples. They all talked about Jesus, telling each other what they had seen.

Then Jesus appeared to them and said, "Peace to all of you." He stood in the center of the group of disciples. "Why are you troubled?" He asked. "Why are you doubting in your hearts?" Then He showed them His hands and feet and said, "It's really Me. Touch Me and see. A ghost doesn't have flesh and bones, as you see I do."

They all sat down together and ate. Jesus talked to the men again about why He had to suffer on the cross and rise from the dead the third day. He said that repentance and forgiveness of sins should be preached in His name among all nations, beginning at Jerusalem.

Jesus appeared to the disciples more than once. The third time was when some of the disciples had decided to go fishing at the Sea of Galilee. They didn't catch anything all night. The next morning they saw a man on the shore who asked them if

Jesus Appears to His Followers
Luke 24:13–35

Name _____

Write in each blank a rhyming word from the word bank to tell the story.

Word Bank
surprise   loss   miles   stay

1. Our hearts were sad;
   we had lost our smiles.
   We traveled from Jerusalem
   about seven _____ **miles** _____ .

2. We talked of our Lord and
   His death on the cross.
   A man came near, and we
   explained our _____ **loss** _____ .

3. He walked with us;
   many things He did say.
   When we got to the village,
   we asked Him to
   _____ **stay** _____ .

4. When He prayed over bread,
   God opened our eyes.
   It was our Lord!
   Imagine our
   _____ **surprise** _____ !

A Servant's Heart • Lesson 110   163

they had any food. When they said no, the man told them to throw their net into the water on the right side of the boat. The net caught so many fish that the disciples couldn't haul it in.

John recognized that it was Jesus on the shore. When Peter heard Who it was, he jumped into the water and swam to Jesus. The other disciples followed in the boat, dragging the net full of fish. Jesus told them to pull the net onto the shore. They caught 153 fish, but the net didn't break.

Jesus called the disciples to come eat with Him. He gave them fish and bread to eat.

The last time Jesus saw His disciples, He took them to Bethany and blessed them. Then Jesus was taken into heaven. The disciples returned to Jerusalem with great joy, praising and blessing God.

⚜

▶ **Who met Cleopas and the other man on the road to Emmaus?** (Jesus)

▶ **What did they talk about?** (Christ's death and Resurrection)

▶ **How did the men respond when they recognized Jesus?** (They were thrilled and returned to Jerusalem and told others they had talked with Jesus.)

▶ **When Jesus appeared again to the group in the room, what did He show them?** (He showed them the wounds from the nails in His hands and feet.)

▶ **Where did Jesus appear to the disciples a third time?** (at the Sea of Galilee)

▶ **Who jumped into the water and swam to meet Jesus?** (Peter)

▶ **What did Jesus do for the disciples on the shore?** (He gave them bread and fish to eat.)

▶ **Where did Jesus go?** (into heaven) Point out that He has promised to come again.

❤ Memory Verse—Matthew 28:6

Practice the memory verse. Distribute the verse visual cards. Direct the students to line up at the front of the classroom, showing the words in sequence. Tell them to hold the cards with just the letters facing the class. Call on individual students to say the verse, using the first-letter clues.

✍ Worktext page 163

Identify the correct rhyming word to complete the rhyme. Read aloud the directions and the word choices. Allow the students to complete the page independently. Remind them that Jesus promised to return some day. Explain that although we cannot see God, Christians can have fellowship with God because of Christ's death and Resurrection. Point out the importance of trusting Christ as Savior, then confessing sin, praying, and reading God's Word daily.

LESSON 111 Jesus Christ, Our Mediator

Materials
• Hymn: "What a Wonderful Savior!"

🎵 Hymn: "What a Wonderful Savior!"
Sing the first four verses (Worktext page 220). Play the recording.

❤ Memory Verse—Matthew 28:6
Practice the memory verse. Call on volunteers to recite the verse. Place each puzzle piece on the bulletin board, pausing for the students to say each part before continuing.

Introducing the Application Story
Define the words *mediator* and *intercede*. Read **Mark 16:19** aloud.

▶ **Where is Jesus now?** (He is in heaven in His Resurrection body.)

Write the word *mediator* for display. Direct the students to find the word *mediator* in their glossary. Read the definition aloud. (*person who acts as a go-between*)

Write the word *intercede* for display. Direct the students to find this word in their Worktext glossary. Read the definition together. (*to plead on behalf of another*)

💡 **Who is our mediator—the One Who pleads on our behalf or goes between sinful man and the holy God?** (Jesus)

💡 **What did Jesus do for all people?** (He died for our sins.)

💡 **What does Jesus ask God to do for people?** (forgive our sins)

Application Story

Read or tell the following. Listening question: **Who intercedes in this story?** (*Ryan's younger brother*)

Ryan and the Prize Melon

My brother Ryan is the fastest kid in our neighborhood. He can go around the bases and reach home plate in the time it takes me to get to second. He wins the fifty-yard dash every year.

Ryan is a fourth grader—he is two years older than I am. But now and then, he needs some help from me.

I guess I need to tell you that Ryan is deaf. He understands sign language, and he reads lips fairly well. He had to learn how to do all that when he was really little. But he can't hear at all, and he can't talk in a way that people understand. He goes to a special school for the deaf across town from my school.

Last Saturday was one of those times when he needed my help. We rode our bikes to the place in town where farmers sell their produce on weekends. Mom wanted us to buy tomatoes and strawberries.

Ryan and I walked through the crowded market, looking at the brightly colored fruits and vegetables. "Look at the watermelons!" I signed to Ryan. Watermelons are his favorite. Ryan's eyes got big, and he nodded. We walked up to the table where the melons were.

"These are the best melons I've grown in ten years," said the farmer behind the table. "The big ones on the ground there are my prize melons. They're not for sale—just for show."

Ryan had already stooped down to admire the big melons. The farmer stood up and moved to chat with a woman at the next table.

I wandered across the aisle to look for strawberries for Mom. I picked a little square basket full of plump red berries, but I knew I'd better check with Ryan. He's better than I am at telling whether fruit is good or not. I turned to ask him, but he wasn't beside me.

I glanced across the aisle, just in time to see Ryan picking up one of the farmer's big display melons. He was smiling and looking around for me.

I put the berries down and hurried across the aisle, but the melon farmer got to Ryan first, and I could tell by his face that he wasn't happy. He grabbed Ryan roughly by the shoulder and spun him around.

"What do you think you're doing, kid?" His voice was loud and stern, and he was pointing his finger in Ryan's face. "I told you those melons weren't for sale."

"Mister—" I said, but I was too late. Ryan's shocked expression turned to fear. The farmer gave his shoulder a shake, and the jolt made him drop the slippery melon right on the farmer's boots.

The melon split open, and pink juice dribbled out in a little stream on Ryan's tennis shoes.

Ryan took one look at the farmer's angry face and then ran. Up the aisle he went, dodging kids and parents. The farmer took off after him.

"No!" I shouted. "You'll never catch him! Mister, just let me tell you—"

But the farmer didn't listen. There was nothing for me to do but chase along behind both of them. I ran, gasping for breath, trying to keep the farmer's back in sight.

I don't know how long the chase would have lasted if Ryan hadn't tripped over the wheel of a baby stroller and sprawled out on the pavement. The farmer ran up to him and stopped, and I ran into the farmer's back.

"Mister," I said between gasps for air, "my brother wasn't trying to steal your melon. He's deaf, see, and he didn't hear you say they weren't for sale." I knelt beside Ryan, who was sitting up, rubbing his elbow. "Are you okay?" I signed to him.

He nodded and looked away. I looked back up at the farmer. "Please forgive him, sir," I said. "He wouldn't steal from you."

The man rubbed the back of his neck and shuffled his feet a little. "Look, I'm the one who needs to apologize here," he said. "I just thought he was trying to make off with my prize melon. I didn't know the kid was—that he had a—tell the kid I'm sorry, will you?" He offered Ryan a hand to help him up.

I signed the farmer's message to Ryan. He glanced up at the farmer and nodded.

Suddenly the farmer's tanned face crinkled into a smile. "What do you say we go eat that melon, boys? It's not good for much else now."

I signed quickly to Ryan, and his huge grin was all the answer the farmer needed.

- ▶ **What was Ryan's physical disability?** (*He was deaf.*)
- ▶ **Who is telling this story?** (*Ryan's younger brother*)
- ▶ **How does Ryan communicate?** (*He uses sign language and reads lips.*)
- ▶ **Why was the melon farmer angry?** (*He thought Ryan was stealing the melon.*)
- ▶ **How did Ryan's brother help?** (*He explained Ryan's disability and asked the farmer to forgive him.*)
- 💡 **How do you know the farmer forgave Ryan?** (*He helped Ryan up and invited them to eat the melon.*)
- 💡 **How do you know that Ryan forgave the farmer?** (*He let the farmer help him up, he nodded, and he gave him a big grin.*)
- ▶ **Who interceded for Ryan?** (*Ryan's younger brother*)
- 💡 **How was Ryan's brother like Christ our mediator?** (*Christ intercedes and asks God for forgiveness for our sins. Ryan's younger brother interceded for Ryan and asked the farmer to forgive Ryan.*)

Explain that Christ as our Mediator not only pleads with God to forgive sinful people, but He even takes the punishment for the guilty so that God can declare them innocent.

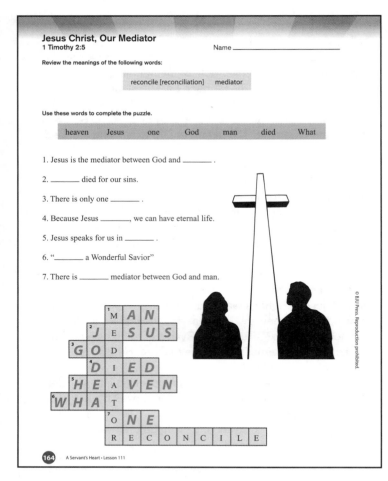

Worktext page 164

Draw conclusions. Review the meaning of *reconcile* and *mediator*. Direct the students to read silently the word choices. Choose a volunteer to read aloud the first sentence, filling in the blank with the correct word. Demonstrate how to write the letters in the crossword puzzle. Continue to complete the puzzle as a class activity. Point out that it is only by God's grace that we can be saved through faith (**Ephesians 2:8–9**).

Reflecting God's Love

Materials
- Hymn: "What a Wonderful Savior!"
- Bicycle reflector
- Flashlight

♫ Hymn: "What a Wonderful Savior!"
Sing the hymn (Worktext page 220).

💡 **What can we do in difficult times or when we are tempted or discouraged?** *(pray, quote Scripture, sing praises to God, talk to other believers)*

Remind the students that when Christians' thoughts are on God, their actions will reflect love for God and God's love for others.

♥ Memory Verse—Matthew 28:6
Review the memory verse. Direct the students' attention to the bulletin board with one piece of the puzzle covered or to the memory verse visual. Invite a volunteer to say the verse filling in the missing phrase. Repeat as time allows.

Picture the Point

Illustrate God's love. Display the bicycle reflector.

▶ **What is this?** *(a reflector)*

💡 **What is it used for?** *(It reflects light from an oncoming or following vehicle and shines the light back to the vehicle so that the bicycle can be seen.)*

Darken the room and demonstrate how the bicycle reflector shines light back from the flashlight. Elicit from the students that God wants us to reflect His love back to Him and to others. Explain that as Christians show love to others, God can use them to bring unbelievers to Him. Read **1 John 4:11, 19** aloud. Encourage the students to mention ways they can show God that they love Him and ways they can show their love and God's love to others.

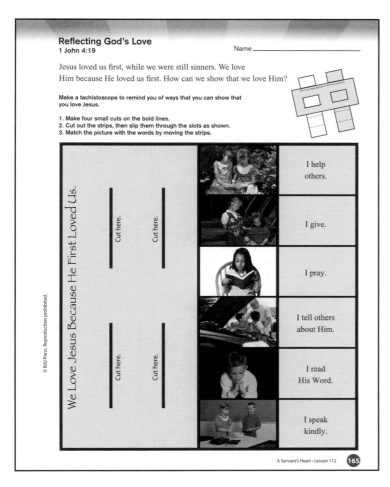

Worktext pages 165–66

Apply Bible knowledge to everyday life. Explain how to make the tachistoscope as described in the Worktext. Guide the students as they make their tachistoscopes. Choose a student's tachistoscope to display the first picture. Demonstrate how to move the words to match the picture. Allow each student to share his with a partner. *(Note:* Some students may find it easier to fold the tachistoscope when cutting the slits.)

Going Beyond

Reinforcement

Remember the Resurrection of Christ. Explain that Christians in the early church greeted each other not with "Hi" or "Hello. How are you?" but with "He is risen!" The usual response was "He is risen, indeed!" Use this heartfelt greeting with the students and encourage them to answer appropriately.

Enrichment

Guide a discussion about witnesses. Read **Luke 24:46–48** aloud. Explain that *a witness* is someone who can report facts about an event. Explain that a credible witness is someone who is an *eyewitness*. For example, a person who sees a car accident happen is an eyewitness. Tell the students that a witness must also have *a good reputation*. Point out that the apostles were men of honor, willing to share their testimonies even when their lives were in danger. Finally, explain that the testimony was supported by the accounts of many others who also saw the risen Lord. Point out that the New Testament records the eyewitness accounts of those who saw and recognized Jesus after the Resurrection.

Guide the students in locating each verse listed below to find out who the witnesses are that are mentioned.

Mark 16:9—Mary Magdalene
Matthew 28:1, 9—Mary Magdalene and the other Mary
Luke 24:33–36—eleven disciples, Simon [Peter] and others
1 Corinthians 15:6–8—five hundred Christians, James, all the apostles, and Paul
John 20:19, 24, 26—the disciples without Thomas, then with Thomas
John 21:1–2—seven disciples: Simon Peter, Thomas, Nathanael, the sons of Zebedee, and two others

Unit 8 Review

Name _____

Fill in the circle next to the correct answer.

1. John cared for Mary, the mother of _____
   - ● Jesus.
   - ○ a thief.

2. Jesus saved the criminal on the cross who _____ Him.
   - ○ spoke evil of
   - ● trusted in

3. When Jesus told some sad believers about the Resurrection, they _____
   - ○ forgot it.
   - ● told others.

4. The women at the tomb were sad because they thought Jesus was _____
   - ● dead.
   - ○ missing.

forgive   saved   separated

Write the word from the word bank that makes each sentence correct.

5. We may enjoy God because He created and _____ *saved* _____ us.

6. Unsaved people are _____ *separated* _____ from God because of sin.

7. Jesus Christ is the only One Who can _____ *forgive* _____ sin.

Circle True or False for each sentence.

8. God is everywhere you go.   (True)   False

9. God knows everything you say, do, and think.   (True)   False

10. God always keeps His promises.   (True)   False

Unit Reviews

Lessons 105–112 • A63

 Unit Review

Materials

- Copy of page A63 ("Unit 8 Review") for each student

Guide a review of Unit 8. Review the people and events in preparation for the Unit 8 Test (optional).

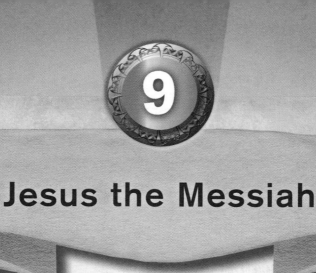

9

Jesus the Messiah

OVERVIEW

Preparing the Teacher

Read **Acts 1:8** and **Jude 1:25**. When talking about miracles, the focus is often on the cosmic and the spectacular (e.g., raising the dead) or the microscopic (e.g., the intricate structure of a snowflake). The real significance of the power of God is often not conveyed. This power has been readily available to His people in every age. It is still manifested in miracles small and great. It cannot be usurped, borrowed, eradicated, or counterfeited by the world. It cannot be used up, misappropriated, hidden, or hoarded by God's people. Sadly, however, a Christian can ignore the power of God due to pride, busyness, or unbelief. Spend some time today meditating on God's omnipotence and its impact on you and your needs. Take a few minutes to praise the Savior Who humbled Himself to bring us salvation and the power of God to live a victorious Christian life.

Preparing the Materials

113—Unit 9 Bookmark [E]; verse visuals; two eight-inch construction-paper circles (one white and one dark)

114—Stapler or two brass fasteners [E]

116—Copy of page A94 ("Miracles Great and Small") [E]

Unit 9a Going Beyond—Copy of page A95 ("What Kind of Man Is This?") [E]; tagboard or construction paper [E]; yarn; transparent tape

119—Strawberry [E, O]

120—Copy of page A96 ("Turning from Temptation") [E]

Unit 9b Going Beyond—2 sheets of construction paper [E]

121—Six 3" × 5" cards; pocket chart [O]

122—Eight pencils; eight coins of the same value; transparency marker

123—Copy of page A97 ("Jesus Died for Me!") [E]; Romans Road bookmark from the Student Materials Packet (CD) [E]

124—Chart paper; two dowel rods

Unit 9c Going Beyond—Playdough [E]; plastic straws [E]; yellow construction paper [E]; transparent tape

127—Invitations of different types [O]

128—Copy of page A98 ("Jesus Shall Reign") [E]; copy of page A64 ("Unit 9 Review") [E]

Unit 9d Going Beyond—Two ten-foot carpentry tape measures; medium-sized basket; small pieces of paper

Unit 9   Jesus the Messiah

Hymn: "Jesus Shall Reign"

Theme, Memory Verse, and Principle	Lesson Number	TE Page	Worktext Page(s)	Appendix Page(s)	Lesson Title	Scripture or Focus
Unit 9a **Jesus Is God** Mark 4:41 *Jesus is God.*	113	248	167–68		Jesus Calms the Storm	Mark 4:35–41
	114	250	169–71		Prayer and Faith	Application Story
	115	252	172		Jesus Raises Lazarus	John 11:1–45
	116	253		A94–95	God's Power	Psalm 126:3
Unit 9b **Jesus Is Man** John 6:38 *Jesus is our example.*	117	255	173		Jesus Was Baptized	Matthew 3; John 1:19–34
	118	257	174		Jesus Was Tempted	Matthew 4:1–11
	119	258	175		The Misery of Sin	Application Story
	120	260	176	A96	Turning from Temptation	1 Corinthians 10:13
Unit 9c **Jesus Is the Savior of the World** 2 Corinthians 5:17 *A saved person is a changed person.*	121	261	177–78		Nicodemus	John 3:1–21
	122	263	179–80		Zacchaeus	Luke 19:1–10
	123	266	181	A97	Tell the Good News	Application Story
	124	267	182		Prophet Focus: Isaiah	Prophet Focus
Unit 9d **Jesus Is the King of Kings** Psalm 24:10 *The Lord Jesus Christ is the King of Glory.*	125	270	183–84		Jesus, the Humble King	Matthew 21:1–11
	126	272	185–86		Jesus Is Coming Again!	Revelation 20–22
	127	274	187		Press On!	Application Story
	128	276	188	A98, A64	Jesus Shall Reign	Luke 1:32–33

Connections	Bible Doctrines	Skills/Applications
L113—Science	**The Doctrine of the Bible**	**Foundational**
	Proofs for Inspiration	• Realize that Jesus Christ is the King of Kings
	The Bible says it is inspired (2 Tim. 3:16–17).	• Realize that Jesus is God and that He is all-powerful
L114—English		
	The Doctrine of God	
	Attributes of God	**Practical**
	God is all-powerful (Jer. 32:27).	• Illustrate a Bible account
	God has shown Himself in nature (Rom. 1:20).	• Identify characters from their speech
L116—Writing		• Read a timeline
	Nature of God	• Identify relevant information
	The Son is God (Heb. 1:8).	• Recall facts and details
		• Complete a picture
	The Doctrine of Man	• Sequence the books in the Old Testament
	Created for God's Glory	• Sequence the books in the New Testament
	God would show His glory and receive glory (Rev. 4:11).	• Identify aspects of the new Jerusalem
		• Identify relevant information
	Condition of Man	• Infer information
	Man is guilty before God (Rom. 3:10–12).	• Record information
		• Infer cause and effect
	Final State of Man	
	Redeemed man lives in the new Jerusalem (Rev. 21:3).	
L120—Writing		**Personal**
	The Doctrine of Salvation	• Share the plan of salvation
	God's Provision	• Realize that God can help us to resist temptations
	Christ became man (incarnation) (John 1:14).	• Write about a personal experience
	Christ did not yield to temptations in His nature (John 14:30).	• Illustrate an experience
L122—Math	Christ did not yield to temptations in His actions (John 8:29).	• Understand and apply Bible knowledge to everyday life
L123—Writing	*Elements of Salvation*	
	God calls men through the Holy Spirit (John 16:7–11).	
	God imparts to the believer spiritual life and a new nature (regeneration) (Eph. 2:4–5; 4:24).	
L124—World History		
	The Doctrine of End Times	
	Spiritual Changes	
L125—English	Earth will be filled with the knowledge of the Lord, but not all will be saved (Rev. 20:4, 8–9).	
L126—TimeLine: John the Apostle		
L128—Writing		

Jesus Is God

Unit 9a

PREVIEW

Doctrines

- God is all-powerful (omnipotent) (Jeremiah 32:27). [Lessons 113, 115]
- God has shown Himself in nature (Romans 1:20). [Lesson 113]
- The Son is God (Hebrews 1:8). [Lesson 115]

Skills and Applications

- Learn Mark 4:41
- Follow directions
- Illustrate an experience
- Identify relevant information
- Recall facts and details
- Realize that Jesus is God and that He is all-powerful
- Write about a personal experience
- Apply Bible knowledge to everyday life

LESSON 113 — Jesus Calms the Storm

Materials

- Chart 24, "What Kind of Man Is This?"
- Hymn: "Jesus Shall Reign"
- Unit 9 Bookmark for each student
- Highlighter for each student (optional)
- Visuals for Science Connection—two eight-inch construction-paper circles, one white and one dark
- Verse visuals: Prepare shapes to represent the wind and waves (see below). Write the first half of Mark 4:41 on the cloud shape and the other half on the wave shape.

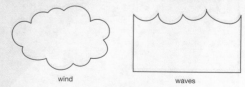

wind   waves

Memory Verse—Mark 4:41

Principle: Jesus is God.
Highlight the memory verse. Direct the students to highlight the verse (optional) and mark the location with the Unit 9 Bookmark. Read **Mark 4:37–41**.

▶ **Why were the disciples afraid?** (*They thought they were going to drown.*)

💡 **Are you ever afraid?** (*Elicit that everyone is afraid at one time or another.*)

💡 **Why did the disciples think Jesus was not like other men?** (*Jesus spoke, and the storm stopped; the wind and waves obeyed Him.*)

💡 **Why was Jesus able to just speak and calm the storm?** (*Jesus is God; He is all-powerful.*)

Practice the memory verse using the verse visuals. Choose two students to come to the front and have each of them hold a verse visual. Lead the class in saying the verse. Direct one group to say the verse; then call on the second group. Next, tell the second group to say the words on the first visual and the first group to say the words on the second visual. Direct the class to stand and recite the verse again.

🔬 Science Connection (optional)

Demonstrate the phases of the moon. Point out the last phrase of the first verse of the hymn. Explain that the words *waxing* and *waning* refer to the process of the moon going through its phases approximately every thirty days. As it does, we see different portions of the moon as different shapes. Discuss how the changes in the moon's shape occur as the moon travels in its orbit, revealing only portions of its

lighted surface. That's why the moon appears to be getting larger or smaller.

Direct attention to the construction-paper circles. *(Note: The directions below assume that you are facing the students with the circles in front of you.)*

[Show the white circle to represent the lighted surface of the moon. Place the dark circle directly over the white circle to cover it completely from view.]

Explain that when the moon is between the earth and the sun, we cannot see the darkened moon. The first phase, or shape, of the moon is called the *new moon.*

[Move the dark circle to the right of the white circle to show a "sliver" of the lighted part of the moon.]

This banana shape is called *a crescent.* Explain that as the moon continues to travel around the earth, it reveals more of its lighted surface. This is called *waxing.*

waxing crescent

[Show the waxing crescent as illustrated. Continue to move the dark circle toward the right of the white circle to reveal more of the moon's lighted surface (waxing). Then remove the dark circle completely to illustrate a full moon.]

Explain that when the earth is closer to the sun than the moon is, we can see all of the moon's surface. This is called a full moon.

[Show the waning crescent as illustrated below. Place the dark circle to the left of the white circle. Slowly move the dark circle to the right over the white circle until the white circle is completely covered from view.]

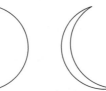

full moon   waning crescent

After the full moon phase, the movement of the moon forms a crescent again, but this time revealing less of the lighted surface. This is called *waning.* As the moon continues to travel, the waning continues to reveal less and less of the moon's surface until we do not see it at all. Then the cycle of the moon begins all over again.

▶ **What is the darkened moon phase called?** *(the new moon)*

💡 **Who controls the waxing and waning of the moon?** *(God)*

Read aloud **Colossians 1:16–17**. Point out that just as God controls the phases of the moon, He also controls the wind, rain, and sea as we will learn in **Mark 4**. If time allows, sing the first verse of the hymn again.

Background Information

Sea of Galilee—The Sea of Galilee is actually a freshwater lake, thirteen miles long and seven and a half miles wide. At times the wind blows across the land and down the hillsides surrounding the lake, stirring up the water. A storm can arise in a

very short time. Waves have been known to be as high as twenty feet. When Jesus and His disciples crossed the lake, they were probably in a Galilean fishing boat. This boat was sturdy enough to withstand the sudden, frequent storms.

Introducing the Bible Account

Guide a discussion about storms. Talk about the results of strong winds on trees and house roofs. Explain the dangers of rising rivers and lightning. Inform the students of safety procedures during storms.

💡 **What are some things a Christian can do to avoid being afraid?** *(Answers will vary. Elicit from the students that they can quote Scripture as a reminder that God is with them, and they may talk to Him.)*

Bible Account

Read Mark 4:35–41 or use the following retelling of the passage. Direct the students to look at the picture on Worktext page 167. Listening question: **Who was afraid?** *(the disciples)*

Jesus Calms the Storm

Jesus was tired. All day crowds of people had tried to force their way to be near Him. They wanted to hear His preaching and be taught by Him. It was now evening, and the crowds were gone.

Jesus told His disciples that they would go across the Sea of Galilee to the other side. The disciples must have thought they would have a pleasant time traveling with Jesus across the lake, but Jesus went to the back of the boat and fell asleep on a pillow.

Suddenly the gentle breeze blew stronger. Clouds formed; the sky grew dark and gray. The waves began to splash wildly against the boat. The disciples were frightened because it was such a violent storm.

The waves were now beating so forcefully against the disciples' boat that the water was coming into the boat. Soon the boat was in danger of sinking. The disciples were afraid that they would be swallowed up by the huge waves. They woke Jesus, and some asked Him if He cared that they were about to drown. Others begged Jesus to save them.

Did Jesus care? He awoke and immediately got up, spoke to the wind, and said to the water, "Peace, be still." Then He turned to the disciples and said, "Why are you so fearful? How is it that you have no faith?"

Once again the disciples were frightened. They could not believe what had just happened! One minute they were in the middle of a raging storm, fearing for their lives, and the next minute it was quiet and peaceful and they were safe. In amazement they asked each other, "Who is this? Even the wind and the waves obey Him!"

Then the boat came safely to the other side of the lake, and Jesus continued to help those in need.

▶ **What did Jesus and His disciples do in the evening?** *(They sailed to the other side of the lake.)*

▶ **What happened as they crossed the sea?** *(A terrible storm swept across the lake.)*

▶ **Where was Jesus?** *(He was asleep in the back of the boat.)*

▶ **What did the disciples think when the storm got worse?** *(They were afraid and thought they would die.)*

▶ **What did the disciples do?** *(They woke Jesus up.)*

▶ **How did Jesus solve the problem?** *(He just spoke, and the storm stopped.)*

💡 **How do you know Jesus wasn't pleased with the way the disciples had reacted?** *(He asked them why they had no faith.)*

Jesus is God. He made the wind and the waves, which always obey Him. He made you and me; we should obey Him too.

InfoScene: "What Kind of Man Is This?"
Display Chart 24 from the Visual Packet as a reference throughout this unit.

🎵 Hymn: "Jesus Shall Reign"

Introduce the hymn (Worktext page 221). Explain that the words of this hymn are based on **Psalm 72**, which talks about God as the perfect King and Ruler. You may want to read Psalm 72 aloud.

Teach the first verse of the hymn. Play the recording of the first verse. Read and discuss the first verse, reminding the students that Christians should glorify God because He made them and takes care of them. Sing the verse with the students several times.

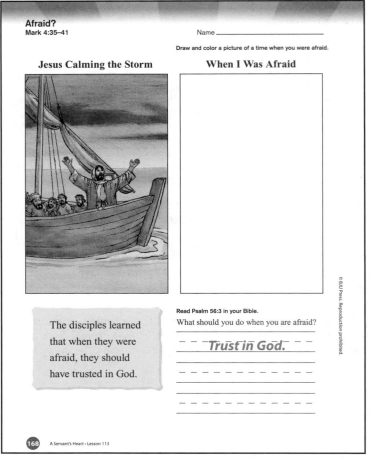

Afraid?
Mark 4:35–41

Name _____

Draw and color a picture of a time when you were afraid.

Jesus Calming the Storm   **When I Was Afraid**

The disciples learned that when they were afraid, they should have trusted in God.

Read Psalm 56:3 in your Bible.
What should you do when you are afraid?

Trust in God.

 A Servant's Heart · Lesson 113

💡 **What does the word *reign* mean?** *(to rule)*

▶ **Who will reign wherever the sun shines?** *(Jesus)*

▶ **How big will Jesus's kingdom be?** *(It will go from shore to shore.)*

▶ **How long will Jesus reign?** *(Read the last phrase of the first verse: "Till moons shall wax and wane no more.")*

💡 **How can a Christian allow Jesus to reign in his life?** *(Elicit that with Christ as his Savior, a Christian should be obedient to Christ and glorify Him in all things.)*

✏️ Worktext page 168

Illustrate an experience with Bibles open to Psalm 56:3. Direct the students to write the answers to the questions. Give them time to draw the picture. Allow several students to show the class their drawings. Point out that we should believe God's promises. He loves all people. God is always with each Christian and will always work the circumstances of each person's life together for his good.

LESSON
114 **Prayer and Faith**

Materials

• Hymn: "Jesus Shall Reign"
• Verse visuals from the previous lesson
• Two brass fasteners for each student or a stapler

⊙ Worktext pages 169–70

Make a song booklet. Tell the students they will make a song booklet from the Worktext pages. Explain that they will use it as they sing the hymn throughout the unit. Guide them as they cut out the pages. Assemble the booklets with either staples or brass fasteners.

♫ Hymn: "Jesus Shall Reign"

Sing the first verse (Worktext page 221). Play the recording and sing the first verse together. Review the meaning of the first verse. Utilize the students' song booklets. (*Note:* Keep the booklets in the classroom until the end of the unit.)

♥ Memory Verse—Mark 4:41

Practice the verse using the verse visuals. Choose two students to hold the verse visuals at the front.

▶ **What does *omnipotent* mean?** *(all-powerful; able to do anything)*

▶ **Why was Jesus able to still the storm?** *(He is God.)*

▶ **Why was Jesus able to raise Lazarus from the dead?** *(He is omnipotent.)*

Introducing the Application Story

Guide a discussion about miracles. Write the word *miracle* for display. Guide the students as they locate it in the glossary of their Worktexts. Read the definition aloud as they read silently.

▶ **What is a miracle?** *(a supernatural event done by the power of God)*

▶ **Where does the power to perform miracles come from?** *(God)*

💡 **Why did Jesus perform miracles?** *(to show the power and work of God; to help people understand or believe)*

▶ **What miracle did Jesus perform in the previous Bible account?** *(He calmed the storm by speaking to the wind and waves.)*

Tell the students that even though Jesus is not here physically, He is omnipresent and still does wonderful miracles every day.

Application Story

Read or tell the following story to your students. Listening questions: **What is an orphan?** *(a child whose parents have died)* **What wonderful thing did God do for Kara, the orphan girl?** *(He provided the missionary with the money to keep her.)*

I Knew He Would Hear Us

   In India there was an orphan girl who was going to be sold as a slave. She begged a missionary from another area to take her home with her. She wanted to live in a missionary house and go to the mission school to learn more about God. The missionary sadly said, "We want you to come, but

we have no money to take care of you. Kara was very sad. The missionary's heart ached for the little girl. The missionary said, "Pray that God will send us money so we can take you in. I will pray too! Remember Jesus said that if we ask God in Jesus's name, we'll receive the answer. Soon we'll be joyfully praising our God together."

Kara excitedly promised that that was exactly what she would do.

When the missionary returned to her home in another town, she found a letter from Christians in America. Along with the letter, they sent some money. It was enough money to take care of Kara! Early the next morning, the missionary sent a messenger to go bring Kara. It was a long day's journey to Kara's village, but in just a couple of hours the messenger returned to the mission house with Kara. Little Kara said, "You prayed that God would send the money, and I asked God to send the money. I knew that He would hear us, so I thought I might as well start walking!" She had already walked halfway to the mission house when the messenger met her.

Kara trusted in God. She prayed with confidence, believing that He would supply her needs. We can trust Him for our needs too.

 Why was Kara's prayer pleasing to the Lord? *(She prayed believing that God would provide the money.)*

 What wonderful things has God done for you? *(Accept any answers, but be sure to point out that God's sending His Son to die for us so we can be saved is the most wonderful gift of all.)*

🔗 English Connection, Worktext page 171

Use the glossary. Direct the students to locate and read again the definition of *miracle* in the glossary of their Worktexts. Guide the students in completing the sentence at the top of Worktext page 171.

Locate verses about the miracles of Jesus. Direct the students' attention to the picture at the top of the Worktext page. Elicit that this is the miracle in which Jesus calmed the storm. After the students have found the references, choose a volunteer to read each passage and complete the sentence. Guide the students in matching the passage with the corresponding picture.

LESSON 115 Jesus Raises Lazarus

Materials
- Hymn: "Jesus Shall Reign"
- Song booklet for each student from Lesson 114
- Verse visuals from Lesson 114

🎵 Hymn: "Jesus Shall Reign"

Sing the first verse (Worktext page 221). Lead the students in singing the first verse as they look at the pictures in their booklets.

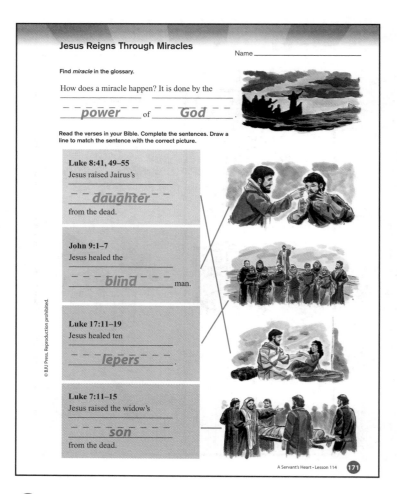

❤ Memory Verse—Mark 4:41

Review the memory verse. Utilize the verse visuals.

Background Information

Raising the Dead—*Jesus raised Lazarus from the dead about one month before His own death and Resurrection. Lazarus lived in Bethany, a town on the road to Jericho, about 2 miles (3 km) from Jerusalem. This was the third time Jesus had raised someone from the dead. He had raised Jairus's daughter (***Mark 5:35–43***) and the widow's son (***Luke 7:11–16***). The miracle of Lazarus's resurrection caused many Jews to believe in Jesus.*

The Sanhedrin—*Lazarus's resurrection brought the Sanhedrin to the final decision to kill Jesus. The Sanhedrin was a council of Jewish leaders who carried out the law under the authority of the Romans. The group normally consisted of seventy-one members, and its leader was the high priest—Caiaphas at that time.*

Preparing the Body for Burial—*Lazarus was buried in a cave. The body was wrapped in strips of linen cloth (with spices between them), and a napkin was placed over the face.*

Introducing the Bible Account

Guide a discussion about death. Discuss how someone feels when a loved one dies. Read aloud **1 Thessalonians 5:9–11**.

- **What happens to a Christian's body and soul at death?** *(The body returns to dust, and the soul goes to either heaven or hell until the resurrection.)*
- **What is heaven?** *(Heaven is a glorious and happy place where the saved will be with the Lord until He makes a new heaven and a new earth, where we will live with Him forever.)*

Bible Account

Read John 11:1–45 or use the following retelling of the passage. Listening question: **What words of comfort did Jesus give to Martha?** *(Jesus told her that whoever believed in Him would never die but would have eternal life.)*

Jesus Raises Lazarus

Lazarus, the brother of Mary and Martha and a close friend of Jesus, was very sick. Lazarus and his sisters lived in the town of Bethany. His sisters sent a messenger to Jesus, Who was teaching and preaching in another region. They hoped that Jesus would come right away because their brother was so sick! They knew how much Jesus loved their brother.

When Jesus received the news from the messenger, He said, "This sickness will not end in death but is meant for the glory of God so that the Son of God may be glorified by it." Jesus stayed where He was for two more days. Jesus's disciples didn't want Him to go back to the Jerusalem area because they were afraid the Jews would try to kill Him. Jesus then told His disciples, "Our friend Lazarus is sleeping, but let's go so that I can wake him up."

Jesus knew Lazarus had already died, but the disciples thought He meant Lazarus was resting. When Jesus and the disciples arrived in Bethany, Lazarus had been in the grave for four days already. Many Jews had come to the sisters' home to comfort them. When Martha heard that Jesus was coming, she hurried out to meet Him. Martha immediately said to Jesus, "Lord, if You had been here, my brother wouldn't have died."

Jesus tried to comfort Martha. He told her that Lazarus would rise again. Martha thought Jesus was talking about the resurrection at the last day. Jesus then told Martha that He is the resurrection and the life. He told her that whoever believes in Him, even if his body is dead, will still live. He told her that whoever believes in Him will never die but have eternal life. He asked Martha whether she believed this.

Martha said to Jesus, "I believe that You are the Christ, the Son of God, Who has come into the world." Then Martha found Mary and told her Jesus wanted to see her. Mary quickly went to meet Jesus. The Jews who were in the sisters' house saw Mary leave. They thought she was going to Lazarus's grave to weep, so they followed her.

When Mary saw Jesus, she fell at His feet and told Him she thought her brother wouldn't have died if Jesus had been there. Jesus saw that Mary and the others were weeping. Jesus cried too.

Jesus knew where Lazarus was, but He asked, "Where have you laid him?" They brought Jesus to the grave. Some of the Jews also thought that Jesus could have kept Lazarus

from dying because they knew about other miracles Jesus had done.

Jesus ordered the stone to be taken away. Martha told Jesus that Lazarus had been dead for four days and his body would smell terrible. Jesus reminded Martha that if she would believe, she would see the glory of God!

What did Jesus do? He gave thanks to God because He wanted those standing around to believe He was sent by God. Then He shouted, "Lazarus, come out." [*Ask the students to call out the same words.*] And Lazarus came out of the cave, wrapped in his grave clothes. Then Jesus said, "Unwrap him and let him go." Jesus had performed another miracle. He is God, and He had raised the dead by the power of God.

- ▶ **Why did Mary and Martha send for Jesus?** *(They thought He could make Lazarus well.)*
- ▶ **Why did Jesus not go to Lazarus right away?** *(He knew God would be glorified by His waiting.)*
- ▶ **Who ran to meet Jesus as He neared Bethany?** *(Martha)*
- ▶ **What did she say to Jesus?** *("My brother would not have died if You had been here.")*
- ▶ **What did Jesus say to her?** *(He told her Lazarus would rise from the dead.)*
- **What did Jesus mean when He said believers will never die but will have eternal life?** *(A believer will never experience anything more than temporary physical death. At death his soul goes to heaven to be with God. Then later his body will be resurrected and reunited with his soul to live on the new earth.)*
- ▶ **What question did Jesus ask Martha?** *(He asked her whether she believed His words.)*
- ▶ **How did Martha answer?** *(She said she believed.)*
- ▶ **Why was Jesus able to raise Lazarus from the dead?** *(Jesus is God. Only God's power can raise the dead.)*
- ▶ **Will you be with Jesus in heaven one day?** *(If you have trusted Christ, He promises that you will be with Him forever. If you haven't yet trusted Christ, you may do so today.)*

Worktext page 172

Locate verses about God's resurrection power. Before the students look at the Worktext page, tell them that God gave others the power to raise the dead. Explain that they are going to see times that God gave Old and New Testament men the power to resurrect certain people. Instruct the class to turn to Worktext page 172. Read the directions and guide them as they complete the page. The students may look up and read one verse for each sentence to find the correct answer or you can choose volunteers to read aloud the verses.

LESSON

116 God's Power

Materials

- Hymn: "Jesus Shall Reign"
- Copy of page A94 ("Miracles Great and Small") for each student

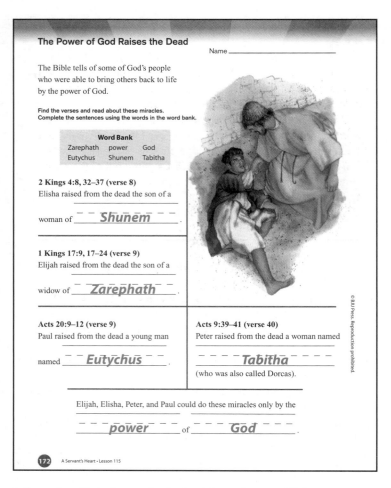

The Power of God Raises the Dead

Name _____

The Bible tells of some of God's people who were able to bring others back to life by the power of God.

Find the verses and read about these miracles. Complete the sentences using the words in the word bank.

Word Bank
Zarephath	power	God
Eutychus	Shunem	Tabitha

2 Kings 4:8, 32–37 (verse 8)
Elisha raised from the dead the son of a

woman of _Shunem_ .

1 Kings 17:9, 17–24 (verse 9)
Elijah raised from the dead the son of a

widow of _Zarephath_ .

Acts 20:9–12 (verse 9)
Paul raised from the dead a young man

named _Eutychus_ .

Acts 9:39–41 (verse 40)
Peter raised from the dead a woman named

Tabitha
(who was also called Dorcas).

Elijah, Elisha, Peter, and Paul could do these miracles only by the

power of _God_ .

172   A Servant's Heart · Lesson 115

© BJU Press. Reproduction prohibited.

- Song booklets for each student from Lesson 114
- Verse visuals from Lesson 114

🎵 Hymn: "Jesus Shall Reign"

Sing the first verse (Worktext page 221). Call several students to the front of the classroom with their song booklets. Allow them to hold up the pictures for the first verse as the class sings the verse with the recording. Repeat the procedure, giving several students a chance to show their booklets in the front of the classroom.

❤ Memory Verse—Mark 4:41

Practice the verse. Read the verse together.

💡 **How did Jesus show that He is God?** *(Answers will vary but may include raising the dead, creating the world, healing the sick, calming the storm, and forgiving sins.)*

Choose two students to hold the verse visuals. Instruct the student holding the first visual to turn it so that the words are *not* showing. Lead the class in saying the verse. Direct the first student to show his visual and the second student to turn his so that the words are *not* showing. Lead the class in saying the verse again. Remove the visuals and call on several individuals to recite the verse.

✎ Writing Connection

Guide a writing activity. Direct the students to locate **Psalm 126:3** in their Bibles. Read the verse together. Share with the class some of the great things that God has done in your life. Explain the directions for page A94 ("Miracles Great and Small") to the students; then elicit examples of God's power in their lives. Write these for display. *(Answers may include salvation, healing, protection, financial provision, encouragement, and guidance.)* After the written testimonies are complete, the students can place them on the starburst shapes on the Unit 9 bulletin board (optional).

▶ Going Beyond

Reinforcement

Materials
- Copy of page A95 ("What Kind of Man Is This?") for each student
- Tagboard or construction paper for each student
- Yarn
- Transparent tape

Make a mobile. Invite students to follow the instructions for making a mobile that shows what happened when Jesus calmed the storm.
  1. Color page A95 ("What Kind of Man Is This?").
  2. Glue page onto tagboard or construction paper.
  3. Cut out the pieces on the heavy lines.
  4. Cut five varying lengths of yarns from 5" to 14".
  5. Cut another piece of yarn 15" long for a hanger.
  6. Punch holes and attach yarn.
     (Pictures can be in any order.)

Encourage the students to use the mobile to retell the account to someone.

Enrichment

Record daily weather information. Remind the students that God *spoke* to create the world (**Hebrews 11:3; Genesis 1:3, 6, 11, 20, 24**). Point out that He still rules over His creation (**Colossians 1:6–17**). Prepare a chart titled "Today's Weather" to record the temperatures (high and low), wind movement (calm or windy, and direction), sky condition (clear or cloudy), and precipitation. You may want to make a wind vane for determining the wind direction by attaching a crepe paper streamer to a stick or ruler.

Direct a storm activity. Instruct the students to follow your motions in listening to the sounds of a storm.
- Snap your fingers alternately (raindrops)
- Rub your palms together (steady rain)
- Tap your fingers on a table or desk (harder rain)
- Clap your hands once (lightning)
- Stomp your feet several times (thunder)

Reverse the sequence to bring the storm to a halt. Point out that the storm in Mark 4 was sudden and fierce.

Jesus Is Man

Unit 9b

PREVIEW

Doctrines

- Christ became man (incarnation) (John 1:14). [Lesson 117]
- Christ did not yield to temptations in His nature (John 14:30). [Lesson 118]
- Christ did not yield to temptations in His actions (John 8:29). [Lesson 118]

Skills and Applications

- Learn John 6:38
- Recall facts and details
- Infer cause and effect
- Realize that God can help us resist temptations
- Write about a personal experience
- Apply Bible knowledge to everyday life

LESSON 117 Jesus Was Baptized

Materials

- Chart 25, "Jesus Was Baptized"
- Chart 39, "Christ's Ministry"
- Hymn: "Jesus Shall Reign"
- Unit 9 Bookmark for each student
- Song booklet from Lesson 114 for each student
- Highlighter for each student (optional)

♪ Hymn: "Jesus Shall Reign"

Teach the second verse (Worktext page 221). Utilize the song booklets.

💡 **What does the word *homage* mean?** *(honor or respect)*

▶ **Who is this homage given to?** *(Jesus)*

Point out that those who *own*, or acknowledge, Jesus as their Lord should take the gospel to those who do not know Him as Savior. Lead the students in singing the first two verses with the recording.

Background Information

John the Baptist—*Elizabeth was a relative of Jesus's mother, Mary. Elizabeth was married to Zachariah, and God gave them a son, John. God called John to be a prophet. John and Jesus probably knew each other as children (**Luke 1:36**). They had possibly been told by their parents of the angels' announcements of their missions. John prepared people for Christ's ministry. He baptized many, including Jesus. He warned sinners to turn away from their sins and be baptized. Some people thought John was the Messiah, but he pointed them to Christ, the true Messiah. The preaching of John the Baptist took place in the wilderness west of the Dead Sea. The word* wilderness *refers to unsettled, uninhabited land. Matthew places John's preaching in the Judean desert.*

John's Message—*John's message was that Jesus, the Lamb of God, was coming and that people were to repent. To repent means to be sorry for your sin, and to turn to Christ for salvation. God's response to repentance is forgiveness. Many came to hear John preach, but he baptized only those who repented and confessed their sins.*

Jesus's Baptism—*The Lord's baptism marked the beginning of His public ministry. At this time, Christ was publicly called the Son of God, the Messiah, and the Savior of the world. Jesus was in*

His early thirties when He was baptized. He came to the Jordan River from Nazareth to be baptized.

Jesus, the Lamb of God—*This name for Jesus Christ shows that by His death He paid the sacrifice for sins, just as a lamb was offered for sin in the Old Testament.*

Jordan River—*This river was the place of Jesus's baptism.* **John 1:28** *says John was baptizing in Bethabara. Most of the Jordan River is below sea level. It runs about seventy-five miles from north to south but winds back and forth for a total length of about two hundred miles. It is the longest river in Palestine.*

Introducing the Bible Account

Guide a discussion about baptism. Allow students who have been baptized since they have been saved to share their experiences. Point out that a person is saved through faith in Christ and not by baptism.

💡 **What does baptism mean?** *(Baptism is an outward sign of a person's union with Christ as Savior and publicly shows his decision to follow Christ.)*

Explain that Jesus was baptized to show obedience to His Father. Display Chart 39, "Christ's Ministry," to show the location of the Jordan River and the place of Jesus's baptism.

Bible Account

Read Matthew 3 and John 1:19–34 or use the following retelling of those passages. Direct the students' attention to Worktext page 173. Choose volunteers to read the information about the Jordan River. Listening question: **What did God say after Jesus was baptized?** *("This is my beloved Son, in whom I am well pleased.")*

Jesus Was Baptized

John did his preaching and teaching near the Jordan River. Many people came to hear him. He told the people to repent of their sins. Then John would baptize in the Jordan River the people who repented. John told the people, "The One Who comes after me is mightier than I am, and I am not worthy to even untie His shoes. He will baptize you with the Holy Spirit."

One day when John saw Jesus coming, he said, "Behold the Lamb of God, Who takes away the sin of the world." Jesus wanted John to baptize Him, but John didn't think he was worthy to baptize Jesus. Jesus wanted to be baptized because He wanted to obey His Father. John baptized Jesus.

When Jesus came up out of the water, an amazing thing happened. The heavens opened, and John saw the Spirit of God coming down in the form of a dove and resting on Jesus. He also heard a voice from heaven say, "This is my beloved Son, in whom I am well pleased." Whose voice do you think this was? It was God's voice.

⚜

Jesus Was Baptized
John 1:19–34; Matthew 3

Unlike other water sources in this part of the world, the Jordan did not dry up completely in the summer. Willow and tamarisk trees grew along its banks, forming a streak of green in the dry, brown land.

The mouth of the Jordan River at the Dead Sea is the lowest spot on earth—about 1,350 feet below sea level.

The Jordan River begins from the snows of Mount Hermon. The river runs about two hundred miles through mountains and desert. It flows into and out of Lake Huleh and the Sea of Galilee and ends in the Dead Sea.

The exact spot where Jesus was baptized is not known. The Scriptures call it "Bethany beyond Jordan," or Bethabara.

A Servant's Heart • Lesson 117 **173**

▶ **What message was John preaching to the people?** *(to repent of their sin and be baptized)*

💡 **What does it mean to repent?** *(to be sorry for your sin and to turn to Christ for salvation)*

💡 **What should people do before being baptized?** *(believe that Christ died for their sins, that He was buried, and that He rose again according to Scripture; repent of their sin and trust in the Lord Jesus Christ as Savior)*

▶ **What did John say when he saw Jesus coming toward him?** *("Behold, the Lamb of God, Who takes away the sin of the world.")*

💡 **Why did John call Jesus the Lamb of God?** *(John was proclaiming Jesus as God's Son, Who was sent to die for sin as the promised Messiah.)*

▶ **Why did John not want to baptize Jesus?** *(John thought that he wasn't worthy or good enough.)*

💡 **Why was Jesus baptized?** *(to be our example and to obey God)*

💡 **Why should a Christian be baptized?** *(to follow Jesus's example, to obey God, to show others one's union with Christ as Savior, and to show one's decision to follow Christ)*

💡 **What does baptism symbolize?** *(Christ's death, burial, and Resurrection; that a Christian is dead to sin and alive in God)*

InfoScene: "Jesus Was Baptized"
Display Chart 25 from the Visual Packet for the students to refer to throughout this unit.

♥ Memory Verse—John 6:38

Principle: Jesus is our example. Direct the students to open their Bibles to John 6:38 and to look at it as you read it aloud.

💡 **Who is speaking these words?** *(Jesus)*

💡 **What examples has Jesus left for Christians to follow?** *(Answers may include that He was baptized, and a Christian should be baptized; He did what was right, and a Christian should do what is right; and that He was humble, and a Christian should be humble.)*

💡 **What does a true follower of Jesus do?** *(not his own will, but God's will)*

💡 **Are you following Christ's example? Are you being obedient to God?** *(Elicit that a Christian should obey Christ and follow His example.)*

Direct them to highlight the verse (optional) and mark the location with the Unit 9 Bookmark.

LESSON 118 Jesus Was Tempted

Materials
- Chart 39, "Christ's Ministry"

Background Information

Christ's Temptation—*Christ was tempted right after His baptism. The Holy Spirit was present, strengthening Jesus. Satan was present, trying to get Jesus to sin. We don't know for sure where in the wilderness the temptation took place, but the traditional site (near the Brook Cherith) is called the Mount of Temptation.*

Fasting—*Fasting is choosing to not eat food for a period of time and is often mentioned in the Bible. Some individuals who fasted were David (when his child became ill) and Ahab (on hearing of his doom). Daniel fasted for three weeks (**Daniel 10:2–3**) as Moses and Elijah did for forty days (**Exodus 34:28; 1 Kings 19:8**). Sometimes people fasted because they wanted to express humility for sin or to show how much they wanted God to hear their prayers.*

Introducing the Bible Account

Guide a discussion. Role-play a situation in front of the class in which someone is tempted and does wrong. Discuss the wrong actions and allow students to tell what choice the person should have made. Use situations such as the following:

A shopper taking something without paying for it
A student cheating on a test
A family member saying unkind words to or about someone

Bible Account

Read Matthew 4:1–11 or use the following retelling of the passage. Display Chart 39, "Christ's Ministry," to point out the Wilderness of Judea and the Mount of Temptation. Listening question: **How many times did Satan tempt Christ on this occasion?** *(three)*

Jesus Was Tempted

After Jesus was baptized, the Spirit of God led Him into the wilderness. There Jesus fasted (went without food) for forty days. He was very hungry.

Then Satan spoke to Jesus and tempted Him. He wanted Jesus to sin. Satan told Jesus that if He was the Son of God, then He should turn the stones into bread.

Jesus answered Satan by quoting Scripture and said that man should not depend only on bread for life, but also on every word from God. Jesus meant that we need not only physical food but also spiritual food from God's Word.

Satan continued to try to get Jesus to yield to his temptations. He took Jesus to Jerusalem and put Him on a high part of the temple. There Satan tempted Christ again. Satan told Jesus that if He was the Son of God, He should jump off and the angels would rescue Him. The angels could have rescued Him, but Jesus didn't give in to Satan. Instead, He answered with Scripture again, quoting the command that says you should never tempt the Lord your God.

Satan came to Jesus a third time. This time he took Jesus up to the top of a very high mountain. He showed Jesus all the kingdoms of the world and how great they were. Then Satan told Jesus he would give Him all these kingdoms if He would just bow down and worship him. Satan was lying; he controls only what God allows him to control.

Jesus told Satan to go away and again quoted Scripture, saying that the Lord God must be worshiped and He is the only One to be served. The Bible tells us that if we resist the Devil, then he will flee from us. Jesus used Scripture to resist Satan, and Satan left Him.

God then provided angels to take care of Jesus.

(*Note:* The Old Testament verses Jesus quoted are **Deuteronomy 8:3, 6:16,** and **6:13.**)

💡 **Who is Satan?** *(Satan was once one of God's greatest angels, but he wanted to be as great as God, so God threw him out of heaven. Satan is now an evil spirit who is the enemy of God and all Christians.)*

💡 **How was Jesus feeling when Satan came to tempt Him?** *(He had been without food for forty days so He was very hungry. Remind the students that Jesus became man to live on earth. He knew physical hunger, pain, and weariness. Yet as God in the flesh He never sinned.)*

▶ **Every time Jesus was tempted by Satan what did He do?** *(He quoted Scripture.)*

▶ **What three temptations did Satan use?** *(He tempted Christ with food, dared Him to jump off the temple so angels could rescue Him, and told Him to bow down and worship him.)*

💡 **What are some ways Satan tempts you?** *(Answers will vary but should include the following: to take things that do not belong to you, to be proud of what you have done instead of giving God the credit for the talents He has given to you, and to think of yourself first and not of others.)*

- **How can a Christian have victory over Satan's temptations?** *(by being filled with the Holy Spirit as Jesus was and quoting Scripture that he has memorized as Jesus did)*
- **Who is stronger, God or Satan?** *(God is stronger.)*
- **Why could Jesus be tempted with earthly temptations?** *(because Jesus was human)*

Review the title of this unit—"Jesus the Messiah." Point out that each person chooses whether or not to sin, but the Christian has God's power to resist. In **Ephesians 6:10–18**, God tells the Christian how to prepare for spiritual battles. Stress the importance of reading and knowing God's Word.

Worktext page 174

Infer cause and effect. Read the top portion of the page to the students. Explain that when Satan tempted Jesus, he thought Jesus would use His power to meet His need for food and to prove to Satan that He was in fact God. Satan's temptations didn't have the effect he wanted. Direct the students to locate **Matthew 4:1–10** in their Bibles, read the verses telling about Satan's temptations and Christ's answers, and complete each sentence.

Memory Verse—John 6:38

Practice the memory verse.

- **How can you learn to love and follow Jesus?** *(You can read the Bible, listen to Bible preaching, and confess and forsake sin. God makes a Christian holy in heart and behavior through the Holy Spirit.)*

LESSON
119 The Misery of Sin

Materials
- Hymn: "Jesus Shall Reign"
- Song booklet for each student from Lesson 114
- A strawberry for each student (optional)

Hymn: "Jesus Shall Reign"

Sing the first and second verses (Worktext page 221). Point out that God wants all people everywhere to come to Him through faith in Jesus Christ.

Memory Verse—John 6:38

Practice the memory verse.

Introducing the Application Story

Guide a discussion about food. Elicit from the students that fruits and vegetables provide vitamins and minerals for their bodies. Call on volunteers to name some of their favorite fruits and vegetables. Explain that the following story is about strawberries. Give each student a strawberry to eat before telling the story (optional).

Jesus Was Tempted
Matthew 4:1–11   Name _____

Jesus was the only perfect person. He was tempted, but He did not sin. He obeyed God's Word and trusted God's power to keep from sinning.

Use the word bank to complete the sentences. The Bible verses will help you.

Word Bank
bread   world   worship
God   angels   stones

Satan Tempted

You are hungry. Make __stones__ into bread.

Matthew 4:3–4

Jump from the top of the temple. God will send __angels__ to catch you.

Matthew 4:6–7

All the kingdoms of the __world__ will be yours if you worship me.

Matthew 4:8–10

Jesus Answered

Man shall not live by __bread__ alone, but by everything that God says.

You shall not tempt [test] __God__.

You should __worship__ and serve only God.

© BJU Press. Reproduction prohibited.

174   A Servant's Heart • Lesson 118

Application Story

Read or tell the following story. Listening question: **What were the results of Billy's sin?** *(He had a stomachache; he was miserable and unhappy; he was afraid to tell his parents where he had been; he had to work to pay for what he had stolen.)*

The Misery of Sin

Billy was so happy when he woke up on Saturday. He was going biking with his friend Zach. He got dressed, ate breakfast, and went to meet his friend.

They rode by Mrs. Hinkley's house. She grew strawberries to sell. Billy and Zach looked at the field of berries turning bright red.

Billy said, "We could take a few. Who would miss them?"

Zach thought for a while and then shook his head. "No, it's wrong—even if no one sees us. Besides, somebody *will* see us. God is always watching. And because I'm a Christian, I'm His servant and I want to serve Him every day in everything I do."

Billy didn't reply, but the boys kept riding around until almost noon. When Zach left to go home for lunch, Billy went by Mrs. Hinkley's house again.

Bright red berries hung on the plants. Billy liked strawberries better than any other fruit.

He laid his bike down out of sight and went into the field. He meant to eat only a few berries, but they were so rich and juicy, he just kept eating. When he finally decided to leave, he realized that he had an awful stomachache.

When Billy got home, he went to his room and lay down. Then his mother called him to come for lunch, and he tried to look cheerful. "Did you have a good morning biking, son?" asked his father.

"Uh, yes, sir," answered Billy.

"Where did you go?" asked his mother.

Billy felt like he was going to be sick. He managed to say, "Oh, to the bridge and back." His father said, "Did you stop anywhere?"

Billy just shook his head no. He thought about the lie he had just told and felt even sicker.

Finally his mother asked him, "Billy, is anything wrong? You've hardly touched your food."

Billy hung his head and said, "I'm just tired and not too hungry."

Then his mother said, "Well, I have something that will make you feel better in a jiffy!" She went into the kitchen and brought out and set before him a big, heaping dish of strawberry shortcake. Billy's stomach gave a funny jump, and before he could stop himself, tears were running down his face.

His mother felt his forehead. "What's wrong, Billy? Are you sick?"

Billy nodded.

His father got up to help him from the table. "Why, Billy, you should have said something. Let me help you, Son."

Billy let his father take him to his room. He didn't know which made him feel worse—the stomachache or deceiving his parents.

"Dad, I . . . I have to tell you something."

And Billy told what he had done. "I'm so sorry."

His father said, "I am too. When you feel a little better, we'll talk about this."

That evening, Billy and his parents talked. He prayed for forgiveness and apologized to his parents.

Then he went to Mrs. Hinkley and asked her to forgive him too. When he returned home, he said, "Mrs. Hinkley says if I help her pick berries next week, she'll consider me paid up!"

Billy gave a huge sigh of relief. With a clear conscience, he slept very well that night.

Tell the students that God shows believers through His Holy Spirit when they have sinned. Sin makes God's children unhappy and miserable until they confess the sin to God. We know that Satan wants us to sin. Encourage the students to obey the Bible and to listen to the Holy Spirit's guidance instead of following Satan.

 What helped Zach to do right? *(He knew that when he was tempted he should turn the other way. He also remembered that God is always watching us.)*

▶ **What choice did Billy make?** *(He chose to sin; he stole strawberries and then lied to his parents.)*

Jesus Helps Us When We Are Tempted

Name _____

Jesus was tempted as we are. He can help us turn away from temptation.

Find out what God says by reading the Bible verse. Read each of the groups of sentences. Answer the question by coloring the *YES* or *NO* apple.

Satan says	God's Word says	🍎🍎🍎🍎🍎🍎🍎🍎🍎🍎🍎🍎🍎	
steal	Exodus 20:15	Jon put a dollar in his desk until his turn at the snack shop. Mickey saw the money and thought how much he would like to go to the snack shop. He went back to his work. **Did Mickey accept God's help to turn away from temptation?**	YES / NO
disobey	Ephesians 6:1	Sarah was playing in her room. She heard her mother call, "Sarah! Come and set the table." Sarah kept on playing and acted as if she didn't hear. **Did Sarah trust God to turn away from temptation?**	YES / NO
cheat	2 Corinthians 8:21	Ted's class was taking a math test. Ted did not know how to do some of the problems. Ted waited until the teacher walked to the other side of the room, and then he got the answers from Eric's paper. **Did Ted turn away from temptation in God's strength?**	YES / NO
be unkind	Ephesians 4:32	The second-grade girls would not let Sandy join their game. Kylie asked Sandy if she would like to go play on the swings with her. **Did Kylie receive God's help to turn away from temptation?**	YES / NO

© BJU Press. Reproduction prohibited.

A Servant's Heart • Lesson 119 **175**

▶ **How did Billy try to cover his sin of stealing the strawberries?** *(He lied to his parents.)*

▶ **Read Numbers 32:23 aloud. Which sins can we hide and get away with?** *(none)*

💡 **Do you sin?** *(Yes, we break God's commandments every day.)*

💡 **How can we have fellowship with God?** *(Come to Christ for salvation and confess our sin.)*

💡 **What does *confess* mean?** *(to agree with God that you're wrong and tell Him you're sorry for your sin)*

▶ Read **1 John 1:9** aloud. **What happens when we confess our sin to God?** *(God forgives us. Point out that a Christian will still sin sometimes, but he should confess and forsake it.)*

✍ Worktext page 175

Apply Bible knowledge to everyday life. Guide the students as they read about what Satan says and what God says. Choose volunteers to read the verses for each situation. Discuss how the person could turn away from temptation rather than give in to it.

Turning from Temptation

Materials

- Hymn: "Jesus Shall Reign"
- Copy of page A96 ("Turning from Temptation") for each student
- Song booklet from Lesson 114 for each student (optional)
- Charts 2–3, "Books of the Bible: New Testament, Old Testament"

🎵 Hymn: "Jesus Shall Reign"

Sing the first and second verses (Worktext page 221). Utilize the song booklets.

❤ Memory Verse—John 6:38

Review the memory verse.

Tell the students that the Bible lists many specific ways we can follow the example of Christ. Point out that a Christian should always seek to please God and do what is right. Explain that a child of God loves and helps others and tells them about God. When Jesus lived on earth, He realized the reality of eternity and the urgency of preaching the truth.

📖 Bible Study Skills

Review the books of the Bible. Direct the students to locate the contents page for the Old Testament in their Bibles, or display Chart 3, "Books of the Bible: Old Testament" (optional). Lead them in reading the names of the books aloud, then direct them to close their Bibles and recite the Old Testament books. Repeat the procedure with the books of the New Testament. You may want to use Chart 2, "Books of the Bible: New Testament" (optional).

✏ Worktext page 176

Recall facts and details. Guide the students as they complete the sentences. Instruct them to find and circle the words from the word bank in the word search at the bottom of the page.

✒ Writing Connection

Guide a writing activity. Distribute page A96 ("Turning from Temptation") and direct the students to locate **1 Corinthians 10:13** in their Bibles. Read the verse together. Share with the class a time when you were tempted to sin and what helped you to turn away from the sin. Explain that they are to write about a time that they were tempted to sin (take something that did not belong to them, say unkind words, fight with a sibling, etc.) and did not. Remind them to write about what helped them to turn from sin. When their paragraphs are completed, the students can place them on the silhouette shapes on the Unit 9 bulletin board.

▶ Going Beyond

Materials

- 2 sheets of construction paper and crayons (or felt-tip markers) for each student

Reinforcement

Illustrate an experience. Encourage the students to draw a picture illustrating the experience that they wrote about on page A96 ("Turning from Temptation"). Guide them as they find Bible verses to use when Satan tempts them in similar situations. Write the Bible reference at the bottom of the picture or copy the verse on the back of the picture.

Enrichment

Identify examples of being like Jesus Christ. Direct each student to trace around his foot on construction paper with a dark crayon or felt-tip pen. Instruct the students to write a word or phrase that tells how they should follow Jesus's example. *(Answers could include being loving, kind, and honest. Remind them that Christians should strive to be like Christ in their words, thoughts, and actions.)* Display the trail of footprints around the classroom.

Jesus Is the Savior of the World
Unit 9c

PREVIEW

Doctrines

- God calls people through the Holy Spirit (John 16:7–11). [Lesson 121]
- People are guilty before God (Romans 3:10–12). [Lesson 122]
- God imparts to the believer spiritual life and a new nature (regeneration) (Ephesians 2:4–5; 4:24). [Lesson 122]
- The Bible says it is inspired (2 Timothy 3:16–17). [Lesson 124]

Skills and Applications

- Learn 2 Corinthians 5:17
- Illustrate and retell a Bible account
- Recall facts and details
- Identify characters by their speech
- Read a timeline
- Share the plan of salvation
- Realize God can change a sinner's heart
- Apply Bible knowledge to everyday life

LESSON 121 Nicodemus

Materials

- Chart 26, "Nicodemus Meets the Messiah"
- Hymn: "Jesus Shall Reign"
- Unit 9 Bookmark for each student
- Highlighter for each student (optional)
- Pocket chart (optional)
- Verse cards: Prepare six 3" × 5" cards by writing on each card a word or phrase from 2 Corinthians 5:17. Place the cards in a box or basket.

♫ Hymn: "Jesus Shall Reign"

Teach the third verse (Worktext page 221). Utilize the recording as desired throughout the unit.

▶ **What will be made to the Lord?** *(endless prayer)*
▶ **What will crown the Lord's head?** *(endless praises)*
💡 **What does it mean that the prayer and praises will be endless?** *(They will never stop.)*

▶ **What is the Christian's prayer like to God?** *(sweet perfume)*
💡 **How can a Christian give the Lord a sacrifice every morning?** *(by praying and praising Him [**Hebrews 13:15**])*

Explain the *morning sacrifice* by reading Psalm 141:2 aloud. Point out that prayer can be compared to the incense that was offered in the morning and evening throughout the Old Testament by the high priest. The sacrifices and incense given showed obedience, respect, faith, and love toward God. Remind the students that the Old Testament sacrifices pointed to the Lord Jesus Christ, the perfect sacrifice Who came to die to provide salvation for all mankind. Point out that a Christian can come to God in prayer because of Christ's death.

Background Information

Nicodemus—*Nicodemus was a Pharisee (a Jew who was strict in keeping the law) and a member of the Sanhedrin (a council of seventy-one men that served as the supreme court of Israel). He spoke with Jesus privately one night, coming after dark probably because he didn't want his acquaintances to know he was meeting with Jesus. However, prior to Christ's Crucifixion, Nicodemus*

---

*tried to defend Jesus by telling the Sanhedrin that the law says a man should have the opportunity to defend himself before being judged. The sad thing is that Nicodemus wasn't consistent. He apparently remained silent later when others turned against Christ. It is believed that Nicodemus was a believer because John 3 tells us he believed Jesus had come from God. He also helped Joseph of Arimathaea bury Jesus's body (**John 19:38–40**). Jesus used the following legal terms that were familiar to Nicodemus: judge, condemned, testify, and witness.*

Introducing the Bible Account

Guide a discussion about taking a stand. Call on volunteers to tell about a time when they needed to take a stand and do or say what was right when others were not in agreement. Tell them that in today's lesson a man named Nicodemus comes to Jesus at night to ask several questions.

Bible Account

Read John 3:1–21 or use the following retelling of that passage. Direct attention to the picture on Worktext page 177. Listening question: **Why did God send Jesus into the world?** *(so that people could have eternal life through faith in Christ)*

Nicodemus

In the darkness of evening, a visitor came to Jesus. His name was Nicodemus, and he was a Pharisee. He called Jesus *Rabbi,* which means "teacher." Nicodemus told Jesus that he knew Jesus couldn't perform miracles unless God was with Him.

Although Nicodemus had come to speak with Jesus, Jesus had a very important message for Nicodemus. Jesus said, "I tell you truly that if a person isn't born again, he cannot enter the kingdom of God." Nicodemus didn't understand what Jesus meant. Nicodemus had been born once and couldn't understand how, now that he was old, he could be born a second time.

Jesus explained to Nicodemus the way of salvation and how the Holy Spirit can cause a person to be born spiritually so that he's a whole new person on the inside. He asked Nicodemus, "If you don't understand when I tell you about earthly things, how can you believe if I talk about heavenly things?" No one has ever been up to heaven and come back to earth to tell about it. Only the Son of God (Jesus) has been in heaven and come down to earth.

He reminded Nicodemus that Moses had lifted up the serpent in the wilderness, and those who had been bitten by snakes could look at it and not die. Jesus said God would lift up the Son of Man the same way. He told Nicodemus that if he would trust in Him (Jesus) he would not perish but have eternal life (live forever with God).

John 3:16 says that God loved the people of the world so much that He gave His only Son so that whoever trusts in Him won't die spiritually but have eternal life. Jesus went on to explain that He wasn't sent by God to condemn the world, but to save it. He told Nicodemus that the person who doesn't trust in Him (Jesus) is condemned. Although God sent Light

Nicodemus Meets the Messiah
John 3:1–21

Nicodemus defended Jesus when the others were trying to find a way to get rid of Him (John 7:45–53).

Nicodemus helped to prepare the body of Jesus for burial (John 19:39–40).

A Servant's Heart • Lesson 121 **177**

(His Son) into the world, people loved darkness because their deeds were evil. Before Nicodemus left, Jesus told him that the one who does the truth comes to the light so that it may be clearly shown that his deeds are done in God.

This is what Nicodemus had done. He had come to Jesus. He had come to the Light. We know that Jesus explained the way of salvation to Nicodemus, but the Bible doesn't tell us whether he trusted Jesus as his Savior.

Later Nicodemus spoke up to defend Jesus Christ (**John 7:50–51**) and helped bury His body (**John 19:38–40**).

▸ **What did Nicodemus not understand?** *(how someone could be born twice)*

▸ **What did Jesus tell him?** *(Jesus was explaining how to be born again, to have a spiritual new birth. Accept several responses but be sure to point out the way of salvation.)*

 What does the word *condemned* mean? *(declared guilty)*

▸ **Who did Jesus say was condemned?** *(those who do not trust in Him for salvation)*

▸ **Who can save us?** *(The only Savior is the Lord Jesus Christ.)*

▸ **What does God require of a person before he can go to heaven?** *(He requires that a person be born again. The Holy Spirit can bring this about.)*

- **Have you accepted the Light, God's Son Jesus, as your Savior?** *(Note: You may want to invite those students who haven't trusted Jesus as their Savior to come see you at a specific time.)*

InfoScene: "Nicodemus Meets the Messiah"

Display Chart 26 from the Visual Packet for the students to refer to throughout this unit.

♥ Memory Verse—2 Corinthians 5:17

Principle: A saved person is a changed person. Direct the students to open their Bibles and to highlight the verse (optional) and mark the location with the Unit 9 Bookmark. Give the students a demonstration of being in Christ. Tell them to close their Bibles. Explain that the bookmark placed in the Bible is like their being in Christ. Just as the bookmark is covered by the Bible and safely tucked away, they too, after they have trusted Christ, are covered, protected, and kept safe in Him.

- **What does it mean to be "in Christ"?** *(It means a person is saved.)*
- ▶ **What is one indication that a person has become a Christian?** *(He is a new person on the inside. His words and actions show that he wants to be like Jesus.)*
- **What do you think are the "old things" in a Christian's life?** *(the sins, the habits, and the way of life before the person became a Christian)*
- **Name some things that should "become new" when a person becomes a child of God.** *(Answers will vary but may include such things as wanting to be obedient, being kind, reading the Bible, thinking more of others and putting them first, and depending on the Holy Spirit.)*

Practice the memory verse. Choose a student to take one of the cards from the memory verse basket. Instruct the student to read the word or phrase that is written on the card. Lead the class in reciting the whole verse. Repeat the procedure until all of the cards have been chosen. Tell the students with the cards to put them in order, either by holding them in the front of the classroom or by placing them in a pocket chart. Read the verse again.

✎ Worktext page 178

Identify characters by their speech. Read the directions to the students and allow them to complete the page independently.

LESSON 122 Zacchaeus

Materials
- Hymn: "Jesus Shall Reign"
- Song booklets for each student from Lesson 114
- Verse cards (and basket from the previous lesson)
- Eight pencils
- Eight coins of the same value
- Transparency marker

♫ Hymn: "Jesus Shall Reign"

Sing the third verse (Worktext page 221). Utilize the students' song booklets. Call on volunteers to tell what each illustration reminds them of in the third verse.
- Praying hands—A Christian can pray to God because of Jesus's death and Resurrection.
- Musical note and crown—Prayer and praises will be given to Jesus continually. Jesus will reign forever.
- The name Jesus—His precious name will be used in praise to God as a Christian prays in the morning.

Call several students to the front of the classroom to hold up their booklets as you lead the class in singing the third verse. Repeat this procedure with other students.

Background Information

Zacchaeus—*Zacchaeus was a short man who climbed a sycamore tree in order to see Jesus. He was a chief publican (a tax collector for the Roman government). Tax collectors were disliked by the people because they were often dishonest. Zacchaeus lived in Jericho, a city known for its priests. However, Jesus chose to go to the tax collector's house rather than a priest's house.*

Sycamore Tree—*In the Bible, sycamore refers to a type of fig tree. Its small, round, nontasty figs were about an inch in diameter. The strong, wide branches of the tree made it easy to climb.*

Jericho—*This city was located west of the Jordan River, about five miles (eight kilometers) from the north end of the Dead Sea. Many palm trees grew in the warm climate, and it was known*

as "The City of the Palms." Jericho *may mean "The Perfumed,"* *getting its name from the sweet-scented balsam tree that grows* *there.*

Repayment—*Roman law required those who had overcharged* *or cheated someone to pay back four times as much as was taken.* *Jewish law required only what was taken plus one-fifth of that* *amount. Apparently Zacchaeus repaid according to Roman law.*

Introducing the Bible Account

Discuss tree climbing. Encourage the students to share any of their experiences of climbing trees. Announce that you are going to tell about a man who climbed a tree for a very special reason.

Bible Account

Read Luke 19:1–10 or use the following retelling of that passage. Listening question: **How much did Zacchaeus choose to pay back to those he had cheated?** *(four times the amount he had stolen)*

Zacchaeus

One day Jesus was passing through Jericho. There were many people trying to get a glimpse of Him. A short tax collector named Zacchaeus was one of them. He was a rich man from that town, but he had few friends. The people usually didn't like tax collectors because most tax collectors were dishonest and got rich by cheating the people, making them pay more taxes than they owed.

Zacchaeus realized that if he was going to see Jesus in such a crowd he would have to do something different. He had an idea: he would run ahead of the crowd and climb a tree so he could see. That's exactly what he did! He climbed a sycamore tree.

Jesus walked along the road with the people following. When He came to the very tree that Zacchaeus had climbed, He looked up and said, "Zacchaeus, come down right away because today I will stay at your house."

Zacchaeus couldn't believe it. Jesus knew his name and wanted to go to his house. Zacchaeus quickly came down and joyfully joined the Lord.

The people were amazed. Jesus was going to the house of a wicked, sinful tax collector! The people began murmuring among themselves.

Zacchaeus spoke to Jesus. He told Him that he was going to give half of what he owned to the poor and restore four times as much as he had falsely taken. Zacchaeus truly wanted to make things right and follow God.

Jesus then told Zacchaeus, "This day salvation has come to this house." Christ told Zacchaeus that He, the Lord, had come to seek and to save those who were lost (not in Christ). Zacchaeus had trusted Christ, and he was a changed man. He would no longer cheat the people but start giving to them.

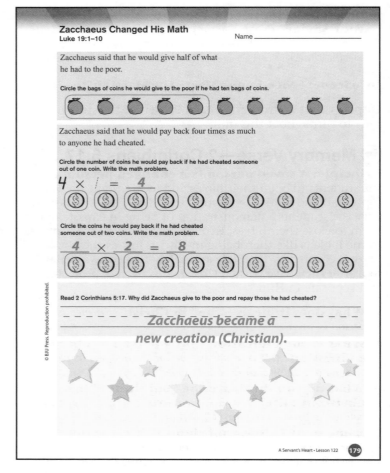

- ▶ **Why was Zacchaeus disliked by the people?** *(He was a tax collector who took their money dishonestly.)*
- 💡 **How did Jesus treat Zacchaeus?** *(He was a friend to him and went to his house to spend time with him.)*
- ▶ **What did Zacchaeus do after meeting with Jesus?** *(He turned from his wrongdoing and trusted Jesus as his Savior.)*
- 💡 **What purpose did Jesus have in coming to earth?** *(He came to seek and to save the lost. Explain that God is holy. We cannot fellowship with God because of sin, but God sent Jesus to pay the penalty for sin. Whoever will accept Jesus's death as payment for his sins and Christ's Resurrection as life-giving will never face eternal punishment for sin.)*
- ▶ **What did the crowd think when Jesus went with Zacchaeus?** *(They didn't like it. They didn't think He should be with this tax collector.)*
- 💡 **How should a Christian treat others?** *(A Christian should treat people with love as Jesus did and be willing to reach out to the unsaved and tell them about Jesus so that they can turn to Christ.)*

❤ Memory Verse—2 Corinthians 5:17

Practice the memory verse. You may use the cards in the basket from the previous lesson. Remind the students that the Holy Spirit changes a sinner's heart when that person comes to Jesus Christ as his Savior.

✏️ Math Connection, Worktext page 179

Guide an activity to solve Zacchaeus's math problems. Point out that when God changed Zacchaeus's heart, the old ways and habits were gone. Not only did Zacchaeus want to give back to the people what he had wrongfully taken, but he also gave back *more* than he had taken from them. Call on a student to tell why Zacchaeus wanted to make things right with others. *(He was a new creation.)* Instruct the students to complete the sentence at the bottom of Worktext page 179.

Display eight pencils side by side on the overhead projector. Choose two students to stand on either side of the overhead projector. Explain that each student will get half of the pencils. Demonstrate giving one pencil at a time to each student, dividing the pencils equally between the two students. Remove the pencil from the left and give it to the student on that side. Repeat, taking a pencil from the right and giving it to the other student. Continue until all of the pencils are removed. Ask each student how many pencils he is holding. *(4 pencils)*

Direct attention to the top of Worktext page 179. Instruct the students to divide the ten bags of coins equally between Zacchaeus and the poor. Direct them to circle the number of bags to show half. *(5 bags)*

Choose a volunteer to stand at the front of the classroom, representing a citizen of Jericho. Give the example that if Zacchaeus took 1 coin, then he gave back *4 times* what he took. Explain that you will represent Zacchaeus returning what is owed. Give the student 1 coin and write *1* on the transparency. Tell the students to circle one coin each time you give the student one coin. Give another coin to the student and write *+ 1* on the transparency. *(1 + 1)* Repeat with another coin and write *+ 1* on the transparency. Tell the students to circle another coin. *(1 + 1 + 1)* Then do this again. *(1 + 1 + 1 + 1)*

Ask the volunteer how many coins he has. *(4)* Ask the students how many coins they should circle. *(4)* Complete the equation. *(1 + 1 + 1 + 1 = 4)* Write $4 \times 1 = 4$ below the equation on the transparency, explaining that the equations mean the same thing. Point out that there were *4 sets of 1 coin.*

Direct attention to the example in the middle of Worktext page 179. Tell the students to complete the equation and circle the coins to represent what Zacchaeus would pay back. *(4 × 1 = 4, 4 coins)*

$$1 + 1 + 1 + 1 = 4$$
$$4 \times 1 = 4$$

Repeat the procedure to show what Zacchaeus would pay back if he had taken 2 coins. Place 2 coins on the overhead projector, write *2* on the transparency. Continue this to show *4 sets of 2 coins* on the transparency, each time continuing the equation. Tell the students to circle two coins each time you place two coins on the overhead projector. Count the number of sets on the overhead projector *(4)* and the number in each set *(2)* to complete the equation. *(8)* Instruct the students to complete the equation on their Worktext page and circle the total number of coins Zacchaeus would pay back. *(4 × 2 = 8, 8 coins)*

$$2 + 2 + 2 + 2 = 8$$
$$4 \times 2 = 8$$

Zacchaeus, Come Down!
Luke 19:1–10

Name _____

1. Place your palm on the page and spread your fingers apart.
2. Trace along each side of the fingers (but not the fingertips).
3. Extend the lines below the fingers to make a tree trunk.
4. Extend the finger lines into branches.
5. Draw leaves behind and between the branches.
6. Draw a road near the tree.
7. Cut out the figures below and glue them onto the picture.

(180) A Servant's Heart • Lesson 122

✏️ Worktext page 180

Illustrate the Bible account of Zacchaeus. Tell the students to cut out the figures at the bottom of the page. Explain that they will illustrate the scene in Jericho the day Zacchaeus met Jesus. Guide the students in drawing a tree on the Worktext page, following the directions as you draw a similar tree for display.

1. Place one hand (palm down) on the Worktext page or a sheet of paper with fingers spread apart.
2. Trace along each side of the fingers (not around the fingertips).
3. Extend the lines below the fingers to make a tree trunk.
4. Extend the finger lines into branches.
5. Draw leaves behind and between the branches.

Tell the students to draw a road near the tree and color their pictures. Then they may glue the figures of Jesus, Zacchaeus, and the crowd to the picture. Encourage the students to show their picture to someone and retell the story of Zacchaeus.

LESSON 123 Tell the Good News

Materials
- Hymn: "Jesus Shall Reign"
- Copy of page A97 ("Jesus Died for Me!") for each student
- Romans Road Bookmark from the Student Materials Section of the CD for each student
- Song booklet for each student from Lesson 114
- Verse cards from Lesson 121

♫ Hymn: "Jesus Shall Reign"
Sing the first three verses (Worktext page 221). Utilize song booklets.

♥ Memory Verse—2 Corinthians 5:17
Practice the memory verse. The verse cards may be helpful.

Introducing the Application Story
Guide a discussion about witnessing. Call on students to share opportunities that they have had, or someone they know has had, to tell others about the Lord. Point out the importance of being willing to tell others about Jesus and His love for them. Emphasize the importance of prayer when witnessing.

Application Story

Read or tell the following story. Listening question: **How did Sandy prepare before witnessing to Michelle?** (*She prayed.*)

The Extra Worksheet

Sandy sat at the table, with the phone in one hand and the papers ready. Mrs. Page had handed these out to her class just two weeks before on the last day of school. Sandy remembered the smile on her teacher's face as she had explained what the papers were.

"Class, these are some extra Bible worksheets I found while I was cleaning out my file drawers. I know many of you enjoy playing school with your friends during the summer, so I wanted to share the extras with you. Who would like some?"

Sandy raised her hand high. Mrs. Page laid three worksheets on Sandy's desk. Sandy noticed that one of the worksheets had the Romans Road on it. It showed a picture of a road leading to heaven, and along the road were signs with Bible verses from the book of Romans.

"You know, class," Mrs. Page was saying, "maybe you could even share these worksheets with other children in your neighborhood who need to know Jesus. Jesus could help you use the worksheets to be a witness this summer. Let's pray about that right now."

As Mrs. Page prayed, Sandy began thinking about her neighbor Michelle, who wasn't saved. School was dismissed, and for the next two weeks in family devotions, Sandy's mom

and dad prayed with her that God would give her an opportunity to witness to Michelle.

Just before Sandy made the call, she prayed again. "Please help me, Lord, to be able to tell Michelle about You."

She punched in the number, and a moment later she heard Michelle answer. "Hi, Michelle. This is Sandy. Can you come over and play with me today?"

Michelle's mom agreed, and right after lunch the doorbell rang. Michelle bounced in, her ponytail bobbing up and down. "I have an idea, Sandy," she said. "Let's play school."

Sandy smiled. "I had the same idea."

The girls sat down in Sandy's room, and Sandy handed Michelle the Romans Road worksheet. "This is your assignment," she said. "You may work on it during class time."

"Are these verses from the Bible?" asked Michelle.

"Yes," said Sandy. Suddenly she forgot all about being the teacher. "Do you want to use my Bible? I can help you look them up."

As they looked up the verses, Sandy explained to Michelle that everyone is a sinner, that the payment for sin is punishment in the lake of fire forever, and that the gift God gave is eternal life through His Son Jesus.

Michelle looked ahead at the next verses and said, "Oh, I know Christ was raised from the dead, and I confess my sins to Him every week. I must be saved." Sandy smiled and explained, "I'm glad you do that, but it's not just knowing facts about Jesus that saves us but trusting that Jesus took the punishment for our sin by His death on the cross. And because He was the perfect sacrifice for our sin," Sandy continued, "God showed how satisfied He was with Christ's payment by raising Him from the dead. Michelle, if you put your trust in Christ as your Savior and ask Him to save you, He will!"

Then Sandy excitedly told Michelle how she had asked Jesus to save her the year before and that now she knew that she would spend eternity with Him.

"Can I do that too?" asked Michelle.

As the two girls bowed their heads, Sandy glanced at the Romans Road worksheet. Silently she thanked God that Mrs. Page had not thrown the extra worksheets away.

- ▶ **Why was Sandy excited that her teacher was giving away extra worksheets?** (*She knew she could use them when she played school.*)
- ▶ **What did Sandy notice about one of the Bible worksheets?** (*It had verses from Romans that showed the way of salvation.*)
- ▶ **What did the teacher pray about when she gave out the papers?** (*that God would use them in some way to bring people to Jesus*)
- ▶ **What did Sandy do the first two weeks of vacation?** (*She prayed that God would give her an opportunity to witness to Michelle.*)
- ▶ **How did God answer her prayer?** (*He worked things out for Michelle to come over and play school with her.*)

✍️ Worktext page 181

Share the plan of salvation. Guide the students as they look up and read the following verses: **Romans 3:23; 6:23; 5:8; 10:9–10; 10:13–14a**.

▶ **Who will be saved?** *(Whoever repents and trusts in the Lord Jesus Christ will be saved.)*

Read **John 3:36** to the students. Explain that those who choose God's way of salvation will have eternal fellowship with Him. Instruct the students to color the signs at the bottom of Worktext page 181 to indicate the correct answers.

Distribute a Romans Road Bookmark to each student. Direct the students to place them in their Bibles. Encourage them to use the bookmark to share the way of salvation with an unsaved person. *(Note: This is a good opportunity to explain the way of salvation to any unsaved students and provide an opportunity for them to make a decision.)*

🖋️ Writing Connection (optional)

Guide the writing of a thank-you note. Distribute copies of page A97 ("Jesus Died for Me!") and direct the students to find **Romans 5:8** in their Bibles. Read the verse together. Share with the class your salvation experience and tell why you are thankful Jesus died for you. Encourage the students to write a thank-you note to Jesus, telling why they are thankful that He died to provide a way for all to be saved. Display the finished notes on the cross shape on the Unit 9 bulletin board. *(Note: Encourage students that are not saved to talk with you or with a parent.)*

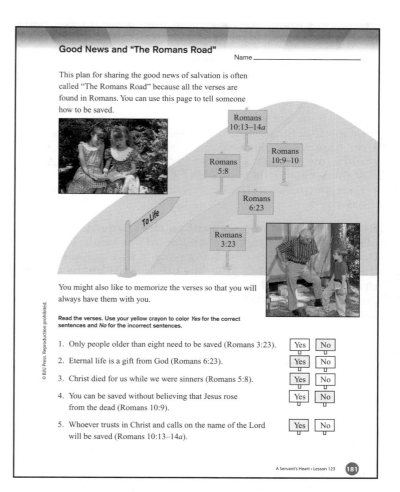

Good News and "The Romans Road"   Name _____

This plan for sharing the good news of salvation is often called "The Romans Road" because all the verses are found in Romans. You can use this page to tell someone how to be saved.

You might also like to memorize the verses so that you will always have them with you.

Read the verses. Use your yellow crayon to color *Yes* for the correct sentences and *No* for the incorrect sentences.

1. Only people older than eight need to be saved (Romans 3:23). Yes No
2. Eternal life is a gift from God (Romans 6:23). Yes No
3. Christ died for us while we were sinners (Romans 5:8). Yes No
4. You can be saved without believing that Jesus rose from the dead (Romans 10:9). Yes No
5. Whoever trusts in Christ and calls on the name of the Lord will be saved (Romans 10:13–14a). Yes No

A Servant's Heart • Lesson 123   181

LESSON 124 Prophet Focus: Isaiah

Materials
- Chart 37, "Divided Kingdom"
- Hymn: "Jesus Shall Reign"
- TimeLine
- Chart 35, "Christ's Birth" (optional)
- A scroll made from chart paper with handwriting lines and two sticks: Fold a piece of chart paper (see diagram), then cut on the fold. Write the verse with the reference (**Isaiah 53:6**) on the top half of the chart paper. Attach that piece of the chart paper to the two dowel rods and roll it to make a scroll.

a.
Cut on fold.
[unused portion of chart paper]
chart paper

b.
Isaiah 53:6
scroll

❤️ Memory Verse—2 Corinthians 5:17
Review the memory verse.

Background Information
Prophets—*See the background information in Lesson 24. Other prophets during Isaiah's time were Hosea (to Israel) and Micah (to Judah).*

Isaiah—*He was a prophet who lived about a hundred years before Jeremiah. Isaiah is called the messianic prophet because the book of Isaiah records more prophecies about the Messiah than any other book in the Bible except Psalms. He is quoted more in the New Testament than any other prophet. He may have been a first cousin of King Uzziah and a grandson of King Joash. The kings during Isaiah's time were Uzziah, Jotham, Ahaz, and Hezekiah. The vision Isaiah saw the year that King Uzziah died was his call to be a prophet, but it is recorded in Isaiah 6 rather than in the first chapter of the book.*

Scope of Isaiah's Warning—*Isaiah warned the people of Judah about God's judgment for sin, but he also spoke against other nations. He preached about God's desire for all people to come to Him. God's judgment is pronounced against those who reject God, but Isaiah tells of eternal peace for those who humbly turn to God.*

Introducing the Prophet Focus
Guide a discussion about a scroll. Display the scroll. Ask the students whether anyone knows what it is. Explain that in Bible times God's Word was written on scrolls. They could be made of *parchment,* a material made of animal skins. Call on a student to unroll the scroll and read the reference and the verse. Write the reference for display. Discuss the verse.

▶ **Where in the Bible would you find this verse?** *(Old Testament)*

Direct students to open their Bibles to the contents page and locate the book of Isaiah.

Prophet Focus

Point to Isaiah on the TimeLine. Explain that today's account comes from the Bible book of Isaiah. Hold an open Bible as you tell the students the following:

- Isaiah was a prophet who lived about seven hundred years before Jesus Christ.
- He foretold the coming of the Messiah, Jesus Christ.
- He is known as the messianic prophet because he spoke and wrote so much about the person, work, and kingdom of the Messiah (the Lord Jesus Christ).
- The name *Isaiah* in the Hebrew language means "Jehovah has saved."

Read the following account to the students. Display Map 37, "Divided Kingdom," and point out Judah. Explain that Isaiah prophesied for many years in this land during the eighth century BC. Listening question: **What was the greatest danger facing the Jewish people?** *(It was their sin and disobedience to God. Elicit that this is also the greatest danger for believers today.)*

Isaiah

At the time Isaiah prophesied in Judah, the Assyrians were strong enemies of the Jews. Isaiah told the people, however, that their sin was a greater danger to them than the Assyrians.

Isaiah warned the people that they should trust Jehovah (God) and not earthly powers. He told King Ahaz (of Israel) to trust God and not heathen (unbelieving) princes, but Ahaz rejected the prophet's warning.

The Bible also tells us that God sent Isaiah to the king of Judah, King Hezekiah (2 Kings 20:1–11). God used Isaiah the prophet to tell Hezekiah that he (Hezekiah) was going to die. Hezekiah began to pray. Isaiah left the house but returned when God told him to go back. This time, God told Isaiah to tell Hezekiah that he would live for fifteen more years.

God used Isaiah to bring other good news to the people. He gave many prophecies to the people about Jesus the Messiah. The amazing thing was that Isaiah told facts about Jesus Christ *seven hundred years* before Christ was born. He told them that Jesus is God and that He would come to earth, minister in Galilee, suffer and die for our sins, and someday rule on earth.

Before Isaiah died, Jerusalem was delivered from Assyria, and the Assyrians didn't attack Jerusalem again. Isaiah was used by God to remind the people that God keeps His promises and that they should pray to Him, love Him, and obey Him.

⚜

▶ **What message did Isaiah give Ahaz?** *(He told him to trust God.)*

▶ **How did Ahaz and Hezekiah respond differently to Isaiah's message?** *(Ahaz rejected the warning; Hezekiah prayed.)*

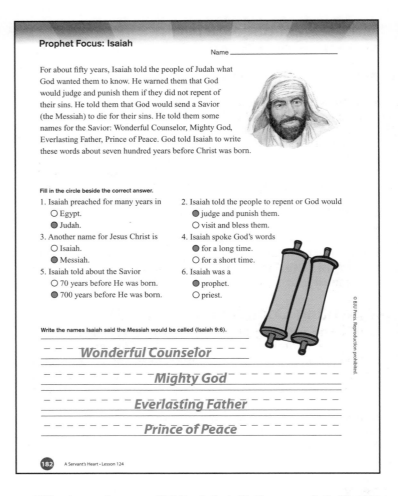

Prophet Focus: Isaiah

Name _____

For about fifty years, Isaiah told the people of Judah what God wanted them to know. He warned them that God would judge and punish them if they did not repent of their sins. He told them that God would send a Savior (the Messiah) to die for their sins. He told them some names for the Savior: Wonderful Counselor, Mighty God, Everlasting Father, Prince of Peace. God told Isaiah to write these words about seven hundred years before Christ was born.

Fill in the circle beside the correct answer.

1. Isaiah preached for many years in
   ○ Egypt.
   ● Judah.

2. Isaiah told the people to repent or God would
   ● judge and punish them.
   ○ visit and bless them.

3. Another name for Jesus Christ is
   ○ Isaiah.
   ● Messiah.

4. Isaiah spoke God's words
   ● for a long time.
   ○ for a short time.

5. Isaiah told about the Savior
   ○ 70 years before He was born.
   ● 700 years before He was born.

6. Isaiah was a
   ● prophet.
   ○ priest.

Write the names Isaiah said the Messiah would be called (Isaiah 9:6).

Wonderful Counselor

Mighty God

Everlasting Father

Prince of Peace

182   A Servant's Heart • Lesson 124

▶ **What good news did Isaiah tell the people?** *(He told them that Jesus would come to die for sinners, and His eternal kingdom would be one of peace. Isaiah spoke of God's love and forgiveness and God's desire for people to repent.)*

Guide a discussion about the message Isaiah proclaimed. Tell the students that the prophets always acknowledged that their words were from God. Read **Isaiah 9:6** aloud and write the following titles for display.
The Mighty God
The Everlasting Father
The Prince of Peace

Call on a volunteer to tell Who the Child mentioned is. *(Jesus Christ)*

Read **Isaiah 65:17, 25** aloud.

▶ **How does Isaiah describe the new heaven and new earth where the saved will live forever?** *(Elicit from the students that God says there will be peace when He reigns on the earth; even the lamb and the wolf will be side by side, and the wolf will not eat the lamb!)*

📝 Worktext page 182

Recall details. Review the events about the prophet Isaiah listed at the top of the page. Instruct the students to complete the page independently, referring to the information at the top of the page.

World History Connection (optional)

Discuss the Dead Sea Scrolls. Call on students to tell whether they have ever found something they would consider a treasure. Display Chart 35, "Christ's Birth," pointing to the Dead Sea. Explain to the students that in 1947, some men came upon a "treasure" in a cave near the Dead Sea while searching for a lost goat. A scroll of the Book of Isaiah, sealed in a jar, was found.

💡 **How old do you think this scroll was?** *(It was written two thousand years ago.)*

The scroll had seventeen sheets of parchment sewn together and was about twenty-four feet long. The writing on the scroll was ancient Hebrew. The scrolls that were discovered at that time, and ten more at a later date, contained parts of all the books of the Old Testament except Esther.

▶ Going Beyond

Reinforcement

Direct role-playing. Choose volunteers to represent Zacchaeus and the citizens of Jericho. Guide the students as they act out what happened after Zacchaeus saw Christ *(returning four times what he had taken and telling others what had happened to him).* Review the account as needed. If time permits, role-play it again, allowing other students to portray Zacchaeus and the citizens.

Enrichment

Materials
- Playdough for each student
- Two-inch length of plastic straw for each student
- Yellow construction paper for each student
- Transparent tape

Make model of an oil lamp. Tell the students that Nicodemus's meeting with Jesus at night may have been lighted by a Roman oil lamp. Explain that the oil was squeezed from olives and poured into a center hole in the lamp. A wick was put in the front hole, which was then lit to give light.

Draw a simple illustration (see below) for display or make a model for the students to follow as they make their own oil lamps out of playdough. Instruct the students to place the plastic straw (wick) at the front of their lamp, and attach the piece of yellow construction paper as the flame. *(Note:* You may reproduce the following art for use in this lesson.)

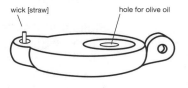

wick [straw]   hole for olive oil

construction paper flame

Jesus Is the King of Kings
Unit 9d

PREVIEW

Doctrines

- God will show His glory and receive glory (Revelation 4:11). [Lesson 125]
- Redeemed humans will live with God forever (Revelation 21:3). [Lesson 126]
- Earth will be filled with the knowledge of the Lord, but not all will be saved (Isaiah 2:3–4; Revelation 20:8–9). [Lesson 126]

Skills and Applications

- Learn Psalm 24:10
- Read a timeline
- Complete a picture
- Sequence the books in the Old Testament
- Sequence the books in the New Testament
- Recognize character development through speech and actions
- Use a glossary
- Describe aspects of the new earth
- Identify relevant information
- Apply Bible knowledge to everyday life

LESSON 125

Jesus, the Humble King

Materials

- Chart 27, "Jesus, the Humble King"
- Chart 41, "City of Jerusalem"
- Hymn: "Jesus Shall Reign"
- Unit 9 Bookmark for each student
- Highlighter for each student (optional)

♫ Hymn: "Jesus Shall Reign"

Teach the fourth verse (Worktext page 221). Point out that the word *realms* refers to kingdoms. Explain that the expression *infant voices* may refer to the voices of young Christians or small children.

▶ **What will all the people and kingdoms do?** *(sing about God's great love)*

▶ **What will the infant voices bless?** *(God's name)*

Background Information

The Donkey—*The donkey was commonly used for travel in Palestine. It was well suited to the steep, narrow, rocky roads.*

The View—*Jesus would have seen the temple as He rode into Jerusalem. He would have crossed the Xystus Bridge, 450 feet above the Kidron Valley, and entered through what is now known as the Golden Gate or East Gate.*

Introducing the Bible Account

Discuss ways of travel. Allow the students to share ways they or people they know have traveled.

▶ **How do important people travel today?** *(Answers will vary, but you may want to suggest that the president of the United States travels in a special jet called Air Force One. Some important or wealthy people sometimes travel in limousines.)*

Remind the students that in Bible times most people walked to get from one place to another. However, kings usually rode in wheeled vehicles. Explain that the following Bible

account tells about an important person who traveled in a different way.

Bible Account

Read Matthew 21:1–11 or use the following retelling of that passage. Listening question: **How did Jesus show His humility?** *(by riding a donkey)* Direct the students to look at Worktext page 183. Point out the route that Jesus took into Jerusalem on Chart 41, "City of Jerusalem," as you retell the events.

The Triumphal Entry

Jesus had been preaching and healing those who had been brought to Him. Now there was something He wanted two of His disciples to do for Him. He told them to go to a nearby village and find a donkey tied up. He told them to bring the donkey and her colt to Him. He also told His disciples that if anyone asked what they were doing with the animals they were to say that the Lord needed them.

The Bible tells us that all this was what the prophet Zechariah hundreds of years before had said would happen. Zechariah 9:9 says, "Rejoice greatly, O daughter of Zion; shout, O daughter of Jerusalem: behold, thy King cometh unto thee: he is just, and having salvation; lowly, and riding upon [a donkey]."

The disciples immediately went and did as Jesus had commanded. They brought the donkey to Jesus and put their robes on its back. Then Jesus got on the donkey. Jesus was the coming King; but He was the humble King and would ride into Jerusalem on a donkey. That's what Zechariah was talking about.

The crowds along the road were very excited. Some people threw their robes on the roadway while others cut down palm branches and spread them along the way to make a "carpet" for the King. People were running in front of and behind Christ as He rode toward Jerusalem. They cried out and praised God, saying, "Hosanna to the Son of David! Blessed is the One Who comes in the name of the Lord! Hosanna in the highest!"

Ask the students to praise God the way they think the people did that day. Tell them to shout, "Hosanna to the Son of David!" and "Hosanna in the highest!" Explain to the students that *hosanna* is a one-word prayer to God for help and was also a praise.

Jesus's ride into Jerusalem took Him through the Garden of Gethsemane, across the bridge over the Kidron Valley, and into the city through the Golden Gate. The people who were praising Him thought He was going to make Himself King of Israel at that time, but Jesus knew when the right time for that would be. First, He would die for the sins of His people and make a way to God possible for all of us. Christ is the King of Kings, but the people praising Him didn't know that He wouldn't take the throne and rule at that time. One week later, Christ was crucified.

Jesus, the Humble King
Matthew 21:1–11

There are several varieties of domesticated donkeys. The smaller, faster ones are used for riding. Larger, heavier ones are used to pull or carry loads. Donkeys have long ears and small feet. Their color varies from gray to almost black with darker hair on the back, mane, and tail.

There are more than 2,800 kinds of palm trees in the world. The date palm is the most common type found in Palestine. A crown of leaves grows out of a straight, branchless trunk. The fruit is good either fresh or dried.

Bethphage (where the disciples found the colt) was a small village on the Mount of Olives. It was close to Bethany on the way from Jericho to Jerusalem. No trace of it is left today.

A Servant's Heart • Lesson 125 **183**

- ▶ **What did Jesus ask His disciples to do?** *(to bring a donkey and its colt from a nearby village)*
- ▶ **What did the disciples do after they brought the donkey to Him?** *(They put their robes across the young donkey's back so Jesus could sit on them.)*
- ▶ **What did the people do as Jesus started toward Jerusalem?** *(They threw clothes and palm branches on the ground in front of Him.)*
- ▶ **How were the people acting?** *(They were very joyful and were shouting, "Hosanna in the highest!")*
- ▶ **What were the people thinking as Christ rode into Jerusalem?** *(They thought Jesus was going to set up a kingdom on earth right then that would free them from the Romans.)*
- 💡 **Were they correct?** *(No. Jesus didn't set up His earthly kingdom at that time, and He still hasn't. He first was crucified to take care of the world's sin problem, but He will come again to rule as King of the whole earth.)*

InfoScene: "Jesus, the Humble King"
Display Chart 27 from the Visual Packet for the students to refer to throughout this unit.

♥ Memory Verse—Psalm 24:10
Principle: The Lord Jesus Christ is the King of Glory. Direct the students to highlight the verse (optional) and mark the location with the Unit 9 Bookmark.

- ▶ **What question is asked in this verse?** *("Who is this King of glory?")*
- ▶ **How does the verse answer the question?** *("The Lord of hosts . . . is the King of glory.")* Explain that the term *host* means an army.
- **Who is this King?** *(Jesus, the Son of God, the Messiah)*

Explain the following key words.

Messiah is an Old Testament name for the promised Redeemer, the Christ. God chose to send Jesus to earth to suffer for our sins .

Selah may mean to pause, to stop and think about what was said.

Practice the verse.

English Connection, Worktext page 184
Guide the using of a glossary. Direct the students to locate *humble* in the glossary. Choose a volunteer to read the definition aloud *(not proud of oneself or boastful; meek or modest)*. Guide the students in completing the top of the page.

Worktext page 184
Identify relevant information. Read aloud the Bible account from the middle of the page. Instruct the students to find the information that will complete each sentence and to write the correct word in the star.

LESSON 126 Jesus Is Coming Again!

Materials
- Hymn: "Jesus Shall Reign"
- TimeLine and picture: John the Apostle
- Song booklets for each student from Lesson 114

Hymn: "Jesus Shall Reign"
Sing the third and fourth verses (Worktext page 221). You may utilize the students' song booklets. Discuss the pictures that go with the fourth verse.
- Faces of different people—people of different ages and nationalities; Jesus came to die for all people even though not all people will receive Him.
- Heart with cross—dwelling (thinking) on His love; Jesus Christ is worthy of our worship.
- Children singing—ways that we bless His name (sing, praise, pray, write poetry and songs, etc.)

Background Information
(Note: This curriculum presents the premillennial, pretribulational position. You may modify the lesson if you choose to teach a differing interpretation of Scripture.)

The Rapture—*The Rapture is Christ's return for the believer. Although we don't know when it will be, God says to be ready all the time. In* **1 Thessalonians 4:16–18**, *Christ tells us that He will "descend from heaven with a shout, with the voice of the archangel, and with the trump of God." The bodies of saved people who have died will rise from their graves and meet the Lord in the air. Then Christians who are alive will go up to meet the Lord.*

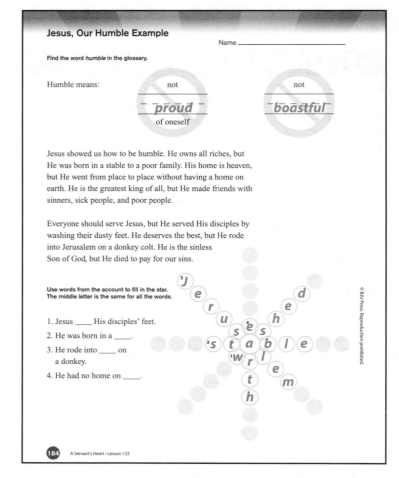

The Judgment Seat of Christ—*This judgment will take place in heaven and will include only saved people, those who have accepted Christ's payment for their sins by the shedding of His blood on the cross. Their faithfulness in serving God will be reviewed and they will be rewarded accordingly.*

The Tribulation—*Christians will not go through the Tribulation. This is the seven-year period following the Rapture. It will be a time of great trouble on earth. During the second half of this period, the Antichrist, who will claim to be God, will command everyone to worship him. God's chosen people, the Jews, will be greatly persecuted. Many will believe on Christ during the Tribulation. They will be called "tribulation saints."*

The Second Coming—*At the end of the Tribulation, the war of Armageddon will take place. As the nations gather to fight against Israel, Christ will return—coming in glory. The wicked armies will all turn against Him. He will bind Satan and cast him and the Antichrist into the lake of fire.*

The Millennium—*Christ will usher in the Millennium with His coming in glory (***Matthew 16, 24–25; Mark 8; Luke 17; Luke 21; John 14***). Jesus Christ will reign on earth for one thousand years of peace. At the end of the Millennium, Satan will be let loose for a short time and will organize a rebellion against Christ and the saved. God will send fire down to destroy all those who follow Satan. Satan will be defeated and cast into the lake of fire forever. God will create a new heaven and a new earth (***Revelation 21***). The new earth will be fresh, beautiful, perfect, and peaceful.*

The Great White Throne Judgment—*After the Millennium, the Lamb's Book of Life will be opened. Because unbelievers (those who have not trusted Christ as their Savior) will not have their names recorded in it, they will be judged for their sin and punished eternally in the lake of fire. There they will be separated from God forever to experience the second death (**Revelation 20**).*

Introducing the Bible Account

Discuss the background information. Discuss some of the background information with the students, as desired. Emphasize that while waiting for Christ's return, a Christian should be working each day for Him. God commands us to tell others the message of salvation (**Matthew 28:18–20; Acts 1:8**).

Bible Account

Read Revelation 20–22 or use the following retelling of that passage. Listening question: **What will it be like when Jesus reigns on earth?** *(Accept any answer, but be sure the students mention that there will be peace on the earth and that it will be a time of increased happiness and joy.)*

The Second Coming

The apostle John was very old. He was a prisoner on the island of Patmos. While he was there, he had an amazing vision. He saw and heard many unusual things that were going to happen. Jesus told John to write everything down. We have what John wrote in the book of Revelation.

John wrote that Jesus will rule on the earth during a future time known as the Millennium. The Lord Jesus will rule all the people in every nation for one thousand years. This is the time that Jesus will take His throne on earth as the King of Kings and Lord of Lords. In his vision John saw Christians sitting on thrones, reigning over and judging the nations with Jesus. These were people who had given their lives for Christ.

John tells us that Satan will be bound in a pit for the thousand years while Christ is ruling. The prophets say the whole earth will be beautiful and peaceful. Wild animals will be tame and gentle. It will be a time of increased joy and happiness.

At the end of the thousand years, Satan will be set free from the pit and will try one more time to attack Jerusalem. However, Christ will utterly defeat Satan and throw him and his angels into the lake of fire forever!

Then the Book of Life will be opened. Those whose names aren't found written there will also be thrown into the lake of fire. They will be separated from God forever.

Next, John saw a new heaven and a new earth. He saw the city of God, the new Jerusalem, coming down from heaven. Those who have their names written in the Lamb's Book of Life will live there. There will be no more tears, no more death, no more pain, sorrow, or crying there. This city was more beautiful than anything John had ever seen. There will be no need for the sun, the moon, or the stars in the city because God is light.

John described a beautiful river flowing through the city and a tree of life growing along its banks. The leaves of the tree will be for the healing of the nations.

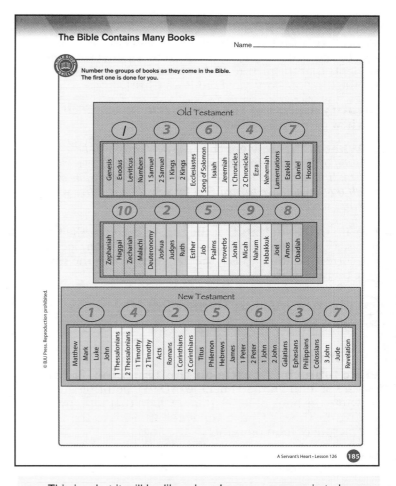

The Bible Contains Many Books

Name _____

Number the groups of books as they come in the Bible. The first one is done for you.

A Servant's Heart • Lesson 126   185

This is what it will be like when Jesus comes again to be the king of the whole earth. Jesus Christ, the Messiah, will be worshiped (**Philippians 2:9–11**). Believers will reign and live with Jesus in perfect harmony and happiness forever.

▶ **Whom did Jesus appear to on the island of Patmos?** *(John)*

▶ **Why was John there?** *(He was a prisoner.)*

▶ **How do we know what John saw?** *(John wrote it down. This account is in the book of Revelation.)*

▶ **Who does John say will rule on earth someday?** *(Christ and Christians)*

▶ **Why will there not be any need for the sun, moon, or stars?** *(God is the light.)*

 What do you think will be the best part of the new heaven and the new earth? *(Answers may vary. Lead the student to understand that being with Christ for all eternity will be the best part.)*

Bible Study Skills, Worktext page 185

Sequence the books of the Old and New Testaments. Lead the students in saying the names of the Old Testament books in order. Instruct them to number the Old Testament books at the top of the page in the correct order. Repeat the procedure with the New Testament books.

⟨✎⟩ Worktext page 186

Complete a picture. Direct the students to count by 2s and connect the dots to form a picture. Discuss with the students that the picture of the throne represents the throne for the King of Glory, the Lord Jesus Christ.

Identify aspects of the new earth. Review briefly what the new earth will be like.

▶ **What is the new earth?** *(The new earth will be a new creation of God after the millennium period. It will be a glorious, beautiful, and peaceful place beyond our imagination, where all those who have trusted God for salvation will live with Him, serving and worshipping Him forever.)*

Explain to the students that they are to cut apart the list of items at the bottom of the page and to place each one under the correct heading. Check their answers before the students glue them in place.

♥ Memory Verse Psalm 24:10

Practice the memory verse.

⟨🕐⟩ TimeLine

Place John the Apostle on the TimeLine. Place the picture of John on the TimeLine (AD 95), pointing out that he wrote the book of Revelation. Explain that John lived during the time of Christ. Guide the students as they glue the picture of John onto their TimeLines.

Review events on the TimeLine. Point to the following symbols on the TimeLine and discuss God's plan.

Creation—God created a perfect world. Adam and Eve sinned. All people choose to sin today. The punishment for sin is death in the lake of fire and separation from God.

The Crucifixion—God sent Jesus to take the guilt and punishment for everybody's sin.

Present Day—Direct attention to the date in the Present Day box. Read **Matthew 24:36** aloud. Ask the students when Christ will come again. *(No one knows.)* Jesus Christ may come now or at any time in the future. The saved will live eternally with Him on the new earth.

LESSON 127 Press On!

Materials
- Hymn: "Jesus Shall Reign"
- Song booklets for each student from Lesson 114
- Different types of printed or written invitations (optional)

⟨♪⟩ Hymn: "Jesus Shall Reign"

Sing all the verses (Worktext page 221). Utilize the song booklets.

♥ Memory Verse—Psalm 24:10

Practice the memory verse.

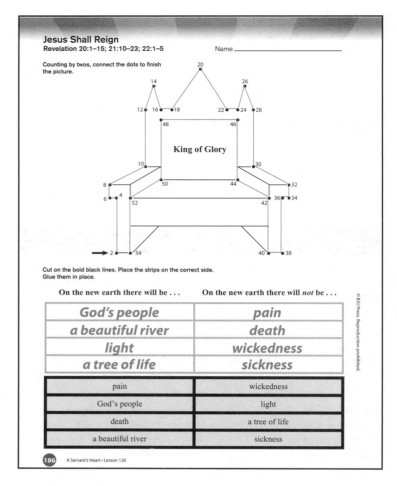

Introducing the Application Story

Discuss invitations. Show the students different types of invitations (optional).

💡 **What kinds of invitations have you or a family member received?** *(Answers may include birthday, wedding, shower, or graduation.)*

💡 **Have you ever been invited somewhere but were unable to attend?** *(Any answer is acceptable.)*

Application Story

Read or tell the following story. Listening question: **Where is the man in the story invited to go?** *(to live in the king's palace)*

An Invitation

Once there was a poor man, a peasant, who lived in a hut. One day a messenger in beautiful clothing knocked at his door. "Good day! I bring good tidings from the king himself. The king commands that you come to his palace and live with him. You may eat at his table for the rest of your life."

The poor man wanted to leave his hut, but he hesitated. "Good sir, how am I to know the way to the king's palace? I have heard it is far away and that there are many dangers to encounter."

"Fear not, peasant. Here is a map drawn by the king himself. It shows all the dangers and how to overcome them. If you follow the instructions here, you will safely arrive at the palace."

The peasant eagerly took the map and thanked the messenger. As he read the map, he saw that it told about the huge, beautiful palace. Its halls and floors were made of pure gold, and its twelve gates were made of pearls. There was a beautiful river flowing from the king's throne.

As the peasant began his journey on the first day, he found that everything was just as the map said. On the second day he met an old man who warned him not to go on. He told the peasant that it was very dangerous and that he should turn back. The peasant glanced at his map. For one second he didn't know what to do. Then he said, "No, I would be a coward to turn back. I want to be with my king. I will follow the instructions on the map and continue."

As the days passed, he met others who warned him to stop and go back. One of them was a man riding a beautiful horse. He too told the peasant to turn back because he had seen fierce lions and the bones of many travelers. This was a little more frightening to the peasant than what he had heard the day before. He sat down by the side of the road to see what his map said. It told him not to be afraid. It said to keep going down the middle of the path, not to turn to the left or to the right. These were the king's words. He would go on.

It seemed that every day he met other travelers. However, some seemed to not care about reaching the king's palace. Some of them even discouraged him by telling him to slow down. He also discovered that there were some who only pretended to be travelers but really were not headed to the palace. Despite facing these discouragements along with the regular sicknesses and troubles of life, the peasant continued on.

Right up to the very end, he met with discouragement. One traveler warned him about more lions, told him not to pay attention to the words on the map, and urged him to turn back. However, the peasant was determined to go on. He told the traveler, "I am on my journey to the king's palace by special invitation, and I won't let those dangers hinder me because I have the king's own promise that I will arrive there safely!" And so he continued.

As he rounded a bend, he saw the ferocious lions. They had a frightening roar! He was so scared he could hardly move, but he fastened his eyes on the map, kept to the middle of the path, and read the king's promises very loudly. Very soon, he was past them and out into a wider part of the road where he was safe.

The peasant was praising the king. He knew that the king had protected him and that the map that he had was better than all the advice of the wisest men in the world. He began to run, and soon he saw the king's palace. It was shining like the sun in all its glory, with servants going in and out singing praises to the king. The peasant was welcomed by the king himself. "Come in, come in! I am pleased that you believed what I told you. Your place at my table is set and your room prepared. Welcome home!"

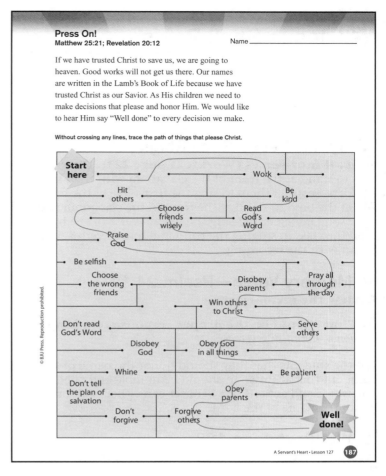

▶ **What was the peasant's goal?** *(to reach the king's palace)*

▶ **How many times was the peasant warned to turn back because there was danger?** *(many times right up to the end)*

💡 **Why did the peasant keep going?** *(He reread the instructions on the map. He believed the king's promises. He wanted to be with his king.)*

▶ **Read Psalm 17:4. What is the Christian's "map"?** *("the word of thy lips"; God's words; the Bible)*

▶ **What was the peasant's reward?** *(He would live in the palace and eat at the king's table.)*

💡 **What should be the goal for a Christian?** *(to do God's will and to live for Him)*

💡 **What will Satan use to try to keep a Christian from that goal?** *(Many answers are acceptable and may include discouragement as well as Satan's attempts to prevent a Christian from reading God's Word, praying, going to church, and telling the truth.)*

💡 **How can a Christian reach God's goal?** *(read and obey God's Word, pray, and trust God)*

✎ **Worktext page 187**

Apply Bible knowledge to everyday life. Read the paragraph at the top of the page to the students. Instruct them to trace the path showing correct choices for living as a Christian should.

Jesus Shall Reign

Materials

- Hymn: "Jesus Shall Reign"
- Copy of page A98 ("Jesus Shall Reign") for each student
- Song booklets for each student from Lesson 114

🎵 Hymn: "Jesus Shall Reign"

Sing all four verses (Worktext page 221). Direct the girls to stand at the front of the classroom with their song booklets. Instruct them to sing the first verse of the hymn. Direct the boys to stand at the front of the classroom with their song booklets and sing the second verse of the hymn. Lead the class in singing the third and fourth verses of the hymn with the recording.

♥ Memory Verse—Psalm 24:10

Review the memory verse.

💡 **What should be the proper response to a king?**
(honor, humility, reverence)

Tell the students that they should honor the name of Jesus. Point out that a Christian should be humble and obedient. The words and actions of a believer can either exalt or dishonor the name of the Lord.

✎ Worktext page 188

Identify relevant information. Remind the students that they have learned about many kings in the Bible. Some kings were good and served God; others were wicked and did not serve God. Instruct the students to find and read the Bible verses given with each description of a king. Tell them to write the correct letter next to each king's description. Direct them to answer the question at the bottom of the page. Discuss with the students who the King of Kings is.

✏ Writing Connection

Guide a writing activity. Distribute copies of page A98 ("Jesus Shall Reign") and direct the students to find **Luke 1:32–33** in their Bibles. Read the verses together. Read the directions at the top of the Activity Page. Encourage the students to think about the words to the hymn before they begin writing. Display some of the students' papers on the crown shapes on the Unit 9 bulletin board.

King of Kings and Lord of Lords
Revelation 19:16   Name _____

God's Word tells about many kings. Some were good and served God; others were wicked and did not serve God. None is greater than the Lord Jesus Christ.

Match the sentence with the king by putting the letter in the correct space. The verses will help you.

___C___ This king was much taller than any of his people (1 Samuel 10:21–23).

___D___ This king was great, and the Lord of hosts was with him (2 Samuel 5:10).

___A___ This king gave a feast that lasted 180 days (Esther 1:1–4).

___E___ This king made a tall image of gold for all to worship (Daniel 3:1).

___B___ This king told the wise men he wanted to worship Jesus (Matthew 2:7–8).

A. Ahasuerus (Xerxes)
B. Herod
C. Saul
D. David
E. Nebuchadnezzar

Who is the King of Kings and Lord of Lords?

_ _ _ _ _ _ _ _ _ _ _ _ _ _ _ _ _ _ _ _
Jesus Christ
_ _ _ _ _ _ _ _ _ _ _ _ _ _ _ _ _ _ _ _

188 A Servant's Heart • Lesson 128

© BJU Press. Reproduction prohibited.

▶ Going Beyond

Reinforcement

Materials

- Two tape measures (or string)
- Medium-sized basket
- Small pieces of paper to place in the basket: On these slips write several examples of things that God's Word tells us to do (pray, read your Bible, give, go to church, tell others about Jesus, etc.) and sins that Satan tempts us with (steal a pencil, hit your brother, cheat on a test, etc.).

Direct a growing game. Choose two groups of five students to stand at the front of the classroom in two lines. Give the leader of each group a tape measure or string. Allow the leaders to choose a piece of paper. Read the words aloud, and direct the students to say whether God tells us to do this or whether Satan tempts us with this sin. They may pass the end of the tape measure to the person behind them only if it is something God tells us to do. Continue with alternating teams until the tape measure is extended to the last person on one of the teams.

Enrichment

Materials

- Questions about the Bible accounts, the hymn, and the memory verse on 3" × 5" cards: If you are using teams, you may want to write these on two different colors of cards. Use questions such as the following.

▸ **I rode into Jerusalem on a donkey. Who am I?**

▸ **You will find the memory verse in this book of the Bible. What's the answer?**

▸ **The princes pay Christ homage. What does *homage* mean?**

Play "What's the answer?" You may record individual points or team points. To record team points, assign each team a color before mixing the cards. Read the questions yourself or allow the students to do so.

Unit Review

Materials

- Copy of page A64 ("Unit 9 Review") for each student

Guide a review of Unit 9. Review the people and events in preparation for the Unit 9 Test (optional).

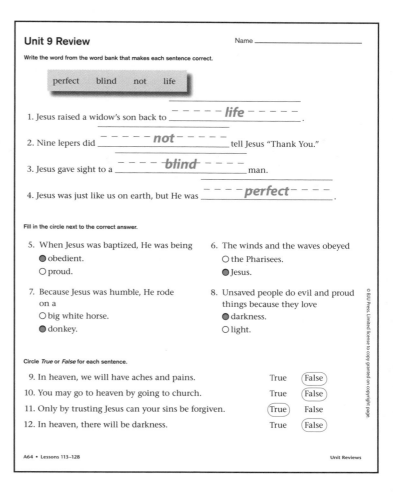

Unit 9 Review　　　　Name _____

Write the word from the word bank that makes each sentence correct.

| perfect | blind | not | life |

1. Jesus raised a widow's son back to _____ *life* _____ .

2. Nine lepers did _____ *not* _____ tell Jesus "Thank You."

3. Jesus gave sight to a _____ *blind* _____ man.

4. Jesus was just like us on earth, but He was _____ *perfect* _____ .

Fill in the circle next to the correct answer.

5. When Jesus was baptized, He was being
   ● obedient.
   ○ proud.

6. The winds and the waves obeyed
   ○ the Pharisees.
   ● Jesus.

7. Because Jesus was humble, He rode on a
   ○ big white horse.
   ● donkey.

8. Unsaved people do evil and proud things because they love
   ● darkness.
   ○ light.

Circle *True* or *False* for each sentence.

9. In heaven, we will have aches and pains.　　True　(False)

10. You may go to heaven by going to church.　　True　(False)

11. Only by trusting Jesus can your sins be forgiven.　　(True)　False

12. In heaven, there will be darkness.　　True　(False)

A64 • Lessons 113–128　　　　　　　　　　Unit Reviews

10

A Generous Heart

OVERVIEW

Preparing the Teacher

Read **John 15:1–7**. Unit 10 introduces students to the twelve disciples and how they served Christ. The students will learn that all believers are to be disciples. Consider God's power available to you as you disciple the students in your classroom. Pray that He will guide your discipling of them so that they will be spiritually fruitful.

Preparing the Materials

129—Unit 10 bookmark [E]

129-44—Copy of the application novel *Pelts and Promises* by Nancy Lohr

130—Piece of drawing paper [E]; American flag (or a picture of one)

131—Animal pelt [O]

135—Piece of drawing paper [E]

Unit 10b Going Beyond—Red construction-paper heart [E]; two white 8½" × 11" sheets of paper [E]; piece of drawing paper, black felt-tip pen, cotton balls, newspaper, cooking oil, and crayons [E]

137—Verse visuals: one piece each of red and yellow poster board or construction paper

Unit 10c Going Beyond—Pictures, photographs, or items to represent the following: money, house, food, shoes, Bible, and toys

141—Map of the United States [O]

142—Toy snake [O]

144—Copy of pages A65–66 ("Unit 10 Review") [E]

Unit 10d Going Beyond—Mural paper; crayons or felt-tip markers; fabric scraps, plastic wrap, crepe paper [O]; boat marker for each team

Unit 10 A Generous Heart

Theme, Memory Verse, and Principle	Lesson Number	TE Page	Worktext Page(s)	Appendix Page(s)	Lesson Title	Scripture or Focus
Unit 10a **I Give Myself to God** Mark 1:17 *Jesus wants to make believers "fishers of men."*	129	282	189–90		John the Baptist	Matthew 11:7–13; 14:3–12
	130	284	191–92		The Disciples Leave All	Mark 1:16–20; 2:13–17; 3:13–19; John 1:43–48
	131	286	193, 256		Beginning and Ending	Application Novel
	132	287	194, 257		Following Jesus	Application Novel
Unit 10b **God Gives to Me** John 14:2b–3 *Jesus is preparing a home for believers.*	133	289	195		Five Thousand Fed	Matthew 14:13–21
	134	291	196		Jesus Promises an Eternal Home	John 13:31–14:6
	135	292	197, 258		Heaven	Application Novel
	136	294	198, 259		Find It Quickly	Application Novel
Unit 10c **I Give My Possessions to God** 2 Corinthians 9:7 *We should give to God joyfully.*	137	296	199–200		The Widow Loves from Little	Mark 12:41–44
	138	298	201–2		Mary Loves from Much	Mark 14:3–9
	139	300	203, 260		Honoring Jesus	Application Novel
	140	301	204, 261		Giving	Application Novel
Unit 10d **I Give Myself to Others** Proverbs 20:11 *Children are known by their deeds.*	141	303	205–6		Dorcas: Doer of Good Deeds	Acts 9:36–43
	142	305	207–8		Paul, the Missionary	Acts 27:1–28:6
	143	307	209, 262		Followers of Jesus	Application Novel
	144	308	210, 263	A65–66	Where Is It?	Application Novel

Connections	Bible Doctrines	Skills/Applications
L130—World History	**The Doctrine of the Bible** *Inspiration* The Holy Spirit worked in the hearts and lives of the writers of the Bible (2 Peter 1:20–21). **The Doctrine of God** *Attributes of God* God is all-powerful (omnipotent) (Matt. 19:26). God is merciful (Ps. 86:15). God is love (1 John 4:8). *Nature of God* The Father, Son, and Spirit are recognized as God (Matt. 28:19). **The Doctrine of Man** *Redemption of Man* Man is a new creation (2 Cor. 5:17). *Final State of Man* Redeemed man will live on the new earth (Rev. 21:3). **The Doctrine of Salvation** *Elements of Salvation* God imparts to the believer spiritual life and a new nature (Eph. 2:4–5; 4:24). **The Doctrine of the Church** *Functions of the Local Church* Oppose sin (Eph. 5:11). Contribute financially (Rom. 15:26). Exhort one another (Heb. 10:25). **The Doctrine of the End Times** *The Tribulation* The giving of rewards to Christians will take place (1 Cor. 3:12–15).	**Foundational** • Realize that Jesus is preparing a home for Christians in heaven • Recognize behavior that honors Jesus **Practical** • Identify parts of a verse • Infer cause and effect • Locate information in a verse • Draw conclusions • Recall facts and details • Interpret pictures • Sequence events • Identify the location of a book in the Bible • Identify characters through dialogue and actions • Follow directions • Read a map **Personal** • Realize that Jesus wants Christians to be "fishers of men" • Understand that we are known by our actions • Understand and apply Bible knowledge to everyday life
L141—Geography		

I Give Myself to God
Unit 10a

PREVIEW

Doctrines

- Oppose sin (Ephesians 5:11). [Lesson 129]
- The giving of rewards to Christians will take place (1 Corinthians 3:12–15). [Lesson 129]
- Redeemed man is a new creation (2 Corinthians 5:17). [Lesson 130]

Skills and Applications

- Learn Mark 1:17
- Identify parts of a verse
- Interpret pictures
- Draw conclusions
- Recall facts and details
- Locate information in a verse
- Realize that Jesus wants all Christians to be "fishers of men"
- Apply Bible knowledge to everyday life

LESSON 129 John the Baptist

Materials

- Chart 39, "Christ's Ministry"
- Hymn: "Living for Jesus"
- Unit 10 Bookmark for each student
- Highlighter for each student (optional)

Memory Verse—Mark 1:17

Principle: Jesus wants to make believers "fishers of men." Explain that Jesus spoke these words to Simon and Andrew when He called them to follow Him.

💡 **What did Jesus mean when He said He would make them "fishers of men"?** (*He would teach them to explain the gospel so that the people would trust Jesus as the Son of God, the Savior.*)

💡 **How are Christians to be "fishers of men"?** (*They are to learn about Jesus and tell others about Him.*)

Direct the students to highlight the verse (optional) and mark the location with the Unit 10 Bookmark. Practice the verse.

Background Information

Herodias's Sin—*Herodias married two of her uncles: Herod Philip I and Herod Antipas. They were both sons of Herod the Great and brothers of her father. Herodias wanted John dead because he condemned her marriages. Salome, Herodias's daughter, danced before her stepfather, Antipas, and she was rewarded with John the Baptist's head.*

Introducing the Bible Account

Guide a discussion about John the Baptist. Call on students to tell what they remember about John the Baptist. (*Answers may vary. Elicit that he preached in a desert region where few people lived, he told men to repent and be baptized, and he lived in the same time period Jesus did.*) Explain that some people thought that Elijah had come back to life in the person of John.

Use a map to introduce the account. Display Chart 39, "Christ's Ministry." Point to the region west of the Dead Sea. Tell the students that John the Baptist preached outside the cities and baptized in the Jordan River. Thus, he is called "the voice of one crying in the wilderness." When Jesus came to be baptized by John, John replied that he could baptize only with water, not with the Holy Spirit.

Bible Account

Read **Matthew 11:7–13** and **14:3–12** or use the following retelling of those passages. Listening question: **Who did Jesus say was the greatest man born in all the world?** *(John the Baptist)*

John the Baptist

Even after Jesus began His ministry, John the Baptist continued to preach to people. John wasn't afraid to tell even King Herod about the king's sin. Herod knew that God wasn't pleased with him for marrying Herodias. John told the king to repent (turn from his sin). Herod didn't like what John said, so he had John put into prison. Herod would have had John killed, but he was afraid because some of the people thought John was a prophet.

Herod's wife, Herodias, was also angry with John the Baptist. She wanted him dead. Herodias had her daughter, Salome, visit King Herod on his birthday. King Herod enjoyed Salome's dancing so much that he told her she could have anything that she wanted. Herodias had already told her what to ask for—the head of John the Baptist.

The king was distressed, but he had to give Salome what she asked for because he had promised. He had John the Baptist killed and gave John's head to Salome.

Some of John's disciples buried his body. John the Baptist was the greatest of the Old Testament prophets. He had the privilege of introducing the prophesied and long-awaited Savior of the world.

When Jesus heard of John's death, He crossed the Sea of Galilee to be alone.

▶ **Why did Herod put John the Baptist into prison?** *(John had said Herod was sinning.)*

▶ **What did Herodias, the queen, do to get rid of John the Baptist?** *(She had her daughter ask for the head of John the Baptist.)*

▶ **Did Herodias get rid of John the Baptist?** *(yes)* Point out that John the Baptist was willing to preach the gospel even though some people hated him.

▶ **Who was sad because of John's death?** *(John's disciples and Jesus)*

John the Baptist Gave His Life to God
Matthew 3:1–17; 11:7–13; 14:3–13   Name _____

Color the circle under *TRUE* if the sentence is true. Color the circle under *FALSE* if the sentence is false.

		TRUE	FALSE
1.	John told people to be baptized and then to repent of their sins.	○	●
2.	Some people thought John was Elijah who had come back to life.	●	○
3.	John said that he could baptize with the Holy Spirit of God.	○	●
4.	John asked Jesus if he could baptize Him.	○	●
5.	Herod had John put into prison for saying Herod was wrong to marry his brother's wife.	●	○
6.	The daughter of Herodias asked to have John's head.	●	○
7.	Jesus was glad to hear that John had been killed.	○	●
8.	Jesus said that John was the greatest man born.	●	○

© BJU Press. Reproduction prohibited.

Riddle: John the Baptist liked to eat
Something not sugar, but just as sweet.

To find the answer, mark out every other letter beginning with the first.

honey

A Servant's Heart · Lesson 129   189

🔊 Worktext page 189

Recall facts and details. Instruct the students to read each sentence, decide whether it is true or false, then color as indicated. Choose a volunteer to read the riddle at the bottom of the page. Read the directions and allow the students to complete the riddle independently.

🎵 Hymn: "Living for Jesus"

Teach the first verse (Worktext pages 222–23). Explain that as the students sing this verse, they are saying they want to live their lives for Jesus as true Christians should, trying to please Jesus. Explain that God will bless Christians who take the right path and yield joyfully to Him.

▶ **What names are given for Jesus?** *(Lord and Savior; Master; Christ)*

Point out that these names remind us that Jesus died for us. Explain that Christians should allow God to rule in their hearts and should live only for Christ. Sing the verse several times.

The Disciples Leave All
Mark 1:16–18

Name _____

Add the vowels to make the correct word.

1. Jesus tells us to **follow** Him.

2. What does this mean?

_____
Answers will vary but should include to do
_____
what Jesus says and to be like Him.
_____

3. Jesus tells us that He will make us

fishers of men

4. What does this mean?

_____
Answers will vary but should include
_____
telling others about Him.
_____

190   A Servant's Heart • Lesson 129

© BJU Press. Reproduction prohibited.

Worktext page 190

Locate information in a verse. Direct the students to open their Bibles to **Mark 1:16–18.** Read the verses together and discuss what it means to follow Jesus. *(to listen and obey what He says, to be like Jesus in attitudes and in actions)*

▶ **What was the occupation (job) that Simon and Andrew left?** *(fishing)*

Point out that before this the disciples had sought fish to catch, but now they would be looking for people to declare the gospel to. Their work now would be to learn about God through Jesus and then to go tell others about Him. Allow the students to complete the page independently.

LESSON 130 The Disciples Leave All

Materials
- Chart 28, "Jesus Chooses His Disciples"
- Hymn: "Living for Jesus"
- Piece of drawing paper for each student
- An American flag (or a picture of one)

🎵 Hymn: "Living for Jesus"
Sing the first verse (Worktext pages 222–23). Utilize the recording as necessary throughout the unit. Review the meaning of the first verse of the hymn.

💡 **Name something we pledge allegiance to.** *(the flag)*
💡 **What does *allegiance* mean?** *(loyalty, devoted attachment, and love to someone or something)*

Point out that Christians serve God because they love Him.

🌐 History Connection (optional)
Explain the meaning of the American flag. Display the flag (or a picture). Discuss the following representations:
the color red—*valor*
the color white—*purity*
the color blue—*justice*
fifty stars—*the fifty states*
thirteen stripes—*the thirteen original colonies*

Background Information
Fishing Business—*Some of Jesus's disciples were in the fishing business. Bethsaida, Peter's hometown, means "house of fish." Fish were sold fresh or dried. Much of the fishing was done with a "cast net," a net that was thrown from a boat into the water and then pulled to shore with fish in it.*

Jesus's Galilean Ministry—*Early in His ministry, Jesus moved from Nazareth to Capernaum because people in His hometown would not receive Him. Except for trips to Judea to attend the Passover feasts in Jerusalem, Jesus ministered in this small area of northern Palestine called Galilee.*

Introducing the Bible Account
Use the background information to introduce the account. Display Chart 39, "Christ's Ministry." Point out Bethsaida and then Capernaum as you share the background information.

Bible Account

Read Mark 1:16–20, 2:13–17, 3:13–19, and John 1:43–48 or use the following retelling of those passages. Direct the students to look at Worktext page 191. Listening question: **What was the name of Philip's friend?** *(Nathanael)*

The Disciples Leave All

After John the Baptist was put into prison, Jesus began His public ministry of preaching. He came into Galilee preaching the kingdom of God. His message was that the kingdom of God was at hand. He urged the people to repent and believe in the gospel, "the good news."

As Jesus walked along the shore of the Sea of Galilee, He saw some men fishing from a boat with a net. The men would throw the net in the water and let it sink to the bottom. When they pulled it back up, it would have fish in it. Jesus said to these men, two brothers named Simon and Andrew, "Follow Me, and I will make you fishers of men." These men already knew what Jesus was doing and had already accepted Him as the Messiah. They were ready to follow Him as disciples.

As soon as they heard these words, the brothers brought their fishing boat to shore, left their nets to follow Jesus, and began learning from Him.

Jesus Chooses His Disciples

Mark 3:13–19

Philip

James, son of Alphaeus

Andrew

John

Simon

Thomas

Matthew

Peter

Judas (Thaddaeus)

Nathanael (Bartholomew)

Judas Iscariot

James

© BJU Press. Reproduction prohibited.

A Servant's Heart • Lesson 130 **191**

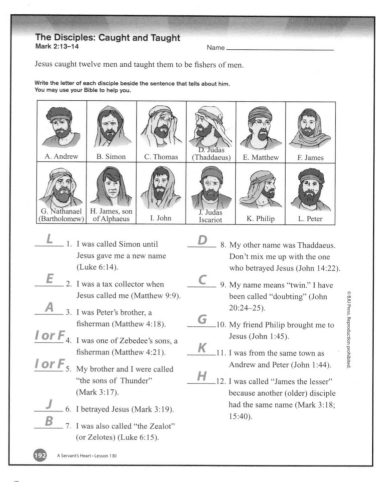

The Disciples: Caught and Taught
Mark 2:13–14   Name _____

Jesus caught twelve men and taught them to be fishers of men.

Write the letter of each disciple beside the sentence that tells about him.
You may use your Bible to help you.

A. Andrew	B. Simon	C. Thomas	D. Judas (Thaddaeus)	E. Matthew	F. James
G. Nathanael (Bartholomew)	H. James, son of Alphaeus	I. John	J. Judas Iscariot	K. Philip	L. Peter

L 1. I was called Simon until Jesus gave me a new name (Luke 6:14).

E 2. I was a tax collector when Jesus called me (Matthew 9:9).

A 3. I was Peter's brother, a fisherman (Matthew 4:18).

I or F 4. I was one of Zebedee's sons, a fisherman (Matthew 4:21).

I or F 5. My brother and I were called "the sons of Thunder" (Mark 3:17).

J 6. I betrayed Jesus (Mark 3:19).

B 7. I was also called "the Zealot" (or Zelotes) (Luke 6:15).

D 8. My other name was Thaddaeus. Don't mix me up with the one who betrayed Jesus (John 14:22).

C 9. My name means "twin." I have been called "doubting" (John 20:24–25).

G 10. My friend Philip brought me to Jesus (John 1:45).

K 11. I was from the same town as Andrew and Peter (John 1:44).

H 12. I was called "James the lesser" because another (older) disciple had the same name (Mark 3:18; 15:40).

© BJU Press. Reproduction prohibited.

192 A Servant's Heart • Lesson 130

As Jesus, Andrew, and Simon (later called Peter) continued to walk along the shore of the lake, they came to two other brothers. These men were mending their fishing nets with their father, Zebedee. James and John also knew Jesus. They too had accepted Him as the Messiah. When Jesus called them, they left their nets and their father's business and followed Jesus Christ. They, too, became fishers of men. The four men walked with Jesus into the town of Capernaum.

One day, some time later, after Jesus had healed a man who was paralyzed, He was back at the lakeside, teaching His disciples and the people who were following Him. There, Levi sat by a tent and waited for caravans to come by so that he could collect their tax money. When Jesus said, "Follow me," Levi (later called Matthew) got up, left his tax-collecting job, and went with Jesus.

Jesus now had five followers. Later, Jesus met and called Philip, who was from the town of Bethsaida, where Andrew and Peter also lived. Philip then went to Nathanael (Bartholomew) and said, "We have found him . . . Jesus of Nazareth." When Nathanael saw Jesus, he too believed Jesus to be the Messiah and wanted to follow Him. Philip and Nathanael became the sixth and seventh disciples.

The rest of the twelve disciples were Thomas, James of Alphaeus, Thaddaeus (later called Judas, not Iscariot), Simon the Canaanite (Simon the Zealot), and Judas Iscariot.

💡 **How much time did Simon, Andrew, James, John, and Levi take to decide to follow Jesus?** *(None; they followed Him immediately.)*

▶ **Andrew's brother had his name changed. His name was Simon; what did the Lord change it to?** *(Peter)*

▶ **What was Levi's name changed to?** *(Matthew)*

💡 **Do you think Jesus had more followers than just the twelve named in this account?** *(Any answer is acceptable, but explain that Luke 10:1 indicates that Jesus had at least seventy other disciples. He chose the twelve to be His apostles.)*

💡 **What do you think would have been best about following Jesus?** *(Any answer is acceptable.)*

💡 **What do you think these men missed when they followed Jesus?** *(Any answer is acceptable, but suggest that they missed family, friends, jobs, and their homes. **Luke 14:26** emphasizes that love for Jesus Christ must surpass love for anybody or anything else. Because of this, they were willing to do whatever the Lord asked.)*

InfoScene: "Jesus Chooses His Disciples"
Display Chart 28 from the Visual Packet for the students to refer to throughout this unit.

💗 **Memory Verse—Mark 1:17**
Practice the verse.

🔖 Worktext page 192

Recall the names of the disciples. Explain to the students that when Jesus was on earth and even before that time, fewer names were used, and no last names were used. To identify one man from another, a person would use the phrase "the son of." For instance, calling James "the son of Zebedee" distinguished him from James the son of Alphaeus. Guide the students in identifying the twelve disciples, sharing information from the following chart.

Disciple	Background
Simon	• also called Peter • brother of Andrew • a fisherman from Bethsaida before Jesus called him • walked on water to Jesus • was called both a "stone" and "Satan" by Jesus • denied knowing Jesus • spoke for and led the disciples • wrote 1 and 2 Peter • was crucified for his faith
Andrew	• brother of Simon Peter • a follower of John the Baptist • a fisherman from Bethsaida before Jesus called him • brought Peter to Christ • brought Jesus five loaves and two fishes to feed five thousand men
John	• son of Zebedee and brother of James • he and James were called "Sons of Thunder" • was called the "disciple whom Jesus loved" • caught fish with his brother James before following Jesus • took care of Jesus's mother after His Crucifixion • wrote the books of John; 1, 2, and 3 John; and Revelation
James	• son of Zebedee and brother of John • he and John were called "Sons of Thunder" • suffered and died for his faith in Christ
Matthew	• also called Levi • wrote the book of Matthew • was a tax collector (a publican) before Jesus called him • considered a traitor by the Jews because he taxed them
Philip	• lived in Bethsaida as did Peter and Andrew • told Nathanael about Jesus • asked by Jesus where they would get bread to feed five thousand people • asked Jesus to let the disciples see God, not yet grasping that Jesus was God
Nathanael	• also called Bartholomew • said Jesus was the Son of God and King of Israel • called an honest man by Jesus
Thomas	• also called Didymus, meaning *twin* • suggested that the disciples die with Jesus • doubted that Jesus had risen until he could touch the scars in His hands
James	• also known as the son of Alphaeus, James the Less, and James the younger
Judas	• known as Judas, son of James; Judas, not Iscariot; Thaddaeus; or Lebbaeus
Simon	• called the Canaanite or Zelotes, which is a transliteration of the Aramaic term meaning *zealot* • wanted to free Israel from Roman rule
Judas	• also called Iscariot or the son of Simon • betrayed Jesus • returned the betrayal money and killed himself

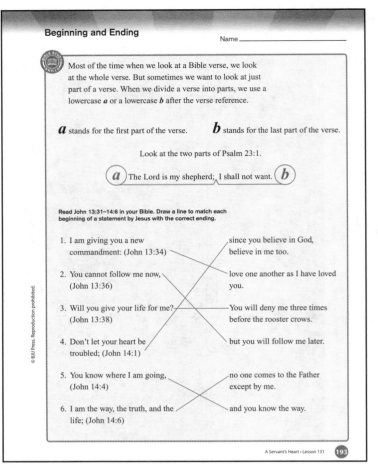

A Servant's Heart • Lesson 131 **193**

LESSON 131 Beginning and Ending

Materials
- Hymn: "Living for Jesus"
- Novel: *Pelts and Promises* for the teacher
- A pelt (optional)

🎵 Hymn: "Living for Jesus"
Sing the first verse (Worktext pages 222–23).
Utilize the recording as necessary throughout the unit. Read **1 Thessalonians 4:1** aloud. Call on students to tell how they can please Jesus. (*trust Him as Savior; love and obey Him*)

❤ Memory Verse—Mark 1:17
Practice the memory verse.

📖 Bible Study Skills, Worktext page 193
Identify parts of a verse. Write "**Psalm 23:1a**" for display. Read the explanation at the top of the Worktext page. Guide the students as they find **John 13:34** in their Bibles. Read the first part of the verse. Choose a volunteer to identify the second part of the verse. Work together to complete each verse on the page.

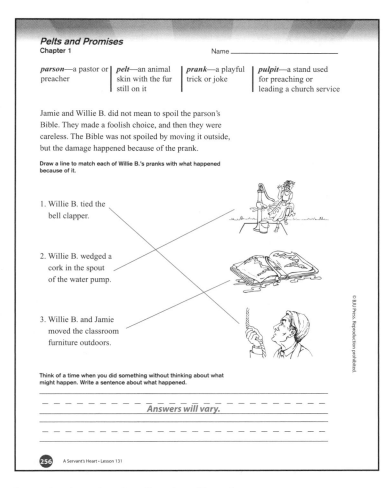

Pelts and Promises
Chapter 1   Name _____

| *parson*—a pastor or preacher | *pelt*—an animal skin with the fur still on it | *prank*—a playful trick or joke | *pulpit*—a stand used for preaching or leading a church service |

Jamie and Willie B. did not mean to spoil the parson's Bible. They made a foolish choice, and then they were careless. The Bible was not spoiled by moving it outside, but the damage happened because of the prank.

Draw a line to match each of Willie B.'s pranks with what happened because of it.

1. Willie B. tied the bell clapper.

2. Willie B. wedged a cork in the spout of the water pump.

3. Willie B. and Jamie moved the classroom furniture outdoors.

Think of a time when you did something without thinking about what might happen. Write a sentence about what happened.

_____
———————— *Answers will vary.* ————————
_____
_____

256   A Servant's Heart • Lesson 131

Introducing the Application Novel

Guide a discussion. Display the novel. Show the cover and ask the students to tell who the author is. *(Nancy Lohr)* Share the information about the author, found on the back cover. Show the pictures on pages 4 (potbelly stove) and 43 (horse-drawn wagon). Discuss the time period in which this story takes place. Display the pelt (optional) and ask the class what they know about it.

Define the following key words.
- **parson**—a pastor or preacher
- **pulpit**—a stand used for preaching or leading a church service
- **prank**—a playful trick or joke
- **pelt**—an animal skin with the fur still on it
- **inventor**—someone who designs or makes a new device or product

Application Novel

Introduce Chapter 1 of *Pelts and Promises*. Call on students to tell whether they have ever played a prank on someone and what happened. Explain that the teacher in this story, Mr. Golde, had been telling his students about inventors. Call on students to name some inventors or inventions. *(Answers may vary.)* Listening question: **What prank did Jamie and Willie B. play?** *(They moved the schoolroom furniture outside.)*

Read Chapter 1 to the students.

▶ **What kind of knife did Jamie have?** *(a deerfoot knife)* Show the picture on pages 104–5.
▶ **Why did Mr. Golde not see Jamie and Willie B. moving the furniture?** *(He was busy showing a handkerchief trick to children under the pecan tree.)*
 Why do you think Mr. Golde suspected Willie B. right away? *(Answers may vary.)*
▶ **Why did Mr. Golde laugh?** *(Willie B. said he was just changing his world—like the inventors.)*
▶ **What punishment did the boys receive from Mr. Golde?** *(They had to sweep the floor and put the furniture back.)*
▶ **What had the boys forgotten to do?** *(close the windows)*
 Why do you think the parson's Bible was all wet? *(The rain came in the open window.)*

✎ Worktext page 256

***Pelts and Promises*, Chapter 1.** Review the key words at the top of the page. Discuss the consequences of Jamie and Willie B.'s actions. Read the directions and instruct the students to complete the page independently.

LESSON 132 Following Jesus

Materials
- Novel: *Pelts and Promises* for the teacher

♥ Memory Verse—Mark 1:17
Practice the memory verse. Read **Romans 12:1** to the students. Point out that when a Christian gives his life to serve God, he demonstrates his love for God and God's love for others.

✎ Worktext page 194
Interpret pictures and draw conclusions. Discuss again what Jesus meant when He said, "I will make you fishers of men." Read the directions and allow the students to complete the page independently. Provide help as needed.

Background Information
Winchester—*a type of rifle*

Application Novel

Introduce Chapters 2 and 3 of *Pelts and Promises*. Discuss what punishment might be given to Jamie and Willie B. by their parents. Listening question: **What plan did the boys come up with to earn money to replace the Bible?** *(They would hunt rabbits, skin them, and take the pelts to sell in Madison.)*

Read the chapters aloud.

▶ **What happened to the Bible?** *(It was ruined.)*

Following Jesus
Mark 1:17

Name _____

Look at each picture. Decide whether the second grader is following Jesus and learning to be a fisher of men. Color a fish to show your answer.

Lisa goes with her mother to hand out tracts. Is Lisa following Jesus?
⬡ Yes   ⬡ No

Karen rides her bike instead of going to church. Is Karen following Jesus?
⬡ Yes   ⬡ No

Jason explains God's Word to Martin. Is Jason following Jesus?
⬡ Yes   ⬡ No

Vicky and Peggy whisper during church. Are Vicky and Peggy following Jesus?
⬡ Yes   ⬡ No

Pelts and Promises
Chapters 2–3

Name _____

vow—a serious promise

Find and read Ecclesiastes 5:5. Fill in the spaces, using your Bible.

It is better not to ___ *vow (promise)* ___ than to ___ *vow (promise)* ___ and not pay.

What promise did Jamie and Willie B. make to Mr. Golde? (p. 15)

They promised to buy a new Bible.

How will they make money to keep their promise? (p. 22)

They will sell pelts.

What do they need to buy before they can start earning money? (p. 22)

They need to buy bullets.

Do you think it will be easy for them to keep their promise? Why or why not?

Answers will vary.

💡 **How do you think Mr. Golde felt about the ruined Bible?** *(Answers may vary.)*

▶ **What did Mr. Golde say to the boys at recess time?** *(He was disappointed in them, but he accepted their apology. He told them they would have to settle the matter with their parents and the parson.)*

▶ **When was the parson returning?** *(October)*

▶ **What special possession did each boy have?** *(Jamie had the deerfoot knife, and Willie B. had Dog.)*

▶ **What punishment did each boy receive from his father to remind him of his wrongdoing?** *(a spanking)*

💡 **Why do you think their fathers did this?** *(Answers may vary.)* Read **Proverbs 29:15** if desired.

▶ **What promise had the boys made to Mr. Golde?** *(They would buy a new Bible.)*

✎ **Worktext page 257**

Recall facts and details. Direct the students to open their Bibles to **Ecclesiastes 5:5**. Read the verse together. Discuss the definition at the top of the page. Instruct the students to complete the sentence explaining the verse. Point out that it is better not to make a vow (promise) than to make one and not keep it. You may want to remind the students about Herod's regret over his vow to Herodias's daughter and her request for the head of John the Baptist. Guide the students in answering the remaining questions on the page.

▶ **Going Beyond**

Reinforcement

Use descriptive words in writing. Write the following words for display: *quick, caring, selfish, helpful, compassionate,* and *doubtful.* Read the list of words. Ask the students to choose one of the words and tell which disciple they would associate with that word and why. Then guide them in writing a sentence about that disciple, using the word.

Enrichment

Make a prayer reminder. Guide a discussion about how believers can be fishers of men as the disciples were. *(telling others about Jesus, being a good testimony, praying for the unsaved, writing letters to unsaved family members and friends)* Direct the students to draw a fish outline on a piece of paper. Instruct them to write the name of someone they can pray for to trust Christ as Savior. Allow them to decorate the fish. They may want to use the fish as a bookmark so they will remember to pray for the person.

God Gives to Me
Unit 10b

PREVIEW

Doctrines

- God is merciful (Psalm 86:15). [Lesson 133]
- God is love (1 John 4:8). [Lesson 134]
- Redeemed man will live on the new earth (Revelation 21:1–3). [Lesson 134]
- The Father, Son, and Spirit are recognized as God (Matthew 28:19). [Lesson 134]

Skills and Applications

- Learn John 14:2*b*–3
- Identify characters through dialogue
- Identify the location of a book in the Bible
- Illustrate Bible scenes
- Sequence events
- Interpret pictures
- Draw conclusions
- Realize that Jesus is preparing a home for Christians in heaven
- Apply Bible knowledge to everyday life

LESSON 133 · Five Thousand Fed

Materials

- Chart 39, "Christ's Ministry"
- Hymn: "Living for Jesus"
- Unit 10 Bookmark for each student
- Highlighter for each student (optional)

Hymn: "Living for Jesus"

Teach the second verse (Worktext pages 222–23).

💡 **What is God's attitude toward us?** (*God loves us even though we are sinners.*)

Explain that the hymnwriter is saying that Christians should live for Jesus because He took our place on the cross, bearing our sin. He loves us so much that we should return that love, dying to self and following Him. Lead the class in singing the verse several times with the recording.

Background Information

Five Thousand Fed—*This is the only miracle Jesus did that is recorded in all four Gospels. The pattern Jesus followed in performing this miracle is one that can be seen in many of His other miracles too. First, there was a great need—something that was beyond human ability. Second, Christ said something that sounded strange to His hearers. Third, the miracle produced a reaction from the people.*

Basket—*When Jesus fed the five thousand, twelve baskets of food were left over. Baskets were used quite often in Bible times for holding bread as well as for gathering fruit. They came in all sizes and shapes. Some were even large enough to hold a person. Paul was let down from the city wall of Damascus in a basket. Most baskets were woven from reeds, ropes, leaves, or twigs.*

Introducing the Bible Account

Use a map to introduce the account. Display Chart 39, "Christ's Ministry," pointing out the Sea of Galilee and Bethsaida. Tell how the people followed Jesus everywhere, bringing their sick and listening to His teaching.

Read **Matthew 14:13–21** or use the following retelling of that passage. Listening question: **What did Jesus do for the crowd?** *(fed them, healed the sick)*

Five Thousand Fed

When Jesus heard that John the Baptist had been killed by Herod, Jesus wanted to have some time alone with His disciples. They got into boats and headed out across the Sea of Galilee. People had been following Jesus, trying to hear what He was telling His disciples. Crowds of people walked along the north shore of the lake and arrived before the boats reached the other side.

Jesus had sailed away to be by Himself, but when He saw the crowds, He felt compassion for them. These people needed Him. Jesus got out of the boat and let the people bring their sick friends and relatives to Him so that He could heal them.

When evening came, the disciples became worried about the people, who were so far away from their homes. They asked Jesus to send the people away so that they could find food. Jesus told them that the people didn't need to go away. He told the disciples, "You give them something to eat." When He said that, He emphasized the word *you*.

The disciples looked around for food to feed the people. They were perplexed. They could find only five loaves of bread and two fish to bring to Jesus. The disciples could see no way that this was enough for five thousand men plus many women and children.

In the hands of God, the Creator, this small amount of food was enough. The disciples made the people sit down in groups of fifty. As they took the food from Jesus and gave it to the groups, God continually multiplied the food.

When all were fed, the disciples collected twelve baskets of leftovers—one for each of them. These disciples would doubt Christ again, but they would later believe so strongly that Jesus was God that they would tell the whole world.

❖

▶ **Why did Jesus want to be away from the people?** *(He had just learned of the death of John the Baptist.)*
▶ **Did the people allow Jesus to be alone with His disciples?** *(No. They followed Him.)*
▶ **How did Jesus feel when he looked at the crowds of people?** *(He felt compassion for them.)*
▶ **When evening came, what did the disciples want Jesus to do with the people?** *(send them away to find food)*
💡 **What would you have suggested for feeding the people?** *(Answers may vary.)*
▶ **Instead of sending them away, what did Jesus tell the disciples to do?** *(feed the people)*

▶ **How did the disciples obey Jesus?** *(They organized the people into groups, distributed the food, and picked up the leftovers.)*
▶ **How could Jesus multiply the food?** *(He is God.)*

Remind the students that God made and takes care of each of us. He alone gives us each breath; He sent His Son to die for us; He gives us food and clothes; He can heal our sicknesses; He is preparing a place for the saved to live forever. Challenge the students to be thankful for all that God gives us.

🖊 Worktext page 195

Illustrate Bible scenes. Read the directions to the students. Guide them in reading the sentence in each box before allowing them to complete the page independently.

♥ Memory Verses—John 14:2b–3

Principle: Jesus is preparing a home for believers.
Practice the memory verse.

▶ **Who is speaking in these verses?** *(Jesus)*
💡 **Who do you think He is speaking to?** *(the disciples and all believers)*
▶ **What does Jesus say He is going to prepare for them in His Father's house?** *(a place)*
💡 **Why do you think He told His disciples about the place He is preparing?** *(Answers will vary but elicit that it was to comfort them. Point out that this is also a comfort to Christians today.)*

▶ **What promise does Jesus give in John 14:3?** *(He will come again to receive the saved.)*

▶ **Where does Jesus say Christians will live forever?** *(with Him)*

▶ **What does God require of a person in order to live with Him forever?** *(No one can live with Jesus forever unless he has been saved and had his heart changed. Explain that a person can be saved only by Christ.* **Romans 3:28** *makes it clear that good works are not a basis for salvation.)*

LESSON 134 — Jesus Promises an Eternal Home

Materials
- Chart 39, "Christ's Ministry"
- Hymn: "Living for Jesus"

🎵 Hymn: "Living for Jesus"
Sing the second verse (Worktext pages 222–23).

Background Information
The Night of the Passover Supper—*Jesus and His disciples celebrated Passover at the house of an unidentified man (**Matthew 26:18–20**). There, Jesus revealed that one of the disciples would betray Him. Then they ate bread, which represented the body of Christ, and drank wine, which represented His blood. Christ told them that eating bread and drinking wine was in remembrance of His body and blood (**1 Corinthians 11:24–25**). Then they sang a hymn and went out.*

Introducing the Bible Account
Guide a discussion about the Passover Supper. Introduce the scene the night Jesus took His last Passover supper with His disciples. Remind the students that only Jesus and His disciples were present. Share the background information.

Bible Account

Read John 13:31–14:6 or use the following retelling of that passage. Listening question: **What did Jesus say He would do for the disciples the next time He came?** *(take them with Him)*

In My Father's House

Jesus was sitting at the table with His disciples. Jesus told them that in a little while He would go away. When Peter asked Jesus where He was going, He answered that they could not yet go where He was going.

Peter said that he would go anywhere with Jesus. Jesus asked Peter, "Will you lay down your life for My sake?" Jesus said that before the rooster crowed the following morning, Peter would deny knowing the Lord Jesus three times. Peter didn't realize how weak and sinful he was.

Jesus told the disciples not to be troubled about His leaving. Christ said that in His Father's house were many dwelling places. The Lord Jesus was going to heaven to prepare a home for His disciples and for all Christians.

Jesus promised to come back again. He told the disciples that when He came back, He would take them away with Him.

Thomas wanted to know how they could know the way if they didn't know where Jesus was going.

Jesus answered Thomas, "I am the way, the truth, and the life. Nobody comes to the Father, except through me."

Although Jesus was going to leave the disciples, He told them many other wonderful things to encourage them. He said that He would rise again—and we know that He did. Jesus said that they could pray to God and that they would have God's presence and peace even in the middle of difficulties. All these things that Jesus told His disciples are true for Christians today.

When Jesus finished saying all this, He and the disciples left the house and went to a garden near a brook named Kidron. Judas betrayed Jesus to the soldiers in that garden. Jesus was arrested and put to death on the cross.

▶ **Who was with Jesus at His last Passover supper?** *(the disciples)*

▶ **Which disciple told Jesus that he would follow Him anywhere?** *(Peter)*

▶ **What did Jesus say to that?** *(He said Peter would deny knowing Him three times that night.)*

💡 **Have you ever told Jesus that you would do something but did not do it?** *(Accept any answer, but point out that many people make promises to God that they don't keep. We must live by God's grace, daily depending on His power to please Him.)*

▶ **What did Jesus tell the disciples that made them sad?** *(He was going away.)*

💡 **What did Jesus tell the disciples that should have made them glad?** *(He said He was going to His Father to prepare a dwelling place for them.)*

▶ **According to Jesus, how could Thomas and the other disciples go to His Father's house?** *(Jesus said that He is the Way, the Truth, and the Life, and that no one could get to His Father except by Him.)*

💡 **Why should those words of Jesus make *us* glad?** *(His words are for all those who believe in Him.)*

▶ **What happened to Jesus in the garden?** *(He was arrested.)*

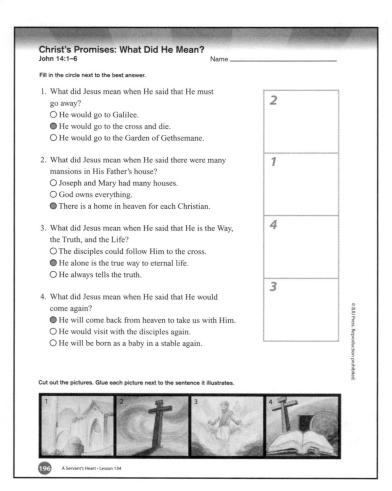

Christ's Promises: What Did He Mean?
John 14:1–6   Name _____

Fill in the circle next to the best answer.

1. What did Jesus mean when He said that He must go away?
   - ○ He would go to Galilee.
   - ● He would go to the cross and die.
   - ○ He would go to the Garden of Gethsemane.

2. What did Jesus mean when He said there were many mansions in His Father's house?
   - ○ Joseph and Mary had many houses.
   - ○ God owns everything.
   - ● There is a home in heaven for each Christian.

3. What did Jesus mean when He said that He is the Way, the Truth, and the Life?
   - ○ The disciples could follow Him to the cross.
   - ● He alone is the true way to eternal life.
   - ○ He always tells the truth.

4. What did Jesus mean when He said that He would come again?
   - ● He will come back from heaven to take us with Him.
   - ○ He would visit with the disciples again.
   - ○ He will be born as a baby in a stable again.

| 2 |
| 1 |
| 4 |
| 3 |

Cut out the pictures. Glue each picture next to the sentence it illustrates.

| 1 | 2 | 3 | 4 |

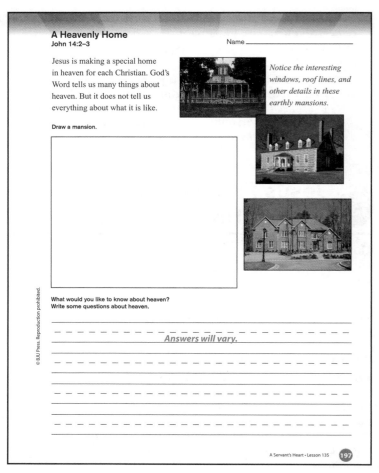

A Heavenly Home
John 14:2–3   Name _____

Jesus is making a special home in heaven for each **Christian**. God's Word tells us many things about heaven. But it does not tell us everything about what it is like.

Notice the interesting windows, roof lines, and other details in these earthly mansions.

Draw a mansion.

What would you like to know about heaven? Write some questions about heaven.

Answers will vary.

Worktext page 196
Interpret pictures and draw conclusions. Discuss the title and the questions on the page. Instruct the students to fill in the circle next to the correct answer. Discuss what the pictures at the bottom of the page represent. Direct the students to cut out the pictures and glue them in the correct places. Provide help as needed.

Memory Verses—John 14:2*b*–3
Practice the memory verses.

LESSON 135 Heaven

Materials
- Hymn: "Living for Jesus"
- Novel: *Pelts and Promises* for the teacher
- Piece of drawing paper for each student

Draw the outline of five jewels for display using different colors.

Hymn: "Living for Jesus"
Sing the first and second verses (Worktext pages 222–23). Discuss with the students how they can live for Jesus by being *fishers of men*.

Memory Verses—John 14:2*b*–3
Practice the memory verses.

▶ **What is heaven?** (*Heaven is a glorious and happy place where the saved dwell with the Lord, awaiting the resurrection of their bodies.*)

Our eternal dwelling place with the Lord will be the new earth and the new Jerusalem (**John 14:3; Revelation 21:1–3**). Remind the students that eternity with the Lord is a time with no sorrow, no tears, no death, and no pain. Point out that the Bible describes the beauty of the new Jerusalem, telling of pearls, gold, and precious stones (**Revelation 21**).

Direct attention to the drawing of the jewels. Tell the students that every time you point to a jewel they will say the verses. Point to a jewel as the class recites the verses. Choose a student to color one jewel. Repeat this procedure as time permits, or recite the verses throughout the day. (*Note:* You may want to read **Revelation 21:1–22:6** and review the description of the new Jerusalem.)

Worktext page 197
Apply Bible knowledge to everyday life. Guide the students as they illustrate a mansion. Instruct them to write at the bottom of the page some questions that they have about heaven.

Application Novel

Introduce Chapters 4 and 5 of *Pelts and Promises*. Allow the students to tell about times that they may have had to do work to earn money for a specific goal. Remind them that God gives us bodies that are able to do work.

Call on students to tell about times when they have had to tell someone about something they did that was wrong and how they felt about it.

▸ **What were Jamie's thoughts at the end of Chapter 3?** *(He told Willie B. that this was the worst trouble he had ever been in, and he wanted to put it behind him as fast as possible.)*

💡 **Why didn't the parson come back until October?** *(He was a circuit riding preacher.)*

💡 **What does that mean?** *(He traveled from church to church.)*

▸ Listening question: **What happens when Jamie and Willie B. have to tell the parson what had happened?** *(The parson was busy with other people.)*

Read the chapters.

▸ **What did Willie B. ask Mr. Olefson, the store keeper?** *(He asked how much it would cost to buy a new Bible.)*

▸ **What did he tell Willie?** *(It would cost $10.98.)*

▸ **What did Jamie think about the price?** *(He thought that was a fortune and they would never be able to come up with it—his father had paid thirteen dollars for Ma's cook stove.)*

▸ **Who helped the boys hunt rabbits?** *(Dog)*

▸ **How many shots did Willie B. use to get two rabbits?** *(five)*

▸ **How many rabbits did Jamie get?** *(one)*

▸ **Ask a student to explain the process the boys went through when they got the rabbits to Willie B.'s.** *(They cut the skins open, cleaned out the animals, and peeled the skins off. Then they cleaned and trimmed the pelts. The pelts were then nailed to the barn wall to dry.)*

▸ **How did the boys feel when they were done?** *(They were discouraged thinking about how long it would take to get the money if they could get even twenty cents apiece for the three pelts they did have.)*

▸ **The first time Jamie told the parson that the Bible was gone, what did the parson think had happened to it?** *(He thought Jamie had taken it home to begin work on his Christmas reading.)*

▸ **Why was there a problem with the boys saying they would have the money for the new Bible by the end of the school term?** *(It was needed sooner so the boys portraying the wise men could read from it for the Christmas pageant.)*

▸ **If the boys did not have it by then, what did the parson say would happen?** *(They would need to tell the whole matter to the church.)*

Worktext page 258

Identifying characters through dialogue. Call on volunteers to identify each person shown on the page *(the parson, Jamie, Willie B., and the storekeeper)*. Read the directions to the students and allow them to complete the page independently.

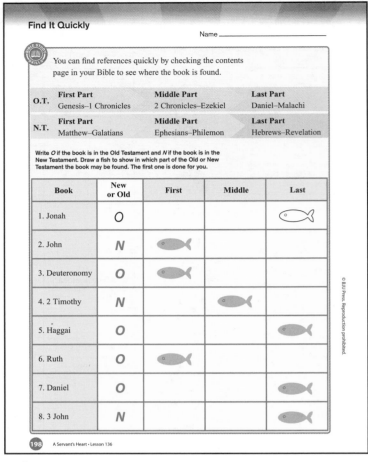

Find It Quickly

Name _____

You can find references quickly by checking the contents page in your Bible to see where the book is found.

O.T.	**First Part** Genesis–1 Chronicles	**Middle Part** 2 Chronicles–Ezekiel	**Last Part** Daniel–Malachi
N.T.	**First Part** Matthew–Galatians	**Middle Part** Ephesians–Philemon	**Last Part** Hebrews–Revelation

Write *O* if the book is in the Old Testament and *N* if the book is in the New Testament. Draw a fish to show in which part of the Old or New Testament the book may be found. The first one is done for you.

Book	New or Old	First	Middle	Last
1. Jonah	O			🐟
2. John	N	🐟		
3. Deuteronomy	O	🐟		
4. 2 Timothy	N		🐟	
5. Haggai	O			🐟
6. Ruth	O	🐟		
7. Daniel	O			🐟
8. 3 John	N			🐟

198   A Servant's Heart • Lesson 136

Find It Quickly

Materials
- Hymn: "Living for Jesus"
- Novel: *Pelts and Promises* for the teacher

 Bible Study Skills, Worktext page 198
Identify the location of the books of the Bible.
Say the books of the Old and New Testaments. Review the concept that words starting with a letter from the first part of the alphabet (*a–l*) are in the first half of the dictionary and words starting with a letter from the last part (*m–z*) are found in the second half of the dictionary.

Direct attention to Worktext page 198. Read and discuss the explanation at the top of the page. Tell the students to turn to the contents page in their Bibles. Call on volunteers to locate the name of the book on the contents page and tell whether it is found in the first, middle, or last part of the Old or New Testament.
- Deuteronomy *(first part of the OT)*
- Acts *(first part of the NT)*
- 2 John *(last part of the NT)*

Continue as time permits. Guide the students as they complete the page.

Locate verses. Write the following references for display one at a time. Guide the students as they locate the verses. Remind them to think about where the verse is found (the first, middle, or last part of the Old or New Testament) when looking for it on the contents page. Call on a volunteer to read the verse(s).
- **1 John 5:13** *(last part of the NT)* Elicit that we can know that we are saved and have eternal life.
- **Matthew 6:31–32** *(first part of the NT)* Point out that God takes care of our needs for food and clothes.
- **Psalm 92:1** *(middle part of the OT)* Remind the students to thank God for all things.

(*Note:* You may want to read **Psalms 100** and **103** when considering God's goodness. You may also encourage an attitude of thankfulness by reading from the book of Psalms each day throughout the next week).

🎵 Hymn: "Living for Jesus"
Sing the second verse (Worktext pages 222–23).

♥ Memory Verses—John 14:2*b*–3
Practice the memory verses. Remind them that Christ will come again and that the saved will live forever with the Lord (**Revelation 21:3**).

Application Novel
Introduce Chapter 6 of *Pelts and Promises*. Review what has happened so far in the story. Read the Chapter 6 title to the students and ask them what they think the boys will trade. Listening question: **What did the boys trade?** *(pelts for money)*

Read the chapter.

- ▶ **How many pelts did the boys need before they could go to Madison?** *(twenty)*
- ▶ **Who took the boys to Madison?** *(Willie B.'s father)*
- ▶ **How much did the storekeeper offer for the twenty pelts?** *($5.00)*
- ▶ **Who said that they would take the offer?** *(Jamie)*
- ▶ **Under what conditions did Willie B. say he would accept the offer?** *(if the storekeeper agreed to buy more pelts when they came again)*
- 💡 **Do you think the boys made a good deal?** *(Answers may very.)*
- ▶ **Did the storekeeper like the boys' workmanship?** *(yes)*

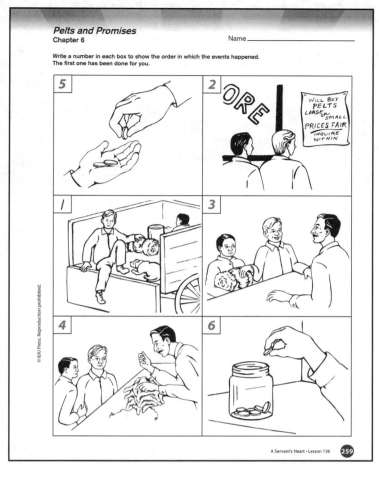

Pelts and Promises
Chapter 6

Name _____

Write a number in each box to show the order in which the events happened. The first one has been done for you.

A Servant's Heart • Lesson 136   259

 Worktext page 259

Sequence events. Direct attention to the pictures on the page. Review the events pictured, then let the students order the events. Point out that the first box is already numbered.

▶ Going Beyond

Reinforcement

Materials

- Red construction-paper heart for each student
- Two white 8½" × 11" sheets of white paper for each student
- Scissors, stapler, glue

Review the Bible accounts studied in Unit 9a and Unit 9b. Discuss how others gave themselves to God. *(John the Baptist gave his life; the disciples left their jobs.)*

▶ **What does God give to us?** *(Some possible answers may be food, clothes, our life, parents, church, salvation, time, and money.)*

▶ **What can you give to God?** *(Answers may vary, but could include money, thankfulness, praise, and time.)*

Make a booklet to show a generous heart. After distributing the materials to the students, tell them to cut their white sheets in half and staple the pages in the upper left-hand corner. Instruct the students to write the title "A Generous Heart" on the first page, then glue the last page to the heart shape. Tell them to draw a picture on each page showing what God gives to them and how they can use that to show God's love to others.

Enrichment

Materials

- A piece of drawing paper, black felt-tip pen, cotton ball, newspaper, cooking oil, and crayons for each student

Make a "stained glass" picture. Distribute the materials to the students and tell them to draw a scene with the black felt-tip pen about one of the Bible accounts. Then instruct them to dip the cotton ball in oil and spread it lightly over the picture. Direct them to press hard as they color the picture, using brightly colored crayons or felt-tip pens. Fasten their pictures to a window pane for the "stained glass" effect.

I Give My Possessions to God

Unit 10c

PREVIEW

Doctrines

- Contribute financially (Romans 15:26). [Lesson 137]
- Exhort one another (Hebrews 10:25). [Lesson 137]
- God is love (1 John 4:8). [Lesson 138]

Skills and Applications

- Learn 2 Corinthians 9:7
- Identify characters through dialogue
- Infer cause and effect
- Follow directions
- Recall facts and details
- Understand the principle of giving
- Apply Bible knowledge to everyday life

LESSON 137 The Widow Loves from Little

Materials

- Chart 29, "The Widow Loves from Little"
- Hymn: "Living for Jesus"
- Unit 10 Bookmark for each student
- Highlighter for each student (optional)
- Verse visuals: Cut out a heart from red posterboard or construction paper. On the back, write the first part of the memory verse. Cut a yellow piece of posterboard or construction paper in half, and draw a happy face on one half and an unhappy face on the other half. On the back of the unhappy face, write the second part of the verse. On the back of the happy face, write the last part of the verse.

♫ Hymn: "Living for Jesus"

Teach the third verse (Worktext pages 222–23). Point out that this verse says a Christian can serve Jesus Christ no matter where he is or what act of obedience he is doing. Point out that everything a Christian does should bring honor and glory to God (**1 Corinthians 10:31**).

▶ **What does it mean to "suffer affliction or loss"?** *(to go through hard times)*

💡 **Does the Lord use the hard times in our lives to help us or hurt us?** *(to help us)* See **Romans 8:28**.

Lead the students in singing the verse several times.

Background Information

The Treasury—*The Bible mentions a treasury as far back as the battle of Jericho in **Joshua 6:19**. The temple in Jerusalem had a treasury with thirteen chests. The people dropped their tithes and offerings into trumpet-shaped tubes attached to the chests. Jesus saw a poor widow place her last two coins into the temple treasury. The widow had given all that she had. He used this example to teach His disciples that believers should be willing to give their all to God.*

What the Widow Gave—*A mite was a small Greek copper coin. It was worth 1/128 of the denarius, which was a day's wage. If a laborer worked an eight-hour workday today, what he would earn in seven and a half minutes is equivalent to the amount the widow gave.*

Introducing the Bible Account

Present background information. Share as much of the background information as you think would be useful in understanding the account. Explain that a *widow* is a woman whose husband has died and who has not remarried, and that a *treasury* is a special place where money and other valuables are stored.

Bible Account

Read Mark 12:41–44 or use the following retelling of the passage. Direct the students to look at the picture on Worktext page 199. Listening question: **What was important about the possession that the widow gave to God?** *(She gave all of the money that she had.)*

The Widow Loves from Little

Jesus had been speaking to groups of Gentiles, Sadducees, and Pharisees. He decided to go with His disciples into the temple. He went into the part of the temple that had the collection containers.

Jesus sat down where He could watch the people. Soon He saw a very poor widow come with her offering. Since Jesus is God, He knows everything. He knew how much she gave as well as her cheerful attitude in giving it. The woman put a small amount of money in the container, but it was all that she had.

Jesus called to His disciples and said, "I tell you truly." When Jesus used this phrase, it stressed the importance of the lesson He was about to teach. Jesus went on to say, "This poor widow has put in more than all the others who have put money into the treasury."

Jesus explained that others who gave had a lot of money and the widow had very little. When the rich gave, they had lots of money left, but when the widow gave her two coins, she gave all that she had, leaving herself nothing. Her gift left her with none of this world's wealth, but she had stored up treasure in heaven.

This was exactly what Jesus wanted His disciples to learn: God does not measure how much we give by the amount of our giving, but by what percentage our giving represents of all that we own. Of course, any gift given to God with the right heart attitude is an everlasting treasure in heaven.

▶ **Where was Jesus when He saw the widow?** *(in the temple)*

▶ **Who went to the temple with Jesus?** *(His disciples)*

▶ **What did Jesus notice about the rich people?** *(They gave many coins.)*

▶ **What did the poor widow give?** *(all she had: two of the least valuable coins)*

▶ **Why did Jesus call His disciples to Him?** *(to teach them a lesson)*

▶ **What did Jesus say about what the widow and what the rich people gave?** *(He said the widow gave more than all the rich.)*

The Widow Loves from Little
Mark 12:41–44

Shofar

The temple had offering containers called shofar chests because they were shaped like shofars, the horns the priests blew.

Bowen Bible Lands Collection, Bob Jones University

Mite

Front

Back

The widow's two copper coins (called mites) were together worth less than one fourth of an hour's wage.

Photos: Bowen Bible Lands Collection, Bob Jones University

© BJU Press. Reproduction prohibited.

A Servant's Heart • Lesson 137 **199**

▶ **What did Jesus mean when He said she gave more?** *(She gave all that she had; she had nothing left.)*

Point out that the widow might have gone hungry until she could get some money again, but she was willing to give out of her love for God. Explain that her giving everything meant that she was depending completely on God's care and protection.

💡 **What did the rich have left?** *(Jesus said they gave out of their abundance, so they had plenty left.)*

▶ **How does God judge the giving of Christians?** *(by how they give, not what they give)*

💡 **What possessions do you have?** *(Answers will vary.)*

💡 **How can Christians give their money for eternal rewards?** *(Answers will vary but could include giving money to missionaries or the local church.)*

Point out that everything we have belongs to God. It could be gone in a moment. Explain that God intends for us to use material things to glorify Him.

InfoScene: "The Widow Loves from Little"
Display Chart 29 from the Visual Packet for the students to refer to throughout this unit.

❤ Memory Verse—2 Corinthians 9:7

Principle: We should give to God joyfully. Direct the students to open their Bibles to the memory verse. Read the verse to them three or four times. Lead them in reading it aloud with you. Display the heart visual. Tell the students

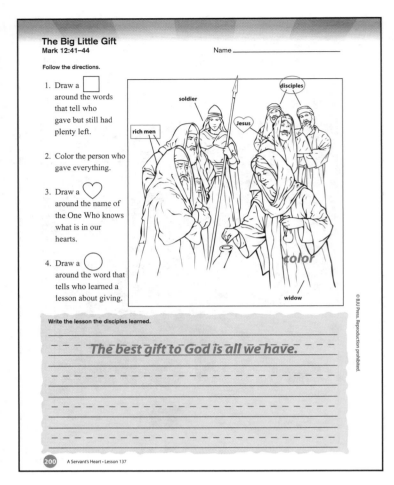

The Big Little Gift
Mark 12:41–44

Name _____

Follow the directions.

1. Draw a ☐ around the words that tell who gave but still had plenty left.

2. Color the person who gave everything.

3. Draw a ♡ around the name of the One Who knows what is in our hearts.

4. Draw a ◯ around the word that tells who learned a lesson about giving.

Write the lesson the disciples learned.

The best gift to God is all we have.

_____

_____

_____

_____

200   A Servant's Heart • Lesson 137

---

that *to purpose* means to do something by choice or to plan to do something. Elicit that each person makes his or her own choice of what to give and how to give it.

Display the *unhappy face* visual and discuss that the verse says giving is not to be forced. Show the *happy face* visual. Point out that God loves a cheerful giver.

▶ **What are the two ways we can give?** (*cheerfully or grudgingly*)

Practice the verse. Choose three students to hold the visuals at the front of the classroom. Point to each visual and lead the students in saying the corresponding part of the verse. Allow various students to hold the verse visuals as you practice several times. Invite the students to highlight the verse (optional) and mark the location with the Unit 10 Bookmark.

⟲ Worktext page 200

Follow directions while recalling facts and details. Guide the students as they complete each step of the instructions. Direct the students' attention to the bottom of the page. Allow them to write their answers and then discuss what they wrote.

LESSON 138 Mary Loves from Much

Materials
- Chart 30, "She Has Done a Good Thing"
- Chart 39, "Christ's Ministry"
- Hymn: "Living for Jesus"
- Verse visuals from the previous lesson

♥ Memory Verse—2 Corinthians 9:7

Practice the memory verse. Choose three students to hold the visuals at the front of the classroom. Instruct each of the students holding a visual to say his part of the verse. Lead the class in saying the verse. Direct the students to open their Bibles to the memory verse. Read the verse together, and then read the verse to the students, pausing to show the corresponding visual for each phrase.

Background Information

Bethany—*Today Bethany is called al-Azariyya, which means "the place of Lazarus." Because of His close friendship with Mary, Martha, and Lazarus, Jesus apparently made Bethany His base of operations when He was in Judea. Simon the leper also lived in that village since it was at his house that Mary anointed Jesus's feet with ointment. The Lord ascended to heaven not far from Bethany.*

The Alabaster Cruse of Ointment—*The word for this container is translated "box," but it was a small, white bottle used to hold ointment or perfume. Its name comes from the alabaster marble stone out of which it was carved. The vessel had a thin neck that could be broken to get the perfume out.*

John 12:1–11—*John names Mary as the woman referred to and Judas Iscariot as the man who complained about the waste of the ointment. John also gives the time as six days before the Passover.*

Introducing the Bible Account

Introduce the account. Point out the city of Bethany on Chart 39, "Christ's Ministry," noting how close it is to Jerusalem, where Jesus was crucified. Share the background information as desired.

Bible Account

Read Mark 14:3–9 or use the following retelling of the passage. Direct the students' attention to Worktext page 201 as they listen. Listening question: **What did Mary give to Jesus to show her love?** (*expensive perfume*)

Mary Loves from Much

Jesus and His disciples were eating supper at the house of Simon the leper in the town of Bethany. Jesus's friends Mary, Martha, and Lazarus lived there too.

While Jesus was eating, a woman came into the house with a beautiful bottle of expensive perfume. She went to Jesus, broke the thin neck of the bottle, and poured the perfume on His head to show her love for Jesus as her Savior.

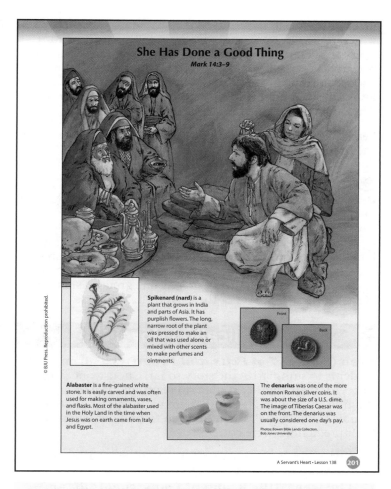

She Has Done a Good Thing

Mark 14:3–9

Spikenard (nard) is a plant that grows in India and parts of Asia. It has purplish flowers. The long, narrow root of the plant was pressed to make an oil that was used alone or mixed with other scents to make perfumes and ointments.

Alabaster is a fine-grained white stone. It is easily carved and was often used for making ornaments, vases, and flasks. Most of the alabaster used in the Holy Land in the time when Jesus was on earth came from Italy and Egypt.

Front

Back

The **denarius** was one of the more common Roman silver coins. It was about the size of a U.S. dime. The image of Tiberias Caesar was on the front. The denarius was usually considered one day's pay.

Photos: Bowen Bible Lands Collection, Bob Jones University

A Servant's Heart • Lesson 138   201

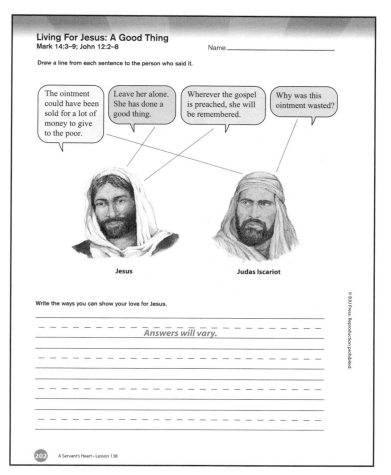

Living For Jesus: A Good Thing
Mark 14:3–9; John 12:2–8   Name _____

Draw a line from each sentence to the person who said it.

The ointment could have been sold for a lot of money to give to the poor.

Leave her alone. She has done a good thing.

Wherever the gospel is preached, she will be remembered.

Why was this ointment wasted?

Jesus

Judas Iscariot

Write the ways you can show your love for Jesus.

_____
- -
Answers will vary.
_____
- -
_____
- -
_____

202   A Servant's Heart • Lesson 138

Judas Iscariot, the treasurer for the disciples, complained that this was a huge waste of money. He said that the costly perfume could have been sold for a lot of money, which could have been given to the poor.

Jesus replied that they would always have poor people with them, but they would not always have Him with them.

The woman who poured out her perfume for Christ was the one who loved to sit and listen to Jesus talk. Her name was Mary.

Jesus said that Mary had done a good thing. She was anointing His body for burial because she wanted to show her love for Him. Jesus said that what Mary had done would be known wherever the gospel is preached and that she would be remembered for her love for Him.

❦

▶ **Why did Mary bring her expensive perfume and pour it on Jesus's head?** *(to show her love)*
▶ **Who complained about it?** *(Judas Iscariot)*
💡 **Whose example should we follow, Mary's or Judas's?** *(Mary's)*

This story has been spread all over the world by the followers of Jesus. Today the Bible has been translated into many languages so that every person who reads it can know how Mary showed her love to Jesus. Mary shows us how intensely we ought to love Him.

💡 **Name some ways that you can show your love to Jesus and worship Him.** *(Many answers are acceptable.)*

InfoScene: "She Has Done a Good Thing"
Display Chart 30 from the Visual Packet for the students to refer to throughout this unit.

✍ **Worktext page 202**
Identify characters through dialogue. Read the directions to the students and call on volunteers to read each statement. Then have the students mark their answers before a volunteer identifies the correct character. Instruct the students to write in their own words ways they can show love for Jesus.

🎵 **Hymn: "Living for Jesus"**
Sing the third verse (Worktext pages 222–23). Review the meaning of the verse and the chorus. Explain the line "I own no other Master," pointing out that many times we try to please ourselves or others rather than God. Explain that a Christian must daily put aside selfish desires and wants. Joyful service follows a willing heart and humility.

Honoring Jesus with Love, Worship, and Respect

Name _____

Read each of the four stories. Draw a circle around the name of the person who is honoring Jesus.

1. Amanda does not like to learn verses for Bible club. She does not think the prizes are very good, and she does not think it's important to learn the verses. (Melissa) learns all her verses and says them on time. She knows the verses when she tells others about Jesus.

2. The other children on the street make fun of Peter and David for going to church. They call them "goody, goody" when they walk past on their way to Sunday school. (Peter) keeps walking. David yells back and throws pebbles at them.

3. Kevin's mother and father sing in the church choir, so Kevin sits with Jake and his family. Jake always tells his parents that he has to go to the restroom, and then he plays outside until church is over. He wants Kevin to go with him. (Kevin) sits quietly and listens to the pastor. He sings the songs he knows and talks to God at prayer times.

4. Tina and Sandi joined the children's choir at church. They do not know any of the songs. The choir leader makes everyone work hard. Tina doesn't listen to the leader. She whispers and giggles. She says she will stop coming as soon as her parents will let her. (Sandi) listens and tries very hard to learn the songs. She is looking forward to the time when they can sing praises in the church service.

A Servant's Heart • Lesson 139   203

LESSON 139 Honoring Jesus

Materials

- Hymn: "Living for Jesus"
- Novel: *Pelts and Promises* for the teacher

✏ Worktext page 203

Recognize behavior that honors Jesus. Read and explain the directions for the Worktext pages. Allow the students to work independently. Discuss the stories after students complete their work.

🎵 Hymn: "Living for Jesus"

Sing the first two verses (Worktext pages 222–23). Sing the first verse again and guide the students to find the meaning for *atone* in the Worktext glossary. Read and review the phrase from the chorus, "For Thou, in Thine atonement / Didst give Thyself for me." Explain the word *atonement*.

💡 **Why did Jesus take the punishment for sin?** *(God loves us and sent Jesus Christ to die in our place. There is nothing that we as sinful people can do to save ourselves.)*

Remind the students that God is holy. Adam chose to sin, which results in everyone being born with a sinful nature. Every sin deserves God's wrath and punishment. Only Jesus, because He is God, could pay the penalty for sin. We must choose to come to God through faith in Christ; believing in Jesus's death, burial, and Resurrection is the only way our sins can be forgiven. Present the plan of salvation.

Lead the students in singing the second verse and chorus of the hymn.

♥ Memory Verse—2 Corinthians 9:7

Practice the memory verse. Read the verse together. Call on a student to name the person in the previous lesson who gave Jesus the very expensive perfume. *(Mary)* Divide your class into three or four groups. Let each group devise sign language motions for the verse, practice it, and then present it to the whole class. *(Note:* You will have three or four versions of signs for the same verse.) As one group is signing the verse, let the remainder of the class recite the verse.

Application Novel

Read Chapter 7 of *Pelts and Promises*. Call on several students to summarize the story so far. Choose one student to begin, then another student to continue, and so on. Read the title of Chapter 7 and ask them what they think the trouble could be. Tell them to listen to find out whether their predictions were correct.

▸ **Why did all the students turn when Willie B. did not answer at roll call?** *(He never missed school.)*

▸ **Why was Willie B. absent from school?** *(He was home with Dog because she was having pups.)*

▸ **Why did Willie B. not call Doc?** *(His family did not have money to pay Doc.)*

▸ **Why did he not use the money he and Jamie had to pay for the doctor?** *(That money was set aside for the new Bible.)*

▸ **What punishment did Ma give Jamie for being late?** *(additional chores for one week)*

▸ **What was the real reason Mr. Golde asked Jamie to fill the water bucket?** *(He wanted Jamie to see Willie B.)*

▸ **What news did Willie B. have?** *(Dog had two puppies.)*

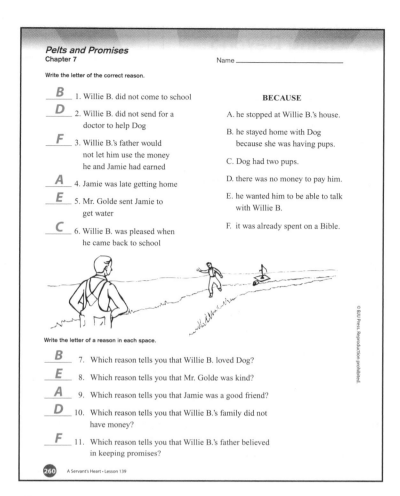

Pelts and Promises
Chapter 7

Name _____

Write the letter of the correct reason.

B 1. Willie B. did not come to school

D 2. Willie B. did not send for a doctor to help Dog

F 3. Willie B.'s father would not let him use the money he and Jamie had earned

A 4. Jamie was late getting home

E 5. Mr. Golde sent Jamie to get water

C 6. Willie B. was pleased when he came back to school

BECAUSE

A. he stopped at Willie B.'s house.

B. he stayed home with Dog because she was having pups.

C. Dog had two pups.

D. there was no money to pay him.

E. he wanted him to be able to talk with Willie B.

F. it was already spent on a Bible.

Write the letter of a reason in each space.

B 7. Which reason tells you that Willie B. loved Dog?

E 8. Which reason tells you that Mr. Golde was kind?

A 9. Which reason tells you that Jamie was a good friend?

D 10. Which reason tells you that Willie B.'s family did not have money?

F 11. Which reason tells you that Willie B.'s father believed in keeping promises?

A Message for Givers
2 Corinthians 9:7

Name _____

Is it possible to give and not please God?

Follow the directions to find what attitude pleases God when we give.

Use your favorite color to shade the following:

☐ All the Ys and Zs in the puzzle

☐ Line 1—the name of an insect *bee*

☐ Line 2—a color word *blue*

☐ Line 3—a number word *fifteen*

☐ Line 4—the name of a flying animal *bat*

☐ Line 5—the name of a kind of pet *cat*

If you have followed the directions, you will see the message from 2 Corinthians 9:7 in the white boxes.

1.	Z	Y	Z	G	O	D	Y	Y	Z	Y	Z	B	E	E	Z
2.	Y	Z	B	L	U	E	Z	Z	Y	L	O	V	E	S	Z
3.	Z	A	Z	Z	Y	Y	Z	Y	F	I	F	T	E	E	N
4.	Y	B	A	T	C	H	E	E	R	F	U	L	Z	Y	Z
5.	Z	G	I	V	E	R	Y	Z	C	A	T	Y	Z	Y	Y

✍ Worktext page 260

Match effect to cause. Direct attention to the phrases on the right side of the page. Explain that each of these phrases completes a sentence on the left and tells why it happened. Tell the students that you will read a phrase, the word *because,* and then choose a volunteer to complete the sentence.

Direct the students to write the letter of the reason in the blank.

Direct attention to the questions at the bottom of the page. Point out that the reasons already given will also answer these questions. Call on students to read the questions and tell the answers. Discuss how God always keeps His promises. Call on students to tell some promises God makes to Christians. *(Answers may vary but could include He will never leave us, He will prepare a place in heaven, and He will come again.)*

LESSON

140 Giving

Materials

• Hymn: "Living for Jesus"
• Novel: *Pelts and Promises* for the teacher

✍ Worktext page 204

Follow directions. Read and discuss the question at the top of the page. Guide the students as they complete each step of the instructions. Lead the students as they recite **2 Corinthians 9:7** together.

♫ Hymn: "Living for Jesus"

Sing the first three verses (Worktext pages 222–23). Play the recording and sing all three verses of the hymn.

♥ Memory Verse—2 Corinthians 9:7

Practice the memory verse.

Application Novel

Read Chapter 8 of *Pelts and Promises*. Review what happened in Chapter 7. Show the picture on page 62.

💡 **How does a mother dog act around her new puppies?** *(She is protective.)*

Tell the class that in this chapter the boys return to the storekeeper with twenty pelts. Allow students to predict whether they think the boys will be able to sell the pelts. *(The boys sell half of them.)*

Worktext page 261 reproduction

Pelts and Promises
Chapter 8

Name _____

Answer the questions.

How many pelts did Jamie and Willie B. have to sell this time?

5 rows × 4 pelts in each row = **20** pelts

What disappointment did they have when Jamie tried to sell the pelts?

The storekeeper did not need any more.

Color the pelts that Jamie was able to sell.

How many were they not able to sell?

20 pelts − 10 pelts = **10** pelts

What do you think Jamie and Willie B. will do now?

Answers will vary.

A Servant's Heart · Lesson 140 **261**

▶ **Why did Jamie have extra chores to do for his mother?** *(It was punishment for not coming home and doing his chores the day he stopped to see Willie B. and Dog.)*

▶ **How does the author describe the softness of the pups?** *(softer than corn silk, softer than the boys' best pelt)*

▶ **Why do the boys nail the pelts in rows of four?** *(They receive one dollar for four pelts; the rows make it easier to count how many dollars they will make.)*

▶ **Did the storekeeper like their pelts?** *(yes)*

▶ **Why did he not buy all twenty pelts?** *(He needed only ten for his shipment.)*

▶ **What else did the storekeeper want to buy?** *(Willie B.'s puppies)*

💡 **What do you think Willie B. and Jamie will do to earn more money?** *(Answers will vary.)*

Worktext page 261

Recall facts and details. Allow the students to complete the page independently. Provide help as needed. Call on students to tell ways that they can earn money. You may want to discuss money management (tithing, saving, and spending). Encourage the students to be willing to work. Challenge them to give their tithe and gifts to God cheerfully.

Going Beyond

Reinforcement

Play a review game. Write for display the two Bible account titles as headings: *The Widow Loves from Little* and *Mary Loves from Much.* Choose two teams. Call on a student from Team A to mention a person, place, or thing from one of the Bible accounts. Choose a student from Team B to come to the front and point to the corresponding heading. If he is correct, his team receives a point. If he is incorrect, the other team receives the point. Repeat this procedure, reversing the team roles.

Enrichment

Materials

- Pictures, photographs, or items to represent the following: money, a house, food, shoes, a Bible, and toys
- The following fill-in-the-blank statement written for display: *I will please God with my _____. How?*

Identify possessions to give to God. Call on students to choose a picture and then complete the sentence you wrote for display. Challenge them to explain how they could please God by their use of the item. Discuss the possible choices that they might make to please God or to please themselves. *(Note:* You may choose to adapt the activity for a learning center. Place the items at the back of the classroom with handwriting paper.)

I Give Myself to Others
Unit 10d

PREVIEW

Doctrines
- God is all-powerful (omnipotent) (Matthew 19:26). [Lesson 141]
- God imparts to the believer spiritual life and a new nature (Ephesians 2:4–5; 4:24). [Lesson 142]
- The Holy Spirit worked in the hearts and lives of the writers of the Bible (2 Peter 1:20–21). [Lesson 142]

Skills and Applications
- Learn Proverbs 20:11
- Read a map
- Locate information in a verse
- Sequence events
- Match characters to actions
- Recall facts and details
- Follow directions
- Understand that we are known by our actions
- Realize how God used Paul to spread the gospel
- Apply Bible knowledge to everyday life

LESSON 141 A Good-Deed Doer

Materials
- Hymn: "Living for Jesus"
- Unit 10 Bookmark for each student
- Map of the United States (optional)
- Highlighter for each student (optional)

♫ Hymn: "Living for Jesus"
Teach the fourth verse (Worktext pages 222–23). Discuss the meaning of the key words and phrases.

▶ **How long do we live on earth?** *(a little while)*

💡 **What is a treasure?** *(something important)*

▶ **What is the hymnwriter's dearest treasure?** *(the light of Jesus's smile)*

💡 **Name some things Christians can say or do that would make Jesus smile.** *(Any appropriate answer is acceptable.)*

Explain that a Christian should explain the gospel to the unsaved and encourage other Christians to follow Christ. Point out that singing is one way to both share the gospel and strengthen other believers (**Colossians 3:16–17**). Remind the students that it's a Christian's duty and joy to glorify God (**Matthew 5:16**). Lead the class in singing the verse several more times.

♥ Memory Verse—Proverbs 20:11
Principle: Children are known by their deeds. Direct the students to open their Bibles to the memory verse. Read the verse to them. Lead the students in reading it aloud.

▶ **Whom is this verse talking about?** *(children)*

▶ **How will people know what you are like?** *(by what you do)*

▶ **According to the memory verse, what should be pure and right?** *(our actions)*

💡 **What is the only way a person can live a life that is right and pleasing to God?** *(only by being saved by Christ and being filled with the Holy Spirit)*

Practice the verse. Direct the students to highlight the verse (optional) and mark the location with the Unit 10 Bookmark.

Background Information

Joppa—*This natural seaport is located on the Mediterranean coast of Israel, ten miles west of Lydda. It was the prophet Jonah's departing port when he tried to run from the will of God. This city is called Jaffa today.*

Introducing the Bible Account

Locate Joppa on a map. Direct the students' attention to the map on Worktext page 205. Share the background information as you choose.

Bible Account

Read Acts 9:36–43 or use the following retelling of the passage. Listening question: **How did Tabitha (Dorcas) treat the widows?** *(She was always doing good to them and helping them.)*

A Good-Deed Doer

Tabitha, who was also called Dorcas, lived in the city of Joppa and was a disciple of Jesus. The Bible says that she was always doing good and helping the poor, especially widows.

Tabitha got sick and died. Some other Christians in Joppa had heard that the apostle Peter had healed a paralyzed man in the nearby town of Lydda (about ten miles from Joppa). They had an idea. Two men went to Lydda and urged Peter to come quickly to Joppa.

When Peter got there, the people took him into the room where Tabitha's body was. The weeping widows showed Peter all the coats and garments that Tabitha had made for them.

Peter asked all the people in the room to leave. He knelt down beside Tabitha and prayed, and then he told her to get up. Tabitha opened her eyes. When she saw Peter, she sat up.

Peter took her hand and helped her stand up. Then he called for the other disciples and the widows to come back into the room.

When news of Peter's raising Tabitha from the dead got around town, people came to see for themselves. Many people believed in the Lord Jesus Christ because of the miracle.

❦

▶ **Where did Tabitha live?** *(Joppa)*
▶ **What had happened to Tabitha?** *(She got sick and died.)*
▶ **What was special about Tabitha?** *(She spent her time helping others.)*
 Was Tabitha's work pure and right? *(yes)*
▶ **Who did the Christians think could help them after their friend had died?** *(Peter)*
▶ **What caused them to think of Peter?** *(He had healed a man in the nearby town of Lydda.)*

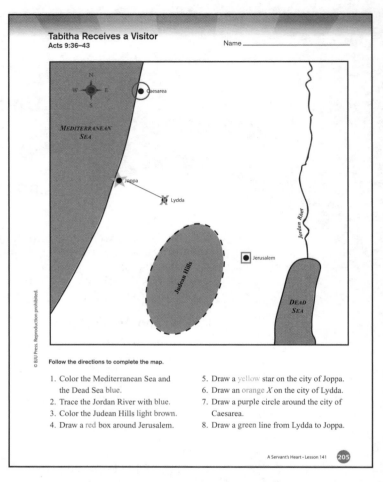

Tabitha Receives a Visitor
Acts 9:36–43

Name _____

Follow the directions to complete the map.

1. Color the Mediterranean Sea and the Dead Sea blue.
2. Trace the Jordan River with blue.
3. Color the Judean Hills light brown.
4. Draw a red box around Jerusalem.
5. Draw a yellow star on the city of Joppa.
6. Draw an orange X on the city of Lydda.
7. Draw a purple circle around the city of Caesarea.
8. Draw a green line from Lydda to Joppa.

A Servant's Heart • Lesson 141 **205**

▶ **How did Peter show that he was willing to help others?** *(He healed the paralyzed man in Lydda, and he came to Joppa at the men's request.)*
▶ **What did Peter do?** *(He had everyone leave the room; then he prayed and told Dorcas to get up, and she did.)*
▶ **How did the miracle affect the people of Joppa?** *(Many of them believed on Jesus as Savior.)*
💡 **Whose power really raised Tabitha from the dead?** *(God's)*

📝 Worktext page 205

Read a map. Direct the students to study the map. Remind them that walking ten miles from Lydda to Joppa could take half a day. Instruct the students to read and follow the directions on the page.

🧭 Geography Connection (optional)

Locate waterways and seaports on a map. Explain that throughout history any city located by a major waterway was likely to be more important. Display the map of the United States. Explain that the first cities were established by the waterways (a lake, a river, or the ocean). Locate the following cities, pointing out their location along the coasts: New York, San Francisco, and New Orleans. Locate these inland cities on major waterways: Minneapolis, Chicago, St. Louis, and Kansas City.

Tell the students to look again at Worktext page 205.

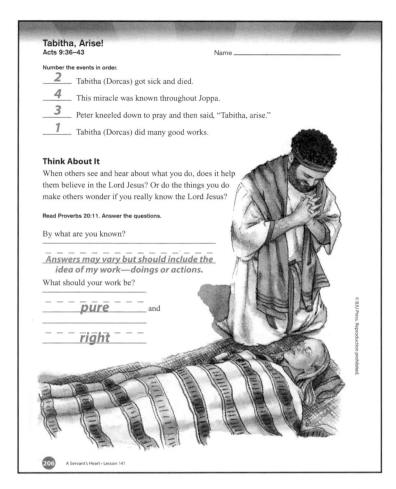

Tabitha, Arise!
Acts 9:36–43   Name _____

Number the events in order.

  _2_ Tabitha (Dorcas) got sick and died.

  _4_ This miracle was known throughout Joppa.

  _3_ Peter kneeled down to pray and then said, "Tabitha, arise."

  _1_ Tabitha (Dorcas) did many good works.

Think About It

When others see and hear about what you do, does it help them believe in the Lord Jesus? Or do the things you do make others wonder if you really know the Lord Jesus?

Read Proverbs 20:11. Answer the questions.

By what are you known?
_____

Answers may vary but should include the idea of my work—doings or actions.

What should your work be?

____ _pure_ ____ and

____ _right_ ____

206   A Servant's Heart • Lesson 141

▶ **What body of water is near Joppa and Caesarea?**
(the Mediterranean Sea)

Point out that these coastal cities were important for trade and transportation. Explain that Herod the Great made Caesarea an important seaport during his reign.

Worktext page 206

Sequence events. Read aloud the sentences at the top of the page. Allow time for students to number the events in order. Choose a volunteer to look up and to read aloud **Proverbs 20:11**. Read and discuss the questions at the bottom of the page. Remind the students that God is holy and that He tells believers to do what is right. Instruct the students to complete the page.

LESSON

142 Paul, the Missionary

Materials
- Chart 40, "The Roman Empire in Paul's Day"
- Hymn: "Living for Jesus"
- Toy snake (optional)

Hymn: "Living for Jesus"

Sing the fourth verse (Worktext pages 222–23).
Review the meaning of the key words and phrases in the fourth verse.

❤ Memory Verse—Proverbs 20:11

Practice the memory verse. Relate the verse to the theme *I Give Myself to Others*. Discuss the students' *doings* as they relate to helping others.

Background Information

Saul—*Born in Tarsus, Saul was a Jew, but through his father he was also a Roman citizen. He became a Pharisee and dedicated himself to stopping the spread of Christianity. On his way to Damascus to arrest Christians, Saul saw a bright light in the sky and heard the voice of Jesus. Saul was blind for three days after that. Saul was saved and baptized, and then he went out to be a missionary for God.*

Introducing the Bible Account

Introduce the Bible account. Direct the students' attention to the map on Worktext page 207. Introduce Saul using background information about his birth and his conversion. Guide the students in finding the cities on the map as you mention them. Tell them that Saul began using his Greek name, Paul, as he went out to spread the gospel. Explain that the following account takes place after Paul took three long missionary journeys. He was now a prisoner being taken to Rome, the center of world government at the time. When he was arrested for spreading the message of Jesus Christ, Paul had insisted that he had the right as a Roman citizen to be put on trial in front of Caesar in Rome, Italy. Paul continued to preach the gospel of Christ as he traveled westward.

Hold the toy snake in your hand (optional). Ask the students whether they think God could use a snake to fulfill His purpose. Tell them that in the following account, God used a viper (snake) for His glory.

Bible Account

Read Acts 27:1–28:6 or use the following retelling of the passage. Display Chart 40, "The Roman Empire in Paul's Day." Direct the students' attention to the map on Worktext page 207 so they may follow Paul's journey to Rome as you speak. Pause to identify on the maps each italicized location from the account. Provide help as needed. Listening question: **How long did Paul stay at Malta?** *(three months)*

Paul the Missionary

Paul, as a Roman prisoner, had been on a ship to *Rome* for a long time. The ship had left *Caesarea*, sailed around the island of *Cyprus* and then around to *Fair Havens* on the island of *Crete*. From Crete, the ship sailed out into the *Mediterranean Sea*. As it sailed toward Italy, the ship was caught in a strong storm.

Paul had warned those in charge not to leave Crete, but they had ignored his warnings. Now that the ship was out of control, the wind carried them to the island of *Clauda* (Cauda), where they tried to reinforce the ship. After leaving Clauda, they sailed out into the deep water where they faced another storm. They were tossed by the storm and could not find their directions because they could not see the stars. They thought that there was no hope. Far from land and without food, everybody was frightened; then Paul spoke up

again. He told them that the angel of God had told him not to fear. God said that Paul was to stand trial before Caesar, so they should not worry; God would get them to Rome.

They went on, driven by the big storm. Soon the ship was in trouble again with strong winds. The storm caused the ship to run aground on a reef. The bow got stuck, and the ship couldn't move. Meanwhile the waves pounded the stern until it began to break apart.

The soldiers wanted to kill the prisoners so that they wouldn't escape, but the centurion who was in charge told everyone to try to get ashore. Coming to land, they discovered they were on an island called *Melita* (Malta). The natives of the island were kind to the 276 shipwrecked men. They built a fire to keep the travelers warm. As Paul laid the sticks he had gathered on the fire, a viper (snake) came out of the fire and grabbed Paul's hand.

When the natives saw the snake on Paul's hand, their superstitions led them to believe that he must be a murderer and that he would now die. Paul shook the snake off, but not before it bit him.

The natives expected Paul to die immediately. Instead, they saw that he was fine and now thought that he must be a god.

The people of the island treated their visitors very well. Paul and the others were on the island for three months until after winter when another ship left.

This is just one of the incidents that happened when Paul was being taken to Rome. Many of Paul's journeys and the things that happened to him are written down in the Bible, in the book of Acts.

When Paul got to Rome, he was kept under guard for over two years. Some of books of the New Testament are letters that Paul wrote from this prison.

Sometime later, he wrote his last letter. It was to Timothy, his son in the faith. He testified that he was ready to die, knowing that he had fought a good fight.

❦

▶ **Why was Paul on a ship headed for Rome?** (He had been arrested for preaching and was going to be put on trial in front of Caesar, the leader of the Roman Empire.)

💡 **What was Paul's trip to Rome like?** (a dangerous journey with storms, a shipwreck, and a snakebite)

Point out that Paul continued to serve the Lord even as he faced many dangers throughout his life (**2 Corinthians 11:23–33**).

▶ **What sea was the ship traveling across?** (the Mediterranean Sea)

▶ **What island were they shipwrecked on?** (Malta)

▶ **How long did Paul stay at Malta?** (three months)

▶ **What bit Paul?** (a snake)

💡 **Name some books of the New Testament that were letters written by the apostle Paul. *Note:* Not all were written from prison.** (Romans through Philemon)

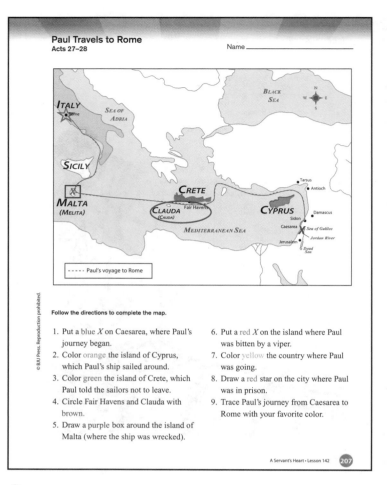

Paul Travels to Rome
Acts 27–28

Name _____

---- Paul's voyage to Rome

© BJU Press. Reproduction prohibited.

Follow the directions to complete the map.

1. Put a blue *X* on Caesarea, where Paul's journey began.
2. Color orange the island of Cyprus, which Paul's ship sailed around.
3. Color green the island of Crete, which Paul told the sailors not to leave.
4. Circle Fair Havens and Clauda with brown.
5. Draw a purple box around the island of Malta (where the ship was wrecked).
6. Put a red *X* on the island where Paul was bitten by a viper.
7. Color yellow the country where Paul was going.
8. Draw a red star on the city where Paul was in prison.
9. Trace Paul's journey from Caesarea to Rome with your favorite color.

A Servant's Heart • Lesson 142 207

💡 **Who led Paul in his conversion, his missionary journeys, and his trial in Rome?** (God. Explain that God used Paul to take the gospel to other parts of the world.)

💡 **Even though Paul ended up in prison for telling others the gospel, do you think he was glad he helped others know how to have eternal life?** (Answers will vary but direct the students to understand that Paul was thrilled to serve God.)

🖉 Worktext page 207

Read a map. Guide the students as they locate each place on the map and color it accordingly.

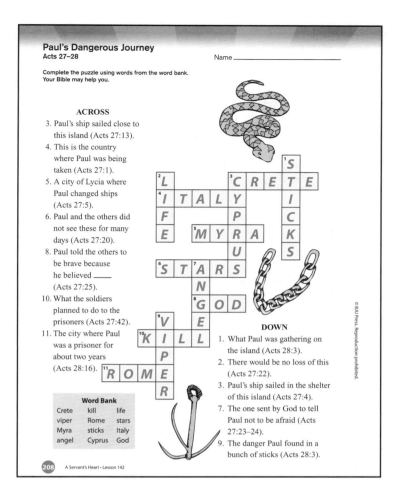

Paul's Dangerous Journey
Acts 27–28

Name _____

Complete the puzzle using words from the word bank.
Your Bible may help you.

ACROSS
3. Paul's ship sailed close to this island (Acts 27:13).
4. This is the country where Paul was being taken (Acts 27:1).
5. A city of Lycia where Paul changed ships (Acts 27:5).
6. Paul and the others did not see these for many days (Acts 27:20).
8. Paul told the others to be brave because he believed _____ (Acts 27:25).
10. What the soldiers planned to do to the prisoners (Acts 27:42).
11. The city where Paul was a prisoner for about two years (Acts 28:16).

DOWN
1. What Paul was gathering on the island (Acts 28:3).
2. There would be no loss of this (Acts 27:22).
3. Paul's ship sailed in the shelter of this island (Acts 27:4).
7. The one sent by God to tell Paul not to be afraid (Acts 27:23–24).
9. The danger Paul found in a bunch of sticks (Acts 28:3).

Word Bank		
Crete	kill	life
viper	Rome	stars
Myra	sticks	Italy
angel	Cyprus	God

Puzzle answers:
ACROSS: 3. CRETE, 4. ITALY, 5. MYRA, 6. STARS, 8. GOD, 10. KILL, 11. ROME
DOWN: 1. STICKS, 2. LIFE, 3. CYPRUS, 7. ANGEL, 9. VIPER

208 A Servant's Heart • Lesson 142

We Followed Jesus

Name _____

Cut out the pictures on the bold lines. Glue each one beside the right description of the person who followed Jesus.

widow	Jesus knew my heart when I put two coins in the offering.	Tabitha (Dorcas)	Many people followed Jesus after Peter prayed and raised me from the dead.
John the Baptist	I came preaching, baptizing, and telling that Jesus would come.	Matthew	I was a tax collector before Jesus called me to follow Him.
Paul	I made many trips to tell people about Jesus. My last trip was to Rome.	John	My brother James and I left our fishing nets to follow Jesus.
Mary of Bethany	I poured precious oil on Jesus to show that I loved and honored Him.	Peter	My brother Andrew and I went with Jesus and became fishers of men.

Matthew | John | Tabitha (Dorcas) | widow
Paul | Mary of Bethany | John the Baptist | Peter

A Servant's Heart • Lesson 143 209

Worktext page 208

Recall facts and details. Call on students to read the word bank choices at the bottom of the page. Guide them as they complete the clues going *Across* and then the clues going *Down*. Choose volunteers to find and read aloud the verses beside each clue. Direct the students' attention to the word bank to help with the spelling of the words in the puzzle.

LESSON 143 — Followers of Jesus

Materials
• Hymn: "Living for Jesus"
• Novel: *Pelts and Promises* for the teacher

Worktext page 209

Match characters to actions. Review each Bible character pictured on the page. Explain the directions for matching and let the students work independently. Remind them to put the pictures in the boxes before gluing them in place.

♪ Hymn: "Living for Jesus"

Sing the third and fourth verses (Worktext pages 222–23). Sing or play the recording of the chorus as you introduce the following motions.
• *O Jesus, Lord and Savior, I give myself to Thee*—Reach your arms to heaven, point to yourself and reach your arms to heaven again.
• *For Thou, in Thine atonement, didst give Thyself for me*—Make a cross with your fingers, reach your hands to heaven, and point to yourself.
• *I own no other Master, my heart shall be Thy throne*—Point to yourself, shake your head no, and place your hands over your heart; reach your hands to heaven.
• *My life I give, henceforth to live, O Christ, for Thee alone*—Run your hands along your body from your head down, and then reach your hands to heaven.

Lead the students in singing the third and fourth verses of the hymn, including the motions for the chorus.

♥ Memory Verse—Proverbs 20:11

Practice the memory verse.

Application Novel

Read Chapters 9 and 10 of *Pelts and Promises*.
Remind the students about the time period when this story takes place.

💡 **How did people get their food?** *(They had to grow gardens and hunt for food. Elicit from the students that guns were necessary because the people had to hunt for food.)*

Allow students to tell the class about any family members who go hunting. Show the picture on page 76 and ask the students how the boy looks. Listening question: **What makes Willie B. look like that?** *(He accidentally shoots Dog.)* Read Chapter 9.

▶ **How much money do the boys need to buy the Bible?** *($3.91)*

▶ **Why did Jamie's dad think that getting the money was not a problem?** *(money was coming in)*

▶ **What did Pa say Jamie must learn?** *(to always keep his word)*

▶ **What had Willie B.'s father told him to do with Dog?** *(chain her)*

▶ **What did Willie B. do instead?** *(He tied her.)*

▶ **Why did Jamie try to stop Willie B. from firing the gun?** *(He saw that it was Dog.)*

▶ **How had Dog gotten loose?** *(She had chewed through the rope.)*

▶ **Why did the boys take Dog to Jamie's house?** *(It was closer than Willie B.'s.)*

Read Chapter 10. Listening question: **Does Dog get better or not?** *(Yes, she does.)*

▶ **Why was Jamie relieved when he saw Ma working on Dog?** *(He knew that she was caring and gentle.)*

▶ **What did Pa say about what had happened?** *(Things that hurt, teach.)*

▶ **How do you know that Willie B. and the pup were glad to see Dog?** *(Willie B. was rolling on the ground, hugging Dog, as the pup jumped and danced on top of them.)*

▶ **Where was the lady pup?** *(She had been sold for one dollar.)*

▶ **How did they earn another $1.25 for the Bible?** *(one dollar for the sale of the pup and twenty-five cents to train her)*

▶ **What did Willie B. say he would give Jamie?** *(the black pup)*

Pelts and Promises
Chapters 9–10   Name _____

Put an *X* in the box next to the answer that is *not* true.

1. After Jamie sold 10 pelts, he felt
☐ worried. ☒ happy. ☐ angry.

2. The boys still needed
☐ more pelts. ☒ $10.98. ☐ $3.91.

3. Jamie's father said that Jamie and Willie B. could
☐ keep hunting. ☒ break the promise. ☐ find another way to earn money.

4. The game hunt ended badly because
☒ they found no rabbits. ☐ Dog followed them. ☐ Dog was hurt.

What do you do when things do not go well for you?
What should you do? Write your answer.

_____
_____ *Answers will vary.* _____
_____
_____
_____
_____

262 A Servant's Heart • Lesson 143

✍ Worktext page 262

Read the directions to the students. Remind them to look for the *one* ending for each sentence that is *not* true. Allow the students to complete the page independently; then discuss the last two questions with them. Elicit that Christians can pray to God for any need. Discuss how right attitudes and actions can have good results. Point out how Jamie accepted responsibility for his wrong actions and tried to make things right. Explain that we can also be unhappy because of a wrong attitude.

LESSON 144 Where Is It?

Materials
- Charts 2 and 3, "Books of the Bible"
- Hymn: "Living for Jesus"
- Novel: *Pelts and Promises* for the teacher

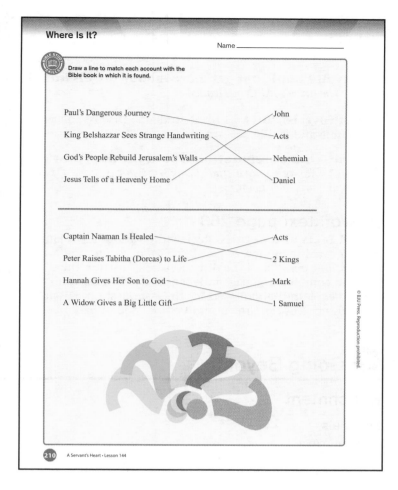

Where Is It?

Name _____

Draw a line to match each account with the Bible book in which it is found.

Paul's Dangerous Journey — John

King Belshazzar Sees Strange Handwriting — Acts

God's People Rebuild Jerusalem's Walls — Nehemiah

Jesus Tells of a Heavenly Home — Daniel

Captain Naaman Is Healed — Acts

Peter Raises Tabitha (Dorcas) to Life — 2 Kings

Hannah Gives Her Son to God — Mark

A Widow Gives a Big Little Gift — 1 Samuel

210   A Servant's Heart • Lesson 144

Application Novel

Read Chapters 11 and 12 of *Pelts and Promises*.
Review what has happened so far in the story.

💡 **Do you think Jamie and Willie B. will earn enough to buy the Bible?**

💡 **How do you think they will get the rest of the money?** *(Any answer is acceptable.)*

Tell the students to listen to find out whether they are correct as you read Chapter 11 to them.

▸ **What did Jamie have to do to keep the pup?** *(train it to guard the chickens and to hunt)*

▸ **What did Jamie name the pup?** *(Loyal) You may choose to discuss this name.*

▸ **How much time did they have till Christmas?** *(two weeks)*

▸ **What idea did Jamie get for making money?** *(selling pecans)*

▸ **Why did the pecan business not work out?** *(The insides of the pecans weren't any good.)*

▸ **How much money did they make from the pecans?** *(twenty cents)*

Read the title of Chapter 12.

💡 **What does this title mean?** *(Jamie and Willie B.'s last chance to make money)*

💡 **What would it be like for Jamie and Willie B. if they have to go before the church and tell what happened?** *(Any answer is acceptable.)* Discuss the importance of being responsible and honest.

📖 **Bible Study Skills, Worktext page 210**

Recite the names of the books of the Bible in order.
Direct the students to turn to the contents page in their Bibles, or display Charts 2 and 3, "Books of the Bible." Lead the students in reading and then reciting the names of the books of the Old and New Testaments in order.

Direct attention to Worktext page 210. Guide the students as they match the people and accounts to the books where they appear. Review briefly the people listed on the page who showed a servant's heart *(Paul, Daniel in the account of King Belshazzar, Nehemiah in rebuilding Jerusalem's wall, John, Naaman and the servant girl, Peter and Dorcas, Hannah and Samuel, and the widow)*. Emphasize the necessity of surrender, humility, and obedience to follow God.

🎵 **Hymn: "Living for Jesus"**

Sing the hymn (Worktext pages 222–23). Practice the hymn with the motions for the chorus.

💗 **Memory Verse — Proverbs 20:11**
Practice the memory verse.

Pelts and Promises
Chapters 11–12

Name _____

Fill in the space next to the correct answer.

1. Why was Jamie not able to sell the pelts?
   - ● The company out east did not need them.
   - ○ Mr. Hardwell did not want them.
   - ○ They were not trimmed right.

2. Why did the boys not sell many pecans?
   - ○ The squirrels got most of them.
   - ○ The trees were too tall to climb.
   - ● There were not many nut meats in the shells.

3. Why was Jamie not able to cut wood for Mr. Hardwell?
   - ○ His father would not let him stay in town.
   - ● Mr. Hardwell cut his own wood.
   - ○ Jamie did not have an axe.

4. Why did Jamie not buy the Bible that cost $8.00?
   - ● It was not like the one they ruined.
   - ○ He had to ask Willie B.
   - ○ His father would not let him.

5. How was Jamie able to keep Loyal and still buy the Bible?
   - ○ His father gave him $2.46.
   - ● He sold his deerfoot knife.
   - ○ Willie B. sold Dog.

What do you think Jamie meant when he said that he finally changed his world for good?

Answers will vary.

A Servant's Heart • Lesson 144 **263**

Read Chapter 12 aloud.

▶ **Who went to Madison on Saturday?** *(Jamie, his dad, and Loyal)*

▶ **How much did the boys still need to buy the Bible?** *($2.46)*

▶ **When the storekeeper asked Jamie, "What can I do for you?" what did Jamie say?** *(He had hoped the storekeeper would buy the rest of the pelts.)*

▶ **What idea did Jamie get after the storekeeper said the company didn't need any more pelts?** *(splitting wood)*

▶ **What had Jamie thought about all night?** *(selling Loyal)*

💡 **If Mr. Hardwell bought Loyal, would Jamie and Willie B. have enough money to buy a Bible like the one they had ruined?** *(no)*

▶ **What two reasons did Jamie give for not wanting to buy the eight-dollar Bible?** *(It wasn't like the one he and Willie B. had ruined, and they had promised Mr. Olefson they would buy the Bible from him.)*

▶ **How did Jamie finally get the $2.46 he needed to replace the Bible?** *(He sold his deerfoot knife.)*

💡 **Do you think that it was hard for Jamie to sell his knife?** *(Any answer is acceptable.)*

Point out that what we have belongs to God. It is not hard to give something away if it belongs to someone else. Explain that a Christian should be willing to share what he has with

others, while being thankful to God. Challenge the students to share their time, money, possessions, and the gospel with others.

▶ **Why did Jamie not get more money for his knife?** *(The sheath needed to be cleaned.)*

Recite **Proverbs 20:11** with the students. Discuss the lessons Jamie and Willie B. learned.

💡 **What kind of reputation would the boys now have?** *(Answers may include being trustworthy, honest, hard working, and sacrificial.)*

✎ Worktext page 263

Recall facts and details. Review the various ideas Jamie had for earning money. *(selling pelts, selling pecans, splitting wood, selling pups)* Read the directions and instruct the students to complete the page independently. Call on volunteers to explain their answers for the last question. Discuss how our choices can affect our lives for good or bad.

▶ Going Beyond

Enrichment

Materials
- Mural paper
- Crayons or felt-tip markers
- Fabric scraps, plastic wrap, crepe paper (optional)

Make a mural about Paul's journey to Rome. Divide a long sheet of paper into sections. Assign each section to one or more students and let them illustrate a segment about Paul's journey.

Reinforcement

Materials
- Boat marker for each team

Guide a review game, "Journey to Rome." Divide the class into two or more teams. Draw a course of equal spaces for each team for display. Provide a boat marker for each team. Place tape or magnets behind the markers so that they can be advanced for each correct answer. Explain that the goal is to reach Rome. Sample questions are provided on the next page. (You may reproduce the following art for use in this lesson or for a learning center.)

Questions for "Journey to Rome" Game

1. How many loaves and fish did Jesus use to feed the more than five thousand people (Matthew 14:17)? *(five loaves and two fish)*
2. Whom did Jesus ask to baptize Him (Matthew 3:13–15)? *(John the Baptist)*
3. What did John the Baptist tell people to do before they were baptized (Matthew 3:2)? *(repent)*
4. Why did Herod have John the Baptist put in prison (Matthew 14:3–4)? *(John had said Herod was wrong to marry his brother's wife.)*
5. Who asked to have the head of John the Baptist (Matthew 14:6–8)? *(Herodias's daughter)*
6. What did Peter and Andrew do for a living before Jesus called them (Mark 1:16)? *(They fished.)*
7. What was Peter's name before Jesus changed it (Mark 3:16)? *(Simon)*
8. What did Jesus tell the disciples that He would make them (Mark 1:17)? *(fishers of men)*
9. Jesus called two more brothers from their fishing business. One was James. Who was the other (Mark 1:19)? *(John)*
10. Jesus called a tax collector whose name was Levi to be His disciple. What was Levi's other name (Matthew 10:3; Mark 2:14)? *(Matthew)*
11. Which two disciples were called "the Sons of Thunder" (Mark 3:17)? *(James and John)*
12. Who brought Nathanael (Bartholomew) to Jesus (John 1:45–46)? *(Philip)*
13. Which disciple was called the son of Alphaeus because there was another disciple who had the same name (Mark 3:18)? *(James)*
14. Which disciple's name means "twin"? *(Thomas)*
15. Why did Jesus say that the poor widow who gave two mites gave the most of all (Mark 12:41–44)? *(She gave everything; she had nothing left.)*
16. What did Mary do with her expensive perfume to show that she loved and worshiped Jesus (Mark 14:3–9)? *(She poured it on His head.)*
17. What did one of the disciples say should have been done with Mary's perfume (Mark 14:3–9)? *(It should have been sold and the money given to the poor.)*
18. Why did Jesus tell the disciples to leave Mary alone (Mark 14:3–9)? *(She had done a good thing; she had anointed His body for burial—accept either answer.)*
19. Why was Dorcas [Tabitha] special to the disciples at Joppa (Acts 9:36)? *(She did many good things; she made clothes for the poor, especially widows—accept either answer.)*
20. Why did Peter travel to Joppa (Acts 9:36–38)? *(The disciples sent for him because Dorcas [Tabitha] had died.)*
21. What did Peter do when he got to Joppa (Acts 9:40)? *(prayed, raised Dorcas [Tabitha] from the dead)*
22. Why did many people in Joppa believe in the Lord (Acts 9:41–42)? *(They had heard that Peter had raised Dorcas [Tabitha] from the dead.)*
23. Where in Italy was Paul being taken as a prisoner (Acts 28:14)? *(Rome)*
24. What kept the ship from getting Paul to Italy for a long time (Acts 27:9, 14, 18)? *(The sailing was dangerous; there were rocks; there were rough winds—accept any of these answers.)*
25. How did Paul know that he, the soldiers, and the sailors wouldn't die in the storm (Acts 27:23–24)? *(God sent an angel to tell him not to be afraid.)*
26. What finally happened to Paul's ship (Acts 27:41)? *(It was wrecked on a reef.)*
27. How did the people on the island treat Paul and the others who were shipwrecked (Acts 28:2)? *(They were kind to them.)*
28. What was Paul gathering on the island (Acts 28:3)? *(sticks for the fire)*
29. What happened to Paul as he put wood on the fire (Acts 28:3)? *(A viper [snake] bit him.)*
30. Why were the other people surprised after the snake bit Paul (Acts 28:6)? *(He didn't die as they thought he would.)*

(*Note:* You might also like to have members of each team say the memory verses from this unit to advance their marker on the game board.)
Mark 1:17
John 14:2b–3
2 Corinthians 9:7
Proverbs 20:11

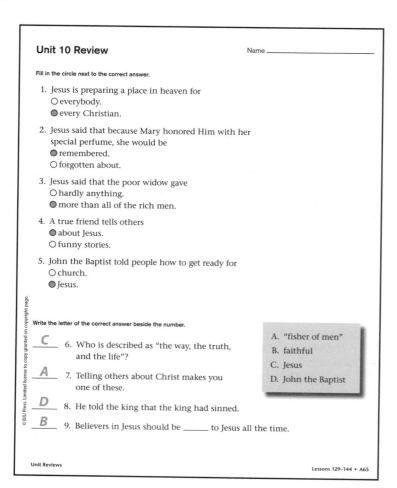

Unit 10 Review

Name _____

Fill in the circle next to the correct answer.

1. Jesus is preparing a place in heaven for
   ○ everybody.
   ● every Christian.

2. Jesus said that because Mary honored Him with her special perfume, she would be
   ● remembered.
   ○ forgotten about.

3. Jesus said that the poor widow gave
   ○ hardly anything.
   ● more than all of the rich men.

4. A true friend tells others
   ● about Jesus.
   ○ funny stories.

5. John the Baptist told people how to get ready for
   ○ church.
   ● Jesus.

Write the letter of the correct answer beside the number.

__C__ 6. Who is described as "the way, the truth, and the life"?

__A__ 7. Telling others about Christ makes you one of these.

__D__ 8. He told the king that the king had sinned.

__B__ 9. Believers in Jesus should be _____ to Jesus all the time.

A. "fisher of men"
B. faithful
C. Jesus
D. John the Baptist

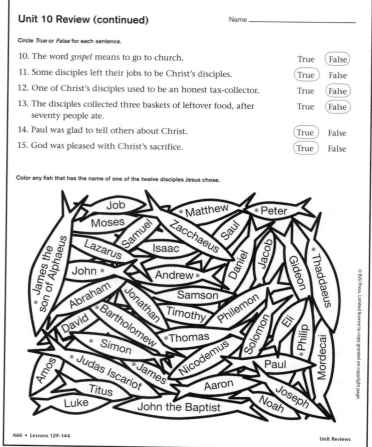

Unit 10 Review (continued)

Name _____

Circle *True* or *False* for each sentence.

10. The word *gospel* means to go to church. True (False)

11. Some disciples left their jobs to be Christ's disciples. (True) False

12. One of Christ's disciples used to be an honest tax-collector. True (False)

13. The disciples collected three baskets of leftover food, after seventy people ate. True (False)

14. Paul was glad to tell others about Christ. (True) False

15. God was pleased with Christ's sacrifice. (True) False

Color any fish that has the name of one of the twelve disciples Jesus chose.

Unit Review

Materials

• Copy of pages A65–66 ("Unit 10 Review") for each student

Guide a review of Unit 10. Review the people and events in preparation for the Unit 10 Test (optional).

Hymns

Note: All the unit hymns (titles in bold) except for the Thanksgiving MiniUnit appear on pages 211–23 in the Student Worktext and are recorded on the Bible 2 Music CD (sold separately).

Unit 1
Praise Ye the Lord, the Almighty* (Tracks 1–4)   **A3**
For the Beauty of the Earth*   A4
My God Is So Great†   A5

Unit 2
Lead On, O King Eternal* (Tracks 5–7)   **A6**
Yield Not to Temptation*   A7
Obedience†   A8–9

Unit 3
Be Thou Exalted† (Tracks 8–10)   **A10–11**
A Tender Heart†   A12
Take Time to Be Holy*   A13

Unit 4
Joy to the World!* (Tracks 11–14)   **A14**
Once in Royal David's City*   A15
O Come, All Ye Faithful*   A16

Unit 5
Joy in Serving Jesus† (Tracks 15–18)   **A17**
Take My Life, and Let It Be Consecrated*   A18

Unit 6
Am I a Soldier of the Cross* (Tracks 19–22)   **A19**
Faith of Our Fathers*   A20
Dare to Be a Daniel*   A21

*May be reproduced
†May not be reproduced except for overhead transparencies or PowerPoint slides for classroom use

Hymns (continued)

*May be reproduced
†May not be reproduced except for overhead transparencies or PowerPoint slides for
  classroom use

Praise Ye the Lord, the Almighty

Joachim Neander
Trans. by Catherine Winkworth

Stralsund Gesangbuch, 1665
Arr. in *Praxis Pietatas Melica*, 1668

1. Praise ye the Lord, the Al - might - y, the King of cre - a - tion! O my soul, praise Him, for He is thy health and sal - va - tion! All ye who hear, Now to His tem - ple draw near; Join me in glad ad - o - ra - tion!

2. Praise ye the Lord, who o'er all things so won - drous - ly reign - eth, Shel - ters thee un - der His wings, yea, so gen - tly sus - tain - eth! Hast thou not seen How thy de - sires e'er have been Grant - ed in what He or - dain - eth?

3. Praise ye the Lord, who with mar - vel - ous wis - dom hath made thee! Decked thee with health, and with lov - ing hand guid - ed and stayed thee; How oft in grief Hath not He brought thee re - lief, Spread - ing His wings for to shade thee!

4. Praise ye the Lord! O let all that is in me a - dore Him! All that hath life and breath, come now with prais - es be - fore Him! Let the A - men Sound from His peo - ple a - gain: Glad - ly for aye we a - dore Him.

For the Beauty of the Earth

Folliott S. Pierpoint

Conrad Kocher

1. For the beau - ty of the earth, For the glo - ry of the skies,
2. For the won - der of each hour Of the day and of the night,
3. For the joy of hu - man love, Broth - er, sis - ter, par - ent, child,
4. For Thy Church that ev - er - more Lift - eth ho - ly hands a - bove,

For the love which from our birth O - ver and a - round us lies:
Hill and vale, and tree and flow'r, Sun and moon, and stars of light:
Friends on earth, and friends a - bove, For all gen - tle thoughts and mild:
Of - fering up on eve - ry shore Her pure sac - ri - fice of love:

Lord of all, to Thee we raise This our hymn of grate - ful praise.

My God Is So Great

Ruth Harms Calkin

Ruth Harms Calkin

My God is so great, so strong and so might-y— There's noth-ing my God can-not do! My God is so great, so strong and so might-y— There's noth-ing my God can-not do! The moun-tains are His. The riv-ers are His. The stars are His hand-i-work, too. My God is so great, so strong and so might-y—There's noth-ing my God can-not do!

Lead On, O King Eternal

Ernest W. Shurtleff

Henry T. Smart

1. Lead on, O King E - ter - nal, The day of march has come!
2. Lead on, O King E - ter - nal, Till sin's fierce war shall cease,
3. Lead on, O King E - ter - nal, We fol - low, not with fears!

Hence - forth in fields of con - quest Thy tents shall be our home;
And ho - li - ness shall whis - per The sweet A - men of peace;
For glad - ness breaks like morn - ing Wher - e'er Thy face ap - pears;

Through days of prep - a - ra - tion Thy grace has made us strong,
For not with swords loud clash - ing, Nor roll of stir - ring drums,
Thy cross is lift - ed o'er us; We jour - ney in its light:

And now, O King E - ter - nal, We lift our bat - tle song.
With deeds of love and mer - cy We watch till Je - sus comes.
The crown a - waits the con - quest; Lead on, O God of might.

Yield Not to Temptation

Horatio R. Palmer

Horatio R. Palmer

1. Yield not to temp - ta - tion, For yield-ing is sin, Each vic - t'ry will
2. Shun e - vil com - pan-ions, Bad lan-guage dis-dain, God's name hold in
3. To him that o'er-com-eth God giv - eth a crown, Thro' faith we shall

help you Some oth-er to win; Fight man-ful-ly on-ward,
rev - 'rence, Nor take it in vain; Be thought-ful and ear - nest,
con - quer, Though of-ten cast down; He, who is our Sav - ior,

Dark pas - sions sub - due, Look ev-er to Je - sus, He will car-ry you through.
Kind-heart - ed and true, Look ev-er to Je - sus, He will car-ry you through.
Our strength will re - new, Look ev-er to Je - sus, He will car-ry you through.

Ask the Sav - ior to help you, Com - fort, strength - en, and keep you,

He is will-ing to aid you, He will car - ry you through.

Obedience

Mike and Ruth Greene   Mike and Ruth Greene

1. O - bed - i - ence is the ver - y best way to show that you be - lieve.
2. We want to live pure, we want to live clean, we want to do our best;

Do - ing ex - act - ly what the Lord com - mands, Do - ing it hap - pi - ly.
Sweet - ly sub - mit - ting to au - thor - i - ty, Leav - ing to God the rest.

Ac - tion is the key, Do it im - med - i - ate - ly. Joy you will re - ceive.
Walk - ing in the light, keep - ing our at - ti - tude right, On the nar - row way;

O - bed - i - ence is the ver - y best way to show that you be - lieve.
For if we be - lieve the Word we re - ceive, we al - ways will o - bey.

O - B - E - D - I - E - N - C - E,

O - bed - i - ence is the ver - y best way to show that you be - lieve.

Be Thou Exalted

Fanny Crosby

Al Smith

1. Be Thou ex - alt - ed for - ev - er and ev - er,
2. Be Thou ex - alt - ed, O Son of the high - est,
3. Be Thou ex - alt - ed, O Spir - it of pow - er,

God of e - ter - ni - ty, the An - cient of Days!
Sav - ior of sin - ful men, Re - deem - er and King!
Dwell - ing with - in our hearts to keep us from sin.

Won - drous in wis - dom, ma - jes - tic in glo - ry,
One with the Fa - ther, co - e - qual in glo - ry,
God of the a - ges, and Lord of Sal - va - tion,

Per - fect in ho - li - ness, and wor - thy of praise.
Hum - bly we come to Thee our hom - age to bring.
Rul - er of heav'n and earth, Thy prais - es we sing!

A Tender Heart

Ron Hamilton

Ron Hamilton

1. Take me now, Lord Je-sus, take me; I would give my heart to Thee.
2. Use me now, Lord Je-sus, use me, As I tell of Cal-va-ry.
3. Send me now, Lord Je-sus, send me, Lead me in Thy per-fect way.

Thy de-vot-ed ser-vant make me, On-ly Thine to be.
May Thy Spir-it move with-in me, Bring-ing souls to Thee.
Thy com-mand shall al-ways guide me; Glad-ly I o-bey.

Sav-ior, while my heart is ten-der, I would give Thee eve-ry part.

All my tal-ents I sur-ren-der; I am Thine, Lord, here's my heart.

Take Time to Be Holy

William D. Longstaff

George C. Stebbins

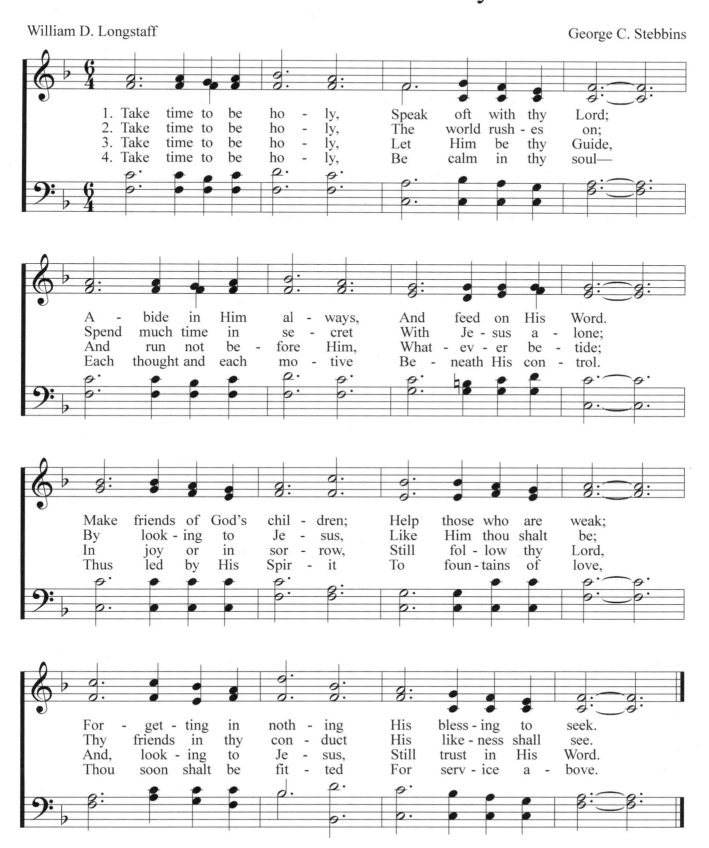

1. Take time to be ho - ly, Speak oft with thy Lord;
2. Take time to be ho - ly, The world rush - es on;
3. Take time to be ho - ly, Let Him be thy Guide,
4. Take time to be ho - ly, Be calm in thy soul—

A - bide in Him al - ways, And feed on His Word.
Spend much time in se - cret With Je - sus a - lone;
And run not be - fore Him, What - ev - er be - tide;
Each thought and each mo - tive Be - neath His con - trol.

Make friends of God's chil - dren; Help those who are weak;
By look - ing to Je - sus, Like Him thou shalt be;
In joy or in sor - row, Still fol - low thy Lord,
Thus led by His Spir - it To foun - tains of love,

For - get - ting in noth - ing His bless - ing to seek.
Thy friends in thy con - duct His like - ness shall see.
And, look - ing to Je - sus, Still trust in His Word.
Thou soon shalt be fit - ted For serv - ice a - bove.

Joy to the World!

From Psalm 98
Isaac Watts

G. F. Handel
Arr. by Lowell Mason

1. Joy to the world! the Lord is come: Let earth re-ceive her
2. Joy to the earth! the Sav-ior reigns: Let men their songs em-
3. No more let sins and sor-rows grow, Nor thorns in-fest the
4. He rules the world with truth and grace, And makes the na-tions

King; Let eve-ry heart pre-pare Him
ploy; While fields and floods, rocks, hills, and
ground; He comes to make His bless-ings
prove The glo-ries of His right-eous-

room, And heav'n and na-ture sing, And heav'n and na-ture
plains Re-peat the sound-ing joy, Re-peat the sound-ing
flow Far as the curse is found, Far as the curse is
ness, And won-ders of His love, And won-ders of His

sing, And heav'n, and heav'n and na-ture sing.
joy, Re-peat, re-peat the sound-ing joy.
found, Far as, far as the curse is found.
love, and won-ders, won-ders of His love.

Once in Royal David's City

Cecil F. Alexander

Henry J. Gauntlett

1. Once in roy - al Da - vid's cit - y Stood a low - ly cat - tle shed, Where a moth - er laid her ba - by In a man - ger for his bed: Ma - ry was that moth - er mild, Je - sus Christ, her lit - tle Child.

2. He came down to earth from heav - en, Who is God and Lord of all, And His shel - ter was a sta - ble, And His cra - dle was a stall: With the poor, and mean, and low - ly Lived on earth our Sav - ior ho - ly.

3. Je - sus is our child - hood's pat - tern, Day by day like us He grew; He was lit - tle, weak, and help - less, Tears and smiles like us He knew; And He feel - eth for our sad - ness, And He shar - eth in our glad - ness.

4. And our eyes at last shall see Him, Thro' His own re - deem - ing love, For that Child so dear and gen - tle Is our Lord in heav'n a - bove, And He leads His chil - dren on To the place where He is gone.

O Come, All Ye Faithful

Latin hymn, 18th century
Trans. by Frederick Oakeley

From Wade's *Cantus Diversi*, 1751

1. O come, all ye faith - ful, joy - ful and tri - um - phant,
2. Sing, choirs of an - gels, sing in ex - ul - ta - tion,
3. Yea, Lord, we greet Thee, born this hap - py morn - ing:

Come ye, O come ye to Beth - le - hem!
Sing all ye cit - i - zens of heav'n a - bove;
Je - sus, to Thee be all glo - ry giv'n;

Come and be - hold Him, born the King of an - gels!
Glo - ry to God, all glo - ry in the high - est:
Word of the Fa - ther, now in flesh ap - pear - ing:

O come, let us a - dore Him, O come, let us a - dore Him, O

come, let us a - dore Him, Christ the Lord!

Joy in Serving Jesus

Oswald J. Smith

Bentley D. Ackley

1. There is joy in serv-ing Je-sus, As I jour-ney on my way,
2. There is joy in serv-ing Je-sus, Joy that tri-umphs o-ver pain;
3. There is joy in serv-ing Je-sus, As I walk a-lone with God;
4. There is joy in serv-ing Je-sus, Joy a-mid the dark-est night,

Joy that fills the heart with prais-es, Eve-ry hour and eve-ry day.
Fills my soul with heav-en's mu-sic, Till I join the glad re-frain.
'Tis the joy of Christ, my Sav-ior, Who the path of suf-fering trod.
For I've learned the won-drous se-cret, And I'm walk-ing in the light.

There is joy, joy, Joy in serv-ing Je-sus, Joy that throbs with-

in my heart; Eve-ry mo-ment, eve-ry hour, As I draw up-

on His power, There is joy, joy, Joy that nev-er shall de-part.

I Don't Have to Wait

Harold Deal

Harry Dixon Loes

1. I don't have to wait un-til I'm grown up, To be lov-ing and
2. Eve-ry day my bod-y is made strong-er, As I eat, play, and
3. If I'm old e-nough to love my par-ents, I can know Je-sus'

true; There are man-y lit-tle deeds of kind-ness That each
sleep; And I'll dai-ly grow more like the Sav-ior, If His
love; I can learn to trust Him and o-bey Him, For He

day I can do. I can read my Bi-ble and
Word I will keep.
watch - es a - bove.

pray, Be a lov-ing help-er al - way;

Am I a Soldier of the Cross?

Isaac Watts

Thomas A. Arne

1. Am I a sol-dier of the cross? A fol-l'wer of the Lamb?
2. Must I be car-ried to the skies On flow-'ry beds of ease,
3. Are there no foes for me to face? Must I not stem the flood?
4. Sure I must fight if I would reign— In-crease my cour-age, Lord;

And shall I fear to own His cause, Or blush to speak His name?
While oth-ers fought to win the prize And sailed thru blood-y seas?
Is this vile world a friend to grace, To help me on to God?
I'll bear the toil, en-dure the pain, Sup-port-ed by Thy Word.

Faith of Our Fathers!

Frederick W. Faber

Henri F. Hemy
Alt. by James G. Walton

Dare to Be a Daniel

Philip P. Bliss

Philip P. Bliss

1. Stand - ing by a pur - pose true, Heed - ing God's com - mand,
2. Man - y might - y men are lost, Dar - ing not to stand,
3. Man - y gi - ants, great and tall, Stalk - ing thro' the land,
4. Hold the gos - pel ban - ner high! On to vic - t'ry grand!

Hon - or them, the faith - ful few! All hail to Dan - iel's Band!
Who for God had been a host, By join - ing Dan - iel's Band!
Head - long to the earth would fall, If met by Dan - iel's Band!
Sa - tan and his host de - fy, And shout for Dan - iel's Band!

Dare to be a Dan - iel, Dare to stand a - lone!

Dare to have a pur - pose firm! Dare to make it known!

Cleanse Me

J. Edwin Orr

Maori melody

1. Search me, O God, and know my heart to - day;
2. I praise Thee, Lord, for cleans - ing me from sin;
3. Lord, take my life, and make it whol - ly Thine:
4. O Ho - ly Ghost, re - viv - al comes from Thee;

Try me, O Sav - ior, know my thoughts, I pray.
Ful - fill Thy Word, and make me pure with - in.
Fill my poor heart with Thy great love di - vine.
Send a re - viv - al— start the work in me.

See if there be some wick - ed way in me;
Fill me with fire, where once I burned with shame;
Take all my will, my pas - sion, self and pride;
Thy Word de - clares Thou wilt sup - ply our need;

Cleanse me from eve - ry sin, and set me free.
Grant my de - sire to mag - ni - fy Thy name.
I now sur - ren - der, Lord, in me a - bide.
For bless - ings now, O Lord, I hum - bly plead.

Nothing But the Blood

Robert Lowry

Robert Lowry

1. What can wash a-way my sin? Noth-ing but the blood of Je-sus;
2. For my par-don this I see— Noth-ing but the blood of Je-sus;
3. Noth-ing can for sin a-tone— Noth-ing but the blood of Je-sus;
4. This is all my hope and peace— Noth-ing but the blood of Je-sus;

What can make me whole a-gain? Noth-ing but the blood of Je-sus.
For my cleans-ing, this my plea— Noth-ing but the blood of Je-sus.
Naught of good that I have done— Noth-ing but the blood of Je-sus.
This is all my right-eous-ness— Noth-ing but the blood of Je-sus.

Oh! pre-cious is the flow That makes me white as snow;

No oth-er fount I know, Noth-ing but the blood of Je-sus.

What a Wonderful Savior!

Elisha A. Hoffman

Elisha A. Hoffman

1. Christ has for sin a - tone - ment made, What a won - der - ful Sav - ior!
2. I praise Him for the cleans - ing blood, What a won - der - ful Sav - ior!
3. He cleansed my heart from all its sin, What a won - der - ful Sav - ior!
4. He gives me o - ver - com - ing pow'r, What a won - der - ful Sav - ior!
5. To Him I've giv - en all my heart, What a won - der - ful Sav - ior!

We are re - deemed! the price is paid! What a won - der - ful Sav - ior!
That rec - on - ciled my soul to God; What a won - der - ful Sav - ior!
And now He reigns and rules there - in; What a won - der - ful Sav - ior!
And tri - umph in each try - ing hour; What a won - der - ful Sav - ior!
The world shall nev - er share a part; What a won - der - ful Sav - ior!

What a won - der - ful Sav - ior is Je - sus, my Je - sus!

What a won - der - ful Sav - ior is Je - sus, my Lord!

When I Survey the Wondrous Cross

Isaac Watts

From a Gregorian chant
Arr. by Lowell Mason

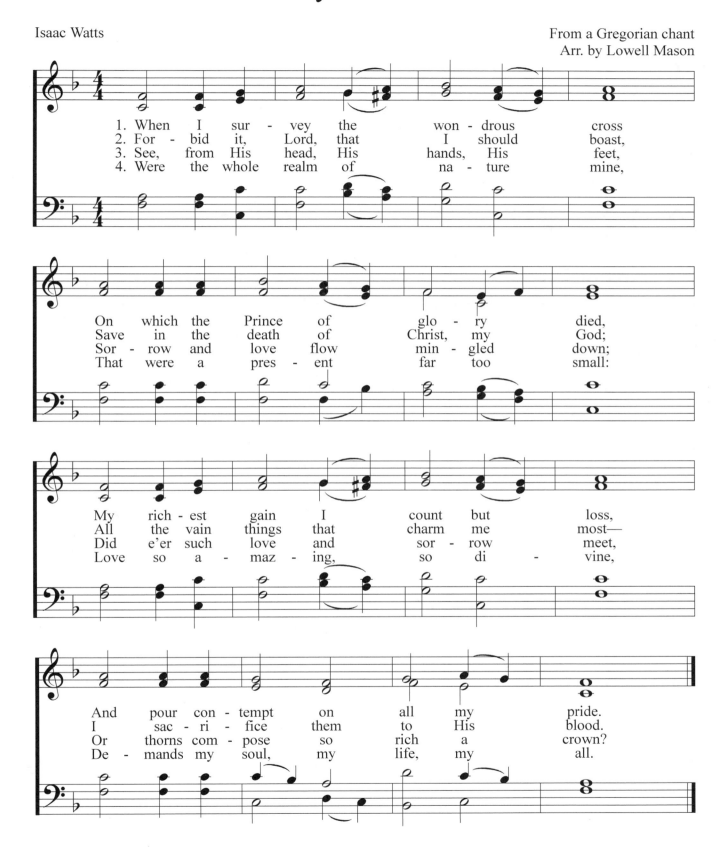

1. When I sur - vey the won - drous cross
2. For - bid it, Lord, that I should boast,
3. See, from His head, His hands, His feet,
4. Were the whole realm of na - ture mine,

On which the Prince of glo - ry died,
Save in the death of Christ, my God;
Sor - row and love flow min - gled down;
That were a pres - ent far too small:

My rich - est gain I count but loss,
All the vain things that charm me most—
Did e'er such love and sor - row meet,
Love so a - maz - ing, so di - vine,

And pour con - tempt on all my pride.
I sac - ri - fice them all to His blood.
Or thorns com - pose so rich a crown?
De - mands my soul, my life, my all.

Easter Hymn

Eileen Berry

Karin Wiley

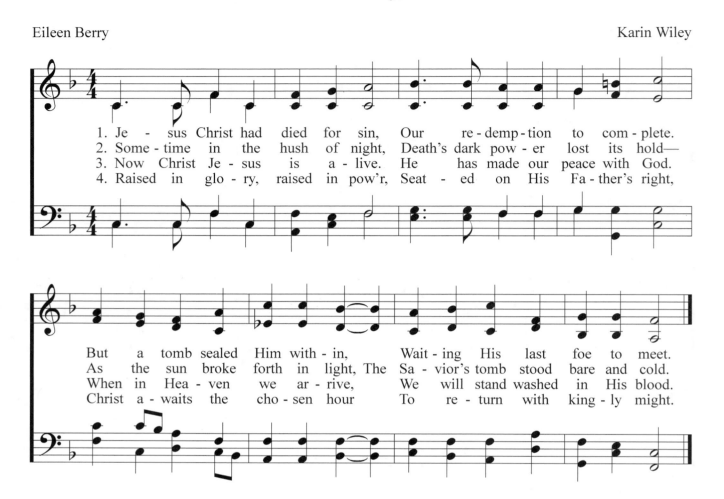

1. Je - sus Christ had died for sin, Our re - demp - tion to com - plete.
2. Some - time in the hush of night, Death's dark pow - er lost its hold—
3. Now Christ Je - sus is a - live. He has made our peace with God.
4. Raised in glo - ry, raised in pow'r, Seat - ed on His Fa - ther's right,

But a tomb sealed Him with - in, Wait - ing His last foe to meet.
As the sun broke forth in light, The Sa - vior's tomb stood bare and cold.
When in Hea - ven we ar - rive, We will stand washed in His blood.
Christ a - waits the cho - sen hour To re - turn with king - ly might.

Jesus Shall Reign

From Psalm 72
Isaac Watts

John Hatton

1. Je - sus shall reign wher - e'er the sun
2. From north to south the princ - es meet
3. To Him shall end - less prayer be made,
4. Peo - ple and realms of eve - ry tongue
5. Let eve - ry crea - ture rise and bring

Does His suc - ces - sive jour - neys run;
To pay their hom - age at His feet;
And end - less prais - es crown His head;
Dwell on His love with sweet - est song,
Hon - or and glo - ry to our King;

His king - dom spread from shore to shore,
While west - ern em - pires own their Lord,
His name like sweet per - fume shall rise
And in - fant voic - es shall pro - claim
An - gels de - scend with songs a - gain,

Till moons shall wax and wane no more.
And sav - age tribes at - tend His word.
With eve - ry morn - ing sac - ri - fice.
Their ear - ly bless - ings on His name.
And earth re - peat the loud "A - men!"

Ye Must Be Born Again

William T. Sleeper

George C. Stebbins

1. A rul-er once came to Je-sus by night To ask Him the way of sal-va-tion and light; The Mas-ter made an-swer in words true and plain,
2. Ye chil-dren of men, at-tend to the word So sol-emn-ly ut-tered by Je-sus the Lord; And let not this mes-sage to you be in vain,
3. O ye who would en-ter that glo-ri-ous rest, And sing with the ran-somed the song of the blest; The life ev-er-last-ing if ye would ob-tain,
4. A dear one in heav-en thy heart yearns to see, At the beau-ti-ful gate may be watch-ing for thee; Then list to the note of this sol-emn re-frain,

"Ye must be born a-gain."

"Ye must be born a-gain, Ye must be born a-gain; I

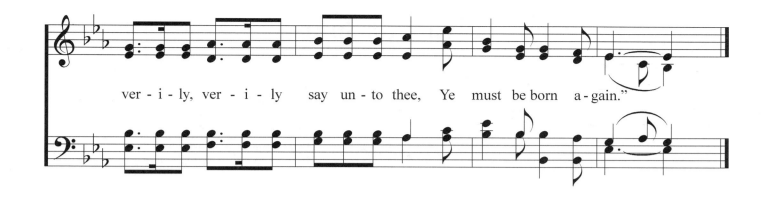

ver - i - ly, ver - i - ly say un - to thee, Ye must be born a - gain."

Fairest Lord Jesus

From the German, 17th Century
4th Verse Trans. by Joseph A. Seiss

Silesian folksong
Arr. by Richard S. Willis

1. Fair - est Lord Je - sus, Rul - er of all na - ture,
2. Fair are the mead - ows, Fair - er still the wood - lands,
3. Fair is the sun - shine, Fair - er still the moon - light,
4. Beau - ti - ful Sav - ior! Lord of the na - tions!

O Thou of God and man the Son: Thee will I cher - ish,
Robed in the bloom - ing garb of spring: Je - sus is fair - er,
And all the twin - kling star - ry host: Je - sus shines bright - er,
Son of God and Son of Man! Glo - ry and hon - or,

Thee will I hon - or, Thou my soul's glo - ry, joy, and crown.
Je - sus is pur - er, Who makes the woe - ful heart to sing.
Je - sus shines pur - er Than all the an - gels heav'n can boast.
Praise, ad - o - ra - tion, Now and for - ev - er - more be Thine!

Living for Jesus

Thomas O. Chisholm

C. Harold Lowden

1. Liv - ing for Je - sus a life that is true,
2. Liv - ing for Je - sus who died in my place,
3. Liv - ing for Je - sus wher - ev - er I am,
4. Liv - ing for Je - sus through earth's lit - tle while,

Striv - ing to please Him in all that I do;
Bear - ing on Cal - vary my sin and dis - grace;
Do - ing each du - ty in His ho - ly name;
My dear - est treas - ure, the light of His smile;

Yield - ing al - le - giance, glad - heart - ed and free,
Such love con - strains me to an - swer His call,
Will - ing to suf - fer af - flic - tion and loss,
Seek - ing the lost ones He died to re - deem,

This is the path - way of bless - ing for me.
Fol - low His lead - ing and give Him my all.
Deem - ing each tri - al a part of my cross.
Bring - ing the wea - ry to find rest in Him.

O Je - sus, Lord and Sav - ior, I give my - self to Thee,

For Thou, in Thine a - tone - ment, Didst give Thy - self for me;

I own no oth - er Mas - ter, My heart shall be Thy throne;

My life I give, hence - forth to live, O Christ, for Thee a - lone.

I'll Go Where You Want Me to Go

1—Mary Brown
2, 3—Charles E. Pryor

Carrie E. Rounsefell

1. It may not be on the moun-tain's height Or o - ver the storm-y
2. Per - haps to-day there are lov-ing words Which Je - sus would have me
3. There's sure - ly some-where a low-ly place In earth's har-vest fields so

sea, It may not be at the bat - tle's front My
speak, There may be now, in the paths of sin, Some
wide, Where I may la - bor thru life's short day For

Lord will have need of me; But if by a still, small
wan - d'rer whom I should seek; O Sav - ior, if Thou wilt
Je - sus the Cru - ci - fied; So, trust - ing my all un -

voice He calls To paths I do not know, I'll an - swer, dear Lord, with my
be my Guide, Tho dark and rug-ged the way, My voice shall ech - o the
to Thy care— I know Thou lov - est me— I'll do Thy will with a

hand   in Thine,   I'll   go   where You want   me   to   go.
mes - sage sweet, I'll   say   what You want   me   to   say.
heart   sin - cere, I'll   be   what You want   me   to   be.

I'll   go where You want me to go, dear Lord, O'er moun-tain or plain   or sea;

I'll   say what you want me to say,   dear Lord, I'll be what you want me to   be.

There Were Twelve Disciples

Unknown

George A. Minor

There were twelve dis - ci - ples Je - sus called to help Him: Si - mon Pe - ter, An - drew,

James, his bro - ther John; Phil - ip, Thom - as, Mat - thew,

James the son of Al - pheus, Thad - deus, Si - mon, Ju - das, And Bar - thol - o - mew.

1.
He has called us too, He has called us too; We are His dis - ci - ples,

2.
I am one, are you? We are His dis - ci - ples, We His work must do.

We Praise Thee, O God, Our Redeemer

Julia C. Cory

Netherlands melody
Arr. by Edward Kremser

1. We praise Thee, O God, our Re-deem-er, Cre-a-tor—
2. We wor-ship Thee, God of our fa-thers, we bless Thee—
3. With voic-es u-nit-ed our prais-es we of-fer—

In grate-ful de-vo-tion our trib-ute we bring;
Thru life's storm and tem-pest our Guide hast Thou been;
To Thee, great Je-ho-vah, glad an-thems we raise;

We lay it be-fore Thee, we kneel and a-dore Thee,
When per-ils o'er-take us, es-cape Thou wilt make us,
Thy strong arm will guide us, our God is be-side us—

We bless Thy ho-ly Name, glad prais-es we sing.
And with Thy help, O Lord, our bat-tles we win.
To Thee, our great Re-deem-er, for-ev-er be praise!

Thanksgiving MiniUnit

OVERVIEW

Preparing the Teacher

God is the great God from Whom all blessings flow. How often we're saddened to hear our students complaining about minor inconveniences when instead they should be constantly praising God for all the huge, innumerable blessings He has poured abundantly into their lives! Yet we must consider how many times God is grieved by our own complaining about inconveniences and perceived injustices. Ask God to convict you of the times when your spirit rises up in ungratefulness, and instead thank God, remembering what we really deserve in light of His holiness and our sinfulness.

The Lord readily recognizes that we have needs we should pray about. But in **Philippians 4:6**, where God instructs us to pray, He also commands us to give thanks to Him in the middle of those very situations we feel such a burden to pray about. As we do submit those things to Him with gratitude, trusting Him to work out each situation for His glory and our good, the result will be that in place of anxiety we will have perfect peace.

At this time of the year, our hearts turn to God in thankfulness. Teach your students that our thanksgiving to God should include both the things we so often overlook and the things that we would not naturally be thankful for.

Preparing the Materials

Lesson A—Copy of pages A48–49 ("Make a Booth" and "Booth Parts") on heavy-weight paper [E]; sheet of 9" × 12" neutral-colored construction paper [E]; overhead transparency of page A37 ("We Praise Thee, O God, Our Redeemer"); overhead transparency or large poster of pages A46–47 ("Choral Reading: Psalm 148"); copies of page A45 ("Grape and Pomegranate Markers") to make one marker for each student

Lesson B—Choral reading poster or transparency; grape or pomegranate marker [E]; copy of page A50 ("Thanks for the Things God Has Given") [E]; materials and ingredients for grape salad snack [O]

Lesson C—Choral reading poster or transparency; grape or pomegranate marker [E]; copy of page A51 ("Thanks a Bunch!") and page A52 ("Thanksgiving Napkin Ring") [E]; wilted plant; watering can with water; container; references and sentences written for display

God's People Give Him Thanks and Praise

PREVIEW

Doctrines

- God is righteous (Psalm 116:5). [Lesson A]
- God is merciful (Psalm 86:15). [Lesson A]
- The Bible presents standards of living and a way of life that are of God (Titus 2:11–12). [Lesson B]

Applications

- Speak God's praises in a choral reading
- Demonstrate a thankful attitude toward God
- Learn about how God's people praised Him in Bible times

LESSON A Feast of Tabernacles

Materials

- Hymn: "Praise Ye the Lord, the Almighty"
- Copy of pages A48–49 ("Make a Booth" and "Booth Parts") on heavy-weight paper for each student
- Sheet of 9" × 12" neutral-colored construction paper for each student
- Overhead transparency of page A37 ("We Praise Thee, O God, Our Redeemer")
- Overhead transparency or large poster of pages A46–47 ("Choral Reading: Psalm 148")
- Copies of page A45 ("Grape and Pomegranate Markers") on colored paper. If desired, color the pictures, cut out, and laminate for future use. Each student will need either a grape marker or a pomegranate marker.

♩ Hymn: "Praise Ye the Lord, the Almighty"

Review the Unit 1 hymn (Worktext page 212). Play the recording of the first verse to help students remember the tune.

♩ Hymn: "We Praise Thee, O God, Our Redeemer"

Sing the first verse. Display on the overhead projector the transparency of page A37 ("We Praise Thee, O God, Our Redeemer").

💡 **What is the meaning of *tribute*?** (*a gift given with gratitude, respect, and honor*)

Sing the first verse. (*Note:* Students may recognize the melody if they have previously heard or sung "We Gather Together.")

Choral Reading

Guide a choral reading. Explain that a choral reading is performed as a choir would perform a piece of music, giving attention to when to speak and when to be silent. Like singing, it is a way of praising and worshiping God.

Show the transparencies or poster made from pages A46–47 ("Choral Reading: Psalm 148"). Distribute the markers made from page A45 ("Grape and Pomegranate Markers") randomly so that those speaking each part are scattered throughout the room. Instruct them to leave the markers lying on their desks to remind them of which part they are to say. Point out that sometimes all of the girls or all of the boys will speak regardless of their markers. Explain that sometimes the entire group will speak. Tell them to watch carefully as you point to the lines from the choral reading. Encourage them to speak clearly and pleasantly when it is their turn.

Practice with one or two lines. Emphasize and model a worshipful attitude. Explain each of the hand signals described. Demonstrate how the claps should sound (brisk, definite) and how the accompanying actions should be executed (cleanly, gracefully).

Direct the students in a choral reading of Psalm 148. This may be prepared for performance as a Thanksgiving program. Make large cutouts of the grapes, the pomegranates, a boy, and a girl plus a placard with the word *All*. Once the students have memorized their assigned parts, you can direct the choir by holding up the cutouts for the appropriate lines instead of pointing to them on the transparency or poster.

Background Information

Thanksgiving Celebration—*As a holiday, Thanksgiving was added to the American calendar relatively recently (in the nineteenth century). The idea, however, of a celebration for giving thanks and praise to God is centuries old. God's people, the Israelites, actually celebrated two feasts that correspond roughly to our celebration of Thanksgiving—the Festival of Weeks (Pentecost) and the Festival of Tabernacles (Ingathering).*

Festivals—*The Festival of Weeks was a one-day celebration at the end of the barley harvest, which came in the middle of the wheat harvest. The other festival, the Festival of Tabernacles, was a whole week long and marked the end of the harvest season, grapes being the last crop harvested.*

Grape Harvest—*Vintage (grape gathering) began in July and lasted until September. The people of a village often shared a vineyard. The whole village usually moved out to the vineyard and camped there until the work was done. The grapes were picked and placed in huge baskets. Some of them were pressed to make grape juice. The press was a cistern cut out of rock with a drain hole in the bottom. Several people would get into the cistern and mash the grapes with their feet so the juice would run down into collecting vessels. The rest of the grapes were dried to make raisins. They were laid on mats in the sun and sprinkled with olive oil. They had to be turned again and again. When they had dried, they were compressed into blocks for storage. The people responded to God's provision with a lot of singing, dancing, and feasting throughout the harvest and the Festival of Ingathering.*

Because of the lack of refrigeration in the ancient world, grape juice fermented into wine. Unlike modern times, however, when wine producers seek to raise the alcoholic levels, people in Bible times typically diluted wine, which had a lower alcohol content than modern beverages to begin with. Thus the wine consumed in Bible times was very different from the wine consumed today. In ancient times wine could be safely consumed in moderation without any loss of mental, spiritual, ethical, or behavioral discernment.

Introducing the Bible Account

Discuss Thanksgiving traditions. Write the word *thanksgiving* for display.

💡 **What words make up the compound word?** *(thanks* and *giving)*

💡 **Who is most worthy of being given our thanks and praise?** *(God, our Creator and Redeemer)*

💡 **How does your family celebrate Thanksgiving?** *(Answers will vary.)*

💡 **Can you imagine building a tent-like shelter in your yard and living in it for a whole week while you celebrate Thanksgiving?** *(Explain that this is what the Israelites did.)*

Read Exodus 23:14–16, 34:22, Leviticus 23:33–43, and Deuteronomy 16:13–15 or use the following retelling. Listening question: **What did the Israelites do during their thanksgiving celebration?** *(lived in booths, made sacrifices, sang, feasted, and worshiped God)*

Feast of Tabernacles

God's people sat resting in their booths made of palm and willow branches. They smelled the pleasant aroma of the fruits they had hung among the leaves. They looked out at the vines from which all the grapes had been picked. The celebration was called the Festival of Ingathering. It was also called the Feast of Tabernacles (tents) or Booths. The harvest work was completed for another year. The grapes were the last of the crops to be gathered.

As they rested, they must have thought about God's goodness to their nation in the years after He brought them out of Egypt. They told their children the stories of how He had provided all that they needed and had driven enemies out of their land. Living in booths for the weeks of harvest reminded them of the years that Israel had wandered in the wilderness, living in tents until God said they were ready to enter the Promised Land. God had commanded them to hold this special celebration to help them remember the lessons He had taught them. Besides learning that He would take care of them and supply their needs, they had learned that they must worship only Him and obey Him in all things.

For seven days, the priests offered sacrifices to God. This showed that His people were thankful and that all things, including their good harvest, belonged to Him. There was a lot of happy singing and feasting. Families made sure that no one was left out. The widows, the orphans, and those who were strangers were all made welcome. Everyone was invited to join in the celebration.

At the end of the seven days, there was another day of rest before the Israelites went back to their homes.

Discussion Questions

💡 **How is this celebration of thanksgiving a pattern for us as we celebrate Thanksgiving in America?** *(Possible answers include thinking about God's goodness, praising Him, feasting, resting, and getting together with God's people.)*

💡 **How was it different?** *(Possible answers include priests offering sacrifices, living in booths, and everyone helping in the harvest, not just the farmers.)*

💡 **What did the Israelites do at the beginning and end of the Festival of Ingathering?** *(They rested.)*

💡 **What were their booths like?** *(like tents, made of branches, hung with fruits)*

▶ **What did the priests do for seven days?** *(They offered sacrifices.)*

▶ **Why did the Israelites have this special celebration?** *(God commanded them to have it.)*

▶ **Why did God command them to do this?** *(to remember the lessons they had learned in the wilderness)*

▶ **What lessons had God taught them?** *(that He would take care of them and supply their needs; that they must worship only Him and obey Him in all things)*

Emphasize that these are still important lessons for God's people to learn and remember. God warns against forgetting the great things He has done. To avoid the sin of their forgetting His greatness and graciousness, God commanded the Israelites to continually keep His Word in their minds and vision as well as to speak His Word to others. Read **Deuteronomy 6:4–12** to the students.

📖 Bible Study

Locate Bible verses that reinforce these lessons. Direct students in using the contents page in their Bibles to find the location of each book. Guide them in locating and reading the following verses.
Joshua 24:17–18—God did great things for Israel.
Psalm 150:2—God is worthy of praise for Who He is and what He does.
Exodus 20:1–3—God's people are to worship and serve only Him.

🖌 Art Connection

Make a booth model. Distribute a copy of page A49 ("Booth Parts") and a sheet of construction paper to each student. Allow time for students to color each piece on the handout and cut out the pieces. Following the directions on page A48 ("Make a Booth"), demonstrate how to fold, cut, and decorate the paper booth. Invite the students to take the models home and explain the Israelites' celebration of thanksgiving to their families.

The Israelites Learn Their History

Materials

- Hymn: "Praise Ye the Lord, the Almighty"
- Copy of page A50 ("Thanks for the Things God Has Given") for each student
- Transparency of page A37 ("We Praise Thee, O God, Our Redeemer") from the previous lesson
- Choral reading poster or transparency from the previous lesson
- Grape and pomegranate markers from the previous lesson
- Materials and ingredients for grape salad snack (see Food Connection in this lesson; optional)

🎵 Hymn: "Praise Ye the Lord, the Almighty"
Sing the first verse (page 212).

🎵 Hymn: "We Praise Thee, O God, Our Redeemer"

Sing the first and second verses. Display on the overhead projector the transparency of A37 ("We Praise Thee, O God, Our Redeemer"). Explain the key words in the second verse:
Fathers—*those who were before us, not just dads*
Tempest—*another word for storm*
Perils—*dangers*

Sing the second verse.

Choral Reading

Guide the choral reading. Distribute the grape and pomegranate markers and follow the same procedure as in the previous lesson. Emphasize and model a worshipful attitude.

Background Information

The Captivity and Return—*Because the Israelites had turned away from worshiping and serving only God, He caused His people to be conquered and carried away to Babylon. Ezra the priest had returned with a group to rebuild the temple in Jerusalem. About fourteen years later, Nehemiah led a group back to rebuild the wall of the city.*

Introducing the Bible Account

Discuss the harvest celebrations of God's people. Review the previous account.

💡 **What did God tell His people to do to remember His goodness to them after the harvest?** *(They were to celebrate the Feast of Tabernacles for seven days; they were to stay in booths to remind them of living in tents during their days in the wilderness.)*

▶ **Do God's people always do what He commands?** *(no)*

After a time, the Israelites forgot to celebrate as God commanded them. They also forgot His goodness to them. They forgot the lessons He had taught them. God caused them to be captured and taken away by their enemies. In time, He allowed them to return to their land.

Bible Account

Read Deuteronomy 31:9–13 and Nehemiah 8:13–18 or use the following retelling. Share the background information. Listening question: **What did Ezra tell the Israelites and how did the people react?** *(Ezra read the Word of God and explained their history of being guided by a great, gracious, and loving Lord. The people enjoyed praising the Lord.)*

The Israelites Learn Their History

God's people gathered together to listen to Ezra the priest read from God's Word. They heard a commandment that God had given Moses and the children of Israel, telling them how to celebrate a special time of thanksgiving to Him.

This had been neglected for some time. As soon as they heard this, they went out rejoicing and gathered branches from olive trees, myrtle trees, palm trees, and other leafy trees. They used the branches to build booths (shelters) on the flat roofs of their houses, in their yards, and in the open places of the city. They lived in the booths for seven days while they celebrated as God's Word had told them they should. Every day they gathered together to listen to the Word of God being read. They learned more and more about worshiping God and serving Him. This was a time of joy and gladness for them. They feasted and enjoyed praising God. It had been centuries, reaching back to the time of Joshua, since this special time of thanksgiving had been celebrated with such detail, seriousness, and joy.

Discussion Questions

💡 **What happened when God's people forgot the lessons He had taught them?** *(They were captured and taken away by their enemies.)*

▶ **Why did the Israelites come together?** *(to listen to Ezra read from God's Word)*

▶ **What did they hear that they joyously obeyed?** *(God had commanded them to have a special time of thanksgiving.)*

▶ **What did the people do as soon as they heard about the Festival of Booths?** *(They went out and gathered branches, built booths, and celebrated the festival.)*

▶ **What did they do at the festival?** *(feasted, praised God, and listened to His Word)*

💡 **How are Christians today sometimes like the Old Testament saints in Ezra's time?** *(Emphasize that God's people still sometimes forget to worship and thank Him. Remind students that we need to look again and again at God's Word so that we will not forget what He has told us. As soon as we realize that we are not pleasing God, we should do what the Israelites did—repent, ask Him to forgive us, and begin immediately to do what is right.)*

📖 Bible Study

Locate Bible verses that tell about thanksgiving. Direct students to use the contents page in their Bibles to find the location of each book. Guide them in locating and reading the following verses.

Psalm 34:1—We should continually give thanks and praise to God.

Psalm 67:3—Everyone should praise God.

Psalm 95:2—We should thank God in prayer and sing songs of thanksgiving to Him.

Reinforce this truth by solving a thanksgiving puzzle. Give each student a copy of page A50 ("Thanks for the Things God Has Given"). Allow the students to complete the puzzle independently. *(The command spelled out in the boxes is PRAISE GOD.)*

🍴 Food Connection (optional)

Prepare and eat a fruit snack or sample Palestinian fruits.

Grape Salad—For each student you will need the following:
- one canned pear half
- one ounce of whipped cream cheese
- seedless grapes (cut in half)
- fresh mint leaves, celery leaves, parsley, or other edible greenery
- a disposable plate and fork

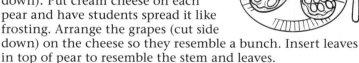

Put a pear half on each plate (flat side down). Put cream cheese on each pear and have students spread it like frosting. Arrange the grapes (cut side down) on the cheese so they resemble a bunch. Insert leaves in top of pear to resemble the stem and leaves.

Palestinian fruits—Provide enough pomegranates, figs (fresh or dried), grapes, raisins, and dates for students to sample.

LESSON C — Jesus at the Feast of Tabernacles

Materials

- Hymn: "Praise Ye the Lord, the Almighty"
- Transparency of page A37 ("We Praise Thee, O God, Our Redeemer") from previous lessons
- Choral Reading poster or transparency from previous lessons
- Grape and pomegranate markers from previous lesson
- Copy of page A51 ("Thanks a Bunch!") for each student
- Copy of page A52 ("Thanksgiving Napkin Ring") for each student
- Wilted plant
- Watering can with water
- Container
- The following references and sentences written for display:
  Deuteronomy 6:5
  1 Samuel 16:7
  Psalm 9:1
  Psalm 16:8–9
  Matthew 15:8
  Philippians 4:7
  My ___ is ___.
  ___ God with all your ___.
  God's ___ will keep your ___.
  Praise God with your ___ ___.
  Man looks on the outside; God ___ at the ___.
  Some honor God with their lips, but their ___ are ___ from Him.

🎵 Hymn: "Praise Ye the Lord, the Almighty"

Sing the hymn (Worktext page 212). Sing all four verses together.

🎵 Hymn: "We Praise Thee, O God, Our Redeemer"

Sing the hymn. Display the transparency of page A37 ("We Praise Thee, O God, Our Redeemer"). Sing the first two verses. Read the third verse and explain the meaning of ***anthem*** *("hymn of praise")*. Sing the third verse together.

Choral Reading

Guide the choral reading. Distribute the grape and pomegranate markers and follow the same procedure as in the previous lessons. Emphasize and model a worshipful attitude.

Picture the Point

Introduce the Bible account with an illustration of true worship. Show students a wilted plant.

▶ **What does this plant need?** *(water)*

Pour some water into a container next to the plant pot.

▶ **Does the plant look better now?** *(no)*
▶ **Did the water help?** *(no)* **Why not?** *(The water wasn't poured into the plant's soil.)*

Explain that many of the priests and religious leaders in the time Jesus was on earth did not tell people how to really know God and worship Him. They did all kinds of religious things that looked like worshiping God, but in their hearts they did not love and serve Him.

Bible Account

From history we understand that at the time of the Feast of Booths (tabernacles or shelters), many people would come to the temple in Jerusalem to celebrate. All around the city, they would build their shelters on rooftops and in the gardens and courtyards. There was music and feasting. At night, the light from huge lampstands in an outer court of the temple could be seen from even far away.

Every day two groups of priests paraded out of the temple gates. One group went to gather leafy branches to build a booth for the temple altar. The other group went to the Pool of Siloam in the southeastern part of the city to bring back water for a thanksgiving ceremony.

Read John 7:2 and 37–53 or use the following retelling. Listening question: **What was wrong with what the priests did?** *(They taught the people the rituals but not the meanings.)*

Jesus at the Feast of Tabernacles

Jesus and His disciples came to the Feast of Booths. On the last day of the festival, Jesus stood on the steps of the temple and said, "If anyone is thirsty, let him come to me, and drink. He who believes on me, as the Scripture has said, rivers of living water will flow out of his innermost being." By this He meant that He would give to anyone who believed on Him eternal life, resulting in a purposeful Christian life in the Spirit, benefiting both the believer and others.

Some people did believe, but the priests and other religious leaders didn't. They were very careful to celebrate the rituals of the feast exactly right, but they didn't really worship God in their hearts. They didn't lead the people in true worship.

Just as the plant wasn't helped by having water poured next to it, the people weren't helped to know and worship God by the things that the priests did. It's possible for us to be like those religious leaders sometimes. We may go to church and look as if we're worshiping, but our hearts aren't right.

Discussion Questions

▶ **Where did Jesus stand to call out His good news to the people?** *(on the temple steps)*
▶ **What does He promise to those who believe?** *(eternal life, living water)*
▶ **How are Christians today sometimes like the religious leaders?** *(They may go to church and look as if they are worshiping, but in their hearts they aren't worshiping.)*
💡 **Who knows whether people are really worshiping?** *(God)*
💡 **How can we really worship God?** *(First, we need to believe in Jesus Christ and ask Him to give us eternal life. We need to do this only once. After that, we must ask God to give us thankful hearts that truly worship Him.)*

Bible Study

Locate Bible verses that tell about a worshipful heart.

Divide the class into five or six groups, assigning each group one of the verses you wrote for display. Direct the students to use the contents page in their Bibles if they need help finding the location of each reference. They should read the assigned verse, decide which sentence goes with it, and fill in the missing words. When they are done, call on a volunteer from each group to write the missing words in the sentences or write them in yourself as the groups share their answers with the class.

Deuteronomy 6:5—_Love_ God with all your _heart_.
1 Samuel 16:7—Man looks on the outside; God _looks_ at the _heart_.
Psalm 9:1—Praise God with your _whole_ _heart_.
Psalm 16:8–9—My _heart_ is _glad_.
Matthew 15:8—Some honor God with their lips, but their _hearts_ are _far_ from Him.
Philippians 4:7—God's _peace_ will keep your _heart_.

Create a thanksgiving promise. Distribute copies of page A51 ("Thanks a Bunch!"). Each student should write his name on the first line and fill in the other lines with things he is thankful to God for. Then he may color his bunch of "grateful grapes," being careful not to color over the words he wrote. If you wish to display the students' lists, direct them to cut out their bunches of grapes and glue them on a piece of construction paper of a contrasting color.

⊘ Art Connection

Create a napkin ring reminder. Give each student a copy of page A52, ("Thanksgiving Napkin Ring"). Tell the students to follow the directions on the page and take it home for a reminder to give thanks.

Grape and Pomegranate Markers

Duplicate enough copies of this page for each student to have either
a grape marker or a pomegranate marker. Copy on colored paper or color
the symbols as desired. Laminate and cut out for future use.

Thanksgiving MiniUnit

Choral Reading
Psalm 148:1–3, 8–13

All: Praise ye the Lord *[2 quick claps]*.

Praise ye the Lord from the heavens *[point to the sky]*.

Praise Him in the heights *[raise hands upward]*.

Praise ye Him *[1 quick clap]*, all his angels.

Praise ye Him *[1 quick clap]*, all his hosts.

 **:**   Praise ye Him, sun and moon *[form a circle with arms above head]*.

 **:**   Praise Him, all ye stars of light *["twinkle" fingers once on each of the words* stars of light*]*.

Boys: Fire and hail *[swoop arms up in front on* fire *and down again on* hail*]*,

Girls: Snow and vapour *[sweep arms gently down in front on* snow *and up again on* vapour*]*,

All: Stormy wind fulfilling His word *[sweep arms side to side overhead]*,

 **:**   Mountains and all hills *[trace high mountains and lower hills in the air]*,

 **:**   Fruitful trees and all cedars *[spread fingers and arms like tree branches overhead]*,

Choral Reading (continued)
Psalm 148:1–3, 8–13

 : Beasts and all cattle *[make cattle horns on head]*,

 : Creeping things *[creep fingers up arm]* and flying fowl
[flap arms gently],

Boys: Kings of the earth *[make crown on head with hands]*

Girls: And all people *[spread arms out in front from center to indicate audience]*,

All: Princes and all judges of the earth *[pound fist on open hand]*,

Boys: Both young men *[point to self with both thumbs]*

Girls: And maidens *[point to self with both forefingers]*,

Boys: Old men *[stoop as if on a cane]*

Girls: And children *[pantomime holding a baby in arms]*,

All: Let them praise the name of the Lord *[2 quick claps]*.

 : For His name alone is excellent *[2 quick claps]*
[2 more quick claps] *[2 more quick claps]*.

All: His glory is above the earth *[spread hands and arms outward]*
and heaven *[praying hands]*.

Make a Booth

Fold the booth.

① Start with an 8½" × 11" sheet of bond (or construction weight) paper. Make an 8½" × 8½" square by folding the shorter edge to the longer and cutting off the excess.

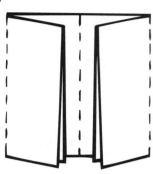

② Fold the square into halves and unfold. Fold the edges to the center. Unfold.

③ Lift the top layer of one quarter section, pull apart, and fold flat. Repeat for the other side.

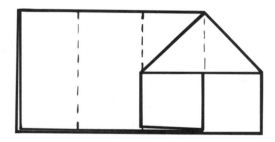

④ Turn the ends so that they are at right angles to the center.

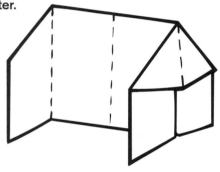

Decorate the booth.

⑤ Color and cut out the branches and fruits on page A49 ("Booth Parts").

⑥ Fold on the dotted lines and glue the branches in place to form the roof. Glue the fruits along the edges.

Add the Israelite family.

⑦ Color and cut out the family on page A49 ("Booth Parts").

⑧ Fold figurines on the dotted lines and stand them in front of the booth.

Booth Parts

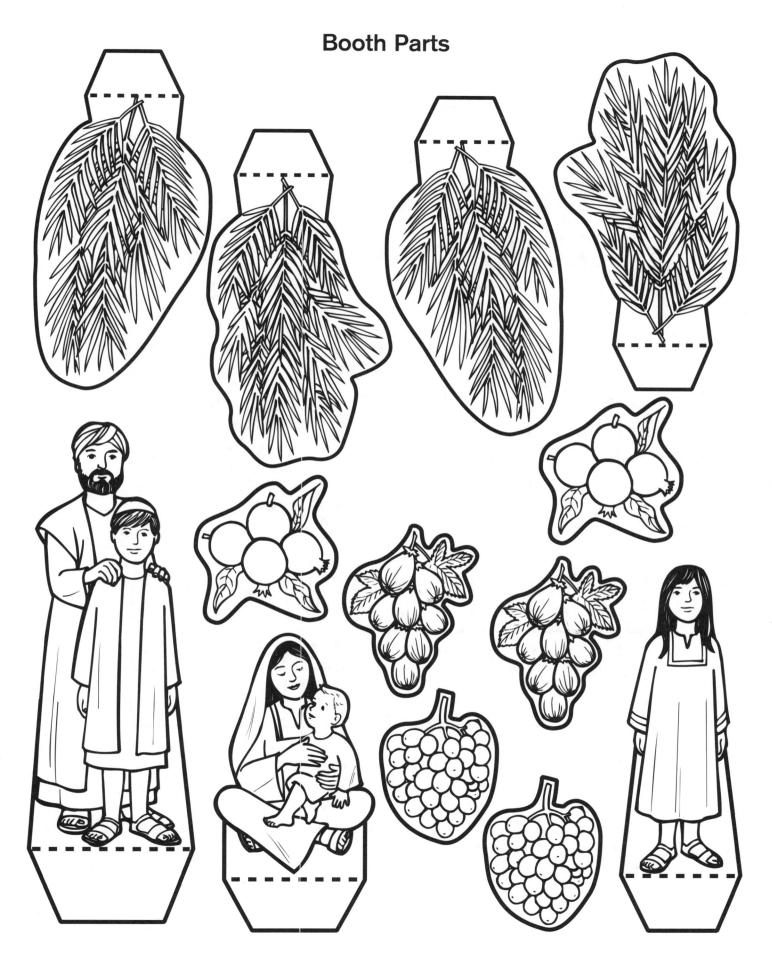

Thanks for the Things God Has Given

Psalm 148:1–3, 8–13

Psalm 148 mentions many things that God has made.
Follow the directions to see what all of them are told to do.

1	2	3	4	5	6	7	8	9	10
_	_	_	_	_	_	_	_	_	_

Directions:

1. Shade box 7 with your pencil.
2. In box 1, write the letter that is on the hill.
3. In box 9, write the letter that is on the king's crown.
4. In box 5, write the letter that is on the sun.
5. In box 2, write the letter that is on the bird in the boy's hand.
6. In box 4, write the letter you see on the cow.
7. In box 3, write the letter that is on the old man's cloak.
8. In box 8, write the letter you see on the boy's tunic.
9. In box 6, write the letter that is beside the moon.
10. In box 10, write the letter you see on one of the sheep.
11. Read the command spelled out in the boxes and color the picture.

Thanks a Bunch!

Write your name on the first line. Make a list of six things you are thankful to God for on the other lines. Color the grapes and leaves, and then cut out the picture.

Offer unto God thanksgiving.
*Psalm 50:14*a

_____

- - - - - - - - - - - - - - - - - - - -

is thankful for

_____

- - - - - - - - - - - - - - - - - - - -

_____

- - - - - - - - - - - - - - - - - - - -

_____

- - - - - - - - - - - - - - - - - - - -

_____

- - - - - - - - - - - - - - - - - - - -

_____

- - - - - - - - - - - - - - - - - - - -

_____

- - - - - - - - - - - - - - - - - .

Thanksgiving Napkin Ring

1. Color the grapes and leaves.
2. Cut on the dark lines.
3. Glue the strip to make a ring.
4. Glue the grapes onto the ring
(being careful not to cover the leaves).
5. Slip a paper napkin through the ring.

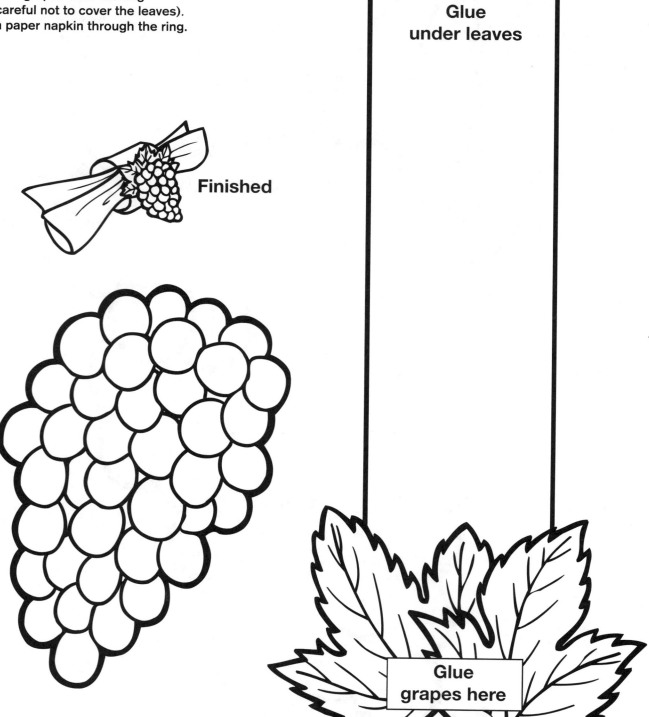

Finished

Glue
under leaves

Glue
grapes here

Unit Reviews

The unit reviews provide students and parents with a study guide for the unit tests published by BJU Press. Permission is granted for the teacher to reproduce a unit review for each student in the class.

Unit 1 Review

Name _____

Write a word from the word bank in each blank.

	image
	ark
	rested
	days

1. God created the world in six _____ .

2. On the seventh day, God _____ .

3. God created man in His own _____ .

4. God told Noah to build an _____ .

Circle the correct word in the parentheses.

5. God spared Noah and his family because they (believed, saw) God.

6. God destroyed the world with a (fire, flood).

7. God promised Abraham a nation of (many, tall) people.

8. Abraham gave his (room, son) to God.

Write your name on the lines.

9. God wants _____ to trust Him.

10. God wants _____ to obey Him.

Unit 2 Review

Name _____

Circle the correct answer in each sentence.

1. The Israelites sinned by worshiping a golden (picture, calf).

2. God spoke to Moses from a burning (boat, bush).

3. God gave His people the land of (Canaan, swamps).

4. The ten plagues came because a leader (did, did not) believe God.

Write the letter of the correct answer from the word bank beside the number.

_____ 5. Pharaoh did not want the Israelites to _____ Egypt.

_____ 6. God wanted His people to _____ His commandments.

_____ 7. God chose Moses and Joshua to be the _____ of Israel.

_____ 8. God used Rahab to hide the spies who were from _____.

A. Israel

B. obey

C. leave

D. leaders

Circle *True* if the statement is true or *False* if the statement is false.

9. God used a donkey and a fish to get Balaam's riches.   True   False

10. God wanted Jonah to preach in Ninevah.   True   False

11. God wanted the people of Ninevah to repent.   True   False

Unit 3 Review

Write the word from the word bank that best completes each sentence.

prayed	see	God	sins

1. God made Samson strong again when Samson _____.

2. Gideon trusted _____ to beat a bigger army.

3. Eli's sons were known for their _____.

4. The Israelites wanted a king they could _____.

Fill in the circle next to the best answer.

5. Who wanted a king so they could be like other nations?
   ○ Samuel
   ○ the Israelites

6. Hannah's great desire was to have
   ○ children.
   ○ riches.

7. What did Hannah give to God?
   ○ her son Samuel
   ○ two coins

8. Because Samson was proud, he lost
   ○ his teeth.
   ○ the power of God.

Circle the correct answer.

9. Ruth loved God and Naomi, her (sister, mother-in-law).

10. Saul was a humble king, but then he became (proud, honest).

Unit 4 Review

Name _____

Circle *True* or *False* for each sentence.

1. God promised Adam and Eve a Savior.   True   False

2. God stopped loving Adam and Eve after they sinned.   True   False

3. The angels told the news of John's birth to the wise men.   True   False

4. King David was related to Jesus.   True   False

5. Immanuel means "God with us."   True   False

6. The wise men called Herod the "King of the Jews."   True   False

7. Herod wanted to worship Jesus.   True   False

8. Only some of the prophecies about Christ's birth came true. True   False

Fill in the circle next to the correct answer.

9. Isaiah told what the name of _____ would be.
   ○ every king
   ○ Jesus

10. Isaiah lived _____ Christ's lifetime.
    ○ before
    ○ during

11. The shepherds praised God and then
    ○ told others.
    ○ went to sleep.

12. The wise men gave gifts to
    ○ Herod.
    ○ Jesus.

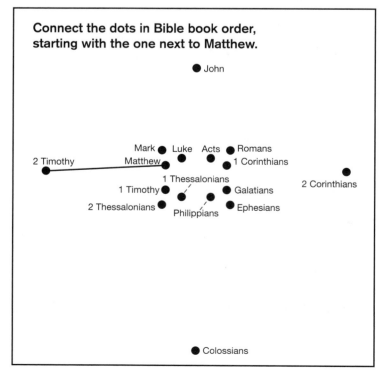

Connect the dots in Bible book order, starting with the one next to Matthew.

- John
- Mark ● Luke ● Acts ● Romans
- 2 Timothy   Matthew ● 1 Corinthians
- 1 Thessalonians
- 1 Timothy ● ● Galatians   2 Corinthians
- 2 Thessalonians ● Philippians ● Ephesians
- Colossians

Unit 5 Review

Name _____

Fill in the circle next to the correct answer.

1. Nehemiah helped to
   ○ give manna.
   ○ build a city's walls.

2. Samuel told God's people to
   ○ obey God.
   ○ please themselves.

3. A servant girl told Naaman's wife about
   ○ the prophet of God.
   ○ Noah's ark.

4. David, the shepherd boy, trusted God when he faced
   ○ a snake.
   ○ Goliath.

Circle the correct word to complete each sentence.

5. Nehemiah honored God by rebuilding the walls of (Jerusalem, his boss's house).

6. Saul disobeyed God, so God (honored, punished) him.

7. The Philistines had (many, a few) soldiers.

8. Naaman obeyed God's prophet and was (beaten, healed).

Circle *True* or *False* for each sentence.

9. David loved God.	True	False
10. Jonathan was mean to David.	True	False
11. Saul's sacrifice honored God.	True	False
12. Jeremiah learned from a potter.	True	False

Unit 6 Review

Name _____

Write the letter of the correct answer in the blank.

1. Living in another country, Daniel still _____ God.

2. Daniel's three friends did not worship _____.

3. Three times a day, Daniel prayed to _____.

> A. the statue
> B. served
> C. God

Circle *True* or *False* for each sentence.

4. The king saw only three men in the fire.   True   False

5. God allowed the fire to burn the three men.   True   False

6. The three men in the fire worshiped an idol.   True   False

7. God had power over the lions.   True   False

Fill in the circle next to the correct answer.

8. The queen who helped the Jews was
   ○ Isaiah's wife.
   ○ Esther.

9. God spared the Jewish nation because they
   ○ prayed.
   ○ fought.

10. Haman, the Jews' enemy, was
    ○ rewarded.
    ○ killed.

Unit 7 Review

Circle *True* or *False* for each sentence.

1. Jesus taught that He answers proud prayers.   True   False

2. Jesus taught about a humble man who was forgiven.   True   False

3. To be like Christ, we must forgive others who sin against us.   True   False

4. All of the lepers Jesus healed thanked Him.   True   False

Fill in the circle next to the correct answer.

5. We should forgive others as much as God forgives
   ○ prisoners.
   ○ us.

6. In the story of the brother who came home, the brother who stayed home was
   ○ humble.
   ○ proud.

7. Paul and Silas were singing and praising God when they were
   ○ in jail.
   ○ well fed.

8. Paul and Silas showed the jailer the joy of
   ○ having lots of things.
   ○ knowing Christ.

Write the letter of the correct answer beside the number.

_____ 9. Jesus said we should _____ many times a day.

_____ 10. Jesus knew that the woman with perfume wanted to _____ Him.

A. please
B. forgive

Name _____

Fill in the circle next to the correct answer.

Through the Roof and Healed

11. Jesus said that the lame man's friends were
    ○ kind.
    ○ forgiven.

12. The Pharisees said that Jesus spoke
    ○ against God.
    ○ the truth.

A Special Gift

13. The woman
    ○ sang to Jesus.
    ○ poured perfume on Jesus.

14. Jesus told the woman that
    ○ her sins were forgiven.
    ○ the perfume was wasted.

Singing in Prison

15. When the earthquake shook the prison,
    ○ Paul and Silas escaped.
    ○ Paul and Silas stayed.

16. The jailer asked,
    ○ "What must I do to be saved?"
    ○ "Why are you still here?"

Unit 8 Review

Name _____

Fill in the circle next to the correct answer.

1. John cared for Mary, the mother of _____
   ○ Jesus.
   ○ a thief.

2. Jesus saved the criminal on the cross who _____ Him.
   ○ spoke evil of
   ○ trusted in

3. When Jesus told some sad believers about the Resurrection, they _____
   ○ forgot it.
   ○ told others.

4. The women at the tomb were sad because they thought Jesus was _____
   ○ dead.
   ○ missing.

| forgive | saved | separated |

Write the word from the word bank that makes each sentence correct.

_____
_ _ _ _ _ _ _ _ _ _ _ _ _ _ _ _
5. We may enjoy God because He created and _____ us.

_____
_ _ _ _ _ _ _ _ _ _ _ _ _ _ _ _
6. Unsaved people are _____ from God because of sin.

_____
_ _ _ _ _ _ _ _ _ _ _ _ _ _ _ _
7. Jesus Christ is the only One Who can _____ sin.

Circle *True* or *False* for each sentence.

8. God is everywhere you go.   True   False

9. God knows everything you say, do, and think.   True   False

10. God always keeps His promises.   True   False

Unit 9 Review

Write the word from the word bank that makes each sentence correct.

perfect	blind	not	life

1. Jesus raised a widow's son back to _____.

2. Nine lepers did _____ tell Jesus "Thank You."

3. Jesus gave sight to a _____ man.

4. Jesus was just like us on earth, but He was _____.

Fill in the circle next to the correct answer.

5. When Jesus was baptized, He was being
   ○ obedient.
   ○ proud.

6. The winds and the waves obeyed
   ○ the Pharisees.
   ○ Jesus.

7. Because Jesus was humble, He rode on a
   ○ big white horse.
   ○ donkey.

8. Unsaved people do evil and proud things because they love
   ○ darkness.
   ○ light.

Circle *True* or *False* for each sentence.

9. In heaven, we will have aches and pains. True False

10. You may go to heaven by going to church. True False

11. Only by trusting Jesus can your sins be forgiven. True False

12. In heaven, there will be darkness. True False

Unit 10 Review

Fill in the circle next to the correct answer.

1. Jesus is preparing a place in heaven for
   ○ everybody.
   ○ every Christian.

2. Jesus said that because Mary honored Him with her special perfume, she would be
   ○ remembered.
   ○ forgotten about.

3. Jesus said that the poor widow gave
   ○ hardly anything.
   ○ more than all of the rich men.

4. A true friend tells others
   ○ about Jesus.
   ○ funny stories.

5. John the Baptist told people how to get ready for
   ○ church.
   ○ Jesus.

Write the letter of the correct answer beside the number.

_____ 6. Who is described as "the way, the truth, and the life"?

_____ 7. Telling others about Christ makes you one of these.

_____ 8. He told the king that the king had sinned.

_____ 9. Believers in Jesus should be _____ to Jesus all the time.

A. "fisher of men"

B. faithful

C. Jesus

D. John the Baptist

Name _____

Circle *True* or *False* for each sentence.

10. The word *gospel* means to go to church.   True   False

11. Some disciples left their jobs to be Christ's disciples.   True   False

12. One of Christ's disciples used to be an honest tax-collector.   True   False

13. The disciples collected three baskets of leftover food, after   True   False
    seventy people ate.

14. Paul was glad to tell others about Christ.   True   False

15. God was pleased with Christ's sacrifice.   True   False

Color any fish that has the name of one of the twelve disciples Jesus chose.

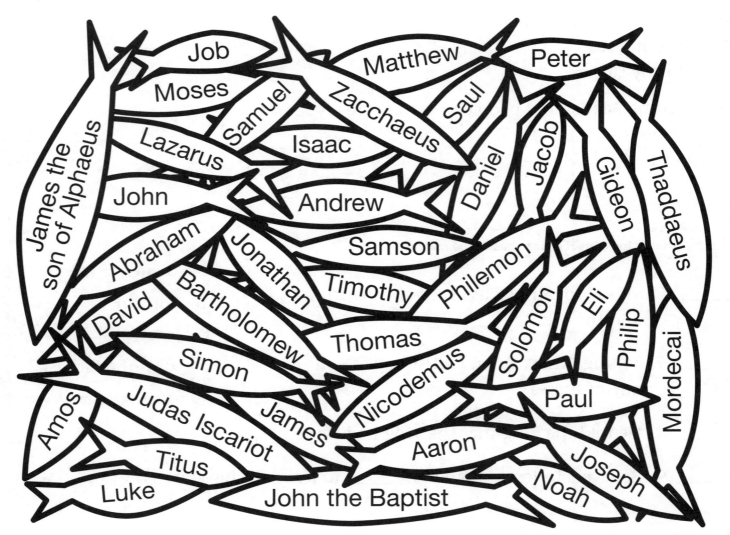

Activity Pages

These activity sheets are designed to help your student visualize, vocalize, or apply knowledge from the lessons. Permission is granted for the teacher to reproduce an activity sheet for each student in the class.

Ancient Middle East

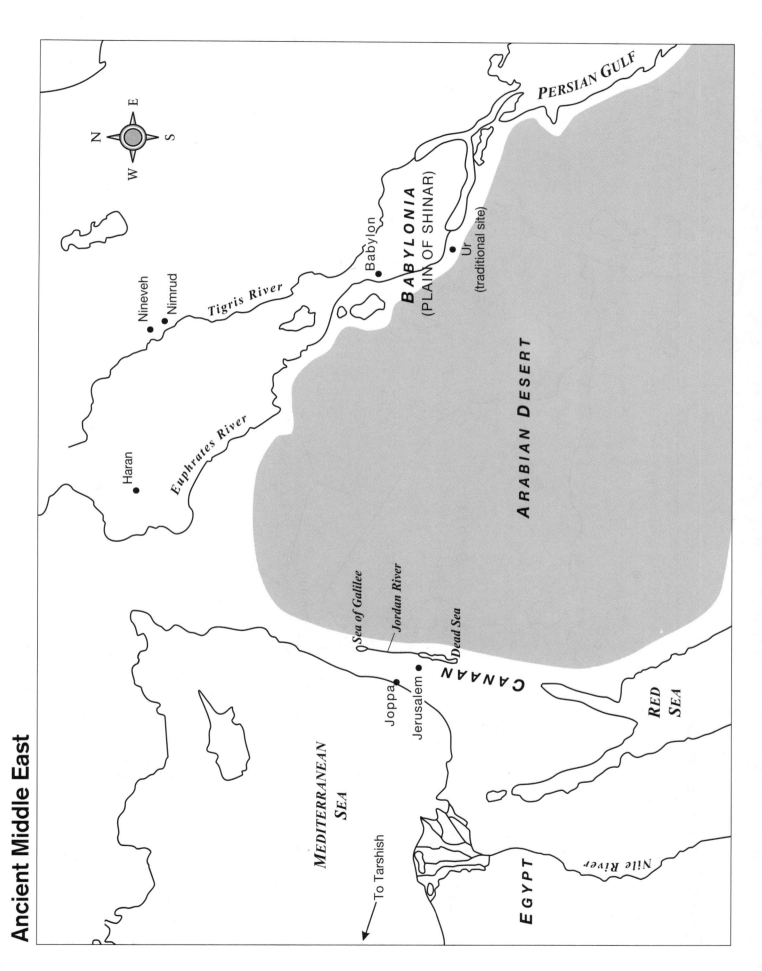

PERSIAN GULF

Tigris River

Babylon

BABYLONIA
(PLAIN OF SHINAR)

Ur
(traditional site)

Nineveh   Nimrud

ARABIAN DESERT

Haran

Euphrates River

Sea of Galilee

Jordan River

Dead Sea

CANAAN

Joppa

Jerusalem

*MEDITERRANEAN
SEA*

*RED
SEA*

To Tarshish

EGYPT

Nile River

The Middle East Today

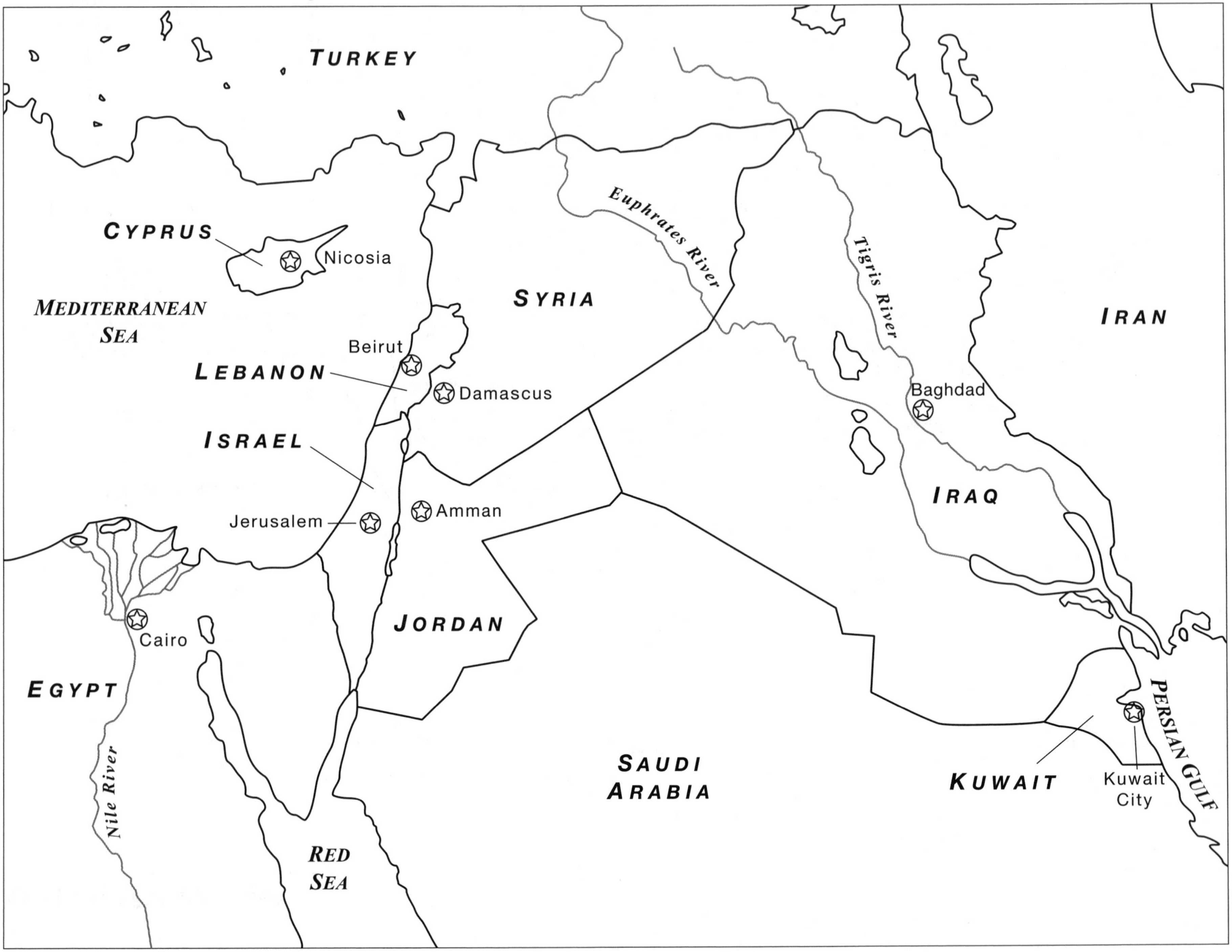

PERSIAN GULF

IRAN

IRAQ

Baghdad

Tigris River

Euphrates River

KUWAIT

Kuwait City

SAUDI ARABIA

SYRIA

Damascus

JORDAN

Amman

TURKEY

CYPRUS

Nicosia

Beirut

LEBANON

ISRAEL

Jerusalem

MEDITERRANEAN SEA

RED SEA

Cairo

EGYPT

Nile River

Name _____

God created! I'm glad!

Draw something that you are thankful that God created.

God created _____, and I'm glad!

God Designed the Ark

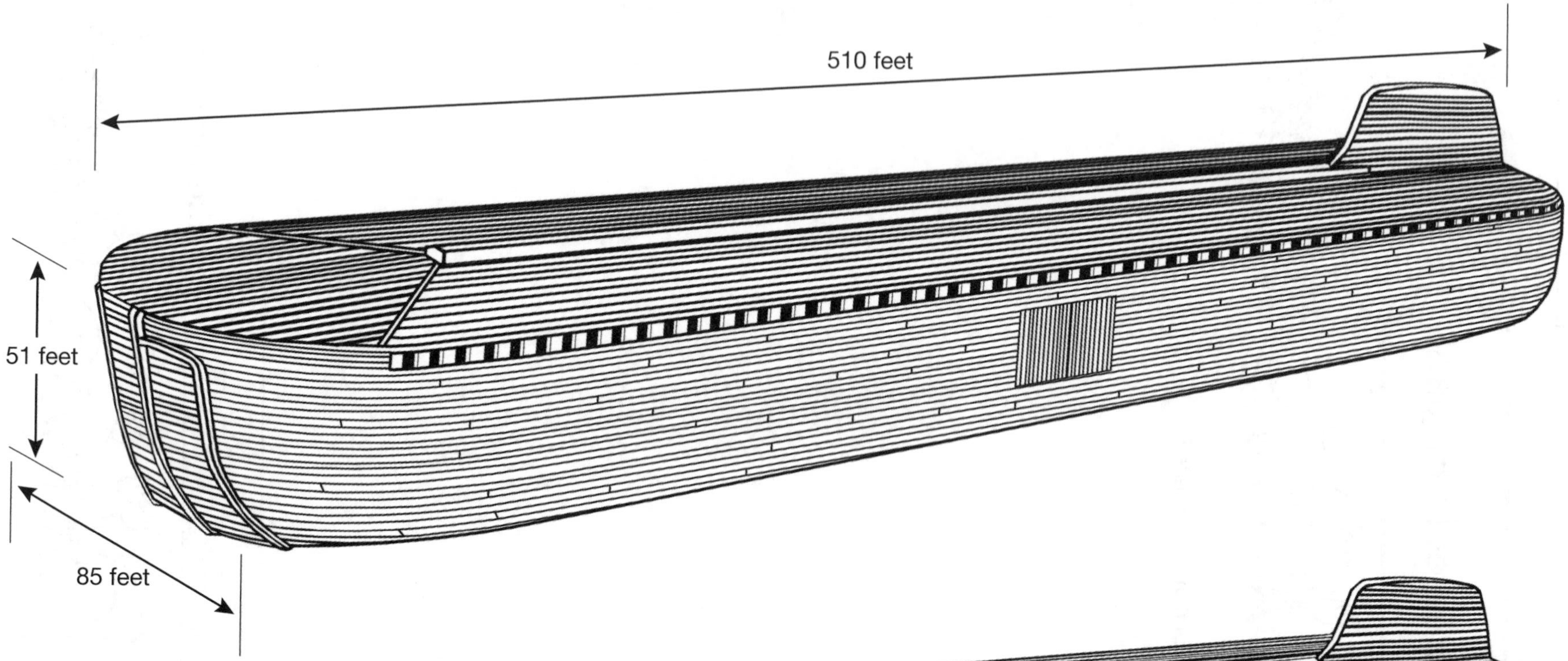

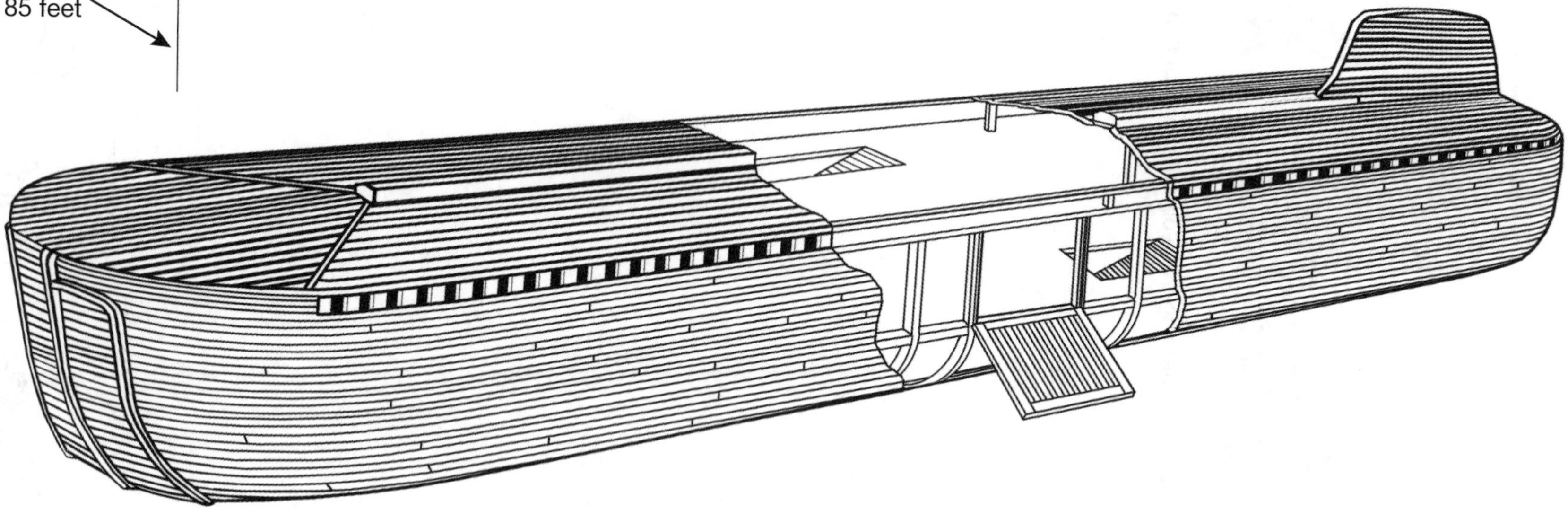

510 feet

85 feet

51 feet

God Is in Control

Draw something that you are thankful that God controls.
Complete the sentence below.

God controls _____ .

Name _____

God Rules Families

Draw your family. Be sure to put yourself in the picture.

Write the names of the people in your family.

_____   _____
_____   _____
_____   _____
_____   _____
_____   _____

God Rules Me

God rules creation. God rules nature. God rules families.
Does He rule you?

Draw a picture of yourself obeying God.
Complete the sentence below.

I obey God when I _____
_____ .

Words of Encouragement

God tells us to **edify** [encourage] one another.
1 Thessalonians 5:11

Think of someone you would like to encourage.
Make a flip-up card for that person using these directions.

Fold an 8½" × 11" piece of paper in half.

Fold the top corner of the folded side down.

Fold it toward you and away from you several times.

Open the card, decorate it, and write an encouraging message.

Close the card, pulling the triangle shape down and inward.

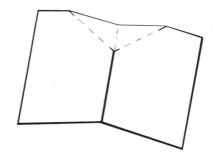

Give the card away!

Draw a picture of a time when Gideon obeyed God.

Complete the sentence below.

Gideon obeyed God when he _____
_____
_____ .

Trusting God

Draw a picture of what Samson was able to do when he asked God for help.

Complete the sentence below.

Samson prayed, and God helped him to _____

_____

_____ .

Name _____

Draw a picture of yourself doing
something for someone else.

Complete the sentence below.

I humbly serve when I _____
_____
_____ .

Name _____

Draw a picture of a time when Samuel obeyed God.

Complete the sentence below.

Samuel obeyed God when he _____

_____

_____ .

The Genealogy of Jesus, from Adam to Isaac

(Genesis 5:3)   Adam
↓
Seth
↓
Enosh
↓
Kenan
↓
Mahalalel
↓
Jared

(Genesis 5:19)   Enoch
↓
Methuselah
↓
Lamech

(Genesis 5:28–29)   Noah
↓
Shem

(Genesis 11:11)   Arpachshad
↓
Shelah
↓
Eber
↓
Peleg
↓
Reu
↓
Serug
↓
Nahor
↓
Terah

(Genesis 11:27)   Abram

(Genesis 21:2–3)   Isaac

Christmas Card

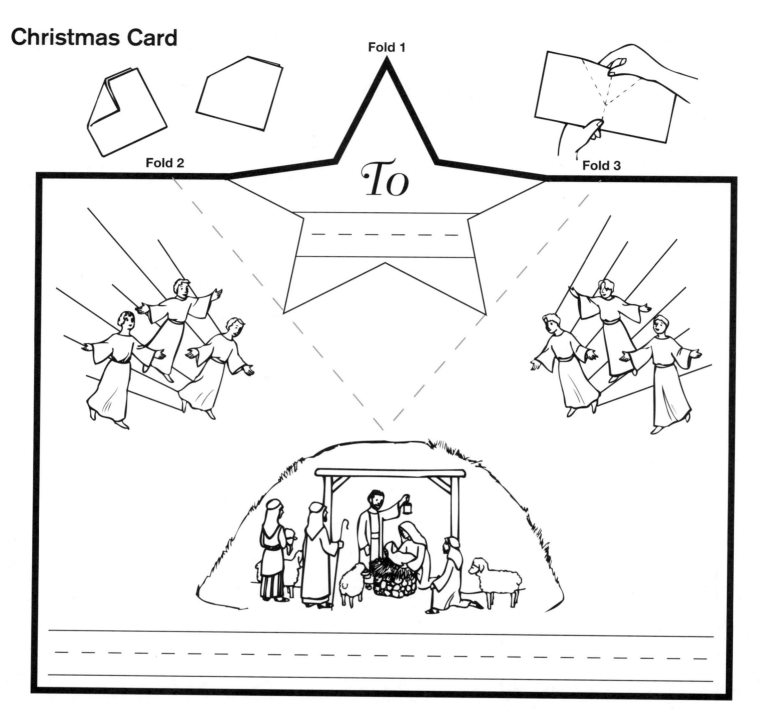

Fold 1

To

Fold 2

Fold 3

Share the good news of the Savior's birth by giving or sending the card to someone.

Write on the handwriting lines as follows:
(top) the name of a person with whom you want to share the good news
(bottom) The Savior is born!
Color the picture.
Cut on the heavy cutting line.
Fold 1: Fold in half from the top point of the star to the bottom of the card.
Fold 2: Fold a triangle down at the top corner of the folded side. Fold it toward you and then away.
Fold 3: Open the card. Close the card, pulling the triangle forward and inward.
Give the card away.

Serving One Another

Dear parents,

In the Bible lessons this week, your child is learning that God's people are to serve one another in love. Your child has been instructed to think of two or three things to do on his own initiative to help someone. These should not be chores your child is told to do. He is to look for opportunities for service. After he has performed the service, direct him to write what he did in the spaces below. Please sign each section to verify the deed.

Please return this sheet by _____ .

Thank you.

I showed a servant's heart by _____

_____

_____ .

Parent's signature _____

I showed a servant's heart by _____

_____

_____ .

Parent's signature _____

I showed a servant's heart by _____

_____

_____ .

Parent's signature _____

A Faithful Servant

Dear parents,

We are studying a Bible unit about serving God. We have learned that God's servants need to know God, serve Him in love, help others, and work together. Encourage your child to be a faithful servant like Nehemiah. Please supervise the tasks that are to be completed each day, oversee the coloring of the stones (which represent his responsibilities), and then return this sheet on _____.

Thank you for your participation in this project.

Start on Monday at the bottom of the wall. Build it strong by doing the tasks and coloring the stones. Answer the questions at the end of the week.

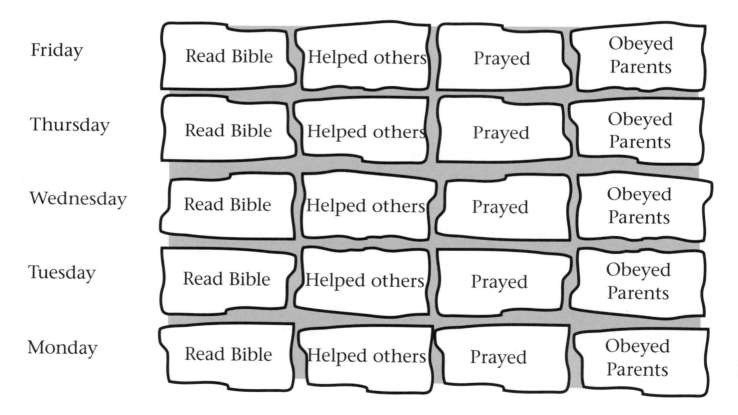

Friday	Read Bible	Helped others	Prayed	Obeyed Parents
Thursday	Read Bible	Helped others	Prayed	Obeyed Parents
Wednesday	Read Bible	Helped others	Prayed	Obeyed Parents
Tuesday	Read Bible	Helped others	Prayed	Obeyed Parents
Monday	Read Bible	Helped others	Prayed	Obeyed Parents

Did you build a strong wall?   yes   no

Have you been a good and faithful servant?   yes   no

Verse Visual Paper Doll

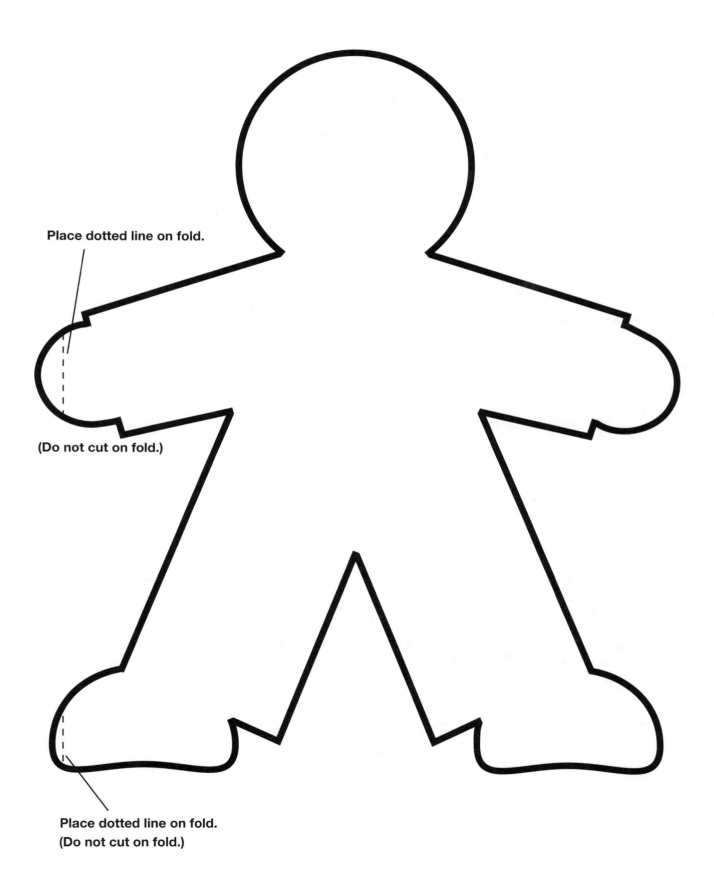

Place dotted line on fold.

(Do not cut on fold.)

Place dotted line on fold.
(Do not cut on fold.)

Kings of Persia

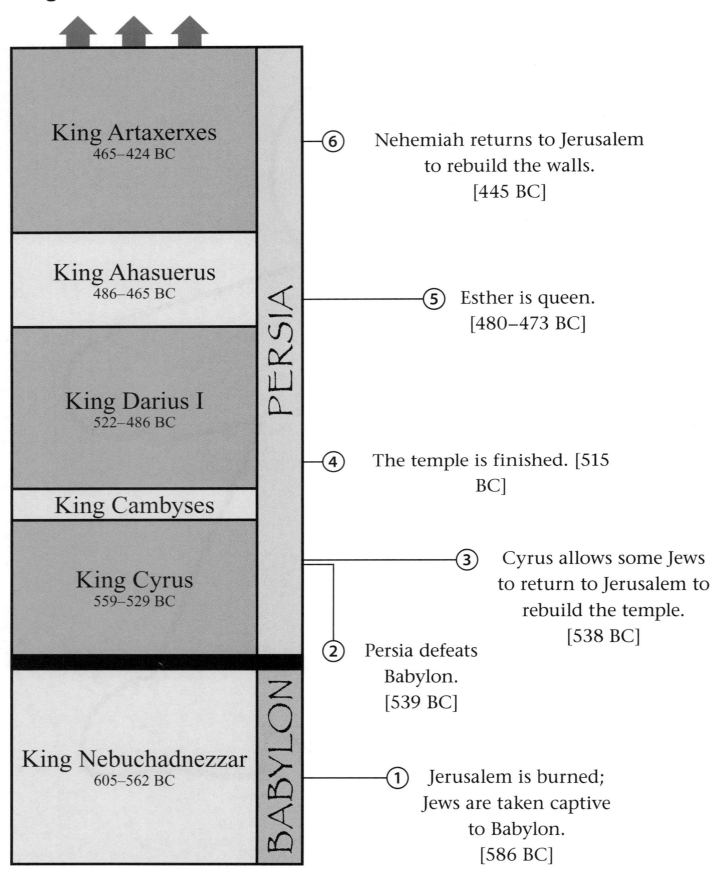

King Artaxerxes
465–424 BC

⑥ Nehemiah returns to Jerusalem
to rebuild the walls.
[445 BC]

King Ahasuerus
486–465 BC

⑤ Esther is queen.
[480–473 BC]

PERSIA

King Darius I
522–486 BC

④ The temple is finished. [515 BC]

King Cambyses

King Cyrus
559–529 BC

③ Cyrus allows some Jews
to return to Jerusalem to
rebuild the temple.
[538 BC]

② Persia defeats
Babylon.
[539 BC]

BABYLON

King Nebuchadnezzar
605–562 BC

① Jerusalem is burned;
Jews are taken captive
to Babylon.
[586 BC]

News! News!
Read All About It!

Write a story about the person whose name the teacher
wrote for display. Write the person's name on the top line.
Draw a picture to go with your story.

A Question of Yams—A Mini-Play
adapted from the book by Gloria Repp

Characters:

❖ **Narrator**

❈ **Kuri**—a boy of New Guinea

✫ **His Father**

✩ **His Mother** (non-speaking part)

✚ **Sakoso**—one of the Head Men of the village

✜ **Other Head Men** (non-speaking parts)

✛ **The thin man**—a stranger to Kuri and his family (non-speaking part)

Scene I

❖ **Narrator:** Kuri's father planted yams so that the family would have food.
(Kuri is hiding. His father is digging with a stick and planting yams. The Head Men approach, looking angry).

✚ **Sakoso:** You must pray to the spirits before you plant yams. If you don't, you will be sorry. Something bad will happen to your garden!
(The Head Men nod their heads and frown.)

✫ **Father:** I will plant our yams in the name of Jesus Christ.
(He bows his head. The Head Men shake their heads and go away angrily.)

Scene II

❖ **Narrator:** The Christians prayed. The yams began to grow.
One day Kuri went fishing. He heard voices.
(Kuri is hiding.)

✚ **Sakoso:** . . . and he must be punished . . .
(He whispers to the thin man, and they go away. Kuri is still hiding.)

❖ **Narrator:** Kuri kept hiding until the sun began to set.
(Kuri yawns and stretches, still hiding.)

A Question of Yams—A Mini-Play (continued)

(The thin man comes back with a stick and begins beating the yams.)

✽ **Kuri:** No! No! Stop it!
(Kuri pantomimes throwing stones at the thin man.)
Come everyone! Come and see the wicked man in our garden!
(The thin man runs away. Father runs up).

✽ **Kuri:** That man tried to beat down our yams! Sakoso told him what to do!
(Father bows his head and prays in a loud voice. Kuri looks surprised.)

✩ **Father:** Mighty God, You have seen the men who want to do this wicked thing. Show them Your power.
(to Kuri) Thank God that you were here, my son.

Scene III

(Much later)

❖ **Narrator:** Kuri was bitten by a snake, but God healed him. The rains did not come, but the Christians carried water to the yam vines. The missionary taught Kuri to read God's Word. Kuri's father called it "God's Carving." At last the yams were ready to eat.
(Kuri, Father, and Mother sit down to eat.)

✩ **Father:** *(praying)* Thank You, God, for how You have taken care of our family. Thank You for the crop of yams. Thank You that Sakoso is asking about Your Carving. Amen.
(Father, Mother, and Kuri all smile at each other and start to eat soup.)

✩ **Father:** Thank God for such good soup.

✩✽ **Father and Kuri:** Behold, God is mighty!

Forgiveness Booklet

Make a copy on heavy paper or tag board for each student. Cut out the covers.
Cut 5 or 6 pieces (3" × 4½") of lined paper for each student.
Staple each student's pages between the covers to make a booklet.
Complete the activity as directed in the lesson.

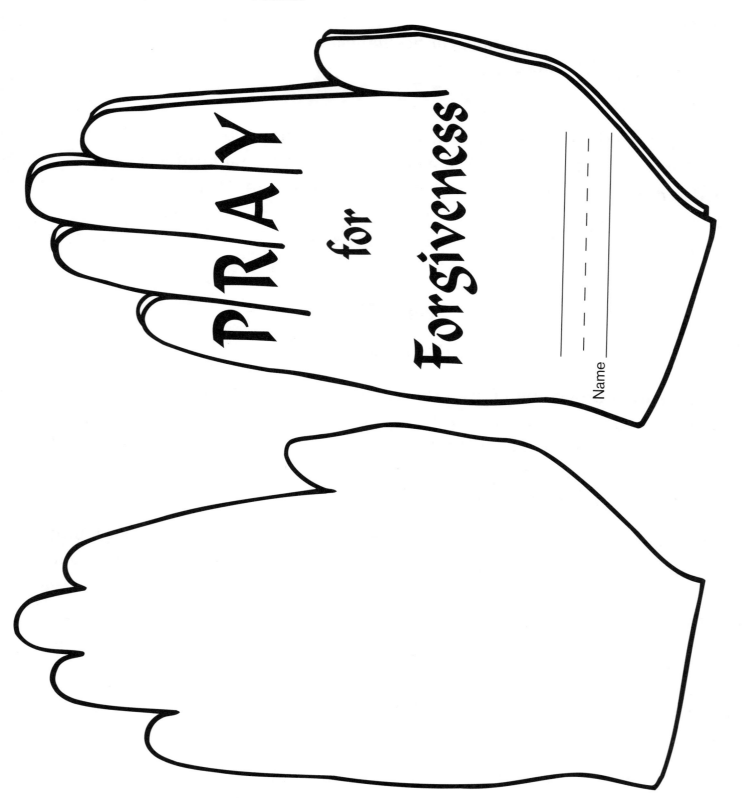

PRAY for Forgiveness

Name

Forgiven and Healed
An Echo Play Based on Mark 2:1–12

One day	*Hold up index finger.*
Four friends	*Hold up four fingers.*
Got up	*Stand up.*
And stretched.	*Stretch.*

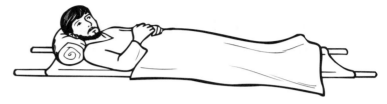

"Our friend can't get up	*Stretch.*
And stretch.	*Chin on one hand, then two hands.*
What to do? What to do?	*Snap fingers of one hand. Smile.*
We know!	*Put hand on heart. Smile.*
Jesus!"	

They ran to their friend's house,	*Slap right thigh [right hand], left thigh [left hand], left shoulder [right hand], right shoulder [left hand]—fast.*
Picked up his bed,	*Pantomime picking up bed.*
And carried him to Jesus.	*Repeat running motions but walking pace.*

"What a crowd!	*Palms open to sides of face in dismay.*
Pardon us!	*Part crowd with right hand,*
Pardon us!	*left hand,*
One side, please!	*both hands.*
What to do? What to do?"	*Chin on one hand, two hands.*
*Repeat previous five lines.	*Repeat parting the crowd.*

"We know!	*Snap fingers.*
The roof!"	*Look up and point.*
They climbed up.	*Running/walking motions—much slower.*
"Easy now. Easy now."	

They made a hole.	*Circle arms in front.*
One tile. Two tiles.	*Pantomime reaching down*
Three tiles. Four.	*and moving tiles right to left.*
Five tiles. Six tiles.	
What a chore!	*Wipe perspiration from brow.*

Forgiven and Healed
(continued)

They lowered their friend.	*Pantomime lowering ropes hand over hand.*
"Steady. Steady.	
Don't let him fall!"	
Jesus knew what the man needed.	*Smile.*
"Your sins are forgiven."	*Point to man on stretcher.*
The scribes thought,	*Frown.*
"What's this? What's this?	*Pound fist on palm twice.*
Only God forgives sins!"	*Fold hands and look heavenward piously.*

Jesus knew what they thought.	*Nod head and smile.*
"Which is easier:	*Gesture both palms up in a question.*
Your sins are forgiven,	*Gesture one palm up,*
Or rise up and walk?	*then the other.*
"Just so you know	*Turn and shake finger at scribes.*
The Son of man has power	*Point upward with index finger.*
On earth to forgive sins.	

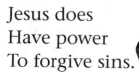

"Get up.	*Gesture to rise.*
Take up your bed.	*Point to bed.*
Walk."	*Point away.*
The man got up,	*Pantomime getting up,*
Took up his bed,	*taking bed,*
And walked—	*and walking.*
Glorifying God.	*Look up, raise hands heavenward, and*
	mouth the words "Thank You."
Jesus does	*Look up,*
Have power	*raise hands heavenward,*
To forgive sins.	*and mouth the words "Thank You."*

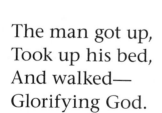

Create a Mobile

1. Color the frame of each circle a different color.
2. Cut out the circles on the outside solid lines and fold them on the dotted lines.
3. Glue each circle onto one end of the strings your teacher gives you.
4. On the tag board your teacher gives you, write Jesus paid for my sins, but I must . . .
5. Decorate the tag board, but do not cover the letters you wrote.
6. Glue or staple the tag board into a circle so that the short ends overlap.
7. Fold each string in half. Leave five inches above the tag board for hanging the mobile. Staple the strings on the inside of the tag board at the top edge and the bottom edge. (Each string is stapled twice.)
8. Hook the paperclip your teacher gives you to the strings at the top.
9. Take the mobile home. Hang it where you will see it often and remember to ask for forgiveness.

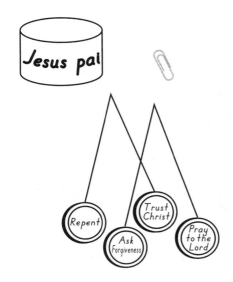

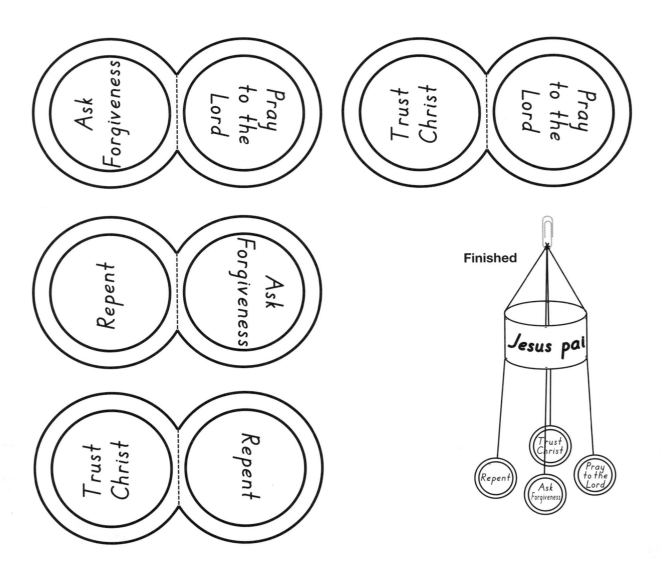

Finished

Name _____

Miracles Great and Small

Find and read Psalm 126:3

God loves us and uses His power to help us every day.
He does many things for us that no one else can do.

Write about something great that God has done for you.

_____

_ _

_____

_ _

_____

_ _

_____

_ _

_____

_ _

_____

_ _

_____

_ _

_____

_ _

_____

What kind of man is this?

Name _____

Turning from Temptation

Find and read 1 Corinthians 10:13.

Jesus lived on earth as a man. He was tempted in every way that we are, but He did not sin. He can always show us a way and help us to turn away from temptation if we ask Him.

Think about a time when you were tempted to sin.
What helped you to turn away from the temptation? Write about it here.

_____

- -

_____

_____

- -

_____

_____

- -

_____

_____

- -

_____

_____

- -

_____

_____

- -

_____

_____

- -

_____

Did you remember to thank Jesus for helping you?

Name _____

Jesus Died for Me!

Read Romans 5:8.

Before you were born,
Jesus knew you would need a Savior.
He loved you perfectly and died so that He could
be your Savior. Do you remember to thank Him?

Write a thank-you note to Jesus.
Thank Him for being your Savior.*

_____
- -
_____

_____
- -
_____

_____
- -
_____

_____
- -
_____

_____
- -
_____

_____
- -
_____

_____
- -
_____

*If you have not asked Jesus to save you, find and read again the verses on the Romans Road (Worktext page 181) and ask your parent or teacher to talk with you about them.

Name ______________________

Jesus Shall Reign

Read Luke 1:32–33.
Read the verses of "Jesus Shall Reign" from your song booklet. Your teacher has told you what each verse means. Choose one of the verses and write how it shows what a wonderful King Jesus is.

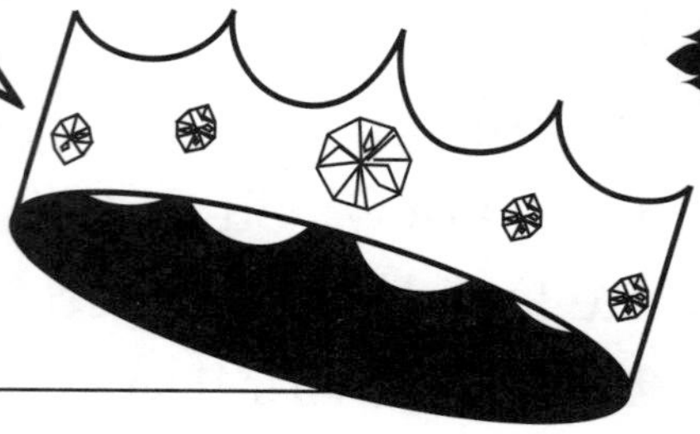

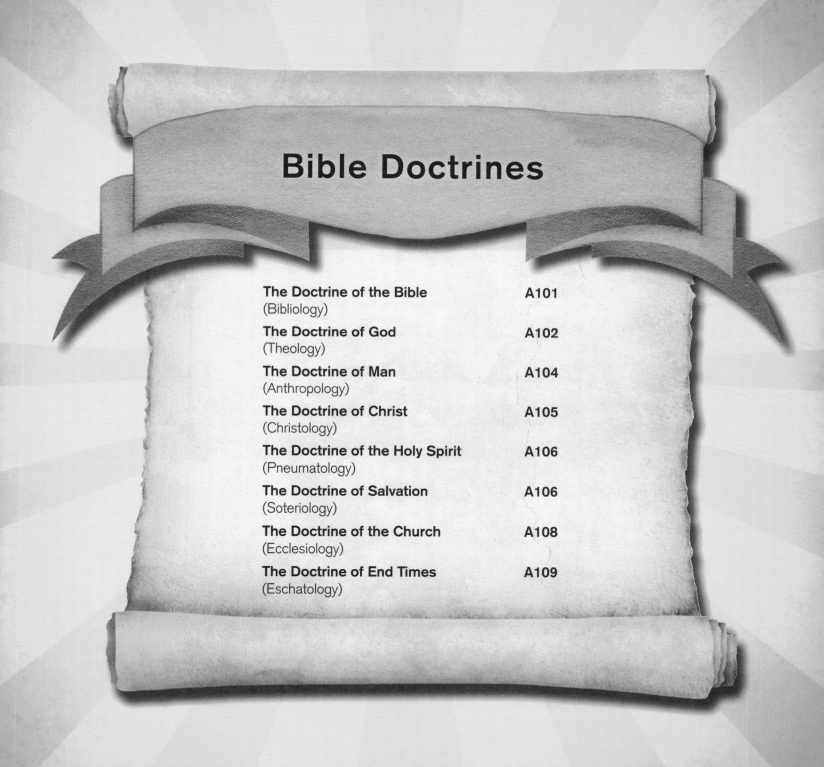

Bible Doctrines

An Outline of Bible Doctrines

Doctrines may be taught as they correlate with a particular lesson. The overview chart for each unit lists the doctrines related to the material in the unit. The preview for each subunit identifies specific doctrines by lesson. In presenting the Bible account in these lessons, you may wish to read the Scripture references given to discuss with students the specific aspect of the doctrine emphasized. You may use the outline on these pages for personal reference or to further develop ideas with the students (*Note:* Not all doctrines receive equal emphasis in the curriculum.)

The Doctrine of the Bible (Bibliology)

I. Inspiration
  A. Definition
    Inspiration is the supernatural influence of the Holy Spirit on the writers of the Bible so that what they wrote was exactly what God wanted written.
  B. The fact of inspiration
    1. The Bible claims to be the Word of God.
      a. The Bible writers use the phrase "thus saith the Lord" hundreds of times (e.g., Exod. 5:1; Josh. 24:2; 2 Sam. 7:5; Isa. 7:7).
      b. The apostle Peter said that the Holy Spirit led the Old Testament writers to write what they wrote (2 Pet. 1:20–21).
      c. The apostle Paul stated that all Scripture is inspired by God (2 Tim. 3:16).
    2. The Holy Spirit shows believers that the Bible is God's Word.
      a. The things of God are discerned through the Spirit and not through natural ability (1 Cor. 2:14).
      b. Those who belong to Christ recognize His words when they read them (John 10:27).
    3. The Bible is self-attesting.
      a. Since the Bible is the Word of God, its own testimony regarding its origin is the most powerful testimony. There is no evidence or testimony greater than that.
      b. Other evidence for the Bible's inspiration is helpful but not as convincing as the Bible's testimony concerning itself.
        (1) The Bible is historically accurate.
        (2) Many of the Bible prophecies have already come true.
        (3) The Bible unfolds a unified message even though it was written by many authors over many centuries.
        (4) The Bible has influenced human history more than any other book.
        (5) The Bible has changed millions of lives.
  C. Results of inspiration
    1. Inerrancy
      Because the Bible writers wrote what God wanted written, the Bible—in its original writings—is completely without error (2 Sam. 7:28; Ps. 12:6; John 17:17; Heb. 6:18).
    2. Authority
      Since the Bible is the Word of God, it has the same authority that God Himself possesses. To doubt the Bible is to doubt God; to disobey the Bible is to disobey God (Luke 24:25; John 15:20; 1 Thess. 2:13; 2 Pet. 3:2).
    3. Sufficiency
      As the Word of our loving, all-knowing, and holy God, the Bible is sufficient to lead believers to godliness. We have no need of another word from heaven (Ps. 119:11, 50, 66, 89, 130; 2 Tim. 3:16–17; Rev. 22:18–19).

II. Canonicity
  A. Definition
    Canon refers to the books of the Bible that Christians have recognized as Scripture.
  B. Criteria for canonicity
    1. Inspiration
      a. Inspiration is the most important criterion for canonicity. Only words breathed out by God qualify to be included in the canon (2 Tim. 3:16).

b. Not every inspired prophecy was canonical. Scripture reveals that God breathed out some words that were not recorded or preserved (2 Cor. 12:4; Rev. 10:4).

2. Orthodoxy
No book that contradicts other Scripture can be part of the canon (Isa. 8:20).

3. Antiquity
a. God gave revelation to explain His redemptive acts and to guide His people.
b. The apostles and prophets were the ones to whom God entrusted the revelation concerning Christ and the founding of the church (John 16:12–15; Eph. 2:20). Therefore, no book subsequent to the generation of the apostles is considered canonical (Heb. 1:1–2; Jude 1:3).

C. Evidences of canonicity
1. The New Testament recognizes the Old Testament books as canonical (Matt. 21:42; John 10:35–36; Acts 15:14–18; 17:11; 2 Tim. 3:16–17; 1 Pet. 1:23–25).
2. Certain New Testament books recognize other New Testament books as canonical (cf. 1 Tim. 5:18; Luke 10:7; 2 Peter 3:15–16).
3. The Bible's self-attestation has led orthodox Christians to recognize the same books as canonical.

D. Reasons for rejecting the apocrypha and pseudepigraphal books
1. Apocrypha (a group of Jewish books written during the intertestamental period)
a. The Jews of that day did not recognize them as Scripture.
b. Christ did not recognize the Apocryphal books as authoritative. Jesus spoke of the Law, the Prophets, and the Psalms as Scripture (Luke 24:44). These three labels stood for the thirty-nine books of our Old Testament. Jesus also indicated that the canon began with Genesis and ended with 2 Chronicles. In the first century, 2 Chronicles was the thirty-ninth book in the Jewish canon (Luke 11:51).
c. The writers of the New Testament often quoted from the Old Testament but never from the Apocrypha. This implies they did not recognize the Apocrypha as Scripture.
d. The Apocrypha contains both factual errors (Judith 1:1) and doctrines contrary to the Old and New Testaments (Sirach 3:30).

2. Pseudepigrapha
a. The pseudepigraphal books (such as the Gospel of Thomas or the Gospel of Judas) falsely claim to be written by apostles or other prominent early Christians even though they were actually written long after these men were dead.
b. The pseudepigraphal books contain teaching that contradicts the Old Testament Scripture recognized by Jesus and the New Testament Scripture produced by His apostles and prophets.

The Doctrine of God (Theology)

I. Existence of God
A. God testifies to His existence in the Bible (Gen. 1:1).
B. God testifies to His existence in the created order (Rom. 1:20).

II. Attributes of God
A. Spirituality
God is a spirit being. He does not have a body. For this reason He is free of all the limitations that hinder physical beings. He is also completely self-sufficient. There is nothing in the world that God needs (John 4:24; Acts 17:24–25; 1 Tim. 1:17).

B. Infinity
God is infinite, or unlimited. The Bible emphasizes that God is not limited in His relationship to space, knowledge, power, or time.

1. Omnipresence
God is independent of space. God's entire being is present in every place (Ps. 139:7–10).

2. Omniscience
God is infinite in His knowledge. He knows everything that has happened, is happening, and ever will happen. He also knows what may happen but never does happen (1 Sam. 23:12; Ps. 147:5; Isa. 46:9–10; Heb. 4:13).

3. Omnipotence
God is all powerful. He is able to do whatever His perfect will has determined to do (Gen. 18:14; Ps. 115:3; Matt. 19:26).

4. Eternality
God is not limited by time. He has never had a beginning, and He will never cease to exist (Deut. 33:27; Ps. 90:2; 102:26–27).

C. Immutability
God is unchangeable in His attributes and His purposes. He will never cease to be what He is. (Ps. 33:11; Mal. 3:6; James 1:17).

D. Holiness
God is separate from His creation. He is the most glorious being in the universe, infinitely exalted above all that He has made. God is also separate from all sin and evil in this world. God is both glorious and pure (Lev. 22:32; Isa. 6:1–5; 40:25; Hab. 1:13; 1 John 1:5).

E. Truthfulness
God is completely reliable. He cannot lie, and He will keep all His promises (Num. 23:19; Jer. 10:9–10; Tit. 1:2).

F. Justice
God is righteous. He perfectly lives the moral standard that His character establishes for the world. He always does what justice demands. He also holds His creatures accountable to do what justice demands. When His creatures fail to meet their obligations, He punishes them (Exod. 34:6–7; Deut. 32:4; Rom. 2:6–8).

G. Love
God is a loving God. He is patient with sinners. He is kind and merciful to all. And He is gracious—He shows favor even to those who deserve punishment. In a fallen world, God's love seems to conflict with His justice. However, because Jesus Christ died in the sinner's place, there is no conflict between God's justice and His love (Exod. 34:6; Ps. 86:5; Acts 14:17; Rom. 3:24–26; Eph. 2:7–9; 2 Pet. 3:9; 1 John 4:8).

III. Tri-unity of God
The doctrine of the Trinity is the biblical teaching that although God is singular in His essence, He exists in three distinct persons: the Father, the Son, and the Holy Spirit. The Bible teaches this in the following ways.

A. There is only one God (Deut. 4:35; 6:4; Isa. 45:5; James 2:19).

B. Three persons are identified as God.
1. The Father is God (John 6:27; 1 Cor. 8:6).
2. The Son is God.
   a. The Son is called God (Isa. 9:6; John 1:1; 20:28; Heb. 1:8).
   b. The Son is worshiped as God (Ps. 2:10–12; Matt. 8:2; John 5:21–23; Phil. 2:9–10; Heb. 1:6; Rev. 5:8–14).
   c. The Son does the works that are unique to God (John 1:1–3; Col. 1:16–17; Heb. 1:3, 10; John 5:22, 25).
3. The Holy Spirit is God.
   a. *Spirit* is used interchangeably with *God* (John 14:16–17, 23; Acts 5:3–4).
   b. The Spirit has a status exalted above that of any created thing (Matt. 12:30–31; 28:19).
   c. The Spirit has divine attributes (1 Cor. 2:11–16; Heb. 9:14) and does divine works (Gen. 1:2; John 3:8; 16:8; Rom. 8:14).

C. These three persons are distinct.
1. Jesus taught that He was distinct from the Father (John 5:31–40).
2. Jesus spoke of the Father, the Son, and the Spirit as distinct persons (Matt. 28:19).

D. The doctrine of the Trinity is a mystery. God's being and character are so great that we can never understand Him fully. Accepting that He is ultimately unknowable is essential to knowing Him truly.

IV. Works of God
A. Creation
1. Biblical evidence
   a. God created the world out of nothing (Gen. 1:1–26; Ps. 33:6–9; John 1:3; Heb. 11:3).
   b. God created everything for His own glory (Rom. 11:36).
   c. God created everything in six days (Gen. 1; Exod. 20:11).
   d. God created the world good (Gen. 1:10, 12, 18, 21, 25, 31).
2. Implications
   a. God owns everything because He made everything out of nothing.
   b. Everything exists to declare the glory of God.
   c. Evolutionary theory should be rejected because it contradicts biblical teaching.

d. God's creation brought Him pleasure, and He still values what He has made.

B. Providence
Providence is the work of God by which He continually preserves His world and governs it for the fulfillment of His plan.
1. Preserving
   a. God preserves His world by continuously holding it together (Col. 1:17; Heb. 1:3).
   b. God preserves His world by constantly caring for His creatures (Ps. 104:10–13; 145:15).
2. Governing
   a. God's governing work extends over every part of His world, including nature, the nations of the earth, and even the choices of individuals (Ps. 135:6–7; Dan. 4:17, 34; Acts 4:28; Eph. 1:11).
   b. The purpose of God's governing work is to establish His kingdom on earth so that He may receive glory forever (1 Cor. 15:28).

The Doctrine of Man (Anthropology)

I. Original state of man
A. God created man in His own image (Gen. 1:26–27).
   1. God made humans to be like Himself in many ways. These include spiritual nature, moral sensitivity, reasoning capacity, and the ability to interact with other persons.
   2. God made humans to be His great masterpiece. The rest of creation is remarkable in its beauty, complexity, and grandeur. However, only humans are said to be made in God's own image.
   3. God made humans to love and serve Him. Because humans are made in God's image, they need to have a relationship with God in order to find fulfillment.
B. God created man good (Gen. 1:31).
   1. Originally humans were morally perfect. They loved God entirely and loved each other as much as self (cf. Mark 12:30–31).
   2. Originally humans were free of pain, sorrow, and death.
C. God created man with the responsibility to exercise dominion (Gen. 1:26, 28).

1. Man is able to manage God's world under God's authority because he was made in God's image.
2. Although humans are part of God's creation, they stand above the created order as the representatives of God.
3. Humans declare God's glory by exercising good and wise dominion over the earth.

II. Fallen state of man
A. Man's temptation and sin
   1. God's prohibition (Gen. 2:16–17)
      a. God told Adam and Eve not to eat from the tree of the knowledge of good and evil.
      b. God promised that if they did eat from this tree, they would die.
   2. The serpent's temptation (Gen. 3:1–6)
      a. Satan, the enemy of God, presented himself as a serpent (cf. Rev. 12:9).
      b. Satan cast doubt on the goodness of God's character (Gen. 3:1).
      c. Satan directly denied God's word (Gen. 3:4).
      d. Satan appealed to the God-given desire to be like God (cf. Gen. 1:27 and 3:5; cf. Gen. 2:9 and 3:6).
      e. Satan told a half-truth regarding the consequences of disobeying God (Gen. 3:5).
   3. Man's first sin (Gen. 3:6)
      a. Eve ate from the forbidden tree when she decided to trust Satan's word instead of God's word (cf. Gen. 2:17; 3:4, 6).
      b. Adam ate from the tree when Eve offered him the fruit (Gen. 3:6).
B. Results of man's sin
   1. The image of God in man was marred (Gen. 3:12–13).
      a. The affections became depraved (Gen. 3:12; Rom. 1:23–32).
      b. The mind was darkened (1 Cor. 2:14; Eph. 4:17–18).
      c. The will was debilitated (Jer. 13:23; Rom. 3:10–12).
   2. The work of dominion was frustrated (cf. Gen. 3:16–19).
      a. The physical world resists human attempts at dominion (Gen. 3:16–19; Rom. 8:22).
      b. Human relationships are characterized by selfishness and strife (Gen. 3:16).

c. Humans are cursed to die (Gen. 3:19).
3. The first sin damaged the entire human race (Rom. 5:12, 19).
   a. All humans are sinful in nature, have lost fellowship with God, and commit sinful deeds.
   b. All humans naturally serve Satan's purposes.
   c. All humans suffer death and deserve eternal judgment.
4. God promised to deliver His people (Gen. 3:15).
   a. Salvation from death and rescue from Satan's bondage is possible only through Christ's death and Resurrection.
   b. God cursed Satan to experience humiliation and defeat.
   c. God promised that His people would triumph over evil.
      (1) God predicted that throughout history Satan and his followers ("the seed of the serpent") would be the enemies of God's people ("the seed of the woman").
      (2) God predicted that in the end His people would have dominion over Satan and his followers.

The Doctrine of Christ (Christology)

I. Person of Christ
   A. Jesus Christ is God.
      See *The Doctrine of God, III. B. 2.*
   B. Jesus Christ is human.
      1. Jesus had a human conception and birth (Matt. 1:18, 20, 24; Luke 1:30–35; Gal. 4:4).
      2. Jesus grew and developed physically, mentally, and spiritually (Luke 2:52).
      3. Jesus experienced hunger (Matt. 4:2), thirst (John 19:28), and fatigue (John 4:6).
      4. Paul compares and contrasts Jesus with Adam, the first man (1 Cor. 15:21–22).
      5. Jesus depended on God's Spirit and His Word, as all humans should (Matt. 4:1–11; 26:39; Mark 1:35).
      6. Jesus had to be human in order to be the sacrificial substitute for humans (Heb. 2:16–17).

7. The salvation of humans leads to their becoming like Jesus (2 Cor. 3:18; Rom. 8:29).
   C. The union of Jesus Christ's two natures is a mystery.
      Jesus in the incarnation took on a human nature so that Jesus is one person with a fully divine nature and a fully human nature. He is not a divine spirit in a human body. He is not a divine person and a human person. He is not a mixture of a divine nature and a human nature into a third, blended nature. Jesus is one person with a divine nature and a human nature.
II. Work of Christ
   A. Jesus Christ fulfills His work through His three offices.
      1. Jesus Christ is the perfect Prophet.
         a. Christ declared the gospel to the Jewish people (Mark 1:14–15, 38).
         b. Christ declared God's word to the nations (Isa. 42:1–4; 49:6; 50:4; Matt. 12:18–20; Heb. 1:2).
         c. Jesus is the prophet Who is greater than Moses (Deut. 18:15–19; Acts 3:19–26; Heb. 1:2; Rev. 1:1).
         d. Jesus is the Word of God the Father (John 1:1–18).
      2. Jesus Christ is the sinless Priest.
         a. Christ offered Himself as the perfect sacrifice for sinners (Isa. 53:10–11; Acts 8:32–35; 1 Cor. 5:7; Rom. 3:25; Heb. 2:17; 7:26–27; Rev. 5:6).
         b. As a better priest of a better covenant, Christ fulfills and surpasses the priesthood of the Mosaic Law (Heb. 7:18–19; 8:1–6).
         c. Christ intercedes for His people (Rom. 8:34; Heb. 7:25).
      3. Jesus Christ is the eternal King.
         a. Christ has complete authority and ability to exercise good and wise dominion over all things (Gen. 49:8–12; Matt. 28:18–20; Luke 1:26–33; Heb. 2:5–9; Rev. 1:5).
         b. Christ will restore humans to the work of exercising dominion over the earth (Rev. 5:9–10; 22:5).
   B. Jesus Christ fulfills His work in two stages.
      1. Jesus Christ humbled Himself by submitting to His Father's will (Phil. 2:5–8).

a. Active obedience
Jesus Christ became a man and perfectly obeyed all of God's law. Therefore, He earned eternal life for Himself as a man (Lev. 18:5; Matt. 3:15; Rom. 8:3; Gal. 4:4).

b. Passive obedience
Instead of claiming eternal life for Himself, Jesus Christ obeyed God the Father and died on the cross, receiving God's wrath so that sinners may receive the eternal life He had earned (Rom. 3:25; 5:19; Phil. 2:8; Col. 2:13–14).

2. God the Father has exalted Jesus Christ for His complete obedience (Phil. 2:9–11).

a. Resurrection
God the Father raised Jesus Christ from the dead, giving Him and His people victory over the power of sin and death. (Acts 2:24; 1 Cor. 6:14; 15:54–56; Rev. 1:18).

b. Enthronement
God the Father has made Jesus Christ the King over all creation in fulfillment of His promises to David (2 Sam. 7:12–16, 18–19; Ps. 2:7–12; Acts 2:22–36).

The Doctrine of the Holy Spirit (Pneumatology)

I. Person of the Holy Spirit
   A. The Holy Spirit is God.
      See *The Doctrine of God, III. B. 3.*
   B. The Holy Spirit is a person.
      The Spirit is not a force. He possesses the characteristics of a person (Isa. 11:2; John 14:26; 15:26; Rom. 15:30; 1 Cor. 12:11; Eph. 4:30).

II. Work of the Holy Spirit
   A. Creation and preservation
      The Holy Spirit was involved in creating the world (Gen. 1:2; Job 26:13; 33:4; Ps. 33:6; 104:30) and continues to be involved in preserving the creation (Gen. 6:3; Job 34:14–15; Ps. 104:29–30).
   B. Empowerment for service
      The Holy Spirit is the member of the Trinity Who empowers people for service to God.
      1. The Holy Spirit enabled people to prophesy (Num. 11:25; 24:2; 1 Sam. 10:6, 10; 19:20; 2 Sam. 23:2; Neh. 9:20,

30). He is responsible for the inspiration of Scripture (1 Tim. 3:16; 2 Pet. 1:21).
      2. The Holy Spirit empowered Israel's leaders for political and military service (Num. 11:16–29; Deut. 34:9; Jud. 6:34; 11:29; 13:25; 1 Sam. 16:13; Ps. 51:11) and for the construction of the tabernacle and the temple (Exod. 28:3; 31:1–11; 1 Chron. 28:12; Hag. 2:5; Zech. 4:6).
      3. The Holy Spirit empowered Jesus for His ministry on earth (Matt. 4:1; 12:28; Mark 1:10; Luke 4:18–21).
      4. The Holy Spirit endows the members of the church with spiritual gifts so that they are able to fulfill their ministry to others (John 7:39; Acts 2:16–18; Rom. 12:3–8; 1 Cor. 12:1–31; Eph. 4:4–14; 1 Pet. 4:10–11).
   C. Salvation of sinners
      The Spirit of God gives new life to the sinner and makes him part of the church, the body of Christ.
      1. The Holy Spirit is involved in regeneration (Ezek. 36:25–27; John 3:5–8).
      2. The presence of the Spirit in a person's life evidences the person's salvation (Rom. 8:16).
   D. Sanctification of believers
      1. In the New Covenant, God promised to put His Spirit within His people in order to solve their sin problem (Ezek. 36:25–27).
      2. The indwelling Spirit enables Christians to live as children of God rather than as slaves to their flesh (Gal. 5:16–26; Rom. 8:9–17).

The Doctrine of Salvation (Soteriology)

I. Election
   A. Definition
      Election is God's gracious choice to favor some people with the salvation that Jesus Christ purchased (Eph. 1:3–5; Acts 13:48; 2 Thess. 2:13).
   B. Timing
      God chose His people before He created the world (Eph. 1:4; 2 Thess. 2:13).
   C. Certainty
      The people God has chosen will not fail to receive His salvation. God does not change His mind, so His elect will remain His elect for all eternity (John 6:37; 15:16; Rom. 8:29–30; 9:15–16; 11:29).

II. Divine calling
  A. God's command to repent
     God commands all people everywhere to repent and trust Christ for salvation (Acts 17:30).
  B. God's displeasure
     God does not take pleasure in the death of the wicked (Ezek. 18:23, 32; 33:11; 2 Pet. 3:9).
  C. God's command to preach
     God commands His people to present the gospel to everyone (Matt. 28:18–20).
III. Conversion
   The doctrine of salvation primarily concerns what God does for the sinner. The doctrine of conversion concerns how the sinner is to receive the gospel message. There are two aspects to conversion.
  A. Repentance
     1. Repentance is the sinner's change of mind regarding sin. It involves godly sorrow for sin and a turning away from it (2 Chron. 7:14; Ezek. 33:11; Matt. 3:8; 2 Cor. 7:9–10; Heb. 12:17).
     2. Repentance is a gift from God to the sinner (Acts 11:18; 2 Tim. 2:25).
     3. Repentance is necessary for conversion. Without repentance, there is no salvation (Matt. 4:17; Luke 24:46–47; Acts 17:30).
  B. Faith
     1. Genuine faith is more than mere mental assent to the facts of the gospel. The true believer trusts in Jesus's death and Resurrection to save him from sin (John 1:12; 2:23–25; Acts 10:43; Rom. 4:5; 1 John 5:13).
     2. Repentance and faith are inseparable. Turning away from sin and trusting in God for pardon are two aspects of one action (Isa. 55:6–7; Mark 1:15; Acts 20:21; Heb. 6:1).
IV. Regeneration
  A. Definition
     Regenerated literally means "born again." Regeneration is God's work of changing the nature of the sinner so that he loves what is good and hates what is evil (Ezek. 11:19–20; John 3:3–8, 19–21).
  B. Need for regeneration
     Because of the Fall, humans love sin and hate God. They do not want to commune with God, and they are not able to obey Him. If sinners are to experience God's salvation, they must receive a new heart (Rom. 3:9–20; 1 Cor. 2:14; Eph. 2:1–3).
  C. Result of regeneration
     God's work of regeneration produces a new life. The believer dies to sin so that he is no longer enslaved to it. He becomes alive to God and capable of obeying Him (Rom. 6:1–11; 2 Cor. 5:15, 17; Eph. 2:4–10; 1 John 2:29).
V. Justification
  A. Definition
     Justification is God's work of declaring the believing sinner righteous because of what Christ has done (Rom. 3:24–25).
  B. Need for justification
     God is just. He punishes the guilty and rewards the innocent. But all humans are guilty before God. God cannot forgive sinners unless their standing before Him is changed (Gen. 18:25; Prov. 17:15; Rom. 3:19–20).
  C. Basis of justification
     God pronounces the believing sinner righteous based on Christ's work. In particular, God gives the believer the righteousness of Christ. God, therefore, considers the believer to be as righteous as Jesus Christ (Matt. 3:15; Rom. 3:21–25; 5:17–19; Gal. 4:4).
  D. Condition for justification
     There is only one condition for experiencing justification. The sinner must believe the gospel. Although many have claimed that justification is by faith and works, the Bible clearly teaches that faith alone is the condition for justification (John 3:18; Rom. 3:28; 4:4–5; Gal. 2:16).
  E. Results of justification
     Because of justification the believer is completely forgiven. God is no longer angry with him because He considers him to be righteous (Rom. 4:6–8; 8:1, 33–34). Also, because of justification God remains just even though He forgives the guilty and saves them from sin (Rom. 3:26, 31).
VI. Sanctification
  A. Definition
     Sanctification is God's ongoing work of making the believer more like Himself. In justification, God declares the sinner righteous. In sanctification, He enables the believer to live righteously (Rom. 6:17–19; 8:1–5).

B. Process of sanctification
   1. Ongoing
      Unlike justification and regeneration—which happen in a moment—God's work of sanctification is a process. From regeneration until death, the believer becomes less given to sin and more given to obeying God and delighting in Him (2 Cor. 3:18; Phil. 1:6).
   2. Cooperative
      Sanctification is a cooperative work. The Holy Spirit (through the Bible and other means) directs, encourages, and empowers the believer to grow spiritually. But the believer also has responsibility. He must submit to the leading of the Spirit and follow His direction (John 17:17; Rom. 6:1–12; 8:1–17; Gal. 5:16–26; 1 Thess. 4:1–3; Phil. 2:12–13; 1 Pet. 1:15).
C. Goal of sanctification
   The purpose of sanctification is to make the believer like Jesus Christ, Who in His humanity, empowered by the Holy Spirit, was the perfect image-bearer of God (Rom. 8:28–29; Col. 3:10; Heb. 1:2–3). The process of sanctification is not complete in this life. Only when the believer leaves this life and is united with his Savior is he fully sanctified (Heb. 12:23; 1 John 1:8; 3:2).

VII. Glorification
A. Definition
   Glorification is God's exaltation of the believer to be freed from all the effects of sin and restored completely to the work of exercising dominion over the earth (Rom. 8:18–30; Eph. 1:13–14; 1 Pet. 1:3–5).
B. Timing
   God will glorify believers at the second coming of Christ (1 Cor. 15:12–23; 1 Pet. 1:13; 1 John 3:2).
C. Aspects of glorification
   1. Moral perfection
      All believers who have not died will be completely delivered from all aspects of sin (1 Cor. 15:55–57; Titus 2:11–14; 1 Pet. 1:13; 1 John 3:2).
   2. Resurrection
      Dead believers will be resurrected, and living believers will be given new bodies. These bodies will be free from pain, sorrow, and death (1 Cor. 15:42–45; Rom. 8:18, 23).
   3. Renewal of all creation
      God will fully restore man's dominion over the created order. Creation will be redeemed to its original glory and goodness (Heb. 2:5–9; Rev. 21:4; 22:5).

The Doctrine of the Church (Ecclesiology)

I. Definition of the church
   The church is the assembly of believers who are brought together through the baptism of the Holy Spirit to serve as the body of Christ and the present manifestation of His kingdom (Matt. 16:18–19; Acts 2:41–47; 1 Cor. 12:13; Col. 1:13).
II. Origin of the church
   It is reasonable to conclude that the church began at Pentecost.
   A. Subsequent to the ministry of Christ
      Jesus prophesied that the church was a coming entity that He would found through His apostles and prophets (Matt. 16:18; Eph. 2:20).
   B. Founded by the gift of the Holy Spirit
      The church is the New Covenant community formed through the promised indwelling of the Holy Spirit.
      1. The church is a new entity, established by the New Covenant, and it includes both Jews and Gentiles (Eph. 2:14–16).
      2. Whereas Israel worshiped at a temple, the church is the temple of the Holy Spirit (1 Cor. 3:16; Eph. 2:22).
      3. The Spirit's indwelling of believers forms the people of God into the body of Christ (1 Cor. 12:13).
   C. Day of Pentecost
      Jesus Christ poured out His Spirit on His followers on the day of Pentecost. Until that time His followers were commanded to wait for the Spirit's coming (Acts 1:4–5; 2:1–42).
III. Manifestations of the church
   A. Visible and invisible
      1. Visible church
         The visible church consists of local churches, comprising those who profess faith in Christ. Not all in the visible church are truly regenerated (1 Cor 1:2; cf. Acts 20:29–30; Rev. 2–3).
      2. Invisible church
         The invisible church consists of all who are truly regenerated by the Spirit (1 Cor. 12:13; Col. 1:13).

B. Local and universal
  1. Local church
     Paul refers to a church that meets in a house (Rom. 16:5).
  2. Regional church
     One can refer to the church of Judea, Galilee, and Samaria (Acts 9:31), though the church of that region is made up of many smaller assemblies.
  3. Universal church
     Paul sometimes speaks of the church as a single community (Eph. 4:4; 5:25).
IV. Government of the church
  A. Head
     Jesus Christ is the head of the church. Therefore, all church leadership is subject to His authority (Eph 1:22; 4:15; 5:23; Col. 1:18; 2:10, 19). Practically, this means that His Word (the Bible) is the standard by which the church is governed.
  B. Pastors
     1. *Overseer* (*bishop*), *elder*, and *pastor* are different titles for the same office (Acts 20:17, 28).
     2. The elders are to oversee and shepherd the people entrusted to their care (Acts 20:28; 1 Tim. 3:1; Titus 1:7; 1 Pet. 5:2). The elders have the responsibility of preaching the Bible and praying for God's church (Acts 6:4).
     3. An elder is to be a man who is gifted in teaching and whose character is above reproach (1 Tim. 3:1–7).
  C. Deacons
     1. The deacons were chosen to focus on meeting material needs of church members (Acts 6:1–6).
     2. The deacons are designated to free the elders to focus on preaching the Word and prayer (Acts 6:1–6).
     3. Deacons must meet certain qualifications (1 Tim. 3:8–13).
  D. Congregation
     1. The entire congregation should be involved in choosing its leadership (Acts 1:13–26; 6:1–6).
     2. The congregation is to decide who will extend the influence of the church in missionary endeavors (Acts 13:1–3).
     3. The entire congregation is to be involved in the work of church discipline (Matt 18:15–17; 1 Cor. 1:2; 5:4–5).

V. Work of the church
  A. Ministry of the Word
     Central to the church's mission is the reading of Scripture and the preaching of the Word (Acts 2:42; 1 Tim. 4:13; 2 Tim. 4:2). Through the reading and exposition of Scripture, the church is built up and the lost are evangelized (Eph. 5:12; Rom. 10:14).
  B. Administration of the ordinances
     Ordinances are actions of obedience, commanded and explained in Scripture and practiced by the New Testament church. Believers carry out the ordinances, not to obtain grace, but rather to testify that they have already received grace.
     1. Baptism
        Baptism is the ordinance that symbolizes our union with Christ in His death, burial, and Resurrection, which is accomplished through the baptism of the Holy Spirit which brings people into the body of Christ (Rom. 6:3–4; Col. 2:12; 1 Cor. 12:13).
     2. Lord's Supper
        The Lord's Supper is the ordinance by which believers are to remember that Christ instituted the New Covenant through His sacrifice on the cross for them as they anticipate his Second Coming (1 Cor. 11:23–26).
  C. Fellowship
     In the church, believers are to encourage, edify, and help one another. This work is an essential part of Christians showing the love of Christ (Acts 2:42; John 13:35; Eph. 4:15–16).
  D. Prayer
     Prayer is an essential part of the church's activity, both corporately and individually (Acts 2:42).
     1. Praise honors God by ascribing to Him the glory He deserves.
     2. Intercession honors God by demonstrating the church's dependence on Him for all that it does. Intercession is also a key way for the church to love and help the members of the body.
     3. Confession of sin is a means for the church to progress in sanctification.

The Doctrine of the End Times (Eschatology)

I. Second Coming of Christ
  A. Rapture
    1. At the Rapture the dead in Christ will rise first, and those who are still alive will be caught up with them to meet Christ in the air (1 Thess. 4:13–18).
    2. The Rapture will occur before the Tribulation.
      a. Christ has promised to keep His church from the hour of trial that is coming on the whole world (Rev. 3:10).
      b. Christ has promised that He will come suddenly and unexpectedly (Matt. 24:36–39, 42–44; 35:13; Luke 12:40; 1 Thess. 5:2).
  B. Tribulation
    1. The Tribulation will be a seven-year period of God's judgment on the world (Dan. 9:24–27; 12:11–12; Rev. 11:2–3; 12:14).
    2. During this time Satan will exercise extensive control over the earth through the Antichrist and False Prophet (2 Thess. 2:3–4; Rev. 13; 17–18).
    3. The Tribulation will be a time of great persecution against God's people (Rev. 11:7–8; 13:17).
    4. The Tribulation will be a time of fruitful evangelism (Rev. 7:4, 9).
  C. Christ's return to earth
    1. When Christ returns, the kingdoms of this earth will become the kingdom of God (Rev. 11:15).
    2. Christ will conquer His enemies, bind Satan for one thousand years, and fully establish His rule on earth (Rev. 19:11–20:3).

II. Millennium
God will restore the earth to a condition that foreshadows the full restoration of the new creation. The earth will be an abundantly fruitful place in which drought and disaster are confined to specific judgments (Isa. 65–66; Zech. 14; Rev. 20).
  A. Long life
  Death will become a rare event, and long life will be considered normal. Anyone who dies at the age of one hundred will be considered a child (Isa. 65:20).
  B. Reigning with Christ
  God's people will reign with Christ over the earth for one thousand years (Rev. 20:4–6).
  C. Final Judgment
    1. At the end of the Millennium, Christ will defeat Satan's final rebellion against His rule (Rev. 20:7–10).
    2. The unsaved dead will be raised from Hades to stand with the unsaved living to be judged by Christ at the Great White Throne (Rev. 20:11–15).

III. Eternal State
  A. Lake of Fire
  The Lake of Fire/Gehenna (often translated *hell*) is a place of torment that God has prepared for the Devil, his angels, and all those who do not repent of their sin (Matt. 25:41; Mark 9:43–48; Rev. 21:8).
    1. Punishment of the wicked is eternal (Isa. 66:24; Matt. 25:41; Mark 9:43–48; Rev. 14:11; 20:10).
    2. Punishment of the wicked is conscious (Rev. 14:11).
    3. Punishment of the wicked is just (Isa. 66:24; Rev. 19:1–3).
  B. New heavens and the new earth
    1. The Old Testament predicted the coming of the Messiah, Who will rule over the earth from Zion. This new earth will be an abundantly fruitful place in which sin and its effects do not exist (Pss. 2:6; 14:7; 53:6; 110:2; Isa. 2:1–4; 11–12; 65:17–19; Jer. 31:1–12; Joel 3:17–18).
    2. The future hope of an earthly kingdom ruled by the Messiah remained the expectation of the disciples. Though Christ told them they could not know the time of the visible arrival of the kingdom, He did not deny their understanding of its nature (Acts 1:6–8). The New Testament also speaks of resurrected believers ruling with Christ (2 Tim 2:12; Rom 5:17; Rom 4:13; 1 Cor. 6:2–3).
    3. The New Testament promises new heavens and a new earth (2 Pet. 3:13; Rev. 21:1). Romans 8:18–25 teaches that the creation is awaiting redemption also. When our bodies are redeemed, the creation will itself be set free from its corruption. Also, the meek will inherit the earth (Matt. 5:5), and Abraham will be heir of the world (Rom. 4:13).

Bible Truths for Christian Growth

The Bible Teaches Us About . . .

Bible Truths for Christian Growth

Bible Truths for Christian Growth are short questions and answers designed to highlight truths from the Word of God, thereby enhancing memorization for the purpose of practical Christian living for the glory of God. The 164 questions and answers have been organized by topic into ten groups. Each group contains from five to thirty-three questions and answers.

The second grade curriculum utilizes eighty-nine of these questions (the seventy-five questions from first grade plus fourteen new ones). Each year additional question/answer pairs are studied to broaden the student's understanding.

Grade Level	BTCG Questions
1	1–75
2	76–89
3	90–108
4	109–127
5	128–146
6	147–164

The selected questions that each grade studies are included in the Student Worktext for that grade. Each grade's Teacher's Edition and Support Materials CD both contain the full set of Bible truths. Teachers may choose to study all the questions and answers or only some of them.

When introducing a question, explain the meaning of unfamiliar words, relate the question to the Bible lessons when appropriate, and apply the truth to the students' lives. The verse references are the basis for the answers and are to help you explain the particular Bible truth. To practice the Bible Truths for Christian Growth, repeat each question and answer several times before expecting the students to begin saying it with you. After the students become familiar with the questions and answers, a variety of games can be played for review. Learning these great scriptural truths can be a vital teaching tool resulting in lifelong changes. Bible Truths for Christian Growth are offered as an optional part of this curriculum.

The Bible Teaches Us About God
(15 questions)

1. **Who is God?** *God is the eternal and holy creator and keeper of the universe and the Savior of mankind (Genesis 1:1; Psalm 90:2; Hebrews 1:3; John 3:16).*
2. **What is God like?** *God is infinite, loving, and unchangeable (Psalm 139:7–10; 1 John 4:8; James 1:17).*
3. **Where is God?** *God is everywhere (Psalm 139:7–12; Proverbs 15:3).*
4. **Can you see God?** *No, I cannot see God, but He always sees me (Jeremiah 23:23–24; John 1:18; 1 Timothy 6:16).*
5. **Why can we not see God?** *We cannot see God because He is a spirit and does not have a body (John 4:24).*
6. **Does God know all things?** *Yes, God knows all things (Job 34:21; Psalm 147:5; Hebrews 4:13).*
7. **Can God do all things?** *Yes, God can do all His holy will (Matthew 19:26; Psalm 135:6).*
8. **Does God ever do evil?** *No, God is always righteous (Deuteronomy 32:4; James 1:13).*
9. **Is there more than one God?** *No, there is only one God (Isaiah 44:6; 45:6, 22; 1 Timothy 2:5).*
10. **In how many persons does this one God exist?** *God exists in three persons (Matthew 3:16–17; 2 Corinthians 13:14).*
11. **Who are the three persons of God?** *The three persons of God are the Father, the Son, and the Holy Spirit (Matthew 28:19).*
12. **Who made God?** *Nobody made God (Psalm 90:2).*
13. **Has God ever had a beginning?** *No, God has always existed (Psalm 93:2; Revelation 4:8).*
14. **Will God ever die?** *No, God lives forever (Deuteronomy 33:27).*
15. **What is God's attitude toward us?** *God loves us even though we are sinners (Jeremiah 31:3; John 3:16; Romans 5:8).*

The Bible Teaches Us About God's Creation
(16 questions)

16. **Who made you?** *God made me (Genesis 1:27; Job 33:4).*
17. **What else did God make?** *God made all things (Genesis 1:1–31; John 1:3).*
18. **Why did God make you and all things?** *God made me and all things for His own glory (Isaiah 6:3; Romans 11:36; 1 Corinthians 6:20; 10:31).*
19. **How can you glorify God?** *I can glorify God by loving Him and doing what He commands (Micah 6:8; John 15:8; 1 John 5:3).*
20. **Why ought you to glorify God?** *I ought to glorify God because He made me and takes care of me (Psalms 104:14–23; 146:5–10; Revelation 4:11).*

21. **Where do you learn how to love and obey God?** *I learn how to love and obey God in the Bible alone (Deuteronomy 30:11–16; Joshua 1:8).*

22. **Who wrote the Bible?** *Holy men who were taught by the Holy Spirit wrote the Bible (2 Timothy 3:16; 2 Peter 1:21).*

23. **What does the Bible reveal?** *The Bible reveals Who God is and how He is redeeming His fallen world through the death, burial, and Resurrection of Jesus Christ (Genesis 3:15; Mark 1:15; 1 Corinthians 15:1–4; Revelation 21:1–4).*

24. **For what purpose does God redeem His creation?** *God redeems His creation so that all who believe in Him will live with Him forever in the kingdom of God (Revelation 21:1–4).*

25. **Who were our first parents?** *Adam and Eve were our first parents (Genesis 2:7, 18–22; 3:20).*

26. **What were our first parents made of?** *God made Adam out of the dust of the ground and formed Eve from Adam's body (Genesis 2:7, 21–22).*

27. **What did God make Adam and Eve to be like?** *God made them in His own image (Genesis 1:26–27).*

28. **What does it mean for humans to be in the image of God?** *God made us eternal beings that are able to reason, to have fellowship with Him, and to understand what is right and wrong (Revelation 14:11; 22:5; Isaiah 1:18; Psalm 27:8; Proverbs 28:5).*

29. **Why did God make Adam and Eve?** *God made them to populate the earth and have dominion over it (Genesis 1:26–28).*

30. **What does it mean for humans to have dominion over the earth?** *We are to manage every part of our lives for the benefit of others and for the glory of God.*

31. **When God made Adam and Eve, what condition were they in?** *God made them sinless and happy (Genesis 1:27–31).*

The Bible Teaches Us About Sin
(11 questions)

32. **Did Adam and Eve remain in their sinless and happy condition?** *No, Adam and Eve chose to disobey God (Genesis 3:6).*

33. **What is sin?** *Sin is transgressing (or breaking) the law of God (1 John 3:4).*

34. **How did God punish Adam's disobedience?** *Adam's punishment was death and separation from God (Genesis 2:17; 3:17–24).*

35. **What was the sin of our first parents?** *Adam and Eve disobeyed God and ate the fruit that God told them not to eat (Genesis 2:17; 3:6).*

36. **What led to the first sin?** *Eve believed a lie instead of God's word (Genesis 2:16–17; 3:1–6).*

37. **Who tempted Adam and Eve to sin?** *Satan tempted Eve, and she gave the fruit to Adam (Genesis 3:1–6).*

38. **What happened to our first parents when they sinned?** *Instead of being sinless and happy, they became sinful and miserable (Genesis 3:8–24).*

39. **What effect did Adam's sin have on all mankind?** *Because of Adam's sin, every person is born with a sinful nature that wants to do evil and has no fellowship with God (Psalm 51:5; Romans 5:12).*

40. **How do we disobey God's law?** *We disobey God's law by not doing what God commands or by doing what God forbids (Matthew 15:3–6).*

41. **What does every sin deserve?** *Every sin deserves to be punished by God (Psalm 89:30–32; Galatians 3:10).*

42. **What is God's final judgment on unbelievers?** *All people who do not trust in Christ for salvation deserve the punishment of the lake of fire forever (Revelation 20:14–15; 21:8).*

The Bible Teaches Us About Satan
(9 questions)

43. **Did God create anyone before He created Adam?** *Yes, God created angels before He created Adam (Job 38:4–7).*

44. **Are all angels good?** *No, some angels are holy, but others are evil (Matthew 25:31; Revelation 12:9).*

45. **What do the good angels do?** *The good angels serve God (Hebrews 1:14).*

46. **Who is Satan?** *Satan is an evil spirit who is the enemy of God and all Christians (John 8:44; 1 Peter 5:8).*

47. **Was Satan ever good?** *Yes, Satan was once one of God's greatest angels (Ezekiel 28:12–14).*

48. **Why is Satan not one of God's angels today?** *Satan became proud, sinned, and tried to fight against God, so God cast him out of heaven (Ezekiel 28:15–16; Revelation 12:3–4, 7–9).*

49. **Who is stronger, God or Satan?** *God is stronger (1 John 3:8; 4:4).*

50. **Does Satan want God's will to be done?** *No, Satan always wants people to disobey God (1 Chronicles 21:1; Ephesians 6:11–12, 16).*

51. **What does Satan do?** *Satan causes us to doubt God's Word, tempts us to sin, and destroys lives (Genesis 3:1; 3:4; Matthew 4:3, 9; John 10:10).*

The Bible Teaches Us About Christ's Work
(33 questions)

52. **Who can save us?** *The Lord Jesus Christ is the only Savior (John 14:6; Acts 4:12).*

53. **What does God require before a person can go to heaven?** *God requires that a person be born again to go to heaven (John 3:3, 16; Acts 4:12).*

54. **What is another word for being born again?** *Regeneration is another word for being born again (Ezekiel 36:26–27; Titus 3:5–6).*

55. **What is regeneration?** *Regeneration is a change of heart whereby God's desires become the sinner's delight.*

56. **Who can change a sinner's heart?** *The Holy Spirit can change a sinner's heart (Titus 3:5).*

57. **How is a heart changed?** *A heart is changed by the Holy Spirit because of the grace of God shown in the work of Christ (Titus 3:4–7).*

58. **What is grace?** *Grace is God's kindness to us when we deserve punishment (Deuteronomy 7:6–9; Ephesians 2:8–9).*

59. **What was the work of Christ?** *The work of Christ was to keep the law of God perfectly and to suffer the penalty for our sins (2 Corinthians 5:21; Hebrews 9:11–14).*

60. **Can anyone be saved by his own works?** *No one can be saved by his own works (Ephesians 2:8–9; Titus 3:4–7).*

61. **Did Christ ever sin?** *No, Christ was holy, sinless, and undefiled (2 Corinthians 5:21; Hebrews 7:26).*

62. **How was it possible for the Son of God to suffer?** *Christ, the Son of God, became human so that He could obey and suffer in our place (Philippians 2:7–8; Hebrews 2:9).*

63. **What is meant by the atonement?** *The atonement is Christ's satisfying divine justice by His sufferings and death in the place of sinners (Romans 5:8–11; 1 Peter 3:18).*

64. **What do we gain from the work of Christ?** *God regenerates, justifies, and sanctifies those who trust in Christ (1 Corinthians 6:11; Titus 3:5–7).*

65. **What is justification?** *Justification is God's forgiving me and treating me just as if I had never sinned. (Romans 3:24–25; Romans 8:1).*

66. **Why can God treat me just as if I had never sinned?** *God can treat me just as if I had never sinned because He has given me Christ's righteousness (Matthew 3:15; 2 Corinthians 5:19, 21; Galatians 4:4–5).*

67. **How am I justified?** *I am justified by faith in the work of Christ (Romans 3:25–28; Galatians 2:16).*

68. **What is sanctification?** *Sanctification is the process by which God transforms saved people to be like Christ in heart and behavior (1 Corinthians 6:19–20; Romans 12:1–2).*

69. **What are the two parts of sanctification?** *The two parts of sanctification are dying to sin and living to righteousness (Romans 8:13; 6:11, 13; Galatians 2:20).*

70. **For whom did Christ obey and suffer?** *Christ obeyed and suffered for sinners (Romans 5:8).*

71. **What kind of death did Christ die?** *Christ died the painful and shameful death of being nailed to a cross (Luke 23:33–38; Philippians 2:8).*

72. **Who will be saved?** *Whoever repents and trusts the Lord Jesus Christ will be saved (Isaiah 55:7; John 3:16).*

73. **What does it mean to repent?** *To repent is to be sorry for my sin because it displeases God (2 Chronicles 7:14; Psalm 38:18; Jeremiah 44:4).*

74. **What is saving faith in Christ?** *Saving faith is trusting only in Christ's death and Resurrection for salvation (1 Corinthians 15:1–4; Romans 10:13).*

75. **Can you repent and believe in Christ by your own power?** *No, I cannot repent and believe in Christ without the help of God's Holy Spirit (John 3:5–6; Titus 3:5).*

76. **Can children repent and trust Christ for salvation?** *Yes, He welcomes them to come to Him (Mark 10:14).*

77. **How long has it been since Christ died?** *Christ died nearly two thousand years ago.*

78. **How were people saved before Christ came?** *People were saved by trusting in the Savior to come (Isaiah 43:11; Hebrews 11:13).*

79. **What in the Old Testament pointed forward to the Savior's sacrifice for sin?** *Animals sacrificed on God's altar pointed to the Savior's sacrifice (Leviticus 4:32–35; Hebrews 9:11–12).*

80. **What did the sacrifices represent?** *The sacrifices represented Christ, the Lamb of God, Who was to die for sinners (John 1:29, 36; Hebrews 9:11–14).*

81. **What are Christ's three offices?** *Christ's offices are that of prophet, priest, and king (Acts 3:22; Hebrews 5:5–6; Revelation 19:16).*

82. **How is Christ *the* prophet?** *Christ revealed God to us and teaches us the will of God (John 1:18; Luke 4:18; John 15:15; Hebrews 1:2).*

83. **How is Christ *the* priest?** *Christ offered Himself as the Lamb of God and pleads with God for us (Romans 3:26; Hebrews 7:25–27).*

84. **How is Christ *the* king?** *Christ rules over us, defends us, and will establish His kingdom on earth (Isaiah 33:22; 1 Corinthians 15:25; Revelation 19:16).*

The Bible Teaches Us About Christ's Resurrection

(5 questions)

85. **On which day of the week do Christians gather for worship?** *Most Christians worship on Sunday, the first day of the week, which Scripture calls the Lord's Day (Acts 20:7; 1 Corinthians 16:1–2; Revelation 1:10).*

86. **Why is Sunday called the Lord's Day?** *Sunday is called the Lord's Day because Christ rose from the dead on that day (Matthew 28:1–6; Mark 16:1–6).*

87. **How should the Lord's Day be spent?** *The Lord's Day should be spent in prayer and praise, in hearing and reading God's Word, and in doing good to other people (Luke 13:10–13; Acts 15:21; 16:13).*

88. **Did Christ remain in the tomb after His Crucifixion?** *No, Christ rose bodily from the tomb on the third day after His death (Matthew 16:21; 28:1–6; 1 Corinthians 15:3–4).*

89. **Where is Christ now?** *Christ is in heaven, interceding for us (Acts 1:9; Ephesians 1:19–21; Hebrews 4:14–16; 7:25).*

The Bible Teaches Us About God's Commandments

(31 questions)

90. How many commandments did God give on Mount Sinai? *God gave ten commandments (Exodus 20:1–17).*

91. What are the Ten Commandments sometimes called? *They are called the Decalogue, which means "ten words."*

92. What do the first four commandments teach? *The first four commandments teach our duty to God (Exodus 20:1–11; Matthew 22:37–38).*

93. What is the usefulness of the law for all people? *The law teaches us that God is holy, that all people ought to live according to His holiness, and that no one is able to keep the law perfectly (Romans 3:20; Galatians 3:19, 21–22).*

94. What does the law teach us about righteousness? *The law teaches that Christ and His perfect obedience are needed if anyone is to be considered righteous before God (Romans 3:28; Galatians 2:16, 21).*

95. What is the usefulness of the law for Christians? *Christians are to use the law to understand God's standard of holy living, which they are to strive toward by the Holy Spirit (Matthew 5:17–48; 22:36–40; Galatians 5:22–25).*

96. What is the first commandment? *The first commandment is "Thou shalt have no other gods before me" (Exodus 20:3).*

97. What does the first commandment teach us? *The first commandment teaches us to worship only God (Matthew 4:10).*

98. What is the second commandment? *The second commandment is "Thou shalt not make unto thee any graven image, or any likeness of any thing that is in heaven above, or that is in the earth beneath, or that is in the water under the earth" (Exodus 20:4–6).*

99. What does the second commandment teach us? *The second commandment teaches us to worship God in a proper manner and to avoid idolatry (Exodus 20:23; Deuteronomy 6:13–18; Ephesians 5:5; Colossians 3:5).*

100. What is the third commandment? *The third commandment is "Thou shalt not take the name of the Lord thy God in vain; for the Lord will not hold him guiltless that taketh his name in vain" (Exodus 20:7).*

101. What does the third commandment teach us? *The third commandment teaches us to reverence God's name (Psalm 29:2).*

102. What is the fourth commandment? *The fourth commandment is "Remember the sabbath day, to keep it holy" (Exodus 20:8–11).*

103. What does the fourth commandment teach us? *The fourth commandment teaches us to set one whole day aside for God (Leviticus 19:30; Deuteronomy 5:12).*

104. What do the last six commandments teach? *The last six commandments teach our duty to our fellow man (Exodus 20:12–17; Matthew 22:39).*

105. What is the fifth commandment? *The fifth commandment is "Honour thy father and thy mother: that thy days may be long upon the land which the Lord thy God giveth thee" (Exodus 20:12).*

106. What does the fifth commandment teach us? *The fifth commandment teaches us that God blesses those who love, honor, and obey their parents (Romans 13:1; Ephesians 6:1–3).*

107. What is the sixth commandment? *The sixth commandment is "Thou shalt not kill" (Exodus 20:13).*

108. What does the sixth commandment teach us? *The sixth commandment teaches us to avoid anger and injury to others (Genesis 9:6; 1 John 3:15).*

109. What is the seventh commandment? *The seventh commandment is "Thou shalt not commit adultery" (Exodus 20:14).*

110. What does the seventh commandment teach us? *The seventh commandment teaches us to be pure in heart, language, and conduct (Matthew 5:27–30; Ephesians 4:29; 5:3–4).*

111. What is the eighth commandment? *The eighth commandment is "Thou shalt not steal" (Exodus 20:15).*

112. What does the eighth commandment teach us? *The eighth commandment teaches us to respect the property of others and to be fair in all of our dealings (Leviticus 6:1–5; Proverbs 11:1; Romans 12:11; Ephesians 4:28; 2 Thessalonians 3:10–12).*

113. What is the ninth commandment? *The ninth commandment is "Thou shalt not bear false witness against thy neighbor" (Exodus 20:16).*

114. What does the ninth commandment teach us? *The ninth commandment teaches us to tell the truth (Proverbs 14:5; Zechariah 8:16; 1 Peter 3:16).*

115. What is the tenth commandment? *The tenth commandment is "Thou shalt not covet thy neighbour's house, thou shalt not covet thy neighbour's wife, nor his manservant, nor his maidservant, nor his ox, nor his ass, nor any thing that is thy neighbour's" (Exodus 20:17).*

116. What does the tenth commandment teach us? *The tenth commandment teaches us to be content with what we have (Galatians 5:26; Philippians 4:11; Hebrews 13:5).*

117. What commandments does God command us to obey first of all? *God commands us to obey the two great commandments (Matthew 22:37–40).*

118. What is the first great commandment? *The first great commandment says, "Thou shalt love the Lord thy God with all thy heart, and with all thy soul, and with all thy mind" (Matthew 22:37).*

119. What is the second great commandment? *The second great commandment says, "Thou shalt love thy neighbour as thyself" (Matthew 22:39).*

120. Who is your neighbor? *All people are my neighbors (Luke 10:25–37; Galatians 6:10).*

The Bible Teaches Us About Church Ordinances

(12 questions)

121. What is an ordinance? *An ordinance is a way of remembering Christ's death, burial, and Resurrection (Romans 6:3–10; 1 Corinthians 11:23–26).*

122. How many ordinances are there in the Bible? *There are two ordinances in the Bible (Matthew 28:19; 1 Corinthians 11:23–26).*

123. What are the two ordinances? *The two ordinances are baptism and the Lord's Supper (Matthew 26:26–28; 28:19).*

124. Who appointed these ordinances? *The Lord Jesus Christ appointed them (Matthew 26:26–28; 28:18–19).*

125. Why did Christ appoint these ordinances? *Christ appointed these ordinances to encourage His disciples to separate from worldliness and to look forward to His return (Acts 2:40–42; 1 Corinthians 11:24–31).*

126. What element is used in baptism? *The element used in baptism is water (Matthew 3:6, 11, 14–17).*

127. What does baptism mean? *Baptism is an outward sign of our union with Christ and our decision to follow Him (Romans 6:3–11; Galatians 3:27).*

128. In Whose name are we baptized? *We are baptized in the name of the Father and of the Son and of the Holy Spirit (Matthew 28:19).*

129. What is the Lord's Supper? *The Lord's Supper is a remembrance of Christ's death for us on the cross and a looking forward to His return (Matthew 26:26–28; 1 Corinthians 11:23–26).*

130. Who is to partake of the Lord's Supper? *All those who have trusted Christ as their Savior, are living for Him, and have confessed and forsaken all sin may partake of the Lord's Supper (1 Corinthians 11:27–31).*

131. What are the elements used in the Lord's Supper? *The elements used in the Lord's Supper are bread and the fruit of the vine (Matthew 26:26–28; Mark 14:22–25).*

132. What do the bread and the fruit of the vine symbolize? *The bread symbolizes Christ's body, which was crucified for us, and the cup symbolizes His blood, which was shed for us (Matthew 26:26–28; Mark 14:22–25; Luke 22:17–20).*

The Bible Teaches Us About Prayer

(18 questions)

133. What is prayer? *Prayer is talking to God (Psalm 10:17; Philippians 4:6).*

134. In Whose name should we pray? *We should pray only in the name of Christ, our intercessor (John 16:23).*

135. What does it mean to pray "in Jesus's name"? *To pray in Jesus's name is to pray for the same kind of things that Jesus our intercessor is praying for and to pray in the same spirit (1 John 5:14).*

136. What guide has Christ given us to teach us how to pray? *Christ has given us the Lord's Prayer (Matthew 6:9–13).*

137. How should we pray? *We should pray after this manner: "Our Father which art in heaven, Hallowed be thy name. Thy kingdom come. Thy will be done in earth, as it is in heaven. Give us this day our daily bread. And forgive us our debts, as we forgive our debtors. And lead us not into temptation, but deliver us from evil: For thine is the kingdom, and the power, and the glory, for ever. Amen" (Matthew 6:9–13).*

138. How many petitions are there in the Lord's Prayer? *There are six petitions in the Lord's Prayer (Matthew 6:9–13).*

139. What is the first petition? *The first petition is "Hallowed be thy name" (Matthew 6:9).*

140. What do we pray for in the first petition? *We say that God is holy and that we want to honor Him (Psalm 145:1–13; Romans 11:36).*

141. What is the second petition? *The second petition is "Thy kingdom come" (Matthew 6:10).*

142. What do we pray for in the second petition? *We pray that Christ will rule over all the earth and that all people will praise God (Psalm 67:1–3; Matthew 28:19–20; Philippians 2:10–11).*

143. What is the third petition? *The third petition is "Thy will be done in earth, as it is in heaven" (Matthew 6:10).*

144. What do we pray for in the third petition? *We pray that the will of God will be done in the life of everyone on earth (Psalm 103:22; Romans 12:2).*

145. What is the fourth petition? *The fourth petition is "Give us this day our daily bread" (Matthew 6:11).*

146. What do we pray for in the fourth petition? *We pray that God will provide everything we need (Proverbs 30:8; Philippians 4:19).*

147. What is the fifth petition? *The fifth petition is "And forgive us our debts, as we forgive our debtors" (Matthew 6:12).*

148. What do we pray for in the fifth petition? *We pray that God will pardon our sins for Christ's sake and enable us to forgive those who have sinned against us (Psalm 51:1; Matthew 6:14–15).*

149. What is the sixth petition? *The sixth petition is "And lead us not into temptation, but deliver us from evil" (Matthew 6:13).*

150. What do we pray for in the sixth petition? *We pray that God will keep us from sin when we are tempted (Psalm 51:10, 12; Matthew 26:41).*

The Bible Teaches Us About the Future
(14 questions)

151. Will Christ come again? *Yes, Christ has promised to return to take us to be with Him (John 14:1–3; Acts 1:11).*

152. When will Christ return? *No one knows when Christ will return (Matthew 24:42, 50; 25:13).*

153. What are the two parts of the Second Coming? *The Second Coming includes the Rapture and the glorious appearing (1 Corinthians 15:51–52; Revelation 19:11–16).*

154. What will happen at the Rapture? *At the Rapture, Christ will resurrect the Christians who have died and change those who are living, giving each of them a body that will never die (1 Corinthians 15:51–52; 1 Thessalonians 4:15–17).*

155. What will happen after the Rapture? *After the Rapture, a seven-year period of judgment will take place on earth, ending with the glorious appearing. (Revelation 6–19)*

156. What will happen at the glorious appearing? *Christ will return to earth, remove all the wicked, and establish His millennial kingdom with His people (2 Thessalonians 1:7–10; Revelation 19:11–16).*

157. What is the Millennium? *Following the Tribulation, the Millennium is a thousand-year period when Christ rules His kingdom on earth (Revelation 20:1–6).*

158. What will happen after the Millennium? *At the end of the Millennium, Christ will defeat and judge all His enemies and establish the new earth and the new Jerusalem (Revelation 20:7–15; 21:1–4).*

159. What happens to people at death? *The body returns to dust, and the spirit goes to either heaven or hell (Genesis 3:19; Psalm 9:17; Luke 16:22–23; Romans 6:23).*

160. What will happen to the wicked in the day of judgment? *The wicked will be thrown into the lake of fire (Revelation 20:11–15).*

161. What is the lake of fire? *The lake of fire is a place of eternal fire and endless torment (Matthew 25:41; Mark 9:43; Luke 16:19–26; Revelation 20:10, 13–15).*

162. What happens to the righteous when they die? *The righteous go to heaven when they die (Matthew 5:11–12; 25:46; John 10:28).*

163. What is heaven? *Heaven is a glorious and happy place where the saved live with the Lord, awaiting the resurrection of their bodies (Luke 23:43; 2 Corinthians 5:8; Philippians 1:23).*

164. What is the eternal dwelling place of the righteous? *Our eternal dwelling place with the Lord will be the new earth and the new Jerusalem (John 14:3; Revelation 21:1–3).*

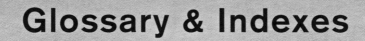

Glossary & Indexes

almighty all-powerful

Almighty one of God's names

angel spirit who lives with God in heaven; messenger sent by God to earth

apostle (ə pŏs'əl) man chosen by Jesus to see the events of His life and His Resurrection and to tell others about Him

ark large boat built by Noah

ark of the covenant the sacred box that contained the Ten Commandment tablets, a jar of manna, and Aaron's rod

ascension (ə sĕn'shən) Christ's going up into heaven forty days after His Resurrection

assurance condition of knowing for sure; certainty

atone (ə tōn') to give a satisfactory payment for a sin, wrongdoing, or injury

baptism a believer's act of obedience using water as a testimony of having trusted Christ

begotten being the child of

beseech to beg or plead

blasphemy attributing evil to God; denying good that should be attributed to God; giving God's attributes to something or someone other than God

blessed holy; having God's favor

blessing a gift from God

born again referring to one who has experienced the new birth (See *new birth*.)

Bread of Heaven a name for Christ, Who provides physical and spiritual food

burnt offering Old Testament offering to God that was burned on an altar

caesar (sē'zər) a title given to Roman emperors

Calvary "the place of a skull"; the place near Jerusalem where Jesus was crucified; Golgotha

Canaan (kā'nən) the land that God promised to give to the Israelites in the Old Testament

centurion (sĕn tŏŏr'ē ən) Roman commander of about one hundred soldiers

charity love

cherub (chĕr'əb) a kind of angel (plural: *cherubim*)

Christian a person who trusts Christ as Savior

church all of those who trust Christ and are saved

cleanseth (klĕnz'əth) frees from guilt; purges or clears

Comforter the Holy Spirit

commandment an order

commend to show or prove

condemn to declare guilty of wrongdoing

confess to admit to doing wrong; to admit one's guilt; saying what God says about sin

corrupt evil and dirty; wicked; sinful

countenance (koun'tə nəns) expression of a person's face; the face itself

covenant (kŭv'ə nənt) a solemn promise or agreement between two or more persons

covet to have a strong desire for something belonging to someone else; to wish something was yours

create to make something from nothing

creator one that makes something new

Creator God

crucify to put to death by nailing or binding to a cross

Day of Atonement (ə tōn´ mənt) a day once a year when the high priest entered the holy of holies to offer sacrifices as payment for the people's sins

death separation of the body and spirit; separation from God

demon an evil spirit

descend (dĭ sĕnd´) to come down; to pass down from parent to child

devil an evil spirit; a demon

Devil another name for Satan

disciple one who follows and serves another; a follower of a certain belief

divine having to do with God; holy and sacred

doctrine a teaching, belief, or principle

draught (drăft) quantity of fish caught in a net

edify to build up spiritually

Elohim (ĕl´ō hēm) a Hebrew name for God indicating His power and authority

Emmanuel (ĭ măn´yōō ĕl) (See *Immanuel*.)

epistle (ĭ pĭs´əl) letter or written message

eternity time without beginning or end

eunuch (yōō´nək) man in charge of a royal household

evangelize (ĭ văn´jə līz) to spread the gospel

everlasting without end; going on forever

exalt to speak highly of; to praise and glorify

exhort (ĭg zôrt´) to encourage

faith trust in God; firm belief without physical proof

false prophet one who preaches or teaches religious ideas against those found in God's Word; deceiver

fellowship being together as friends; enjoying each other's company

firmament (fûr´ mə mənt) sky between the heavens and the earth

fisher of men person who leads others to trust Christ as Savior

follower one who believes and lives by another's teachings; disciple

forerunner person who goes before to prepare the way for another or to tell of another's coming

foretold predicted; told about future happenings

forgiveness act of excusing or pardoning someone for a wrongdoing

fornication (fôr nĭ kā´shən) immoral or evil behavior; idolatry

frankincense (frăng´kĭn sĕns) gum from certain trees that gives off a spicy, sweet smell when burned

fruit anything yielded or produced

genealogy (jē nē ŏl´ə jē) record of ancestors; family tree

generation all the people born in a certain time period

Gentile (jĕn´tīl) any person who is not Jewish

girdle belt worn around the waist

glorify to praise or worship

Good Shepherd a name for Christ showing He leads and guides us

gospel the truth of the good news of Christ's coming to earth, dying for our sins, and being seen after rising from the dead

grace God's kindness to us even though we do not deserve it

Great Commission Christ's command to His disciples to teach the gospel worldwide (Matthew 28:19–20)

guilty having done wrong and deserving punishment

harlot (här´ lət) immoral woman

heart center of human thinking and feelings

heathen person who does not know about or believe in God

heaven glorious and happy place where God and His angels live; where saved people go after death

Hebrew Jewish language; Jewish person

hell place of dreadful torment where the unsaved are punished after death

high priest head or chief of the Jewish priests with the responsibility of overseeing the temple and administering religious ceremonies

holy attribute of God: sinless, perfect, and righteous; set apart

holy of holies room in the tabernacle where the ark of the covenant was kept

Holy Spirit one of the three persons of the Trinity, Who lives in the hearts of Christians; the Holy Ghost, God

homage (hŏm´ĭj or ŏm´ĭj) special respect shown to honor someone

honor *n.* glory and praise; honesty; *vb.* to treat with love, admiration, and respect

household of faith the collective group of believers born into the family of God through faith in Jesus Christ

humble not proud of oneself or boastful; meek or modest

humility state of being without self-pride or boastfulness

I Am one of the names for God showing His eternal existence "apart from" creation

idol statue worshiped as a god; person or thing loved more than God

image likeness; something that is like another in form or nature; idol

Immanuel (ĭ măn´yo͞o ĕl) a name of Jesus, meaning "God with us"

impute (ĭm po͞ot´) to transfer (righteousness or guilt) from one person to another

incarnate (ĭn kär´nĭt) the Son of God in human flesh

incense substance that gives off a sweet smell when it is burned

incorruptible (ĭn kə rŭp´tə bəl) clean and perfect; without error

infinite very great; without boundary; endless

iniquity sin and wickedness

inspiration God's breathing out of the Scriptures using holy men

intercede (ĭn tər sēd´) to ask or pray on behalf of another

Israel God's chosen people; the Jews; the land of the Jews

Jehovah (jĭ hō´və) the personal name of God in the Old Testament

Jew a person of the Hebrew race, God's chosen people

Jubilee Year (jōō´bə lē) a celebration the Jews observed every fifty years

judgment act of hearing and deciding a case; decision given by a judge

just right, fair, and honest; good and righteous

justify to declare righteous

lake of fire the place of unimaginable eternal punishment where the unbelievers in hell are sent after being judged for their sin

Lamb name used for Jesus Christ that shows that by His death He paid the sacrifice for our sins just as a lamb was sacrificed in Old Testament times for the sins of the Israelites

laver (lā´vər) large bowl used for washing sacrifices in the Jewish tabernacle or temple

law rule made by God or by human authority

leaven (lĕv´ən) substance such as yeast that causes dough to rise; often used as a symbol of sin in the Bible

leper (lĕp´ər) person who has leprosy

leprosy (lĕp´rə sē) skin disease that attacks the nerves, causes weakening and wasting away of muscles, and is characterized by white, scaly scabs; a picture of sin

Levite (lē´vīt) member of the tribe of Levi from which the Jewish priests were chosen

longsuffering patience; perseverance; slow to avenge wrongs

Lord God; Jesus Christ

Lord's Supper a church ordinance by which we remember Christ's sacrifice on the cross; the last meal that Jesus had with His disciples

lots (casting) using stones or sticks to decide an outcome or determine the portion of something given to each person

magistrate (măj´ĭ strāt) officer of a government, such as a judge or president

malefactor (măl´ə făk tər) one who does evil; criminal

Man of Sorrows a name for Jesus, showing His sorrow and suffering for the sins of the world

mediator (mē´dē ā tər) person who acts as a go-between

mercy God's withholding of the punishment we deserve

mercy seat the gold plate covering the ark of the covenant on which the high priest sprinkled the blood for a sin offering

Messiah (mə sī´ə) the Old Testament name for the promised Redeemer; Christ

might power

Millennium (mĭ lĕn´ē əm) period of a thousand years following the Tribulation when Christ will reign on earth

millstone one of two round, flat stones used for grinding grain

miracle supernatural event done by the power of God that shows His works

missionary person who goes out to tell the story of Jesus and God's plan of salvation

moneychanger person who exchanges one kind of money for another kind

myrrh (mûr) fragrant extract from the wood and bark of a common Palestinian bush

Nazarene (năz ə rēn´) a person from Nazareth; another name for Jesus

Nazirite (năz´ər īt) a Hebrew who had taken certain religious vows; he could not drink wine, cut his hair, or touch a ceremonially unclean thing

new birth when God gives eternal life to a sinner who confesses his sins and trusts Christ

new heaven and new earth future heaven and earth that will be created by God; eternal dwelling place of the redeemed

obey to do what one is told to do

observance act of keeping customs, laws, or religious ceremonies

offering something given as an act of worship to God

omnipotent (ŏm nĭp´ə tənt) all-powerful; almighty

omnipresent (ŏm nə prĕz´ənt) always present; existing everywhere at the same time

omniscient (ŏm nĭsh´ənt) all-knowing; having complete knowledge of everything

ordinance a way of remembering Christ's death and Resurrection

palsy (pôl´zē) disease that causes paralysis

parable short story that teaches a lesson; earthly story with a heavenly meaning

paradise heaven; dwelling place of God and His angels

pardon forgiveness

Passover when the death angel passed over the Hebrew homes that had blood sprinkled on the doorpost (Exodus 12:13)

Passover Feast an eight-day Jewish celebration in remembrance of the Israelites' escape from Egypt

patriarch (pā´trē ärk) father, ruler, or founder of a family, tribe, or group

Pentecost (pĕn´tĭ kôst) a Jewish celebration (feast) held fifty days after Passover to remember the harvest and the giving of the Ten Commandments; the time when the Holy Spirit was given to the early Christians

pharaoh (fâr´ō) title given to the kings of ancient Egypt

Pharisee (făr´ĭ sē) member of a Jewish group that was strict in keeping Jewish law

Philistines (fĭ lĭs´tēnz; fĭl´ĭ stēnz) enemies of the Jews who lived in Palestine during Old Testament times

plague (plāg) suffering or trouble sent from God; rapid spreading of a deadly disease

potter's field cemetery for poor or friendless people

praise to express the worth or value of something or someone through words or songs

prayer act of speaking to God

priest Old Testament servant of God chosen by God to offer sacrifices

proclaim to make known to the public

prodigal (prŏd´ĭ gəl) wasteful and careless

prophecy (prŏf´ĭ sē) a prediction; usually from God

prophesy (prŏf´ĭ sī) to tell about future events; to proclaim God's will

prophet a preacher in Bible times who told of God's will and future events

propitiation (prō pĭsh ē ā´shən) act of appeasing wrath; our means of salvation through Christ's death

proud feeling pleased over something done, made, or owned; honored; dignified

providence God's guidance of all things to accomplish His purpose and plan

province section of a kingdom or an empire; in Roman times, a section of the empire ruled by a governor

psalm religious song, poem, or hymn of praise to God

publican tax collector of ancient Rome

R

rabbi "teacher" or "master"; a Jewish religious leader

ram's horn trumpet made of a curved horn from a male sheep

ransom price paid to free captives

Rapture taking of the saved to heaven when Christ returns

reconcile (rĕk´ən sīl) to bring together again in peace and friendship after being separated

redeemer one who buys something back that was lost; one who saves or sets free

Redeemer Jesus Christ

Redemption Christ's act of rescuing us and freeing us from sin; our salvation

regeneration (rĭ jĕn ə rā´shən) act of receiving a new spiritual life; salvation; new birth

remission forgiveness of sin

repent to be sorry for, ask forgiveness for, and turn away from sin

repentance act of being sorry for, asking forgiveness for, and turning away from sin; a change of mind about sin

resurrection (rĕz ə rĕk´shən) act of coming to life again

righteous doing that which is right in the sight of God; hating sin and loving good

Sabbath (săb´əth) the seventh day of the week; the day used for worship and rest in the Old Testament and the Gospels

sackcloth rough cloth made from the hair of goats and camels and worn as a sign of sadness

sacrifice an offering given to God for the forgiveness of sin

Sadducees (săj´ə sēz) group of Jews who did not believe in angels or resurrection

saint person who is saved

salvation God's saving us from the punishment of sin

sanctification (săngk tə fĭ kā´shən) the process in which God makes saved people holy in heart and behavior

sanctuary (săngk´chōō ĕr ē) holy place set apart for the worship of God

Sanhedrin (săn hē´drĭn) the Jews' seventy-one-member supreme court for religious and government cases

Satan another name for the Devil; an evil spirit who is the enemy of God and all Christians

saved the condition of one who has trusted Christ and asked forgiveness for sins; set free from sin's power and punishment

savior (sāv´yər) one who saves others from trouble or disaster

Savior (sāv´yər) Jesus Christ our Lord

scapegoat one who takes the blame for others; in Old Testament times a goat that was taken into the wilderness, symbolically taking the blame for the sins of the people, similar to the way Jesus took the blame for our sins

Scripture holy writings of God; the Bible

separation being set apart; living differently from the unsaved in a total and noticeable way

sepulcher or **sepulchre** (sĕp´əl kər) tomb or cave used for burial

seraph (sĕr´əf) angel of important position believed to lead in the worship of God, described as having six wings (Isaiah 6:2)

servant person who works for someone else

Sheol (shē´ōl) a Hebrew name for hell

shofar or **shophar** (shō´fär) ancient Hebrew trumpet made of a ram's horn and used for giving signals

sin disobedience to the law of God

slothful lazy

smite to hit or slap; to destroy or kill

sojourn (sō´jərn) to stay in one place for a time

soothsayer one who tells the future, or pretends to; a fortuneteller

sorcerer person who practices magic and claims to have the help of evil spirits

soul part of the person that thinks, acts, feels, and lives forever

sow (sō) to spread or plant seed

surety (shoor´ĭ tē) person who agrees to be responsible for the debts or faults of another

swaddling clothes strips of cloth wrapped around a newborn baby

synagogue (sĭn´ə gŏg) Jewish congregation or a place to meet for worship

tabernacle (tăb´ər năk əl) tent used by the Israelites as a place of worship while they were wandering in the wilderness and until the temple was built

tablet small flat piece of stone used for writing

talent unit of weight for gold or silver; ability to do something well

tares harmful weeds that grow in grain fields

temple building used for worship

temptation act of trying to make a person do something wrong; attraction

Ten Commandments the ten rules for living that God gave to Moses on Mt. Sinai (Exodus 20)

testament will or promise; one of the two divisions of the Bible

testify to give evidence for; to tell about what one has seen or heard

testimony open statement of one's beliefs or faith in God

thresh to separate the grain or seeds from a plant such as wheat

till to plow or cultivate the ground

tithe (tīTH) small part; small tax; offering to God of one-tenth of all that a person earns

transfiguration

transfiguration (trăns fĭg yə rā´shən) the changed appearance of Christ on the mountain (Matthew 17:1–13)

transform to change the appearance, shape, or nature of a thing

transgression sin; act of doing what God forbids

translate to take to heaven without death; to express in another language

trespass to disobey; to sin

tribe any one of the twelve groups of the Hebrews, each of which descended from one of the sons of Jacob

tribute tax; expression of thanks or respect

Trinity God the Father, God the Son, and God the Holy Spirit in one divine nature

trust *n.* firm, unchanging belief in the power, love, or truthfulness of a person or thing; faith and confidence; *vb.* to have faith in, to depend on

twinkling quick wink of the eye; very short time; moment

unbelief thinking that something is not true

undefiled clean and pure; not corrupted or made dirty

unfaithful not keeping one's promises

ungodly sinful and wicked

unrighteousness wickedness; sinfulness

vainglory great pride in oneself; boastful display or "showing off"; arrogance; opposite of humility

vengeance (věn´jəns) punishment or injury in return for a wrong

vessel large boat or ship; container for holding liquids

viper type of poisonous snake

virgin pure, unmarried female

watchtower high tower or high place from which to watch for enemy ships, forces, etc.

wayside side of a path or road

wilderness region of land with no people; dry, bare land

wise men the men who followed the star from the East to Bethlehem seeking Jesus

witness a person who tells about an event he has seen; *vb.* to tell others about Christ and the way of salvation

Word the way God speaks to humans; in Scripture, referring to both the Bible (the written Word) and Jesus Christ (the living Word)

worship to show honor, love, and respect

yoke wooden frame that links two oxen or horses together for pulling a plow or heavy load; a burden

Zion (zī´ən) a name for Jerusalem; a hill in Jerusalem that represents the whole city

Cumulative Index for Bible 1–Bible 6 (by unit number)

Entry	1	2	3	4	5	6
Aaron						
speaks for Moses		2		1		3
makes the golden calf		2		1		
murmurs against Moses			2			
disobedience of sons, Nadab and Abihu			2			
Abijah (King)						5
Abimelech (King)	3					
Abram/Abraham						
receives Abrahamic covenant	2	1	1		1	2
leaves homeland	2	1	1		1, 6	2
journeys to Egypt	2			1		2
rescues Lot						2
receives new name	2		1		1	2
birth of Ishmael			1		1	
receives his promised son, Isaac	2	1	1		1, 6	2
sacrifices Isaac	2	1			1, 6	2
dies					1	
Achan						
steals and receives punishment		2				
Adam and Eve						
live in the Garden of Eden	1	1	1		1	1
disobey God (the Fall)	1	4	1		1	1
Adoniram Judson: God's Man in Burma	9					
Aeneas					7	
Agabus						
prophesies about famine				9		
Ahab (King)						
challenged by Elijah before the altar of Baal	10		3		2	
receives warning from Elijah	10		3			
pouts about not getting his own way			3		2	
Ahasuerus (King)		6			3	6
Ahaziah (King)						5
Amaziah (King)						5
Amon (King)						5
Amos				10		
Ananias						
helps Saul with his blindness	9		9	6	7	
Ananias and Sapphira						
lie to God			9			
die for their sin			9			
Anna	4				4	7
Apollos						
fellowships with Paul			9			

Entry	1	2	3	4	5	6
Application Novels						
Captive Treasure		2				
Pelts and Promises		10				
Songbird					3	
Stuart's Run to Faith						3
Aquila and Priscilla						
fellowship with Paul		9				
Ark of the Covenant	5				3, 6	
Asa (King)					5	
Athaliah (Queen)					6	
Babel (Tower of)					1	
Balaam						
hears the donkey speak		2				
blesses Israel		2				
Barabbas						8
Barak					2	
Barnabas						
travels with Paul to Cyprus	9		7	6		9
gives to the cause of Christ			7			
Bathsheba					5	5
Belshazzar (King)						
holds a feast		6				6
sees handwriting on the wall		6				
Bible Study Skills						
Bible-reading habit				1–10	1–10	1–10
complete a Bible study					6, 9	2–5
identify book abbreviations			5	2, 7		
identify books			9	1–2, 9	1	
identify divisions					1–3, 5–7, 9–10	1–10
identify location	6, 9–10	2–3, 5–7, 10	2	1–3, 7, 10	1, 6	1–10
identify parallel Bible accounts			8		8	
identify parts of a reference	3, 5, 8					
identify parts of a verse		10	9			
locate information in a verse	9–10					
outline Scripture					9	
read names of New Testament books	10	10				
sequence books		1, 3, 5–6, 8–9	8–9	1–3, 7	1–3, 5–7, 9–10	1–10
understand scope of a reference				10	9	
use a Bible dictionary					1, 10	

	Grade Level					
	1	2	3	4	5	6
use a concordance					2, 7	
use cross-references			7	2, 7	2, 5	
use strategy to memorize Scripture					1	
use contents page	1–2, 4–7	1–2, 5–6, 9–10	1–2, 6			
use topical headings					9	
Cain and Abel						
born to Adam and Eve			1		1	1
give offerings to God			1		1, 6	1
Cain kills Abel			1		1	1
Caleb						
gives a good report about Canaan	5			1		
Captive Treasure				2		
Carey, William					7	
Christmas						
man's need of a Savior		4				4
Isaiah's prophecy of a promised Savior		4		4		4
appearance of angel to Zachariah			4			
Zachariah unable to speak			4			
birth of John the Baptist			4			
Gabriel's message to Mary	4					
journey to Bethlehem	4				4	4
birth of Christ	4	4	4	4	4	4
visits from the shepherds and the wise men	4	4	4	4	4	4
presentation of Jesus at the temple	4		4		4	7
Anna and Simeon see the Christ child	4		4		4	7
Cornelius						
has a dream	9			7		9
receives the Lord	9			7		9
Creation						
days of	1	1	1			1
of man	1	1	1			1
Crosby, Fanny					10	
Daniel						
selected to learn in Babylon						6
survives the lions' den		6				6
interprets handwriting on the wall		6				6
tells about the last days			10			6
Darius (Governor)						
signs decree		6			3	6
sends Daniel to the lions' den		6			3	6
declares everyone will worship the living God		6				6

	Grade Level					
	1	2	3	4	5	6
Darius (King)						
commands that the temple construction continue					6	
David						
becomes next in line to be the king of Israel	6	5		2		
plays his harp for King Saul	6					
fights Goliath	6	5		2		
flees from Saul	6	5		2	5	
Saul and Jonathan killed in battle	6	5				
sits on the throne of Israel	6	5		2	5	5
rules as king of Israel	6			2	5	5
sins with Bathsheba					5	5
writes psalms					10	
Dead Sea Scrolls	10		10			
Deborah				2		
Disciples (Apostles)						
leave all to follow Jesus	7	10	9	6		
eat Last Supper with Christ	8		8	8	8	8
encourage other Christians	9	7				9
tell others the gospel of Christ	9	7				9
Divided Kingdom				2		
Dorcas (Tabitha)		10		7		
Easter						
prophecies		8		8	8	8
anointing by Mary			8		8	
triumphal entry	8	8		8	8	
cleansing of the temple	8	8		8	8	
betrayal by Judas	8			8	8	8
Jesus's trial and Crucifixion	8	8		8	8	8
Jesus's death and burial	8	8		8	8	8
Jesus's Resurrection	8		8	8	8	8
empty tomb	8	8		8	8	8
appearances after death	8	8		8	8	8
Eglon (King)				2		
Ehud				2		
Eli				3		
Elijah						
tells Ahab there will be no rain			3	2		
trusts God by the Brook Cherith			3	2		
eats at the widow's house			3	2		
defeats prophets of Baal on Mount Carmel	10		3	2		
calls down fire from heaven	10			2		
doesn't trust God to take care of him			3			
anoints Elisha			3	2		

	Grade Level					
	1	2	3	4	5	6
Knox, John				9		
Livingstone, David						7
Luther, Martin						9
Kuyper, Abraham		7				
Merle d'Aubigné, Jean Henri				4		
Moody, D. L.			2			
Occom, Samson						8
Polycarp						2
Spurgeon, Charles Haddon						1
Taylor, J. Hudson			7			
Tindley, Charles				8		
Tyndale, William			6			
Wang, Mingdao			5			
Watts, Isaac						3
Wesley, John			8			
Whitefield, George					9	
Zwingli, Ulrich					8	
Hezekiah (King)						
prays for recovery from illness				2		5
prays for God's leading				2		5
Historical Novel						
Morning Star of the Reformation						7
Hophni and Phinehas					3	
Hosea				3		
Huss, John					4	
Hymn History Stories						
Babcock, Maltbie						
"This Is My Father's World"	1					
Baxter, Lydia						
"Take the Name of Jesus with You"			7			
Bliss, Philip						
"Jesus Loves Even Me"	10					
Brooks, Phillips						
"O Little Town of Bethlehem"			4			
Buell, Harriet						
"A Child of the King"	6					
Chisholm, Thomas O.						
"Great Is Thy Faithfulness"						5
Crosby, Fanny						
"Be Thou Exalted"		3				
Lathbury, Mary						
"Break Thou the Bread of Life"				2		
Neander, Joachim						
"Praise Ye the Lord, the Almighty"		1				
Oatman, Johnson						
"Count Your Blessings"				6		

	Grade Level					
	1	2	3	4	5	6
Scriven, Joseph						
"What a Friend We Have in Jesus"			9			
Spafford, Horatio						
"It Is Well with My Soul"				10		
Stone, Samuel						
"The Church's One Foundation"				9		
Thompson, Will						
"Jesus Is All the World to Me"	7					
Towner, Daniel and John Sammis						
"Trust and Obey"	3					
Walter, Howard						
"I Would Be True"				3		
Watts, Isaac						
"Am I a Soldier of the Cross?"		6				
"I Sing the Mighty Power of God"				1		
"Joy to the World"		4				
Isaac						
goes to Mount Moriah to be sacrificed	2	1			1	2
marries Rebekah	2				1	2
receives sons, Jacob and Esau	3				1	2
gives Jacob the blessing	3				1	2
Isaiah		9				
Ishmael					1	
Israelites						
released from Egypt	5			1		3
cross the Red Sea	5			1	6	
receive manna from heaven	5		2			
receive quail from heaven	5		2			
receive the Ten Commandments from God through Moses	5		2	1		3
worship the golden calf	5			1		
receive instructions for the tabernacle				1		3
send spies to Canaan	5			1		
Jabin (King)					2	
Jacob						
receives birthright from Esau	3				1	
deceives his father	3				1–2	
dreams	3					
works for a wife	3					
reunites with Esau	3					
Jael					2	
James						7
Jehoahaz (King)						5
Jehoiachin (King)						5

	Grade Level					
---	1	2	3	4	5	6
Uzziah (King)						5
Watts, Isaac						3
Whitefield, George					9	
Widow						
cheerfully gives all she has		10				
Wise Men						
see the star	4	4	4	4		4
seek for the Christ child	4	4	4	4		4
ask Herod about the child born to be king	4	4	4	4		4
give gifts and worship Jesus	4		4	4		4
Woman at the Well						
trusts Christ as her Savior			5			
tells friends about Jesus			5			

	Grade Level					
---	1	2	3	4	5	6
Woman of Shunem						
receives son as a blessing from God			3			
Zacchaeus						
climbs a tree to see Jesus		9				
meets Jesus		9				
repays those he cheated		9				
Zechariah					7	10
Zedekiah (King)						5
Zephaniah						5
Zerubbabel					6	
Zwingli, Ulrich					8	

Bible 2 Index (by lesson number)

Memory Verse List

Verses are listed by their lesson range within each Unit.

Unit 1

1–4	Genesis 1:1
5–8	Genesis 6:8, 22
9–12	Deuteronomy 6:5
13–16	Genesis 15:6

Unit 2

17–20	Exodus 14:31
21–24	Exodus 32:26
25–28	John 14:15
29–32	Micah 6:8*b*

Unit 3

33–36	Isaiah 45:22
37–40	2 Chronicles 7:14
41–44	Galatians 6:10
45–48	1 John 1:7

Unit 4

49–52	Isaiah 9:6
53–56	Luke 2:11

Unit 5

57–60	Mark 10:45
61–64	1 Samuel 12:24
65–68	1 Chronicles 28:20*a*
69–72	Psalm 133:1

Unit 6

73–76	Romans 8:28
77–80	Deuteronomy 31:6
81–84	Romans 1:16
85–88	Psalm 56:11

Unit 7

89–92	Romans 3:10–11
93–96	Ephesians 1:7
97–100	Psalm 103:12
101–104	Matthew 6:14–15

Unit 8

105–108	Romans 5:8
109–112	Matthew 28:6

Unit 9

113–116	Mark 4:41
117–120	John 6:38
121–124	2 Corinthians 5:17
125–128	Psalm 24:10

Unit 10

129–132	Mark 1:17
133–136	John 14:2*b*–3
137–140	2 Corinthians 9:7
141–144	Proverbs 20:11

Photo Credits

The following agencies and individuals have furnished materials to meet the photographic needs of the Student Worktext. We wish to express our gratitude to them for their important contribution.

Suzanne R. Altizer
Bowen Bible Lands Collection,
  Bob Jones University
George Collins
Tim Davis

Getty Images
iStockphoto.com
JupiterImages Corporation
PhotoDisc/Getty Images
Unusual Films

Unit 1
© iStockphoto.com/Blue_Cutler 15 (left); © iStockphoto.com/Kativ 15 (right); Unusual Films 21 (all)

Unit 3
Unusual Films 49

Unit 5
PhotoDisc/Getty Images 86 (top left, bottom right); Suzanne R. Altizer 86 (center left, top right); © 2009 JupiterImages Corporation 86 (bottom left), 104; Getty Images/Dorling Kindersley 86 (center right); Unusual Films 95 (all)

Unit 8
Unusual Films 165 (first, second, fifth, and sixth images); © iStockphoto.com/ princessdlaf 165 (third image); © 2009 JupiterImages Corporation 165 (fourth image)

Unit 9
Unusual Films 181

Unit 10
Tim Davis 197 (top); George Collins 197 (center); Suzanne R. Altizer 197 (bottom); Bowen Bible Lands Collection, Bob Jones University 199 (all), 201 (all); Unusual Films 204 (all)

CD Instructions

How to Use the Teacher's Toolkit CD

Contents

The Teacher's Toolkit CD contains the following materials:
• Visuals
• Student Materials
• Activity Pages
• Hymns
• Unit Reviews
• Bible Truths for Christian Growth
• Bulletin Boards

Getting Started

Viewing the Teacher's Tookit materials requires Adobe® Reader® 7.0 or higher. The most recent version of Adobe Reader may be downloaded at no charge from the Adobe website at www.adobe.com. An Internet connection is required to download Reader.

Windows

Insert the CD. If it does not start automatically, open the CD's file listing and launch the file "Startup.exe." Read and accept the license agreement to begin using the Teacher's Toolkit materials. Navigate within the CD using the bookmarks on the left side of the screen.

Mac

Insert the CD, click on the CD icon, and open the file "main.pdf" to begin using the Teacher's Toolkit materials.

Minimum System Requirements

Component	*Specification*
Processor (CPU)	Pentium IV
Operating System	Windows XP or later; Mac OS Leopard
RAM	256Mb
Display Size (pixels)	1024 × 768
Application	Adobe Reader 7 or later

Additional Help

For more detailed instructions, including how to print files and insert visuals into presentations, please refer to the file "CD_info.pdf" on the CD. For further assistance, call BJU Press Customer Service at 1-800-845-5731.